Quantitative Techniques for Competition and Antitrust Analysis

Quantitative Techniques for Competition and Antitrust Analysis

Peter Davis and Eliana Garcés

Princeton University Press
Princeton and Oxford

Published by Princeton University Press,
41 William Street, Princeton, New Jersey 08540

In the United Kingdom: Princeton University Press,
6 Oxford Street, Woodstock, Oxfordshire OX20 1TW

Library of Congress Cataloging-in-Publication Data

Davis, Peter J. (Peter John), 1970–
Quantitative techniques for competition and antitrust analysis / Peter Davis, Eliana Garcés.
p. cm.
Includes bibliographical references and index.
ISBN 978-0-691-14257-9 (alk. paper)
1. Consolidation and merger of corporations. 2. Antitrust law.
3. Econometrics. I. Garcés, Eliana, 1968– II. Title.

HD2746.5.D385 2010
338.8′2015195–dc22 2009005675

British Library Cataloging-in-Publication Data is available

This book has been composed in Times using TEX Typeset
and copyedited by T&T Productions Ltd, London

press.princeton.edu

10 9 8 7 6 5 4 3 2 1

For Lara, Adrian, and Tristan

For Sara

Contents

Preface

The use of quantitative analysis by competition authorities is increasing around the globe. Whether the quantitative analysis is submitted by external experts, or the competition authority itself undertakes the analysis, empirical analysis is now a vitally important component of the competition economist's toolkit. Much of the empirical analysis submitted to, or carried out by, investigators is fairly straightforward. This is partly because simple tools are often very powerful and partly because the need to communicate with nonexperts sometimes places a natural boundary on the degree of sophistication which can comfortably be used. Of course, one person's "cutting-edge" method is another's basic tool and this difference drives the normal process of diffusion of new methods from basic research to applied work. The tools we discuss in this book are broadly the result of the ideas and methods which have developed over the past twenty years in the empirical industrial organization literature and which are either gradually diffusing into practice or, no doubt in a small number of cases, gradually diffusing into obscurity.

While the aim of this book is to examine empirical techniques, we cannot stress enough that any empirical analysis in a competition investigation needs to be evaluated together with the factual, documentary, and qualitative evidence collected during the case. An empirical analysis will usually be one albeit important element in a broader evidence base. Only in a small minority of cases will quantitative analysis alone be sufficiently clear-cut, precise, and robust enough to support a finding, though it will provide one important plank of evidence in a wider range of cases. Even in cases where quantitative analysis is important, a solid qualitative analysis and a good factual knowledge of the industry will provide both a necessary basis for quantitative work and a source for vital reality checks regarding the conclusions emerging from empirical work.

With those caveats firmly in mind, in this book we discuss the most useful and most promising empirical strategies available to antitrust and merger investigators. Some of these techniques are tried and tested, others are more sophisticated and not yet widely embraced by practitioners. Throughout we try to take a careful practitioner's eye to tools that have often been proposed by the academic community. The fact is that practitioners need to understand both the potential uses and the important limitations of the available methods before they will, indeed before they should, choose to apply them. We do that by closely tying the empirical models and empirical strategy used to answer our competition policy questions to the underlying economic theory. Specifically, economic theory allows us to define the assumptions required for a given piece of empirical work to be meaningful. Indeed, no solid empirical analysis is entirely disconnected from economic theory and thus theory usually has a very important role in providing guidance and discipline in the design of empirical work.

The purpose of this book is not theory for itself but rather the aim is to help competition economists answer very practical questions. For this reason the structure of the book is broadly based around potential competition issues that need to be addressed. The first two chapters provide a review of basic theory and econometrics. Specifically, the first chapter reviews the determinants of market outcomes, i.e., demand, costs, and the competitive environment, since those are the fundamental elements that need to be very well-understood before any competition policy analysis is possible. The second chapter reviews the basic econometrics of multiple regression with a particular emphasis on the crucially important problem of "identification." Identification—the data variation required to enable us to tell one model apart from another—is a theme which emerges throughout the book. The subsequent chapters guide the reader through issues such as the estimation of cost and demand functions, market definition, the link between market structure and price, the scope for identifying firms' competitive conduct, damage estimation, merger simulation, and we end with the developing approaches to the quantitative assessment of the effects of vertical restraints. Each chapter critically discusses the empirical techniques that have been used to address that competition policy issue. The book does not aim to be comprehensive, but we do aim to provide practical guidance to investigators.

Naturally, sometimes tools which are too simple for the job at hand can result in the investigator getting a radically wrong answer. On the other hand, sophisticated tools poorly understood will be poorly applied and are more likely to act as a black box from which a decision emerges instead of providing a great deal of insight. Such is the challenge faced by antitrust agencies in choosing an appropriate economic methodology. In some instances, we will discuss empirical techniques that an individual agency may well currently judge to be too complicated, too theoretical, or too time-consuming to be of immediate practical use for time-constrained investigators. The approach of this book is that these techniques can still be useful in that they will at least signal the difficulty or complexity of a particular question and even an abstract discussion still provides guidance on the relevant empirical questions that need to be investigated if we want to have conclusions on a particular topic. In addition, the requisite expertise may be built gradually within an institution rather than within the remit of, say, a particular merger inquiry with a statutory deadline. The ultimate objective of this book is not to have economists in competition authorities replicate the examples discussed in these chapters but to help them develop a way of thinking about empirical analysis which will help them design their own original answers to the specific problems they will face given the data that they have. We also hope that the book will help reduce the amount of concurrent rediscovery of strengths and weaknesses of particular approaches currently undertaken in agencies across the world.

Finally, it is important to note that while this book explores the variety of methods available to analysts, the right tool for any particular inquiry will depend on the context of that inquiry. This book does not aim to explicitly or implicitly set any requirements as to how competition questions should be addressed empirically in any particular jurisdiction. We do, however, aim to raise awareness among empirical economists of the underlying econometric and economic theory that inevitably underpins all empirical techniques. Our hope is that increased awareness will both promote high-quality work in the relatively simple empirical exercises and also reduce the entry barriers hindering the use of more sophisticated approaches where such methods are appropriate.

Acknowledgments

Dr. Peter Davis currently serves as Deputy Chairman of the U.K. Competition Commission. While he is a principal author of the text, he writes as an individual and the views expressed in this text are solely those of the author and should not be taken to reflect the views of the U.K. Competition Commission. Indeed, this text has evolved from a project undertaken, before his current appointment, by Applied Economics Ltd (www.appliedeconomics.com) for the European Commission.

Dr. Eliana Garcés previously worked for the Chief Economist team at DG Competition before taking on her current role as a Member in the Cabinet of European Commissioner for Consumer Protection Meglena Kuneva. The contribution to this work is her own and does not represent the opinions of the European Commission.

This book began life as a project in the European Commission to disseminate practical knowledge and good practices in empirical analysis. We would like to thank the European Commission and, in particular, the EC's Competition Chief Economists who served during the making of this book, Lars Hendrik Röller and Damien Neven, for their continued support of the project.

The book has benefited in numerous ways from contributors. The authors would like to thank Richard Baggaley from Princeton University Press for his support, encouragement, and patience and Jon Wainwright from T&T Productions Ltd for his tireless efforts to typeset the book in the face of numerous corrections and amendments. Enrico Pesaresi provided valuable support throughout the process. We also thank Frank Verboven and Christian Huveneers for their detailed comments on the draft version. And, of course, the anonymous reviewers for their important contributions. This work builds heavily on the work of many authors who have each contributed to the literature. The authors would, however, like to thank, in particular, Douglas Bernheim and John Connor for allowing them to draw extensively from their work on cartel damage estimation. Last but by no means least, the book incorporates in substantial part updated and expanded content from classes and lectures Peter has taught at MIT and LSE over the best part of a decade and a substantial debt of gratitude is due to former students and colleagues at those institutions as well as to his former classmates and teachers at Yale and Oxford. In particular, thanks are due to Ariel Pakes, Steve Berry, Lanier Benkard, Ernie Berndt, Sofronis Clerides, Philip Leslie, Mark Schankerman, Nadia Soboleva, Tom Stoker, and John Sutton.

1

The Determinants of Market Outcomes

A solid knowledge of both econometric and economic theory is crucial when designing and implementing empirical work in economics. Econometric theory provides a framework for evaluating whether data can distinguish between hypotheses of interest. Economic theory provides guidance and discipline in empirical investigations. In this chapter, we first review the basic principles underlying the analysis of demand, supply, and pricing functions, as well as the concept and application of Nash equilibrium. We then review elementary oligopoly theory, which is the foundation of many of the empirical strategies discussed in this book. Continuing to develop the foundations for high-quality empirical work, in chapter 2 we review the important elements of econometrics for investigations. Following these first two review chapters, chapters 3–10 develop the core of the material in the book. The concepts reviewed in these first two introductory chapters will be familiar to all competition economists, but it is worthwhile reviewing them since understanding these key elements of economic analysis is crucial for an appropriate use of quantitative techniques.

1.1 Demand Functions and Demand Elasticities

The analysis of demand is probably the single most important component of most empirical exercises in antitrust investigations. It is impossible to quantify the likelihood or the effect of a change in firm behavior if we do not have information about the potential response of its customers. Although every economist is familiar with the shape and meaning of the demand function, we will take the time to briefly review the derivation of the demand and its main properties since basic conceptual errors in its handling are not uncommon in practice. In subsequent chapters we will see that demand functions are critical for many results in empirical work undertaken in the competition arena.

1.1.1 Demand Functions

We begin this chapter by reviewing the basic characteristics of individual demand and the derivation of aggregate demand functions.

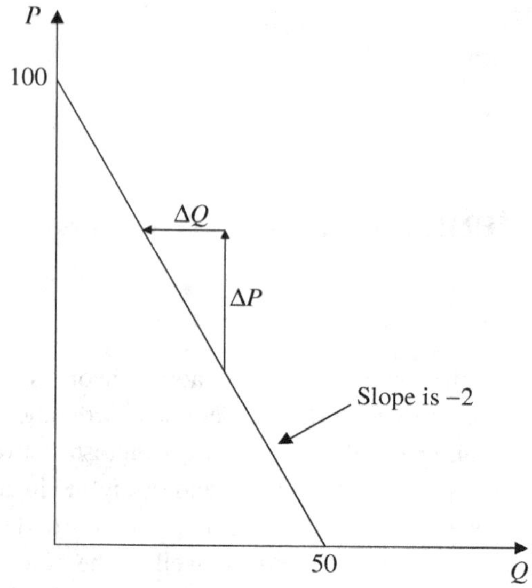

Figure 1.1. (Inverse) demand function.

1.1.1.1 The Anatomy of a Demand Function

An individual's demand function describes the amount of a good that a consumer would buy as a function of variables that are thought to affect this decision such as price P_i and often income y. Figure 1.1 presents an example of an individual linear demand function for a homogeneous product: $Q_i = 50 - 0.5P_i$ or rather for the inverse demand function, $P_i = 100 - 2Q_i$. More generally, we may write $Q_i = D(P_i, y)$.[1] Inverting the demand curve to express price as a function of quantity demanded and other variables yields the "inverse demand curve" $P_i = P(Q_i, y)$. Standard graphs of an individual's demand curve plot the quantity demanded of the good at each level of its own price and take as a given the level of income and the level of the prices of products that could be substitutes or complements. This means that along a given plotted demand curve, those variables are fixed. The slope of the demand curve therefore indicates at any particular point by how much a consumer would reduce (increase) the quantity purchased if the price increased (decreased) while income and any other demand drivers stayed fixed.

In the example in figure 1.1, an increase in price, ΔP, of €10 will decrease the demand for the product by 5 units shown as ΔQ. The consumer will not purchase any units if the price is above 100 because at that point the price is higher than the value that the customer assigns to the first unit of the good.

One interpretation of the inverse demand curve is that it shows the maximum price that a consumer is willing to pay if she wants to buy Q_i units of the good. While a

[1] This will be familiar from introductory microeconomics texts as the "Marshallian" demand curve (Marshall 1890).

consumer may value the first unit of the good highly, her valuation of, say, the one hundredth unit will typically be lower and it is this diminishing marginal valuation which ensures that demand curves typically slope downward. If our consumer buys a unit only if her marginal valuation is greater than the price she must pay, then the inverse demand curve describes our consumer's marginal valuation curve.

Given this interpretation, the inverse demand curve describes the difference between the customer's valuation of each unit and the actual price paid for each unit. We call the difference between what the consumer is willing to pay for each unit and what he or she actually pays the consumer's surplus available from that unit. For concreteness, I might be willing to pay a maximum of €10 for an umbrella if it's raining, but may nonetheless only have to pay €5 for it, leaving me with a measure of my benefit from buying the umbrella and avoiding getting wet, a surplus of €5. At any price P_i, we can add up the consumer surplus available on all of the units consumed (those with marginal valuations above P_i) and doing so provides an estimate of the total consumer surplus if the price is P_i.

In a market with homogeneous products, all products are identical and perfectly substitutable. In theory this results in all products having the same price, which is the only price that determines the demand. In a market with differentiated products, products are not perfectly substitutable and prices will vary across products sold in the market. In those markets, the demand for any given product is determined by its price and the prices of potential substitutes. In practice, markets which look homogeneous from a distance will in fact be differentiated to at least some degree when examined closely. Homogeneity may nonetheless be a reasonable modeling approximation in many such situations.

1.1.1.2 The Contribution of Consumer Theory: Deriving Demand

Demand functions are classically derived by using the behavioral assumption that consumers make choices in a way that can be modeled as though they have an objective, to maximize their utility, which they do subject to the constraint that they cannot spend more than they earn. As is well-known to all students of microeconomic theory, the existence of such a utility function describing underlying preferences may in turn be established under some nontrivial conditions (see, for example, Mas-Colell et al. 1995, chapter 1). Maximizing utility is equivalent to choosing the most preferred bundle of goods that a consumer can buy given her wealth.

More specifically, economists have modeled a customer of type (y_i, θ_i) as choosing to maximize her utility subject to the budget constraint that her total expenditure cannot be higher than her income:

$$V_i(p_1, p_2, \dots, p_J, y_i; \theta_i) = \max_{q_1, q_2, \dots, q_J} u_i(q_1, q_2, \dots, q_J; \theta_i)$$
$$\text{subject to } p_1 q_1 + p_2 q_2 + \cdots + p_J q_J \leqslant y_i,$$

where p_j and q_j are prices and quantities of good j, $u_i(q_1, q_2, \dots, q_J; \theta_i)$ is the utility of individual i associated with consuming this vector of quantities, y_i is the disposable income of individual i, and θ_i describes the individual's preference type. In many empirical models using this framework, the "i" subscripts on the V and u functions will be dropped so that all differences between consumers are captured by their type (y_i, θ_i).

Setting up this problem by using a Lagrangian provides the first-order conditions

$$\frac{\partial u_i(q_1, q_2, \dots, q_J, y_i; \theta_i)}{\partial q_j} = \lambda p_j$$
$$\iff \frac{\partial u_i(q_1, q_2, \dots, q_J, y_i; \theta_i)/\partial q_j}{p_j} = \lambda \quad \text{for } j = 1, 2, \dots, J,$$

together with the budget constraint which must also be satisfied. We have a total of $J + 1$ equations in $J + 1$ unknowns: the J quantities and the value of the Lagrange multiplier, λ.

At the optimum, the first-order conditions describe that the Lagrange multiplier is equal to the marginal utility of income. In some cases it will be appropriate to assume a constant marginal utility of income. If so, we assume behavior is described by a utility function with an additively separable good q_1, the price of which is normalized to 1, so that $u_i(q_1, q_2, \dots, q_J; \theta_i) = \tilde{u}_i(q_2, \dots, q_J; \theta_i) + q_1$ and $p_1 = 1$. This numeraire good q_1 is normally termed "money" and its inclusion provides an intuitive interpretation of the first-order conditions. In such circumstances a utility-maximizing consumer will choose a basket of products so that the marginal utility provided by the last euro spent on each product is the same and equal to the marginal utility of money, i.e., 1.[2]

More generally, the solution to the maximization problem describes the individual's demand for each good as a function of the prices of all the goods being sold and also the consumers' income. Indexing goods by j, we can write the individual's demands as

$$q_{ij} = d_{ij}(p_1, p_2, \dots, p_J; y_i; \theta_i), \quad j = 1, 2, \dots, J.$$

A demand function for product j incorporates not only the effect of the own price of j on the quantity demanded but also the effect of disposable income and the price of other products whose supply can affect the quantity of good j purchased. In figure 1.1, a change in the price of j represents a movement along the curve while a change in income or in the price of other related goods will result in a shift or rotation of the demand curve.

[2] This is called a quasi-linear demand function and gives the result because the first-order condition for good 1 collapses to

$$\lambda = \frac{\partial u_i(q_1, q_2, \dots, q_J, y_i; \theta_i)/\partial q_1}{p_1} = \frac{\partial u_i(q_1, q_2, \dots, q_J, y_i; \theta_i)}{\partial q_1},$$

which is the marginal utility of a monetary unit. That in turn is equal to one.

The utility generated by consumption is described by the (direct) utility function, u_i, which relates the level of utility to the goods purchased and is not observed. We know that not all levels of consumption are possible because of the budget constraint and that the consumer will choose the bundle of goods that maximizes her utility. The *indirect* utility function $V_i(p, y_i; \theta_i)$, where $p = (p_1, p_2, \dots, p_J)$, describes the maximum utility a consumer can feasibly obtain at any level of the prices and income. It turns out that the direct and indirect utility functions each can be used to fully describe the other.

In particular, the following result will turn out to be important for writing down demand systems that we estimate.

For every indirect utility function $V_i(p, y_i; \theta_i)$ there is a direct utility function $u_i(q_1, q_2, \dots, q_J; \theta_i)$ that represents the same preferences over goods provided the indirect utility function satisfies some properties, namely that $V_i(p, y_i; \theta_i)$ is continuous in prices and income, nonincreasing in price, nondecreasing in income, quasi-convex in (p, y_i) with any one element normalized to 1 and homogeneous degree zero in (p, y_i).

This result sounds like a purely theoretical one, but it will actually turn out to be very useful in practice. In particular, it will allow us to retrieve the demand function $q_i(p; y_i; \theta_i)$ without actually explicitly solving the utility-maximization problem.[3] Computationally, this is an important simplification.

1.1.1.3 Aggregation and Total Market Size

Individual consumers' demand can be aggregated to form the market aggregate demand by adding the individual quantities demanded by each customer at any given price. If $q_{ij} = d_{ij}(p_1, p_2, \dots, p_J; y_i; \theta_i)$ describes the demand for product j by individual i, then aggregate (total) demand is simply the sum across individuals:

$$Q_j = \sum_{i=1}^{I} q_{ij} = \sum_{i=1}^{I} d_{ij}(p_1, p_2, \dots, p_J, y_i; \theta_i), \quad j = 1, 2, \dots, J,$$

where I is the total number of people who might want to buy the good. Many potential customers will set $q_{ij} = 0$ at least for some sets of prices $p_1, p_2, \dots, p_J$ even though they will have positive purchases at lower prices of some products. In some cases, known as single "discrete choice" models, each individual will only buy at most one unit of the good and so $d_{ij}(p_1, p_2, \dots, p_J, y_i; \theta_i)$ will be an indicator variable taking on the value either zero or one depending on whether individual i buys the good or not at those prices. In such models, the total number of people

[3] This result is known as a "duality" result and is often taught in university courses as a purely theoretical equivalence result. For its very practical implications, see chapter 9, where we describe the use of Roy's identity to generate empirical demand systems from indirect utility functions rather than the direct utility formulation.

who may want to buy the good is also the total potential market size. (We will discuss discrete choice models in more detail in chapter 9.) On the other hand, when individuals can buy more than one unit of the good, to establish the total potential market size we need to evaluate both the total potential number of consumers and also the total number of goods they might buy. Often the total potential number of consumers will be very large—perhaps many millions—and so in many econometric demand models we will approximate the summation with an integral.

In general, total demand for product j will depend on the full distribution of income and consumer tastes in the population. However, under very special assumptions, we will be able to write the aggregate market demand as a function of aggregate income and a limited set of taste parameters only:

$$Q_j = D_j(p_1, p_2, \dots, p_J, Y; \theta),$$

where $Y = \sum_{i=1}^{I} y_i$.

For example, suppose for simplicity that $\theta_i = \mu$ for all individuals and every individual's demand function is "additively separable" in the income variable so that an individual's demand function can be written

$$d_{ij}(p_1, p_2, \dots, p_J, y_i; \theta_i) = d_{ij}^*(p_1, p_2, \dots, p_J; \mu) + \alpha_j y_i,$$

where α_j is a parameter common to all individuals, then aggregate demand for product j will clearly only depend on aggregate income. Such a demand function implies that, given the prices of goods, an increase in income will have an effect on demand that is exactly the same no matter what the level of the prices of all of the goods in the market. Vice versa, an increase in the prices will have the same effect whatever the level of income.[4]

The study of the conditions under which we can aggregate demand functions and express them as a function of characteristics of the income distribution such as the sum of individual incomes is called the study of aggregability.[5] Lessons from that literature motivate the use of particular functional forms for demand systems in empirical work such as the almost ideal demand system (AIDS[6]). In general, when building empirical models we may well want to allow market demand to depend on other statistics from the income distribution besides just the total income. For example, we might think demand for a product depends on total income in the population but also the variance, skewness, or kurtosis of the income distribution. Intuitively, this is fairly clear since if a population were made up of 1,000 people

[4] If consumer types are heterogeneous but are not observed by researchers, then an empirical aggregate demand model will typically assume a parametric distribution for consumer types in a population, $f_\theta(\theta; \mu)$. In that case, the aggregate demand model will depend on parameters μ of the distribution of consumer types. We will explore such models in chapter 9.

[5] For a technical discussion of the founding works, see the various papers by W. M. Gorman collected in Gorman (1995). More recent work includes Lewbel (1989).

[6] An unfortunate acronym, which has led some authors to describe the model as the nearly ideal demand system (NIDS).

making €1bn and everyone else making €10,000, then sales of €15,000 cars would be at most 1,000. On the other hand, the same total income divided more equally could certainly generate sales of more than 1,000. (For recent work, see, for example, Lewbel (2003) and references therein.)

1.1.2 Demand Elasticities

Elasticities in general, and demand elasticities in particular, turn out to be very important for lots of areas of competition policy. The reason is that the "price elasticity of demand" provides us with a unit-free measure of the consumer demand response to a price increase.[7] The way in which demand changes when prices go up will evidently be important for firms when setting prices to maximize profits and that fact makes demand elasticities an essential part of, for example, merger simulation models.

1.1.2.1 Definition

The most useful measurement of the consumer sensitivity to changes in prices is the "own-price" elasticity of demand. As the name suggests, the own-price elasticity of demand measures the sensitivity of demand to a change in the good's own-price and is defined as

$$\eta_{jj} = \frac{\%\Delta Q_j}{\%\Delta P_j} = \frac{100(\Delta Q_j/Q_j)}{100(\Delta P_j/P_j)}.$$

The demand elasticity expresses the percentage change in quantity that results from a 1% change in prices. Alfred Marshall introduced elasticities to economics and noted that one of their great properties is that they are unit free, unlike prices which are measured in currency (e.g., euros per unit) and quantities (sales volumes) which are measured in a unit of quantity per period, e.g., kilograms per year. In our example in figure 1.1 the demand elasticity for a price increase of 10 leading to a quantity decrease of 5 from the baseline position, where $P = 60$ and $Q = 20$, is $\eta_{jj} = (-5/20)/(10/60) = -1.5$.

For very small variations in prices, the demand elasticity can be expressed by using the slope of the demand curve times the ratio of prices to quantities. A mathematical result establishes that this can also be written as the derivative with respect to the logarithm of price of the log transformation of demand curve:

$$\eta_{jj} = \frac{P_j}{Q_j}\frac{\partial Q_j}{\partial P_j} = \frac{\partial \ln Q_j}{\partial \ln P_j}.$$

[7] The term "elasticity" is sometimes used as shorthand for "price elasticity of demand," which in turn is shorthand for "the elasticity of demand with respect to prices." We will sometimes resort to the same shorthand terminology since the full form is unwieldy. That said, we do so with the caveat that, since elasticities can be both "with respect to" and "of" anything, the terms elasticity or "demand elasticity" are inherently ambiguous and therefore somewhat dangerous. We will, for example, talk about the elasticity of costs with respect to output.

Demand at a particular price point is considered "elastic" when the elasticity is bigger than 1 in absolute value. An elastic demand implies that the change in quantity following a price increase will be larger in percentage terms so that revenues for a seller will fall all else equal. An inelastic demand at a particular price level refers to an elasticity of less than 1 in absolute value and means that a seller could raise revenues by increasing the price provided again that everything else remained the same. The elasticity will generally be dependent on the price level. For this reason, it does not usually makes sense to talk about a given product having an "elastic demand" or an "inelastic demand" but it should be said that it has an "elastic" or "inelastic" demand at a particular price or volume level, e.g., at current prices. The elasticities calculated for an aggregate demand are the market elasticities for a given product.

1.1.2.2 Substitutes and Complements

The *cross-price elasticity* of demand expresses the effect of a change in price of some other good k on the demand for good j. A new, higher, price for p_k may, for instance, induce some consumers to change their purchases of product j. If consumers increase their purchases of product j when p_k goes up, we will call products j and k demand *substitutes* or just substitutes for short.

Two DVD players of different brands are substitutes if the demand for one of them falls as the price of the other decreases because people switch across to the now relatively cheaper DVD player. Similarly, a decrease in prices of air travel may reduce the demand for train trips, holding the price of train trips constant.

On the other hand, the new higher price of k may induce consumers to buy less of good j. For example, if the price of ski passes increases, perhaps fewer folk want to go skiing and so the demand for skiing gear goes down. Similarly, if the price of cars increases, the demand for gasoline may well fall. When this happens we will call products j and k demand *complements* or just complements for short. In this case, the customer's valuation of good j increases when good k has been purchased:[8]

$$\eta_{jk} = \begin{cases} \dfrac{P_k}{Q_j}\dfrac{\partial Q_j}{\partial P_k} > 0 \quad \text{and} \quad \dfrac{\partial Q_j}{\partial P_k} > 0 & \text{if products are substitutes,} \\[2ex] \dfrac{P_k}{Q_j}\dfrac{\partial Q_j}{\partial P_k} < 0 \quad \text{and} \quad \dfrac{\partial Q_j}{\partial P_k} < 0 & \text{if products are complements.} \end{cases}$$

[8] Generally, this terminology is satisfactory for individual demand functions but can become unsatisfactory for aggregate demand functions, where it may or may not be the case that $\partial Q_j/\partial P_k = \partial Q_k/\partial P_j$ since in that case the complementary (or substitute) links between the products may be of differing strengths. See, in particular, the discussion in the U.K. Competition Commission's investigation into Payment Protection Insurance (PPI) at, for example, www.competition-commission.org.uk/inquiries/ref2007/ppi/index.htm. In that case, some evidence showed that loans and insurance covering unemployment, accident, and sickness were complementary only in the sense that the demand for insurance was affected by the credit price while the demand for credit appeared largely unaffected by the price of the accompanying PPI. That investigation (chaired by one of the authors) found it useful to introduce a distinction between one-sided and two-sided complementarity. An analogous distinction could be made for asymmetric demand substitution patterns.

1.1.2.3 Short Term versus Long Term

Most demand functions are static demand functions—they consider how consumers allocate their demand across products at a given point in time. In general, particularly in markets for durable goods, or goods which are storable, we will expect to have important intertemporal linkages in demand. The demand for cars today may depend on tomorrow's price as well as today's price. If so, demand elasticities in the long run may well be different from the demand elasticities in the short run. In some cases the price elasticity of demand will be higher in the short run. This happens for instance when there is a temporary decrease in prices such as a sale, when consumers will want to take advantage of the temporarily better prices to stock up, increasing the demand in the short run but decreasing it at a later stage (see, for example, Hendel and Nevo 2006a,b). In this case, the elasticity measured over a short period of time would overestimate the actual elasticity in the long run. The opposite can also occur, so that the long-run elasticity at a given price is higher than the short-run elasticity. For instance, the demand for petrol is fairly inelastic in the short run, since people have already invested in their cars and need to get to work. On the other hand, in the long run people can adjust to higher petrol prices by downsizing their car.

1.1.3 Introduction to Common Demand Specifications

We often want to estimate the effect of price on quantity demanded. To do so we will typically write down a model of demand whose parameters can be estimated. We can then use the estimated model to quantify the impact of a change in price on the quantity being demanded. With enough data and a general enough model our results will not be sensitive to this choice. However, with realistic sample sizes, we often have to estimate models that impose a considerable amount of structure on our data sets and so the results can be sensitive to the demand specification chosen. That unfortunate reality means one should choose demand specifications with particular care. In particular, we need to be clear about the properties of the estimated model that are being determined by the data and the properties that are simply assumed whatever the estimated parameter values. An important aspect of the demand function will be its curvature and how this changes as we move along the curve. The curvature of the demand curve will determine the elasticity and therefore the impact of a change in price on quantity demanded.

1.1.3.1 Linear Demand

The linear demand is the simplest demand specification. The linear demand function can be written $Q_i = a - bP$ with analogous inverse demand curve

$$P = \frac{a}{b} - \frac{1}{b} Q_i.$$

In each case, a and b are parameters of the model (see figure 1.2).

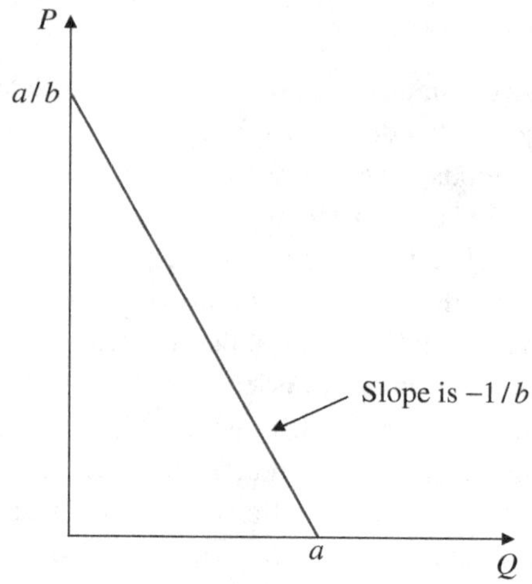

Figure 1.2. The linear demand function.

The slope of the inverse demand curve is

$$\frac{\partial P}{\partial Q} = \frac{-1}{b}.$$

The intercepts are a/b at $Q = 0$ and a at $P = 0$. The linear demand implies that the marginal valuation of the good keeps decreasing at a constant rate so that, even if the price is 0 the consumer will not "buy" more than a units. Since most analysis in competition cases happens at positive prices and quantities of the goods, estimation results will not generally be sensitive to assumptions made about the shape of the demand curve at the extreme ends of the demand function.[9] The elasticity for the linear demand function is

$$\eta = (-b)\frac{P}{Q}.$$

Note that, unlike the slope, the elasticity of demand varies along the linear demand curve. Elasticities generally increase in magnitude as we move to lower quantity levels because the variations in quantity resulting from a price increase are larger as a percentage of initial sales volumes. Because of its lack of curvature, the linear demand will sometimes produce higher elasticities compared with other demand specifications and therefore sometimes predicts lower price increases in response to mergers and higher quantity adjustments in response to increases in price. As an extreme example, consider an alternative inverse demand function which asymptotes as we move leftward in the graph toward the price axis where $Q = 0$. In that case, only very large price increases will drive significant quantity changes at low levels of

[9] We rarely get data from a market where goods have been sold at zero prices. As we discuss below, calculations such as consumer surplus on the other hand may sometimes be very sensitive to such assumptions.

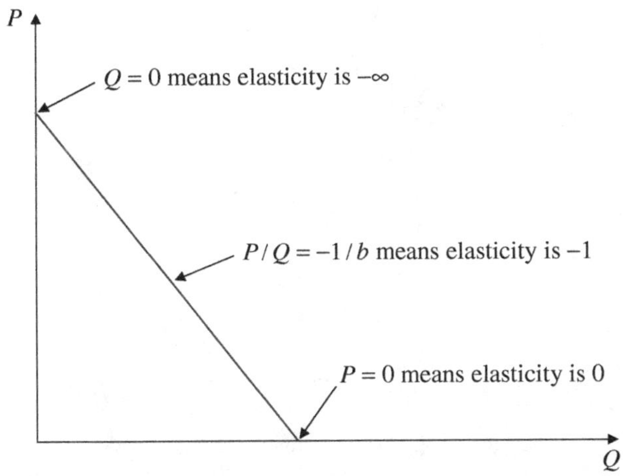

Figure 1.3. Demand elasticity values in the linear demand curve.

output or, analogously, small price changes will drive only small quantity changes, i.e., a low elasticity of demand. An example in the form of the log-linear demand curve is provided below. In contrast, the linear demand curve generates an arbitrarily large elasticity of demand (large in magnitude) as we move toward the price axis on the graph (see figure 1.3).

1.1.3.2 Log-Linear Demand

The one exception to the rule that elasticities depend on the price level is the log-linear demand function, which has the form

$$Q = D(P) = e^{a} P^{-b}.$$

Taking natural logarithms turns the expression into a demand equation that is linear in its parameters:

$$\ln Q = a - b \ln P.$$

This specification is particularly useful because many of the estimation techniques used in practice are most easily applied to models which are linear in their parameters. Expressing effects in terms of percentages also provides us with results that are easily interpreted. The inverse demand which corresponds to figure 1.4 can be written

$$P = P(Q) = (e^{-a} Q)^{-1/b}.$$

When prices increase toward infinity, if $b > 0$ then the quantity demanded tends toward 0 but never reaches it. An assumption embodied in the log-linear model is that there will always be some demand for the good, no matter how expensive it is. Similarly, the demand tends to infinity when the price of the good approaches 0.

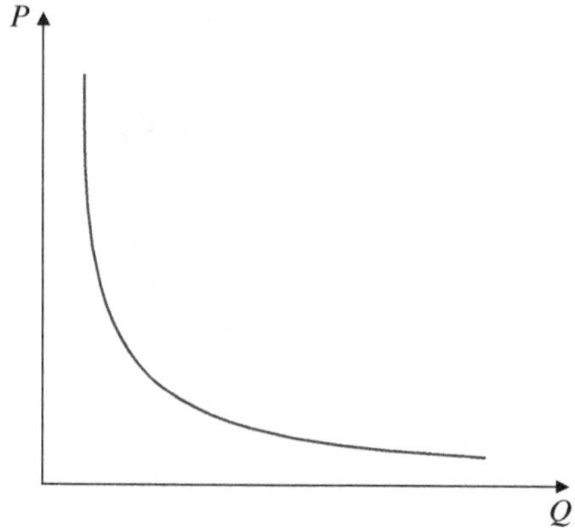

Figure 1.4. The log-linear demand curve.

As a product approaches the zero price, consumers are willing to have an unlimited amount of it:

$$\lim_{P\to\infty} D(P) = e^{a} \lim_{P\to\infty} P^{-b} = 0,$$

$$\lim_{Q\to\infty} P(Q) = \lim_{Q\to\infty} (e^{-a}Q)^{-1/b} = 0.$$

The log-linear demand also has a constant elasticity over the entire demand curve, which is a unique characteristic of this functional form:

$$\eta = \frac{\partial \ln Q}{\partial \ln P} = -b.$$

As a result the log-linear demand model is sometimes referred to as the constant elasticity or iso-elastic demand model. Price changes do not affect the demand elasticity, which means that if we have one estimate of the elasticity, at a given price, this estimate will—rather conveniently but perhaps optimistically—be the same for all price points. Of course, if in truth the price sensitivity of demand does depend on the price level, then this iso-elasticity assumption will be a strong one imposed by the model whatever values we estimate its parameters a and b to take on. Empirically, given enough data, we can tell apart data generated by the linear demand model and the log-linear model since movements in supply at different price levels will provide us with information about the slope of demand and hence elasticities. Formally, we can use a "Box–Cox" test to distinguish the models (see, for example, Box and Cox 1964).

1.1.3.3 Discrete Choice Demand Models

Consumer choice situations can be sometimes best represented as zero–one "discrete" decisions between different alternative options. Consider, for example, buying a car. The choice is "which car" rather than "how-much car." In such situations, a discrete choice demand model is typically used to capture consumer behavior. These models allow utility maximization to take place over existing options. One of the most popular discrete choice demand models is the multinomial logit (MNL) demand model, sometimes called "logit" for brevity (see McFadden 1973).

The MNL demand model assumes that the utility provided to a consumer who chooses to buy product j takes the form[10]

$$U_{ij} = \alpha x_j + \beta p_j + \varepsilon_{ij},$$

where $j = 1, \dots, J$ indicates the product and i indicates a particular individual. The utility provided is determined by the good's characteristics x_j, the price p_j, and by an element of utility ε_{ij} which indicates the particular taste of individual i for good j. Product attributes provide utility to the consumer while higher prices reduce utility so β will typically be negative. As before, each individual is assumed to pick the option which provides her with the most utility, $\max_{j=1,\dots,J} U_{ij}$. As before, aggregate demand in such situations is the sum of all individual demands. The MNL model simply makes a particularly convenient set of assumptions about the form of "consumer heterogeneity," i.e., the way in which one consumer is different from others in the population. In the MNL model, consumers are assumed to be identical except for the random additively separable terms ε_{ij}. A more detailed discussion of the logit model and other discrete choice models of demand is presented in chapter 9.

For now we note that we will see that in some cases estimation of MNL amounts to running a linear regression. Elasticities on the other hand generally need to be calculated as a second step once the parameters have been estimated. Discrete choice demand models are typically nonlinear and although some of them are mathematically intractable others are highly tractable.

1.1.4 Consumer Welfare

Many competition authorities around the world, at least in principle, use a "consumer welfare" standard to evaluate policy and firm behavior. Such a standard is not uncontroversial since some economists argue that there should be equal (or at least some) weight assigned to producer and consumer welfare with redistributions if desired achieved by other means such as taxation.[11] Whichever welfare standard

---

[10] More precisely, these are called "conditional indirect utilities." The reason is that it is the indirect utility obtained if product j is chosen, i.e., conditional on choosing product j. We will see in chapter 9 that these choice models can be motivated by using our familiar (utility maximization subject to a budget constraint) model by imposing constraints on the consumer's choice set. The "indirect" comes from the fact that the utility is specified as a function of price.

[11] We do not discuss the relative merits of arguments in this debate here, though it is certainly an important and interesting one. The proponents of consumer surplus standards usually cite a political economy reason: that consumers are large in number and have only very diffuse incentives to intervene individually in making markets work for them while large firms have far less diffuse incentives to extract surplus. The economics of Harbinger triangles suggests that pure static deadweight losses are sometimes "small." Putting deadweight losses to one side, standard monopoly pricing results in a transfer of surplus

is used, we must say what we mean by "consumer welfare" and generally, in practice, competition authorities often mean an approximation to consumer welfare, "aggregate consumer surplus," a term which we define below.[12] Generally, actions that permanently result in an increase of market output, a decrease in prices, or an increase in the customers' valuation of the product will increase "consumer surplus" and so are deemed beneficial for consumers. If firms provide tax revenue that is subsequently redistributed in part, or individuals invest in companies either directly or via pension funds, then the distinction between individual (rather than consumer) welfare and producer welfare is less clear cut than the consumer–producer distinction. Democratic governments that enact competition laws presumably ultimately care (at least) about all their citizens, which some argue means there should be at least some weight for shareholders via a weight on producer surplus. Such weight would probably lead to a less interventionist approach than a "pure" consumer welfare standard. Even within a consumer welfare standard, there are significant choices to be made. For example, to operationalize a "true" consumer welfare measure, an agency would need to decide how careful to be when weighting individuals' utilities by their respective marginal utilities of income. Doing so, or not, could lead to profoundly different practical outcomes in a competition agency. In particular, weighing consumers according to their marginal utilities of income may lead an agency to be involved in more intervention to protect poorer consumers, even potentially at the cost of richer consumers. Some in the competition policy world consider such income redistributions to be more in the realm of social policy than competition policy. Others disagree that an easy distinction is possible. For a concrete example where such issues might arise consider price discrimination for a good where inelastic demanders tend to be poorer. If so, price discrimination could involve poor customers paying high prices while rich consumers pay lower prices. A recent example, is electricity in the United Kingdom, where many poorer customers are, to an extent, "locked in" to prepay meters and hence are charged more per unit than their richer neighbors who pay monthly and can change provider. A competition agency acting to stop price discrimination would typically result in richer customers paying more and poorer customers paying less. Absent clear governmental instructions on the framework for analysis, an important question is whether a competition agency is in a suitable position to make such (distributional and hence political) judgments.

---

from consumers to producers. In addition, the evidence suggests that there are potentially important dynamic effects of competition on productivity, including cost reductions and also welfare gains resulting from increased variety and improved quality. Quantifying such effects is tremendously difficult but also potentially tremendously important. Efforts to do so include Nickell (1996) and more recently Aghion and Griffith (2008). The link between competition and productivity is important in competition policy but also in international trade and so much of the available evidence comes from that field. See, for example, the contributions and literature surveyed by Jensen et al. (2007).

[12] Many current authors attribute "consumer surplus" to Marshall (1890). However, Hotelling (1938) attributes "consumer surplus" to an engineer, Jules Dupuit, in his work of 1844. See the discussion in Hotelling (1938).

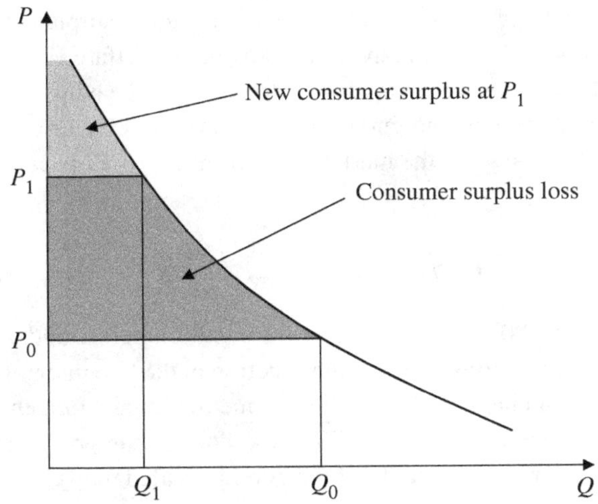

Figure 1.5. Reduction in consumer surplus following a price increase.

We note that some regulators do have legal obligations to protect consumers generally but also vulnerable consumer groups specifically (e.g., the water regulator in the United Kingdom, Ofwat).

1.1.4.1 Consumer Surplus

The consumer surplus derived from a unit of consumption is the difference between the price that a consumer would be willing to pay for it and what she actually pays, i.e., the market price. Since the demand curve describes the maximum that a consumer would have been willing to pay for each unit, the consumer surplus is simply the difference between the demand curve and the price actually paid. Every unit being consumed generates consumer surplus and so the total consumer surplus is the area below the demand curve that falls above the price paid for the good. Figure 1.5 represents the loss of consumer surplus after prices increase from P_0 to P_1, reducing demand.

1.1.4.2 Quantification of Consumer Surplus

If $P(Q)$ denotes the inverse demand curve, calculation of consumer surplus at price P_0 and quantity Q_0 involves the following calculation:

$$\mathrm{CS}_0 = \int_0^{Q_0} (P(Q) - P_0)\,\mathrm{d}Q = \int_0^{Q_0} P(Q)\,\mathrm{d}Q - P_0 Q_0.$$

Welfare measurements can be very sensitive to the demand specification chosen, so in practical circumstances one will sometimes need to examine several plausible specifications and describe the range of potential outcomes given assumptions about demand. In particular, the behavior of the inverse demand curve $P(Q)$ close to

$Q = 0$ can have a large impact on the value of consumer surplus obtained and it is something about which we will rarely have any data. Welfare estimates of changes within the realm of experience will tend to rely less heavily on our underlying assumptions about the demand curve (e.g., whether it is linear or log-linear). The welfare effect of a change in the market price from P_0 to P_1 is calculated by

$$\begin{aligned}\Delta\mathrm{CS} &= \mathrm{CS}_1 - \mathrm{CS}_0 \\ &= \int_0^{Q_1} P(Q)\,\mathrm{d}Q - P_1 Q_1 - \int_0^{Q_0} P(Q)\,\mathrm{d}Q + P_0 Q_0,\end{aligned}$$

where the subscripts "0" and "1" indicate the situation before and after the change. For some policy evaluations, the demand function in the two integrals will be different. For example, in chapter 10 we will examine the impact of a change in vertical ownership arrangements in the cable TV market on consumer welfare. Theory suggests that both the price and quality of the good provided may change as a result of the change in market structure.

One approach to estimating consumer surplus is to estimate the demand curve. However, there are also alternatives when evaluating welfare outcomes. For example, a simple technique for approximating deadweight loss in practice involves the method originally used by Harberger (1954) in his classic cross-industry study of the magnitude of deadweight loss. Deadweight loss is the surplus that is lost to consumers and not transferred to producers when prices increase, and is sometimes known as the Harberger triangle. Since consumers lose the surplus and producers do not gain it, it represents a fall in total welfare. In that study Harberger observed

(i) a measure of "excess" profits allowing for a 10.4% "normal" rate of return on capital in the calculation of total costs, $C(Q)$, $\Pi = P(Q)Q - C(Q)$, and

(ii) a measure of sales $R = P(Q)Q$ for each industry.

Our data tell us that

$$\frac{\Pi}{R} = \frac{P(Q)Q - C(Q)}{P(Q)Q} = \frac{P(Q) - AC(Q)}{P(Q)}$$

so that the "return on sales" ratio gives us the percentage monopolistic price markup (the Lerner index) under either the assumption that all industries neither benefit from economies of scale nor suffer from diseconomies of scale so that average and marginal costs were equal or alternatively if we measure monopoly distortions only relative to a "second best" welfare outcome where firms must price to make nonnegative returns because lump-sum transfers are not possible.

The elasticity of demand then tells us how much sales will fall following such a percentage price increase. The deadweight loss (Harberger triangle) is then estimated as one half of the price change times the predicted quantity change, each in levels rather than percentages, i.e.,

$$\text{Deadweight Loss} = \frac{(P - AC)\Delta Q}{2} = \frac{\Pi^2(-\eta)}{2(PQ)},$$

where the former is just the definition of deadweight loss from monopolistic pricing under our assumptions while the latter involves only our "data." The equality can be seen by expanding and canceling terms since[13]

$$\frac{(P - AC)\Delta Q}{2} = \frac{((P - AC)Q)^2}{2(PQ)} \frac{(-\Delta Q/Q)}{(P - AC)/P} = \frac{\Pi^2 \eta}{2(PQ)}.$$

Harberger assumed that all industry price elasticities of demand η were -1. One can also evaluate the transfer involved from consumers to firms as simply the "excess" profits being earned. Thus, for example, Harberger had an estimate of the excess profits (averaged over the period 1924–28) for the bakery products industry of \$17 million and an estimate of excess profits/sales, and therefore markups above average costs, of $100\Pi/R = 5.3\%$. Reverse engineering Harberger's calculation we learn that revenues were $R = \Pi/0.053 = \$320.8$ million and we can then calculate that

$$\text{Deadweight Loss} = \frac{\Pi^2(-\eta)}{2(PQ)} = \frac{17^2(1)}{2(320.8)} = 0.45 \text{ million},$$

about half a million dollars on sales of \$321 million. The transfer from consumers to firms of course involves all the \$17 million in "excess" profits, so that the order of magnitude of consumer surplus loss is greater than that of the deadweight loss. Notice finally that the more elastic demand is, for a given level of excess profits, the greater the expected deadweight loss.[14]

Such an exercise is not easy in a cross-industry study and, for example, it is striking that many of Harberger's estimates of excess profits (and prices) were in fact negative, suggesting that prices in many industries were "too low" rather than "too high." He derives the "normal" profit rate by allowing for a 10.4% return on capital employed, which he calculates by using the simple average of profit rates across industries in his study. In a modern application we would usually want to use a more sophisticated approach to the "cost of capital" which adjusts for risk across the various industries. (See, for example, the discussion on the weighted average cost of capital (WACC) in chapter 3.)

Consumer welfare calculations can be a useful tool for a rough approximation of an effect but given the crucial importance of assumptions, for which there is sometimes little factual evidence, the impact on consumer welfare is currently sometimes not actively quantified during investigations but rather qualitatively assessed in view of the conduct's expected impact on prices, output, and other variables relevant for consumer valuation.

---

[13] In this formula, η is measured as the percentage change in quantities that results from the percentage change in prices above cost, i.e., $(P - AC)/P$.

[14] In the U.K. Competition Commission's investigation into payment protection insurance, excess profits from PPI were estimated to be £1.4 billion on sales of £3.5 billion. If the price elasticity of demand were -1.5, then such a calculation suggests a deadweight loss of $(1{,}400)^2(1.5)/(2 \times 3{,}500) =$ £420 million. Harberger triangles need not always be small.

There are a number of related notions of consumer welfare in addition to consumer surplus and in fact consumer surplus is best considered an imperfect approximation for an "exact" welfare measure for a given individual. We may alternatively use equivalent variation (EV) or compensating variation (CV) to measure welfare "exactly" in a continuous choice demand context, while researchers also use expected maximum utility (EMU) in the discrete choice demand context. Compensating variation calculates the change in income that must be given to or taken from a consumer *after* a price change in order to bring her back to her previous utility level. The equivalent variation is the change in income (positive or negative) that one should give to or take from our consumer *before* a price change to give her the same utility level before and after a price change.[15] Marshall showed that consumer surplus will equal compensating variation if a consumer has a constant marginal utility of income.

In some cases, these objects are easy to calculate directly, for example, among other results Hausman (1981) provides analytic expressions for CV that arise from a single inside good (and one outside good) linear demand curve of the form we graphed in figure 1.3 (Hausman 1981; Hurwicz and Uzawa 1971).[16] This debate around approximating consumer welfare measures for a given individual is at one level only for the perfectionist; the consensus from the literature appears to be that measures of consumer surplus changes from price rises do not typically appear particularly sensitive to the approximation which motivates the use of consumer surplus. On the other hand, the approximation error can be a significant amount relative to a deadweight loss calculation. Of course, in interpreting such results it is important to keep in mind that authors will often assume that market demand curves can be rationalized as if they were a representative consumer's demand curve. As we have described, representative agent demand models require strong and probably unrealistic assumptions. In a more general model where aggregate demand depends on the distribution of income (and perhaps also on other elements of consumer heterogeneity), CV and EV measures can be calculated for each individual and then aggregated across individuals. One interpretation of this "result" is that authors must be very careful with deadweight loss calculations. Another far more controversial interpretation is that the classical deadweight losses are only of a similar order

[15] To illustrate the difference for the classic continuous choice demand case, readers may recall the difference between Marshall's demand curve, which is a function of price for a given level of income $d(p, y)$ and the Hicksian demand, which is described as a function of price for a given level of utility, $d(p, u)$ (Hicks 1956). See the discussion in, for example, Deaton and Muellbauer (1980b, chapter 7). For more on practical methods to compute exact welfare measures, see Vartia (1983). We follow practice rather than theory in this section, but also point the reader to Breslaw and Smith (1995), who very usefully provide computer code for approximating CV using Aptech's GAUSS matrix programming language using a method which avoids solving differential equations (à la the method suggested in Hausman (1981)).

[16] In looking at Hausman (1981) it is important to recall that a numerical error means he was far more negative about consumer surplus as an approximation than the actual results suggested (see Irvine and Sims 1998). See also Hausman and Newey (1995).

to our approximation error for welfare calculations and perhaps are therefore best considered typically small.[17]

This brings to a conclusion our brief review of the concepts from demand theory that are used daily in competition policy analysis. We will discuss each of these concepts in greater depth in future chapters, but next we turn to costs and production.

1.2 Technological Determinants of Market Structure

Firm decisions are an important driver of market structure, performance, and conduct and so, if we are to understand market outcomes, we must first understand firm decisions. In turn, if profits are an important driver of firm decisions, then we must understand the drivers of profits, namely revenues and costs. Demand analysis provides a toolbox for analyzing firm revenues. We now turn to the economists' toolbox for analyzing information on the cost side of the market.

Economists examining firms' cost structure, efficiency, and productivity have found three interrelated types of models particularly useful: production functions, cost functions, and input demand equations. We describe each below. We will see that each contains information about both technological possibilities for combining inputs into outputs and also about the cost of doing so. Along the way these tools facilitate an analysis of firm efficiency and productivity.

1.2.1 Production Functions

To produce output the firm must combine inputs according to a technological and/or managerial process. A production function describes the output that can be achieved by efficiently combining inputs.[18] It reflects technological reality and is expressed as $Q = f(K_1, \dots, K_n; \alpha_1, \dots, \alpha_m, u)$, where K_i are inputs, α_j are technological parameters, and u is a firm-specific (or plant- or occasionally process-specific) productivity indicator. The causes of the unknown (to the researcher) productivity indicator u are often of great interest as well as the differences in productivity across firms or plants. Whatever the causes, a firm with a higher u can for some reason combine inputs to produce more output than a firm of lower productivity. Reasons

[17] If competition authorities operated a total welfare standard, one might conclude that these short-run effects are small and antitrust intervention should therefore be highly limited. On the other hand, even if this were true, if competition authority interventions affect the incentives to reduce costs or to compete by introducing new or better products, then the relevant consumer (and total) surplus gains can be extremely large in the longer term. Moreover, there are examples where even the short-run measures of deadweight losses will be large.

[18] Recall that production possibility sets capture the ways in which inputs can feasibly be turned into outputs. In contrast, production frontiers capture the ways in which inputs can efficiently be turned into output, that is, the smallest levels of inputs required to produce a given level of output. Under technical assumptions, production functions capture the information in the production possibility frontier, that is, they describe the efficient ways of combining inputs to produce output.

might include the firms' respective levels of know-how and the managerial quality of their production processes.

When choosing a specification for a production function, it is important to be aware of the implications of a given functional form in terms of assumptions being made about the actual production process. Some functional forms are more flexible than others in that different values for the parameters can accommodate many different technological realities. Other functional forms, on the other hand, describe very specific production processes. Obviously, we are attempting to capture reality so our production function specification should be capable of doing so. To illustrate, in this section we first introduce some terminology and then we present two classic examples: the fixed-proportions technology and the Cobb–Douglas production function.

1.2.1.1 Terminology

Isoquants. The extent to which technology allows different inputs to substitute for one another is important for both the mix of inputs a firm will choose and also the amount of output a firm can produce. We call a contour describing the combinations of inputs that produce any given level of output an isoquant, where "iso" means "same" (so isoquant means same quantity). An example of an isoquant is provided in figure 1.6.

Marginal Product. The marginal product of an input is the increase in output due to an increase in that input alone. For example, the marginal product of input K_i is defined as $\text{MP}_{K_i} = \partial Q/\partial K_i$.

Marginal Rate of Technical Substitution. The slope of an isoquant tells us how much we need to increase one input to compensate for the decrease in another input if we want to maintain the same output level. This is called the marginal rate of technical substitution (MRTS):

$$\text{MRTS}_{jk} = \frac{\partial Q/\partial K_j}{\partial Q/\partial K_k}.$$

Returns to Scale. We sometimes consider what happens to the amount of output produced, $f(\lambda K_1, \dots, \lambda K_n; \alpha_1, \dots, \alpha_m, u)$, when all inputs are increased by a factor λ. For example, we might perhaps consider $\lambda = 2$ in which case we are considering what happens to output if we double all inputs. If output also increases by λ, then we say that the production function exhibits constant returns to scale (CRS). If output increases by more than λ, we say there are increasing returns to scale (IRS), and if output increases by less than λ, we say there are decreasing returns to scale (DRS).

There are increasing returns to scale in the transportation of oil and that is why supertankers exist. To see why, consider that an approximate formula for the volume

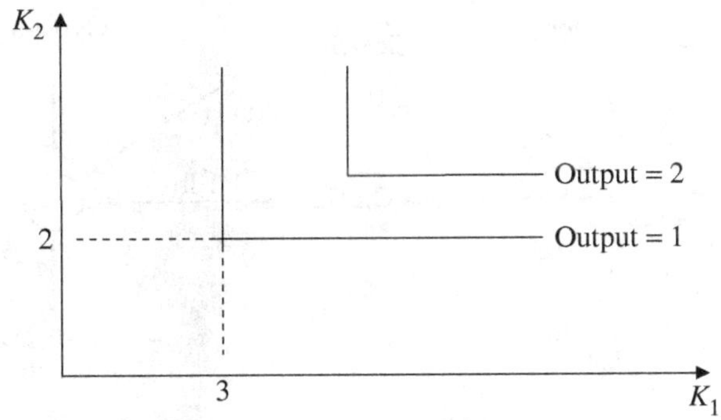

Figure 1.6. Isoquants for the fixed-proportions technology.

of oil that an oil tanker can carry is length × height × width. That means to double the volume of oil carried we need to double either the length, the height, or the width but definitely not all three. That in turn means we do not need to double the amount of steel used to build the oil tanker if we want to double the amount of oil that can be carried from one place to another. Similarly, we may not need to double the size of the crew.

Industries which will tend to exhibit CRS include those where we can build identical plants next to each other.

On the other hand, if it takes more and more inputs to produce a single extra unit of output, then we say there are DRS. Continuing our previous example, even if in principle there are CRS available from building identical plants next to one another, if management and coordination of all those plants become ever more complex as the firm grows, we may nonetheless suffer from DRS at the firm level.

Formally, assume a production function $Q = f(K_1, K_2; u)$.

If $f(\lambda K_1, \lambda K_2; u) = \lambda f(K_1, K_2; u)$, there are CRS.

If $f(\lambda K_1, \lambda K_2; u) > \lambda f(K_1, K_2; u)$, there are IRS.

If $f(\lambda K_1, \lambda K_2; u) < \lambda f(K_1, K_2; u)$, there are DRS.

The nature of returns to scale can differ at different levels of production. Indeed, one reason economies of scale can be important in competition policy is that returns to scale determine the minimum efficient scale of operation and so may help evaluate an "efficiency" defense in a merger. Alternatively, a monopoly may argue that it is a natural monopoly and therefore should not be broken up during a competition investigation.

1.2.1.2 Fixed-Proportions Technology

The fixed-proportions production technology provides an important if somewhat extreme example. It implies that to produce output we need to use inputs in fixed

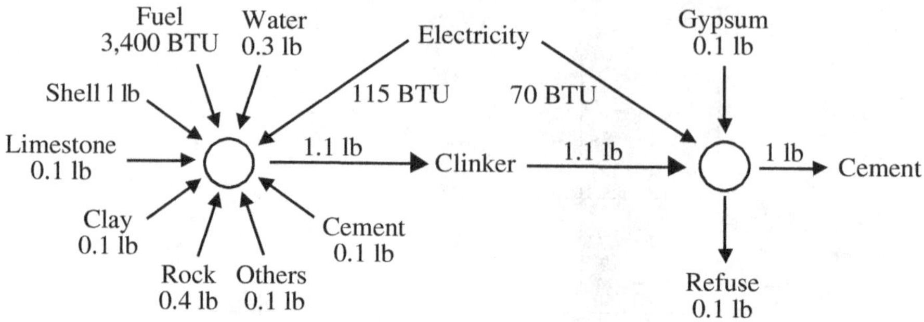

Figure 1.7. Zero substitution between inputs: an approximate recipe for portland cement. (Cement kilns are easy to spot—they are usually long cylindrical tubes which can be 750 feet long.) *Source*: Derived from a graph provided by Tom Stoker, MIT. Numbers amended to protect confidentiality.

proportions, that is, there is no way to substitute among the inputs to produce output. Suppose, for instance, a unit of output Q can only be produced with three units of K_1 and two units of K_2, where K_1 and K_2 are inputs. The production function is expressed by

$$Q = \min\{\tfrac{1}{3}K_1; \tfrac{1}{2}K_2\}.$$

The isoquants are shown in figure 1.6.

We see that in this example unless we have additional K_1 available we cannot increase production no matter how much available K_2 there is as there is no substitutability between the inputs. Such a production function could be that of the perfect martini, where gin and vermouth are combined in fixed proportions: with each martini requiring 75 ml of gin and 5 ml of vermouth.[19]

Another example of such a production function is provided by the recipe for portland cement (see figure 1.7). In this case, the mapping of isoquants is not possible on a two-dimensional scale but the characteristics of the production function are similar. Whenever a production process involves following a fixed "recipe" one must increase all inputs by a given factor to increase output.

Note that in this example of zero substitution among inputs, the marginal product of an extra unit of input holding fixed the amount of all other inputs is zero. When working with a fixed-coefficients production technology, to produce some more output we need more of each of the inputs.

1.2.1.3 The Cobb–Douglas Production Function

The Cobb–Douglas production function is frequently used for its flexibility and convenient properties. This function is named after C. W. Cobb and P. H. Douglas, who introduced it in 1928 in a study on the evolution of output, capital, and labor

[19]Winston Churchill is reputed to have had a slightly different fixed-proportions production function for the perfect dry martini, one which involved only a "glance" at the vermouth.

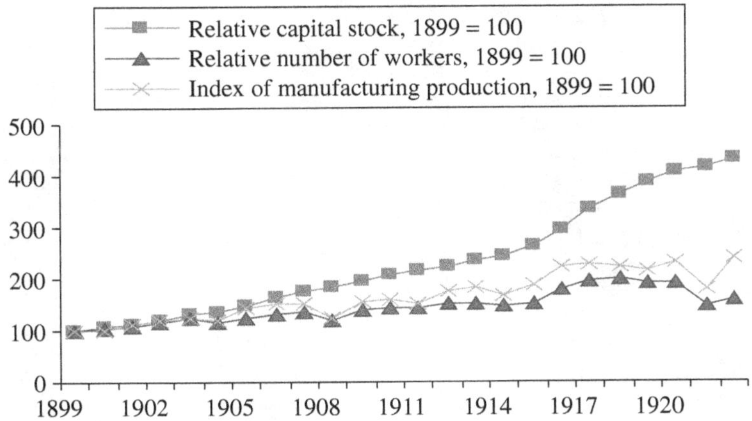

Figure 1.8. A plot of Cobb and Douglas's data.

in the United States between 1899 and 1924. Their time series evidence examines the relationship between aggregate inputs of labor and capital and national output during a period of fast growing U.S. labor and even faster growing capital stock. Their data are plotted in figure 1.8.[20]

Cobb and Douglas designed a function that could capture the relationship between output and inputs while allowing for substitution and which could be both empirically relevant and mathematically tractable. The Cobb–Douglas production function is defined as follows:

$$Q = a_0 L^{a_L} K^{a_K} u \quad \Longrightarrow \quad \ln Q = \beta_0 + a_L \ln L + a_K \ln K + v,$$

where $v = \ln u$, $\beta_0 = \ln a_0$, and where the parameters (a_0, a_L, a_K) can be easily estimated from the equation once it is log-linearized. As figure 1.9 shows, the isoquants in this function exhibit a convex shape indicating that there is a certain degree of substitution among the inputs.

Marginal products, the increase in production achieved by increasing one unit of an input holding other inputs constant, are defined as follows in a Cobb–Douglas function:

$$\mathrm{MP}_L \equiv \frac{\partial Q}{\partial L} = a_0 a_L L^{a_l - 1} K^{a_K} F^{a_F} u = a_L \frac{Q}{L},$$

$$\mathrm{MP}_K \equiv \frac{\partial Q}{\partial K} = a_0 L^{a_l} a_K K^{a_{K-1}} F^{a_F} u = a_K \frac{Q}{K},$$

so that the marginal rate of technical substitution is

$$\mathrm{MRTS}_{LK} = \frac{\partial Q / \partial L}{\partial Q / \partial K} = \frac{a_L}{a_K} \frac{K}{L}.$$

[20] In their paper (Cobb and Douglas 1928), the authors report the full data set they used.

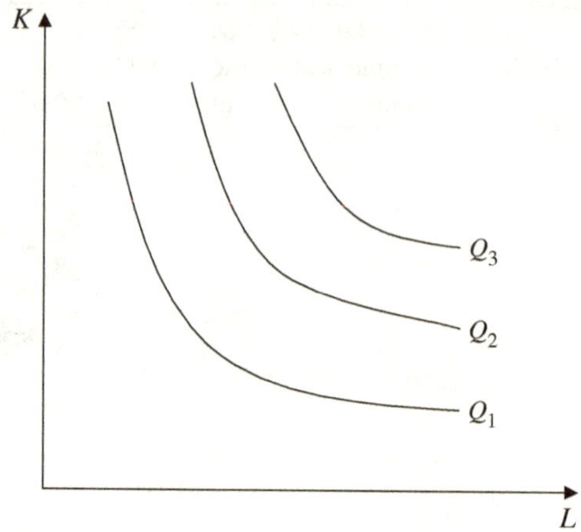

Figure 1.9. Example of isoquants for a Cobb–Douglas function.

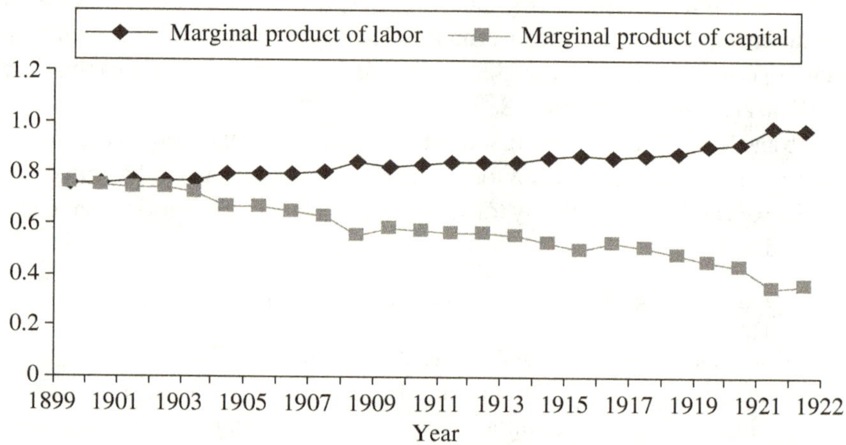

Figure 1.10. Cobb and Douglas's implied marginal products of labor and capital.

Cobb and Douglas's econometric evidence suggested that the increase in labor and particularly capital over time was increasing output, but not proportionately. In particular, as figure 1.10 shows their estimates suggested that the marginal product of capital was declining fast. Naturally, such a conclusion in 1928 would have profound implications for the likelihood of continued large capital flows into the United States.

1.2.2 Cost Functions

A production function describes how much output a firm gets if it uses given levels of inputs. We are directly interested in the cost of producing output, not least to decide how much to produce and as a result it is quite common to estimate cost functions.

Rather surprisingly, under sometimes plausible assumptions, cost functions contain exactly the same information as the production function about the technical possibilities for turning inputs into outputs but require substantially different data sets to estimate. Specifically, assuming that firms minimize costs allows us to exploit the "duality" between production and cost functions to retrieve basically the same information about the nature of technology in an industry.[21]

1.2.2.1 Cost Minimization and the Derivation of Cost Functions

In order to maximize profits, firms are commonly assumed to minimize costs for any given level of output given the constraint imposed by the production function with regards to the relation between inputs and output. Although the production function aims to capture the technological reality of an industry, profit-maximizing and cost-minimizing behaviors are explicit behavioral assumptions about the ways in which firms are going to take decisions. As such those behavioral assumptions must be examined in light of a firm's actual behavior.

Formally, cost minimization is expressed as

$$C(Q, p^L, p^K, p^F, u; \alpha) = \min_{L,K,F} p^L L + p^K K + p^F F \quad \text{subject to} \quad Q \leqslant f(L, K, F, u; a),$$

where p indicates prices of inputs L, K, and F, u is an unobserved cost efficiency parameter, and α and a are cost and technology parameters respectively. Given input prices and a production function, the model assumes that a firm chooses the quantities of inputs that minimize its total cost to produce each given level of output. Thus, the cost function presents the schedule of quantity levels and the minimum cost necessary to produce them.

An amazing result from microeconomic theory is that, if firms do indeed (i) minimize costs for any given level of output and (ii) take input prices as fixed so that these prices do not vary with the amount of output the firm produces, then the cost function can tell us everything we need to know about the nature of technology. As a result, instead of estimating a production function directly, we can entirely equivalently estimate a cost function. The reason this theoretical result is extremely useful is that it means one can retrieve all the useful information about the parameters of technology from available data on costs, output, and input prices. In contrast, if we were to learn about the production function directly, we would need data on output and input quantities.

This equivalency is sometimes described by saying that the cost function is the dual of the production function, in the sense that there is a one-to-one correspondence

[21] This result is known as a "duality" result and is often taught in university courses as a purely theoretical equivalence result. However, we will see that this duality result has potentially important practical implications precisely because it allows us to use very different data sets to get at the same underlying information.

between the two if we assume cost minimization. If we know the parameters of the production function, i.e., the input and output correspondence as well as input prices, we can retrieve the cost function expressing cost as a function of output and input prices.

For example, the cost function that corresponds to the Cobb–Douglas production function is (see, for example, Nerlove 1963)

$$C = kQ^{1/r} p_L^{\alpha_L/r} p_K^{\alpha_K/r} p_F^{\alpha_F/r} v,$$

where $v = u^{-1/r}$, $r = \alpha_L + \alpha_K + \alpha_F$, and $k = r(\alpha_0 \alpha_L^{\alpha_L} \alpha_K^{\alpha_K} \alpha_F^{\alpha_F})^{-1/r}$.

1.2.2.2 Cost Measurements

There are several important cost concepts derived from the cost function that are of practical use.

The *marginal cost* (MC) is the incremental cost of producing one additional unit of output. For instance, the marginal cost of producing a compact disc is the cost of the physical disc, the cost of recording the content on that disc, the cost of the extra payment on royalties for the copyrighted material recorded on the disc, and some element perhaps of the cost of promotion. Marginal costs are important because they play a key role in the firm's decision to produce an extra unit of output. A profit-maximizing firm will increase production by one unit whenever the MC of producing it is less than the marginal revenue (MR) obtained by selling it. The familiar equality MC = MR determines the optimal output of a profit-maximizing firm because firms expand output whenever MC < MR thereby increasing their total profits.

A *variable cost* (VC) is a cost that varies with the level of output Q, but we shall also use the term "variable cost" to mean the sum of all costs that vary with the level of output. Examples of variable costs are the cost of petrol in a transportation company, the cost of flour in a bakery, or the cost of labor in a construction company. *Average variable cost* (AVC) is defined as AVC = VC/Q. As long as MC < AVC, average variable costs are decreasing with output. Average variable costs are at a minimum at the level of output at which marginal cost intersects average variable cost from below. When MC > AVC, the average variable costs is increasing in output.

Fixed costs (FC) are the sum of the costs that need to be incurred irrespective of the level of output produced. For example, the cost of electricity masts in an electrical distribution company or the cost of a computer server in a consulting firm may be fixed—incurred even if (respectively) no electricity is actually distributed or no consulting work actually undertaken. Fixed costs are recoverable once the firm shuts down usually through the sale of the asset. In the long run, fixed costs are frequently variable costs since the firm can choose to change the amount it spends. That can make a decision about the relevant time-horizon in an investigation an important one.

Sunk costs are similar to fixed costs in that they need to be incurred and do not vary with the level of output but they differ from fixed costs in that they cannot be recovered if the firm shuts down. Irrecoverable expenditures on research and development provide an example of sunk costs. Once sunk costs are incurred they should not play a role in decision making since their opportunity cost is zero. In practice, many "fixed" investments are partially sunk as, for example, some equipment will have a low resale value because of asymmetric information problems or due to illiquid markets for used goods. Nonetheless, few investments are literally and completely "sunk," which means informed judgments must often be made about the extent to which investments are sunk.

In antitrust investigations, other cost concepts are sometimes used to determine cost benchmarks against which to measure prices. *Average avoidable costs* (AAC) are the average of the costs per unit that could have been avoided if a company had not produced a given discrete amount of output. It also takes into account any necessary fixed costs incurred in order to produce the output. *Long-run average incremental cost* (LRAIC) includes the variable and fixed costs necessary to produce a particular product. It differs from the average total costs because it is product specific and does not take into account costs that are common in the production of several products. For instance, if a product A is manufactured in a plant where product B is produced, the cost of the plant is not part of the LRAIC of producing A to the extent that it is not "incremental" to the production of product B.[22] Other more complex measures of costs are also used in the context of regulated industries, where prices for certain services are established in a way that guarantees a "fair price" to the buyer or a "fair return" to the seller.

In both managerial and financial accounts, variable costs are often computed and include the cost of materials used. Operating costs generally also include costs of sales and general administration that may be appropriately considered fixed. However, they may also include depreciation costs which may be approximating fixed costs or could even be more appropriately treated as sunk costs. If so, they would not be relevant for decision-making purposes. The variable costs or the operating costs without accounting depreciation are, in many cases, the most relevant costs for starting an economic analysis but ultimately judgments around cost data will need to be directly informed by the facts pertinent to a particular case.

---

[22] For LRAIC, see, for example, the discussion of the U.K. Competition Commission's inquiry in 2003 into phone-call termination charges in the United Kingdom and in particular the discussion of the approach in Office of Fair Trading (2003, chapter 10). In that case, the question was how high the price should be for a phone company to terminate a call on a rival's network. The commission decided it was appropriate that it should be evaluated on an "incremental cost" basis as it was found to be in a separate market from the downstream retail market, where phone operators were competing with each other for retail customers. In a regulated price setting, agencies sometimes decide it is appropriate for a "suitable" proportion of common costs to be recovered from regulated prices and, if so, some regulatory agencies may suggest using LRAIC "plus" pricing. Ofcom's (2007) mobile termination pricing decision provides an example of that approach.

1.2.2.3 Minimum Efficient Scale, Economies and Diseconomies of Scale

The minimum efficient scale (MES) of a firm or a plant is the level of output at which the long-run average cost (LRAC $=$ AVC $+$ FC$/Q$) reaches a minimum. The notion of long run for a given cost function deals with a time frame where the firm has (at least some) flexibility in changing its capital stock as well as its more flexible inputs such as labor and materials. In reality, cost functions can of course change substantially over time, which complicates the estimation and interpretation of long-run average costs. The dynamics of technological change and changing input prices are two reasons why the "long run" cannot in practice typically be taken to mean some point in time in the future when cost functions will settle down and henceforth remain the same.

We saw that average variable costs are minimized when they equal marginal costs. MES is the output level where the LRAC is minimized. At that point, it is important to note that MC $=$ LRAC. For all plant sizes lower than the MES, the marginal cost of producing an extra unit is higher than it would be with a bigger plant size. The firm can lower its marginal and average costs by increasing scale. In some cases, plants bigger than the MES will suffer from diseconomies of scale as capital investments will increase average costs. In other cases average and marginal costs will become approximately constant above the MES and so all plants above the MES will achieve the same levels of these costs (and this case motivates the "minimum" in the MES). Figure 1.11 illustrates how much plant 1 would have to increase its plant size to achieve the MES. In that particular example, long-run costs increase beyond the MES. Even though MES is measured relative to a "long-run" cost measure, it is important to note that the "long run" in this construction refers to a firm's or plant's ability to change input levels holding all else equal. As a result, this intellectual construction is more helpful for an analyst when attempting to understand costs in a cross section of firms or plants at a given point in time than as an aid to understanding what will happen to costs in some distant time period. As we have already noted, over time both input prices and technology will typically change substantially.

We say a cost function demonstrates *economies of scale* if the long-run average cost decreases with output. A firm with a size lower than the MES will exhibit economies of scale and will have an incentive to grow. *Diseconomies of scale* occur when the long-run average variable cost increases with output.

In the short run, economies and diseconomies of scale will refer to the behavior of average and marginal costs as output is increased for a given capacity or plant size. Mathematically, define

$$S = \frac{\text{AC}}{\text{MC}} = \frac{C}{Q\partial C/\partial Q} = \frac{1}{\partial \ln C/\partial \ln Q}.$$

Thus we can derive a measure of the nature of economies of scale S directly from an estimated cost function by calculating the elasticity of costs with respect to

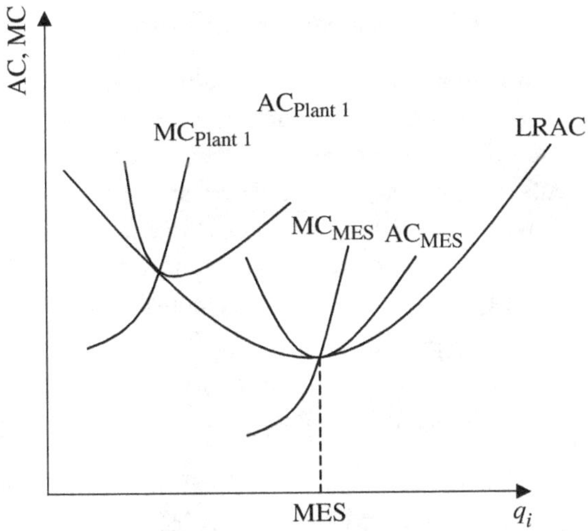

Figure 1.11. The minimum efficient scale of a plant.

output and computing its inverse. Alternatively, one can also use $S^* = 1 - \text{MC}/\text{AC}$ as a measure of economies of scale, which obviously captures exactly the same information about the cost function. If $S > 1$, we have economies of scale because AC is greater than MC. On the other hand, if $S < 1$, we have diseconomies of scale.

There are many potential sources of economies of scale. First, it could be that one of the inputs can only be acquired in large discrete quantities resulting in the firm having lower unit costs as it uses all of this input. An example would be the purchase of a passenger plane with several hundred available seats or the construction of an electricity grid. Also, as size increases, there may be scope for a more efficient allocation of resources within a firm resulting in cost savings. For example, small firms might hire generalists good at doing lots of things while a larger firm might hire more efficient, but indivisible, specialized personnel. Sources of economies of scale can be numerous and a good knowledge of the industry will help uncover the important ones.

If we have substantial economies of scale, the minimum efficient size of a firm may be big relative to the size of a market and as a result there will be few active firms in that market. In the most extreme case, to achieve efficiency a firm must be so large that only one firm will be able to operate at an efficient scale in a market. Such a situation is called a "natural" monopoly, because a benevolent social planner would choose to produce all market output using just one firm. Breaking up such a monopoly would have a negative effect on productive efficiency. Of course, since breaking up such a firm may remove pricing power, we may gain in allocative efficiency (lower prices) even though we may lose in productive efficiency (higher costs).

1.2.2.4 Scale Economies in Multiproduct Production

Determining whether there are economies of scale in a multiproduct firm can be a fairly similar exercise as for a single-product firm.[23] However, instead of looking at the evolution of costs as output of one good increases, we must look at the evolution of costs as the outputs of all goods increase. There are a variety of possible senses in which output can increase but we will often mean "increase in the same proportion." In that case, the term "economies of scale" will capture the evolution of costs as the scale of operation increases while maintaining a constant product mix.

Ray economies of scale (RES) occur when the average cost decreases with an increase in the scale of operation, or, equivalently, if the marginal cost of increasing the scale of operations lies below the average cost of total production.

In order to formalize our notion of economies of scale in a multiproduct environment, let us first define the multiproduct cost function, $C(q_1, q_2)$. Next fix two quantities q_1^0 and q_2^0 and define a new function

$$\tilde{C}(Q \mid q_1^0, q_2^0) \equiv C(Qq_1^0, Qq_2^0),$$

where Q is therefore a scalar measure of the scale of output which we will vary while holding the proportion of the two goods produced fixed. Total production can be expressed as

$$(q_1, q_2) = Q^*(q_1^0, q_2^0).$$

Graphically, if we trace a ray through all the points (Qq_1^0, Qq_2^0), $Q > 0$, our multiproduct measure of economies of scale will measure the economies of scale of the cost function above the ray (see figure 1.12).

The slope of the cost function along the ray is called the directional derivative by mathematicians, and provides the marginal cost of increasing the scale of operations:

$$\begin{aligned}\widetilde{\text{MC}}(Q) &= \frac{\partial \tilde{C}(Q)}{\partial Q} = \frac{\partial C(Qq_1^0, Qq_2^0)}{\partial Q} \\ &= \frac{\partial C(q_1, q_2)}{\partial q_1}\frac{\partial q_1}{\partial Q} + \frac{\partial C(q_1, q_2)}{\partial q_2}\frac{\partial q_2}{\partial Q} \\ &= \sum_{i=1}^{2} \text{MC}_i q_i^0.\end{aligned}$$

Given

$$\text{RES} = \frac{\widetilde{\text{AC}}}{\widetilde{\text{MC}}} = \frac{\tilde{C}(Q)/Q}{\widetilde{\text{MC}}(Q)} = \left(\frac{\partial \ln \tilde{C}(Q)}{\partial \ln Q}\right)^{-1},$$

RES > 1 implies that we have ray economies of scale,
RES < 1 implies that we have ray diseconomies of scale.

[23] For a very nice summary of cost concepts for multiproduct firms, see Bailey and Friedlander (1982).

1.2.2.5 Economies of Scope

Although economies of scale in multiproduct firms mirror the analysis of economies and diseconomies of scale in the single-output environment, important features of costs can also arise from the fact that several products are produced. The cost of producing one good may depend on the quantity produced of the other goods. Indeed, it may actually decrease because of the production of these other goods. For example, nickel and palladium are two metals sometimes found together in the ground. One option would be to build separate mines for extracting the nickel and palladium, but it would obviously be cheaper to build one and extract both from the ore.[24] Similarly, if a firm provides banking services, the cost of providing insurance services might be less for this firm than for a firm that only offers insurance. Such effects are referred to as economies of scope. Economies of scope can arise because certain fixed costs are common to both products and can be shared. For instance, once the reputation embodied in a brand name has been built, it can be cheaper for a firm to launch other successful products under that same brand.

Formally, *economies of scope* occur when it is cheaper to produce a given level of output of two products $(\tilde{q}_1, \tilde{q}_2)$ together compared with producing the two products separately by different firms (see Panzar and Willig 1981). To determine economies of scope we want to compare $C(\tilde{q}_1, \tilde{q}_2)$ and $C(\tilde{q}_1, 0)+C(0, \tilde{q}_2)$. If there are economies of scope, we want to understand the ranges over which they occur. For instance, we want to know the set of $(\tilde{q}_1, \tilde{q}_2)$ for which costs of joint production are lower than individual production:

$$\{(\tilde{q}_1, \tilde{q}_2) \mid C(\tilde{q}_1, \tilde{q}_2) < C(\tilde{q}_1, 0) + C(0, \tilde{q}_2)\}.$$

In addition, we will say *cost complementarities* arise when the marginal cost of production of good 1 is declining in the level of output of good 2:

$$\frac{\partial}{\partial q_2}\left(\frac{\partial C(q_1, q_2)}{\partial q_1}\right) = \frac{\partial^2 C(q_1, q_2)}{\partial q_2 \partial q_1} < 0.$$

An example of a cost function with economies of scope is the multiproduct function shown in figure 1.12. In the figure the cost of producing both goods is clearly lower than the sum of the costs of producing both goods separately. In fact, the figure shows there is actually a "dip" so that the cost of producing the two goods together is lower than the cost of producing them each individually. Clearly, this cost function demonstrates very strong form of economies of scope.[25]

---

[24] For example, the Norilsk mining center in the Russian high arctic produces nickel, palladium, and also copper. In that case, nickel mining began before the others at the surface, and underground mining began later.

[25] Note that it is sometimes important to be careful in distinguishing "economies of scope" from "subadditivity" where a single-product cost function satisfies $C(q_1 + q_2) < C(q_1 + 0) + C(0 + q_2)$.

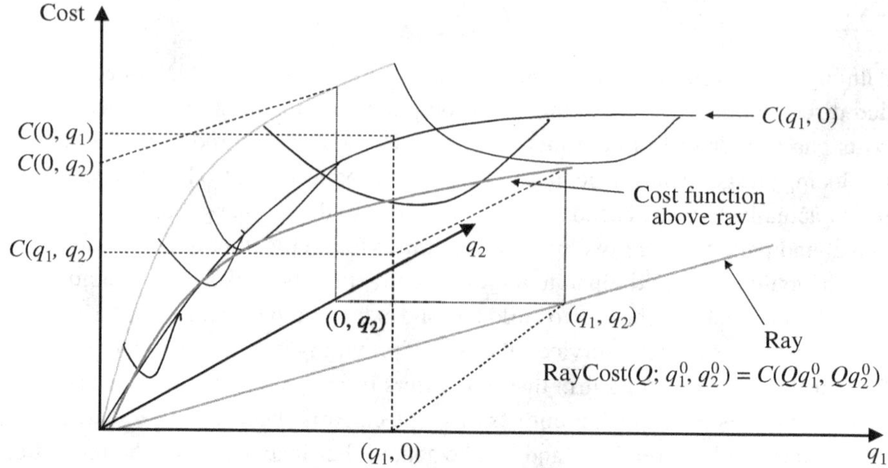

Figure 1.12. A multiproduct cost function. No unique notion of economies of scale in multiproduct environment, so we consider what happens to costs as expand production keeping output of each good in proportion. *Source*: Authors' rendition of a multiproduct cost function provided by Evans and Heckman (1984a,b) and Bailey and Friedlander (1982).

Economies of scope can have an effect on market structure because their existence will promote the creation of efficient multiproduct firms. When considering whether to break up or prohibit a multiproduct firm, it is in principle informative to examine the likely existence or relevance of economies of scope. In theory, it should be easy to evaluate economies of scope, but in practice when using estimated cost functions one must be extremely careful in assessing whether the cost estimates should be used. Very often one of the scenarios has never been observed in reality and therefore the hypothesis used in constructing the cost estimates can be speculative and with little possibility for empirical validation. A discussion of constructing cost data in a multiproduct context is provided in OFT (2003).[26]

In a multiproduct environment, conditional single-product cost functions tell us what happens to costs when the production of one product expands while maintaining constant the output of other products. Graphically, the cost function of product 1 conditional on the output of product 2 is represented as a slice of the cost function in figure 1.13 that, for example, is above the line between $(0, q_2)$ and (q_1, q_2).[27]

Conditional cost functions are useful when defining the *average incremental cost* (AIC) of increasing good 1 by an amount Δq_1, holding output of good 2 constant. This cost measure is commonly used to evaluate the cost of a firm's expansion in a particular line of products.

[26] See, in particular, chapter 6, "Cost and revenue allocation," as well as the case study examples in part 2.

[27] These objects are somewhat difficult to visualize in what is a complex graph. The central approach is to consider the univariate cost functions that result when the appropriate "slice" of the multivariate cost function is taken.

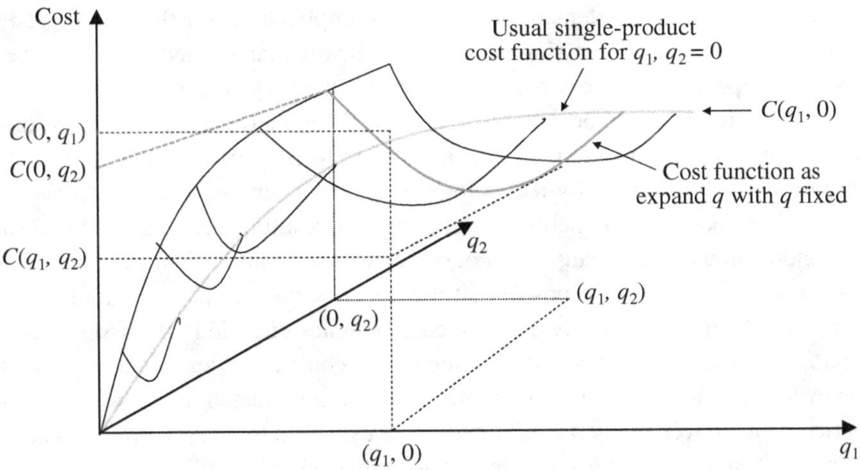

Figure 1.13. Conditional product cost function in multiproduct environment. We can still consider what happens to costs as the firm expands production of a single output at any fixed level of output of the other good.

Formally, the conditional average incremental cost function is defined as

$$\text{AIC}_1(q_1 \mid q_2) = \frac{C(q_1 + \Delta q_1 \mid q_2) - C(q_1 \mid q_2)}{\Delta q_1}.$$

The conditional single-output marginal cost is defined as

$$\text{MC}_1(q_1 \mid q_2) = \frac{\partial C(q_1, q_2)}{\partial q_1}.$$

Product-specific economies of scale can also be evaluated. Economies of scale in product 1, holding output of product 2 constant, are defined as

$$S_1(q_1 \mid q_2) = \frac{\text{AIC}(q_1 \mid q_2)}{\text{MC}(q_1 \mid q_2)}.$$

As usual, $S_1 > 1$ indicates the presence of economies of scale in the quantity produced of good 1 conditional on the level of output of good 2, while $S_1 < 1$ indicates the presence of diseconomies of scale.

1.2.2.6 *Endogenous Economies of Scale*

The discussion above has centered on economies of scale that are technologically determined. We discussed inputs that were necessary to production and that entered the production function in a way that was exogenously determined by the technology. However, firms may sometimes enhance their profits by investing in brands, advertising, and design or product innovation. The analysis of such effects involves important demand-side elements but also has implications on the cost side. For example, if R&D or advertising expenditures involve large fixed outlays that are largely independent of the scale of production, they will result in economies of scale. Since firms will choose their level of R&D and advertising, these are often called "endogenous" fixed costs.[28] The decision to advertise or create a brand is not imposed exogenously by technology but rather is an endogenous decision of the firm in response to competitive conditions. The resulting economies of scale are also endogenous and, because the consumer welfare contribution of such expenditures may or may not be positive, it may or may not be appropriate to include them with the technologically determined economies of scale in the assessment of economies of scale and scope, depending on the context. For example, it would be somewhat odd for a regulator to uncritically allow a regulated monopoly to charge a price which covered any and all advertising expenditure, irrespective of whether such advertising expenditure was in fact socially desirable.

1.2.3 Input Demand Functions

Input demand functions provide a third potential source of information about the nature of technology in an industry. In this section we develop the relationship between profit maximization and cost minimization and describe the way in which knowledge of input demand equations can teach us about the nature of technology and more specifically provide information about the shape of cost functions and production functions.

1.2.3.1 The Profit-Maximization Problem

Generally, economists assume that firms maximize profits rather than minimize costs per se. Of course, minimizing the costs of producing a given level of output is a necessary but not generally a sufficient condition for profit maximization. A profit-maximizing firm which is a price-taker on both its output and input markets will choose inputs to solve

$$\max_{L,K,F} \Pi(L,K,F,p,p^L,p^k,p^F,u;\alpha) = \max_{L,K,F} pf(L,K,F,u;\alpha) - p^L L - p^K K - p^F F, \qquad (1.1)$$

where L denotes labor, K capital, F a third input, say, fuel, and $f(L,K,F,u;\alpha)$ the level of production; p denotes the price of the good produced and the other prices (p^L, p^K, p^F) are the prices of the inputs. The variable u denotes an unobserved efficiency component and α represents the parameters of the firm's production function.

[28] Sutton (1991) studies the case of endogenous sunk costs. In his analysis, he assumes that R&D and advertising expenditures are sunk by the time firms compete in prices although in other models they need not be.

If the firm is a price-taker on its output and input markets, then we can equivalently consider the firm as solving a two-step procedure. First, for any given level of output it chooses its cost-minimizing combination of inputs that can feasibly supply that output level. Second, it chooses how much output to supply to maximize profits.

Specifically,

$$C(Q, p^L, p^K, p^F, u; \alpha) = \min_{K,L,F} p^L L + p^K K + p^F F \quad \text{subject to} \quad Q \leqslant f(K, L, F, u; \alpha) \tag{1.2}$$

and then define

$$\max_Q \Pi(Q, p, p^L, p^K, p^F, u; \alpha) = \max_Q pQ - C(Q, p^L, p^K, p^F, u; \alpha). \tag{1.3}$$

With price-taking firms, the solution to (1.1) will be identical to the solution of the two-stage problem, solving (1.2) and then (1.3).

If the firm is not a price-taker on its output market, the price of the final good p will depend on the level of output Q and we will write it as a function of Q, $P(Q)$, in the profit-maximization problem. Nonetheless, we will still be able to consider the firm as solving a two-step problem provided once again that the firm is a price-taker on its input markets. Profit-maximizing decisions in environments where firms may be able to exercise market power will be considered when we discuss oligopolistic competition in section 1.3.[29]

1.2.3.2 Input Demand Functions

Solving the cost-minimization problem

$$C(Q, p^L, p^K, p^F, u; \alpha) = \min_{K,L,F} p^L L + p^K K + p^F F \quad \text{subject to} \quad Q \leqslant f(K, L, F, u; \alpha)$$

---

[29] If the firm is not a price-taker on its input markets, the price of the inputs may also depend on the level of inputs chosen and, while we can easily define the firm's cost function as

$$C(Q, u; \alpha, \vartheta_L, \vartheta_K, \vartheta_F) = \min_{K,L,F} p^L(L; \vartheta_L)L + p^K(K; \vartheta_K)K + p^F(F; \vartheta_F)F \quad \text{subject to} \quad Q \leqslant f(K, L, F, u; \alpha),$$

the resulting cost function should not, for example, depend on the realized values of the input prices but rather on the structure of the input pricing functions, $C(Q, u; \alpha, \vartheta_L, \vartheta_K, \vartheta_F)$. This observation suggests that estimation of cost functions in environments where firms can get volume discounts from their suppliers are certainly possible, but doing so requires both careful thought about the variables that should be included and also careful thought about interpretation of the results. In particular, in general the shape of the cost function will now capture a complex mixture of incentives generated by (i) substitution possibilities generated by the production function and (ii) of the pricing structures faced in input markets.

produces the conditional input demand equations, which express the inputs demanded as a function of input prices, conditional on output level Q:

$$L = L(Q, p^L, p^K, p^F, u; \alpha),$$
$$K = K(Q, p^L, p^K, p^F, u; \alpha),$$
$$F = F(Q, p^L, p^K, p^F, u; \alpha).$$

Conveniently, Shephard's lemma establishes that cost minimization implies that the inputs demanded are equal to the derivative of the cost function with respect to the price of the input:

$$L = L(Q, p^L, p^K, p^F, u; \alpha) = \frac{\partial C(Q, p^L, p^K, p^F, u; \alpha)}{\partial p^L},$$
$$K = K(Q, p^L, p^K, p^F, u; \alpha) = \frac{\partial C(Q, p^L, p^K, p^F, u; \alpha)}{\partial p^K},$$
$$F = F(Q, p^L, p^K, p^F, u; \alpha) = \frac{\partial C(Q, p^L, p^K, p^F, u; \alpha)}{\partial p^F}.$$

The practical relevance of Shephard's lemma is that it means that many of the parameters in the cost function can be retrieved from the input demand equations and vice versa. That means we have a third type of data set, data on input demands, that will potentially allow us to learn about technology parameters.[30]

Finally, if firms are price-takers on output markets, solving the profit-maximizing problem produces the unconditional input demand equations that express input demand as a function of the price of the final good and the prices of the inputs:

$$L = L(p, p^L, p^K, p^F, u; \alpha),$$
$$K = K(p, p^L, p^K, p^F, u; \alpha),$$
$$F = F(p, p^L, p^K, p^F, u; \alpha).$$

Note that both conditional (on Q) and unconditional factor demand functions depend on productivity, u. Firms with a higher productivity will tend to produce more but will use fewer inputs than other firms in order to produce any given level of output. That observation has a number of important implications for the econometric analysis of production functions since it can mean input demands will be correlated with the unobservable productivity, so that we need to address the endogeneity of input

[30] For a technical discussion of the result, see the section "Duality: a mathematical introduction" in Mas-Colell et al. (1995). In the terminology of duality theory, the cost function plays the role of the "support function" of a convex set. Specifically, let the convex set be $S = \{(K, L, F) \mid Q \leqslant f(K, L, F, u; \alpha)\}$ and define the "support function" $\mu(p_L, p_K, p_F) = \min_{(K,L,F)}\{p_L L + p_K K + p_F F \mid (L, K, F) \in S\}$, then roughly the duality theorem says that there is a unique set of inputs (L^*, K^*, F^*) so that $p_L L^* + p_K K^* + p_F F^* = \mu(p_L, p_K, p_F)$ if and only if $\mu(p_L, p_K, p_F)$ is differentiable at (p_L, p_K, p_F). Moreover, $L^* = \partial\mu(p_L, p_K, p_F)/\partial p_L$, $K^* = \partial\mu(p_L, p_K, p_F)/\partial p_K$, and $F^* = \partial\mu(p_L, p_K, p_F)/\partial p_F$.

demands in the estimation of production functions (see, for example, the discussion in Olley and Pakes 1996; Levinsohn and Petrin 2003; Ackerberg et al. 2005). The estimation of cost functions is discussed in more detail in chapter 3.

1.3 Competitive Environments: Perfect Competition, Oligopoly, and Monopoly

In a perfectly competitive environment, market prices and output are determined by the interaction of demand and supply curves, where the supply curve is determined by the firms' costs. In a perfectly competitive environment, there are no strategic decisions to make. Firms spend their time considering market conditions, but do not focus on analyzing how rivals will respond if they take particular decisions. In more general settings, firms will be sensitive to competitors' decisions regarding key strategic variables. Both the dimensions of strategic behavior and the nature of the strategic interaction will then be fundamental determinants of market outcomes. In other words, the strategic variables—perhaps advertising, prices, quantity, or product quality—and the specific way firms in the industry react to decisions made by rival firms in the industry will determine the market outcomes we observe. The primary lesson of game theory for firms is that they should spend as much time thinking about their rivals as they spend thinking about their own preferences and decisions. When firms do that, we say that they are interacting strategically. Evidence for strategic interaction is often quite easy to find in corporate strategy and pricing documents.

In this section, we describe the basic models of competition commonly used to model firm behavior in antitrust and merger analysis, where strategic interaction is the norm rather than the exception. Of course, since this is primarily a text on empirical methods, we certainly will not be able to present anything like a comprehensive treatment of oligopoly theory. Rather, we focus attention on the fundamental models of competitive interaction, the models which remain firmly at the core of most empirical analysis in industrial organization. Our ability to do so and yet cover much of the empirical work used in practical settings suggests the scope of work yet to be done in turning more advanced theoretical models into tools that can, as a practical matter, be used with real world data.

While some of the models studied in this section may to some eyes appear highly specialized, we will see that the general principles of building game theoretic economic (and subsequently econometric) models are entirely generic. In particular, we will always wish to (1) describe the primitives of the model, in this case the nature of demand and the firms' cost structures, (2) describe the strategic variables, (3) describe the behavioral assumptions we make about the agents playing the game, generally profit maximization, and then, finally, (4) describe the nature of equilibrium, generally Nash equilibrium whereby each player does the best they can given the choice of their rival(s). We must describe the nature of equilibrium as each firm has its own objective and these often competing objectives must be reconciled if a model is to generate a prediction about the world.

1.3.1 Quantity-Setting Competition

The first class of models we review are those in which firms choose their optimal level of output while considering how their choices will affect the output decisions of their rivals. The strategic variable in this model is quantity, hence the name: quantity-setting competition. We will review the general model and then relate its predictions to the predicted outcomes under perfect competition and monopoly.

1.3.1.1 The Cournot Game

The modern models of quantity-setting competition are based on that developed by Antoine Augustin Cournot in 1838. The Cournot game assumes that the only strategic variable chosen by firms is their output level. The most standard analysis of the game considers the situation in which firms move simultaneously and the game has only one period. Also, it is assumed that the good produced is homogeneous, which means that consumers can perfectly substitute goods from the different firms and implies that there can only be one price for all the goods in the market. To aid exposition we first develop a simple numerical example and then provide a more general treatment.

For simplicity suppose there are only two firms and that total and marginal costs are zero. Suppose also that the inverse demand function is of the form

$$P(q_1 + q_2) = 1 - (q_1 + q_2),$$

where the fact that market price depends only on the sum of the output of the two firms captures the perfect substitutability of the two goods. As in all economic models, we must be explicit about the behavioral assumptions of the firms being considered. A probably reasonable, if sometimes approximate, assumption about most firms is that they attempt to maximize profits to the best of their abilities. We shall follow the profession in adopting profit maximization as a baseline behavioral assumption.[31] The assumptions on the nature of consumer demand, together with the assumption on costs, which here we shall assume for simplicity involve zero

[31] Economists quite rightly question the reality of this assumption on a regular basis. Most of the time we fairly quickly receive reassurance from firm behavior, company documents, and indeed stated objectives, at least those stated to shareholders or behind closed doors. Public reassurances and marketing messages are, of course, a different matter and moreover individual CEOs or other board members (and indeed investors) certainly can consider public image or other social impacts of economic activity. For these reasons and others there are always departures from at least a narrow definition of profit maximization and we certainly should not be dogmatic about any of our assumptions. And yet in terms of its predictive power, profit maximization appears to do rather well and it would be a very brave (and frankly irresponsible) merger authority which approved, say, a merger to monopoly because the merging parties told us that they did not maximize profits but rather consumer happiness.

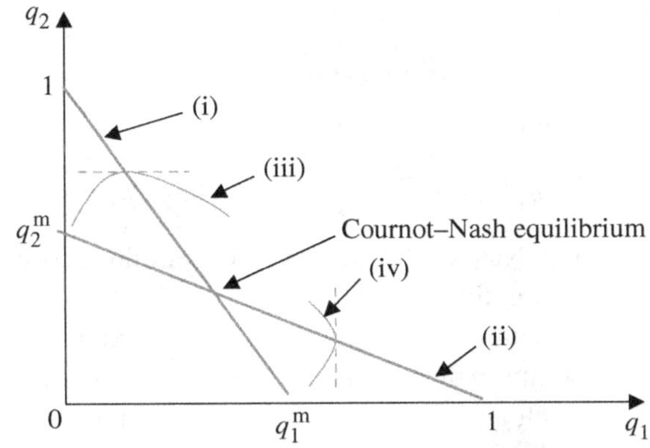

Figure 1.14. Reaction functions in the Cournot model. (i) $R_1(q_2)\colon\ q_1 = \frac{1}{2}(1-q_2)$; (ii) $R_2(q_1)\colon\ q_2 = \frac{1}{2}(1-q_1)$; (iii) $\bar{\pi}_1 = q_1(1-q_1-q_2)$ (isoprofit line for firm 1); (iv) $\bar{\pi}_2 = q_2(1-q_1-q_2)$ (isoprofit line for firm 2).

marginal costs, $c_1 = c_2 = 0$, allow us to describe the way in which each firm's profits depend on the two firms' quantity choices. In our example,

$$\pi_1(q_1, q_2) = (P(q_1+q_2) - c_1)q_1 = (1-q_1-q_2)q_1,$$
$$\pi_2(q_1, q_2) = (P(q_1+q_2) - c_2)q_2 = (1-q_1-q_2)q_2.$$

Given our behavioral assumption, we can define the reaction function, or best response function. This function describes the firm's optimal quantity decision for each value of the competitor's quantity choice. The reaction function can be easily calculated given our assumption of profit-maximizing behavior. The first-order condition from profit maximization by firm 1 is

$$\frac{\partial \pi_1(q_1, q_2)}{\partial q_1} = (1-q_2) - 2q_1 = 0.$$

Solving for the quantity of firm 1 produces firm 1's reaction function

$$q_1 = R_1(q_2) = \tfrac{1}{2}(1-q_2).$$

If both firms choose their quantity simultaneously, the outcome is a Nash equilibrium in which each firm chooses their optimal quantity in response to the other firm's choice. The reaction functions of firms 1 and 2 respectively are

$$R_1(q_2)\colon\quad q_1 = \tfrac{1}{2}(1-q_2) \qquad \text{and} \qquad R_2(q_1)\colon\quad q_2 = \tfrac{1}{2}(1-q_1).$$

Solving these two linear equations describes the Cournot–Nash equilibrium

$$q_1 = \tfrac{1}{2}(1-q_2) = \tfrac{1}{2}(1-\tfrac{1}{2}(1-q_1)) = \tfrac{1}{2}(\tfrac{1}{2}+\tfrac{1}{2}q_1) = \tfrac{1}{4}+\tfrac{1}{4}q_1,$$

so that the equilibrium output for firm 1 is

$$\tfrac{3}{4}q_1^{\mathrm{NE}} = \tfrac{1}{4} \quad \Longrightarrow \quad q_1^{\mathrm{NE}} = \tfrac{1}{3}.$$

The equilibrium output for firm 2 will then be

$$q_2^{\text{NE}} = \tfrac{1}{2}(1 - \tfrac{1}{3}) = \tfrac{1}{3}.$$

The resulting profits will be

$$\pi_1^{\text{NE}} = \pi_2^{\text{NE}} = \tfrac{1}{3}(1 - \tfrac{1}{3} - \tfrac{1}{3}) = \tfrac{1}{9}.$$

Graphically, the Cournot–Nash equilibrium is the intersection between the two firms' reaction curves as shown in figure 1.14.

The reaction function is the quantity choice that maximizes the firm's profits for each given quantity choice of its competitor. The profits for the different combinations of output choices in a Cournot duopoly are plotted in figure 1.15.

Isoprofit lines show all quantity pairs (q_1, q_2) that generate any given fixed level of profits for firm 1. These lines would be represented by horizontal slices of the surface in figure 1.15. We can define a given fixed level of profit $\bar{\pi}_1$ as

$$\bar{\pi}_1 = (1 - q_1 - q_2)q_1.$$

Note that given a level of profits and quantity chosen by firm 1, the output of firm 2 can be inferred as

$$q_2 = 1 - q_1 - \frac{\bar{\pi}_1}{q_1}.$$

Isoprofit lines can be drawn in a contour plot as shown in figure 1.16. Firm 1's best response to any given q_2 is where it reaches highest isoprofit contour. The figure reveals an important characteristic of the model: for a fixed output of firm 1, firm 1's profits increase as firm 2 lowers its output. If the competitor chooses not to produce, the profit-maximizing response is to produce the monopoly output and make monopoly profits. That is, if $q_2 = 0$, then $q_1 = \frac{1}{2}(1 - q_2) = 0.5$ and the profit will be

$$\bar{\pi}_1 = (1 - q_1 - q_2)q_1 = (1 - 0.5 - 0)0.5 = 0.25.$$

More generally, the first-order conditions in the Cournot game produce the familiar condition that marginal revenue is equated to marginal costs. Given the profit function

$$\pi_i(q_i, q_j) = P(q_1 + q_2)q_i - C_i(q_i),$$

the first-order conditions are

$$\frac{\partial \pi_i(q_1, q_2)}{\partial q_i} = \underbrace{P(q_1 + q_2) + q_i P'(q_1 + q_2)}_{\text{Marginal revenue}} - \underbrace{C_i'(q_i)}_{\text{Marginal cost}} = 0,$$

which in general defines an implicit function we shall call firm i's reaction curve, $q_i = R_i(q_{-i})$, where q_{-i} denotes the output level of the other firm(s).[32] In our

[32] That is, we can think of the first-order condition defining a value of q_i which, given the quantities chosen by other firms, will set the first-order condition to zero.

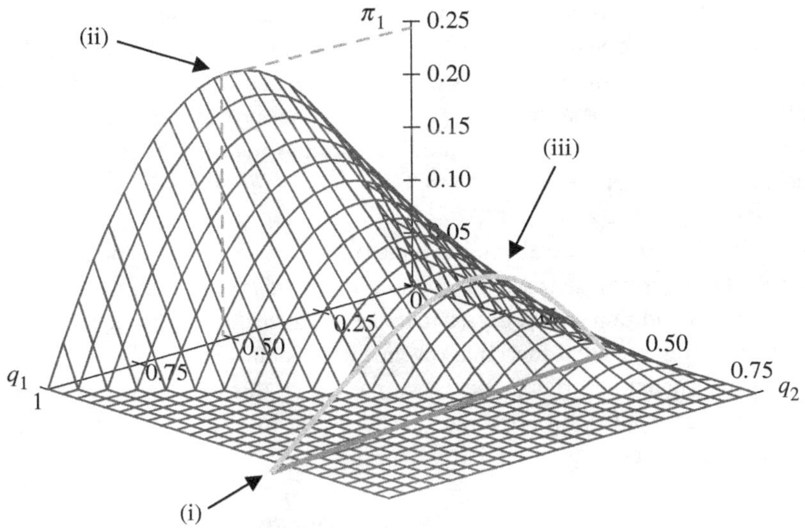

Figure 1.15. Profit function for a two-player Cournot game as a function of the strategic variables for each firm. (i) For each fixed q_2, firm 1 chooses q_1 to maximize her profits; (ii) the q_1 that generates the maximal level of profit for fixed value of q_2 is firm 1's best response to q_2; (iii) profits if firm 1 is a monopoly: $q_2 = 0, q_1 = 0.5, \Pi_1 = 0.25$.

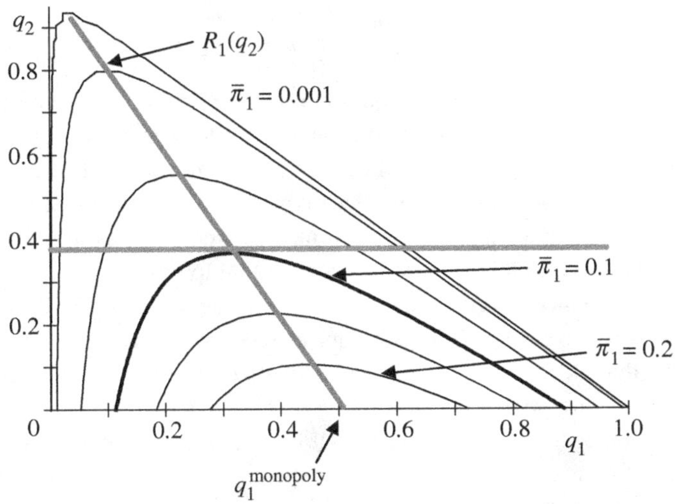

Figure 1.16. Isoprofit lines in simple Cournot model.

two-player case, we have two first-order conditions to solve, which can each in turn be used to define the reaction functions $q_1 = R_1(q_2)$ and $q_2 = R_2(q_1)$. In general, with N active firms we will have N first-order conditions to solve. Nash equilibrium is the intersection of the reaction functions so that solving the reaction functions can involve solving N nonlinear equations. Our numerical example makes these equations linear (and hence easy to solve analytically) by assuming that inverse demand curves are linear and marginal costs constant. In general, however, computers can usually solve nonlinear systems of equations for us provided a solution exists.[33] Ideally, we would like a "unique" prediction about the world coming out of the model and we will get one only if there is a unique solution to the set of first-order conditions.[34]

Note that since profits are always revenues minus costs, marginal profitability can as always be described as marginal revenue minus marginal cost. At a maximum, the first-order condition will be zero and hence we have the familiar result that profit maximization requires that marginal revenue equals marginal cost.

To see the impact of strategic decision making, at this point it is worth taking a moment to relate the Cournot optimality conditions, with perhaps the more familiar results from perfect competition and monopoly.

1.3.1.2 Quantity Choices under Perfect Competition

In an environment with price-taking firms, the first-order condition from profit maximization leads to equating the marginal cost of the firm to the market price, provided, of course, that there are no fixed costs so that we can ignore the sometimes important constraint that profits must be nonnegative:

$$\pi_i(q_i) = pq_i - C_i(q_i) \implies \frac{\partial \pi_i(q_i)}{\partial q_i} = p - C_i'(q_i) = 0 \implies p = C_i'(q_i).$$

Evidently, if the price is €1 and the marginal cost of producing one more unit is €0.90, then my profits will increase if I expand production by that unit. Similarly, if the price is €1 while the marginal cost of production of the last unit is €1.01, my profits will increase if I do not produce that last unit. Repeating the calculation makes clear that quantity will adjust until marginal cost equals marginal revenue, which by assumption in this context is exactly equal to price.

Going further, since all firms face the same price, all firms will choose their quantities in order to help price equal marginal cost so that $C_i'(q_i) = C_j'(q_j) = p$. In particular, that means marginal costs are equalized across firms because all firms face the same selling price.

Note that joint cost minimization also implies that the marginal costs are equated across active firms. Consider what happens when we minimize the total cost of producing any given level of total output:

$$\min_{q_1,q_2} C_1(q_1) + C_2(q_2) \quad \text{subject to} \quad q_1 + q_2 = Q.$$

[33] For the conditions required for existence of a solution to these nonlinear equations and hence for Nash equilibrium, see Novshek (1985) and Amir (1996).

[34] In general, a system of N nonlinear equations may have no solution, one solution, or many solutions. In economic models the more commonly problematic situation arises when models have multiple equilibria. We discuss the issue of multiple equilibria further in chapter 5.

In particular, note that such a problem yields the following first-order optimality conditions,

$$C_1'(q_1) = C_2'(q_2) = \lambda,$$

where λ is the Lagrange multiplier in the constrained minimization exercise. Clearly, minimizing the total costs for any given level of production will involve equalizing marginal costs.

Intuitively, if we had firms producing at different marginal costs, the last unit of output produced at the firm with higher marginal costs could have been more efficiently produced by the firm with lower marginal costs. Perfect competition, and in particular the price mechanism, acts to ensure that output is distributed across firms in a way that ensures that all units in the market are as efficiently produced as possible given the existing firms' technologies. It is in this way that prices help ensure *productive efficiency*.

In perfectly competitive markets, prices also act to ensure that the marginal cost of output is also equal to its marginal benefit, so that we have *allocative efficiency*. To see why, recall that the market demand curve describes the marginal value of output to consumers at each level of quantity produced. At any given price, the last unit of the good purchased will have a marginal value equal to the price. The supply curve of the firm under perfect competition is the marginal cost for each level of quantity since firms adjust output until $p = \text{MC}(q)$ in equilibrium. Therefore, when price adjusts to ensure that aggregate supply is equal to aggregate demand, it ensures that the marginal valuation of the last unit sold is equal to the marginal cost of its production. In other words, the market produces the quantity such that the last unit is valued by consumers as much as it costs to produce. It is this remarkable mechanism that ensures that the market outcome under perfect competition is socially efficient.

1.3.1.3 Quantity Setting under Monopoly

In a monopoly, there is only one firm producing and therefore the market price will be determined by this one firm when it chooses the total quantity to produce. As usual, the firm's profit function is

$$\pi_i(q_i) = P(q_i)q_i - C_i(q_i)$$

and the corresponding first-order condition is

$$\frac{\partial \pi_i(q_i)}{\partial q_i} = \underbrace{P(q_i) + P'(q_i)q_i}_{\text{Marginal revenue}} - \underbrace{C_i'(q_i)}_{\text{Marginal cost}} = 0.$$

Note that the first-order condition from monopoly profit maximization is a special case of the first-order condition under Cournot where the quantity of the other firms is set to zero. The monopolist, like any profit-maximizing firm in any of the scenarios analyzed, chooses its quantity in order to set marginal revenue equal to marginal cost.

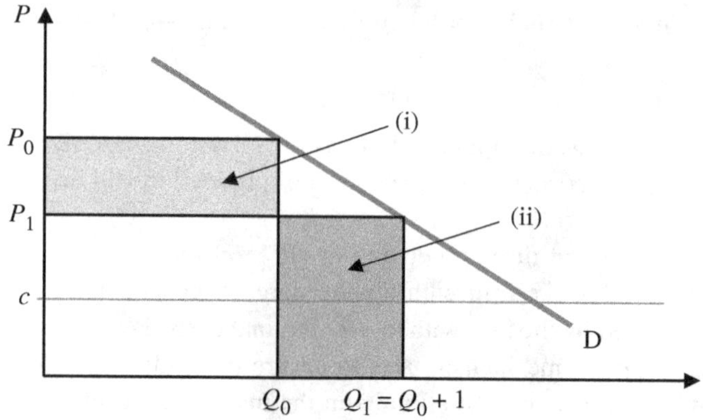

Figure 1.17. Demand, revenue, and marginal revenue.
(i) Loss of revenue $Q_0 \Delta P \to QP'(Q)$. (ii) Increase of revenue P_1.

Note that the slope of the inverse demand function $P'(q_i)$ is negative. That means that the marginal revenue generated by an extra unit sold is smaller than the marginal valuation by the consumers as represented by the inverse demand curve $P(q_i)$. Graphically, the marginal revenue curve is below the inverse demand curve for a monopolist. The reason for this is that the monopolist cannot generally lower the price of only the last unit. Rather she is typically forced to lower the price for all the units previously produced as well. Increasing the price therefore increases the revenue for each product which continues to be sold at the higher price, but reduces revenue to the extent that the number of units sold falls. Figure 1.17 illustrates the marginal revenue when the monopolist increases its sales by one unit from Q_0 to Q_1. To sell Q_1, the monopolist must reduce its selling price to P_1, down from P_0. The marginal revenue associated with selling that extra unit is therefore

$$\begin{aligned}\text{MR} &= P_1 Q_1 - P_0 Q_0 = P_1(Q_1 - Q_0) + Q_0(P_1 - P_0)\\ &= P_1 \times 1 + Q_0 \Delta P = P_1 + Q_0 \Delta P.\end{aligned}$$

Under a profit-maximizing monopoly, marginal revenue of the last unit sold is lower than the marginal valuation of consumers. As a result, the monopoly outcome is not socially efficient. At the level of quantity produced, there are consumers for whom the marginal value of an extra unit is greater than the marginal cost of supplying it. Unfortunately, even though some consumers are willing to pay more than the marginal cost of production, the monopolist prefers not to supply them to avoid suffering from lower revenues from the customers who remain. The welfare loss imposed by a monopoly market is illustrated in figure 1.18.

1.3.1.4 Comparing Monopoly and Perfect Competition to the Cournot Game

In all competition models, profit maximization implies that the firm will set marginal revenue equal to marginal cost: MR = MC. Whereas in perfect competition, firms'

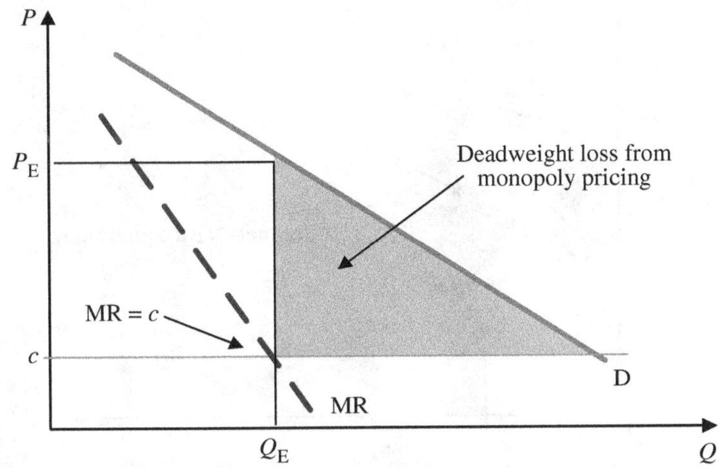

Figure 1.18. Welfare loss from monopoly pricing compared with perfect competition.

marginal revenue is the market price, in a monopoly market the marginal revenue will be determined by the monopolist's choice of quantity. In a Cournot game, the marginal revenue depends on the firm's output decision as well as on the rivals' output choices.

Specifically, in a Cournot game, we showed that the first-order condition from profit maximization,

$$\text{Max}_{q_i} \pi_i(q_i, q_j) = P(q_1 + q_2)q_i - C_i(q_i),$$

is

$$\frac{\partial \pi_1(q_1, q_2)}{\partial q_1} = P(q_1 + q_2) + q_1 P'(q_1 + q_2) - C_1'(q_1) = 0.$$

As always, the firm equates marginal revenue to marginal cost. As in the monopolist case, the marginal revenue is smaller than the marginal valuation by the consumer. In particular, because of the negative slope of the demand curve, we have

$$\text{MR}_1(q_1, q_2) = P(q_1 + q_2) + q_1 P'(q_1 + q_2) < P(q_1 + q_2).$$

Graphically, the marginal revenue curve is below the demand curve.

First notice that under Cournot, the effect of the decrease in price $P'(q_1 + q_2)$ is only counted for the q_1 units produced by firm 1, while under monopoly the effect is counted for the entire market output.

Second, under Cournot, the marginal revenue of each firm is affected by its output decision *and* by the output decisions of competing firms, outputs which do affect the equilibrium price. The result is a negative externality across firms. When firm 1 chooses its optimal quantity, it does not take into account the potential reduction in profits that other firms suffer with an increase in total output. This effect is called a "business stealing" effect. As a result Cournot firms will jointly produce and sell

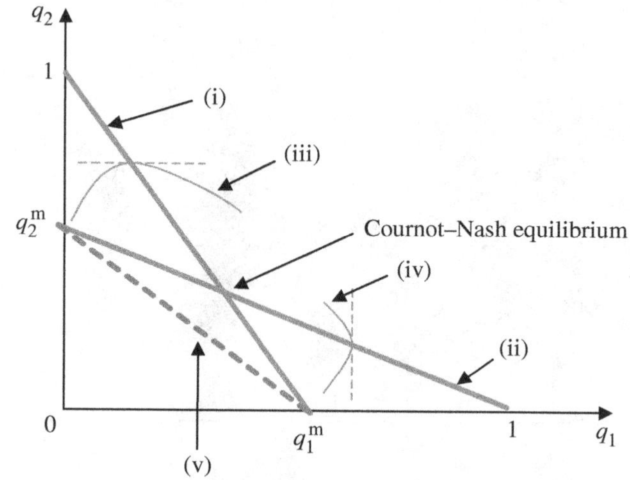

Figure 1.19. Cournot equilibrium versus monopoly: (i)–(iv) as in figure 1.14; (v) output combinations that maximize joint profits.

at a lower price than an equivalent (multiplant) monopolist. Figure 1.19 illustrates the joint industry profit-maximizing output combinations and the Cournot–Nash equilibrium. If firms have the same constant marginal cost, any output allocation among the two firms such that the sum of their output is the monopoly quantity, i.e., any combination fulfilling $q_1 + q_2 = Q^{\text{monopoly}}$, will maximize industry profits. The industry profit-maximizing output levels are represented by the dashed line in the figure. The Cournot–Nash equilibrium is reached by each firm maximizing its profits individually. It is represented by the intersection of the two firms' reaction function. The total output in the Cournot–Nash equilibrium is larger than under monopoly. At a very basic level, competition authorities which apply a consumer welfare standard are aiming to maintain competition so that the negative externalities across firms are preserved. In so doing they ensure that firms endow positive externalities on consumers, in the form of consumer surplus.

Under perfect competition, social welfare is maximized because the market equates the marginal valuations with the marginal cost of production. A monopolist firm will decide not to produce units that are valued more than their costs in order not to decrease total profits and therefore social welfare is not maximized. That said, production costs are still minimized.[35] Social welfare is not maximized with Cournot competition but the loss of welfare is less severe than in the monopoly game thanks to the extra output produced as a result of the Cournot externalities. Output and social welfare will be higher than in the monopolist case since the firm does not factor in the effect of lower prices on the other firms' revenues. When

[35] Experience suggests that monopolies will often, among other things, suffer from X-inefficiency as well as restricting output, so this result should probably not be taken too literally. (See the literature on X-inefficiency following Leibenstein (1966).)

a firm's output expansion only has a small effect on price, the Cournot outcome becomes close to the competitive outcome. This is the case when there are a large number of firms and each firm is small relative to total market output. In a Cournot equilibrium, marginal cost can vary across firms and so industry production costs are not necessarily minimized unless firms are symmetric and marginal costs are equal across firms.

In summary, Cournot equilibrium will be bad for the firms' profits but good for consumer welfare relative to the monopoly outcomes. On the other hand, Cournot will be good for the firms' profits but bad for consumer welfare relative to a market with price-taking firms.

The Cournot model has had a profound impact on competition analysis and it is sometimes described as the model that antitrust practitioner's have in mind when they first consider the economics of a given situation. As we discuss in chapter 6, the model is, among other things, the motivation for considering the commonly used Herfindahl–Hirschman index (HHI) of concentration.

1.3.2 Price-Setting Competition

Oligopoly theory was developed to explain what would happen in markets when there were small numbers of competing firms. Cournot's (1838) theory was based on a form of competition in which firms choose quantities of output and the construction appeared to fit with the empirical evidence that firms seemed to price above marginal cost, the price prediction of the perfect competition model. While Cournot was successful in predicting price above marginal cost, some unease remains about whether firms genuinely choose the level of output they produce or determine their selling price and sell whatever demand there is for the product at that price. This observation motivated the analysis of what became one of the most important theoretical results in oligopoly theory, Bertrand's paradox.

1.3.2.1 The Bertrand Paradox

Bertrand (1883) considered that Cournot's model embodied an unrealistic assumption about firm behavior. He suggested that a more realistic model of actual firm behavior was that firms choose prices and then supply the resulting demand for their product. If so, then price rather than quantity would be the relevant strategic variable for the firms. Bertrand's model does indeed seem highly intuitive since firms do frequently set prices for their products. Thus from the point of view of the description of actual firm behavior, it seems to fit reality better than Cournot's model. Nonetheless, we now treat Bertrand's model as important because it produces paradoxical, counterintuitive results.[36] Like many results in economics, Bertrand's results are

[36] A paradox is defined in the Oxford English Dictionary as a statement or tenet contrary to received opinion or belief; often with the implication that it is marvelous or incredible; sometimes with unfavorable connotation, as being discordant with what is held to be established truth, and hence absurd or fantastic.

usually considered important because they force us to ask carefully which of his assumptions are violated.[37]

Bertrand considers a duopoly in a homogeneous products market with a market demand curve $Q = D(p)$. If firm 1 prices above its competitors, customers will only buy from the cheaper firm and firm 1's demand will be 0. If firm 1 prices below its competitor, it will supply the whole market since no customer will want to buy from firm 2. If firm 1 and firm 2 offer the same price, then demand will be split between the two firms, we shall assume equally (the exact split is not crucial). The demand curve for firm 1 will be as follows:

$$q_1 = D_1(p_1, p_2) = \begin{cases} D(p_1) & \text{if } p_1 < p_2, \\ D(p_1)/2 & \text{if } p_1 = p_2, \\ 0 & \text{if } p_1 > p_2, \end{cases}$$

where demand is assumed to be split evenly if the two firms charge identical prices. Assuming constant marginal costs c for both firms, Bertrand showed that there is a unique Nash equilibrium: $p_1^* = p_2^* = c$.

The proof is based on the following arguments. If firm 2 prices above marginal costs, $p_2 > c$, then firm 1 can undercut slightly by setting $p_1 = p_2 - \varepsilon$, where ε is very small, and take the whole market. Provided that p_1 is above marginal cost, firm 1 will still make positive profits. However, firm 2 also has the incentive to undercut firm 1 by a slight amount and for as long as the prices are above marginal costs firms will have an incentive to undercut each other. No firm has an incentive to price below marginal costs because that would imply that they would make losses. Therefore, the only possible stable outcome is the Nash equilibrium, where both firms are pricing at marginal cost. In this situation, both firms make zero profits.

The Bertrand game has a very important, strong implication. Namely, Bertrand's result implies that as long as there is more than one player in the market, prices for all firms will be set to marginal cost and profits will be zero. In other words, as long as there are at least two firms in the market for a homogeneous product and no fixed costs, the market will produce the perfect competition equilibrium. Such a result occurs despite the fact that both firms would be better off if they both increased their prices! Bertrand's result is considered to be a paradox because intuitively, neither business people nor economists usually expect a duopoly to produce the same results as we would get from a perfectly competitive market. Moreover, the data substantiate such intuition: the vast majority of oligopolies have positive markups and the firms involved do not generally price at, or often even close to, marginal cost.

[37] Another example of such a result is the Modigliani and Miller theorem (1958). These authors showed that under certain—on the face of it highly plausible—assumptions, the capital structure of a firm does not matter for the value of the firm. Of course, most practitioners and academics believed and believe that the proportions of debt and equity do matter and so for fifty years corporate finance has studied violations of Modigliani and Miller's assumptions, which include the absence of taxes and bankruptcy costs as well as the presence of full information and efficient markets.

How do we react to Bertrand's paradox? Well, if you have a theory with well-defined assumptions which gives you implausible predictions, it is time to look at the assumptions. Following Bertrand's results, economists have examined a large variety of alternative assumptions in order to obtain predictions that conform better to reality.

In the next three sections we discuss three further important examples which, along with others we will discuss later in the book, have been found to modify Bertrand's model in a way that relaxes his strong conclusions. First, fixed costs can be introduced into the model. Second, product differentiation can be introduced. Product differentiation gives a certain degree of pricing power to each firm. Third, capacity constraints, which put a limit to the percentage of the market that any firm can supply, have been incorporated. We discuss each model in turn.

1.3.2.2 Bertrand Competition with Fixed Costs

First note that the Bertrand result that price equals marginal cost only applies in cases where fixed costs are zero. If fixed costs are nonzero, then firms maximize profits subject to the nonnegativity constraint that profits must be nonnegative while profits may well be negative if prices were set at marginal cost. Firm one's problem can be written as follows:

$$\max_{p_1}(p_1 - c_1)D_1(p_1, p_2) - F_1 \quad \text{subject to} \quad (p_1 - c_1)D_1(p_1, p_2) - F_1 \geqslant 0$$

and in a two-firm game, firm 2 will solve the analogous problem. If $F_1 = 0$, then the profit constraint is always there but under normal conditions does not constrain the profit-maximizing choice of price so that in informal analyses (e.g., in classrooms) it is usually ignored. However, if $F_1, F_2 > 0$, price undercutting will force the profit constraint to bind for at least one firm in equilibrium. Suppose firm 2's constraint binds first as prices are driven down by price undercutting. Firm 1 will then face a choice between (i) sharing the market (by setting its price equal to that charged by firm 2 when it makes zero profits at equal prices $D_1(p_1, p_2) = D(p_1)/2$ if $p_2 = p_1$) or (ii) slightly undercutting that price which will keep its rival out of the market so that $D_1(p_1, p_2) = D(p_1)$, where $p_1 = p_2 - \varepsilon$, with ε a small increment.[38] Generally, the latter will be more profitable and therefore this version of Bertrand competition with fixed costs results in the prediction that prices will be driven down to levels sufficient to keep the less efficient rival out of the market (see Chowdhury 2002). Slight changes to the game can, however, change this result. For example, a two-stage game with entry involving sinking a fixed cost and then price

[38] There is an easily overcome technical problem arising in this setting because firm 1 would want to be as close to firm 2's price as possible but still smaller than it, which can result in there being no solution to the firm's optimization problem. Technically, the optimization is over the open set $[0, p_2)$ and so need not have a solution. The problem is easily overcome by assuming that price increments occur in small discrete steps, perhaps pennies or cents.

competition will result in only one firm entering and that firm charging a monopoly price. The reason is that if two firms enter, thereby sinking their respective fixed costs, they would compete à la Bertrand at the second stage. That in turn means they would not recover their fixed costs and hence one of the firms will decide it is better not to enter the market. Finally, we note that such situations are also sometimes expected to experience "Edgeworth" cycles, where firms go through a process of undercutting each other until prices are so low that one firm prefers to jump back up to a high price, thereby beginning the cycle again (see Maskin and Tirole 1988b; Noel 2007; Castanias and Johnson 1993; Doyle et al. 2008).

1.3.2.3 Price Competition with Differentiated Products

Models with product differentiation assume that firms' products differ and so are imperfect substitutes for consumers. If so, then each product has a degree of uniqueness and certain consumers may be willing to pay a premium to get each particular product. The differentiation can come due to differences in concrete attributes such as product quality or location or in consumers' subjective perceptions such as those that may result from a brand's image.

Suppose we face a market with two differentiated goods and the following linear demand system:

$$\text{Demand for good 1:} \qquad q_1 = a_1 - b_{11}p_1 + b_{12}p_2,$$
$$\text{Demand for good 2:} \qquad q_2 = a_2 - b_{22}p_2 + b_{21}p_1.$$

First note that good 1 is a substitute for good 2 if an increase in the price of good 2 increases the demand for good 1, which is equivalent to saying that $\partial q_1/\partial p_2 = b_{12} > 0$. Good 1 is a complement for good 2 if an increase in the price of good 2 decreases the demand for good 1 meaning that $\partial q_1/\partial p_2 = b_{12} < 0$.

Assuming firms choose prices, the profit-maximizing firm will choose its best response to the rivals' choices of price. Define the best response function of firm i as[39]

$$R_i(p_{-i}) = \underset{p_i}{\text{argmax}}\, \pi_i(p_i, p_{-i}).$$

If we assume constant marginal costs, the profit function can be expressed as

$$\pi_i(p_i, p_{-i}) = (p_i - c)D_i(p_i, p_{-i}).$$

Differentiating with respect to own price, the first-order condition for profit maximization will be

$$\frac{\partial \pi_i(p_i, p_{-i})}{\partial p_i} = D_i(p_i, p_{-i}) + (p_i - c)\frac{\partial D_i(p_i, p_{-i})}{\partial p_i} = 0,$$
$$\Longleftrightarrow \qquad (a_i - b_{ii}p_i + b_{ij}p_j) + (p_i - c)(-b_{ii}) = 0,$$

[39] The notation "argmax" may be new to some readers. It is shorthand for the "argument which maximizes" the function. Here, the price of firm i. The optimal price for firm i will depend on the prices charged by rivals and that dependence is captured in the statement of the reaction function as $p_i = R_i(p_{-i})$.

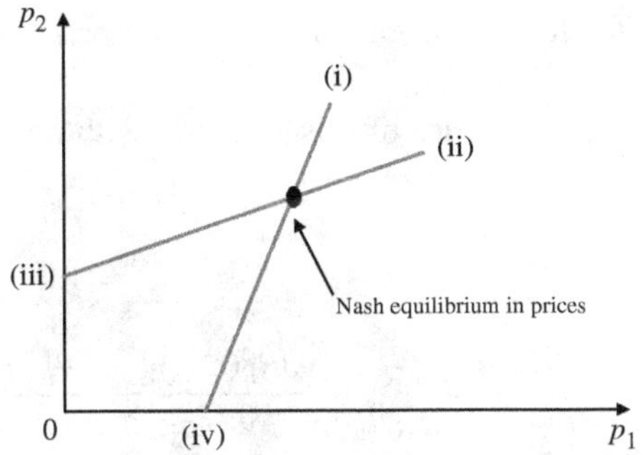

Figure 1.20. Best response curves in price competition with differentiated substitute products. (i) $R_1(p_2) = c/2 + (a_1 + b_{12}p_2)/2b_{11}$; (ii) $R_2(p_1) = c/2 + (a_2 + b_{21}p_1)/2b_{22}$; (iii) $c/2 + a_2/2b_{22}$; (iv) $c/2 + a_1/2b_{11}$.

or, more concisely,

$$a_i + b_{ij}p_j = (2p_i - c)b_{ii}.$$

Rearranging gives the best response function for the producer of product i to a given announcement of price p_j by i's rival firm j:

$$R_i(p_{-i}): \quad p_i = \frac{c}{2} + \frac{a_i + b_{ij}p_j}{2b_{ii}}.$$

Note that the slope of reaction function is $b_{ij}/2b_{ii}$, which, in particular, depends on b_{ij}. In fact, since b_{ii} will be positive, whether the reaction function slopes up or down depends only on the sign of b_{ij}. That in turn means that it depends directly on whether the goods are complements or substitutes.

In a differentiated product price game with demand substitutes ($b_{ij} > 0$), the reaction curves slope up. If firm i increases prices, the best response for firm j is also to increase prices. Graphically, our two-firm example can be represented with each firm pricing according to the best response curves pictured in figure 1.20.

Formally, a generic noncooperative game involves firm i choosing some strategic variable a_i to maximize its profits. The game produces a best reaction function: $a_i^* = R_i(a_{-i}) = \text{argmax}_{a_i}\, \pi_i(a_i, a_{-i})$, where "argmax" means the argument which maximizes the objective function, here the action a_i which maximizes firm i's profits.

Differentiating gives the following equality:

$$\left.\frac{\partial \pi_i(a_i^*, a_{-i})}{\partial a_i}\right|_{a_i^* = R_i(a_{-i})} = \pi_i^i(R_i(a_{-i}), a_{-i}) = 0$$

by definition of the best response function, where the notation "$|_{a_i^* = R_i(a_{-i})}$" denotes that the first-order condition is evaluated at the point where player i is playing a best response to its rival's strategies, a_{-i}. Intuitively, if I am at my optimal choice of action, say, for example, output, then my marginal profit is zero as required by the optimization process.

Totally differentiating both sides of this equation with respect to another player j's action gives

$$\begin{aligned}\frac{\mathrm{d}\pi_i^i(R(a_{-i}),a_{-i})}{\mathrm{d}a_j} &= \left.\frac{\partial\pi_i^i(a_i,a_{-i})}{\partial a_i}\right|_{a_i^*=R_i(a_{-i})}\frac{\partial R_i(a_{-i})}{\partial a_j}+\left.\frac{\partial\pi_i^i(a_i,a_{-i})}{\partial a_j}\right|_{a_i^*=R_i(a_{-i})}\\ &= 0.\end{aligned}$$

Using double superscripts to indicate double derivatives, this equation can be expressed as

$$\frac{\mathrm{d}\pi_i^i(R_i(a_{-i}),a_{-i})}{\mathrm{d}a_j} = \pi_i^{ii}(r_i(a_{-i}),a_{-i})\frac{\partial R_i(a_{-i})}{\partial a_j}+\pi_i^{ij}(R_i(a_{-i}),a_{-i})=0,$$

which in turn can be rearranged to provide an expression for the slope of the reaction curve:

$$\frac{\partial R_i(a_{-i})}{\partial a_j}=\frac{-\pi_i^{ij}(R_i(a_{-i}),a_{-i})}{\pi_i^{ii}(R_i(a_{-i}),a_{-i})}.$$

(Alternatively, we could obtain this expression directly by applying the implicit function theorem to the first-order condition which implicitly defines firm i's reaction function. See your favorite mathematics or economics textbook, e.g., Mas-Colell et al. (1995, pp. 940–43).) The reaction curve describes the action that maximizes firm i's profits given its competitors' choices. Thus, the second-order condition requires that the second own derivative is negative at the profit-maximizing choice of action a_i, $R(a_{-i})$. That is, $\pi_i^{ii}(R_i(a_{-i}),a_{-i})<0$.

Thus this result says that the sign of the slope of the reaction function will then depend on the cross derivative of the firm profit function $\pi_i^{ij}(a_i,a_{-i})$ evaluated at the point $(R_i(a_{-i}),a_{-i})$. Intuitively, we said that at an optimum the marginal profitability of a firm given your action is zero. Now suppose a rival's action a_j goes up. We consider what happens to my optimal choice of action. Clearly, if $\pi_i^{ij}(R_i(a_{-i}),a_{-i})<0$ then my (firm i's) marginal profitability is falling in your action. That means, when you increased a_j, my marginal profitability fell below zero. The question of i's best response to the new a_j is the question of how to restore my marginal profitability back up to zero, i.e., how do I increase my marginal profitability. If $\pi_i^{ii}(a_i,a_{-i})<0$, then we know that decreasing my action a_i will increase my marginal profitability. In summary, when you increased a_j, then I optimally decreased my action a_i. Thus, if $\pi_i^{ij}(R_i(a_{-i}),a_{-i})<0$, my best response will be decreasing in your choice of action and my reaction function will be downward sloping. Analogously, if $\pi_i^{ij}(R_i(a_{-i}),a_{-i})>0$, then my best response will be increasing in your choice of action and my reaction function will be upward sloping.

As an example, we showed that in the model the first-order conditions are

$$\pi_i^i(p_i, p_{-i}) = D_i(p_i, p_{-i}) + (p_i - c)D_i^i(p_i, p_{-i})$$

so that the cross derivative is

$$\pi_i^{ji}(p_i, p_{-i}) = D_i^j(p_i, p_{-i}) + (p_i - c)D_i^{ji}(p_i, p_{-i}).$$

With linear demands such as those described at the beginning of this section, the second term is zero $D_i^{ij}(p_i, p_{-i}) = 0$ and hence

$$\pi_i^{ji}(p_i, p_{-i}) = D_i^j(p_i, p_{-i}) = b_{ij}.$$

Whether the reaction functions are upward or downward sloping will depend on the sign of b_{ij}. If b_{ij} is positive so that the goods are substitutes, the reaction function will be upward sloping. If b_{ij} is negative and the goods are complements, the reaction functions will be downward sloping.

If reaction functions are downward sloping, then we will say the game is one of *strategic substitutes*. Returning to the material on the Cournot game, one can easily check that a Cournot game is a game of strategic substitutes, where we write the firm's action, or strategic variable, as quantity q. In Cournot games, competitors will react to a unilateral increase in quantity by decreasing their quantity. In price-setting games, if the goods are demand complements, then reaction curves will also slope downward and the game will also be one of strategic substitutes: firms will react to the increase in the price of a rival's complementary good by decreasing their own price. For this reason, price games among complementary goods will have many properties similar to Cournot-style quantity games.

If reaction functions are upward sloping, then we will say the game is one of *strategic complements*. This is the case in most pricing games such as differentiated products Bertrand pricing games, where the products are demand substitutes. In such cases, firms will react to a rival's unilateral increase in price by increasing their own price(s).

The introduction of product differentiation allows for a model of strategic interaction based on price-setting competition that allows for prices to be above marginal costs. Price competition in a market with differentiated products has become the most generally used model for differentiated product industries. It is, for example, used in particular to model competition in markets for branded consumer goods.

1.3.2.4 Price Competition with Capacity Constraints

One important attempt to reconcile Cournot and Bertrand while making apparently reasonable assumptions on behavior and maintaining consistency with empirically observed outcomes was formulated in Kreps and Scheinkman (1983). They describe a two-stage game in which firms choose capacity in the first stage and then play a Bertrand competition game in the second stage, given their installed capacity. Kreps and Scheinkman show that, provided customers are allocated to the different producers according to the rule of "efficient rationing" in the second stage, the subgame perfect equilibrium of this two-stage game can be similar to the one-shot Cournot game.

When there are capacity constraints, the total supply can be less than the total demand for a given price. This means we must be concerned with "rationing rules." Rationing rules are assumptions about the way the good is assigned to consumers. It determines (i) who gets the good and who does not, and (ii) which firms supply to which customers. Common rationing assumptions are (i) efficient rationing, where the consumers who value the good most are served first by the lowest-price firm until the firm's capacity is exhausted, and (ii) proportional (random) rationing, where each consumer has an equal probability of being served by any of the existing firms.

With efficient rationing the residual demand of the lowest price firm looks as shown in figure 1.21 since the very highest valuation customers—those at the top-left of the market demand curve—are all served by the lowest price firm. Only when the lowest price firm's capacity is exhausted does the higher price firm begin to experience positive demand for its product.

Suppose firm 1 is the low-cost firm with capacity k_1. Under efficient rationing, the first k_1 units are always bought from firm 1. Firm 2's demand curve is then just a downward-sloping demand curve where at each price firm 2 faces the residual demand, that is, the market demand minus k_1. There is one more wrinkle, that firm 2 cannot sell more than its own capacity k_2. Kreps and Scheinkman show that when the total demand is larger than the sum of capacities in the market, the equilibrium of their two-stage (capacity then price competition) game will correspond to the solution of a one-stage Cournot game where the strategic variable is capacity instead of output produced.[40]

We follow Kreps and Scheinkman to solve for the equilibrium of the two-stage game, we proceed by backward induction, solving stage two first. At stage two, firms are playing a Bertrand price competition game with their capacities k_1 and k_2 for firm 1 and firm 2 respectively fixed. Sales for any firm will be

$$q_i(p_i, p_j; k_i, k_j) = \begin{cases} \min\{D(p_i), k_i\} & \text{if } p_i < p_j, \\ \min\{\max\{D(p_i) - k_j, 0\}, k_i\} & \text{if } p_i > p_j, \\ \min\{(k_i/(k_i + k_j))D(p), k_i\} & \text{if } p_i = p_j. \end{cases}$$

To see why, notice first that the firm gets all the market demand up to its full capacity when it prices below competitors. On the other hand, if a firm prices above

[40] As capacities increase, the nature of the equilibrium changes. In particular, one must use mixed strategies for medium capacities and with very large capacities the equilibrium is a Bertrand equilibrium.

its competitor, it will supply any positive residual demand up to its own capacity. The efficient rationing assumption is thus also embodied in the firm's assumed demand curve in the term $\max\{D(p_i) - k_j, 0\}$. If prices are the same across competitors, we assume that each firm will supply their share of the total capacity available at that price.

At the second stage of our game, the firms take capacities as given and choose their price to maximize their own profits, for each possible price of rivals. The best response function for each firm at stage 2 is therefore

$$\begin{aligned} R_i(p_j; k_i, k_j) &= \operatorname*{argmax}_{p_i} \pi_i(p_i, p_j; k_i, k_j) \\ &= \operatorname*{argmax}_{p_i} (p_i - c) q_i(p_i, p_j; k_i, k_j). \end{aligned}$$

There are two possible scenarios. If capacities are large, so large that capacities are not an effective constraint on sales, then the sales of each firm are

$$q_i(p_i, p_j; k_i, k_j) = \begin{cases} D(p_i) & \text{if } p_i < p_j, \\ 0 & \text{if } p_i > p_j, \\ (k_i/(k_i + k_j))D(p) & \text{if } p_i = p_j. \end{cases}$$

In this case, the firm's demand curve is exactly the one obtained in a Bertrand game with homogeneous products, except for the minor difference in the "splitting rule" when prices are equal. As a result, in this case the equilibrium of the subgame will involve setting price equal to marginal costs, $p^* = mc$. Since this case is less interesting than that of small capacities we focus on that case.

If capacities are small so that capacity constraints are binding, we have

$$0 \leqslant k_i \leqslant D(p_i) - k_j \leqslant D(p_i).$$

The first inequality follows since capacities are positive. The second illustrates that capacity constraints are binding and then capacity is smaller than residual demand at the current price while the latter inequality follows simply since k_j is positive. Rearranging the middle inequality gives that total capacity is no larger than demand:

$$k_i + k_j \leqslant D(p) \quad \Longleftrightarrow \quad k_i \leqslant \left(\frac{k_i}{k_i + k_j}\right) D(p)$$

and in that case sales will be

$$q_i(p_i, p_j; k_i, k_j) = \begin{cases} k_i & \text{if } p_i < p_j, \\ \min\{k_i, D(p_i) - k_j\} = k_i & \text{if } p_i > p_j, \\ k_i & \text{if } p_i = p_j. \end{cases}$$

Now assuming that equilibrium price adjusts to equate total industry capacity to market demand, we have that $k_i + k_j = D(p^*)$ or, inverting the demand equation, $p^* = P(k_i + k_j)$.

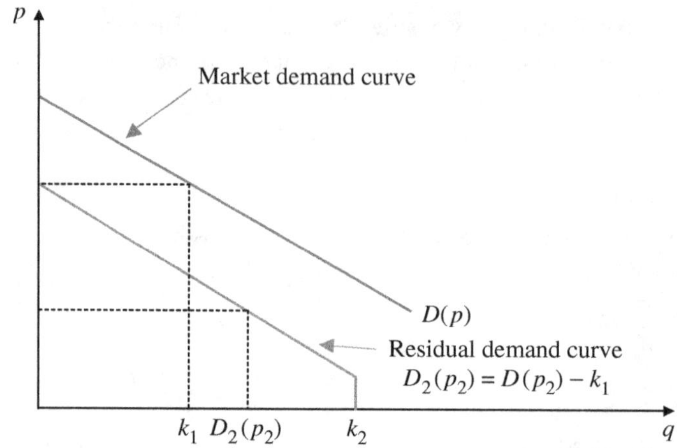

Figure 1.21. Residual demand curve with efficient rationing.

If so, then to solve for the equilibrium of the game in stage one, we need to substitute the optimal prices p^* into the reaction function of the capacity setting game. That is, each firm solves

$$\begin{aligned} R_i(k_j) &= \underset{k_i}{\operatorname{argmax}}\, \pi_i(p_i^*, p_j^*; k_i, k_j) \\ &= \underset{k_i}{\operatorname{argmax}} (p_i^* - c) q(p_i^*, p_j^*; k_i, k_j) \\ &= \underset{k_i}{\operatorname{argmax}} (P(k_i + k_j) - c) k_i. \end{aligned}$$

Clearly, since the objective function is the same as that used in the Cournot model, with qs replaced by ks, the reaction functions derived for the subgame perfect equilibrium of the two-stage game look exactly like the one-shot Cournot game profit function with the choice variable being capacity k instead of output q, and with the inverse demand function $P(k_i + k_j)$.

Deneckere and Davidson (1986) show that the Kreps and Scheinkman result is sensitive to the exact rationing rule used (see figure 1.21). They argue first that the "efficient rationing" is not very likely since under that rule the most highly valued units must be bought from the low-price firm. Second, they note that if, for example, consumers are randomly distributed between the two firms, then the Kreps and Scheinkman result disappears. On reflection, perhaps the fact that this result is sensitive is not really terribly surprising: Kreps and Scheinkman are trying to 'compress' a two-stage game into a simpler and yet equivalent one-stage game—clearly an endeavor which is, at least in general, only going to work under strong and restrictive assumptions.

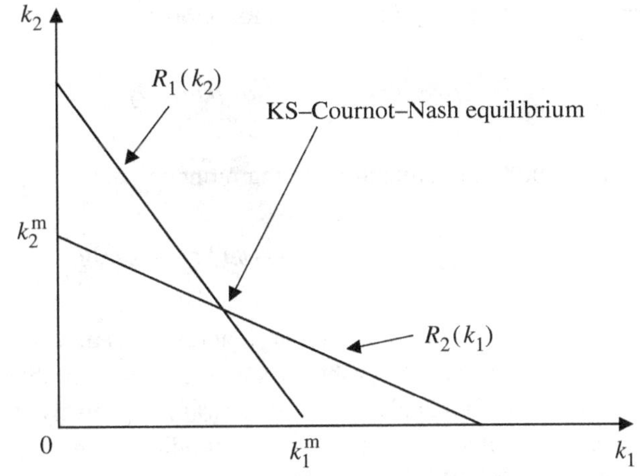

Figure 1.22. Reaction functions in Kreps and Scheinkman two-stage game.

1.3.3 The Monopoly and Dominant-Firm Models

In this section we first briefly revisit the monopoly model and then discuss a variant of that model in which a dominant firm faces a competitive fringe which acts nonstrategically.

1.3.3.1 Monopoly Models

The clearest "dominant" firm model is one in which a firm is a monopoly. Our baseline model of such a situation is that a monopolist will simply maximize profits in a way that is unconstrained by rivals. However, a monopolist may be a price-setting monopolist, a quantity-setting monopolist, a multiplant quantity-setting monopolist or a multiproduct quantity-setting monopolist or indeed a multiplant, multiproduct, price- or quantity-setting monopolist. Thus there is no single model of a monopoly. In order of complexity static monopoly models of the firm assume that they solve problems including:

1. Price-setting monopolist: $\max_p (p - c)D(p)$.
2. Quantity-setting monopolist: $\max_q (P(q) - c)q$.
3. Multiplant, quantity-setting monopolist:

$$\max_{q_1,\dots,q_J} \sum_{j=1}^{J} (P(q_1 + q_2 + \cdots + q_J) - c_j(q_j))q_j.$$

4. Multiproduct, price-setting monopolist:

$$\max_{p_1,\dots,p_J} \sum_{j=1}^{J} (p_j - c_j)D_j(p_1, \dots, p_J).$$

5. Multiproduct, multiplant, price-setting monopolist:

$$\max_{p_1,\dots,p_J} \sum_{j=1}^{J} (p_j - c_j(D_j(p_1,\dots,p_J)))D_j(p_1,\dots,p_J).$$

6. Multiproduct, multiplant, quantity-setting monopolist:

$$\max_{q_1,\dots,q_J} \sum_{j=1}^{J} (P_j(q_1,\dots,q_J) - c_j(q_j))q_j.$$

Single-product monopolists will act to set marginal revenue equal to marginal cost. In those cases, since the monopoly problem is a single-agent problem in a single product's price or quantity, our analysis can progress in a relatively straightforward manner. In particular, note that single-agent, single-product problems give us a single equation (first-order condition) to solve. In contrast, even a single agent's optimization problem in the more complex multiplant or multiproduct settings generates an optimization problem is multidimensional. In such single-agent problems, we will have as many equations to solve as we have choice variables. In simple cases we can solve these problems analytically, while, more generally, for any given demand and cost specification the monopoly problem is typically relatively straightforward to solve on a computer using optimization routines.

Naturally, in general, monopolies may choose strategic variables other than price and quantity. For example, if a single-product monopolist chooses both price and advertising levels, it solves the problem $\max_{p,a}(p-c)D(p,a)$, which yields the usual first-order condition with respect to prices,

$$\frac{p-c}{p} = -\left(\frac{\partial \ln D(p,a)}{\partial \ln p}\right)^{-1},$$

and a second one with respect to advertising,

$$(p-c)\frac{\partial D(p,a)}{\partial a} = 0.$$

A little algebra gives

$$\frac{p-c}{p} p \frac{D(p,a)}{a} \frac{\partial \ln D(p,a)}{\partial \ln a} = 0$$

and substituting in for $(p-c)/p$ using the first-order condition for prices gives the result:

$$\frac{a}{pD(p,a)} = \left(\frac{\partial \ln D(p,a)}{\partial \ln a}\right) \bigg/ \left(-\frac{\partial \ln D(p,a)}{\partial \ln p}\right),$$

which states the famous Dorfman and Steiner (1954) result that advertising–sales ratios should equal the ratios of the own-advertising elasticity of demand to the own-price elasticity of demand.[41]

[41] For an empirical application, see Ward (1975).

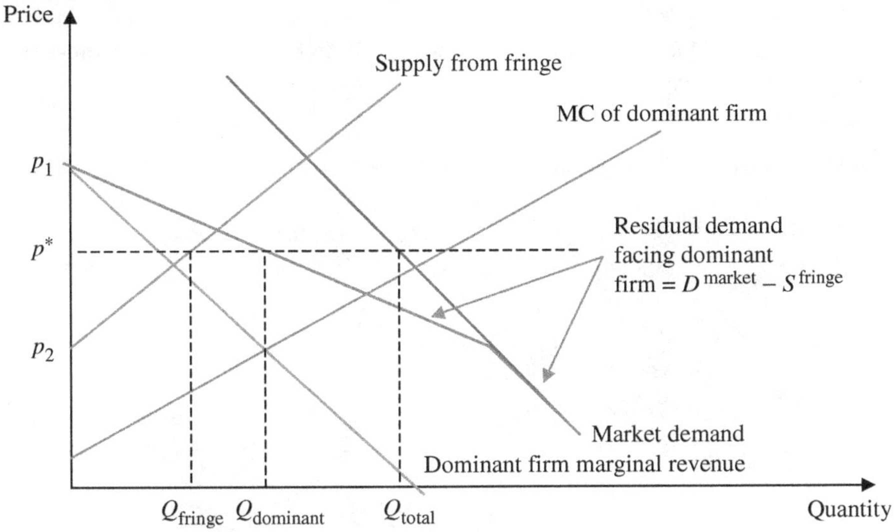

Figure 1.23. Deriving the residual demand curve.

1.3.3.2 The Dominant-Firm Model

The dominant-firm model supposes that there is a monopoly (or collection of firms acting as a cartel) which is nonetheless constrained to some extent by a competitive fringe. The central assumption of the model is that the fringe acts in a nonstrategic manner. We follow convention and develop the model within the context of a price-setting, single-product monopoly. Dominant-firm models analogous to each of the cases studied above are similarly easily developed.

If firms which are part of the competitive fringe act as price-takers, they will decide how much to supply at any given price p. We will denote the supply from the fringe at any given price p as $S^{\text{fringe}}(p)$. Because of the supply behavior of the fringe, if they are able to supply whomever they so desire at any given price p, the dominant firm will face the residual demand curve:

$$D^{\text{dominant}}(p) = D^{\text{market}}(p) - S^{\text{fringe}}(p).$$

Figure 1.23 illustrates the market demand, fringe supply, and resulting dominant-firm demand curve. We have drawn the figure under the assumption that (i) there is a sufficiently high price p_1 such that the fringe is willing to supply the whole market demand at that price leaving zero residual demand for the dominant firm and (ii) there is analogously a sufficiently low price p_2 below which the fringe is entirely unwilling to supply.

Given the dominant firm's residual demand curve, analysis of the dominant-firm model becomes entirely analogous to a monopoly model where the monopolist faces the residual demand curve, $D^{\text{dominant}}(p)$. Thus our dominant firm will set prices so that the quantity supplied will equate the marginal revenue to its marginal cost of supply. That level of output is denoted Q_{dominant} in figure 1.23. The resulting price will be p^* and fringe supply at that price is $S^{\text{fringe}}(p^*) = Q_{\text{fringe}}$ so that total supply (and total demand) are

$$Q_{\text{total}} = Q_{\text{dominant}} + Q_{\text{fringe}} = S^{\text{fringe}}(p^*) + D^{\text{dominant}}(p^*) = D^{\text{market}}(p^*).$$

A little algebra gives us a useful expression for understanding the role of the fringe in this model. Specifically, the dominant firm's own-price elasticity of demand can be written as[42]

$$\begin{aligned}\eta_{\text{demand}}^{\text{dominant}} &\equiv \frac{\partial \ln D^{\text{dominant}}}{\partial \ln p}\\ &= \frac{\partial \ln(D^{\text{market}} - S^{\text{fringe}})}{\partial \ln p}\\ &= \frac{1}{D^{\text{market}} - S^{\text{fringe}}} \frac{\partial (D^{\text{market}} - S^{\text{fringe}})}{\partial \ln p}\end{aligned}$$

so that we can write

$$\eta_{\text{demand}}^{\text{dominant}} = \frac{1}{D^{\text{market}} - S^{\text{fringe}}} \left[\left(\frac{D^{\text{market}}}{D^{\text{market}}} \right) \frac{\partial D^{\text{market}}}{\partial \ln p} - \left(\frac{S^{\text{fringe}}}{S^{\text{fringe}}} \right) \frac{\partial S^{\text{fringe}}}{\partial \ln p} \right]$$

and hence after a little more algebra we have

$$\begin{aligned}\eta_{\text{demand}}^{\text{dominant}} &= \left(\frac{D^{\text{market}}}{D^{\text{market}} - S^{\text{fringe}}} \right) \frac{\partial \ln D^{\text{market}}}{\partial \ln p}\\ &\quad - \left(\frac{S^{\text{fringe}}/D^{\text{market}}}{(D^{\text{market}} - S^{\text{fringe}})/D^{\text{market}}} \right) \frac{\partial \ln S^{\text{fringe}}}{\partial \ln p}\\ &= \frac{1}{\text{Share}^{\text{dom}}} \eta_{\text{demand}}^{\text{market}} - \left(\frac{\text{Share}^{\text{fringe}}}{\text{Share}^{\text{dom}}} \right) \eta_{\text{supply}}^{\text{fringe}},\end{aligned}$$

where η indicates a price elasticity. That is, the dominant firm's demand curve—the residual demand curve—depends on (i) the market elasticity of demand, (ii) the fringe elasticity of supply, and also (iii) the market shares of the dominant firm and the fringe. Remembering that demand elasticities are negative and supply elasticities positive, this formula suggests intuitively that the dominant firm will therefore face a relatively elastic demand curve when market demand is elastic or when market demand is inelastic but the supply elasticity of the competitive fringe is large and the fringe is of significant size.

---

[42] Recall from your favorite mathematics textbook that for any suitably differentiable function $f(x)$ we can write

$$\frac{\partial \ln f(x)}{\partial \ln x} = \frac{1}{f(x)} \frac{\partial f(x)}{\partial \ln x}.$$

1.4 Conclusions

- Empirical analysis is best founded on economic theory. Doing so requires a good understanding of each of the determinants of market outcomes: the nature of demand, technological determinants of production and costs, regulations, and firm's objectives.
- Demand functions are important in empirical analysis in antitrust. The elasticity of demand will be an important determinant of the profitability of price increases and the implication of those price increases for both consumer and total welfare.
- The nature of technology in an industry, as embodied in production and cost functions, is a second driver of the structure of markets. For example, economies of scale can drive concentration in an industry while economies of scope can encourage firms to produce multiple goods within a single firm. Information about the nature of technology in an industry can be retrieved from input and output data (via production functions) but also from cost, output and input price data (via cost functions) or alternatively data on input choices and input prices (via input demand functions.)
- To model competitive interaction, one must make a behavioral assumption about firms and an assumption about the nature of equilibrium. Generally, we assume firms wish to maximize their own profits, and we assume Nash equilibrium. The equilibrium assumption resolves the tensions otherwise inherent in a collection of firms each pursuing their own objectives. One must also choose the dimension(s) of competition by which we mean defining the variables that firms choose and respond to. Those variables are generally prices or quantity but can also include, for example, quality, advertising, or investment in research and development.
- The two baseline models used in antitrust are quantity- and price-setting models otherwise known as Cournot and (differentiated product) Bertrand models respectively. Quantity-setting competition is normally used to describe industries where firms choose how much of a homogeneous product to produce. Competition where firms set prices in markets with differentiated or branded products is often modeled using the differentiated product Bertrand model. That said, these two models should not be considered as the only models available to fit the facts of an investigation; they are not.
- An environment of perfect competition with price-taking firms produces the most efficient outcome both in terms of consumer welfare and production efficiency. However, such models are typically at best a theoretical abstraction and therefore they should be treated cautiously and certainly should not systematically be used as a benchmark for the level of competition that can realistically be implemented in practice.

2
Econometrics Review

Throughout this book we discuss the merits of various empirical tools that can be used by competition authorities. This chapter aims to provide important background material for much of that discussion. Our aim in this chapter is not to replicate the content of an econometrics text. Rather we give an informal introduction to the tools most commonly used in competition cases and then go on to discuss the often practical difficulties that arise in the application of econometrics in a competition context. Particular emphasis is given to the issue of identification of causality. Where appropriate, we refer the reader to more formal treatments in mainstream econometrics textbooks.[1]

Multiple regression is increasingly common in reports of competition cases in jurisdictions across the world. Like any single piece of evidence, a regression analysis initially performed in an office late at night can easily surge forward and end up becoming the focus of a case. Once under the spotlight of intense scrutiny, regression results are sometimes invalidated. Sometimes, it is the data. Outliers or oddities that are not picked up by an analyst reveal the analysis was performed using incorrect data. Sometimes the econometric methodology used is proven to provide good estimates only under extremely restrictive and unreasonable assumptions. And sometimes the analysis performed proves—once under the spotlight—to be very sensitive in a way that reveals the evidence is unreliable. An important part of the analyst's job is therefore to clearly disclose the assumptions and sensitivities at the outset so that the correct amount of weight is placed on that piece of econometric evidence by decision makers. Sometimes the appropriate amount of weight will be a great, on other occasions it will be very little.

In this chapter we first discuss multiple regression including the techniques known as ordinary least squares and nonlinear least squares. Next we discuss the important issue of identification, particularly in the presence of endogeneity. Specifically, we consider the role of fixed-effects estimators, instrumental variable estimators, and "natural" experiments. The chapter concludes with a discussion of best practice

[1] A very nice discussion of basic regression analysis applied to competition policy can be found in Fisher (1980, 1986) and Finkelstein and Levenbach (1983). For more general econometrics texts, see, for example, Greene (2007) and Wooldridge (2007). And for an advanced and more technical but succinct discussion of the econometric theory, see, for example, White (2001).

in econometric projects. The aim in doing so is, in particular, to help avoid the disastrous scenario wherein late in an investigation serious flaws in econometric analysis are discovered.

2.1 Multiple Regression

Multiple regression is a statistical tool that allows us to quantify the effect of a group of variables on a particular outcome. When we want to explain the effect of a variable on an outcome that is also simultaneously affected by several other factors, multiple regression will let us identify and quantify the particular effect of that variable. Multiple regression is an extremely useful and powerful tool but it is important to understand what it does, or rather what it can and cannot do. We first explain the principles of ordinary least-squares (OLS) regression and the conditions that need to hold for it to be a meaningful tool. We then discuss hypothesis testing and finally we explore a number of common practical problems that are frequently encountered.

2.1.1 The Principle of Ordinary Least-Squares Regressions

Multiple regression provides a potentially extremely useful statistical tool that can quantify actual effects of multiple causal factors on outcomes of interest. In an experimental context, a causal effect can sometimes be measured in a precise and scientific way, holding everything else constant. For example, we might measure the effect of heat on water temperature. On the other hand, budget or time constraints might mean we can only use a limited number of experiments so that each experiment must vary more than one causal factor. Multiple regression could then be used to isolate the effects of each variable on the outcomes. Unfortunately, economists in competition authorities cannot typically run experiments in the field. It would of course make our life far easier if we could just persuade firms to increase their prices by 5% and see how many customers they lose; we would be able to learn about their own-price elasticity of demand relatively easily. On the other hand, chief executives and their legal advisors may entirely reasonably suggest that the cost of such an experiment would be overly burdensome on business.

More typically, we will have data that have been generated in the normal course of business. On the one hand, such data have a huge advantage: they are real! Firms, for example, will take actions to ameliorate the impact of price increases on demand: they may invest in customer retention strategies, such as marketing efforts aimed at explaining to their customers the cost factors justifying a price increase; they might change some other terms of the offer (e.g., how many weeks of a magazine subscription you get for a given amount) or perform short-term retention advertising targeted at the most price-sensitive group of customers. If we run an experiment in a lab, we will have a "pure" price experiment but it may not tell us about the elasticity of demand in reality, when real consumers are deciding whether to spend their own real money given the firm's efforts at retaining their business. On the other hand, as this example suggests, a lot will be going on in the real world, and most importantly none of it will be under the control of the analyst while much of it may be under the control of market participants. This means that while multiple regression analysis will be potentially useful in isolating the various causes of demand (prices, advertising, etc.), we will have to be very careful to make sure that the real-world decisions that are generating our data do not violate the assumptions needed to justify using this tool. Multiple regression was, after all, initially designed for understanding data generated in experimental contexts.

2.1.1.1 Data-Generating Processes and Regression Specifications

The starting point of a regression analysis is the presumption, or at least the hypothesis, that there is a real relationship between two or more variables. For instance, we often believe that there is a relation between price and quantity demanded of a given good. Let us assume that the true population relationship between the price charged, P, and the quantity demanded, Q, of a particular good is given by the following expression:[2]

$$P_i = a_0 + b_0 Q_i + u_i,$$

where i indicates different possible observations of reality (perhaps time periods or local markets) and the parameters a_0 and b_0 take on particular values, for example 5 and -2 respectively. We will call such an expression our "data-generating process" (DGP). This DGP describes the inverse demand curve as a function of the volume of sales Q and a time- or market-specific element u_i, which is unknown to the analyst. Since it is unknown to the analyst, sometimes it is known as a "shock"; we may call u_i a demand shock. The shock term includes everything else that may have affected the price in that particular instance, but is unknown and hence appears stochastic to the analyst. Regression analysis is based on the idea that if we have data on enough realizations of (P, Q), we can learn about the true parameters (a_0, b_0) of the DGP without even observing the u_is.

If we plot a data set of sample size N, denoted $(P_1, Q_1), (P_2, Q_2), \ldots, (P_N, Q_N)$ or more compactly $\{(P_i, Q_i); i = 1, \ldots, N\}$, that is generated by our DGP, we will obtain a scatter plot with data spread around the picture. An ideal situation for estimating a demand curve is displayed in figure 2.1. The reason we call it ideal will become clear later in the chapter but for now note that in this case the true DGP, as illustrated by the plotted observations, seems to correspond to a linear relationship

[2] It is perhaps easier to motivate a demand equation by considering the equation to describe the price P which generates a level of sales Q. If Q is stochastic and P is treated as a deterministic "control" variable, then we would write this equation the other way around. For the purposes of illustration and since P is usually placed on the y-axis of a classic demand and supply diagram, we present the analysis this way around, that is, in terms of the "inverse" demand curve.

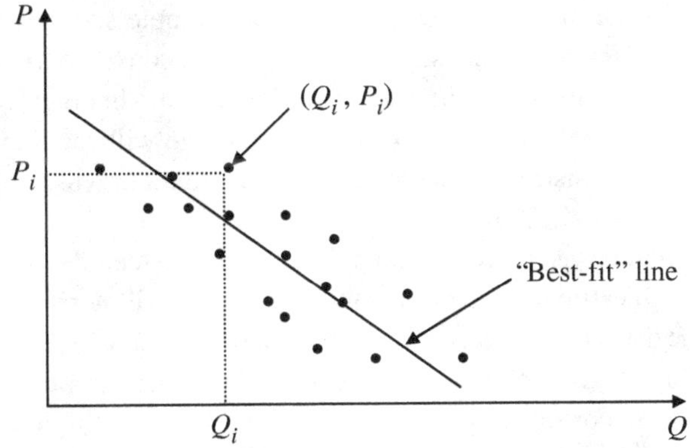

Figure 2.1. Scatter plot of the data and a "best-fit" line.

between the two variables. In the figure, we have also drawn in a "best-fit" line, in this case the line is fit to the data only by examining the data plot and trying to draw a straight line through the plotted data by hand.

In an experimental context, our explanatory variable Q would often be non-stochastic—we are able to control it exactly, moving it around to generate the price variable. However, in a typical economics data set the causal variable (here we are supposing Q) is stochastic. A wonderfully useful result from econometric theory tells us that the fact that Q is stochastic does not, of itself, cause enormous problems for our tool kit, though obviously it changes the assumptions we require for our estimators to be valid. More precisely, we will be able to use the technique of OLS regression to estimate the parameters (a_0, b_0) in the DGP provided (i) we consider the DGP to be making a conditional statement that, given a value of the quantity demanded Q_i and given a particular "shock" u_i, the price P_i is generated by the expression above, i.e., the DGP, (ii) we make an assumption about the relationship between the two causal stochastic elements of the model, Q_i and u_i, namely that given knowledge of Q_i the expected value of the shock is zero, $E[u_i \mid Q_i] = 0$, and (iii) the sequence of pairs (Q_i, u_i) for $i = 1, \dots, n$ generate an independent and identically distributed sequence.[3] The first assumption describes the nature of the DGP. The second assumption requires that, whatever the level of Q, the average value of the shock u_i will always be zero. That is, if we see many markets with high sales, say of 1 million units per year, the average demand shock will be zero and similarly if we see many markets with lower sales, say 10,000 units per year, the average demand shock will also be zero. The third assumption ensures that we

[3] Note that the technique does not need to assume that Q and u are fully independent of each other, but rather (i) that observations of the pairs (Q_1, u_1), (Q_2, u_2), and so on are independent of each other and follow the same joint distribution and (ii) satisfy the conditional mean zero assumption, $E[u_i \mid Q_i] = 0$. In addition to these three assumptions, there are some more technical "regularity" assumptions that primarily act to make sure all of the quantities needed for our estimator are finite—see your favorite econometrics textbook for the technical details.

obtain more information about the process as our sample size gets bigger, which helps, for example, to ensure that sample averages will converge to their population equivalents.[4] We describe the technique of OLS more fully bellow. Other estimators will use different sets of assumptions, in particular, we will see that an alternative estimation technique, instrumental variable (IV) estimation, will allow us to handle some situations in which $E[u_i \mid Q_i] \neq 0$.

In most if not all cases, there will be a distinction between the true DGP and the model that we will estimate. This is because our model will normally (at best) only approximate the true DGP. Ideally, the model that we estimate includes the true DGP as one possibility. If so, then we can hope to learn the true population parameters given enough data. For example, suppose the true DGP is $P_i = 10 - 2Q_i + u_i$ and the model specification is $P_i = a - bQ_i + cQ_i^2 + e_i$. Then we will be able to reproduce the DGP by assigning particular values to our model parameters. In other words, our model is more general than the DGP. If on the other hand the true DGP is

$$P_i = 10 - 5Q_i + 2Q_i^2 + u_i$$

and our model is

$$P_i = a - bQ_i + e_i,$$

then we will never be able to retrieve the true parameters with our model. In this case, the model is misspecified. This observation motivates those econometricians who favor the general-to-specific modeling approach to model specification (see, for example, Campos et al. 2005). Others argue that the approach of specifying very general models means the estimates of the general model will be very poor and as a result the hypothesis tests used to reduce down to more specific models have an extremely low chance of getting you to the right answer. All agree that the DGP is normally unknown and yet at least some of its properties must be assumed if we are to evaluate the conditions under which our estimators will work. Economists must mainly rely on economic theory, institutional knowledge, and empirical regularities to make assumptions about the likely true relationships between variables. When not enough is known about the form of the DGP, one must be careful to either design a specification that is flexible enough to avoid misspecified regressions or else test systematically for evidence of misspecification surviving in the regression equation.

Personally, we have found that there are often only a relatively small number of really important factors driving demand patterns and that knowledge of an industry (and its history) can tell you what those important factors are likely to be. By important factors we mean those which are driving the dominant features of the data. If those factors can be identified, then picking those to begin with and then

[4] The third assumption is often stated using the observed data (P_i, Q_i) and doing so is equivalent given the DGP. For an introduction to the study of the relationships between the data, DGP, and shocks, see the Annex to this chapter (section 2.5).

refining an econometric model in light of specification tests seems to provide a reasonably successful approach, although certainly not one immune to criticism.[5] Whether you use a specific-to-general modeling approach or vice versa, the greater the subtlety in the relationship between demand and its determinants, the better data you are likely to need to use any econometric techniques.

2.1.1.2 *The Method of Least Squares*

Consider the following regression model:

$$y_i = a + bx_i + e_i .$$

The OLS regression estimator attempts to estimate the effect of the variable x on the variable y by selecting the values of the parameters (a, b). To do so, OLS assigns the maximum possible explanatory power to the variables that we specify as determinants of the outcome and minimizes the effect of the "leftover" component, e_i. The value of the "leftover" component depends on our choice of parameters (a, b) so we can write $e_i(a, b) = y_i - a - bx_i$. Formally, OLS will choose the parameters a and b to minimize the sum of squared errors, that is, to solve

$$\min_{a,b} \sum_{i=1}^{n} e_i(a, b)^2.$$

The method of least squares is rather general. The model described above is linear in its parameters, but the technique can be more generally applied. For example, we may have a model which is not linear in the parameters which states $e_i(a, b) = y_i - f(x_i; a, b)$, where, for example, $f(x_i; a, b) = ax^b$. The same "least-squares" approach can be used to estimate the parameters by solving the analogous problem

$$\min_{a,b} \sum_{i=1}^{n} e_i(a, b)^2.$$

If the model is linear in the parameters, the technique is known as "ordinary" least squares (OLS). If the model is nonlinear in the parameters, the technique is called "nonlinear" least squares (NLLS).

In the basic linear-in-parameters and linear-in-variables model, a given absolute change in the explanatory variable x will always produce the same absolute change in the explained variable y. For example, if $y_i = Q_i$ and $x_i = P_i$, where Q_i and P_i represent the quantity per week and price of a bottle of milk respectively, then an increase in the price of milk by €0.50 might reduce the amount of milk purchased by, say, two bottles a week. The linear-in-parameters and linear-in-variables assumption implies that the same quantity reduction holds whether the initial price is €0.75 or €1.50. Because this assumption may not be realistic in many cases, alternative

---

[5] An example of this approach is examined in more detail in the demand context in chapter 9.

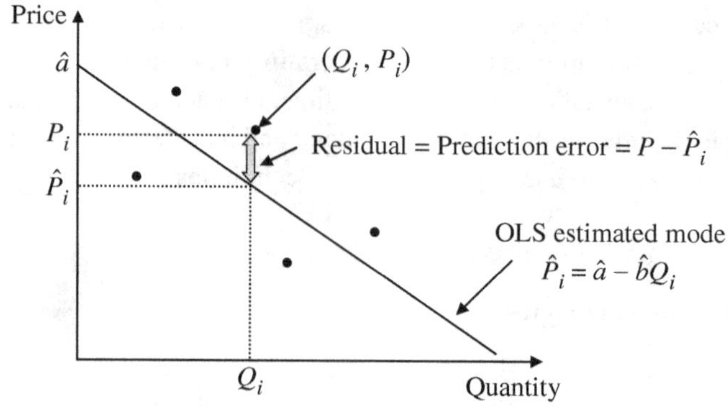

Figure 2.2. Estimated residuals in OLS regression.

specifications may fit the data better. For example, it is common to operate a log transformation on price and quantity variables so that the constant estimated effect is measured in terms of percentages, $y_i = \ln Q_i$ and $x_i = \ln P_i$. In that case, $\partial \ln Q_i / \partial \ln P_i = b$ while $\partial Q_i / \partial P_i = bQ_i / P_i$ so that the absolute changes depend on the level of both quantity demanded and price. Such variable transformations do not change the fact that the model is linear in its parameters, and so the model remains amenable to estimation using OLS.

We first discuss the single-variable regression to illustrate some useful concepts and results of OLS and then generalize the discussion to the multivariate regression. First we introduce some terminology and notation. Let $(\hat{a}, \hat{b})$ be estimates of the parameters a and b. The predicted value of y_i given the estimates and a fixed value for x_i is

$$\hat{y}_i = \hat{a} + \hat{b}x_i.$$

The difference between the true value y_i and the estimated $\hat{y}_i$ is the estimated error, or the residual e_i. Therefore, we have

$$e_i = y_i - \hat{y}_i.$$

Figure 2.2 shows the estimated residuals for our inverse demand curve, where $y_i = P_i$ and $x_i = Q_i$. We see that positive residuals are above the estimated line and negative residuals are below it. OLS estimation of the inverse demand curve minimizes the total sum of squares of the "vertical" prediction errors.[6] If the model nests the true DGP and the parameters of the estimation are exactly right, then the residuals will be exactly the same as the true "errors," i.e., the true random shocks that affect our explained variable.

[6] In contrast, if we estimated this model on the demand curve, we would be minimizing the "horizontal" prediction errors on this graph: imagine rotating the graph in order to flip the axes. The assumptions required would be different, since they would require, for instance, that $E[e_i \mid P_i] = 0$ rather than $E[e_i \mid Q_i] = 0$ and the estimates we obtain will also be different, even if we plot the two lines on the same graph.

Mathematically, finding the OLS estimators involves solving the minimization problem:

$$\min_{a,b} \sum_{i=1}^{n} e_i(a,b)^2 = \min_{a,b} \sum_{i=1}^{n} (y_i - a - bx_i)^2.$$

The first-order conditions, also known as the normal equations, are given by setting the first derivatives with respect to a and b respectively to 0:

$$\sum_{i=1}^{n} 2(y_i - \hat{a} - \hat{b}x_i)(-1) = 0 \quad \text{and} \quad \sum_{i=1}^{n} 2(y_i - \hat{a} - \hat{b}x_i)(-x_i) = 0.$$

If the model is linear in the parameters, then the minimization problem is quadratic in the parameters and hence the first-order conditions are linear in the parameters. As a result, the first-order conditions provide us with a system of linear equations to solve, one for each parameter. Linear systems of equations are typically often easy to solve analytically. In contrast, if we write down a nonlinear (in parameters) model, we may have to solve the minimization problem numerically, but conceptually the approach is no different.[7]

In the two-parameter case, the first normal equation can be solved to give $\hat{a} = \bar{y} - \hat{b}\bar{x}$, where $\bar{y}$ and $\bar{x}$ denote sample averages, as shown below:

$$\begin{aligned} &\sum_{i=1}^{n} 2(y_i - \hat{a} - \hat{b}x_i)(-1) = 0 \\ &\iff \sum_{i=1}^{n} y = \hat{a}n + \hat{b}\sum_{i=1}^{n} x_i \\ &\iff \hat{a} = \frac{1}{n}\sum_{i=1}^{n} y_i - \hat{b}\frac{1}{n}\sum_{i=1}^{n} x_i. \end{aligned}$$

The estimated value of the intercept is a function of the other estimated parameter and the average value of the variables in the regression. If the estimated parameter $\hat{b}$ is equal to 0 so that our explanatory variables have no explanatory power, then the estimated parameter $\hat{a}$ (and the predicted value of y) is just the average value of the dependent variable.

Given the expression for $\hat{a}$, we can solve

$$\begin{aligned} &\sum_{i=1}^{n} 2(y_i - \hat{a} - \hat{b}x_i)(-x_i) = 0 \\ &\iff \sum_{i=1}^{n} (y_i - \hat{a} - \hat{b}x_i)x_i = 0 \end{aligned}$$

[7] Programs such as Matlab and Gauss provide a number of standard tools to allow nonlinear problems to be solved. Solving nonlinear systems of equations can sometimes be very easy in practice, but can also be very difficult even with the very good computational algorithms now easily accessible to analysts.

$$\Longleftrightarrow \quad \sum_{i=1}^{n}(y_i - (\bar{y} - \hat{b}\bar{x}) - \hat{b}x_i)x_i = 0$$

$$\Longleftrightarrow \quad \sum_{i=1}^{n}(y_i - \bar{y})x_i - \hat{b}\sum_{i=1}^{n}(x_i - \bar{x})x_i = 0$$

$$\Longleftrightarrow \quad \hat{b} = \sum_{i=1}^{n}(y_i - \bar{y})x_i \Big/ \sum_{i=1}^{n}(x_i - \bar{x})x_i.$$

The estimated parameter $\hat{b}$ is thus the ratio of the sample covariance between the dependent and explanatory variable (numerator) to the variance of the explanatory variable (denominator).

More generally, we will want to estimate regression equations where the dependent variable is explained by a number of explanatory variables. For example, sales may be determined by both price and advertising levels. Alternatively, a "second" explanatory variable may be a lower- or higher-order term such as a square root or squared term meaning that such a specification can account for both multiple variables and also particular types of nonlinearities in variables. Retaining the linear-in-parameters specification, a multivariate regression equation takes the form:

$$y_i = a + b_1x_{1i} + b_2x_{2i} + b_3x_{3i} + e_i.$$

For given parameter values, the predicted value of y_i for given estimates and values of (x_{1i}, x_{2i}, x_{3i}) is

$$\hat{y}_i = \hat{a} + \hat{b}_1x_{1i} + \hat{b}_2x_{2i} + \hat{b}_3x_{3i}$$

and so the prediction error is $e_i = y_i - \hat{y}_i$.

In this case, the minimization problem is the same as the case with two parameters except that it involves more parameters to minimize over:

$$\min_{a,b_1,b_2,b_3} \sum_{i=1}^{n} e_i(a, b_1, b_2, b_3)^2.$$

Fortunately, as in the two-parameter case, provided the model is linear in the parameters this minimization problem is a quadratic program and so will have first-order conditions which are also linear in the parameters and admit analytic solutions.

To find those solutions, however, it is usually easier to use matrix notation, following the unifying treatment provided by Anderson (1958). To do so, simply stack up observations for the regression equation above to define the equivalent matrix expression

$$\begin{bmatrix} y_1 \\ y_2 \\ \vdots \\ y_n \end{bmatrix} = \begin{bmatrix} 1 & x_{11} & x_{21} & x_{31} \\ 1 & x_{12} & x_{22} & x_{32} \\ \vdots & \vdots & \vdots & \vdots \\ 1 & x_{1n} & x_{2n} & x_{3n} \end{bmatrix} \begin{bmatrix} a \\ b_1 \\ b_2 \\ b_3 \end{bmatrix} + \begin{bmatrix} e_1 \\ e_2 \\ \vdots \\ e_n \end{bmatrix} = \begin{bmatrix} x_1' \\ x_2' \\ \vdots \\ x_n' \end{bmatrix} \beta + \begin{bmatrix} e_1 \\ e_2 \\ \vdots \\ e_n \end{bmatrix},$$

which can in turn be more simply expressed in terms of vectors and matrices as

$$y = X\beta + e,$$

where y is an $(n \times 1)$ vector and X is an $(n \times k)$ matrix of data, while β is the $(k \times 1)$ vector of parameters to be estimated and e is the $(n \times 1)$ vector of residuals. In our example, $k = 4$ as there are four parameters to be estimated.

The general OLS minimization problem can be easily solved by using matrix notation. Specifically, note that the OLS minimization problem can be expressed as

$$\min_{\beta} e(\beta)'e(\beta) = \min_{\beta}(y - X\beta)'(y - X\beta),$$

so that the k first-order conditions are the (linear-in-parameters) form:

$$\begin{aligned}\frac{\partial(y - X\beta)'(y - X\beta)}{\partial\beta} &= 2(-X)'(y - X\beta)\\ &= 2(-X'y + X'X\beta)\\ &= 0.\end{aligned}$$

Solving for the vector of coefficients β, we obtain the general formula for the OLS regression estimator in the multivariate case:

$$\hat{\beta}^{\text{OLS}} = (X'X)^{-1}X'y.$$

Note that this formula is the multivariate equivalent of the bivariate results we developed earlier.

The variance of the OLS estimator can be calculated as follows:

$$\text{Var}[\hat{\beta}^{\text{OLS}} \mid X] = E[(\hat{\beta}^{\text{OLS}} - E[\hat{\beta}^{\text{OLS}} \mid X])(\hat{\beta}^{\text{OLS}} - E[\hat{\beta}^{\text{OLS}} \mid X])' \mid X].$$

Now if we suppose that the DGP is of the form $y = X\beta_0 + u$, then

$$\begin{aligned}E[\hat{\beta}^{\text{OLS}} \mid X] &= E[(X'X)^{-1}X'(X\beta_0 + u) \mid X]\\ &= \beta_0 + (X'X)^{-1}X'E[u \mid X]\\ &= \beta_0.\end{aligned}$$

Provided $E[u \mid X] = 0$ and since $\hat{\beta}^{\text{OLS}} - \beta_0 = (X'X)^{-1}X'u$, we have

$$\begin{aligned}\text{Var}[\hat{\beta}^{\text{OLS}} \mid X] &= E[(X'X)^{-1}X'u((X'X)^{-1}X'u)' \mid X]\\ &= (X'X)^{-1}X'(E[uu' \mid X])X(X'X)^{-1}.\end{aligned}$$

If the variance is homoskedastic so that $E[uu' \mid X] = \sigma^2 I_n$, then the formula collapses to the simpler expression,

$$\text{Var}[\hat{\beta}^{\text{OLS}} \mid X] = (X'X)^{-1}\sigma^2 I_n.$$

2.1.2 Properties of OLS

Ordinary least squares is a simple and intuitive method to apply, which explains some of its popularity. However, it is also attractive because the estimators it produces exhibit some very desirable properties provided the assumptions it requires hold. Next we briefly review these properties and the conditions necessary for them to hold.

2.1.2.1 Unbiasedness

An estimator is unbiased if its expected value is equal to the true value, i.e., if the estimator is "on average" the true value. This means that the average of the coefficient estimates over all possible samples of size n, $\{(X_i, Y_i);\ i = 1, \ldots, n\}$, would be equal to the true value of the coefficient. Formally,

$$E[\hat{\beta}] = \beta_0,$$

where β_0 is the true parameter of the DGP. The unbiasedness property is equivalent to saying that, on average, OLS estimation will give us the true value of the coefficient. For OLS estimators to be unbiased, a largely sufficient condition[8] given the DGP $y = X\beta_0 + u$ is that $E[u \mid X] = 0$, meaning that the real error term must be unrelated to the value of our explanatory variables. For instance, if we are explaining the quantity demanded as a function of price and income, it is necessary that the shocks to the demand be uncorrelated with the level of prices or income.

The unbiasedness condition can formally be obtained by applying the law of iterative expectations that states that the expected value of a variable is equal to the expected value of the conditional expectation over the whole set of possible values of the conditions. Formally, it states that $E[\hat{\beta}^{\text{OLS}}] = E_X[E[\hat{\beta}^{\text{OLS}} \mid X]]$. This allows us to write the expected value of the OLS estimator as follows:

$$\begin{aligned} E[\hat{\beta}^{\text{OLS}} \mid X] &= (X'X)^{-1}X'E[y \mid X] = (X'X)^{-1}X'E[X\beta_0 + u \mid X] \\ &= (X'X)^{-1}X'X\beta_0 + (X'X)^{-1}X'E[u \mid X] \\ &= \beta_0 + 0 \quad \text{if } E[u \mid X] = 0. \end{aligned}$$

In general, unbiasedness is a tougher requirement than consistency, which we discuss next. In particular, while we will typically be able to find estimators for linear models which are both unbiased and also consistent, many nonlinear models will admit estimators which are consistent but not unbiased.

---

[8] Strictly, there are in fact other regularity conditions which together suffice. In particular, we will require that $(X'X/n)^{-1}$ exists.

2.1.2.2 Consistency

An estimator is a consistent estimator of a parameter if it tends toward the true population value of the parameter as the sample available for estimation gets large. The property of consistency for averages is derived from a "law of large numbers." A law of large numbers provides a set of assumptions under which a statistic converges to its population equivalent. For example, the sample average of a variable will converge to the true population average as the sample gets big under weak conditions.

Somewhat formally, we can write one such law of large numbers as follows. If $X_1, X_2, \ldots, X_n$ is an independent random sample of variables from a population with mean $\mu < \infty$ and variance $\sigma^2 < \infty$ so that $E[X_i] = \mu$ and $\mathrm{Var}[X_i] = \sigma^2$, then consistency means that as the sample size n gets bigger the sample average converges[9] to the population average:

$$\bar{X}_n = \frac{1}{n}\sum_{i=1}^{n} X_i \to \mu.$$

Note that the necessary conditions for this to happen are that the first and second moments, i.e., the mean and the variance, of the variable exist and are finite. Those are relatively weak requirements as they will tend to hold in the case of almost all economic variables, which generally have a finite range of possible values.[10]

Let us develop the requirements for consistency of OLS. To do so, write the OLS estimator as

$$\begin{aligned}\hat{\beta}^{\mathrm{OLS}} &= (X'X)^{-1}X'y \\ &= (X'X)^{-1}X'(X\beta_0 + u) \\ &= \beta_0 + (X'X)^{-1}X'u.\end{aligned}$$

We have

$$\hat{\beta}^{\mathrm{OLS}} = \beta_0 + \left(\frac{X'X}{n}\right)^{-1}\left(\frac{1}{n}X'u\right).$$

Note that each of the terms in $X'X/n$ and $(1/n)X'u$ are actually just sample averages. The former has, as its jkth element, $(1/n)\sum_{i=1}^{n} x_{ij}x_{ik}$ while the latter has, as its jth element, $(1/n)\sum_{i=1}^{n} x_{ij}u_i$. These are just sample averages which, according to a "law of large numbers," will converge to their respective population means.

---

[9] Econometrics textbooks will often spend a considerable amount of time defining precisely what we mean by "converge." The two most common concepts are "convergence in probability" and "almost sure convergence." These respectively provide the "weak" law of large numbers and the "strong" law of large numbers (SLLN).

[10] A random variable which can only take on a finite set of values (technically, has finite support) will have all moments existing. Possible exceptions (might) be price data in hyperinflations, where prices can go off to close to infinity in extreme cases but even there presumably there is a limit on the amount of money that can be printed and also on the number of zeros that can be printed on any piece of paper. In contrast, occasionally economic models of real world quantities do not have finite moments. For example, Brownian motions are sometimes used in finance as approximations to the real world.

We also require that inverting the matrix $(X'X/n)^{-1}$ does not cause any problems (e.g., division by zero would be bad). In fact, the OLS estimator will be consistent if, for a large enough sample,

(1) $\frac{X'X}{n} \to M_X$, where M_X is a positive definite $(k \times k)$ matrix;

(2) $\frac{X'u}{n} \to \underline{0}$, a $(k \times 1)$ vector of zeros.

In each case, we will require laws of large numbers to hold. That will mean we will require finite first and second moments with, in the case of (2), the first population moment equal to zero. Thus the assumptions required for OLS to converge will involve those which ensure a law of large numbers to hold and then assumptions on the population averages. Specifically, that $E[u_i x_{ij}] = 0$ or, because of the law of iterated expectations, it suffices to assume that $E[u_i \mid x_{ij}] = 0$ since $E_{(u,x)}[u_i x_{ij}] = E_x[(E_{u|x}[u_i \mid x_{ij}])x_{ij}] = E_x[(0)x_{ij}] = 0$.

It should by now be clear that our assumption $E[u_i \mid x_{ij}] = 0$ plays a central role in ensuring OLS is consistent. If this assumption is violated, OLS estimation may well produce estimators that bear no relation to the true value of the parameters of the DGP, even if we fortuitously write down a family of models which includes the DGP. Unfortunately, this crucial assumption is often violated in real world settings. Among others, causes can include (i) misspecification of models, (ii) measurement error, and (iii) endogeneity. We discuss these problems, and in particular the problem of endogeneity, later in this chapter.

2.1.3 Hypothesis Testing

Econometric estimation produces an estimate of one or more parameters. A sample will provide an estimate, not the population value. Hypothesis testing involving a parameter helps us measure the extent to which the estimated outcome is consistent with a particular assumption about the real magnitude of the effect. In terms of a parameter, the hypothesis could be that the parameter takes on a particular value, say 1.[11] Concretely, hypothesis testing helps us explicitly reject or not reject a given hypothesis with a specified degree of certainty—or "confidence." To understand how this is done, we need to understand the concept of confidence intervals.

[11] More generally, we can test whether the assumptions required for our model and econometric estimator are in fact satisfied. In terms of a model, the hypothesis could be that a model is correctly specified (see, for example, any econometric text's discussion of the RESET test). In terms of an estimator, the hypothesis could be that an efficient estimator that requires strong assumptions is consistent and the strong assumptions are true (see any econometric discussion of the Wu–Durbin–Hausman test).

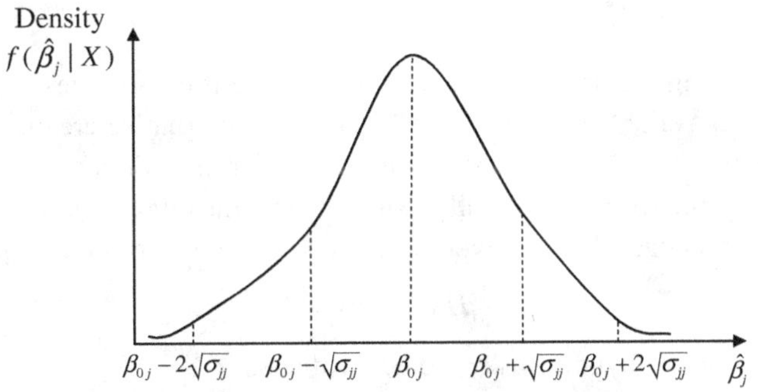

Figure 2.3. The distribution of an OLS estimator: $E[\hat{\beta}_j \mid X] = \beta_{0j}$ and $\mathrm{Var}[\hat{\beta}_j \mid X] = \sigma_{jj}$.

2.1.3.1 *Measuring Uncertainty and Confidence Intervals*

OLS regressions produce estimates for the parameters of our specified model by using the information given by the sample data, and as a result the parameter estimates from an OLS regression are stochastic variables. Estimates are normally based on a sample of the population, not on the entire population. That means that if we had drawn a different sample, we would probably have obtained different estimates.

The unbiasedness property of our OLS estimator tells us that the expected value of our estimated coefficient is the true value of the parameter, $E[\hat{\beta}_j \mid X] = \beta_{0j}$, where "$j$" denotes the jth element of the parameter vector β. Recall also that we can measure the level of uncertainty attached to any estimated coefficient by evaluating its standard deviation, normally called the standard error in this context. Defining $\mathrm{Var}[\hat{\beta}_j \mid X] = \sigma_{jj}$, we can write $\mathrm{s.e.}[\hat{\beta}_j \mid X] = \sqrt{\sigma_{jj}}$. By estimating β_{j0} with different samples of size n, we would end up with a distribution of realized values of the estimator such as that shown in figure 2.3.

In any given sample, we can construct estimates of β_{0j} and σ_{jj}, so that we can obtain information about the distribution of the estimator, even though we only have one sample. Estimating the distribution gives us an idea of how different the estimator could be if we drew a different sample of the same size. If the estimator has a normal distribution (as statistical theory often tells us, it would eventually—if our estimator satisfies a suitable central limit theorem), then 95% of the distribution density will lie within two standard errors of the mean.[12] This means that for 95% of the samples of a given size, the estimator would fall within that interval. Such an interval is called the "95% confidence interval" since we are 95% confident that our estimator would fall within that range.

[12] See, for example, chapter 5 of White (2001) for the conditions under which OLS estimators will satisfy a central limit theorem. Note that introductory texts often talk about "the" central limit theorem (CLT), whereas in truth CLTs are a type of theorem and there are many of them; for instance, not all CLTs involve normal distributions.

2.1.3.2 Hypothesis Testing

Hypothesis testing is important in econometrics and it involves testing an assumption referred to as the "null hypothesis" against an alternative creatively called the "alternative hypothesis." The most common test for an estimator is the test to see whether the estimator is statistically "significant," meaning significantly different from zero. In that case the null hypothesis to be tested is written as

$$H_0: \quad \beta_0 = 0$$

while the alternative hypothesis could be written as

$$H_{10}: \quad \beta_0 = \beta_{\text{alt}}.$$

We want to test whether we can reject the null hypothesis with sufficient confidence. If the null hypothesis is true, the expected value of the estimated parameter is 0 and therefore in 95% of cases (samples drawn from the population) the estimated value for the parameter will fall within the 95% confidence interval given by $(-2\sigma_\beta, 2\sigma_\beta)$. Generally, we consider that falling outside of the 95% confidence interval is unlikely enough (it happens only 5% of the time) to allow us to reject that the null hypothesis is true. Careful analysts will describe such a hypothesis test as having provided an answer with 95% confidence and may also go on to consider whether we can reject the null hypothesis with 99% or higher confidence. Analogously, under the alternative hypothesis that β_0 is some nonzero value β_{alt}, estimating the parameter value to be zero or close to zero will occur with certain probability. We need to assess whether the probability of finding a zero estimate if the alternative hypothesis is true is low enough to let us reject the assumption that the true value is β_{alt}. Figure 2.4 illustrates graphically the values of the estimator for which we would reject or fail to reject that the true value of the coefficient is 0.

Figure 2.4 also illustrates two very important concepts in hypothesis testing, both of which have important implications for policy making. Specifically, since our test relies on some measure of probability, making an error in rejecting or accepting a hypothesis is always a possibility. There are two types of errors, helpfully known as "type I" and "type II":

Type I. An analyst may reject the null hypothesis when it is, in fact, true. This is called making a type I error. We will make type I errors 5% of the time when using a 95% level test (one in twenty tests). In figure 2.4 the probability of making a type I error is depicted by the lighter area plus the area to the left of $-2\sigma_\beta$.

Type II. Alternatively, we can fail to reject our null hypothesis when it is actually false. This is called making a type II error. It is more difficult to know how likely this error is since it will depend on how close the true value of the parameter (let us say β_{alt} in figure 2.4) is to the null hypothesis. In figure 2.4 this probability is depicted by the darker area, which is the area within the 95% confidence interval of the null hypothesis.

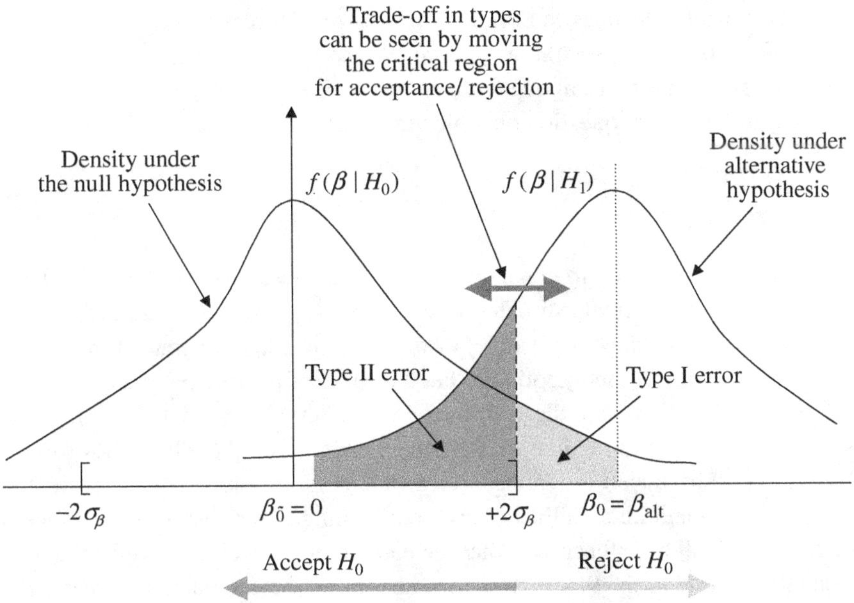

Figure 2.4. Hypothesis testing and the trade-off between type I and type II errors.

Both type I and II errors are undesirable but also unavoidable without collecting more information. Assume that our null hypothesis is that a parameter indicating some kind of competitive abuse is zero. For example, this could be a parameter indicating a cartel overcharge. With a null hypothesis of innocence, a type I error will mean that we decide that there was an abuse when in fact there was none (we find an innocent company guilty). A type II error means that we determine that there was no abuse when in fact there was abuse (we find a guilty company innocent). A decision rule will always have implications for the probability of those two kinds of errors and both errors can be costly. For instance, finding predation when there was none will have the effect of raising prices and may actively impede effective competition that was beneficial for consumers. On the other hand, if we find that prices are competitive when in truth there was predation, we may disturb the competitive process by permitting such foreclosure strategies. Whether we make the type I or the type II error large will therefore be a policy choice. We might decide to apply a criminal standard that "it is better that twelve guilty men go free than an innocent goes to jail," a standard which makes the type I error small but in doing so makes the type II error large. In the figure this trade-off can be seen by moving the critical region for acceptance or rejection; shrinking the type I error makes the type II error larger. Some note that in competition analysis if the hypothesis that a firm is abusing its market power is incorrectly rejected by a competition agency, then the forces of competition may nonetheless correctly redress the error while interventions by government, perhaps in the form of regulation, may persist far longer. Ultimately, the question of the relative size of forces working to correct the system after an error of regulatory judgment, and hence the relative costs of such policy errors, is an empirical question. However, it is probably fair to say that it is an important empirical question on which there is not a great deal of hard empirical evidence.[13]

2.1.3.3 The t-Test

The t-test is the test used to consider the null hypothesis that $H_0 : \beta_{0j} = 0$ when evaluating OLS coefficient estimates. Specifically, suppose our estimate for the true parameter β_{0j} associated with the jth regressor is $\hat{\beta}_{0j}$. We may want to know whether we can reject the hypothesis that the value of the true parameter is 0.

If the value 0 falls within the 95% confidence interval constructed using $\hat{\beta}_{0j}$ and its standard error s. e.$(\hat{\beta}_j)$, then we will not be able to reject the hypothesis that the true value is 0 because the realized value of $\hat{\beta}_{0j}$ is not unlikely enough if 0 was indeed the true magnitude of the effect. If performing a 95% test of significance, we will reject the null hypothesis that the true parameter is equal to a given value if that value falls outside of the 95% confidence interval of the estimated parameter $\hat{\beta}_{0j}$.

The standard way to test the null hypothesis that the true parameter β_{0j} is in fact a particular number β_j (e.g., zero), $H_0 : \beta_{0j} = \beta_j$, is to compute a statistic called the "t-statistic," which takes the following form (Student 1908)[14]:

$$t \equiv \frac{\hat{\beta}_j - \beta_{j0}}{\text{s.e.}(\hat{\beta}_j)}.$$

The t-statistic calculates the difference between the estimator and the value proposed as the null hypothesis value and expresses it as a proportion of the standard deviation of the estimator (its standard error), s.e. $(\hat{\beta}_j) = \sqrt{\text{Var}(\hat{\beta}_j)}$.[15] Testing whether the null hypothesis is true is equivalent to testing whether the t-statistic is equal to 0.

Under standard assumptions, a t-statistic has a probability distribution called Student's t-distribution. For large samples, this distribution approaches the normal distribution and in this case any t value higher than 1.96 in absolute value will have a

---

[13] That said, collecting more information can reduce both type I and type II errors in any given situation. To see why, consider what would happen in figure 2.4 if the variance of the distributions shrinks. With more information, the chance of a type II error falls for a given level of type I error and, also, we can typically reduce type I errors because more data allow higher confidence levels to be used. More information is, however, not a panacea in reality since collecting it costs money. If the burden of evidential proof required of a competition agency on a given case is high, then competition agencies with limited budgets will prioritize their casework. Doing so means reducing the number of cases investigated. That in turn affects the chance of prosecution and hence reduces deterrence. As a result, and quite probably only in principle rather than practice, the optimal size of a competition agency's budget will depend on all these factors.

[14] The development of the t-distribution involved important contributions from Student (actually a pseudonym for Gosset) and Fisher (1925). Their respective contributions are described in Fisher-Box (1981).

[15] For example, for an OLS estimator we have derived the formula: $\text{Var}(\hat{\beta}_j) = \sigma^2(X'X)^{-1}$

probability of less than 5% if the null hypothesis involves $\beta_{0j} = 0$.[16] So, in practice, we reject the null hypothesis $\beta_{0j} = 0$ when the absolute value of the t-statistic is higher than 1.96. Since 2 is, for most practical purposes, sufficiently close to 1.96, as a rule of thumb and for a quick first look, if the estimated coefficient $\hat{\beta}_j$ is more than double its standard error, the null hypothesis that the true value of the parameter is 0 can be rejected and $\hat{\beta}_j$ is said to be significantly different from 0. In general, small standard errors and/or a big difference between the value of the parameter under the null hypothesis and the estimated coefficient will mean that we reject the null hypothesis.

To illustrate let us use the Hausman et al. (1994) demand estimates, presented in table 2.1. The first column of results represents the parameters of an equation characterizing the demand for Budweiser beer.[17] Let us test whether we can reject the hypothesis that the coefficient of the log of price of Budweiser in that equation is equal to zero. The t-statistic will be

$$t = \frac{\hat{\beta}_j - \beta_{j0}}{\sqrt{\hat{\sigma}_{jj}}} = \frac{-0.936 - 0}{0.041} = -22.8.$$

Since $|t| = 22.8 > 1.96$ we can easily reject the null hypothesis that the effect of the price of Budweiser on the quantity demanded for Budweiser is 0 with a 95% degree of confidence. In fact, with a t-statistic of 22.8 we could easily also reject the null hypothesis with a 99% degree of confidence.

2.1.4 Common Problems in Multiple Regressions

Running a regression in a statistical package is extremely simple given modern user-friendly software and fast computers. The results can also often be intuitive. Partly as a result of such progress, the use of regression analysis has become very common in competition policy, as in many other fields. In terms of generating output—"numbers"—OLS and other estimators like instrumental variables (IVs) are very simple to implement, and are potentially very powerful tools. Yet estimators like OLS and IVs rely on strong underlying assumptions, assumptions which are frequently likely to be violated in many economic contexts. As a result, using econometrics to develop numbers that one can confidently "believe" remains a highly skilled job. Weeding out unreliable regression results is easier but even that is not without serious challenges.

A set of regression estimates are only as good as the underlying assumptions used to build and estimate the model. Basically, there are two types of assumptions. First, given a regression model, say a linear regression model, there are econometric

[16] For very small samples, a table indicating the probability distribution of the t-statistic can be used. Such tables are generally available in econometrics books.

[17] In fact these equations are "brand share" equations. We will consider the equations in more detail in chapter 9.

Table 2.1. Estimation for the demand for premium beer brands (symmetry imposed during estimation).

	1 Budweiser	2 Molson	3 Labatts	4 Miller	5 Coors
Constant	0.393	0.377	0.230	−0.104	—
	(0.062)	(0.078)	(0.056)	(0.031)	—
Time	0.001	−0.000	0.001	0.000	—
	(0.000)	(0.000)	(0.000)	(0.000)	—
$\log(Y/P)$	−0.004	−0.011	−0.006	0.017	—
	(0.006)	(0.007)	(0.005)	(0.003)	—
$\log(P_{\text{Budweiser}})$	−0.936	0.372	0.243	0.150	—
	(0.041)	(0.231)	(0.034)	(0.018)	—
$\log(P_{\text{Molson}})$	0.372	−0.804	0.183	0.130	—
	(0.231)	(0.031)	(0.022)	(0.012)	—
$\log(P_{\text{Labatts}})$	0.243	0.183	−0.588	0.028	—
	(0.034)	(0.022)	(0.044)	(0.019)	—
$\log(P_{\text{Miller}})$	0.150	0.130	0.028	−0.377	—
	(0.018)	(0.012)	(0.019)	(0.017)	—
log(number of stores)	−0.010	0.005	−0.036	0.022	—
	(0.009)	(0.012)	(0.008)	(0.005)	—
Conditional own	−3.527	−5.049	−4.277	−4.201	−4.641
Price elasticity	(0.113)	(0.152)	(0.245)	(0.147)	(0.203)

$$\Sigma = \begin{Bmatrix} 0.000359 & -1.436 \times 10^{-5} & -0.000158 & -2.402 \times 10^{-5} \\ & 0.000109 & -6.246 \times 10^{-5} & -1.847 \times 10^{-5} \\ & & 0.005487 & -0.000392 \\ & & & 0.000492 \end{Bmatrix}$$

Source: Hausman et al. (1994).

assumptions required to estimate it. In the heat of a case, sometimes staff economists are tempted to remember the appealing properties of OLS estimators while the assumptions that generate those appealing features are, shall we say, less clearly at the forefront of analytical working papers.

Secondly, there are assumptions that generate a given regression model. Even when no economic model has been explicitly used to derive the form of the regression, the regression will always correspond to a particular implicit model or a family of economic models. Naturally, if the implicit model is materially wrong it may not be appropriate to rely on the regression results. If we do not state the assumptions explicitly, then the interpretation of regression results becomes even harder since the reader (perhaps the judge in a case context) must figure out what those assumptions are and whether they are reasonable. On the other hand, if we state all of our assumptions up-front, we need to be sure that such overt honesty is not inappropriately punished by either the courts of public opinion or whichever judicial body reviews an agency's competition decision. To make any progress in analysis we may have to pick the least undesirable set of assumptions. Of course, every model of the world is inevitably "wrong," and such issues often require quite careful judgment in light of all the evidence available in a given case. On other occasions, formal statistical methods can help inform such judgments powerfully. For example, when the data we have can reject the model we are positing as being the true DGP.

In this section, we will describe the most common problems found to occur during the implementation of regression analysis and outline the ways the literature has attempted to address them. Specifically, we discuss in turn misspecification, endogeneity, multicollinearity, measurement error, and heteroskedasticity.

2.1.4.1 Misspecification

Generally, misspecification occurs when a regression model cannot represent, for any value of the parameters, the true data-generating process (DGP). In other words, the econometric model is not a valid representation of the process in the world which generates the data. This happens because the regression model specified by the analyst has imposed restrictions on the relationship between the variables that is not true. As we have noted, in reality no model is "correctly specified" but, nonetheless, testing to see whether the data we have clearly reject the model we are working with in favor of a more appropriate one is a very useful and important activity. This kind of specification error can result from the imposition of an incorrect functional form in the relation between two variables when the true relationship is nonlinear. For example, we may have included the wrong variable specification in a regression, perhaps x instead of $\ln(x)$.

Another source of specification error can be the omission of an important explanatory variable, a source of error which is equivalent to forcibly setting its coefficient in the regression to zero. For example, we may have omitted a term with a higher order such as the squared value of a regressor. Misspecification due to an erroneous functional form can produce biased estimates. The cost estimation in Nerlove (1963) discussed in chapter 3 presents an illustration of this problem, and its solution.[18] If the omitted variable is important to explain our dependent variable and if it happens to be also correlated with one of the explanatory variables included in the regression, the estimated parameters on the included regressors in our regression will be biased. This problem of "omitted variables" can be considered to be one source of the problem of endogeneity, a problem we discuss below. If the omitted variables are not correlated with any of the other of the regressors, then the problem is not immediately serious since the estimators will often be unbiased. That said, we will get a lower level of explanatory power in our model than if we included all the relevant variables. A very low explanatory power, as represented by a very low R-squared, is a sign that we are missing important determinants of our explained

[18] See the practical examples in chapter 3 for a discussion of the Nerlove (1963) paper.

outcome.[19] This is not always a problem—for example, if we are only interested in the value of a particular coefficient and we are confident that the error term, i.e., what is left out, is uncorrelated with any of our included regressors. On the other hand, if we are trying to model the explained variable, a very low R-squared can be an indication that we are missing important determinants and therefore that our model of the data-generating process is substantially incomplete.

Alternatively, misspecification can result from the omission of an interaction term between variables when the true value of a coefficient is dependent on the level of another one of the variables. For instance, the effect of a price increase on quantity demanded might depend on people's level of income. Interactions might be a good idea when the effect of a variable is measured over a very wide range of the values of the remaining regressors since in that case nonlinearities are more likely to occur.

In some cases, misspecification can be detected by informally checking the behavior of the estimated error term, the residuals. For example, sometimes plotting the residuals versus the explanatory variables reveals some systematic patterns between them. If so, the OLS assumption that $E[u_i \mid x_i] = 0$ is probably violated and the estimates biased. More formally, an econometric literature has evolved to examine specification issues. If the null hypothesis of misspecification can be stated as a parametric restriction on a more general alternative model (e.g., a model with both x and $\ln(x)$), then we can use classical tests to evaluate misspecification (see Godfrey 1989).[20] An early and yet still very useful test for general functional form misspecification is provided by Ramsey (1969).

2.1.4.2 *Endogeneity*

Endogeneity of regressors is probably the argument used most frequently to raise concerns about regression analyses. The reason is that potential endogeneity problems tend to be pervasive in economics and the solutions to endogeneity problems are sometimes few and far between. As a result, endogeneity is sometimes inappropriately ignored even though it can fatally invalidate the results of a regression. Endogeneity means that one of the regressors used in the model is correlated with the "shock" component of the model.

One reason for such a correlation is if we are suffering from an omitted-variable problem (see above). For example, an included regressor might be entirely irrelevant but correlated (for whatever reason) with the true causal factor, which has been

---

[19] Or in the case of IV regression a suitably adjusted R-squared.

[20] Recall that the classical trinity of statistical tests states that you can fit either (1) the unrestricted model and test whether the restrictions are rejected (e.g., true parameters are zero), (2) the restricted model and test whether the derivative of the objective function (e.g., likelihood) with respect to a parameter is nonzero when evaluated at a parameter value associated with the restricted model (usually zero), or (3) the likelihood ratio approach, which involves fitting both the restricted and unrestricted models. These three approaches are known as the Wald, the Lagrange multiplier, and the likelihood ratio approaches, respectively.

unfortunately omitted from the regression. The effect of this regressor will consequently be overstated. Omitted causal variables that are correlated with regressors will therefore cause an endogeneity problem, but are not the only source of them.

Alternatively, our model may also suffer from endogeneity if an included regressor is in fact simultaneously determined with our explained variable. This means that "shocks" affect both the explained and the explanatory variables. Two important examples among several that we will consider in detail in later chapters are:

(a) **Demand estimation** (see chapter 9). In a regression of quantity Q on price P, we often consider P as endogenous since we think (Q, P) pairs tend to be generated by the intersection of demand and a pricing equation (supply curve). In such a situation any demand (or supply) shock will systematically and simultaneously affect both the regressor P and the explained variable Q (see Wright 1928).

(b) **Price-market structure regressions** (see chapter 5). Assume we want to measure the effect of the number of competing firms on the price of a good. We could regress the price of the good on some cost variables, known determinants of demand (season, income, etc.), and the number of firms. One can imagine that in those places where costs are particularly high, we are likely to have a high price *and* a smaller number of firms than in low-cost areas due to lower demand in high-cost areas. If we have controlled completely for cost differences, our estimates will be fine. However, if some cost differences are unobserved, we will appear to find high prices in areas with few firms and might infer market power for these firms when in fact it is just that there are unobserved cost differences affecting both prices and the number of firms.

In such a situation we might want to explicitly model the full system of equations rather than consider estimation of a single equation. For example, in the demand estimation context we might wish to add a pricing equation (i.e., a "supply" curve). Certainly, making explicit a model of the determinants of the endogenous variable will make clear the reasons and possible solutions to an endogeneity problem. For example, we shall see below that movements in the supply curve caused by cost variation can help identify the demand curve and solve the endogeneity problem. Models in which we write down full and explicit models of all of the endogenous variables are known as "full information" models. We discuss how such simultaneous equation models can help us to understand identification strategies later in this chapter.

On the other hand, we may not wish to estimate the full system of equations but rather use a single-equation approach. Such estimators are sometimes called "limited information" estimators since they do not require that we fully specify models for all of the endogenous variables.

For completeness, suppose that we have the following "true" market demand equation,

$$Q_t = \alpha_0 - \beta_0 P_t + u_t,$$

and suppose further that we estimate the following model:

$$Q_t = \alpha - \beta P_t + e_t.$$

For OLS to be consistent, we require

$$E[e_t(\alpha_0, \beta_0) \mid P_t] = E[u_t \mid P_t] = 0,$$

while if P is endogenous, then

$$E[e_t(\alpha_0, \beta_0) \mid P_t] = E[u_t \mid P_t] \neq 0.$$

To see how such a situation can arise, suppose sales are affected by both prices and market drivers that we do not directly observe. For example, suppose as analysts we do not observe periodic advertising campaigns that increase sales. Firms on the other hand may want to charge higher prices in high demand periods and they know they will face higher demand when they advertise. If so, it may appear to us, as analysts, that there was a big positive "shock" u_t, and consequently a high demand, in periods when prices P_t are high.

In such a case, we must have information which allows us to distinguish the direct effect of a movement along a demand curve (higher sales must be associated with low prices) from movement (shifts) of the demand curve caused by factors in u_t. The latter effect will tend to indicate that high demand periods tend to have higher prices. If we use an OLS estimator, we will capture the observed correlation between price and quantity demanded consisting of the "negative" source of correlation associated with the slope of the demand curve and the "positive" source of correlation associated with the rightward shift of the demand curve in high demand periods. An OLS estimator will combine the two effects so that if the latter effect is sufficiently strong, we may well even estimate a significant positive coefficient β and erroneously conclude that demand slopes upward.

Omitted-variable problems can sometimes be corrected by including the relevant variables. In our previous example, if we knew advertising was the omitted variable, we knew advertising campaigns were a fairly rare event and we could identify when they occurred during our sample periods, we may be able to correct for this effect by inserting a dummy variable taking on the value 1 for the periods when the advertising campaigns took place and 0 otherwise. On the other hand, if advertising campaigns occur frequently, or are of materially different magnitudes or in periods we cannot observe, such a technique will not help to correct the endogeneity bias. Similarly, if we do not know that advertising is the source of variation in the demand shock that is causing the endogeneity problem (perhaps it is income variation or an evolution in tastes) then we are unlikely to be able to solve the problem in such a direct fashion. Below and in chapter 5 we discuss the use of "fixed effects" to solve endogeneity problems in a similar fashion.

The alternative limited-information approach is to use IV estimators (see, for example, Krueger and Angrist 2001; Angrist et al. 1996). IV estimators allow us to identify the parameters of a single-equation model even if we believe we have an endogeneity problem caused by $E[u_t \mid P_t] \neq 0$. Even if we do not actually specify an equation for the endogenous variables, economic theory will typically provide at least some guidance over potentially appropriate "instruments" for this technique. An introduction to a variety of IV techniques is provided later in this chapter.

2.1.4.3 Multicollinearity

When the explanatory variables in a regression are highly correlated with each other, we will not be able to separate the effects of the different regressors and the estimators will not represent the true effect of the variable on the outcome. Assume a true DGP is

$$y_i = a_0 + b_{10}x_{i1} + b_{20}x_{i2} + u_i.$$

If $x_{i1} = \lambda x_{i2}$, the DGP can be rewritten as

$$y_i = a_0 + (b_{10} + \lambda b_{20})x_{i2} + u_i.$$

The fundamental problem with this specification is that we simply cannot identify the separate effects of x_{1i} and x_{2i} on y_i. We can only identify the combination $(b_{10}\lambda + b_{20})$ and we will be able to tell apart or "identify" the three parameters $(b_{10}, \lambda, b_{20})$ or even the two marginal effects, $(b_{10}, \lambda b_{20})$.

Technically, in case of perfect collinearity what happens is that the matrix $M_X = X'X/n$ is not invertible because two columns are linear combinations of each other. In practice, a regression package attempting to estimate a specification which includes both x_{1i} and x_{2i} will usually automatically complain if the two variables are perfectly correlated.[21] The coefficients simply cannot be calculated and the computer code will either crash or more sophisticated code will automatically drop one or more variables causing the problem. In practice, what normally happens is that one can get close to an invertibility problem.

Specifically, the two variables may not be exactly a linear combination of each other but rather close enough to cause problems with this condition even though coefficients can be calculated. This can be a particular problem if the sample is small and may arise even where, if we had enough data, the various coefficients would be identified in theory.

A sign that there may be multicollinearity problems is the presence of coefficients that are individually insignificant although they are jointly highly significant. To see why recall that the variance of an OLS estimator depends on $(X'X/n)^{-1}$. If the

[21] Earlier we described the assumption required for OLS that the limit of cross-products of the matrix of regressors $X'X/n$ must converge in an appropriate sense to a "positive definite" matrix M_X. The matrix X is $(n \times k)$ and for M_X to be positive definite X must be of "full column rank," i.e., of rank k. If in a given sample the matrix X is not of full rank, as it will not be if its columns are linearly dependent, then the matrix $X'X/n$ will be of rank less than k and hence will not be invertible. Thus a computer code which attempts to compute $(X'X/n)^{-1}$ will fail.

variables in X are close to collinear, then this inverse will "blow up" becoming close to a division by zero. At least one of the two parameters on the collinear variables will be reported as being estimated very imprecisely. In such a case, reported standard errors on individual parameters will typically be very large indeed.

2.1.4.4 Measurement Error

Measurement error can occur in either dependent or independent variables. If the true "data" y_i^* and x_{i1}^* are each observed with error, we may actually observe only $y_i = (y_i^* + v_i)$ and $x_{i1} = (x_{i1}^* + \varepsilon_i)$.[22] Suppose we write down the data-generating process as

$$y_i^* = a_0 + b_{10}x_{i1}^* + u_i,$$

which we can write as

$$y_i = a_0 + b_{10}x_{i1} + (u_i + v_i - b_{10}\varepsilon_i).$$

If we actually estimate the model

$$y_i = a + b_1x_{i1} + w_i,$$

then, at true parameter values (a_0, b_{10}), the regressor in our model $x_{i1} = (x_{i1}^* + \varepsilon_i)$ is correlated with the error $w_i(a_0, b_{10}) = (u_i + v_i - b_{10}\varepsilon_i)$. Thus even in the event that u_i, v_i, ε_i, and x_{i1}^* are each mutually independent, we have

$$\begin{aligned} E[w_i(a_0, b_{10})x_{i1}] &= E[(u_i + v_i - b_{10}\varepsilon_i)(x_{i1}^* + \varepsilon_i)] \\ &= -b_{10}\,\mathrm{Var}[\varepsilon_i] \\ &\neq 0. \end{aligned}$$

First notice that if we only have measurement error in the dependent variable ($v_i \neq 0$ and $\varepsilon_i = 0$), then our OLS estimator will not suffer from consistency problems. That said, OLS parameter estimates have standard errors that will depend on the variance of the error so that even measurement error in the dependent variable will make our coefficient estimates less precisely estimated. On the other hand, if we only have measurement error in the independent variable ($v_i = 0$ and $\varepsilon_i \neq 0$), then our OLS estimator will be inconsistent. In the special case where there is only one regressor, the resulting bias is known as "attenuation" bias because the OLS estimator is always biased toward zero. However, in general, as soon as we move to multivariate regression, very little can be said about the form and direction of the bias resulting from measurement error (see Reiersol 1950 and references therein). Intuitively, a causal effect is more difficult to capture when there is measurement error in the data blurring the true causal effect of the x variable on the y variable. At first thought, you might think such effects would go away as the sample size

[22] For a slightly less whirlwind survey of estimation under measurement error, we refer the reader to a good graduate econometrics textbook such as Greene (2007).

gets large and yet this result says they do not if there is measurement error in the x variable—the OLS estimator is inconsistent. More optimistically, instrumental variable techniques can be shown to help solve measurement error problems and we discuss their use and application below.

2.1.4.5 Correlated Errors and Heteroskedasticity

Standard errors provide a measure of uncertainty in a set of parameter estimates under the assumption that the data-generating process (DGP) provides the true model of the world. Standard errors typically calculated by default in OLS computer software packages are correct only if (i) the disturbances are uncorrelated across observations and (ii) the variance of the disturbances are the same across observations. In terms of the DGP, $y_i = a_0 + b_{10}x_{i1} + u_i$, these classical assumptions can be stated as (i) $E[u_i u_j] = 0$ for all $i \neq j$ and (ii) $E[u_i^2] = \sigma_u^2$ for all i. These assumptions will not always, or even typically, hold in practical settings.

Correlated errors. Correlation of error terms across observations can arise in a number of contexts. Perhaps the easiest to consider is in time series where shocks take several periods to fade. A positive shock in one period will lead to a positive shock in the next one. For example, in time series models we may approximate such a process using an "autoregressive" model such as the AR(1) model $u_t = \rho u_{t-1} + \varepsilon_t$ so that even if $E[\varepsilon_t \varepsilon_{t-s}] = 0$ for all $s > 0$ we nonetheless have $E[u_t u_{t-s}] = \rho^s$. An extreme form of correlation across observations can be generated by duplicating the data set by recording each observation twice. Doing so, according to the standard OLS formula would dramatically reduce the uncertainty and standard errors of the OLS estimates, yet clearly there is no real new information, just duplicates. The reason one would be misled is that the usual OLS estimates of standard errors rely on the assumption that observations are independent realizations, whereas in this instance the act of duplicating the data has led to a very extreme form of "dependence."

Heteroskedasticity. The assumption that $E[u_i^2] = \sigma_u^2$ for all i is known as the assumption of homoskedasticity. When it fails we will describe ourselves as being in a situation of heteroskedasticity where $E[u_i^2] \neq E[u_j^2]$ for some $i \neq j$. That is, we are in a situation with heteroskedasticity if the variance of the error is different across observations. On the other hand, heteroskedasticity can affect groups of observations, meaning that certain observations will together have a large or small variance of the error. When the variance of the error term is not homoskedastic, the standard errors calculated by OLS regression packages will usually be wrong. Fortunately, as we saw earlier, both unbiasedness and consistency rely largely on the assumption that $E[u_i \mid x_i] = 0$ and do not require assumptions about the second moments of the unobservable, except that they are finite. Thus in contrast to a problem like endogeneity, heteroskedasticity will not bias the coefficients estimated by OLS. Unfortunately, heteroskedasticity will usually bias our estimates of standard errors unless we use the correct formulas and so the analyst must be careful to do so.

Formally, the true variance of the estimator $\hat{\beta}$ has the following expression:

$$\begin{aligned}\operatorname{Var}[\hat{\beta} \mid X] &= E[(X'X)^{-1}X'u((X'X)^{-1}X'u)' \mid X] \\ &= (X'X)^{-1}X'E[uu' \mid X]X(X'X)^{-1} \\ &= (X'X)^{-1}(X'\Omega X)(X'X)^{-1}.\end{aligned}$$

This is different from the formula typically used to estimate the variance of $\hat{\beta}^{\text{OLS}}$ in the case of homoscedasticity where the covariance of the disturbance term across observations is 0 and the variance for each observation is assumed to be the same so that we have $\Omega = \sigma^2 I_n$, where I_n is an $(n \times n)$ identity matrix. Substituting this expression into the general formula yields $\operatorname{Var}[\hat{\beta}^{\text{OLS}} \mid X] = \sigma^2(X'X)^{-1}$.

Unsurprisingly, hypothesis tests that use the wrong standard errors will lead us to the wrong conclusions on hypothesis tests as confidence intervals are built with standard errors (see earlier in the chapter). There are a number of ways to avoid this problem. As described for the AR(1) model, one can model the correlation among error terms. Doing so explicitly imposes some structure to the error term matrix Ω. This technique is common in times series analysis. Alternatively, the simplest way is to use OLS regression while calculating "robust" or heteroskedasticity consistent standard errors (HCSEs) using the Huber–White procedure, since this technique does not require us to make any parametric assumptions about the nature of the correlation between the error terms (Huber 1967; White 1980). We refer the reader to standard econometrics textbooks for a discussion of these procedures, noting only that they involve estimating the term $(X'\Omega X)$, where if X is an $(n \times k)$ matrix, it consists of a $(k \times k)$ matrix of elements each of the form $\sum_{t=1}^{n}\sum_{s=1}^{n}\sigma_{st}x_{sj}x_{tk}$. Since each of these are averages over observations we do not need to estimate each element σ_{st} consistently but rather just the average term. Such estimates are known as Huber–White or HCSE standard errors.

Knowledge of $(X'\Omega X)$ and an analogously estimated $(X'\Omega y)$ can also be used to construct (asymptotically) more efficient estimators. For example, we can use an estimator known as generalized least squares (GLS) estimation, $\hat{\beta}^{\text{GLS}} = (X'\Omega X)^{-1}(X'\Omega y)$, which takes into account the error term structure in the calculation of the coefficient and its standard error. We note that such econometric results are asymptotic in character and in small samples "asymptotically more efficient" estimators can in fact have higher variance than their simpler OLS counterparts.[23]

[23] Intuitively, the GLS estimator weighs the sample using the elements of Ω to construct the following: $\sum_{t=1}^{n}\sum_{s=1}^{n}\sigma_{st}x_{sj}x_{tk}$. Weighing the observations in the sample unequally is great for efficiency if we put lots of weight on those observations containing lots of information.

The reason is that if we have a small sample, we may have in effect a poor estimate of the right weights and hence may be incorrectly weighing the observations in the sample—perhaps even overweighing the observations containing little information.

2.2 Identification of Causal Effects

The ultimate objective of a multiple regression exercise is often to help identify the causal effect of some variable x on some variable y. Such an exercise in finding causation is fundamentally different to an exercise in finding correlations between variables and, in fact, far more difficult. Correlation may be entirely spurious (e.g., it may so happen that the number of priests and murderers both increase over time so the data series are correlated). Positive or negative correlation does not imply causation. Alternatively, correlation may arise because two variables are simultaneously determined by some third factor. For example, while we are delighted that it is often reported that drinking a glass of red wine each day does actually reduce the risk of heart attacks—journalists report that science tells us there is a causal relationship—we have always worried that the relationship is not genuinely causal. If some third factor is at play—perhaps that richer people drink more red wine and also have better access to health care—then we would see a correlation between wine drinking and good health but the relationship would not be causal. The only way to find out whether you genuinely believe the medical study is to look at it and decide whether the researchers used a suitable methodology to identify causal effects. It is important to stress that a regression equation does not distinguish correlation and causality and estimation will usually pick up correlations even if there is absolutely no causal relationship between the variables.

Turning to the case wherein there is (or may be) a true causal relationship between two variables, we often want to find the exact causal relationships so that we can make statements along the lines of, if variable x goes up then variable y will fall. In the case of a unidirectional causal relationship, to identify the extent of the true causal relationship using OLS we showed in the previous section that we must be careful about correlations between the causal variable(s) and any variables that are not observed by analysts. Further complications arise when the true causal relationships are multidirectional. The most famous example of such a situation for economists involves the simultaneous determination of price and quantity by the two causal relationships embodied respectively in demand and supply curves. On the demand side, the quantity demanded is usually causally affected by price while on the supply side the price charged by a supplier for its output may depend on the quantity to be supplied (e.g., if unit production costs change with the volume supplied). In a competitive market the price and quantity will both simultaneously be determined by these two underlying causal relationships. As we will see below, in such situations, we may observe zero, positive, or negative correlations between our price and quantity data even though there are truly causal relationships between the variables. This section explains techniques economists have found useful for identifying causal effects in the presence of potentially multidirectional causal relationships.

2.2.1 Endogeneity and Identification

Earlier in the chapter we discussed the fact that omitted variables and simultaneity can each cause endogeneity problems. Recall that we established that an omitted variable that affects both the explanatory variable of interest and the outcome of interest can create a correlation between the regressor and the error term violating the assumptions we need to hold for an OLS estimator to be consistent. In these cases, we need to use one of several methods that can solve the problems of omitted variables and/or simultaneity. In this section, we introduce the identification problem encountered in empirical analysis generally and we do so in the important context of the econometric identification of demand and supply functions. We then discuss the most commonly used techniques that aid identification, namely fixed-effects regressions, instrumental variable techniques, and evidence from "natural" experiments. Stock market event studies will also be discussed. For a semiformal statistical statement of the problem of identification, the reader is directed to the annex at the end of this chapter (section 2.5).

2.2.2 Identification of Demand and Supply

Much of the empirical work in competition analysis concerns the estimation of demand functions and supply-side relationships (often pricing equations are, in particular circumstances, related to cost functions). Since the basic supply-and-demand model in a competitive market provides a classic identification problem, one no doubt familiar to many readers, it will help us introduce the debate around identification generally. The study of identification is certainly worthy of substantial attention by any economist who intends to work with data, even informally. Elsewhere in the book we build on this discussion when we attempt to use the framework of identification to help distinguish the economic models which are generating market data. For example, we often want to distinguish whether data are generated from firms which are colluding or competing and this is a topic we discuss extensively in chapter 6.

2.2.2.1 Regressions and Market Equilibria

In a classical model of supply and demand both prices and volume of sales (quantity) are determined by the intersection of supply and demand. The data we observe are the outcome of a market equilibrium. A regression equation attempting to estimate the relationship between price and quantity demanded could therefore be either a demand curve or a supply (i.e., pricing) curve. To illustrate this point, let us assume the market demand function is

$$Q_i = Q_i^{\mathrm{D}}(P_i, w_i^{\mathrm{D}}, u_i^{\mathrm{D}}; \theta^{\mathrm{D}}),$$

where P_i denotes prices, w_i^{D} denotes observed factors that affect demand, u_i^{D} denotes combination of the factors that affect demand that we do not observe, and θ^{D} are parameters we wish to estimate. Analogously, we could describe an industry supply equation

$$Q_i = Q_i^{\mathrm{S}}(P_i, w_i^{\mathrm{S}}, u_i^{\mathrm{S}}; \theta^{\mathrm{S}}).$$

Market equilibrium prices and quantities are determined by the requirement that demand is equal to supply in equilibrium. In other words, prices and quantities will equilibrate so as to ensure

$$Q_i^{\mathrm{D}} = Q_i^{\mathrm{S}} \iff Q_i^{\mathrm{D}}(P_i, w_i^{\mathrm{D}}, u_i^{\mathrm{D}}; \theta^{\mathrm{D}}) = Q_i^{\mathrm{S}}(P_i, w_i^{\mathrm{S}}, u_i^{\mathrm{S}}; \theta^{\mathrm{S}}),$$

where i could indicate the markets or time periods from which we have data. The two equations

$$Q_i = Q_i^{\mathrm{D}}(P_i, w_i^{\mathrm{D}}, u_i^{\mathrm{D}}; \theta^{\mathrm{D}}) \quad \text{and} \quad Q_i = Q_i^{\mathrm{S}}(P_i, w_i^{\mathrm{S}}, u_i^{\mathrm{S}}; \theta^{\mathrm{S}})$$

are known as the "structural form" of this two-equation economic model. While if we solve the single equation $Q_i^{\mathrm{D}}(P_i, w_i^{\mathrm{D}}, u_i^{\mathrm{D}}; \theta) = Q_i^{\mathrm{S}}(P_i, w_i^{\mathrm{S}}, u_i^{\mathrm{S}}; \theta)$ for the variable being determined, price, $P_i = P(w_i^{\mathrm{D}}, u_i^{\mathrm{D}}, w_i^{\mathrm{S}}, u_i^{\mathrm{S}}; \theta^{\mathrm{D}}, \theta^{\mathrm{S}})$ and then plug that back into either the supply or the demand curve, we get a second equation $Q_i = Q(w_i^{\mathrm{D}}, u_i^{\mathrm{D}}, w_i^{\mathrm{S}}, u_i^{\mathrm{S}}; \theta^{\mathrm{D}}, \theta^{\mathrm{S}})$. We can have a full description of the two endogenous outcomes of our model, each in terms of only exogenous variables. Namely, the equilibrium price and quantity can be expressed as

$$P_i = P(w_i^{\mathrm{D}}, u_i^{\mathrm{D}}, w_i^{\mathrm{S}}, u_i^{\mathrm{S}}; \theta^{\mathrm{D}}, \theta^{\mathrm{S}}),$$
$$Q_i = Q(w_i^{\mathrm{D}}, u_i^{\mathrm{D}}, w_i^{\mathrm{S}}, u_i^{\mathrm{S}}; \theta^{\mathrm{D}}, \theta^{\mathrm{S}}).$$

Equations describing the determinants of endogenous variables in terms of only exogenous variables are called "reduced-form" equations. Estimating a reduced form for market prices and quantities will require data on equilibrium prices and quantities in that market as dependent variables and then observed demand and supply shifters (perhaps GDP and cost data such as input prices respectively) as variables that will explain the market outcomes. Note that in estimating the reduced-form equations, we are not estimating either a demand function or a supply function but rather the market outcome from a combination of the two.

2.2.2.2 *Identifying Demand and Supply Functions from Market Data*

Much of the time we will want to estimate either the demand or the supply function. In practice, the demand curve, i.e., the quantity demanded at each price, is rarely observed. But what we see are data on the equilibrium prices and quantities—data

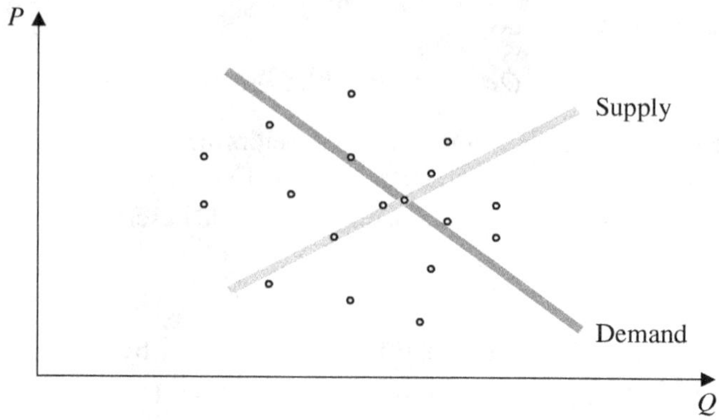

Figure 2.5. Price and quantity data: The intersection of a supply and a demand curve generates our data point (Q_i, P_i).

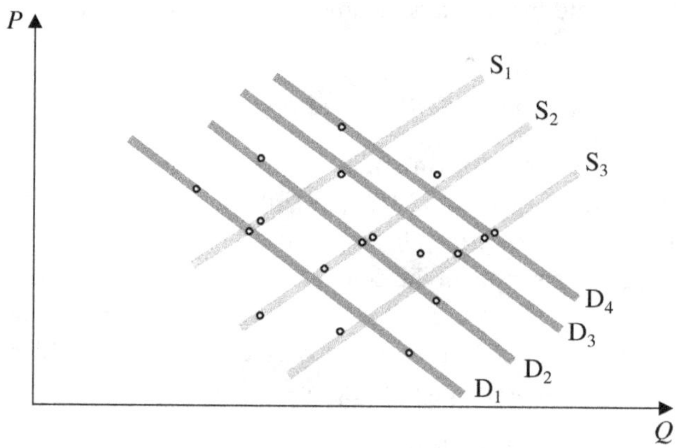

Figure 2.6. Indicative supply and demand curves shifting and generating a data set.

points generated if our model of the world is correct by the intersection of the demand and supply curves.

When we collect price and quantity data and plot them, we might find the results look like the plot in figure 2.5. According to our model, the data scattered across the whole of figure 2.5 are plotting neither a nice demand curve nor a nice supply curve. The reason is precisely because the data are generated as a result of both a supply curve and a demand curve; in fact, they are the result of their intersection. In this case we need the full two equation model to describe the process of data generation. The DGP involves two equations as illustrated in figure 2.6. Such examples clearly demonstrate that a lack of correlation between two variables, here price and quantity, need not imply there is not an underlying causal relationship between the two. Indeed, in this case there are not just one but two underlying causal relationships between them.

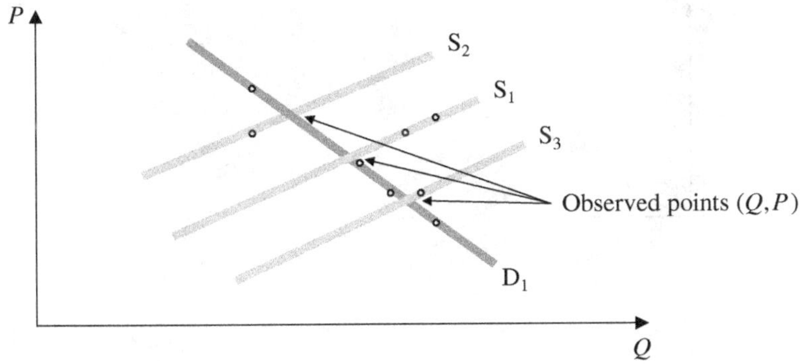

Figure 2.7. Identification of the demand curve using movements of the supply curve.

If all we observe is price and quantity, then we cannot hope to identify either a demand or a supply function even if we assume all shifts are linear shifts of the underlying curves; simply, there are many potential shifting demand or supply curves that could have produced the same set of market outcomes. For example, while we clearly need two equations to generate a single point as the prediction, the location of the point does not constrain the slope of either line. From price and quantity data alone it is impossible to empirically quantify the effect of an increase in prices on the quantity demanded and therefore to extract information such as the demand elasticity.

A major contribution associated with the work of authors such as Wright, Frisch, Koopmans, Wald, Mann, Tintner, and Haavelmo is to understand what is necessary to identify supply and demand curves (or indeed parameters in any set of linear simultaneous equations).[24] Between them they showed that in order to identify the demand function, we will need to be able to exploit shifts in the supply function which leave the demand function unchanged. Figure 2.7 makes clear why: if we know that the observed equilibrium outcomes correspond to a particular demand function, we can simply use the shifts in supply to trace out the demand function. Thus supply shifts will allow us to identify which parameter values (intercept, slope) describe the demand function.

Supply shifters could be cost-changing variables such as input prices or exchange rates. Naturally, for such a variable to actually work to identify a demand curve we need it to experience sufficient variation in our data set. Too little data variation would give an estimate of the demand function only in a very small data range and the extrapolation to other quantity or price levels would likely be inaccurate. Furthermore, in practice the demand curve will itself not usually stay constant, so that we are in fact trying to identify movements in supply that generate movement in price and quantity that we know are due to supply curve movement rather than

[24] For a history of the various contributions from authors, see Bennion (1952).

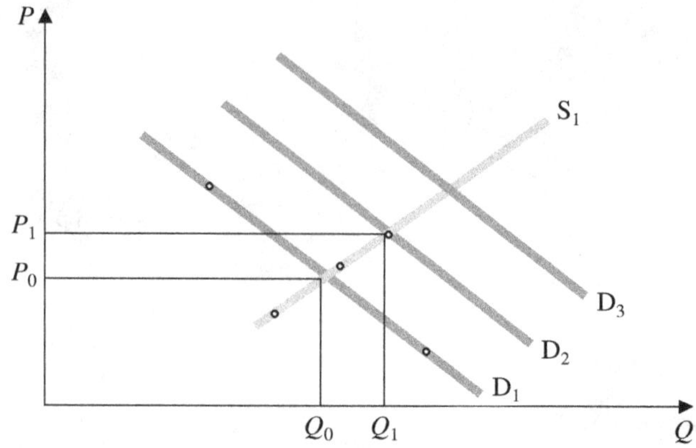

Figure 2.8. Movements in the demand curve can be used to help identify the supply curve.

demand curve movement (as distinct from a situation where all we know is that one of them must have moved to generate a different outcome).

If, on the other hand, the demand is shifting and the supply is constant, we cannot identify the demand function but we could potentially identify the supply function. This situation is represented in figure 2.8.

A shifting demand will, for example, arise when effective but unobserved (by the econometrician) marketing campaigns shift demand outwards, increasing the amount that consumers are collectively willing to buy at any given price. As we described earlier, an OLS estimate of the coefficient on the price variable will in this case be biased. It will capture both the effect of the higher price and the effect of the advertisement. This is because the higher price coincides in this case with surges in the demand that are unexplained by the regression. This induced positive correlation, in this case between unobserved demand shifters and price, generates "endogeneity" bias and in essence our estimator faces an identification problem.

On occasion we will find genuinely upward-sloping demand curves, for example, when analyzing extreme versions of the demand for "snob" goods, known as Veblen goods (expensive watches or handbags, where there may be negative network externalities so that consumers do not want lots of people to own them and actively value the fact that high prices drive out others from the market) (Leibenstein 1950). Another example is when analyzing extreme cases of inferior goods, where income effects actually dominate the direct effects of price rises and again we may believe demand curves actually slope upward. However, these are rare potential exceptions as even in the case of snob and inferior goods the indirect effects must be very strong indeed to actually dominate the direct effect (or the latter must be very weak). In contrast, it is extremely common to estimate apparently positive price coefficients during the early phases of a demand study. Ruling out the obviously wrong upward-sloping demand curves is, however, relatively easy. In many cases, the effect of endogeneity can be far more subtle, causing a bias in the coefficient that is not quite so obviously wrong: suppose we estimate a log–log demand curve and find a slope coefficient of −2. Is that because the actual own-price elasticity of demand is −2 or is that because the actual own-price elasticity of demand is −4 and our estimates are suffering from endogeneity bias? In practical settings ruling out the obviously crazy is a good start, and pushes us in the right direction. In this case, a good economic theory which clearly applies in a given practical context can tell us that the demand curve must (usually) slope down. This is not a very informative restriction, though it may suffice to rule out some estimates. Unfortunately, economic theory typically does not place very strong restrictions on what we should *never* (or even rarely) observe in a data set.[25] As a result, it may be of considerable help but will rarely provide a panacea.

The study of identification[26] establishes sets of theoretical conditions that establish that given "enough" data we can learn about particular parameters.[27] After such an "identification theorem" is proven, however, there remain very important practical questions, namely, (i) how many data constitute "enough" and (ii) in any given empirical project do we have enough data? If we have theoretical identification and the mean independence restrictions between unobservables and exogenous variables hold, we may still not be able to identify the parameters of our model if there is insufficient real data variation in the exogenous variables. In a given data set, if our parameters are not being "well" identified because of lack of data variation, we will find large estimated standard errors. Given enough data these may become small but "enough" may sometimes require a huge amount of data. In practical competition agency decision making where we can collect the best cost data that firms hold, such difficulties are regular occurrences when we try to use cost data from firms to identify their demand equations. Basically, often the cost data are relatively infrequently collected or updated and hence do not contain a great deal of variation and hence information. Such data will in reality often have a hard time identifying demand curves, even if in theory the data should be very useful.

In practical terms, the general advice is therefore the following:

(a) Consider whether the identification assumptions (e.g., conditional mean independence) that the estimator uses are likely to be valid assumptions.

(b) Put a substantial amount of thought into finding variables that industry experience and company documents indicate will significantly affect each of supply and demand conditions.

---

[25] Supply-side theory can be somewhat helpful as well. For instance, every industrial organization economist knows that no profit-maximizing firm should price at a point where demand is inelastic. Between them the restrictions from profit maximization and utility theory (demand slopes down) tell us that own-price elasticities should usually be greater than −1. In relying on such theory it is important to keep in mind whether it fits the industry; for example, we know that when low prices today beget high demand today but also high demand tomorrow (as in experience goods) firms may have incentives to price at a point where static demand elasticities are below 1 in magnitude.

[26] For a further discussion of the formalities of identification, see the annex to this chapter (section 2.5).

[27] A discussion of identification of supply and demand in structural equations can be found in chapter 6.

(c) Pay particular attention to finding variables which are known to affect either supply or demand but not both.

(d) Use estimates of standard errors to help evaluate whether parameters are actually being identified in a given data set. Large standard errors often indicate that you do not have enough information in the sample to actually achieve identification even if in theory (given an infinite sample) your model is well identified. In an extreme case of a complete failure of identification, standard errors will be reported to be either extremely large or even reported as missing values in regression output.

Even if we cannot account for all relevant covariates, identification of demand (or supply) functions is often possible if we correctly use the methods that have developed over the years to aid identification. We now turn to a presentation of the techniques most often used in empirical analysis to achieve identification. For example, we introduce fixed-effects estimators which can account for unobserved shifts correlated with our variables. We also study the important technique of instrumental variables, which instead of using the conditional mean restriction associated with OLS that the regressors be independent of the error term, $E[U \mid X] = 0$, relies upon the alternative moment restriction that another variable Z be uncorrelated with the error, $E[U \mid Z] = 0$, but sufficiently related to X to predict it, so that this prediction of X by Z is what is actually used in the regression. We will also describe the advantages and disadvantages of using "natural experiments" and event studies that attempt to use exogenous shocks to the explanatory variable to identify its causal effect.

2.2.3 Methods Used to Achieve Identification

The study of identifying causal effects is an important one and unsurprisingly a variety of techniques have been developed, some crude others very subtle. At the end of the day we want to do our best to make sure that the estimate of the parameter is not capturing any other effect than the one it is supposed to capture, namely the direct effect of that particular explanatory variable on the outcome. We first discuss the simplest of all methods, the "fixed-effect" technique before moving on to discuss the technique of "instrumental variables" and the technique commonly described as using "natural experiments." Finally, we also introduce event studies, which share the intuition of natural experiments.[28]

2.2.3.1 Fixed Effects

We have said that one reason why identifying causal effects is difficult is that we must control for omitted variables which have a simultaneous effect on one or more

[28] There is an active academic debate regarding the extent of similarity and difference between the instrumental variable and natural experiment approaches. We do not attempt to unify the approaches here but those interested in the links should see, for example, Heckman and Vytlacil (2005).

explanatory variables and on the outcome.[29] One approach is to attempt to control for all the necessary variables, but that is sometimes impossible; the data may simply not be available and anyway we may not even know exactly what we should be controlling for (what is potentially omitted) or how to measure it. In very special circumstances a fixed-effects estimator will help overcome such difficulties.

For example, in production function estimation it is common to want to measure the effect of inputs on outputs. One difficulty in doing so is that firms can generally have quite different levels of productivity, perhaps because firms can have very good or fairly poor processes for transforming inputs into outputs. If processes do not change much over short time periods, then we call α_i firm i's productivity and propose a model for the way in which output is transformed into inputs of the form

$$y_{it} = \alpha_i + w_{it}\beta + u_i,$$

where y_{it} is output from firm i in period t and w_{it} is the vector of inputs. As a profession, economists have a very hard time finding data that directly measures "firm productivity," at least without sending people into individual factories to perform benchmarking studies. On the other hand, if the processes do not vary much in relation to the frequency of our data, we might think that productivity can be assumed constant over time. If so, then we can use the fact that we observe multiple observations on a factory's inputs and output to estimate the factory's productivity α_i.

To emphasize the distinction we might write (more formally but equivalently) the fixed-effects model as

$$y_{it} = \sum_{g=1}^{n} d_{ig}\alpha_g + w_{it}\beta + u_{it},$$

where d_{ig} is a dummy variable taking the value 1 if $i = g$ and zero otherwise. The advantage of this way of writing the model is that it makes entirely clear that d_{ig} is "data" while the α_gs are parameters to be estimated (so that to construct, for example, an OLS estimator we would construct an X matrix with rows $x'_{it} = (d_{i1}, \dots, d_{in}, w_{it})$). The initial formulation is useful as shorthand but some people find it so concise that it confuses.

If we ignored the role of productivity in our model, we would use the regression specification

$$y_{it} = w_{it}\beta + v_{it}$$

so that if the DGP were

$$y_{it} = \alpha_i + w_{it}\beta_0 + u_{it},$$

we would have an unobservable which consisted of $v_{it} = \alpha_i + u_{it}$.

In that case OLS estimators will typically suffer from an endogeneity bias since the error term $v_{it} = \alpha_i + u_{it}$ and variables w_{it} will be correlated because of the

[29] Most econometrics texts have a discussion of fixed-effects estimators. One nice discussion in addition to those in standard textbooks is provided in chapter 3 of Hsiao (1986).

presence of firm i's productivity α_i in the error term. The reason is that firms' productivity levels will typically also affect their input choices, i.e., the value of w_{it}. Indeed, while discussing the relationships between production functions, cost functions, and input demand equations in chapter 1, we showed that firms' input demands will depend on their level of productivity. In particular, to produce any given amount of output, high-productivity firms will tend to use few inputs. There is, however, at least one additional effect, namely that high-productivity firms will also tend to produce a lot and therefore use lots of inputs. As a result, we cannot theoretically predict the direction of the overall bias, although most authors find the latter effect dominates empirically. Specifically, most authors find that OLS estimates of production functions find the parameters on input demands tend to be above fixed-effects estimators because of the positive bias induced by efficient firms producing a lot and hence using lots of inputs.[30]

To use a fixed-effects approach we must have a data set where there are sufficient observations that share unobserved characteristics. For instance, in our example we assumed we had data from each firm on multiple occasions. More generally, we need to be able to "group" observations and still have enough data in the groups to use the "within-group" data variation in independent and dependent variables to identify the causal effects. Continuing our example, it is the fact that we observe each firm on multiple occasions that will allow us to estimate firm-specific fixed effects; the "group" of observations involves those across time on a given firm.

The general approach to applying the fixed-effects technique is to add a group-specific dummy variable that controls for those omitted variables that are assumed constant across members of the same group but that may vary across groups. A group fixed effect is a dummy variable that takes the value 1 for all observations belonging to the group, perhaps a city or a firm, and 0 otherwise. The dummy variable will control for the effect of belonging to such a group so that any group-specific unobserved characteristic that might have otherwise affected both the dependent and the explanatory variable is accounted for. In practice, a fixed-effects regression can be written as

$$y_{it} = \sum_{g=1}^{G} d_{ig}\alpha_g + w_{it}\beta + u_{it},$$

where d_{ig} are series of dummy indicators that take a value of 1 when observation i belongs to group g, where g indexes the G groups, so $g = 1, \dots, G$. The coefficient β identifies the effect of the variables in w_{it} on outcome y_{it} while controlling for the factors which are constant across members of the group g, which are encapsulated in α_g.

The parameters in this model are often described as being estimated using "within-group" data variation, although the term can sometimes be a misnomer since this

[30] See, for example, the comparison of OLS and fixed-effects estimates reported in table VI of Olley and Pakes (1996).

regression would in fact use both within- and between-group data variation to identify β.

To see why, consider the more general model:

$$y_{it} = \sum_{g=1}^{G} d_{ig}\alpha_g + \sum_{g=1}^{G} (d_{ig} w_{it})\beta_g + u_{it},$$

in which there are group-specific intercept and also group-specific slope parameters. Provided the groups of observations are mutually exclusive, the OLS estimates of this model can be shown to be

$$\left.\begin{aligned}\hat{\beta}_g &= \left(\sum_{(i,t)\in I_g} (w_{it} - \bar{w}_g)(w_{it} - \bar{w}_g)'\right)^{-1} \left(\sum_{(i,t)\in I_g} (w_{it} - \bar{w}_g)(y_{it} - \bar{y}_g)'\right) \\ \hat{\alpha}_g &= \bar{y}_g - \hat{\beta}_g \bar{w}_g\end{aligned}\right\} \quad \text{for each } g = 1, \dots, G,$$

where I_g defines the set of i, t observations in group g and where $\bar{w}_g$ and $\bar{y}_g$ are respectively the averages across i, t observations in the group. To see this is true, write the model in matrix form and stack the sets of observations in their groups and note that the resulting matrices X_g and X_h will satisfy $X_g' X_h = 0$ for $g \neq h$ because $d_{ig} d_{ih} = 0$ (see also, for example, Hsiao 1986, p. 13). Recall in a standard panel data context, the group of data will mean all the observations for a given firm over time so the within-group averages are just the averages over time for a given firm. Similarly, the summations in the expression for $\hat{\beta}_g$ involve summations over observations in the group, i.e., over time for a given firm. Note that the estimates of both the intercept and slope parameters for each group g depend only on data coming from within group g and it is in that sense that estimates of this general model are truly only dependent on within-group data variation.

In contrast, when estimating the more specific fixed-effects model first introduced, which restricts the slope coefficients to be equal across groups so that $\beta_1 = \beta_2 = \cdots = \beta_G \equiv \beta$, the OLS estimates of the model become

$$\hat{\beta} = \left(\sum_{g=1}^{G} \sum_{(i,t)\in I_g} (w_{it} - \bar{w}_g)(w_{it} - \bar{w}_g)'\right)^{-1} \times \left(\sum_{g=1}^{G} \sum_{(i,t)\in I_g} (w_{it} - \bar{w}_g)(y_{ig} - \bar{y}_g)'\right),$$

$$\hat{\alpha}_g = \bar{y}_g - \hat{\beta}\bar{w}_g \quad \text{for each } g = 1, \dots, G,$$

which clearly, via the estimator $\hat{\beta}$, uses information from all of the groups of data. Despite the fact that this latter estimator uses information from all groups, this estimator is often known as the "within-group" estimator. The reason is that the estimator is numerically identical to the one obtained by estimating a model using variables in differences from their group means, namely estimating the following model by OLS where the group-specific fixed effects have been differenced out:

$$(y_{it} - \bar{y}_g) = \beta(w_{it} - \bar{w}_g) + e_{it},$$

where $e_{it} = u_{it} - \bar{u}_g$.

Thus, in this particular sense the estimator is a within-group estimator, namely it exploits only variation in the data once group-specific intercept terms have been controlled for. Note that this is not the same as only using within-a-*single*-group data variation, but rather that the OLS estimator uses the variation within *all* of the groups to identify the slope parameters of interest.

Since it involves the ratio of averaged covariance to the averaged variance, the estimator $\hat{\beta}$ can perhaps be understood as an average of the actual "within-group" estimators $\hat{\beta}_g$ over all groups. In the case of the restricted model, where the DGP involves slope parameters that are the same across groups, the parameters $(\alpha_1, \dots, \alpha_G)$ successfully account for all of the between-group data variation in the observed outcomes y_i and a fixed-effects regression will add efficiency compared with using only data variation within a single group, in the way that the more general model did. However, when the true (DGP) slope coefficients are actually different, such an estimator will not be consistent.

The econometric analysis above suggested that fixed effects can be an effective way to solve an endogeneity problem and hence can help identify causal relationships. In doing so the various estimators are using particular dimensions of the variation in our data in an attempt to identify true causal relationships. OLS without any group-specific parameters uses all the covariation between outcome and control variables. In contrast, introducing a full set of group-specific intercepts and slope coefficients will allow us to use only within-group data variation to identify causal effects while the more conventional fixed-effects estimator uses within-group data variation and some across-group data variation to identify the causal effects. Fixed effects are particularly helpful if (i) we have limited data on the drivers of unobserved differences, (ii) we know that the true causal effects, those estimated by $\hat{\beta}$, are common across groups, and (iii) we know that unobserved factors common to a group of observations are likely to play an important role in determining the outcome y. Of course, these latter two assumptions are strong ones. The second assumption requires that the various groups of data must be sufficiently similar for the magnitude of causal effects to be the same while the last assumption requires that members of each group must be sufficiently similar that the group-specific constant term in our regressions will solve the endogeneity problem. These assumptions are rarely absolutely true and so we should rely on fixed-effects estimators only having taken a view on the reasonableness of these approximations. For example, in reality firms' processes and procedures do both differ across firms and also evolve over time. Even if adding labor to each firm causes the firm to be able to produce the same amount of additional output as would be required for the causal effect of labor on output to be the same for every firm, any factor affecting productivity which varies over time for a given firm (e.g., as a result of firms adopting new technology or adapting their production process) would be missed by a fixed effect. Such factors will prevent successful identification if the movement reintroduces a correlation between an explanatory variable and the error in the regression.[31]

Because fixed-effects regression uses within-group data variation, there must be enough variation of the variables x and y *within* each group (or at least some groups) to produce an effect that can be measured with accuracy. When the variation in the explanatory variables is mostly across groups, a fixed-effects approach is unlikely to be produce useful results. In such circumstances the estimated standard errors of the fixed-effects estimator will tend to be very large and the value of the estimator of the slope parameters will be "close" to zero. In the limit, if in our data set $w_{it} \approx \bar{w}_g$ for all i in each group g, so there is little within-group data variation, the reported estimate of β would either be approximately zero, very large, or ill-defined—each of the latter two possibilities occurs if the matrix inverse is reported as close to or actually singular so that we are effectively dividing by numbers very close to zero. The reason is that the fixed-effects estimator is not being well-identified by the available data set even though if we had enough or better data we would perhaps be able to successfully identify the parameters of the model.

Another technique related to the fixed-effects method and often used is the random-effects regression. Random-effects regression treats the common factor within a group α_g as a modeled part of the error term and treats it as a common but random shock from a known distribution rather than a fixed parameter to be estimated. The advantage of this technique is that it does not result in a very large number of regressors, as can be the case in fixed-effects regression, and this can ease computational burdens. On the other hand, it makes the nontrivial assumption that the common characteristics shared by the group are random and not correlated with any of the explanatory variables included in the regression (see, for example, the discussion and potential solution in Mundlak (1978)).[32] The fixed-effects disadvantage of computational constraints is far less important now than it was previously and as a result fixed-effects estimators have tended to be preferred in recent years.

[31] For a proposal for dealing with time-varying situations, see Olley and Pakes (1996) and also the important discussion in Ackerberg et al. (2005). Ensuring that production functions are estimated using data from firms with similar "enough" underlying production technologies will help mitigate concerns that causal effects differ across firms. For example, the same production function is unlikely to be appropriate for both power stations generating hydroelectricity and those using natural gas as a fuel.

[32] If we do have data on measures/causes of firm productivity, we might consider the model with $\alpha_i = \lambda' x_i + e_i$, which also has the advantage that the resulting α_i can be correlated with included w_{it} variables (see Mundlak 1978; Chamberlain 1982, 1984).

For further discussion and examples, see chapter 3, where we examine a fixed-effects approach to production function estimation and chapter 5, where we examine a fixed-effects approach to estimating the effect of market structure on prices charged in a market.

2.2.3.2 *Instrumental Variables*

Instrumental variables are used frequently in the empirical analysis of competition issues.[33] For example, they are the most common solution to endogeneity and identification problems in the estimation of demand functions. Formally, suppose we have the following single-equation regression model:

$$y_i = x_{1i}\beta_1 + x'_{2i}\beta_2 + \varepsilon_i,$$

where $\beta = (\beta_1, \beta_2)$, $x'_i = (x_{1i}, x'_{2i})$, and where the vector of variables x'_{2i} are exogenous and x_{1i} is endogenous. That is, the variable x_{1i} is correlated with the error term ε_i so that an OLS estimator's identification restriction is not valid.[34] Instrumental variable techniques propose using an alternative identifying assumption, namely they suppose that we have a set of variables $z_i = (z_{1i}, x_{2i})$ which are correlated with x_i but uncorrelated with the error term. For example, in a demand equation, where y_i denotes sales and x_{1i} denotes prices we may believe that the DGP does not satisfy the identification assumption used for OLS estimators that unobserved determinants of sales are uncorrelated with prices so that $E[\varepsilon_i \mid x_i] \neq 0$. But we assume the alternative identification assumption needed to apply instrumental variable techniques that there is a variable z_i correlated with price but that does not affect sales in an independent way so that $E[\varepsilon_i \mid z_i] = 0$ and $E[x_i \mid z_i] \neq 0$. It turns out that these assumptions allow us to write down a number of consistent estimators for our parameters of interest β including (i) a first instrumental variable estimator and (ii) the two-stage least-squares (2SLS) estimator.[35]

To define a first IV estimator, stack up the equation $y_i = x'_i\beta + \varepsilon_i$ over $i = 1, \dots, n$ observations so that we can write the matrix form $y = X\beta + \varepsilon$, where y is $(n \times 1)$, X is $(n \times k)$ for our data set and define the $(n \times p)$ matrix of instrumental variables Z analogously. Define a first instrumental variable estimator:

$$\hat{\beta}^{\text{IV}} = [Z'X]^{-1}Z'y = \left[\frac{1}{n}Z'X\right]^{-1}\frac{1}{n}Z'y.$$

---

[33] Instrumental variables as a technique are usually attributed jointly to Reiersol (1945) and Geary (1949). See also Sargen (1958). For more recent literature, see, for example, Newey and Powell (2003). For formal econometric results, see White (2001).

[34] For simplicity we present the case where there is one endogenous variable. If we have more than one endogenous variable in x_{1i}, little substantive changes beyond the fact that we will need at least one variable in z_i, i.e., one instrument, for each endogenous variable in x_{1i} and in the 2SLS regression approach we will have one set of first-stage regression output for each endogenous variable.

[35] We call the former estimator "a" first IV estimator deliberately, since 2SLS is also an IV estimator and, as we shall see, generally a more efficient one.

It can be shown that $\hat{\beta}^{\mathrm{IV}}$ is a consistent estimator β and that under homoskedasticity the variance of the estimator is

$$\mathrm{Var}(\hat{\beta}^{\mathrm{IV}}) = \sigma^2[Z'X]^{-1}[Z'Z][X'Z]^{-1}.$$

While this provides a consistent estimate, Theil (1953) showed that a more efficient estimator (2SLS) is available:[36]

$$\hat{\beta}^{\mathrm{2SLS}} = [X'Z(Z'Z)^{-1}Z'X]^{-1}X'Z(Z'Z)^{-1}Z'y,$$

where $\mathrm{var}(\hat{\beta}^{\mathrm{2SLS}}) = \sigma^2[X'Z(Z'Z)^{-1}Z'X]^{-1}$ if $E[\varepsilon\varepsilon' \mid Z] = \sigma^2 I_n$, i.e., the errors are homoskedastic.

Remarkably, the two-stage least-squares estimator $\hat{\beta}^{\mathrm{2SLS}}$ is entirely equivalent to running two OLS regressions. Looking at the estimator from that perspective provides some useful intuition for why it works. The 2SLS estimator gets its name because the estimator defined above can be obtained in the following two steps:

(1) First-stage regression: $X_1 = Z\delta + u$.

(2) Second-stage regression: $y = \hat{X}_1\beta + X_2\alpha + \nu$.

Here $\hat{X}_1 = Z\hat{\delta}^{\mathrm{OLS}}$ denotes the fitted values obtained from the first-stage regression. Specifically, at the first stage we run an OLS regression of the endogenous variables in X on Z and obtain $\hat{X}_1 = Z\hat{\delta}^{\mathrm{OLS}}$, the fitted values. At the second stage, we run an OLS regression with dependent variable y taking the fitted values from the first-stage regression and using those fitted values in the place of the endogenous explanatory variable in the original model. Originally, this two-stage approach was primarily convenient because computer programs (or earlier formulas applied using hand calculators) that could estimate OLS were standard, while those capable of estimating 2SLS were less common. Today, the computational requirements of estimating a 2SLS model directly are trivial but most experienced analysts will still look at both first- and second-stage regression results nonetheless. The reason is that while the second-stage results are the estimates of interest, the first-stage results are very helpful in evaluating whether the instruments are in fact sufficiently correlated with the endogenous variable being instrumented.

A good instrumental variable will be one that is (1) strongly correlated with the explanatory variable so that there is explanatory power in the first equation which is additional to the included exogenous regressors (which are included in Z as instruments for themselves) and (2) uncorrelated with the unobserved term in the second equation ν. Intuitively, the first-stage regression acts to find the variation in X_1 which is correlated with Z. Since Z is uncorrelated with ε and we can write $\nu = \varepsilon + (X_1 - \hat{X}_1)\beta$, we know that $\hat{X}_1$ will also be uncorrelated with ν so that OLS on the second equation will provide unbiased estimates. Remarkably, the OLS

[36] See your favorite econometrics textbook for more details.

estimates of such a two-stage process provides exactly the 2SLS estimator. To see why, notice that by construction $\hat{X}_1$ and $(X_1 - \hat{X}_1)$ are uncorrelated. For example, to estimate a demand equation we could run a regression of prices on the exogenous variables in X_2 and our instrumental variable—perhaps cost data. In doing so we would be isolating the variation in prices caused by movement in costs (which is in addition to any variation in prices explained by movements in the demand curve caused by the exogenous demand shifting variables X_2).

Standard errors and confidence intervals will tend to be larger in IV regressions than OLS regressions, making it more difficult to reject a null hypothesis of no effect. If in actuality the variable X_1 is exogenous so that OLS is efficient and consistent, then moving to IV will involve a loss of efficiency. If OLS is inconsistent because X_1 is indeed endogenous, then the problem becomes a genuine one, albeit one which may help the search for the best available instruments. Generally, the problem is greater the lower the conditional correlation between the endogenous variable X_1 and the instruments Z_1 (that is, the correlation conditional on the exogenous variables X_2). Thus, highly significant instruments in the first-stage regression equation which explain considerable variation in X_1 in addition to that explained by X_2 is a good indication that the instrument satisfies the requirement that it is appropriately correlated with the endogenous regressor.

When using instrumental variable techniques then, it is important to check the quality of the instruments. Specifically, it is very important to make sure that the instrument is in fact correlated with the endogenous explanatory variable. Fortunately, as we have seen, this is extremely easy to check by examining the first-stage regression output and as a result it is good practice to report the results of the first-stage regression in a 2SLS estimation. Checking that there is no correlation between the instrument and the shock is harder, yet the 2SLS estimator will not be consistent if there is such a correlation. If we have more potential instruments than potentially endogenous regressors (in which case we will call the model "over-identified"), then we can test this assumption to some extent by examining the effect of subsets of the instrumental variables on the parameters. Beyond that we can plot the fitted shock against each of the instruments and see if there are systematic patterns in the graphs which may indicate that $E[\varepsilon_i \mid z_i] \neq 0$. Although the estimator will impose this assumption on average, looking at the plots can be revealing. (See also the discussion in chapter 3.)

IV/2SLS estimators are extremely useful in the presence of endogeneity but they are less efficient estimators than OLS if we do not have an endogeneity problem. OLS will have lower standard errors than IV/2SLS estimates and for this reason IV/2SLS should only be used if the data (or industry knowledge) suggest that it is needed. The Durbin–Wu–Haussman endogeneity test allows us to evaluate whether the instrumental variable technique is actually solving an existing endogeneity problem. One source of intuition for the test is that it basically includes the error term from the first-stage regression in our original regression specification. If the coefficient is significantly different from zero, we reject the null hypothesis of exogeneity. More generally, the Durbin–Wu–Haussman test can be used in any situation where we have two estimators $\hat{\beta}^1$ and $\hat{\beta}^2$ with the properties:

(a) $\hat{\beta}^1$ is consistent and efficient under the null hypothesis H_0 but not consistent under the alternative hypotheses H_1, and

(b) $\hat{\beta}^2$ is consistent under both H_0 and H_1 but only efficient under H_1.

In our example, $\hat{\beta}^1 = \hat{\beta}^{2SLS}$ and $\hat{\beta}^2 = \hat{\beta}^{OLS}$ so that the test with the null hypothesis that all the regressors are exogenous against the alternative that they are not can be recast as a test of whether $\hat{\beta}^1 = \hat{\beta}^2$, i.e., whether the second estimator is consistent.

Instrumental variable techniques are a common way to address endogeneity issues in multiple regression. But their efficacy in avoiding endogeneity bias rests on the quality of the instruments chosen and many instruments are not obviously credible when scrutinized closely. Many instruments come from economic models. However, instruments need not be derived from economic models and one great advantage is that there is no need to specify exactly the mechanism through which an instrument affects the endogenous variable. For example, if we wish to estimate demand we do not need to specify exactly the form of the price-setting model (perfectly competitive, oligopolistic, monopolistic) to know that costs will affect supply (the prices at which firms are willing to supply) and hence are likely to be valid instruments.[37]

Generally, the fewer assumptions we need to make about why and how an instrument should be a determinant of the variable of interest, the less restrictive our underlying identifying assumptions are. Natural experiments provide an extreme example of this principle since they aim to take advantage of random exogenous shocks on the endogenous explanatory variable to identify the effect of that variable.

2.2.3.3 *Natural Experiments (Differences in Differences)*

Biometricians (medical statisticians) evaluate drugs by running experiments where they take a group of individuals and "treat" some of them with a new drug while the others are given a placebo (sugar pill). We say subjects are either given a "treatment" or assigned to the "control" group and the individual subjects are randomly assigned between the two groups. Such experiments provide us with exogenous variation in a variable x, the treatment, which will allow us to measure an outcome y; perhaps the survival rate (see Krueger and Angrist 2001). In particular, the random assignment means that while there is heterogeneity in individuals' propensity to suffer acutely from a disease, such heterogeneity will not—by design—be correlated with actual

[37] There are, of course, limits to such propositions. Prices in upstream markets between retailers and manufacturers sometimes look surprisingly flat and do not vary obviously with costs, perhaps because prices are the outcome of a bargaining situation. Also, in some investigations competition agencies look at situations where competition does not appear to be working very well. In such cases, the link between cost and price variables can be, shall we say, somewhat less than obvious.

drug-taking. In contrast, if we just observed data from the world, then those more prone to seek treatment or need the treatment would take the drugs while others would not.

The implication is that a regression equation estimated using data observed directly from the world would suffer greatly from endogeneity bias—we would incorrectly conclude that there is tendency for a very effective drug to actively cause low survival rates! However, since in our experiment the treatment is assigned to individuals randomly and is not linked to any of the characteristics of individual subjects, either observed or unobserved, any difference in the average outcome between both groups can be assigned to the effect of the treatment.[38]

Controlled experiments are common in medical science and also in social experiments. Even economists, working directly or indirectly for firms and governments can and do run experiments, at least in the sense that we might evaluate demand and advertising elasticities of demand by exogenously varying prices or advertising and observing the impact on sales. Auction design experiments are also frequently used—firms want to understand what happens to their auction revenue if they change the rules. There are, of course, lots of difficulties associated with running such real-world experiments. For example, if markets are large, then "experimenting" with pricing can easily get very expensive if the experiment does not quite work in the way one hopes it will. On the other hand, if there are lots of local markets, then perhaps the cost of getting it wrong in one, or a few, localities may not be so great. For regulators and competition authorities attempting to remedy problems they find in markets (e.g., poor information) running experiments could well be an attractive option. However, at the moment there are plenty of cases where regulators or competition authorities will mandate changes in, say, information provision—e.g., summary boxes on credit card statements—without using experiments to test whether such remedies are effective in terms of the desired outcomes, despite the fact that there are certainly circumstances where this could be done. Many companies have "test and control" systems where at least direct mail advertising success rates are carefully measured and advertising messages are tuned appropriately. Similar systems are sometimes available for testing product design either before full commercial launch or for product redesign afterward. At present, competition authorities do not typically attempt to leverage internal systems when they do exist—in the main (as far as we can tell) because of concerns that the oversight of parties in managing such projects will not be sufficient to ensure unbiased outcomes.

All of that said, it is clearly impossible to use experiments in lots of circumstances. We cannot randomly submit firms to treatments such as mergers or randomly allocate

[38] There would, of course, be serious ethical issues if a biometrician genuinely proposed to run literally this exact experiment—knowingly giving sugar pills to cancer victims would quite probably land you in jail. On the other hand, researchers used to do exactly that. James Lind (1753) is usually described as the inventor of controlled experiments. The story goes that while at sea in 1747 as ship's surgeon he gave some crew suffering from "scurvy" (which we now know is caused by lack of vitamin C) fresh citrus fruit while others continued with what would be their normal rations.

firms to be vertically integrated and nonvertically integrated and see which generates more efficient outcomes. As in the medical world, there are some serious hurdles to overcome in experimental design.

One potential solution is to use "natural" exogenous variation affecting firms. Institutional changes, known demand shifts or known supply shifts that are completely exogenous to the rest of the determinants of the market can sometimes create the equivalent of a laboratory experiment. Empirical analyses that exploit such data variation are for obvious reasons known as "natural experiments."

One significant problem that natural experimenters immediately ran into is that events occur over time. One way to examine the impact of a natural experiment is to consider what happened before the event and compare it with what happened after the event. Such a source of identification faces the serious problem that many other events may occur during the intervening period and we may wrongly attribute causation to the "treatment." If so we will face an identification problem in distinguishing between the many events that occurred between the "before" and "after" period. For example, suppose we wish to evaluate the impact of a new competition regime on concentration, say, the U.K. Enterprise Act (EA). We could look at concentration before and after 2003 when the Act came into force. Unfortunately lots of other events would also have occurred. We might observe that concentration in industry went up between, say, 2000 and 2005 but we could not plausibly argue that because the EA came into force in 2003, EA is the cause of this higher concentration. The singer Kylie Minogue had a number one single in 2003, so perhaps she was the cause? A simple before-and-after regression analysis would happily suggest she was! This example is obviously flippant since all but the most ardent Kylie fans would probably rule her out as a plausible causal force behind the concentration in industry, but the point we hope is clear—there will usually be multiple plausible explanatory events which occur in a given year and we need to be able to identify which was genuinely causal. The bottom line is that this kind of "before-and-after" source of identifying data variation is unlikely to generate reliable results. The exception would be if for some particular reason it is reasonable to assume that nothing else material happened in the interim.

More plausibly, if we want to measure the diversion ratio between two products in order to learn about their substitutability, we might use an unexpected plant closure (due, for instance, to extreme weather conditions) affecting availability of one product.[39] If the plant closure affecting product A results in an increase in the sales or prices of product B, then we might conclude that products A and B are demand substitutes. This experiment uses only time series variation but closing and reopening periods mean we might have multiple relevant events which could help

[39] The diversion ratio (DR) between two products A and B is the proportion of sales that are captured by product B when product A increases its price by some amount. The DR tells us about substitutability between products and it is sometimes approximated by examining the effect of removing product A from the market entirely and seeing if the customers move across to buy product B.

identification somewhat; of course, even multiple events suffer the problem that product B's sales may happen to go up for some reason in the month that A's plant closes and then happen to go down again for some reason in the month that it comes back on stream.

One potential solution to the causality problem is to use the "difference-in-differences" technique.[40] Consider the fixed-effects DGP

$$y_{it} = \alpha_i + \tau_t + \delta d_{it} + \varepsilon_{it},$$

where $i = 1, \dots, N$ and $t = 1, \dots, T$ denotes time and where d_{it} denotes an indicator variable where $d_{it} = 1$ if i is in the treatment group and $t \geqslant t^*$, where t^* denotes the date of the treatment and $d_{it} = 0$ otherwise. For example, if $i = 1, 2$ denotes the state while t^* is the date of a law that passed in one of those states (the treatment group), the other state is used as a control group. Define the difference operator so that, for any variable x, $\Delta x_{it} \equiv x_{it} - x_{it-1}$, then differencing the DGP over time gives

$$\Delta y_{it} = \Delta \tau_t + \delta \Delta d_{it} + \Delta \varepsilon_{it}.$$

Now consider the difference between the control and the treatment group by supposing i is in the control group (so that $\Delta d_{it} = 0$) and j is in the treatment group so that

$$\Delta y_{jt} - \Delta y_{it} = \delta \Delta d_{jt} + (\Delta \varepsilon_{jt} - \Delta \varepsilon_{it}),$$

where $\Delta d_{jt^*} = 1$. We can estimate the parameter δ by using this "difference-in-differences" specification in which all of the time and group fixed effects have dropped out. This specification is helpful primarily because it makes clear that the parameter δ is identified by using the difference in experience over time of the treatment and control groups. The term $(\Delta \varepsilon_{jt} - \Delta \varepsilon_{it})$ is simply an error term, albeit a rather complex one. Of course, we may in fact choose to estimate the fixed-effects specification directly and generally doing so will yield more efficient estimators. The parameter δ is known as the "treatment effect" and captures the average causal effect of treatment on the outcome variable y_{it} (see, for example, Imbens and Angrist 1994; Angrist 2004).[41]

Milyo and Waldfogel (1999), for example, collected data on prices from liquor stores near the border of the two states Rhode Island (RI) and Massachusetts (MA) following the decision known as the "44 Liquormart decision" in which the U.S. Supreme Court overturned an RI ban on advertising the prices of alcoholic drinks. The shops in neighboring MA were able to advertise prices while those in RI could only advertise prices after May 13, 1996. Such a "natural experiment" creates a situation where we have shops in one group (state) which are "treated" by a change in law while the other group is not. If we choose shops in MA which experience

[40] For a discussion of natural experiments in economics, see Meyer (1995).

[41] For an application in the supply and demand context, see also Angrist et al. (2000).

similar other events pre and post the May 1996 event, then we can use those shops in MA as a control group. Milyo and Waldfogel chose to examine shops in RI and MA near the border because they expected the shops—other than the legal change—to experience a similar evolution of trading conditions.

Milyo and Waldfogel collect data on prices on thirty-three widely available beverages (products such as Budweiser beer, Tanqueray gin, Bacardi rum, Jack Daniels whiskey, and so on). They visited the shops quarterly and used the resulting data set (6,480 observations) to run the following regression:

$$\ln p_{sjt} = \sum_{s=1}^{S} d_s \lambda_s + \sum_{j=1}^{J} d_j^{\text{MA}} \tau_j^{\text{MA}} + \sum_{j=1}^{J} d_j^{\text{RI}} \tau_j^{\text{RI}} + \sum_{t=1}^{T} d_t^{\text{MA}} \alpha_t^{\text{MA}} + \sum_{t=1}^{T} d_t^{\text{RI}} \alpha_t^{\text{RI}} + \varepsilon_{sjt},$$

where $s = 1, \dots, S$ indexes stores, $j = 1, \dots, J$ products, and $t = 1, \dots, T$ time periods. The model consists of a store fixed effect d_s with parameter λ_s for each store s and a state-specific product fixed effect d_j^{MA} and d_j^{RI}, where, for example, d_j^{MA} takes on the value 1 for the observation on product j in MA and 0 elsewhere so that the model can explain differences in price levels for each product. State-specific time dummy variables d_t^{MA} and d_t^{RI} are also included in the regression. Since there is a full set of store-specific dummy variables they set $\alpha_1^{\text{MA}} = \alpha_1^{\text{RI}} = 0$. The difference-in-differences approach focuses on the impact of the legal change on the difference between the store prices across different states. The resulting estimates of the state-specific time effects on the prices α_t^{MA} and α_t^{RI} are plotted in figure 2.9. From this graph they conclude the following:

1. Prices are not stable over time, they rose 2–3% in the two states over the period, although most of this occurs in the period after May 1996. Although there is not a clear large price movement either up or down in RI following the relaxation of advertising restrictions, the tendency is for each state's prices to rise after May 1996. That means the "before-and-after" comparison we would have made with only RI data would not control for the fact that prices have risen generally and in particular also in MA, where the law did not change.

2. The prices do appear to move together so that common factors may be affecting both markets and so MA shops may act as a reasonable control group.

3. Moreover, in four out of the five quarterly observations after May 1996 (the period wherein advertising was allowed) RI prices have risen less than those in MA, which perhaps suggests a negative effect of advertising on prices. (Although price increases in RI were also generally lower than in MA before May 1996 as well, albeit by a smaller amount than afterwards.)

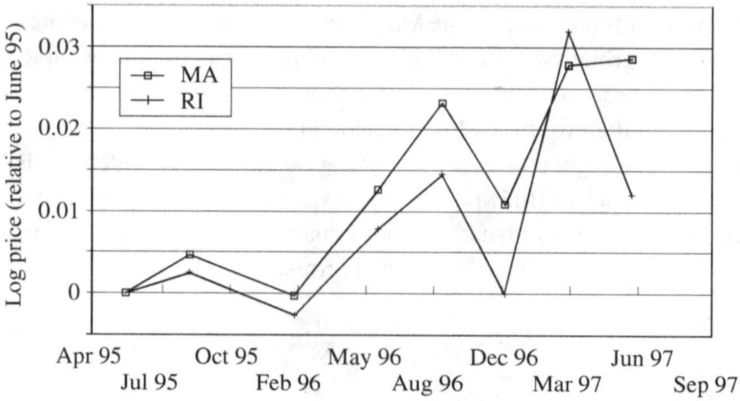

Figure 2.9. Time effects in Rhode Island and Massachusetts (log price). *Source*: Milyo and Waldfogel (1999).

The difference-in-differences approach, although very intuitive, still requires some strong assumptions. First, any covariates included in the regression must not be affected by the "experiment," otherwise our estimate of the effect of exogenous structural change will be biased. Second, we must not omit any variable that may affect the outcome of interest and which may be correlated, even incidentally, with the variable whose effect we are trying to measure, i.e., the regulatory or other structural change. If those conditions are violated, the estimator of the effect of the experiment will be biased.

Unfortunately, these conditions are often violated in competition contexts, which is why very good natural experiments are hard to come by. For example, suppose we wish to evaluate the impact of patents on drug prices and we consider "going off patent" to be a natural experiment. We consider its impact on drug prices relevant to helping us learn about the effect of patent protection on drug prices. Since branded drugs are observed to sometimes increase prices in response to patent expiry, we might incorrectly conclude that the impact of patent protection is to reduce drug prices when in fact we have incorrectly ignored the product repositioning that may accompany the expiry of a patent. In this case, econometric results would be suffering from an omitted-variable problem. Finally, since natural experiments are by definition random, it is not always possible to find an appropriate "natural experiment" in the relevant time period for an investigation. However, when the opportunity presents itself, data variation arising from suitable natural experiments should usually be used since, if properly handled, they can provide as good a way as any other available method of identifying causal effects.[42]

[42] For further discussion of natural experiments, see White (2005).

2.2.3.4 Stock and Bond Market Event Studies

Stock and bond market event studies focus on the effect of an exogenous change in a firm's market conditions on the valuation of that firm. They provide a potentially useful technique for capturing the expected market impact of events such as mergers, new contractual arrangements, or other sudden changes in competitive conditions. Stock and bond market event studies do not look directly at the effect of an event on market outcomes but instead reveal the expected impact on the firm's valuation, which is a market measure of the firm's expected rest-of-lifetime profitability.

A fundamental idea in finance is that markets aggregate information. An implication is that stock or bond market reactions to announced events may provide useful information about the true impact of a change. For example, Eckbo (1983) suggested that mergers for market power (those which increased prices) and mergers which generated synergies (cost reductions) would each increase the stock value of the merging parties but that only mergers for market power would increase the stock price of rivals (Eckbo 1983). If so, then he proposed using the stock market reactions of rivals to merging parties as a form of information useful for merger evaluation. Recent studies in this vein include Duso et al. (2006a,b).

On the other hand, others have argued that the source of identification in such studies is highly problematic, for example, if mergers are strategic complements so that one merger encourages another, then a merger may indicate future mergers in the industry and hence rivals' prices may go up even if a merger results in only cost reductions from the merging parties.[43] Indeed, critics point to the empirical observations that mergers do indeed typically come in waves rather than as single events. For a critique, see McAfee and Williams (1988). The academic debate on this topic is polarized, and for our part we think it is easy to miss the important point. Namely that, as with all other evidence, the results of stock market event studies should not be taken at face value and if rivals' stock market valuations are found to rise, we still have two possible explanations for that fact, explanations that it may be possible to bring at least qualitative data to bear on. For example, contemporary interviews with traders may help decide the question of whether or not this is because market participants believe the merger announcement is signaling future mergers. Such information may help inform whether or not such correlations should be treated as evidence of market power. It is also worth noting in this debate that at least some studies (e.g., Aktas et al. 2007) find that on average rivals in their European data set suffer negative abnormal returns, consistent with the general policy stance of considering most mergers pro-competitive.

The first step of an event study is to identify both the event to be studied and the event window, which is the time period during which the financial markets react to the event. The objective of the methodology is to measure the "abnormal returns"

---

[43] See Eckbo (1983) and also, for a theoretical rationale for why mergers may be strategic complements, Nocke and Whinston (2007).

of the firms during the event window. The change in the price of a stock over some period tells us the *return* to holding the stock. Thus for example, we may measure the overnight return (change in price overnight) or inter-day return (close to close return) or the intra-day return (open to close change in price). Abnormal returns are the difference between the observed returns and a benchmark level of "normal returns" which capture the returns that would have been expected in the market (i.e., required by investors to hold the stock) had the event not occurred. The normal returns are typically estimated using a period unaffected by the event, normally a period preceding the event.

There are several techniques that can be used to estimate the normal returns and each method makes different assumptions about the valuation of the firm or group of firms. The simplest technique is to assume a constant average return. For example, in a simulation study, Brown and Warner (1985) use 250 days of return data. They define day 0 as the date of an event, and the event window as five days before (perhaps to pick up insider trading or "leakage" of information in the form of market rumors) to five days afterward so that the event window is defined as the eleven-day time period $t = -5, \dots, +5$. The period of data $t = -239, \dots, -6$ is the data set used to estimate normal returns and is denoted the "estimation period."[44] Sometimes authors add an "insulation period" so, for example, Aktas et al. use an eleven-day event window but use the 200 daily observations for the period that ends 30 days before the initial announcement of a merger. They describe that the 30-day insulation period is designed to mitigate potential information leakage.

Mean adjusted returns. In the simplest case the company's expected return is assumed to be constant over time and the actual return is only the expected return with some random shocks. The normal return is then calculated using the model

$$R_{it} = \mu_i + \varepsilon_{it}$$

over the estimation periods, where i indicates a particular asset and ε_{it} is a random shock with an expected value of 0. In that case, normal returns can be estimated as

$$\hat{\mu}_i = \bar{R}_i = \frac{1}{239} \sum_{t=-244}^{-6} R_{it}$$

so that the abnormal returns can be evaluated using $R_{it} - \bar{R}_i$.

Market model. Alternatively, one can use a market model that assumes that the return of the firm or group of firms is related to the market return, so that we have

$$R_{it} = \alpha_i + \beta_i R_{mt} + \varepsilon_{it},$$

[44] Some authors introduce an "insulation period" between the estimation period and the event window in order to avoid the effects of information leakage (see, for example, Aktas et al. 2007).

where R_{mt} is the market return or the return of the benchmark portfolio of assets. Testament to the importance of this type of regression is that the finance community will often talk about the "search for alpha," meaning α_i (picking a stock means picking one for which returns are idiosyncratically high) and also the "beta" of stock i, meaning β_i, the part of the return on a given stock which is associated with general market movements. Given estimates of alpha and beta, the residual provides a measure of abnormal returns, $\text{AR}_{it} = R_{it} - (\hat{\alpha}_i + \hat{\beta}_i R_{mt})$.

One can use more sophisticated financial models (asset pricing models) to estimate the abnormal rate of return of the firm. For example, while the capital asset pricing model (CAPM) (Sharpe 1964; Lintner 1965) is a common choice for such an exercise, Fama and French (1993, 1996) show that the cross-sectional variation in returns on stocks (bonds) can be explained by a three-factor model (five-factor model). The Fama and French multifactor model provides a richer description of the normal returns on stocks or bonds. For example, these authors show that, in addition to an overall market factor, a factor relating to firm size and a factor relating to the ratio of book-equity to market equity appears to play a statistically significant role in explaining stock returns. Carhart (1997) suggests an additional factor and the resulting model is known as Fama–French plus momentum. For a fuller discussion of the relative merits of these different alternatives, we refer the interested reader to MacKinlay (1997) and, in particular, Campbell et al. (1997).

Given a method for estimating normal returns, and hence an estimate of the abnormal return we can evaluate the sign, statistical significance, and magnitude of any abnormal return.[45] The cumulative abnormal return (CAR) is simply the summation of the total abnormal return over the event window. Thus, for example with an eleven-day event window,

$$\text{CAR}_{it} = \sum_{t=-5}^{+5} \text{AR}_{it}.$$

A numerical example is provided in chapter 10.

2.3 Best Practice in Econometric Exercises

The array of difficulties described in this chapter that can adversely affect econometric estimates can be addressed by following best practice. Doing so will help avoid unpleasant surprises at critical moments in investigations and should in general help increase the overall quality of the analysis. These practices concern the derivation of the specification to be estimated, the preliminary descriptive analysis of the data used and the use of specification testing and robustness checking to verify the results. No matter which econometric techniques are used, each of these steps is important

[45] A test can be run to evaluate the null hypothesis that the abnormal return is not significantly different from the normal return.

in ensuring you obtain "numbers you can believe" (as distinct from getting numbers in the form of regression output).

2.3.1 Derivation of the Specification

Before you dive in and start running regressions, it is usually helpful to spend some time thinking hard about (1) the question you wish to address, (2) the industry being studied, and (3) the potential economic models you might wish to use to structure your way to finding an answer to your questions. In an ideal academic exercise one might go about deciding (1) then (3) and then go to the "data" to find an interesting context and pick (2). Generically, even in an academic context where question, laboratory, and competing theories must be chosen, it is impossible for ordinary human beings to follow an approach which attempts to sequence these questions and the more usual experience is to iterate back and forth between them.

On the other hand, in the context of antitrust investigations, the question and laboratory may be very well defined. For example, we may need to evaluate the impact of a merger on prices in a particular industry. Even so we will need to think hard about the environment in which our firms operate, the strategic and nonstrategic choices they make, and their objectives in doing so. Doing so is effectively attempting to capture the available qualitative information in the form of a class of economic models that may help structure our understanding. Potentially relevant theory models are usually best first considered under very strong assumptions, which can if needed be later relaxed.

Before running a regression we will, at a minimum, need to know (1) which variable(s) we want our model to explain, (2) which variables are likely to play the role of explanatory variables, and (3) whether theory and industry knowledge suggest that particular variables are likely to be endogenous. We provide a number of examples of this practice in the book but the reader should be in no doubt whatsoever that it is a genuinely challenging activity to do well.

As we will illustrate throughout the book, every regression specification is the reflection of an implicit model so it is a good practice to think about a model that we are comfortable with beforehand (in terms of a reasonable first approximation to behavior in the industry) and then derive a regression specification that at least encompasses that model, i.e., that includes it as a special case. For instance, if we are estimating the effect of determinants of price, we must ask ourselves what the theory predicts those determinants should be. Theory will tell us that price is determined by demand factors, cost factors, and the nature of the interaction between competitors. We may well conclude that we will need data on each of those factors. Before beginning an investigation we must establish an appropriate project plan to ensure that (1) the necessary data are available or that we have found realistic (in terms of what can be achieved in an investigation) and reasonable empirical strategies for compensating for missing information and (2) there is variation in variables whose causal effect you wish to identify. It will, for example, be entirely impossible to estimate a meaningful price elasticity of demand from data generated in an industry where there is no price variation. Of course, the problem is you may not know that until after you have at least looked at the data. Much of the material in this book provides examples of how this process works and we lay out most of the well-known models as well as some less well-known ones. Of course, there is considerable additional difficulty in going beyond the well-known and well-understood set of models and, while you may wish to do so, do not underestimate the difficulty involved in doing so within the context of an ongoing investigation, particularly one with a statutory deadline! Every model is an approximation and short timescales mean the feasible approximations are necessarily rough in character.

2.3.2 Getting to Know the Data

Getting to know the data that will be used in an empirical exercise is an extremely important preliminary step and it is one that often happens at least in part during the important process of "cleaning" a data set.

Data Cleaning. Humans make mistakes and machines break down so whether data are entered by hand or collected automatically they are often "dirty." You will inevitably find a considerable number of obvious mistakes in initial data sets and those observations must be verified and either dropped (if doing so does not itself cause econometric problems) or ideally corrected. You may find, for example, that the price of a product like a single branded chocolate bar will be reported in your data set as having cost thousands of euros; at some point someone made a mistake. Verifying the units of variables is often central. Many weeks into a case, it is extremely unhelpful to realize that in aggregating sales data across package sizes you have added up variables with different units and have subsequently done all your work with the wrong aggregate sales data. Such mistakes are extremely easy to make and have severe implications (e.g., unit sales volumes of 330 ml cans can have been added to volumes of 0.5 l bottles in hundreds of units). Outliers can also be detected by looking at the main descriptive statistics of a value such as the minimum, the maximum, and the average and median values. It is advisable to always present a table with the averages and data range of the variables used in a regression.

Scatter Plots. Plotting the data is usually helpful. Doing so will help you pick up both obviously unreasonable data points during the cleaning process and also help identify any problems with units of the variables. For example, if you plot cost and price data (with labels), it often becomes clear if something has gone amiss in putting together the data set; the data may, for instance, appear to be telling you that all of a company's sales are occurring at a loss, which would be surprising and, shall we say, worth chasing up. Basic plausibility checks are important and too often neglected by inexperienced empirical analysts who often want to jump into regressions before having looked at the data. The result can be that regression results fall apart as soon as someone goes back to look at the data and starts asking perfectly reasonable questions about its quality.

More generally, scatter plots, graphs, and tables are the analyst's constant companion during this phase of a data intensive investigation. Cut the data in a variety of ways and get to know them. Plotting graphs of the relationships between the dependent and the main independent variables will usually save time and trouble further along in the exercise. For instance, plotting the data will tell you at least what the major correlation patterns are in the data. It is usually possible to get a hint at the results of a regression exercise by visually inspecting how the data behave. For example, if you are to estimate a demand curve and the data clearly show both prices and quantities rising, you know immediately that you will estimate an upward-sloping demand curve unless you can understand the causes (e.g., other demand shifters) and find suitable data about them.

Plotting the data also allows you to see whether there is data variation in the relevant dimensions. If the key variables in an analysis exhibit little variation (or indeed variation at the wrong frequency), it will be impossible to measure the causal effect of one variable on another. An insignificant coefficient in a regression analysis will only indicate "no effect" if there is enough information in a sample to pick up an effect if it were there. Evidence of frequency differentials across, say, quantities and prices will raise the question of exactly how the industry works and whether you should be working with daily, weekly, monthly, or quarterly data. For example, if you are observing prices weekly but the company's pricing committee meets monthly to set prices, you are in danger of ignoring the institutional framework in an industry unless you take that appropriately into account. Always remember you are attempting to understand the DGP, the process by which the data you have collected was generated.

Tables and Graphs. Tables or graphs using subsets of the data can be particularly important because, even if they are two dimensional, they allow you to condition on third and fourth variables in a fashion similar to that which will be performed by regression analysis. Many analysts believe that if you cannot present data in a table in a way that replicates the intuition for regression results, then you probably should not believe your findings. "Cutting" the data into "pieces," i.e., examining conditional statements in this way, is often very useful.

Residual Plots. Once you begin estimation, econometric analysis requires the search for an appropriate regression specification. If estimating by OLS, you need to check for major violations of the OLS assumptions, particularly the conditional mean requirement. For now we note that such violations can often be picked up informally by examining plots of residuals. For example, OLS estimation requires $E[u_i \mid x_i] = 0$ and this can be verified (at least partially) by examining a plot of $(\hat{u}_i, x_i)$. (For an example see the discussion of Nerlove (1963) presented in chapter 3.)

Fitted Value Plots. Plotting the data and their fitted values will help identify outliers which may have a disproportionate impact on the coefficients. Outliers are observations with values that are very much above or below that of the rest of the data. Sometimes outliers are the result of data input errors and in the cases where such an error is obvious the value should normally be set to missing, provided you believe such errors are occurring in the sample in an appropriately random way.[46]

Formal Testing. More formally there are a battery of tests for outliers (e.g., Cook's distance), functional form misspecification, heteroskedasticity, endogeneity, autocorrelation, and so on. Ideally, a regression specification should pass them or at least most of them. That said, do remember that if you were using 95% significance tests (and your tests were independent), then you would reject one in twenty tests, even if the model were the true DGP. The impact of statistical dependence between tests performed on a specification is complex. If you are rejecting more than 5% of the tests you run, you are probably examining a model with genuine problems although it could also be that the tests you are using are highly dependent tests, each picking up the same random pattern in the data. On the other hand, if absolutely no tests reject their null hypothesis that may be equally worrying as it can indicate that there is little real information in a data set. These observations suggest that, where possible, joint tests are more desirable than sequences of lots of individual ones. However, the reality with such formal testing is that test statistics are often important primarily because they help flag up that something is going on in the data underlying your estimates and you should try to understand what it is.

Out-of-Sample Prediction. The most challenging specification check is to consider the model's ability to predict out of sample. In OLS, for instance, this may involve assessing the validity of the linearity assumption beyond the range of data used. Is the estimated effect still valid at observed values of the explanatory or explained variables that are different than those used in the model? Are predictions at values that lie outside the sample credible? A genuine out-of-sample prediction using fresh data to verify whether an extrapolation is valid can provide a tremendously powerful check on a model. On the other hand, once the data have been used to improve the model, reported "out-of-sample" tests lose their power. In particular, if an analyst

[46] In other cases, the observation may represent a real phenomenon but one that is unusual enough to justify dropping the observation altogether or more often modeling that element specifically; one-off sources of data variation can always be modeled using an appropriately constructed indicator variable and such an approach may be preferable to either removing the observation or generalizing the model to capture exactly what went on that week. For example, in an interest rate plot from the United Kingdom of data from 1992, September 16, 1992 would stand out because for one day interest rates went up from 10 to 12% (and were announced to go up to 15%) as the government attempted to defend the value of the pound against speculators who considered it overvalued in the European Exchange Rate Mechanism (ERM). The pound left the ERM later that day.

follows a process of iteration by which models are improved following the failure of out-of-sample tests, then to a large extent the iteration effectively brings the data back "in sample." For this reason such "out-of-sample checks" reported in expert reports must be treated with a degree of skepticism unless genuinely new data can be brought into play, perhaps later in an investigation.[47] It is in any case generally prudent not to use an econometric model to predict outcomes under conditions (i.e., values of the explanatory variables) that are very different from that of the sample used in the estimation.

2.3.3 Robustness Checks

Robustness checks involve examining the stability of the results with respect to variations in the model specification or estimation method. Every single model ever estimated can be tested to destruction but, on the other hand, knowing your regression specification is robust to minor (or even major) changes is clearly desirable. For example, an analyst may not be confident that a particular assumption holds so it may be useful to test whether relaxing the assumption, for instance, by allowing nonlinearities or introducing an additional control variable, drastically affects the estimation results. If the results are not robust to particular departures from the favored model presented, then good practice means that that fact should be reported in the description of the results.

For example, we have already described that outliers sometimes emerge in data sets. If an analyst decides to keep extreme values in the sample, it is better to show that those values are not drastically affecting the regression estimates. If the regression is affected by the inclusion of the extreme values, the analyst must be ready to argue why it makes sense to give weight to these observations. Finally, when the regression is run on a sample composed by different groups or distinct time frames, it is useful to test whether the results are robust to the exclusion of some of the groups or time intervals. Since the regression on the whole sample gives us an average of the effect over the sample population, we want to make sure that this average is representative of the effect and is not the average of widely different magnitudes. If excluding a group (such as a country or a firm) or a time period drastically affects the results, this fact should be reported. Particularly, this type of robustness check will help detect whether the results are driven by one small part of the sample as opposed to by the whole sample.

Following these simple practices of knowing your data and checking assumptions and results will save trouble down the line and increase the credibility of econometric results. Increasingly, econometric investigations submitted in the context of antitrust

[47] That is, if the model is constructed to pass the out-of-sample checks, then the out-of-sample checks are not in reality "out of sample," even if they are not in the final reported version used in the estimation of the model. It is not wrong to use the larger data set, but it is a clear misrepresentation to construct a model using the full sample and then reestimate it using half the sample and subsequently "verify" that the model works well on the full sample.

investigations are subject to replication exercises by the opposing party. Ensuring the good quality of the exercise from the outset will save the analysts presenting the work some unnecessary embarrassment later in the process. Of course, all of the above said, not every possible robustness check can be performed and reported. However, this is one important area where increased transparency can greatly enhance quality assurance. Sharing computer code, discussion of regression specifications, and even the use of data rooms (where confidential data can be seen by the professional economic advisors to merging parties) all help drive up quality and avoid the risk of programming or other mistakes surviving long in an investigation.[48]

2.4 Conclusions

- In an investigation, econometric analysis must be given the appropriate amount of evidential weight. The appropriate weight will depend on the reasonableness (or more realistically the degree of unreasonableness) of the economic and econometric assumptions that the analysis required as well as the quality and robustness of the estimation results themselves.
- It is good practice to carefully study the raw data to detect outliers; to evaluate correlations between the explanatory variables; to assess the extent of relevant variation in the explanatory variables; and to examine any relationships that emerge between the error term and the explanatory variables.
- Economic theory and knowledge of the industry must guide the specification of the regression. When little is known or little can reasonably be assumed, the regression specification may need to be flexible enough to encompass a variety of possible forms of DGP. In particular, we want the model to be rich enough to ensure the model can explain the important features of the data.
- Ordinary least-squares estimators are consistent and unbiased under specific assumptions, and depending on the context these may be reasonable or not. The assumptions include that the explanatory variables must be uncorrelated with the unobserved determinants of the outcome, i.e., with the error term. This assumption will be violated if we have misspecification of the model, our data suffer from measurement error, or our regressors are endogenous.
- Hypothesis testing allows us to formally decide whether we can accept or reject, with a given level of confidence (often 95%) the hypothesis that the true value of a coefficient is different from an estimated value. Such testing can be helpful in getting to the point where an analyst understands the extent and nature of the information contained in a given data set, and how that

[48] At the same time, data rooms can be costly in terms of scarce resources during an investigation. Confidentiality agreements—with appropriate punishments for noncompliance–for example, must be negotiated and if one party gets access, then generally all, or at least many, will want it.

information is reflected in the estimates obtained for a particular model using a particular estimation technique.

- The most common problems with OLS regressions are misspecification, endogeneity, multicollinearity, measurement error, and heteroskedasticity. In all but the last case, our estimated coefficients will be biased so that we will draw false conclusions about their true value. Even heteroskedasticity will give us bad estimators for our standard errors and will make our hypothesis testing problematic unless it is appropriately controlled for.
- Identification is a central issue in all empirical work. As a first of many examples in the book, in this chapter we examined the classic problem of identification of supply and demand. In that particular case, an important challenge in the identification of causal effects involves the fact that price and quantity are simultaneously determined. A mixture of economic and econometric theory tells us that, in that case, the solution involves using supply shifters to identify the demand equation and demand shifters to identify the supply equation.
- In the presence of suspected endogeneity, a variety of identification strategies can potentially be used. Fixed-effect estimation facilitates like-with-like comparisons within a sample and therefore allows us to exclude the effect of differentiating factors that affect both the explanatory variables and the outcome. The grouping of "similar" observations is determined by the analyst. Instrumental variable techniques allow us to isolate the variation in endogenous regressors that is not correlated with the error term so that it can be considered exogenous. A good instrument "cleans out" the variation in the endogenous regressor that is introducing a correlation with the error term while leaving the remaining variation, the part that is uncorrelated with the error term. Natural experiments, as well as event studies, use exogenous shocks to the otherwise endogenous variable to identify its effect on the outcome.
- Once the estimation is carried out, robustness and sensitivity tests to changes in the sample or changes in specification are indispensable. In addition, it is often helpful to examine tables and graphs of raw data that capture the mechanism at work in the regression. For example, it is possible to condition on a small range of values for the other explanatory variables and to construct a graph or table of the dependent variable and the central variable(s) of interest. Doing so, may help convince you and your readers that there is "nothing funny" going on in the regression specification. Such exercises are particularly helpful where decision makers are not econometrics experts and so inevitably the actual estimation process may appear to be somewhat of a "black box" exercise, where it is difficult to evaluate competing econometrics experts each claiming that the others are wrong. It is currently an unfortunate fact of antitrust life that much expert econometric advice simply

neutralizes other opposing expert testimony, leading to the decision being made on other grounds. Indeed, one aim of the rest of this book is to help practitioners make their econometric evidence more convincing to the audience (including judges, competition lawyers, CEOs, and other economists and econometricians) who must evaluate it.

2.5 Annex: Introduction to the Theory of Identification

The theoretical study of identification[49] considers a system of equations along the lines of $U = m(X, Y)$, where U describes a vector of unobservables in the model determined by m, an unknown vector function of the K observed exogenous variables X and the G endogenous variables Y (see, for example, Matzkin 2008 and the references therein). The literature usually considers the case that there is one unobservable U per equation so that $m\colon \mathbb{R}^{G+K} \to \mathbb{R}^{G}$. Posed generally, the identification question is, under what conditions can we use the joint distribution of $F_{X,Y}(X, Y)$, which given enough data is what we observe, to learn about the function m and also the joint distribution of the unknown variables, $F_U(U)$? For example, following Angrist et al. (2000), in a general supply-and-demand system we would have the two general equations:

$$Q_i = Q_i^{\rm S}(P_i, w_i^{\rm S}, u_i^{\rm S}) \quad \text{and} \quad Q_i = Q_i^{\rm D}(P_i, w_i^{\rm D}, u_i^{\rm D}).$$

In the supply-and-demand system we studied graphically, these functions were linear in both variables and parameters. More generally, if the supply-and-demand functions are respectively strictly increasing in $u_i^{\rm S}$ and $u_i^{\rm D}$, then we will be able to invert these equations to give a system of equations of the form $U = m(X, Y)$, where $U = (u_i^{\rm S}, u_i^{\rm D})$, $Y = (P_i, Q_i)$, and $X = (w_i^{\rm S}, w_i^{\rm D})$. Suppose now we know (assume) that the true U generated by the true m function is conditionally independent of X. Immediately, we can see that if we propose some function $\tilde{m}$ which generates the random variable $\tilde{U} = \tilde{m}(X, Y)$, in general the conditional distribution $F_{\tilde{U}|X}$ will differ with X. Independence of U and X requires that the whole conditional distribution does not vary with values of X, while an assumption of conditional mean independence such as that typically used in OLS estimators requires that the first moment of the distribution does not vary with X and moreover that it is fixed and equal to zero. Thus independence-type restrictions will act to rule out potential functions $\tilde{m}$ and in so doing help us to find the true m function. Intuitively, this argument tells us that assumptions which impose conditional mean independence restrictions such as $E[U \mid X] = E[m(X, Y) \mid X] = 0$ will help identify the function m.

If our supply-and-demand functions are known to be parametric functions $Q_i = Q_i^{\rm S}(P_i, w_i^{\rm S}, u_i^{\rm S}; \theta^{\rm S})$ and $Q_i = Q_i^{\rm D}(P_i, w_i^{\rm D}, u_i^{\rm D}; \theta^{\rm S})$, then entirely analogously assumptions such as conditional mean independence will help us identify

[49] Some readers will find this material particularly hard and may want to omit it on first reading. The reader who requires a more formal presentation in a general setting is referred to Matzkin (2008).

the true value of those parameters precisely because they will help identify the true m function which in the parametric case boils down to finding the true parameter values, $(\theta^{\mathrm{D}}, \theta^{\mathrm{S}})$. Nonparametric identification results are more general in the sense that they establish identification for a general true m function, whereas parametric identification only establishes a weaker form of identification, namely identification of the true m function (i.e., its parameters) given that we constrain the truth to be within a predefined class of parametric functions. In the supply-and-demand system we studied graphically, for example, econometrics textbook treatments of identification of simultaneous linear equations establishes that each equation can be identified provided there is an omitted variable for each equation which can be used to identify the other equation. Advanced readers will note that such an identification result is a parametric identification result since it holds only within the class of m functions which are linear in parameters. That is, if we write down a two-equation linear system of equations to be the DGP, then an omitted variable for each equation that is included in the other provides (the parametric) identification results presented in econometrics textbooks.

If you wish to challenge yourself greatly, then the literature on identification in instrumental variable estimation for multivariate latent variable models may provide sufficient distraction from casework. In latent variable models we do not observe the Y variables themselves but rather some indicator of them. For instance, in chapter 5 we discuss estimation of entry models where we do not observe profitability but we do observe entry. In such a model, we have $U = m(X, Y^*)$, where the star indicates that we do not observe the variable itself.

3

Estimation of Cost Functions

Costs are a key component of profitability, and as such it should perhaps not be surprising that knowledge of an industry's or a firm's cost function is often very important for competition analysis. While theoretical cost functions will be familiar from introductory economics courses, the aim of this chapter is to describe the tools available for determining the shape of real-world cost functions in order that estimates of them can be used in practical settings.

Before we progress to such practicalities, it is useful to pause briefly to recall Viner's (1931) theory, which may usefully be described as the "cost structure" theory of firm size and hence market structure.[1] Viner and others were exploring the model of perfect competition which had permeated economics both in terms of partial and general equilibrium models. Sraffa (1926) in particular observed that the shape of the cost function mattered for whether firms were likely to be small enough to be considered atomistic and therefore close to the types of firms assumed by proponents of perfect competition as a model of long-run competition.

In a model of price-taking firms with cost function $C(q)$, firms solve

$$\max_q pq - C(q)$$

so that, absent fixed costs, firm size is given by the solution to the equation

$$p = \frac{\partial C(q)}{\partial q}.$$

More generally, output expansion will be profitable as long as $p > \partial C(q)/\partial q$. Unfortunately, if $C(q) = cq$, we have a constant marginal cost, then our condition for output expansion becomes $p > c$, which is either true for all output levels so that firms expand output to the point where price-taking becomes implausible or not true for any output level in which case the firm produces nothing.

Viner (1931) argued that, at least in the short run, firms were in fact likely to have U-shaped average cost curves. Moreover, he argued that even in the long run, if some factor of production such as land were in fixed supply, then cost functions

[1] The Viner paper is reprinted in Stigler and Boulding (1950). The debate around the nature of long-run supply curves is summarized in Aslanbeigui and Naples (1997).

were likely to be U-shaped. A U-shaped cost function means that the firms' scale of supply will be determined by the shape of their cost function and thus firms may be small relative to the size of a market, at least partially restoring price-taking firms as a plausible long-run assumption. If so, in the long run entry will drive prices down until active firms operate at a scale which achieves the minimum of their average cost function, where average cost equals the marginal cost of production (and also price). The reader may also recall the case of natural monopoly, where average costs are always declining so that efficient production always involves a market with just a single active firm. In each case, Viner's theory of market structure attributes a central explanatory role to the shape of firms' cost functions.

In practical terms, sometimes we will see industries with a small number of very large firms. It can be that firms with large market shares are benefiting from barriers to entry and that they are able to use their market power to price far above cost and hurt consumers. However, it may instead be that those large firms are big because they are highly efficient producers. If antitrust authorities act to break up efficient large firms into inefficient small ones, they will usually be hurting rather than helping consumers.

Cost considerations are important in both merger and regulatory contexts. In merger investigations, one reason for approving a merger even if it appears likely to bolster market power can be if unit costs are likely to go down. One reason they might is if a merger generates substantial economies of scale. Similarly, in regulatory contexts, regulators often choose to set prices as a function of some measure of costs. In doing so, regulators face the complex task of getting appropriate and meaningful data, devising a relevant cost measure, and estimating its value.

For some purposes, we may "only" need estimates of the marginal or average cost of production and, if so, such estimates can potentially be retrieved from company records or industry estimates. In such cases there may be no need to actually estimate a cost function. However, on other occasions, we want to know whether the marginal cost varies with the quantity produced, and in particular whether we have economies or diseconomies of scale as firm size varies. In this case, the economists' traditional approach requires making (perhaps weak) assumptions about the potential form of the cost function and estimating the cost model's parameters. We provided a first discussion of the approach in chapter 1. While "econometric" cost function estimation is perhaps most familiar to economists, "engineering" cost estimation can also prove very effective. One way to get engineering estimates is to perform detailed interviews with the technical personnel at plants and firms to get hands-on estimates of costs and scale effects. In the next three sections, we first discuss some important differences between accounting and economic costs. Second, we discuss estimation of traditional production and cost functions. Third, we consider alternative approaches to estimation, in particular, the use of "frontier" models including efficient frontier analysis (EFA), stochastic frontier analysis (SFA), and data envelopment analysis (DEA).

3.1 Accounting and Economic Revenue, Costs, and Profits

To econometrically estimate cost functions an analyst will of course typically need access to cost data (alternatives using production and input demand data were explored in chapter 1). Unfortunately, analysts must tread carefully around cost data since even the most conventional economic measurements of costs are not always easily retrieved from company documents. The most common difficulty is that reported accounting costs can differ, sometimes dramatically, from economic costs.[2]

3.1.1 Reconciling Accounting and Economic Costs

There are some important differences between the definition of costs used by economists and those used in practice in managerial and even more particularly in financial accounting. While such differences are quite generally and regularly stressed by industrial organization economists, following in particular an influential article by Fisher and McGowan (1983),[3] doing so is a somewhat self-serving but not obviously overwhelming concern. Analysts in the financial markets, for instance, regularly attempt to extract useful information, even from published financial accounts. Such information is used, for example, to build or at least inform firm valuation models to price equities. It is therefore possible, indeed probable, that academic industrial organization has somewhat "thrown out the baby with the bathwater" in almost entirely discarding accounting information. A more reasonable view is that accounts may contain useful information, but to use them appropriately one must be rather a sophisticated user, or at least not a naive one. It is rare that an investigator can take accounts at face value. While the measurement aim of economists and accountants is the same, financial accounts attempt to be comparable across firms and are composed using standard techniques which may not reflect the particular circumstances relevant for evaluating economic costs or profits. Management accounts are typically available in competition inquiries and these are often more useful for measuring economic profits than financial accounts, but nonetheless attempts to do so face a number of substantive but sometimes not insurmountable difficulties.

3.1.1.1 Most Common Difficulties

One area for concern is introduced by joint production costs or revenues. Antitrust authorities sometimes attempt to calculate whether one product produced by a mul-

[2] For a more in-depth discussion, see OFT (2003). See also Geroski (2005).

[3] See also Martin (1984), who concludes: "Fisher and McGowan have demonstrated the well known point that accounting measures of capital intensity are likely to be inaccurate. This should be, and has been, considered in carrying out empirical studies of the concentration–profit relationship." Fisher and McGowan were critiquing structure–conduct–performance (SCP) regressions of the form described in chapter 6. As we document there, the criticisms of SCP were not limited to concerns around measurement with accounting data.

tiproduct firm is generating "excessive profits." Doing so in the presence of joint production requires that the authority attempt to allocate costs and revenues among operations. Such attempts at cost or revenue "allocation" are particularly difficult. To see why, consider a firm which spends €100 million digging a mine and then goes about extracting two metals, perhaps platinum and palladium from ore obtained from the mine. An antitrust authority asking whether the mine owner is making "excess profits from palladium" risks ignoring the reality that the firm's objective is to make profits from both activities, not palladium alone. It is striking that theory tells us that a social planner maximizing welfare may well extract "excess" profits from one product and use those profits to cross-subsidize the other activity. The literature on Ramsey pricing develops this result.[4]

A second area for concern arises in vertically integrated firms where transfer pricing can be used to assign a cost to inputs which may not reflect the actual value of that input. Transfer pricing can provide a method of transferring accounting profits between companies which in turn can have important real-world motivations. For instance, if tax liabilities on profits differ between upstream and downstream firms, perhaps because the production occurs in different member states, then a firm may have a strong incentive to report their accounting profits in one member state and not in another.

A third area of difficulty arises from differences in timing. If costs and revenues are either not generated over the same time horizon as either each other, and/or the time horizon for which the accounts are being prepared, there can be important differences between economic and accounting costs. To illustrate, consider a factory which is to be bought and paid for now, that will be useful for the next 30 years, but must be accounted for annually. How much does the factory cost in each of those 30 years? To answer such questions from the economist's perspective we will discuss the concepts of (a) opportunity cost and (b) economic depreciation in the next two sections.

3.1.1.2 *Opportunity Costs*

Opportunity cost is the value of the best alternative use of the input. When there is a market for the input, the value of the best alternative use is the market price of the input and so no additional adjustment is needed to obtain opportunity costs. When there is no market for the input, economists must still value the maximum returns that this input could bring in an alternative use. For example, the opportunity cost of investing in extra production capacity for a good is the return of the amount of capital

[4] Ramsey pricing aims at setting the prices of several products or firms such as to maximize social welfare subject to some prespecified profit constraint. See the original exposition of Ramsey pricing in Ramsey (1927). In practical settings, when evaluating such arguments, it is important to keep in mind that Ramsey pricing is, however, definitively not the same as monopoly pricing! Measures of excess economic profitability can, at least in principle, help distinguish the two situations. In practice, doing so with any degree of precision requires a great deal of very good data and careful analysis. For that reason, and in the face of budgetary constraints, many agencies prefer to make qualitative judgements about whether—or not—prices are justified by Ramsey pricing style arguments.

used if it had been invested in the next best alternative, appropriately adjusted for risk profile. Similarly, the opportunity cost of research and development expenditures is the return that the amount spent would have gained if it had been used in the most profitable alternative, again with a similar risk profile.

Opportunity costs do not just occur with capital goods. An example of noncapital opportunity costs are the opportunity costs for the work of a company owner, that is, the highest income that this person could achieve in another occupation, salaried or not, but again adjusting for risk and effort levels. In common language, opportunity costs are sometimes expressed in qualitative rather than monetary terms. For instance, you might hear a colleague say that the opportunity costs of launching a new product is the forgone improvement in the quality of another product. In a quantitative evaluation, in principle we would then have to calculate the expected return of the alternative investment to put a monetary value to it. Doing so would obviously not be easy and in practice such opportunity-cost calculations will often be substantial approximations using an "appropriate" interest rate times the amount of money being invested; we will say more in a moment.

Another sometimes important arena for opportunity costs is in the valuation of inventories of unsold goods. Accountants sometimes use valuation methods such as first-in-first-out (FIFO) rather than last-in-first-out (LIFO) valuation rules. Using FIFO assigns the cost of using up a unit of inventories to be the historic cost of producing the oldest unit in stock. Naturally, that may well not reflect the opportunity cost of replacing the unit of inventory, which will have more to do with current production costs.

Despite the wide applicability of the concept of opportunity cost, in practice, the issue of calculating opportunity costs probably arises most commonly in the computation of capital expenditures, a process which we describe next.

3.1.1.3 Depreciation and the Cost of Capital

The case of capital is very useful to illustrate the kind of differences that arise between economic and accounting costs. Accountants tend to report the cost of capital goods as a depreciation charge in the accounts, which can be calculated according to various formulas. They may also include a financing charge as interest paid if the firm has borrowed money to finance the purchase of capital goods.

Figure 3.1 illustrates the effect of a constant depreciation rule on capital valuation. Part (a) shows the value of a capital good on the books when using two alternative depreciation schedules. The straight-line depreciation uses a fixed proportion of the value of the good as the cost allocated to that year's profits. The dashed line shows the value of a capital asset using an accelerated depreciation schedule; higher depreciation charges are taken in the early years of an asset's life. Part (b) shows the (constant) depreciation charge taken each year when using the straight-line depreciation method.

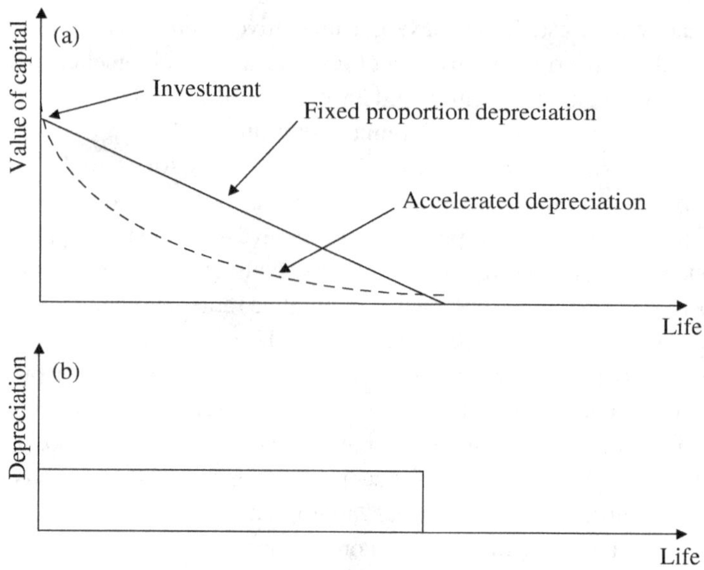

Figure 3.1. Depreciation schedules. *Source*: Tom Stoker, MIT Sloan.

With a constant depreciation rule, the accounting cost of capital will be

$$\text{Cost of capital}_t = \delta K_t,$$

where K_t is the original capital investment.

An economist, on the other hand, would ideally define the user cost of capital (UCC) as the opportunity cost of the capital employed (whether financed by debt or equity) plus economic depreciation:

$$\text{UCC}_t = \text{Opportunity cost}_t + \text{Economic depreciation}_t.$$

The opportunity cost will be an appropriate interest rate times the amount of capital employed so that

$$\text{Opportunity cost}_t = rV_t,$$

where V_t is the value of the capital good at time t. An "appropriate" interest rate r will control for risk since not all investments are equally risky. The question then arises about what we mean by an "appropriate" interest rate. One popular answer to that question is to use the weighted average cost of capital (WACC) for the firm.[5]

[5] At its most basic the WACC takes the various sources of funds (usually debt and equity, but there can be different types of debt and equity: senior and subordinated debt or ordinary and preference shares) and takes the weighted average return required for each source of funds where the weights allocated to each required return are the proportions of debt and equity. An important complication emerges in that tax treatments can differ by source of funds, in particular, in many jurisdictions corporate taxes are paid on profits after interest is deducted as an expense, which means interest is accounted for as an expense while taxes are due on the returns to equity. While we may determine the weights in a WACC calculation by the amount of various sources of funds, the underlying return on each source of funds must, of course,

The second component of the user cost of capital is economic depreciation, which can be calculated as the (expected) change in the value of the asset over the period of use:

$$\text{Economic depreciation}_t = V_t - V_{t+1}.$$

The difference between economic depreciation and accounting depreciation can be a source of substantial differences between economic and accounting profits. In fact, there are many accounting methods used to "write off" capital. In general, the firm deducts each year a share of the value of the investment either at a constant or decreasing rate (see figure 3.1). The choice of the method used to write off the capital can potentially have an enormous impact on the annual cost figures and hence result in substantial reallocations of profits across periods. Accounting depreciation is rarely negative, but economic depreciation certainly can be when assets appreciate in value.

To illustrate the differences, consider a firm which buys a new car. An accounting treatment might calculate the depreciation charge by writing off the value of the investment using a straight-line depreciation charge over ten years, so that depreciation would be one tenth of the purchase price each year. The economist, however, when looking at the economic depreciation might go to a price book for second-hand cars and compare today's price differential between a new car and the identical model of car which is one year old. Doing so would give you an estimate of the economic depreciation—the decline in value of the asset—that results from holding it for one year. Using a 2007 Belgian car magazine, we see, for instance, that a new Volkswagen Passat Variant Comfortline costs €28,050 while a similar one-year-old model can be found for €21,000.[6] We can calculate the economic cost or the UCC as

$$\begin{aligned}\text{UCC}_t &= \text{Opportunity cost}_t + \text{Economic depreciation}_t\\ &= rV_t + (V_t - V_{t+1})\\ &= r \times 28{,}050 + (28{,}050 - 21{,}000),\end{aligned}$$

where V is the market value of the capital good and r is often measured using the WACC.[7] With $r = 10\%$ the user cost of capital is €9,855.

be calculated. Debt costs can often be obtained from accounting statements while obtaining those for equity leads us toward methods such as those associated with the CAPM (see, for example, White et al. 2001).

[6] *Le Moniteur Automobile*, September 2007.

[7] Doing so involves calculating a weighted average of the cost of equity and the cost of debt according to their respective participation in the value of the firm. WACC $= (D/V)(1-t)r^{\mathrm{d}} + (E/V)r^{\mathrm{e}}$, where D/V and E/V are, respectively, the ratio of debt and equity to the value of the firm, r^{d} is the cost of debt, r^{e} is the cost of equity, and t is the marginal corporate tax rate (assuming that tax is not paid on debt). Authors often use the book-value of debt for D and the market value of equity (number of shares outstanding times share price) for E, while by definition $V = E + D$. The cost of debt r^{d} can be obtained as the ratio of interest expenses to debt for a given firm, whereas the cost of equity is often obtained from an asset pricing model, although within the context of a case it may also come from company documents.

One can also perform the equivalent calculation:

$$\text{UCC}_t = (r + \text{Depreciation rate})\,V_t,$$

where

$$\begin{aligned}\text{Depreciation rate} &= \frac{V_t - V_{t+1}}{V_t} = \frac{28{,}050 - 21{,}000}{28{,}050} \\ &= 0.25133, \\ \text{UCC}_t &= (0.10 + 0.25133) \times 28{,}050 \\ &= 9{,}855.\end{aligned}$$

If the new car is expected to last five years, the accounting cost of the firm for the first year might be $28{,}050/5 =$ €5,610. The economic costs will nevertheless be €9,855 given the rapid decline in the market value of the car during its first year of usage, a percentage depreciation rate of 25.1%.

3.1.2 Comparing Costs and Revenues: Discounted Cash Flows

Sometimes, we want to compare the cost of an investment with the value of its expected return. A common method to calculate the flow of revenues is to calculate the discounted cash flow generated by the investment. This means calculating the present value of the future revenue stream generated by the current capital expenditure.

The discounted cash flow is calculated as follows:

$$\text{DCF} = \sum_{t=1}^{T} \frac{R_t}{(1+r)^t} + \text{FV}_T,$$

where R_t is the revenue generated by the investment at time t, r is the discount rate, which is normally the cost of capital of the firm, and FV_T is the final valuation of the investment at the end period of the project T.

Discounted cash flows can be used to compare the value of revenue streams with the value of the cost streams when the time paths are different. In competition investigations such calculations are commonplace. For example, they will be useful when evaluating prices that are cost reflective in investigations of industries where production involves investment in costly durable capital goods (e.g., telecommunications, where firms invest in networks). Another example involves the investigation of predation cases, where many jurisdictions use a "sacrifice" or "recoupment" test. The idea is that a dominant firm charging a low price today to drive out a rival is following a strategy that involves a sacrifice of current profits. The idea of the sacrifice test is that such a sacrifice would only be rational if it were followed by sufficiently higher profits in the future.

3.2 Estimation of Production and Cost Functions

The traditional estimation of cost and production functions can be a complex task that raises a number of difficult issues. In tandem with obtaining appropriate data, one must combine a sound theoretical framework that generates one or more estimating equation(s) with appropriate econometric techniques. We introduce the main empirical issues in cost estimation and proceed to discuss some seminal illustrative examples which help illustrate both the problems and usefulness of the approach.

3.2.1 Principles of Production and Cost Function Estimation

The theory of production and cost functions and the empirical literature estimating them is a significant body of literature. Chapter 1 in this volume covers the basic theoretical framework underlying the empirical estimation of cost functions. We review here the basic conclusions of that discussion and then proceed to present some practical examples of cost function estimation since that is undoubtedly the best way to see how such exercises can be done.

3.2.1.1 Theoretical Frameworks and Data Implications

Intuitively, costs simply add up. However, as we will see, that simple picture is often complicated because firms have input substitution possibilities—they can sometimes, for example, substitute capital for labor. Substitution possibilities mean that we have to think harder than simply adding up a firm's costs for the inputs required to produce output. To see why, let us consider a case when costs do just add up because there are no substitution possibilities, namely the case of producing according to a fixed recipe.

To fix ideas, let us consider an example. To produce a cake, suppose we need 1 kg of flour, six eggs, a fixed quantity of milk, and so on. Ignoring divisibility issues, the cost of producing a cake may simply be the sum of the prices of the ingredients times the quantities they are required in. A fixed-proportions production function has the form

$$Q = \min\left\{\frac{I_1}{\alpha_1}, \frac{I_2}{\alpha_2}, \dots, \frac{I_n}{\alpha_n}\right\},$$

where $I_1, I_2, \dots, I_n$ are inputs such as flour, eggs, and milk, while the parameters $\alpha_1, \dots, \alpha_n$ describe the amount of each input required to produce a single cake. So if we require 1 kg of flour and six eggs $\alpha_1 = 1$ and $\alpha_2 = 6$ and the ratio $\frac{1}{6}I_2$ tells us the number of cakes that we have enough eggs to make. However, now suppose that some capital and labor are required to produce the cake. We could either have a small amount of labor and a cake-mixer or a large amount of labor and a spoon. In this case, we have capital–labor substitution possibilities and depending on the relative prices of capital and labor our cake producer may choose to use them in different proportions. The "fixed-proportions" production function may therefore suffice as a model for the materials piece of the production function, but we will require a production function that embeds that piece into a full production function which allows for substitution possibilities in capital and labor.

In general, we describe a production function as

$$Q = f(I_1, \dots, I_m; \alpha_1, \dots, \alpha_m),$$

where $I_1, I_2, \dots, I_m$ are inputs such as labor, capital, and other materials, and the alphas are parameters. Probably the most famous production function that captures an ability to produce output using capital and labor in different proportions is the Cobb–Douglas production function (Cobb and Douglas 1928):

$$Q = \alpha_0 L^{\alpha_1} K^{\alpha_2}.$$

First note that a Cobb–Douglas production function requires that each firm must have at least some capital and also some labor if it is to produce any output. Second, we note that when writing down an econometric model, we will often suppose that at least one of the "inputs" is a variable which is not observed by the investigator. For clarity of exposition we distinguish the observed and unobserved inputs by introducing an "input" variable over which, in the simplest (static) version of these theories, the firm is typically assumed to have no choice.[8] This unobserved "input" will become our econometric error term and is sometimes described as measuring firms' (total factor) "productivity." We shall denote a firm's (total factor) productivity by u and $\alpha = (\alpha_1, \dots, \alpha_m)$.

Given a production function, we may describe the minimum cost of producing a given level of output as the solution to

$$C(Q; \alpha, u) = \min_{I_1, \dots, I_m} p_1 I_1 + \cdots + p_m I_m \quad \text{subject to } Q \leqslant f(I_1, \dots, I_m, u; \alpha),$$

where $Q \leqslant f(I_1, \dots, I_m, u; \alpha)$ describes the fact that the amount of output must be less than that feasible according to the production function.

Describing the costs of producing output in this way makes it rather clear that costs and technological possibilities—as encapsulated in the production function—are rather fundamentally related. This interrelation is discussed in appropriate depth in chapter 1. That fact has important implications for both the theorist and the researcher interested in eliciting information about the cost structure of firms in an industry, namely that such information can be obtained in several ways. If we want to learn about the way costs vary with output, we can either examine a cost function directly or instead learn about the production function and estimate costs indirectly. Finally, readers may recall that there is a relationship between cost functions and input demand equations, via Shephard's lemma, which states that under sometimes reasonable assumptions, the input demands which solve the cost-minimization

[8] For a model in which the firms do make investments to boost their productivity, see Pakes and Maguire (1994).

program can be described as

$$I_j = \frac{\partial C(Q, p_1, \dots, p_n; \alpha, u)}{\partial p_j}.$$

Thus input demand equations and the cost function are also intimately related and, as a result, much information about technology can also sometimes be inferred from estimates of input demand equations.

An extremely important fact for the investigator is that each of these three approaches to understanding costs requires somewhat different variables to be in our data sets. For example, to empirically estimate a production function such as

$$Q = f(I_1, \dots, I_m, u; \alpha),$$

where $I_1, I_2, \dots, I_m$ are inputs such as labor, capital, and other materials, we need data on input quantities for different levels of quantity produced Q. A cost function, on the other hand, will relate the minimum possible cost to the quantity produced and input prices so will take the form

$$C = C(Q, p_1, \dots, p_m, u; \alpha).$$

Input demand schedules relate the optimal demand for inputs to the quantity produced and the input prices $I_j = D_i(Q, p_1, \dots, p_m, u; \alpha)$. Shephard's lemma makes it clear that the input demand approach contains information about the first derivatives of the cost function rather than the level of costs. For that reason, not all information about costs can be inferred from input demands.

Before discussing some empirical applications, we first discuss four substantive issues that must be squarely faced by the investigator when attempting to learn about costs or technology using econometrics. Each is introduced here and subsequently further explored below.

3.2.1.2 Empirical Issues with Cost and Production Estimation

There are four issues that are likely to arise in cost or production function estimation exercises: endogeneity, functional form, technological change, and multiproduct firms.

First we note that in each of the three estimation approaches described above, we may face a problem with endogeneity. To see why, consider a data set consisting of a large number of firm-level observations on outputs and inputs and suppose we are attempting to estimate the production function $Q = f(I_1, \dots, I_m, u; \alpha)$.

For OLS estimation, even if the true model is assumed linear in parameters and the unobserved (productivity) term is assumed additively separable, productivity must not be correlated with the independent variables in the regression, i.e., the chosen inputs. We will face an endogeneity problem if, for example, the high-productivity firms, those with high unobserved productivity u, also demand a lot of inputs. On the one hand, according to the model, the efficient firms may require fewer inputs to produce any given level of output. On the other hand, and probably dominating, we will expect the efficient firms to be large—they are the ones with a competitive advantage. As a result, efficient firms will tend to be both high productivity and use high levels of inputs. These observations suggest that the key condition required for OLS to provide a consistent estimator will not be satisfied. Namely, OLS requires u_i and I_j to be uncorrelated but these arguments suggest they will not be. If we do not account for this endogeneity problem, our estimate of the coefficient on our endogenous input will be biased upward.[9] To solve this problem by instrumental variable regression we would need to find an identifying variable that can explain the firm's demand for the input but that is not linked to the productivity of a firm. Recent advances in the production function estimation literature have included the methods described in Olley and Pakes (1996), who suggest using investment as a proxy for productivity and use it to control for endogeneity.[10] Levinsohn and Petrin (2003) suggest an alternative approach, but in an important paper Ackerberg et al. (2006) critique the identification arguments in those papers, particularly Levinsohn and Petrin (2003), and suggest alternative methodologies.

A second consideration is that we must carefully specify the functional form to take into account the technological realities of the production process. In particular, the functional form needs to reflect the plausible input substitution possibilities and the plausible nature of returns of scale. If we are unsure about the nature of the returns to scale in an industry, we should adopt a specification that is flexible enough to allow the data to determine the existence of scale effects. It is not uncommon to impose restrictions such as requiring the production function have the same returns to scale over the whole range of output and such potentially restrictive assumptions should only be made when deemed reasonable over the data range of the analysis. Overly flexible specifications, on the other hand, may produce estimated cost or production functions that do not behave in a way that is plausible, for example, by producing negative marginal costs. The reason is that data sets are often limited and unable to identify parameters in overly flexible specifications. Clearly, we want to use any actual knowledge of the production process we have before we move to estimation, but ideally not impose more than we know on the data.

Third, particularly when the data for the cost or production function estimation come from time series data, we will need to take into account technological change going on in the industry—and therefore driving a part of the variation in our data. Technological progress will result in new production and cost functions and the cost

[9] In fact, this intuition, discussed in chapter 2, is really only valid for the case of a single endogenous input. If we have multiple endogeneity problems, establishing the sign of the OLS bias is unfortunately substantially harder.

[10] While capital stock is already in a production function, investment—the change in capital stock—is not, at least provided that the resulting capital stock increases only in the next period.

and input prices associated with the corresponding output cannot therefore immediately be compared over time without controlling for such changes. For this reason, one or more variables attempting to account for the effect of technological progress is generally included in specifications using time series data. Clearly, with a cross section of firms there is less likely to be a direct problem with technological progress but, equally, if firms are using different technologies or the same technologies with different level of aptitude, then it would be important to attempt to account for such differences.

When the firms involved produce more than one product or service, costs and inputs can be hard to allocate to the different outputs and constructing the data series for the different products may turn into a challenge. Estimating multiproduct cost or production functions will also further complicate the exercise by increasing the number of parameters to estimate. Of course, such efforts may nonetheless be well worthwhile.

In the next sections, we use well-known estimation examples to discuss these and other issues as they are commonly encountered in actual cost estimation exercises.

3.2.2 Practical Examples of Cost Function Estimation

Numerous empirical exercises have shown that cost functions can be used to estimate the technological characteristics of the production process and provide information about the nature of technology in an industry. The estimation of cost functions is sometimes preferred to other approaches since, at its best, it subsumes all of the relevant information about production into a single function which is very familiar from our theoretical models. Doing so can of course be done only in cases where firms behave in the manner assumed by the model: they must minimize costs and they must typically be price-takers in the input markets (see the discussion in chapter 1). In what follows we provide a discussion of two empirical exercises. The examples presented are not meant to be comprehensive or to reflect the state of the art in the literature, but rather to introduce the rationale of the methodology and point to the econometric issues that are likely to arise. We also hope that they provide a solid basis for going on to explore more advanced techniques.

3.2.2.1 Estimating Economies of Scale

A wonderful empirical example of an attempt to estimate economies of scale using a cost function is the classic study on the U.S. electric power generation industry by Nerlove (1963). He calculated a baseline regression model derived from the common Cobb–Douglas production function, $Q = \alpha_0 L^{\alpha_L} K^{\alpha_K} F^{\alpha_F} u$, where Q, K, L, and F denote output, capital, labor, and fuel, respectively:

$$\ln C = \beta_0 + \beta_Q \ln Q + \beta_L \ln p_L + \beta_K \ln p_K + \beta_F \ln p_F + V.$$

It can be shown that a Cobb–Douglas production function implies a cost function of the form

$$C = kQ^{1/r} p_L^{\alpha_L/r} p_K^{\alpha_K/r} p_F^{\alpha_F/r} v,$$

where $v = u^{-1/r}$, $r = \alpha_L + \alpha_K + \alpha_F$, and $k = r(\alpha_0 \alpha_L^{\alpha_L} \alpha_K^{\alpha_K} \alpha_F^{\alpha_F})^{-1/r}$. The parameter r can be interpreted as the degree of economies of scale (see the discussion below). The model restricts the economies of scale to be constant for all quantities.

Taking a natural log transformation of this cost function, Nerlove obtained an equation which is linear in the parameters and can be easily estimated using standard regression packages:

$$\ln C = \beta_0 + \beta_Q \ln Q + \beta_L \ln p_L + \beta_K \ln p_K + \beta_F \ln p_F + V,$$

where $\beta_0 = \ln k$, $\beta_Q = 1/r$, $\beta_L = \alpha_L/r$, $\beta_K = \alpha_K/r$, $\beta_F = \alpha_F/r$, and $V = \ln v$.

The cost equation above is an unrestricted model, i.e., there are no restrictions imposed on the parameters of the cost function. On the other hand, cost functions in theory are expected to satisfy some conditions. For example, Nerlove imposes the theoretical "homogeneity" restriction, that cost functions should be homogeneous of degree 1 in input prices, before estimating the equation.[11] That is, he imposes

$$\beta_L + \beta_K + \beta_F = 1, \quad \text{which is equivalent to } \beta_K = 1 - \beta_F - \beta_L.$$

With modern computers we could just estimate the restricted model by telling our regression package to impose the restriction directly. Nerlove, on the other hand, at the time estimated an unrestricted formulation of the restricted model:

$$\ln C - \ln p_K = \beta_0 + \beta_Q \ln Q + \beta_F(\ln p_F - \ln p_K) + \beta_L(\ln p_L - \ln p_K) + V.$$

The restriction results in one parameter less to be estimated, namely β_K, which can be inferred from the other parameters. In practice, intuitively, this may be helpful if such variables as the capital price data are noisy, making estimation of an unrestricted β_K difficult. On the other hand, the parameter restriction has not actually removed the price of capital from the equation since that price is now used to normalize the other input prices and cost. Thus such an argument, while intuitive, does rely rather on the idea that there remains enough information in the relative prices (log differences) to infer β_L and β_F even though we have introduced measurement error in each of the relative price variables remaining in the equation.

Nerlove estimates the model using the OLS using cost and input price data from 145 firms in 1955. His results are presented in table 3.1.

As we have described, OLS is only an appropriate estimation technique for cost functions under strong assumptions regarding the unobserved efficiencies of the firm, particularly that they be conditional mean uncorrelated with choice of quantity

[11] If, for example, we double the price of all inputs, the total cost of producing the same level of output will also double.

Table 3.1. Nerlove's cost function estimation results.

Variable	Parameter	$\|t\|$-Statistic
$\ln Q$	0.72	(41.33)
$(\ln p_L - \ln p_K)$	0.59	(2.90)
$(\ln p_F - \ln p_K)$	0.41	(4.19)
Constant	−4.69	(5.30)
R^2	0.927	—

Source: Estimation results from the model presented in Nerlove (1963). The dependent variable is $\ln C - \ln P_K$. Estimated from data from 145 firms during 1955. The full data set is made available in the original paper.

produced. Note that Nerlove's initial estimates suggest rather surprisingly that $\beta_K = 1 - 0.59 - 0.41 = 0$, a matter to which we shall return.

We can retrieve a measure of economies of scale S as follows:

$$S = \left(\frac{\partial \ln C}{\partial \ln Q}\right)^{-1} = (0.72)^{-1} = 1.39 > 1.$$

As $S > 1$, we conclude that the production function exhibits economies of scale.

To see why, consider that

$$\frac{\partial \ln C}{\partial \ln Q} = \frac{Q}{C}\frac{\partial C}{\partial Q} = \frac{\text{MC}}{\text{AC}},$$

so that

$$S = \left(\frac{\partial \ln C}{\partial \ln Q}\right)^{-1} = \frac{\text{AC}}{\text{MC}}.$$

Thus, the estimated cost function implies $S > 1$ so that AC > MC, i.e., AC is declining so that there are economies of scale.

A log-linear cost function's diseconomies or economies of scale are a global property of the cost function and, as such, do not depend on the exact level of output being considered. We will see below that with more general cost functions, the value of S will depend on the level of output.

Figure 3.2 shows Nerlove's data (in natural logs) and also the estimated costs as a function of output. Note that the model involves prices so the fitted values are not plotted as a simple straight line.

A basic specification check of any estimated regression equation involves plotting the residuals of the estimated regression. The residual is the difference between the actual and the estimated "explained" variable. For consistent estimation using OLS, the residuals need to have an expected value conditional on explanatory variables of zero. In figure 3.3, it is apparent that residuals are dependent on the level of output which violates the requirement for OLS to generate consistent estimates. At both low and high levels of output, the residuals are positive so that true cost is

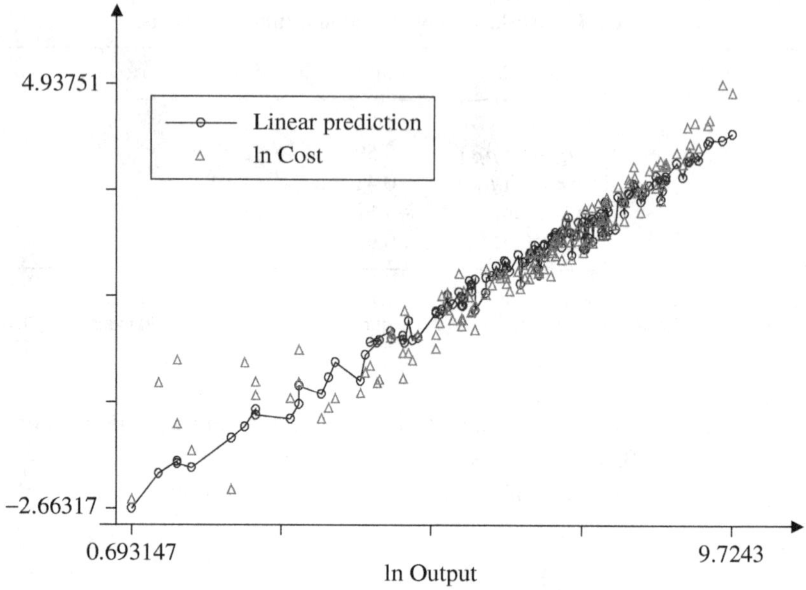

Figure 3.2. Nerlove's first model data and fitted values.
Source: Authors' calculations from data provided in Nerlove (1963).

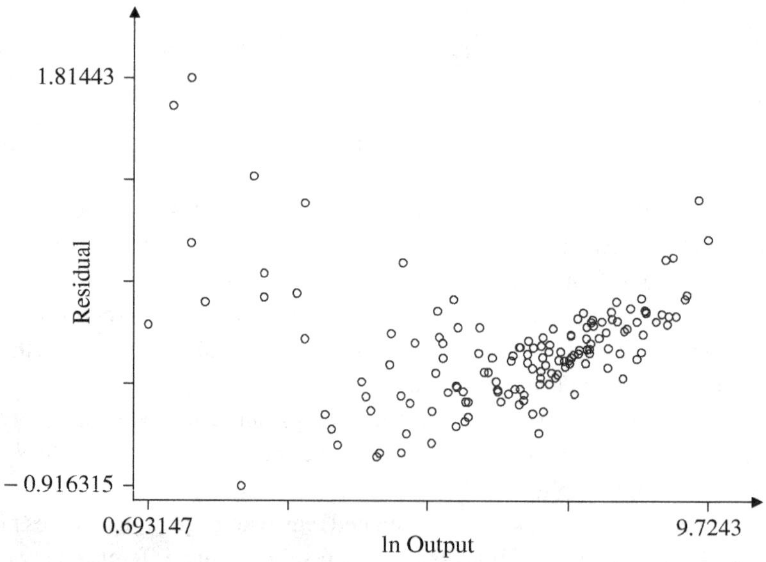

Figure 3.3. Residual plot calculated using Nerlove's data.

systematically higher than the estimated value. On the other hand, for intermediate values of output the true value of costs is lower than the estimated value. A plot of the residuals reveals a clear U-shaped pattern.

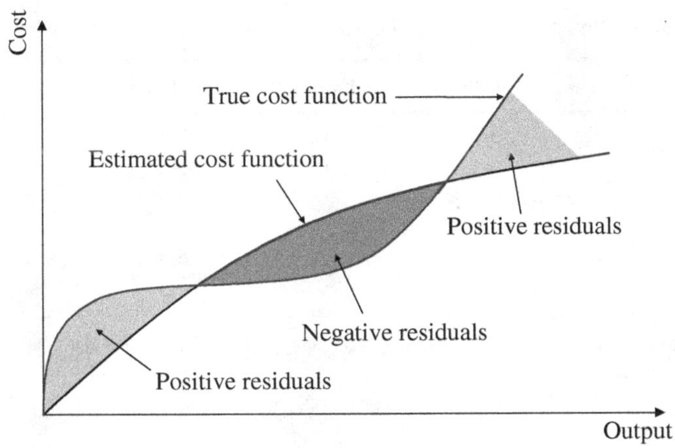

Figure 3.4. Estimated and true cost function approximation.
Source: Authors' rendition of figure 3 in Nerlove (1963).

This diagnosis suggests that the assumed shape of the cost function is incorrect and that the true shape is more likely to have the form as in figure 3.4.

In fact, the data indicate that there are increasing returns to scale that are exhausted at a certain level of output after which there are decreasing returns to scale. Nerlove suggests that the specification can be corrected by introducing a second-order term in the natural log of output as an additional explanatory variable. This generates a more flexible cost function that will allow the cost to vary with level of output in a way that can generate economies of scale followed by diseconomies of scale as output rises. Now we have

$$\ln C = \beta_0 + \beta_Q \ln Q + b \ln Q^2 + \beta_F(\ln p_F - \ln p_K) \\ + \beta_L(\ln p_L - \ln p_K) + \ln p_K + V$$

so that we have $S = (\beta_Q + 2b \ln Q)^{-1}$, which varies with the level of output Q. For example, if $b > 0$ and $\beta_Q < 1$, then

$$S > 1 \iff 1 > (\beta_Q + 2b \ln Q) \\ \iff (1 - \beta_Q) > 2b \ln Q \\ \iff \ln Q < (1 - \beta_Q)/2b$$

so that the cost function will have economies of scale at low output levels and then diseconomies of scale at higher output levels, once $\ln Q > (1-\beta_Q)/2b$. This more flexible revised model produces the results shown in table 3.2.

Note that now $\beta_K = 1 - 0.48 - 0.44 = 0.08$. Figure 3.5 repeats Nerlove's diagnostic check—a graph of residuals against the explanatory variable. In contrast to our earlier findings, the graph shows that the expected value of the residuals from this regression is indeed independent of the level of output and seems to stay around

Table 3.2. Nerlove's cost function estimation results with flexible specification.

Variable	Parameter	$\lvert t \rvert$-Statistic
$\ln Q$	0.15	(2.47)
$(\ln Q)^2$	0.05	(9.42)
$(\ln p_L - \ln p_K)$	0.48	(2.98)
$(\ln p_F - \ln p_K)$	0.44	(5.73)
Constant	−3.76	(5.36)
R^2	0.96	—

Source: Authors' calculations using data from Nerlove (1963). Dependent variable is $\ln C - \ln P_K$. Estimated using data from 145 firms during 1955.

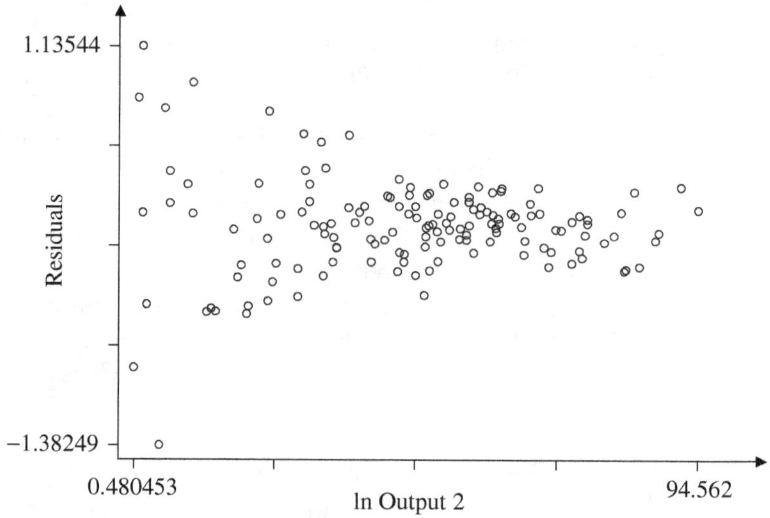

Figure 3.5. Diagnostic residual plot for Nerlove's more flexible functional form.

0 as we look across the graph, as required for consistent estimates in OLS. On the other hand, the variance of the residuals does seem to be related to output, which suggests a heteroskedasticity problem. Heteroskedasticity is less of a problem than functional form misspecification, because it does not imply that our estimates are inconsistent. However, the presence of heteroskedasticity does mean that we will have to be careful when calculating standard errors, the measures of uncertainty associated with our parameter estimates. Specifically, a conventional formula will assume homoskedasticity and will generate inconsistent estimates of the standard errors even though we have consistent estimates of the parameters themselves. Fortunately, it is usually possible to construct heteroskedasticity consistent standard errors (HCSEs), i.e., estimates of standard errors that are robust to the presence of heteroskedasticity. We refer to chapter 2 for a discussion of heteroskedasticity.

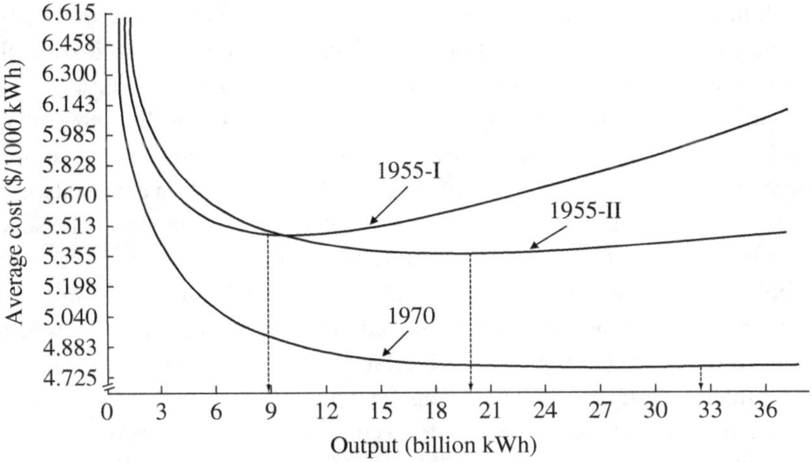

1955-I	88	26	11	7	3	4	2	2		1		1												
1955-II	76	15	8	8	3	7	2	2		2		1												
1970	26	22	7	10	9	1	6	4	3	2	1	4	1	1	1	2	2	1	2	1	1	1	2	1	3

Size distribution of firms

Figure 3.6. The evolution of cost functions. *Source*: Christensen and Greene (1976).

Christensen and Greene (1976) reestimate the same cost function adjusting the 1955 data and adding 1970 data. They try various models, some of which are illustrated in figure 3.6.

The lowest line on the graph is the cost curve estimated using 1970 data while the top two lines are estimates using different model specifications each with data from 1955. First note that the 1955 models differ a great deal at high levels of output. Looking at the table underneath the figure, which reports the number of observations at each scale of output in each data set, it is easy to see why. At high levels of output there are simply very few data points and therefore little information about the shape of the curves at those high output levels. Where there is a substantial amount of data, at lower output levels, the two 1955 regression results seem far more in agreement. A second nice feature of this graph is that it demonstrates very clearly the impact of technological progress over time. First, the technological progress seems to have changed the minimum efficient size (MES) of operations. An increase in MES would be indicated by a movement to the right of the point at which the average cost function reaches a minimum. Secondly, and more dramatically evident in the graph, it is clear that by 1970 technological progress has shifted the average cost function downward. At all levels of output, the average cost of producing a kilowatt hour of electricity is lower in 1970 than it was in 1955.

So far, in presenting Nerlove's study we have carefully examined the econometric results, but to ease exposition we have omitted a crucial step in a proper analysis, one that would ordinarily need to be undertaken before progressing this far down the path in an empirical exercise. Namely, we have not examined the validity the theoretical model's basic assumptions. In this case we would want to know that a plausible view of the firm's activities is that it (1) minimizes costs for a given level of output at a given point of time, and (2) is a price-taker in the input markets. These kinds of basic modeling framework assumptions are usually best considered by developing an understanding of the industry being studied. In electricity generation, it is a fact that the electricity cannot generally be stored and has to be supplied on demand so market dynamics tend to be fairly straightforward.[12] Firms do try to supply the electricity at the lowest possible costs.[13] With regards to the input markets, however, the assumption of price-taking behavior may sometimes be more difficult to motivate. On the one hand, relatively small generators are unlikely to be other than price-takers on the markets for capital and for fuel, although Nerlove notes that fuel was purchased on long-term contracts. Labor, on the other hand, was heavily unionized so that wages were also set via negotiated long-term contracts. Today, many labor economists would not recognize "price-taking" as the relevant assumption for negotiated labor market outcomes, except perhaps as an approximation (see, for example, Manning 2005). On the other hand, if input prices are effectively fixed when firms are deciding how much labor capital and fuel to use—even if they are fixed by long-term contracts rather than fixed to the firm in the "price-taking" sense—then firms will choose the mix of inputs that minimize the cost of producing any given level of output treating input prices as fixed and our assumptions may not be implausible even if they are not motivated in the way the theorists initially envisioned.

In addition to such immediate concerns, a myriad of other factors may also raise issues that need careful consideration. For example, in electricity there could be opportunities in the industry for a strategic withdrawal of capacity by suppliers to exploit bottlenecks resulting in output varying independently of demand and costs.[14] Also, for a study like Nerlove's which uses variation across firms, it will be very important that input prices vary sufficiently across firms to tell us the way costs differ in response to changes in relative input prices. If major inputs are, say, commodities, then we may be unlikely to see sufficient variation in input prices across firms.

---

[12] Current researchers may have a harder time since today there are some exceptions to this general rule available by using hydroelectric generators. While electricity is hard to store, engineers realized that water can be both stored and also used to generate electricity. The Dinorwig power station in Wales, for instance, has used its reversible pump/turbines since 1984. It uses cheap off-peak electricity to pump water up the mountain and then uses that water to move its turbines in order to generate electricity at peak times.

[13] On the other hand, this might not be the case in heavily regulated sectors.

[14] See, for example, the discussion in Joskow and Kahn (2001), who note that during the summer of 2000 wholesale electricity prices in California were almost 500% higher than they were in the same months in 1998 or 1999. See also Borenstein et al. (2002). If supply and demand are inelastic and supply is less than demand, then prices will skyrocket.

3.2.2.2 Estimating Scale and Scale Effects in a Multiproduct Firm

In the case of multiproduct firms, efficiencies can arise not only from economies of scale but also from economies of scope, the efficiency gain from using a unique production entity for several goods or services. In an interesting paper, Evans and Heckman (1984a,b) undertake an empirical estimation of the cost function of the U.S. telecommunications giant AT&T in order to determine whether economies of scale and scope in the production of local and long-distance services justified the existence of a single national carrier.[15]

In 1982, the U.S. government accused AT&T of foreclosing the long-distance toll market by leveraging its monopoly on local exchanges and decided to break up the company into different providers for local exchange and for the long-distance services. This led eventually to the proposal to create the "baby Bells," providers of local toll services which were barred from entering the long-distance market, and of AT&T as a long-distance carrier. AT&T argued that there were significant efficiencies from managing all telecommunications services within one company and that the breakup of the company by region and activity would cause the irremediable loss of those efficiencies.

Evans and Heckman (1984a,b), hereafter EH, try to empirically examine these claims by testing for the "subadditivity" of the cost function, a property implying that the cost of production is lower when production is carried out by one firm compared with when it is carried out by several smaller firms. The property of subadditivity, which we define formally below, suffices to ensure that productive efficiency will be achieved by a single firm rather than multiple firms and therefore could provide a rationale for allowing a single large firm to provide both local and long-distance telecommunications services rather than two more specialized firms.

To proceed, define the following two-product cost function:

$$C = C(q_L, q_T, r, m, w, t),$$

where q_L is the output level of local calls L, q_T is the output level of toll calls T. As usual, cost functions depend on input prices so that r is the rate of return of capital, w is the wage rate, and m is the price of materials. In addition, EH use time series data so they must correct for changes in the cost function over time. For that reason, t is a variable capturing the current trend in technology. EH obtained their output data by dividing the revenues generated with the two different services by the average prices for local and toll services respectively.

The cost function defined above is a two-product cost function. More generally, we can define a J input and M output cost function. For example, EH used a two-product

[15] See Evans and Heckman (1984a,b, 1986). The latter corrects some important errors that crept into the reporting of the authors' results in their initial article.

and three-input variant of the general multiproduct Translog cost function:

$$\begin{aligned}\ln C &= \alpha_0 + \sum_{j=1}^{J} \alpha_j \ln p_j + \sum_{m=1}^{M} \beta_m \ln q_m + \frac{1}{2}\sum_{j=1}^{J}\sum_{k=1}^{J} \gamma_{jk} \ln p_j \ln p_k \\ &+ \frac{1}{2}\sum_{m=1}^{M}\sum_{i=1}^{M} \delta_{mi} \ln q_m \ln q_i + \frac{1}{2}\sum_{j=1}^{J}\sum_{m=1}^{M} \rho_{jm} \ln p_j \ln q_m \\ &+ \Bigg(\sum_{j=1}^{J} \lambda_j \ln p_j \ln \text{RnD} \\ &\quad + \sum_{m=1}^{M} \theta_m \ln q_m \ln \text{RnD} + \mu \ln \text{RnD} + \tau (\ln \text{RnD})^2\Bigg).\end{aligned}$$

Evidently, this cost function is much more general than the Cobb–Douglas cost function used by Nerlove. It shows a greater flexibility and it can be shown to locally approximate any cost function. For EH's application, we will set $J = 3$ as the number of inputs and $M = 2$ as the number of outputs. In addition, we will follow EH and capture technological progress by using lagged research and development expenditure of Bell laboratories, which we shall denote RnD.

The Translog cost function as presented is an unrestricted formulation. In estimation we may wish to impose the restrictions on cost functions that are suggested by theory. For example, in estimation, EH impose the homogeneity restriction in input prices in a strategy analogous to Nerlove's approach discussed above. In addition, they impose symmetry restrictions with respect to input prices.

In fact, EH estimate a system of equations including the Translog cost function and the three-input cost-share equations:

$$s_j = \alpha_j + \sum_{k=1}^{J} \gamma_{jk} \ln p_k + \sum_{m=1}^{M} \rho_{jm} \ln q_m + \lambda_j \ln \text{RnD}.$$

Let us motivate the equations Evans and Heckman actually estimate. To do so, recall Shephard's lemma, which states that one can obtain the input demand functions by taking the derivative of the cost function with respect to input prices.

Define I_j as the input demand function, which by Shephard's lemma is

$$I_j = \frac{\partial C(q_1, q_2, p_1, p_2, p_3, t)}{\partial p_j}$$

so that input j's share of total costs is then

$$s_j = \frac{p_j I_j}{C} = \frac{p_j}{C}\frac{\partial C}{\partial p_j} = \frac{\partial \ln C}{\partial \ln p_j}.$$

Applying Shephard's lemma to the multiproduct Translog model with three inputs, we obtain the three-input cost-share equations:

$$s_j = \alpha_j + \sum_{k=1}^{J} \gamma_{jk} \ln p_k + \sum_{m=1}^{M} \rho_{jm} \ln q_m + \lambda_j \ln \mathrm{RnD}.$$

Note that these input share equations have many parameters in common with the cost function. As a result, we can estimate them together with the Translog cost function:

$$\begin{aligned}\ln C = \alpha_0 &+ \sum_{j=1}^{J} \alpha_j \ln p_j + \sum_{m=1}^{M} \beta_m \ln q_m + \frac{1}{2}\sum_{j=1}^{J}\sum_{k=1}^{J} \gamma_{jk} \ln p_j \ln p_k \\ &+ \frac{1}{2}\sum_{m=1}^{M}\sum_{i=1}^{M} \delta_{mi} \ln q_m \ln q_i + \frac{1}{2}\sum_{j=1}^{J}\sum_{m=1}^{M} \rho_{jm} \ln p_j \ln q_m \\ &+ \Bigg(\sum_{j=1}^{J} \lambda_j \ln p_j \ln \mathrm{RnD} \\ &\quad + \sum_{m=1}^{M} \theta_m \ln q_m \ln \mathrm{RnD} + \mu \ln \mathrm{RnD} + \tau (\ln \mathrm{RnD})^2\Bigg).\end{aligned}$$

Whether or not the theoretical restrictions are imposed, we can estimate the four equations simultaneously using, for example, a seemingly unrelated regression estimator (SURE). Of course, if the data support the theoretical equality across equations of the coefficients γ, ρ, and λ, we can impose these cross-equation restrictions and in doing so gain efficiency in estimation.[16] As always, if the theoretical restrictions do not hold in the data, our efforts at achieving efficiency will, in fact, have sacrificed consistency and our estimates will be biased.

Note also that we can retrieve the factor price elasticities of input demand from the parameters of the cost-share equation by applying Shephard's lemma. In particular, since $s_j = p_j I_j / C$, we have $\ln I_j = \ln s_j - \ln p_j + \ln C$ so that

$$\begin{aligned}\frac{\partial \ln I_j}{\partial \ln p_k} &= \frac{\partial \ln s_j}{\partial \ln p_k} - \frac{\partial \ln p_j}{\partial \ln p_k} + \frac{\partial \ln C}{\partial \ln p_k} = \frac{1}{s_j}\frac{\partial s_j}{\partial \ln p_k} - \frac{\partial \ln p_j}{\partial \ln p_k} + s_k \\ &= \begin{cases} \dfrac{\gamma_{jk}}{s_j} + s_k & \text{if } j \neq k, \\ \dfrac{\gamma_{jk}}{s_j} - 1 + s_k & \text{if } j = k. \end{cases}\end{aligned}$$

[16] There are a number of simultaneous equation techniques that the investigator should consider in such a context. SURE and maximum likelihood are two useful methods, but they are unable to address endogeneity issues. For that reason, a system GMM estimation approach may generally be the most appropriate.

Evans and Heckman wanted to know whether the cost of producing q_L and q_T separately differed from the cost of producing them jointly. Their first test involved comparing $C(q_L, q_T)$ and a restricted cost function which imposed, in fact only approximately, the restriction that $C(q_L, q_T) = C(q_L) + C(q_T)$. In terms of the Translog function, a nontrivial approximation argument suggests that this restriction can be imposed approximately by imposing the parameter restriction $\delta_{mi} = -\beta_m \beta_i$. (See Evans and Heckman (1984a,b) for a discussion of this restriction.) Clearly, this is a parameter restriction that can fairly easily be tested using standard econometric methods for testing nonlinear parameter restrictions.

This joint-production test, if rejected, only establishes that we cannot consider these production activities separately. EH would like to say far more. Specifically, they wish to consider whether productive efficiency can be achieved using a single firm. To do so they apply the following test of "subadditivity." Assume one wants to produce the total industry output $(\tilde{q}_L, \tilde{q}_T)$ but instead of having a single firm producing it all, several smaller firms will produce a part. Call s_{ij} the share of product j produced by firm i. The relevant question is whether it costs more to produce the total output with several firms compared with the case when one firm produces all. If it does cost more to split the production across several firms, then we have a case for AT&T being a natural monopolist, albeit one which produces multiple products.

Specifically, EH test whether

$$C(\tilde{q}_L, \tilde{q}_T) < \sum_{i=1}^{I} C(s_{i1}\tilde{q}_{iL}, s_{i2}\tilde{q}_{iT}),$$

where

$$\sum_{i=1}^{I} s_{ij} = 1, \quad s_{ij} > 0 \quad \text{for } j = L, T.$$

Evans and Heckman propose a local test for subadditivity arguing that failure to find local subadditivity is relevant for rejecting global subadditivity. Such a local test is important since we usually will not see all possible levels of output. Indeed, a major difficulty with the AT&T data is that the data do not contain observations on the data points most directly relevant; before the breakup we simply will not have seen what happens to the costs of producing local and long-distance phone calls separately. Evans and Heckman thus very sensibly argue the case for a local test, using only the region of the cost function for which output combinations have indeed previously been observed, i.e., that for which there are data in the data set.

To do so, EH restrict the levels of total output for each product that fall within the aggregate output levels for which they had data. In other words, the total quantities produced by the hypothetical multiple firms of each product must fall within the range of the aggregate production observed under the actual monopoly. They also imposed that the proportional product mix be within the observed combinations of

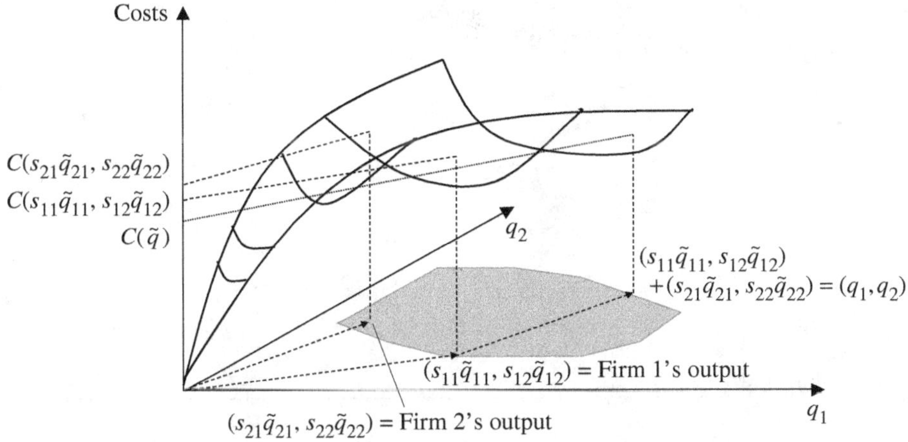

Figure 3.7. Region for acceptable estimation in Evans and Heckman.
Source: Authors' rendition of a figure provided by Evans and Heckman (1984a,b).

(q_L, q_T). Note that if we know the form of the function $C(q_L, q_T)$, it can be simple to run the test simulating the breakup of a monopolist and calculating C for the hypothetical production levels of the smaller firms. However, doing so will usually only tell us about the functional form we have assumed since we usually only have data for some output combinations $(\tilde{q}_L, \tilde{q}_T)$ and their associated costs $C(\tilde{q}_L, \tilde{q}_T)$. Extrapolating beyond the range for which data are available can obviously be very risky.

The shaded area in figure 3.7 illustrates the region defined by EH's restrictions. One set of restrictions defining the shaded area comes from the observed range of relative proportions of the outputs, shown in figure 3.8. Although both output levels increase over time, the long-distance toll calls increase at a faster rate over the whole period. Figure 3.9 shows that there is a clear time trend in the mix of outputs presumably caused by changes in demand and also technological progress. The fact that there is variation in the output mix is helpful but the fact that variation occurs over time makes one wonder whether we are in fact estimating a single cost function. At a minimum it means we must model the movement in the cost function over time and it is that which motivates EH to include an index for technological change in the regression.

Evans and Heckman (1984a,b) provide us with a very nice example of the estimation of economies of scale and scope in a multiproduct context. However, later research pointed out that the cost function that they estimated appears to behave in strange ways and did not satisfy some desirable properties of cost functions. Röller (1990a,b) revisited their subadditivity test, requiring that the cost function estimates satisfied certain properties of a "proper" cost function. In particular, Röller imposed that the cost function be nonnegative and linear homogeneous, concave, and nondecreasing in prices, and having positive marginal costs schedules. He also argued that Translog cost functions are unattractive functional forms in the context

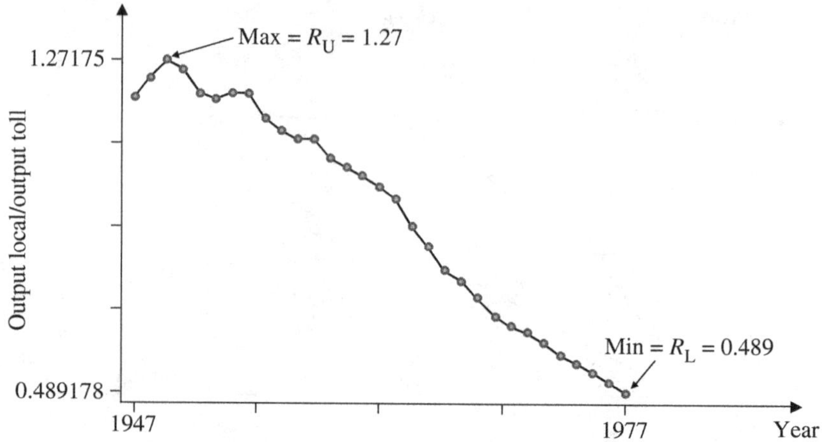

Figure 3.8. Realized local/toll output combinations.
Source: Authors' calculations using data from Evans and Heckman (1984a,b).

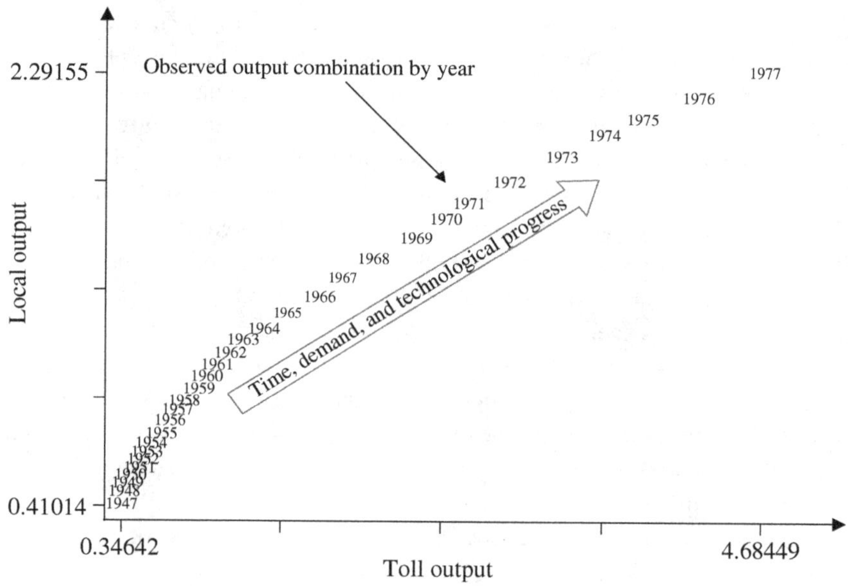

Figure 3.9. Trend in relative weight of local and toll calls.
Source: Authors' calculations using data from Evans and Heckman (1984a,b).

of evaluating breaking up firms. The reason is that they involve natural logs of output(s), and natural logs become minus infinity at zero output levels, which is exactly what breaking up AT&T would have involved (specialism in either long-distance or local telephony). For that reason Röller suggests using a different cost-specification form: he applied a CES-quadratic (constant elasticity of substitution function with quadratic terms) cost function.

A number of interesting discussions and improvements on this methodology have been suggested. Sueyoshi and Anselmo (1986) redefine the acceptable region of estimation by taking into account the need to satisfy the symmetry condition. Shin and Ying (1992) set up a global subadditivity test for local exchange carriers and estimate the model using cross-sectional data. Salvanes and Tjøtta (1998) suggest a procedure to calculate the region where an estimated Translog cost function such as that used by Evans and Heckman meets the requirements of positive costs, positive marginal costs, homogeneity, monotonicity, and concavity in input prices.

3.3 Alternative Approaches

Although traditional cost function estimation as presented above is the approach taken in many empirical investigations, there are a number of related alternative approaches. The first considers cost or production functions as "ideals" or "frontiers" which are to be estimated. Instead of treating deviations from a cost function as random mean zero deviations, efficient frontier analysis (EFA) considers the theoretical construct as an ideal that firms may or may not achieve. Two popular classes of models commonly used particularly in the regulatory context, are data envelopment analysis (DEA) and stochastic frontier analysis (SFA), each of which focus on taking into account firm-specific inefficiencies. In this section we briefly discuss each of these two classes of models and their associated methods. We then go on to discuss a noneconometric approach which focuses on retrieving very detailed specific information from firms by discussing costs with industry experts, perhaps engineers, with direct knowledge of cost and efficiency issues. This approach is sometimes known as producing "engineering" estimates.

3.3.1 Accounting for Firm-Specific Inefficiencies

Farrell (1957) argued that although our theory assumes that firms minimize costs, what we observe in reality may not be exact cost minimization.[17] Naturally, the basic idea that firms only approximate an ideal rather than achieve it is a general one. As a result techniques have been developed so that the ideas we explore in this section can be applied in a variety of contexts: (1) using production and input data to estimate a production frontier, or (2) using cost and output and input price data to either estimate a cost frontier or indeed (3) estimate a profit frontier. In each case, the data used are different but the principles are the same. To illustrate, recall that a production function describes the maximal output achievable for any given level of inputs and in reality firms may not achieve this maximal level of output. If so, we may then wish to estimate an efficient cost or production frontier rather than the cost or

[17] A very good in-depth survey provided in Greene (1997). A comprehensive treatment is also provided in the books by Kumbhakar and Knox-Lovell (2000) and Coelli et al. (2005).

production function described in the previous section of this chapter. This approach is particularly popular in a regulatory context where yardstick competition is used to encourage efficient production but requires an ability to evaluate and compare the relative efficiencies of regulated firms.

When considering potential sources of inefficiency, the literature typically distinguishes three distinct sources of potential inefficiencies, referred to respectively as allocative inefficiency, technical inefficiency, and scale inefficiency.

Allocative inefficiency occurs when firms use the wrong mix of inputs when producing output because they incorrectly adjust to input relative price signals.

Technical inefficiency in contrast will measure the extent to which firms use inputs in the right proportions but are inefficient in the sense that they do not manage to produce as much output as an efficient firm would be able to. As we will see, technical efficiency is measured by the ratio of the minimum feasible input that is needed to produce the output of a given firm and the level of input that the firm actually uses. For instance, if the production function tells us that it is possible to run a given size shop with four sales clerks, a firm employing six clerks for the same output will have a technical efficiency of $\frac{4}{6} = \frac{2}{3}$ or 66%. This implies that the firm could, in theory, save 33% of its costs.

Opportunities for *scale efficiencies* may arise when firms operate at levels of output associated with decreasing returns to scale (production frontiers) or diseconomies of scale (cost frontiers). In a production context, and continuing our example, imagine that our store is now efficiently run with four employees but that it could double the output by adding only two more sales clerks. That means that if it employed six clerks and was technically efficient it would only take three clerks to produce the output that it produces today with four. Scale efficiencies could be measured as $\frac{3}{4}$ or 75%.

This idea that we may be able to estimate systematic firm inefficiency has been operationalized in a number of ways, most popularly through the use of nonparametric models such as DEA and parametric models such as SFA. The authors writing in each of these traditions argue that in reality firms' efficiencies are heterogeneous and yet systematic in the sense that only an entirely efficient firm would achieve the result predicted by the theory. If so, then the real firms in our data sets will tend to be systematically less efficient than the ideal. Indeed, if everything is measured properly, then their cost and output achievements will all lie below the ideal cost function.

In the next two sections we provide a brief introduction to the foundations of those two approaches and discuss their main advantages and limitations.

3.3.1.1 Nonparametric Frontier Methods (DEA)

Production frontiers (*input-oriented models*): a basic one-output and one-input DEA model considers the maximal or frontier output that can be produced for each amount of input available (see figure 3.10(a)).[18] To produce the graph a basic DEA model will find the frontier which encloses (envelops) the data, formally, we find the smallest convex set which encloses all the data points. To examine technical efficiency of the plant or firm whose data are plotted at B we might attempt to measure the ratio AB/AC, which tells us the amount of output our firm is managing to produce with the inputs used relative to the amount of output that our estimate of the production frontier suggests the firm could produce with that level of input.

With multiple outputs and inputs the analysis becomes harder to visualize, but with two outputs and one input (e.g., staff) a DEA analysis may effectively plot output per unit input for a variety of plants or products (see figure 3.10(b)). Consider, for example, that telephone call-center staff can undertake two activities: (i) telephone sales and (ii) after-sales customer service. Since any given operator can clearly only be on the phone with one person at a time, there is a trade-off in the volume of each type of call that can be handled each day. To examine efficiency of call handling, we might begin by plotting sales calls per telephone operator against after-sales calls per staff member for a collection of regional call centers for a company and we may obtain results such as those presented in figure 3.10 (where each data point represents a call center and the frontier has been plotted by finding the smallest convex set which encloses all the data points; the frontier "envelops" the data). The graph shows there are some "technically efficient" call centers (those on the frontier) and some call centers which are below the frontier that may be able to improve their technical efficiency. Sometimes (relative) technical efficiency is measured as the ratio, 100 × OA/OB, where OA and OB are the distance of the ray from O to A and B respectively, so that a call center operating at B would have a technical efficiency rating of 100% while those inside the frontier will be operating at lower technical efficiency levels. In this kind of situation, the analysis could progress largely by hand. In more complex contexts, when we have one output and multiple inputs or when we have both multiple outputs and multiple inputs, the analysis cannot progress using only a graph but the analogous analysis relating the output(s) to input(s) can be undertaken numerically in order to determine the technically efficient production frontier associated with any given level of input(s).

To illustrate, consider the one-output and multiple-input case, where output by firm i is denoted q_i and there is a vector of J inputs used by firm i, $\underline{I}_i = (I_{1i}, \dots, I_{Ji})$. The DEA estimate of efficiency for an individual observation, say,

[18] The development of DEA is often attributed to Charnes et al. (1978). For an overview to the mid 1990s, see Fare et al. (1995). For a comprehensive recent treatment, see Cooper et al. (2007). The relative advantages of DEA and production frontier analysis were discussed in a series of articles following the publication of the original paper by Aigner and Chu (1968). This debate is now largely of historical interest, but the interested reader may like to see Schmidt (1976, 1978) and Chu (1978). A great deal of the distinction arose from the fact that the original DEA methods did not report measures of statistical uncertainty and applications reported no standard errors, t-statistics, or R-squared calculated. DEA methods typically make convexity assumptions while the method known as the Free Disposal Hull (FDH) method allows for nonconvex production sets (see Deprins and Tulkens 1984).

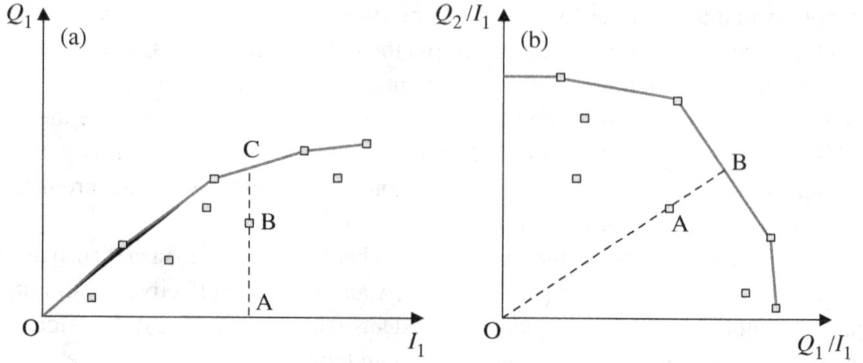

Figure 3.10. (a) A one-output and one-input DEA model. (b) A two-output, single-input DEA analysis.

for firm k, θ_k, could be constructed by solving the minimization problem:

$$\min_{\theta,\gamma_1,\ldots,\gamma_J} \left\{ \theta \;\middle|\; \frac{q_k}{\theta} \leqslant \sum_{i=1}^{n} \gamma_i q_i;\; I_{jk} \geqslant \sum_{i=1}^{n} \gamma_i I_{ji},\; j = 1,\ldots,J; \right.$$
$$\left. \theta > 0;\; \gamma_i \geqslant 0,\; i = 1,\ldots,n \right\}.$$

To understand this minimization problem first note that the observed data are the inputs and output levels for each firm and that the nonnegative weighted sums $\sum_{i=1}^{n} \gamma_i q_i$ and $\sum_{i=1}^{n} \gamma_i I_{ji}$ for $j = 1,\ldots,J$ define a "virtual" company's level of output and inputs. That is, the virtual company is defined by the nonnegative weights γ_i of actual companies' input and output combinations. Second, note that reducing θ in q_k/θ acts to scale up actual output from firm k. Thus the optimization program states that we should scale up actual output from firm k as much as is possible subject to the requirement that we can find the smallest virtual company which could actually have produced that higher level of output given the actual combinations of inputs and outputs observed in the data set. We compute the Farrell efficiency index θ_k for each company, i.e., we solve n optimization programs, one for each company in the data set.[19]

[19] Restrictions on the allowable combinations of companies define the nature of the "virtual" company. For example, we may wish to assume that existing companies can only be contracted but not expanded so that we additionally impose the restriction that $0 \leqslant \gamma_i \leqslant 1$ or we may wish to assume that our virtual companies can only be constructed as weighted combinations of the scale of existing companies, $0 \leqslant \sum_{i=1}^{n} \gamma_i \leqslant 1$. For a detailed discussion, see Banker et al. (1984). It is important to note that we have suppressed the k indices from the program described in the text. Since we get one set of parameters for each firm, the full set of estimates involves efficiency indices θ_k and a set of weights, $\gamma_{1k},\ldots,\gamma_{nk}$ for $k = 1,\ldots,n$.

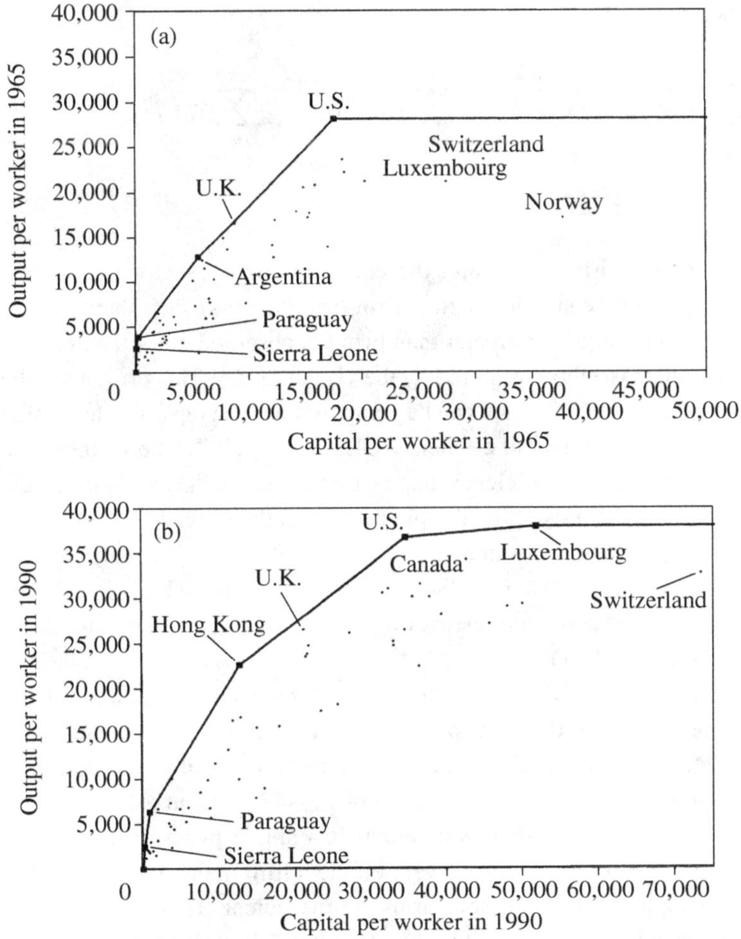

Figure 3.11. The world production frontier.
Source: Figure 6 from Kumar and Russell (2002).

Kumar and Russell (2002) provide a powerful real-world application using aggregate (in fact, country-level) data. Their results are presented in figure 3.11 and show evolution of the world's production frontier over the period 1965–90.[20]

Cost frontiers (*output-oriented models*). The basic methodology described above for determining production frontiers translates directly into cost frontier models. Specifically, if the input price vector is denoted $p_k = (p_{k1}, \dots, p_{kJ})$ for $j = 1, \dots, J$ inputs for firm k, the superscript "obs" denotes that the variable is observed data and we retain our earlier notation for outputs and inputs, an efficient cost frontier

[20] If the reader would like a data set to try such an exercise on, one is provided in table 1 of Thanassoulis (1993). That data set relates to fifteen hypothetical hospitals and was also used in Sherman (1984) and Bowlin et al. (1985).

can be defined as the solution to

$$\min_{\substack{I_{k1},\dots,I_{kJ},\\ \gamma_1,\dots,\gamma_J}} \left\{ \sum_{j=1}^{J} p_{kj}^{\text{obs}} I_{kj} \;\middle|\; q_k^{\text{obs}} \leqslant \sum_{i=1}^{n} \gamma_i q_i^{\text{obs}};\; I_{kj} \geqslant \sum_{i=1}^{n} \gamma_i I_{ij}^{\text{obs}},\; j = 1,\dots,J; \right.$$
$$\left. \gamma_i \geqslant 0,\; i = 1,\dots,n \right\}.$$

That is, for each firm k, we find the cost-minimizing vector of inputs required $(I_{k1},\dots,I_{kJ})$ by the smallest virtual firm (smallest γ_is) such that (1) output from that virtual firm is equal or greater than firm k's observed output, and (2) the inputs paid for are (at least) those required by the virtual firm.[21] This program will yield an optimal level of cost C_k^*, which can be compared with an observed level of cost C_k^{obs} to yield a measure of overall efficiency $\text{OE}_k = C_k^*/C_k^{\text{obs}}$. The method also allows us to measure allocative efficiency since we can observe the extent to which a firm's input mix differs from its optimal input mix given the observed input prices. For an applied example, see, for example, Sueyoshi (1991), who estimates a DEA model using the Evans and Heckman (1984a,b) data set from the AT&T divestiture that we explored within the context of estimating conventional cost functions earlier in this chapter (Sueyoshi 1991).

The proponents of DEA argue that it makes very few assumptions regarding the functional form of the cost (production) frontier, while its critics argue that it can rely heavily on the realized data.[22] The reason is that the basic DEA models use extreme data points to define the set of possible outcomes, for example, what is feasible in terms of cost minimization. If a single piece of data is incorrectly recorded, we may appear to have a very efficient firm in the data so that the frontier incorrectly suggests that the other firms are inefficient. This sensitivity to outliers can raise substantive concerns. On the other hand, this method avoids imposing a specific parametric functional form on the cost or production function. To reconcile DEA models with more standard parametric modeling approaches, the literature has developed a statistical foundation for DEA models. Specifically, one way to view a given DEA model is that it defines a residual for each firm k in the data set. In our cost example we could define u_k as the deviation from the optimal level of cost, $u_k = C_k^{\text{obs}}(1 - \text{OE}_k) = C_k^{\text{obs}} - C_k^*$. Doing so has allowed the introduction of two-sided errors similar to those used in the SFA literature to which we now turn (see, for example, Post et al. 2002).

[21] As with production frontiers it may be appropriate to include a constraint on the set of virtual firms that we consider as our benchmark. As before we might wish to consider adding the constraint that $0 \leqslant \gamma_i \leqslant 1$ or that $0 \leqslant \sum_{i=1}^{n} \gamma_i \leqslant 1$.

[22] For a Monte Carlo evaluation of DEA given the assumption that data are generated in truth by a Cobb–Douglas production frontier, see Pedraja-Chaparro et al. (1999).

3.3.2 Parametric Frontier Models: SFA

Parametric frontier models may provide a more familiar methodology for most readers: building parametric models. Aigner and Chu (1968) are credited with suggesting that to estimate a frontier model we could proceed by minimizing the sum of squared residuals (OLS style) subject to the constraint that the model's predicted output(s) must be greater than the observed output(s). Such a program is easily solved by using standard packages (Gauss, Matlab, Mathematica) if the production frontier model is linear in parameters since it is simply a quadratic program subject to a set of linear constraints. Alternatively, since all the residuals are positive we may simply choose a model's parameters to minimize the sum of the prediction errors, a linear program subject to linear constraints (see also Kumbhakar and Knox-Lovell 2000).

To illustrate, consider the Cobb–Douglas frontier model of the form $\ln Q_i = \beta_0 + \beta_L \ln L_i + \beta_K \ln K_i + \beta_F \ln F_i - u_i$. This model could be fit to a single cross-sectional data set consisting of observations on n firms, $i = 1, \dots, n$, by solving the problem:

$$\min_{\beta_0,\beta_L,\beta_K,\beta_F} \sum_{i=1}^{n} u_i(\beta_0, \beta_L, \beta_K, \beta_F) \quad \text{subject to} \quad u_i(\beta_0, \beta_L, \beta_K, \beta_F) \geqslant 0,\ i = 1, \dots, n,$$

where $u_i(\beta_0, \beta_L, \beta_K, \beta_F) = \beta_0 + \beta_L \ln L_i + \beta_K \ln K_i + \beta_F \ln F_i - \ln Q_i$, which we require to be positive to ensure that the predicted production frontier model always lies above the actual output achieved. This basic model insists that all errors lie to one side of the frontier.

One disadvantage associated with estimated frontiers obtained from techniques like this model (and the basic DEA model) which insist that errors are always one-sided is that they can be very sensitive to values associated with individual observations and therefore measurement error. In practice, since measurement is imperfect we may get a few observations above the "true" production frontier, if only as a result of measurement problems.

In order to circumvent this problem, SFA generalizes the basic parametric frontier model by introducing an additional "two-sided" source of uncertainty due to measurement error. Thus, the SFA model has both a description of (1) unobserved firm-specific heterogeneity in inefficiency and (2) measurement error. This distinction is shown in figure 3.12, where a single data point, the one furthest southeast in the figure, drives the estimation of the "one-sided errors" frontier to indicate substantial diseconomies of scale at high output levels. That may be true, or it may be that the particular observation was measured with error for some reason. Models with "two-sided" errors allow some of the data to lie "below" the cost frontier because it is measured with error.

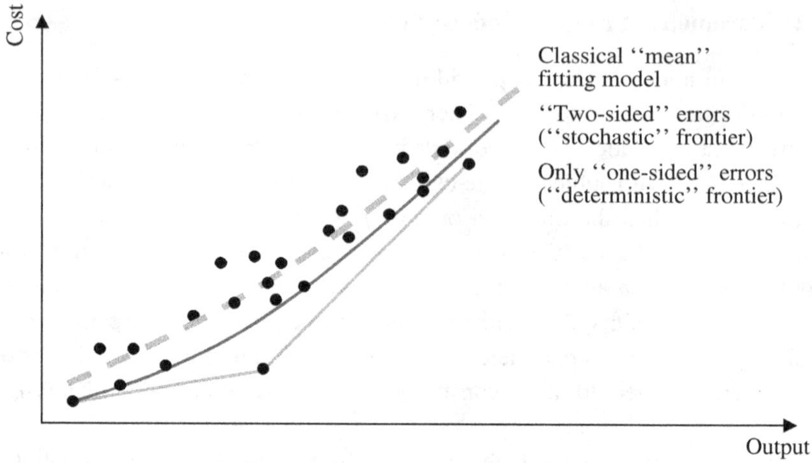

Figure 3.12. Two-sided "stochastic" versus one-sided "deterministic" frontier models.

To illustrate consider the SFA of the cost function where it is specified with two error terms so that our model is $C_i = f(q, p; \alpha) + v_i - |u_i|$, where p denotes input prices, q denotes output, while u_i and v_i are respectively assumed to represent firm-specific inefficiency and measurement error.

One error term represents a firm's particular overall (in)efficiency, u_i. Often this error is assumed to have an exponential, half normal, or truncated normal distribution because it can only take on positive values, indicating, via the minus sign, that firms will be measured to be less efficient than the frontier. The other error term is a random shock v_i that describes measurement error, perhaps normal so that $v_i \sim N(0, \sigma_v)$. Some authors in this literature call a model without the latter error term, i.e., with $\sigma_v = 0$, the "deterministic frontier model" although to do so seems a bit odd since there is still a stochastic element in the model. Hence we have used the term "one-sided error model." In that case, the model forces all differences between firms into differences in predicted efficiency levels. In reality, differences may well also just be due to other random factors (measurement error, unusual number of equipment failures, and so on).

For completeness, consider a production frontier model with an alternative error specification, $\ln q_i = \ln f(I_{1i}, \dots, I_{mi}; \alpha) + \ln u_i + v_i$. If we specify the model of shocks so that $u < 1$, then the log of the technical efficiency term will again be negative, $\ln(u) < 0$. The most common approach to estimation is via maximum likelihood estimation given an assumed distribution for u and v (see, for example, Hall and Stephenson 1990). Many distributions are possible, but one popular one is the half normal model, which assumes $\ln u_i \sim (-1)|N(0, \sigma_v)|$. Since the model breaks down the difference between observed production and the predicted frontier into two error term components, $\ln u_i + v_i$, described respectively as technical inefficiency and measurement, it will always be necessary to make sufficient assumptions to break up the error term in the model into these components. In particular, even if there is no direct information in the data about the amount of measurement error, we may nonetheless be able to disentangle the effects if we assume that measurement error is drawn from a symmetric distribution while technical inefficiency $\ln u_i$ is drawn from a distribution which only takes on negative values.[23]

In sum, SFA differs from traditional cost function analysis only in the way firm-specific unobservables are assumed to differ across firms. Such alternative assumptions about the nature of firm-specific heterogeneity in (in)efficiencies are, in principle, testable. A substantial advantage of a frontier approach is that it allows an investigator or agency to talk about heterogeneous firms and efficiency levels. In allowing such a discussion, one adds an ability to assess the degree of efficiency of particular firms. However, the investigator must always be careful to note that fundamentally we are putting structure and terminology on unobservables. The division between measurement and efficiency in SFA, for example, is only as good as the assumptions used to "break up" the error term into two components.

As a final word, we note that DEA is sometimes presented as being "very" different from SFA methods, since the frontier estimate is typically calculated by solving an optimization problem rather than a standard estimation algorithm. In fact, DEA is sometimes described as the "operations research" approach as distinct from an "econometric" approach. In practice, there are differences but the literature historically appears to overemphasize them and the last twenty years has been a period of substantial convergence (although there certainly was an extensive debate between the proponents of DEA and the proponents of SFA and other model-based frontier methods). For example, the proponents of SFA initially observed that DEA methods did not appear to have a statistical foundation, while more recent authors have shown that is incorrect and it is now standard to calculate standard errors and confidence intervals for DEA models using a class of methods called the "bootstrap" (see Simar and Wilson 1998).[24]

3.3.3 The Engineering Approach

We end this section by discussing a final approach to cost estimation, known as the engineering approach. This approach to determining the nature of scale economies

[23] We are not aware of a result in the literature which states the minimal assumptions which are sufficient to guarantee we can identify the two components that compose the aggregate error term, although that does not mean it does not exist.

[24] The usual idea in a "bootstrap" is to take the data sample we have and then pick at random a "new" sample of the same size from our actual data sample by sampling with replacement and estimating the output desired (e.g., our measure of efficiency). By doing so many times we get lots of different sets of estimates and we can measure the uncertainty of our measure given the data simply by calculating the standard error of our different estimates. If we wish to estimate technical efficiency levels, Simar and Wilson (1998) suggest bootstrapping from the distribution of estimated technical efficiency scores (see below and Simar and Wilson 1998). It turns out that this procedure yields a consistent estimate of the true standard error under fairly general assumptions. For a general introduction to the bootstrap by its inventors, see Efron and Tibshirani (1994).

was pioneered by Bain (1956). It is based on interviews with engineers familiar with the planning and design of plants and produces direct and detailed industry specific data (see also Stennek and Verboven 2001). As the name suggests, the objective is to determine the shape of the cost function or the nature of the production function by collecting specific and detailed information first hand from people knowledgeable of the cost and scale implications of their businesses.

A recent application of the engineering method has been the work on the telecommunication market undertaken by Gasmi et al. (2002). Based on an engineering process model that gathers detailed industry-specific and structure-specific cost data, they estimate various cost functions for a duopoly in the local exchange telecommunications network and proceed to test for the subadditivity of the cost function to examine whether the industry would be more efficient with a monopoly structure. The work undertaken by Ofcom (2007) in order to evaluate the appropriate price for mobile call termination services provides another example.[25] Ofcom's cost model was based on engineering estimates and used to estimate the appropriate mobile call termination rates (prices charged when one mobile phone network terminates a call on another provider's network). Investments in telecommunications equipment tend to be "lumpy" and the same equipment can be used to both originate and terminate phone calls. In essence, Ofcom's model attempted to capture the set of telecommunications assets required to deliver a given volume of incoming and outgoing phone calls, texts, and data services. The model also included a geographic dimension as the amount of telecommunications equipment required depends on whether signals are free to travel across wide open spaces or are more limited by buildings found in urban environments. Given price data for the set of equipment required, and of course the asset requirement, engineers can construct an estimate of the costs associated with any given level of output of each service, in each time period, in each geographic region. Of course, the information requirements for such an exercise are substantial. For example, if assets are lumpy, then the optimal timing of asset purchases will depend on the expected future evolution of asset prices and output levels. One observation is that while fixed coefficient production technologies are highly amenable to engineering exercises, it is more difficult to capture cost structures where firms can substitute between inputs depending on their relative prices.

3.4 Costs and Market Structure

This chapter has discussed a variety of methods for measuring cost functions. While there are many reasons to be interested in costs, we began the chapter by discussing Viner's (1931) cost-based theory of firm size and market structure and so it seems

[25] See also the U.K. Competition Commission's report available at www.competition-commission.org.uk/appeals/communications_act/completed_cases.htm.

natural to finish with a brief discussion of the literature's conclusions on the topic. The basic and striking conclusion is that empirical studies typically find that minimum efficient scale (MES) is not a terribly good predictor of market concentration. Rather, firm size often appears bigger than is necessary to exploit technical efficiencies. Sutton provides a number of examples (Sutton 1991, p. 382, 1998). One classic example is provided by Anderson et al. (1975), who argued that in the U.S. sugar industry at the time an efficient sugar beet processing plant cost about \$30 million to construct. Whether in sugar beet or sugar cane, those authors argued that a firm building a single plant of MES would account for no more than 3–6% of total sales of refined sugar in the average marketing region. In contrast, the authors pointed out that concentration was far higher than could be explained by MES since four (eight) firm concentration ratios across the United States varied from 52.7% (79%) in Chicago–West to 95.3% (100%) in the Lower Pacific region (see the original article or Sutton (1991, table 6.3)).

The reactions to such findings are multifaceted and take us to a range of alternative topics some of which we will explore further in later chapters. Making the puzzle perhaps deeper, Scherer et al. (1975) argue that in many of the industries they consider—such as cigarettes, beer brewing, or petroleum refining—the cost disadvantages at a plant of operating below scale are low.[26] Those authors agree with the conclusion that in many industries the scale of actual operations is not obviously justified by technical efficiencies. More recently, authors such as Foster et al. (2008) have contributed to the literature documenting enormous differences in scale and productivity across firms in a given industry.

Subsequent work, most notably by Sutton has argued that theories of market structure must not just take into account the cost side of a market, but rather take into account features such as the intensity of price competition and the effectiveness of advertising or R&D strategies in response to fragmented (low concentration) industries (see Sutton 1991). If, for example, price competition is very intensive, we will tend to find high concentration. For intuition, think about the incentives for a second firm to enter a market if, when she enters, the two firms will play a pure Bertrand equilibrium. Knowing she will face very intense price competition, a potential entrant who must pay some form of entry cost would never actually enter. Ironically, if firms competed intensely on prices post entry, then we may actually see market outcomes involving a monopoly charging a monopoly price unfettered by the risk of entry! The bottom line is that the literature has rightly concluded that technology—cost structure—can be important for lots of reasons but is by no means the only determinant of either firm size or indeed market structure.

[26] Exceptions include industries such as the cement industry, where it appears to be very costly to operate below scale. The study also considers multiplant economies of scale measuring the efficiencies that result from operating an optimal number of plants.

3.5 Conclusions

- Cost information can be highly relevant for a diverse range of competition policy and regulatory investigations. For example, cost information can shed light on margins and efficiencies.
- Firm's accounting and financial data can provide useful information about both costs and profits. However, the data may need to be carefully adjusted in order to correctly represent economic rather than accounting costs and/or profits. In particular, opportunity costs are an important component of economic costs. Economic depreciation can also substantively differ from accounting depreciation.
- We can operationalize the notions of production and cost functions by estimating them. Doing so is a nontrivial but certainly feasible activity. In doing so we must worry about familiar econometric challenges such as functional forms, endogeneity and heteroskedasticity. When using data with a cross-sectional component such as a cross section of plants or firms, we must ensure that we are learning about firms using an appropriately similar production technology. When using data sets with a time series component, we must worry in particular about the way in which we account for technical change.
- An important limitation when evaluating the nature of scale or scope efficiencies is that we can only reasonably evaluate them within the realm of experience. If there is no data to inform the shape of a single- or multi-product cost function for some output combinations, we will only learn about the shape of our assumed cost function model by proceeding as though there are data available.
- Firm and plant level heterogeneity in efficiency is well-documented in the literature and through experience. A class of alternative approaches which explicitly integrate firm-specific idiosyncrasies and in particular inefficiencies has been developed and the most commonly cited classes of models are the nonparametric data envelopment analysis (DEA) class of models and the parametric stochastic frontier analysis (SFA). Each class of models has expanded significantly in recent years. In addition, our understanding of the linkages and overlap between the models has increased substantially. The appropriate choice from the now rich toolbox of models will, of course, depend on the factual circumstances of the case under investigation.

4
Market Definition

In both EU and U.S. jurisdictions, the courts have stated that competition authorities must define markets before progressing to evaluate competitive effects.[1] In addition, legal statute in numerous jurisdictions uses either market share or concentration thresholds to define safe harbors. Each of these external forces acts to push competition agencies to define markets. These are by no means the only forces at work. Internally, competition agencies often undertake a market definition exercise as the first step in an investigation since firms' market shares are used as a first screening device to give the investigator a first hint of the likelihood of a potential problem. For all these reasons and indeed others, market definition is usually an important step in a competition investigation.

That said, it is generally considered unwise to spend a huge amount of resources to perform a complex analysis of market definition just to have an idea of whether there might possibly be a problem. As a result, methods that are intuitive and relatively easy to apply are often favored over sophisticated methods that require subtlety in application. An exception to this general rule is when small variations in market definition are crucial for the conclusions of the assessment. Moreover, as competition policy investigations move away from the application of "form-based" or "structural" reasoning, where sometimes all that mattered was a market share calculation and hence all that mattered was market definition, toward an analysis more centered on the potential effects of a merger or a conduct on the market, the issue of market definition may play a less prominent role. Indeed, in an "effects-based" analysis it is usually important to keep in mind that market definition is rarely an end in itself. In a merger investigation, for example, while it may be fascinating intellectually to discuss exactly what the right market definition is, the central question is whether when two firms merge prices will go up.

Market definition is an important activity in merger cases but that is one among many contexts in which it is important. For example, all of the techniques presented in this section can be used for determining the degree of dominance of a particular firm or group of firms and will therefore be relevant in analysis geared toward

[1] *Brown Shoe v. United States*, 370 U.S. 294, 344 (1962). *Europemballage Corporation and Continental Can Company Inc. v. Commission of the European Communities*, Case 6-72 (1973). In paragraph 14 of the latter case, the ECJ argues: "The definition of the relevant market is of essential significance..."

investigating potential antitrust abuses. In this chapter, we first explain the main concepts used in market definition and then go on to explore quantitative methods that are used to define the relevant market(s) for a competition investigation. We will review different methods in order of complexity, starting with the use of price correlations, survey techniques, shock analysis, and formal and semiformal tests such as diversion ratio analysis, critical loss analysis, the hypothetical monopolist test—often (incorrectly) equated with and called the small but significant nontransitory increase in prices (SSNIP) test, and the more recently proposed full equilibrium relevant market (FERM) test, originally associated with the U.S. Horizontal Merger Guidelines from 1984.[2]

4.1 Basic Concepts in Market Definition

Market definition is often an important step in a competition assessment and one about which there is often a great deal of debate. When we define the relevant competition policy market, we are attempting to define the set of products that impose constraints on each other's pricing or other dimension of competition (quality, service, innovation). We will call the set of products that compete in that sense the set of products in the market, or more correctly the "competition policy" market. A firm whose product faces close competing substitutes will have only a limited ability to raise its price above that of close substitutes and competition between firms will ensure that its price is driven down close to its cost. Thus market definition for competition policy purposes is directly related to the concept of market power. Indeed, a common description of a competition policy market is one which is "worth monopolizing."

Before presenting the tools for the empirical investigation of market definition, we take the opportunity to refresh some basic theoretical concepts relating to the definition of a market and, in particular, the concept of market power.

4.1.1 Markets and Market Power

Market power is sometimes defined as the ability of a firm to raise the prices of its products above the competitive level. If a firm faces many substitutes for its products, the market power of the firm will be limited. To see why, consider a monopoly provider of electricity. If consumers have no choice and need heat to live, they are likely to be willing to pay whatever it takes to get electricity. In such a situation a monopolist will have a great deal of market power, i.e., freedom to profitably increase prices above the competitive level. In such a situation consumers have no choice and the market is a market for electricity, albeit from just one provider. On the other hand, if consumers can relatively easily switch to alternative energy sources, perhaps gas or coal, the monopoly electricity provider's ability to raise prices profitably will be

[2] The working paper version of Ivaldi and Lorincz (2009) introduced the term FERM and while they subsequently drop it in favor of the term US84, we rather like the more descriptive terminology, so we use it below.

heavily constrained—it cannot raise the price beyond the point where too many consumers would switch. Intuitively, we will argue that if this constraint is large enough to impose a significant restriction on the electricity producer's ability to increase prices, then the market should be defined as the energy market (electricity plus gas or coal) and in this wider market the electricity monopolist will have little market power.

In the paragraph above we have drawn a clear distinction between a world where very few consumers would switch following a price rise and a world where many consumers would switch following a price rise. In practice, of course, the world is often far less black and white and as a result we may ask how much price sensitivity is enough to define a narrow market? When does the ability to differentiate turn into market power? When is substitution "large enough"? How much substitution exactly does one need between two products to put them in the same market? Naturally, theory provides only very partial answers to such questions and as a result practitioners commonly use quantitative benchmarks that are generally accepted and which ensure some consistency in the decision-making process. For example, in much of the discussion that follows, we will consider whether price increases of 5% or 10% are profitable when defining markets. Even then it is important to note that market definition in practice often requires the exercise of evidence-based judgment, where the evidence can be of varying quality.

4.1.2 Supply and Demand Substitutability

The key factors that limit market power—the ability to raise prices above the competitive level—are the extent of demand substitutability and the extent and nature of supply reaction, in particular, of supply substitutability. We describe each of these concepts below since any market definition exercise will examine each of them in detail. We also describe the fact that a market definition exercise usually proceeds along two dimensions: (1) a product market definition dimension and (2) a geographical market definition dimension. Product and geographic market definition should, in principle, be considered together. However, it is common practice as a practical matter to examine first product market substitution on the demand and supply sides and then to go on to consider geographic market substitution, again on the demand and supply sides. In each case, the market definition process usually begins with a single candidate product, or occasionally with a collection of them.

Demand substitutability describes the extent to which buyers respond to a price increase by substituting away to alternative products (product market definition) or alternative locations (geographic market definition). For example, if the price of gold goes up, then consumers may switch their consumption by buying less gold and perhaps more silver. If, when a firm attempts to increase its price, "enough" of her customers switch to substitute goods, then clearly her ability to raise prices is severely constrained. We want to include substitute products in our competition policy market whenever "enough" buyers, in a sense that will be made more precise below, would switch in response to a price increase. Of course, goods to which consumers do not switch in response to a price increase should be excluded from the market. Geographic market definition on the demand side considers the extent to which increasing a price in one area would induce consumers to purchase from alternative localities.

There are numerous difficulties (and therefore fascinations) in such an apparently simple activity as evaluating demand substitutability. One common difficulty faced in practice is that sometimes there are simply no real potential close "substitute" products, or, alternatively, sometimes there are a very large number of them.[3] In the absence of identifiable discrete potential substitutes, a competition authority may capture demand substitution away to a diffuse set of alternatives by ignoring the substitution during the market definition phase of an investigation. In doing so, we must be sure to take proper account of it later during the competitive assessment phase of the investigation. This approach can lead to a relatively narrow market definition, but it does not mean the agency will find competition problems since even a monopolist can face a highly elastic demand curve and therefore have no ability to raise prices. Specifically, that will be the case when attempts to do so would be met by substitution of expenditure to other activities, even if they are only specified generically as an "outside" alternative.

Supplier substitutability describes suppliers' responses to an increase in a product's price. When prices increase, consumers respond but so may rival suppliers since with higher prices available they have greater incentives to produce output. For example, in the market for liquid egg products[4] (such as those used for producing omelettes), the equipment used for processing and putting the product into cartons can also be used to produce cartons of fruit smoothies. That fact means that if the price of liquid egg went up sufficiently, suppliers of smoothies may potentially substitute their production capacity to produce processed egg. Another example might involve red and yellow paint—if it is easy to switch machines from producing red paint to producing yellow paint, the returns to producing these two products can never be far apart. If yellow paint producers were more profitable than red paint producers, then we would soon enough induce some of the red paint producers to switch to producing yellow paint.

As with all apparently simple concepts, there are numerous questions about exactly what is meant by supply substitutability. For example, the current Commission

---

[3] An example of the latter includes the U.K. CC's investigation into a "soft" gambling product known as the "Football Pools." That inquiry received evidence from a survey of consumers who had recently stopped playing the Football Pools about their reasons for doing so. The survey found that 65% of lapsed customers had not switched expenditure to any kind of gambling product, while they had saved the money for a large variety of alternative uses, most of which were not obviously best considered as potential substitutes (see www.competition-commission.org.uk/inquiries/ref2007/sportech/index.htm).

[4] See, for example, the discussion of the liquid egg market in Stonegate Farmers Ltd/Deans Foods Group Ltd (www.competition-commission.org.uk/inquiries/ref2006/stonegate/index.htm).

Notice on Market Definition[5] does not require a case officer to consider potential entrants as a source of supply substitutability for market definition purposes, though such entry might easily be considered in a more general sense a source of supply substitutability. Rather, the guidelines suggest that it is better to leave the analysis of the constraints imposed by potential competition to a later phase of the investigation. The rationale is that, among other things, the effects of entry are unlikely to be immediate. Still, economic theory says that, in some limited circumstances, even potential entrants may impose a price constraint on existing market players (see Baumol et al. 1982; Bailey 1981). This happens, for example, when incumbent's prices are hard to adjust and potential entrants interpret current prices as being the prices for the post-entry situation. In this case, the incumbent needs to maintain a pre-entry price that is low enough to discourage entry. Thus, important judgements are often made around supply substitutability both in individual cases and in the guidance documents from various jurisdictions. To return to our earlier examples, one response to the red and yellow paint example might be to argue that supply substitution implies that the appropriate market definition involves one market for "paint." Such an argument can be compelling, but there are significant limits to the appropriate scope of this type of argument for market definition. To see why, let us turn to the liquid egg and smoothie example. In that case, raw supply-side logic might suggest a market definition would include both liquid egg and smoothies. However, such a conclusion appears to be an odd one since these are patently different products. In fact, agencies would probably take the view that the appropriate response would be to view the potential movement of packaging and processing equipment as a supply response within the market for liquid egg. After all, the constraint arises on the liquid egg producers because machine capacity is moved across to produce liquid eggs and not because liquid eggs and smoothies are really competing, although the firms producing them may well be. The draft 2009 U.K. merger guidelines, for example, follow the U.S. guidelines in using this logic to suggest that demand substitution should play the primary role in defining the market while supply substitutability may tell us about the identity and scale of, in particular, potential competitors within that market. Thus the market would be for liquid egg, but the set of potential competitors may involve liquid egg and (formerly) smoothie producers.

Finally, we note that the responses by rivals can be to enter or expand production following a price rise but theory suggests the response may also be to increase prices since prices are strategic complements. While quantity reactions by rivals may decrease the profitability of attempted price increases, price reactions by rivals to price increases may reinforce their profitability. It would appear to be an odd market definition practice that treated price and quantity responses asymmetrically irrespective of the context. Thus, practice has evolved to recognize the potential role of supply substitution but also to recognize that its role is limited for market

[5] Commission Notice on Market Definition, OJ C 372 9/12/1997.

definition. (See also the EU Notice on the Definition of the Relevant Market for the Purposes of Community Competition Law, which similarly significantly constrains the role of supply substitutability in market definition.)

4.1.3 Qualitative Assessment

Before we progress to consider quantitative approaches to market definition, it is worth emphasizing that much of the time market definition relies at least in part on qualitative assessment. Indeed, qualitative evaluation is universally the starting point of any market definition exercise. Clearly, for example, it is probably not necessary to do any formal market analysis to get to the conclusion that the price of ice cream will not be sensitive to the price for hammers. Indeed, if such qualitative assessments were not possible, it would be necessary to do a huge amount of work in every investigation to check out every possibility—an impossibility at current resource levels in most authorities. In practice, we can narrow down the set of possibilities to those which are plausible and also substantive. Very minor products, for example, may just not make a great difference to a competition evaluation. To do so, it is best to start with the product characteristics and the intended use(s) of the product. Doing so allows the investigator to define a broad and yet plausible set of possible demand substitutes. The products which are substitutes in use are sometimes known as the set of "functional" substitutes.

For our purposes the concept of market definition is designed primarily to describe the set of products which constrain a firm's pricing decisions. Thus, to be included in a market, it is not enough for products to be functional substitutes; they need to be good enough demand or (to the extent appropriate) supply substitutes to actually constrain each other's price. To illustrate the distinction, consider two different seafoods: smoked salmon and caviar. Both will be familiar items at least in terms of existence, even if the latter is not a regular feature of most of our dinner tables. Caviar is potentially a functional substitute for smoked salmon in that it could be served as part of a salad. Would that suffice to put smoked salmon into a broader market that includes caviar? To answer that question we must first consider the extent of demand substitutability at competitive prices, which for present purposes we can take as current prices. At the moment, the retail price of 100 g of smoked salmon in Europe can oscillate around €1.50–2.00. The price of 100 g of caviar can run into hundreds of euros. Intuitively, since the price of the smoked salmon is far below the price of caviar, those customers who consider the two to be close substitutes will be eating smoked salmon in their salads. Similarly, those who do not really like caviar will be eating smoked salmon while only those with a particularly intense taste for caviar will be prepared to pay such a large premium for it.[6] On the other hand, many of the consumers of smoked salmon

[6] The reader will, of course, have picked up that we should probably worry about whether the fact that salmon and caviar need not be consumed in equal quantities is important. To aid discussion we will put

may like caviar and consider it to be a perfectly acceptable functional substitute at least in some uses (e.g., pre-dinner canapes), but would not actually substitute at current price levels. The lesson is that in a world with only those two products, salmon would be considered a market in itself at current price levels, despite the fact that caviar is indeed a functional substitute in many applications for current customers of salmon. Note that the force in this argument relies on the current price differential driving the set of current consumers of salmon to include those consumers for whom caviar may be a perfectly good functional substitute but caviar is so expensive that it is not a demand substitute. Since the extent of demand substitutability between goods depends on their relative price levels, if prices were different, then the appropriate competition policy market definition could also be different.

While such intuitive and unstructured arguments can be helpful, both formal and informal market definition exercises typically use the hypothetical monopolist test (HMT; see section 4.5 below for an extensive discussion) as a helpful framework for structuring decision making. The HMT test suggests that markets should be defined as the smallest set of products which can profitably be monopolized. The basic idea is that firms/products outside such a market cannot be significantly constraining behavior of firms inside the market since they cannot constrain a hypothetical monopolist of all the products in the market. Usually, the HMT is described in terms of price, so we ask whether the hypothetical monopolist would be able to exploit a material degree of market power, that is, to raise the prices of goods inside the candidate market by a small but significant amount. Of course, since firms can compete in quality, service, quantity, or even innovation, in principle the test can be framed using any of these competitive variables.

Qualitative analysis can sometimes be enough to satisfactorily define the relevant market, indeed it is sometimes necessary to rely on purely qualitative analysis. That said, a more explicitly quantitative analysis of market data will often be very helpful for informing and supplementing our judgments in this area.

4.1.4 Supplementing Qualitative Evidence

We will explore in detail a whole array of quantitative techniques for market definition in the rest of this chapter. Before we do so, however, it is worth noting that an important element of the qualitative assessment typically involves an evaluation of the extent to which consumers view products as functional substitutes. While a qualitative assessment of (1) the various product characteristics of goods and (2) the uses to which consumers put the goods is usually helpful and sometimes all that is available, it is often possible to supplement such qualitative evidence with more quantitative evidence.

---

this issue to one side. The key question will remain whether enough consumers will substitute enough volume from salmon to caviar to make increases in the price of salmon unprofitable.

Table 4.1. Characteristics of London airports.

Airports	Distance to center of city (km)	Private car (min)	Public transport: Bus (min)	Public transport: Rail (min)	Airport denomination on Ryanair website; bus service to city promoted on Ryanair website
Stansted	59	85	75	45	London (Stansted); Ryanair bus service
Heathrow	28	65	65	55	Not served by Ryanair
Gatwick	46	85	90	60	London (Gatwick)
Luton	54	44	60	25	London (Luton); Ryanair bus service
London City	14	20	—	22	Not served by Ryanair

Source: Ryanair and Aer Lingus proposed concentration, Case no. COMP/M.4439, p. 33.

To illustrate, consider the evidence provided to the European Commission in its investigation of the proposed merger between Ryanair and Aer Lingus.[7] Ryanair argued that the London airports were not demand substitutes, at least for time-sensitive passengers. Consider table 4.1, which documents the time taken by various transport modes to each London airport from the center of the city, which brings some data to bear on the question of whether these airports are "too different" to be considered functional substitutes for customers who want to go from London to Dublin. Ryanair argued they were, while the Commission noted, among other things, that the U.K. Civil Aviation Authority considers that a "two-hour surface access time" is the relevant benchmark for airport catchment areas for leisure passengers. The Commission concluded that scheduled point-to-point passenger air transport services between Dublin and London Heathrow, Gatwick, Stansted, Luton, and City airports belong to the same market. Note that although the Commission has quantified an important set of characteristics of the potentially substitute products in a manner that helps it understand the extent of substitutability, it must ultimately make a judgment about whether these products are similar enough to be considered in the same market on the basis of this and other evidence.

Analysis of consumers' tastes can also help inform the question of substitutability. Continuing our discussion of the Ryanair and Aer Lingus case, consider, for example, the survey of passengers at Dublin airport that the Commission undertook. A sample of consumers at Dublin airport were asked: "Would you ever consider [a] flight to/from Belfast as an alternative to using Dublin airport?" The results are presented in table 4.2 and suggest that only 15–20% (the survey result is stated as 16.6% but taking the decimal places seriously would probably involve an optimistic view about

[7] Case no. COMP/M.4439, which is available at http://ec.europa.eu/comm/competition/mergers/cases/decisions/m4439_20070627_20610_en.pdf.

Table 4.2. Responses of passengers on airport use in Belfast.

Valid	Frequency	Percent	Valid percent	Cumulative percent
Yes	445	16.6	16.6	16.6
No	1,751	65.5	65.5	82.1
Do not know	388	14.5	14.5	96.6
No answer	90	3.4	3.4	100.0
Total:	2,674	100.0	100.0	—

Source: Ryanair and Aer Lingus proposed concentration, Case no. COMP/M.4439, page 365.

the right level of precision) of passengers view Belfast as a functional substitute for Dublin airport. A pure functional substitute question is quite hard to ask consumers since it may be outside their area of experience but the "ever consider" element of this question appears to make it quite powerful evidence, at least within a range of conditions not too dissimilar from those known to consumers (e.g., price differentials that are within most customers' experience).[8]

We will consider further the use of survey evidence later in the chapter. In the next section we examine the use of price information for market definition. Prices can be thought of as one way in which products will be "similar" or "different" in the eyes of consumers and the competition policy world has traditionally emphasized its importance. In doing so, it is important to note that firms do not always compete on price—they may compete in advertising, service, product quality, quantity, or indeed innovation. If so, then it may be important to analyze markets in those terms rather than price alone. A merger, for example, that leads to no increase in prices but a substantial lessening of service provision can potentially be even less desirable than a merger which leads to price increases.[9]

4.2 Price Level Differences and Price Correlations

Examining price differences and correlations is perhaps the most common empirical method used to establish the set of products to be included in a product market.

[8] It is important to note that such a general and inclusive survey question such as "ever consider" is very useful as evidence when the vast majority of replies are "no." It is, however, distinctly less helpful for market definition when the vast majority of replies are "yes" since we simply would not know whether "ever consider" implied a significant constraint or it is just that, faced with an interviewer, customers could just about imagine situations where they could conceivably use Belfast instead of Dublin airport.

[9] In terms of the welfare analysis of mergers, inward demand shifts caused by service or quality falls will sometimes result in far larger consumer (and/or total) welfare losses than the movement along a demand curve that occurs when prices rise. Deadweight loss triangles, in particular, are sometimes estimated to be small; see the chapter 2 discussion of the classic cross-industry study by Harberger (1954).

Because correlations require only a small amount of data and are very simple to calculate, they are very commonly presented as empirical evidence in market definition exercises. Correlation analysis rests on the very intuitive assumption that the prices of goods that are substitutes should move together, an assumption we shall examine in this section. Despite the simplicity of this proposition, applying correlation analysis is not always straightforward and like any diagnostic tool can be extremely dangerous if applied with insufficient thought to the dangers of false conclusions. In this section, we present the rationale for the use of correlation analysis in market definition and discuss the considerations vital to applying this methodology usefully.

4.2.1 The Law of One Price

The "law of one price" states that active sellers of identical goods must sell them at identical prices. If one seller lowers price, it will get all the demand and the others will sell nothing. If a seller increases price above a rival, she will sell nothing. Since only the firm with the lowest price sells, the equilibrium result is that all active firms sell at the same price and share the customers.

Formally, if goods 1 and 2 are perfect substitutes, the demand schedule of firm 1 is

$$D_1(p_1, p_2) = \begin{cases} 0 & \text{if } p_1 > p_2, \\ D(p_1) & \text{if } p_1 < p_2, \\ \frac{1}{2}D(p_1) & \text{if } p_1 = p_2, \end{cases}$$

where the latter piece of the demand schedule defines the sharing rule; in this case it describes that if prices are equal then demand will be divided equally between the two players.

Even in the case when goods are located in different places and consumers consider the price of "delivered" goods, the generalized law of one price suggests that prices of perfect substitutes will converge to differ only by the difference in transportation costs whenever arbitrage opportunities are exploited. Arbitrageurs are market participants that take advantage of price differentials that allow them to make money by buying wherever a good is relatively cheap and selling where it is relatively expensive. The existence of arbitrageurs both tends to force prices in two locations together and tends to induce a great deal of relative price sensitivity. One should always look for evidence of such arbitrage activities since they can be a strong indication of the bonds between apparently geographically disparate markets. For instance, prices of unregulated commodities or currencies on the world market are kept relatively homogeneous (absent the transport costs) by the presence of active arbitrageurs.

The law of one price applies only to goods which are perfect substitutes, at least once transported to the same location. Of course, most goods are not perfect substitutes but may nonetheless be close enough substitutes to ensure that demand schedules and hence prices are closely interrelated. The intuition from the law of one price is that similarities in the levels of prices can indicate that goods are close substitutes. Taking this idea one step further, price correlation analysis is based on the idea that prices of close substitutes will move together. We will develop this idea using a formal economic model below, but intuitively it means that we expect prices of substitute goods to move together across time or across regions. Thus, both similarity in the level of prices and also co-movement of prices may be helpful when attempting to understand the extent of substitutability between goods.

4.2.2 Examples of Price Correlation

Price correlation analysis involves comparing two price series. The comparison could be across time, in which case we compare the time series of the products' prices. But it could also be a comparison across space, in which case we compare a cross-sectional sample of both products' prices.

4.2.2.1 Nestlé–Perrier

In the Nestlé–Perrier merger, a key question became whether the relevant market was the market for still water, the market for water, or the market for nonalcoholic drinks. Price correlations were calculated between brands in the different categories and produced the results shown in table 4.3. The brands are labeled from A to I. The table reports correlations between prices of goods of individual brands of still water (A–C), sparkling water (D–F), and soft drinks (G–I).

From the results, it appears fairly clear that this evidence suggests that the relevant market is the market for water, including both still and sparkling waters but excluding soft drinks. The price correlation between brands of still water and sparkling water is of similar magnitude as the correlation of brands within the group of still waters, at around 0.9. This is clearly a rather high number and is sufficiently close to 1 so as to appear not to leave a great deal of doubt as to its interpretation. In contrast, the positive correlations between the prices of water and soft drinks is low, between 0 and 0.3. That said, the table produces negative price correlations between soft drinks and water, which might suggest that if the price of water rises, the prices for soft drinks decrease and vice versa. This is a rather odd result and it would be interesting to dig a little deeper to understand the causes of such correlation. Although there are a variety of possible causes, one potential explanation is that soft drinks and water are complementary products. The very low correlation within the group of soft drinks is also worth noting. It might be arguable from these data that branded soft drinks present a market of their own.

Even with a very high price correlation, other evidence could potentially outweigh the correlation analysis. For example, we might also find survey evidence from consumers suggesting that they are clearly segmented by either having a strong preference for either still or sparkling water. Intuitively, supply substitutability seems

Table 4.3. Correlations between prices of brands of still water (A–C), sparkling water (D–F), and soft drinks (G–I).

	A	B	C	D	E	F	G	H	I
A	1								
B	0.93	1							
C	0.91	0.94	1						
D	0.91	0.85	0.86	1					
E	0.94	0.97	0.95	0.92	1				
F	0.93	0.99	0.96	0.88	0.99	1			
G	0.11	0.05	−0.01	0.33	−0.02	0.01	1		
H	−0.57	−0.55	0.25	0.16	0.24	0.27	0.17	1	
I	−0.77	−0.75	−0.81	−0.86	−0.86	−0.79	0.33	−0.11	1

Source: Charles River International (previously Lexecon), "Beyond argument: defining relevant markets," which reports on analysis performed in the EU competition inquiry into the French mineral water market, OL L 356. See www.crai.com/ecp/assets/beyond_argument.pdf, where the table reports fifteen brands rather than the nine selected here. OJ L 356. Case under EEC regulation 4064/89. Case no. IV/M 190 Nestlé/Perrier (1992). While the decision document omits all of the correlation table for confidentiality reasons, paragraph (16) of the decision provides some information regarding the brand identities in the table. In particular, it tells us that: "The coefficient of correlation of real prices among the different brands of waters ranges between a minimum of 0.85 (Badoit and Vittelloise) and 1 (Hépar and Vittel)."

likely in this case but supposing there was evidence from company documents or testimony that the machines for each type of water were impossible to move across to produce the other and we also found evidence that company pricing policies were such that they induced a high correlation in prices for some other reason, perhaps simply that the same person currently prices the two goods. The fact that prices are currently correlated may not reassure us that if it were in fact profitable to raise prices for say sparkling water, then prices would indeed be increased. This concern, for example, was raised in the U.K. Competition Commission's 2007 investigation into the groceries market because most supermarket chains operated a "national" pricing strategy so that prices were perfectly correlated across the country.[10] Nonetheless, the CC decided that it was appropriate to define local markets because there was no evidence of demand substitutability and little evidence of supply substitutability while the CC took the view that firms could potentially abandon such pricing policies if it were profitable to do so.

4.2.2.2 The Salmon Debate

In the United Kingdom, it became relevant for a merger case to establish whether Scottish farmed salmon was a distinct market or whether the market included, in

[10] See the U.K. Competition Commission market inquiry into the groceries market, which is available at www.competition-commission.org.uk/inquiries/ref2006/grocery/index.htm.

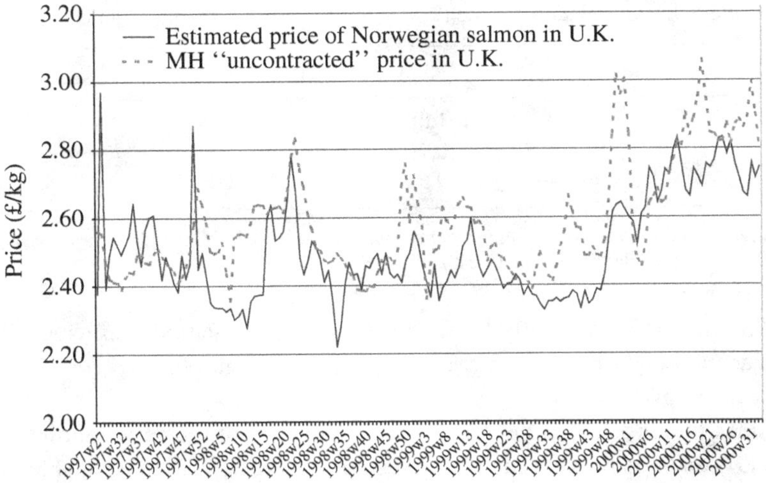

Figure 4.1. The price series for Scottish and Norwegian salmon sold in the United Kingdom (MH: Marine Harvest Scotland Ltd, which is Nutreco's salmon farming operation in Scotland). *Source*: Figure 4.7 (Competition Commission 2000). The CC, in turn, describes the source as a Lexecon report provided during the investigation.

particular, Norwegian farmed salmon.[11] Both salmons are Atlantic salmons but it was unclear whether buyers in the United Kingdom actually had sufficiently similar tastes for the different types of salmon to treat the market as the market for Atlantic salmon sold in the United Kingdom rather than, for example, the market for Scottish salmon sold in the United Kingdom.

Figure 4.1 plots the price series for each of Scottish and Norwegian farmed salmon.

Calculating the correlation coefficient between the price series gives us the result of 0.67. (See appendix 4.4 of the CC report.) Clearly, this figure is more difficult to interpret compared with the result of 0.90 obtained in the previous example. Such situations provide us with a difficult question: clearly, the correlation is positive but is the correlation high enough to suggest these two products are in the same market? In the salmon case, the consultants suggested a "comparability" test that involved comparing the figure obtained with the correlation coefficients of clear substitutes in that market. This seems a very sensible practical approach, though one which introduces some room for flexibility in choosing the comparison. In this case the consultants chose to compare the correlation coefficients with those obtained by comparing U.K. prices of salmon of different weights. The results are presented in table 4.4.

[11] See the U.K. Competition Commission's report "Nutreco Holding NV and Hydro Seafood GSP Ltd: A report on the proposed merger" (2000). See www.competition-commission.org.uk/inquiries/completed/2000/index.htm. The CC subsequently revisited salmon in the proposed merger of Pan Fish and Marine Harvest in 2006. See www.competition-commission.org.uk/inquiries/ref2006/panfish/index.htm.

Table 4.4. Correlation between MH U.K. prices for various weight categories.

	2–3 kg	3–4 kg	4–5 kg
2–3 kg	1.00	—	—
3–4 kg	0.76	1.00	—
4–5 kg	0.52	0.87	100

Source: Lexecon. Table 1 (Competition Commission 2000). The CC, in turn, describes the source as a Lexecon report provided during the investigation.

In this case, 0.67 is slightly lower than the price correlation coefficient obtained for adjacent weight cells but higher than the coefficient obtained for salmon two weight cells apart.

Besides looking at the coefficient itself, the graph of the series allows a visual inspection and it is pretty clear that the two prices are at least somewhat correlated. There is a similar pattern over time both in the level of the prices (the two series are pretty much on top of one another) and also in the way the two series move together with at least some shocks appear to broadly coincide in timing. Naturally, one needs to be rather careful in drawing hasty conclusions from an apparent correlation (visual or numerical) such as these ones. In the next sections we explain why a superficial correlation analysis can go wrong and how not to fall into the most common traps in using price correlations for market definition.

4.2.3 Use and Limitations of Price Correlation Analysis

In order to understand what lies behind price correlations, we need to understand what lies behind the prices of two differentiated products.[12] The prices of products are determined by the costs incurred in their production, the level of the demand they face, and by the availability and prices of substitutes. When we use price correlations to determine whether two goods are in the same market, we are assuming that what determines the co-movement in prices is primarily the influence of differences in the goods' prices on consumer behavior. However, there are other factors, unrelated to consumer substitution between products, which can cause a co-movement and therefore produce a positive correlation in prices. In particular, cost factors may co-move while correlated demand shocks and trends may also produce a false impression that prices are affecting each other. We discuss each of these alternative scenarios below.

Consider a situation where the demand for two differentiated products is captured by the two linear demand equations expressed as

$$q_1 = a_1 - b_{11}p_1 + b_{12}p_2 \quad \text{and} \quad q_2 = a_2 - b_{22}p_2 + b_{21}p_1.$$

Assuming each product is produced by a different firm which respectively maximize

[12] For a critique of the use of price correlation analysis, see, for example, Werden and Froeb (1993a). A response is provided by Sherwin (1993).

profits and compete in prices, we can calculate each firm's reaction function and then we can solve for the Nash equilibrium in prices as the solution to the two reaction function equations. Specifically, under price-setting competition, we showed in chapter 1 that the reaction functions of the firms will be

$$p_1 = \frac{c_1}{2} + \frac{a_1 + b_{12} p_2}{2b_{11}} \quad \text{and} \quad p_2 = \frac{c_2}{2} + \frac{a_2 + b_{21} p_1}{2b_{11}},$$

where c_1 and c_2 are the marginal costs of goods 1 and 2 respectively. After some algebra, Nash equilibrium prices are described by the following formulas:

$$p_1^{\text{NE}} = \left(\frac{4b_{11}b_{22}}{4b_{11}b_{22} - b_{12}b_{21}}\right)\left(\frac{c_1}{2} + \frac{a_1}{2b_{11}} + \frac{b_{12}}{4b_{11}}\left(c_2 + \frac{a_2}{b_{22}}\right)\right),$$

$$p_2^{\text{NE}} = \left(\frac{4b_{11}b_{22}}{4b_{11}b_{22} - b_{12}b_{21}}\right)\left(\frac{c_2}{2} + \frac{a_2}{2b_{22}} + \frac{b_{21}}{4b_{22}}\left(c_1 + \frac{a_1}{b_{11}}\right)\right).$$

First note that the prices depend on the intercepts of the demand equations (a_1 and a_2), the own-price effects (b_{11} and b_{22}), and the cross-price effects (b_{12} and b_{21}). They also depend on the cost of both goods.

Suppose $b_{12} = b_{21} = 0$ so that the products are completely unrelated in terms of demand substitutability. The formulas for the Nash equilibrium prices reduce to

$$p_1^{\text{NE}} = \frac{c_1}{2} + \frac{a_1}{2b_{11}} \quad \text{and} \quad p_2^{\text{NE}} = \frac{c_2}{2} + \frac{a_2}{2b_{22}}.$$

Note that from these expressions we can see that there are several ways in which we can find positive price correlations even though the products are not related on the demand side and are not substitutes.

4.2.3.1 *False Positives: Correlated Inputs or Demand Shocks*

If two products use the same input and its price varies, we will generate a positive correlation in the costs of producing the two products. For instance, both airline travel and rubber are intensive in fuel-based inputs. As the price of oil varies, the costs of producing both airline travel and rubber will covary so that $\text{cov}(c_1, c_2) \neq 0$. Moreover, the equations above capture the intuition that prices vary with marginal costs and so the prices of the outputs, airline travel and rubber, will also be correlated. A (in this case very) naive application of price correlation analysis might therefore find that the prices of rubber and airline travel are correlated and thus argue they are in the same product market. Naturally, such a conclusion would be a mistake—the positive correlation is a "false positive" for market definition since we are not in truth learning from the positive correlation in prices that the products are demand substitutes. Putting it another way one could not plausibly claim that airline travel is a demand substitute for rubber, that if the price of rubber were to go up, people would increase their air travel!

Figure 4.2. Ratio of U.K. to Norwegian feed prices.
Source: U.K. Competition Commission salmon report.

In the "salmon debate" the U.K. Competition Commission (CC) made an attempt to exclude the risk of false positives due to the positive correlation in costs potentially induced by common input prices. In particular, salmon feed may be sold in a global market. If so, then the marginal costs of producing salmon in the United Kingdom and in Norway may positively co-move even if the two products are not in truth demand substitutes. To test this hypothesis the CC looked at the relative prices of salmon feed in Norway and the United Kingdom. Doing so makes it clear that the cost of feed in the United Kingdom was falling with respect to the cost of feed in Norway during the period considered.

Figure 4.2 makes it clear that while the *positive* correlation observed in the price data could be explained by a positive correlation in costs, in this case costs appear to be negatively correlated and so this potential false positive explanation is not supported by the facts.

A related cause of false positives in a price correlation exercise is the occurrence of common demand shocks, when $\text{cov}(a_1, a_2) \neq 0$. To see why, consider any two normal goods, say cars and holidays. When the economy is good we will tend to see high demand, and hence high prices, for both cars and holidays and yet, of course, we would not want to define those two goods as being in the same market. Income is one demand shifter that may show up in common price movements but, of course, there are potentially many others, each of which is a danger for generating a false positive between prices of goods which experience the same demand shifters rather than are demand substitutes. Unsurprisingly, in many cases there will be room for substantial debate about the implications of a positive correlation.

4.2.3.2 Spurious Correlation and Nonstationarity

Another problem which emerges as a term in the debate around price correlations when measuring them with time series is that commonly termed "spurious correlation." Spurious correlation occurs when two series appear to be correlated but are in fact only correlated because each of them has a trend. The correlation in this case is a "coincidence" and is not the product of any genuine interrelation between the two products. This idea was explored in Yule (1926), who showed that the correlation coefficient actually converges toward 1, i.e., perfect correlation, for any two time series that each respectively has an upward trend. Similarly, if one series trends upward while the other trends down, we will find a correlation that tends to -1. These facts can lead to some serious inference problems. For example, the number of pirates over the Atlantic has decreased over the last three centuries while the average height of individuals has increased. These would be two variables that would trend in opposite directions and so, given a long enough time series we would find high levels of negative correlation between the two. As the number of pirates decreased the average height increased, but of course it would be nonsense to argue that the decrease in the number of pirates has anything to do with the increase in the average height of the population.[13] The basic lesson is that one needs to be very careful when dealing with correlations when variables trend. Seemingly highly robust correlations can be completely spurious and the two variables may be in fact completely unrelated.

A formal way to approach this problem is to assess whether a series is "stationary."[14] A series is stationary when, eventually, shocks to the series no longer affect the value of the series.[15] As the simplest example, suppose the series at each point in time is entirely independent of the points in any other time period. In that case, if we know the value of the variable yesterday or the day before, this carries absolutely no information for predicting the value of the variable today. And, in particular, if a shock occurs, it is not at all persistent: in the next period there is absolutely no trace of it. This archetype stationary series is called a form of "white noise." As a concrete example, define $\varepsilon_t \sim \text{Uniform}[-1, 1]$ to be a variable that in each period takes a value randomly between -1 and 1 according to a uniform distribution. The time series produced by such a data-generating process will look like figure 4.3.

---

[13] Yule's original example reported a correlation of 0.95 between the proportion of marriages performed by the Church of England and the mortality rate over the period 1866–1911. The assumption is that the relationship between these two series is not causal—a stance which all but the most ardent of religious conspiracy theorists would probably accept. Granger and Newbold (1974) make a similar point but in the context of "random walks."

[14] For an introduction to nonstationarity see the guide developed when Robert Engle and Clive Granger won the Nobel Prize in Economics partly for their work in this area, available at http://nobelprize.org/nobel_prizes/economics/laureates/2003/ecoadv.pdf. There are also numerous textbooks in this area (see, for example, Stock and Watson (2006) or, for a more advanced discussion, Banerjee et al. (2003), Johansen (1995), and Hendry (1995)).

[15] Formally, a stationary process is a stochastic process whose probability distribution at any fixed point in time does not change over time. That is, if the joint distribution of a time series $(X_{1+s}, X_{2+s}, \dots, X_{T+s})$ does not depend on s. That means we can observe a time series of any length T and the date at which we start observing it will not affect the joint distribution of the data. This property is sometimes known as "strict" stationarity and other forms of stationarity are also possible. For example, we may only require that the first and second moments of the series do not vary over time and this would be a weaker form of stationarity.

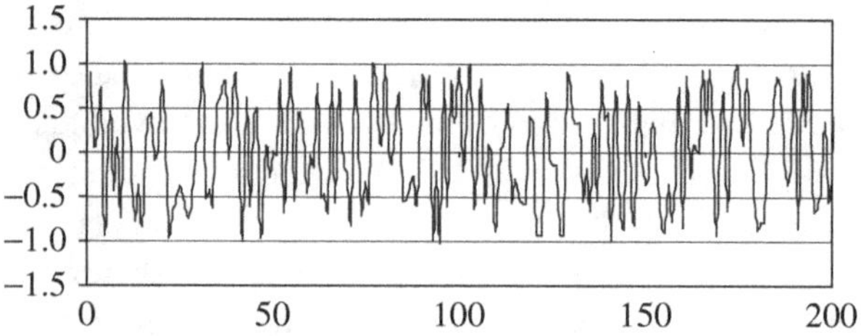

Figure 4.3. White noise series: $\rho = 0$.

Now consider a price series generated by the first-order autoregressive series, $P_t = \rho P_{t-1} + \varepsilon_t$, where we might again suppose that $\varepsilon_t \sim$ Uniform$[-1, 1]$. In this case, today's price is determined by the price in the previous period and a "white noise" shock. It is interesting to see the extent to which the shocks persist in such a series. To do so, substitute in the expression for prices successively to give

$$\begin{aligned} P_t &= \rho P_{t-1} + \varepsilon_t \\ &= \rho(\rho P_{t-2} + \varepsilon_{t-1}) + \varepsilon_t \\ &= \rho^2 P_{t-2} + \rho\varepsilon_{t-1} + \varepsilon_t \\ &= \rho^2(\rho P_{t-3} + \varepsilon_{t-2}) + \rho\varepsilon_{t-1} + \varepsilon_t \\ &= \rho^3 P_{t-3} + \rho^2\varepsilon_{t-2} + \rho\varepsilon_{t-1} + \varepsilon_t, \\ P_t &= \rho^t P_0 + \rho^{t-1}\varepsilon_1 + \cdots + \rho\varepsilon_{t-1} + \varepsilon_t. \end{aligned}$$

Doing so allows us to see that prices today are determined by the price at the beginning of the series, the initial condition, and then all of the shocks that subsequently happened weighted by terms that depend on the parameter ρ. If $\rho < 1$, the effects of both the initial condition P_0 and also all the old shocks die out with time. The smaller the ρ, the faster the effect of the shock dies out, i.e., the less persistent the shocks are. When this happens we say that the series is stationary. In contrast, note that if $\rho = 1$, then shocks to the series will never stop mattering, they will always matter to the value of prices being observed no matter how much time passes. In that case, we say that the shocks are persistent as the past never goes away, always affecting the current value of the price. If $\rho = 1$, we say that the price series follows a "random walk" and such a series is an example of an integrated or a nonstationary process. If a series is integrated of order 1, it means that the first difference of the series, the series $P_t - P_{t-1}$, is stationary. An example of integrated time series and also a number of stationary time series are shown in figure 4.4, which presents an integrated series which puts $\rho = 1$ and three other, stationary, time series which respectively set ρ equal to 0, 0.5, and 0.8.

Unlike the stationary time series, the integrated time series tends to wander off and does not quickly revert to its long-run value. To see why, note that a Uniform$[-1, 1]$ variable will always have a mean zero and so the series will never appear to wander

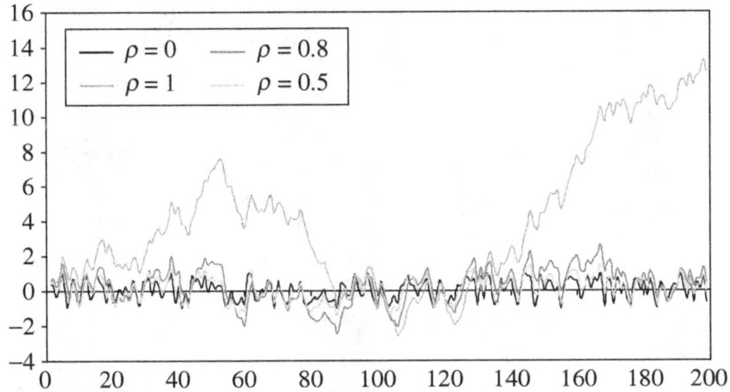

Figure 4.4. Examples of an integrated and a number of stationary time series.

away from that average. A stationary series can wander off a little from the mean, but eventually the past stops mattering and so the behavior of the series between, say, periods 0 and 100 cannot be very different from that between periods 100 and 200. In contrast, an integrated time series has no such mean-reversionary tendency. It turns out that if we have two price series generated with $\rho = 1$, even if the shocks in each series are entirely independent of one another, we will find that $\text{cov}(P_t^1, P_t^2) \to \pm 1$ in a fashion that is highly reminiscent of the results we saw when variables have trends. Thus, in the presence of integrated time series we face an additional danger that we will find highly correlated prices but that the correlation will be entirely spurious.

The salmon example provides an illustration of the kinds of debates that sometimes arise in competition cases. Consider figure 4.5, which plots the U.K. spot market prices for salmon produced in the United Kingdom and in Norway. Note in particular that up to about the year 2000, the time series appear to be characterized by a number of short-term shocks which do not look as though they persist for very long, if at all. Note, for example, the big spikes which last for just one period. In addition, the series behave like stationary series oscillating around their mean values. In contrast, after the year 2000, the series seem to both wander away from their previous mean and so appear to the eye more like nonstationary processes. If the correlations obtained previously are driven by this part of the data, then our result might not be reliable, that is, if the correlation coefficient for this section of the time series is driven purely by spurious correlation. One potential response is to split the sample and calculate the correlation on the first—stationary—section of the data.

Another response is to look at whether two prices are tied together by examining the stationarity of the ratio of prices. Suppose that economic forces ensure that two prices are never too different from one another for long periods of time because supply or demand substitutability forces the “law of one price” to broadly hold. Then we might expect to find that the relative prices for products should have the

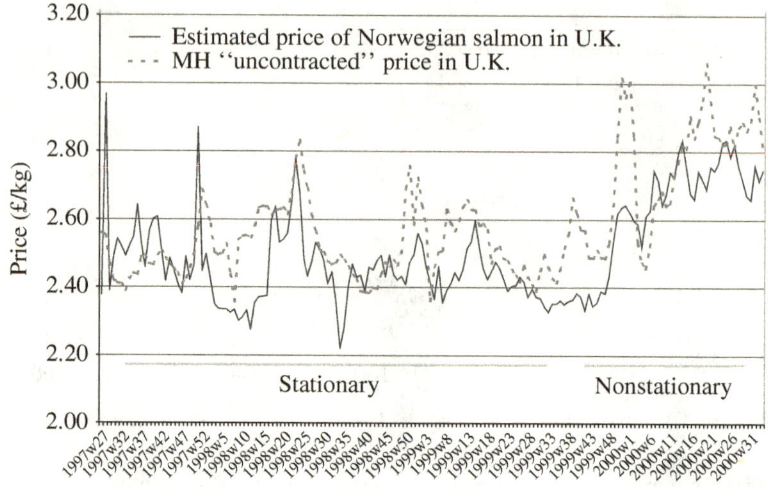

Figure 4.5. Stationary and nonstationary segments of price series. *Source*: U.K. Competition Commission salmon report. *Original source:* Lexecon.

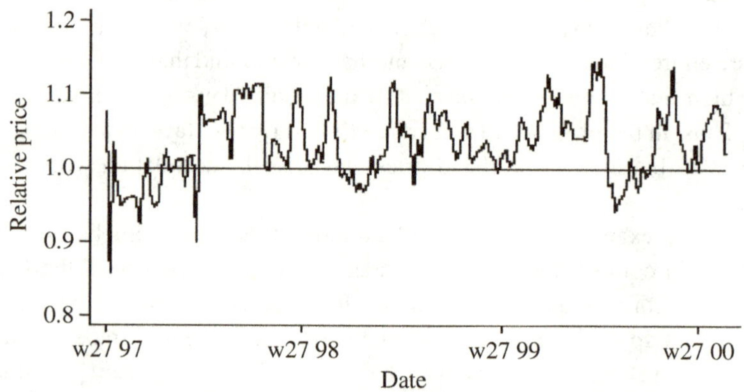

Figure 4.6. Relative prices. *Source*: U.K. Competition Commission salmon report. *Original source:* Lexecon.

long-run reversionary property, i.e., they should be stationary. Using the price series of our salmon example above, define $P_t^{\text{Scottish}}/P_t^{\text{Norwegian}} = \nu_t$, which is graphed in figure 4.6.

A first look seems to indicate that in the first few periods, the price of Scottish salmon is appreciating over time with respect to the price of Norwegian salmon, indicating that they may not be perfect substitutes. For the rest of the sample the ratio generally varies above 1. The claim that the relative price ratio of two goods should be stationary when they are demand substitutes appears plausible but it is in fact a very strong claim. Let us look at its theoretical foundation.

Recall the differentiated product Nash equilibrium in prices defined at the beginning of this section described the ratio of Nash prices as

$$\begin{aligned}
\frac{p_1^{\mathrm{NE}}}{p_2^{\mathrm{NE}}} &= \left(\frac{4b_{11}b_{22}}{4b_{11}b_{22}-b_{12}b_{21}}\right)\left(\frac{c_1}{2}+\frac{a_1}{2b_{11}}+\frac{b_{12}}{4b_{11}}\left(c_2+\frac{a_2}{b_{22}}\right)\right)\Big/ \\
&\quad \left[\left(\frac{4b_{11}b_{22}}{4b_{11}b_{22}-b_{12}b_{21}}\right)\left(\frac{c_2}{2}+\frac{a_2}{2b_{22}}+\frac{b_{21}}{4b_{22}}\left(c_1+\frac{a_1}{b_{11}}\right)\right)\right] \\
&= \left(\frac{c_1}{2}+\frac{a_1}{2b_{11}}+\frac{b_{12}}{4b_{11}}\left(c_2+\frac{a_2}{b_{22}}\right)\right)\Big/ \\
&\quad \left(\frac{c_2}{2}+\frac{a_2}{2b_{22}}+\frac{b_{21}}{4b_{22}}\left(c_1+\frac{a_1}{b_{11}}\right)\right) \\
&\overset{?}{=} v_t,
\end{aligned}$$

where the question mark indicates that we are testing whether the ratio generates a stationary process. Note in particular that $p_1^{\mathrm{NE}}/p_2^{\mathrm{NE}}$ can be stationary, but only under very stringent conditions. In particular, note that even if the products are substitutes, the relative costs of the two products need to remain broadly constant, as will the relative demand intercepts and the own- and cross-price elasticities. Each of these will need to stay broadly constant over the period examined, or somehow fortuitously move together, or else relative prices will not appear as a mean-reverting stationary series. If, for example, we have a persistent shock in cost or demand for one of the products only, we might wrongly conclude that the products are not related.

On the other hand, even if the products are not demand substitutes, so that $b_{ij} = 0$ for $i \neq j$, we could potentially wrongly find stationarity in relative prices when common shocks to costs or demand for the two products appropriately cancel each other out or indeed are themselves stationary.

All that said, when the goods are perfect substitutes, we do expect the "law of one price" to hold and that should act to keep the prices of the two products approximately the same. That is pretty strong intuition, but the lesson of this section is that price correlation exercises are not for the naive and certainly cannot be applied as though they are a panacea for market definition. In this chapter we have seen that lesson a number of times, and here we see again that (1) rejecting stationarity does not imply that the goods are not substitutes and (2) accepting stationarity does not necessarily imply that goods are demand substitutes even with seemingly high correlation coefficients. In general, we will want to substantiate claims about stationarity and correlations by checking what happened to the costs of, and demand for, the products during the period of interest. If such shocks exist they may cause a false negative if only one product is affected and substitution is less than perfect. If the shocks are common to both products, they may cause a false positive and the products can appear to be more related than they really are.

There are several ways in which one can test the existence of stationarity. The first, illustrated in Stigler and Sherwin (1985), looks at the correlation in price changes, i.e., the correlation in the first differences of prices:

$$\text{Corr}(P_t^1 - P_{t-1}^1, P_t^2 - P_{t-1}^2).$$

An alternative method is to statistically test whether nonstationarity might be a problem. To do so we can compute a test called the Dickey–Fuller test for each price series to see whether each price series is nonstationary. Then we use the same test to see whether the relative prices are stationary. If the hypotheses that the two individual series are stationary are rejected but the relative price series does appear stationary, then we can claim that the result is consistent with a connection between the markets which suggests the two products should be in the same market in a way akin to getting correlation in the levels of stationary price series. Of course, whether stationary or nonstationary, correlation analysis runs the substantial risk of false positives or negatives and as a result it is usually a mistake to simply calculate the correlation and accept it at face value as strong evidence about market definition.

We end this section by noting that there is a more formal econometric approach to the question of testing for co-movement in prices which involves testing for "co-integration." This type of analysis involves both complex and sometimes subtle econometric arguments and also is often applied in a way that is insufficiently informed by economic theory. The combination can be extremely dangerous. For example, one result which, on the face of it, suggests that researchers do not need to worry about endogeneity when working with co-integrated series is the result that says OLS estimators of "co-integrating" relations are "superconsistent" and integrated regressors can be correlated with error terms (see Stock 1987). Naive applications of that result argue, for example, that it implies that it is unproblematic to run regressions of price on quantity. Such claims are obviously both dangerous and ultimately "wrong," since, for example, you still would not know whether your regression were a demand or a supply curve.[16] While in principle, under special circumstances, you may not have an endogeneity problem, you certainly will not have escaped the fundamental identification problem that both supply and demand curves depend on prices and quantities. Investigators with limited knowledge in the co-integration arena are therefore advised to proceed with extreme caution when attempting to apply complex econometric arguments with sometimes subtle implications. The risk of being led seriously astray by apparently extremely attractive

[16] Engle and Granger (1987) studied a single "co-integrating" relationship and showed that applying OLS to a regression of the form $Y_t = \alpha X_t + \varepsilon_t$, where Y and X are integrated (of order 1) and ε_t is stationary gives us a "superconsistent" estimator of α. The terminology of "superconsistent" is used to indicate that the estimator is consistent and converges to the true parameter value faster than a normal OLS estimator (at rate T instead of at rate $T^{1/2}$). OLS estimators use the correlation $E[X_t \varepsilon_t]$ to identify the parameter α and the superconsistency result occurs because X_t is integrated while ε_t is stationary so that intuitively the correlation between them will necessarily be small because X wanders away from its initial value while ε_t mean reverts.

econometric theorems is very high. On the other hand, if carefully applied with both economic and econometric theory solidly in mind when doing so, the tools for dealing with integrated and co-integrated time series can sometimes help avoid the problem of spurious correlation.[17]

4.2.3.3 *The Risk of False Negatives*

We have already illustrated how, in a world of imperfect substitutes, asymmetric shocks to demand and costs can cause price series to deviate from one another even when the products are perhaps even fairly close substitutes. We close this section by noting that there are other circumstances when we will underestimate the degree of substitutability of two products by just looking at how their prices move together.

In particular, if the signal-to-noise ratio is low, we will find little correlation between the prices but this result will be driven by random short-lived shocks to the prices of the product and the apparent lack of correlation will not reflect the underlying structural relationship between the products. For instance, suppose the inputs are really different for the two goods and input prices move around a lot. Then the observed correlation in prices will be small due to the variance in the price series caused by shocks to input prices even though the two series may exhibit some limited co-movement. Also, if the data are noisy due to poor quality or measurement problems and the actual prices do not vary much in the period observe, the correlation coefficient will appear small since it will only pick up the noise in the series. When the size of the shocks is large relative to the movement of the price series over the period observed, this problem will be exacerbated since the "signal to noise" ratio will be low.

Similarly, the picture generated by contemporaneous correlations in prices may mislead investigators when, for example, prices respond to changes in market conditions only with a time lag. Even if two products are in fact good long- or medium-term demand substitutes, we may see little contemporaneous correlation in prices and wrongly conclude that the products are not related.

4.2.4 Rival Cost and Demand Data for Price Correlation Analysis

As in all quantitative analysis, one cannot draw more information from the analysis than is already present in the data. If the data are noisy, we will find a low level of

[17] These tools are particularly important and popular in macroeconomics, but not without critics (see, for example, Greenslade and Hall 2002). Those authors argue that "in a common realistic modeling situation of limited data set and the theory requirements of a fairly rich model, the techniques proposed in the existing literature are almost impossible to implement successfully." That quote gives a more pessimistic impression than those authors in fact conclude with, when these tools are appropriately combined with economic theory, but it should nonetheless provide a very useful cautionary note to any investigator. Difficulties of identification, the way in which purely statistical analysis must be supplemented with economic theory, and the appropriate framework for statistical analysis are certainly not unique to the co-integration literature—they are each generic difficulties that must be faced and overcome in any serious econometric analysis.

correlation no matter how related the products really are. If visual inspection shows that the prices co-move, the correlation coefficient will tell you that the prices co-move, although you might derive some additional information about the scale of the co-movement from the number itself and are likely to want to consider the statistical significance of any correlation.[18] Whatever the numerical value of the correlation, a central lesson we have attempted to hammer home is that it can be very important to get underneath the number to identify the source of the co-movement.

In this section we outline a "test" for identifying good sources of co-movement in prices. This test consists of identifying changes in the demand or cost of the potential substitute product that do not affect the original product. This could be changes in the price of an input (i.e., cost movement) used in the substitute product only or a change in the intensity of demand by a group of users that do not want the original product. These changes are likely to affect the price of the potential substitute. Noticing an impact on the price of the original product would indicate that the two are indeed substitutes enough to influence each other's prices.

To see why, recall that economic theory predicts different price-setting mechanisms for prices when in the presence or absence of a substitute. In particular, the expressions for Nash equilibrium prices that we obtained in those two cases were respectively

$$p_1^{\text{NE}} = \left(\frac{4b_{11}b_{22}}{4b_{11}b_{22} - b_{12}b_{21}}\right)\left(\frac{c_1}{2} + \frac{a_1}{2b_{11}} + \frac{b_{12}}{4b_{11}}\left(c_2 + \frac{a_2}{b_{22}}\right)\right)$$

and

$$p_1^{\text{NE}} = \frac{c_1}{2} + \frac{a_1}{2b_{11}}.$$

When analyzing price correlations, we are often interested in knowing whether b_{12} is nonzero. Examining these formulas, it is apparent that a good way to test for such connections is to observe shifts in the other product's demand or costs (a_2 or c_2) provided that variation is not of the form that would contemporaneously shift the product's own demand or cost (a_1 or c_1). If the effect of such a shift is noticeable in p_1, then we will be able to conclude that b_{12} is nonzero, though as with any price correlation analysis it will nonetheless be difficult to decide whether or not b_{12} is truly big enough to justify putting both products in the same market. As with many areas of competition policy, ultimately the decision-making body (regulator,

[18] As we have already mentioned, statistical inference with nonstationary time series data is "nonstandard" in the sense that t-statistics of 2 are generally not enough to establish statistical significance. In fact, while we can, for example, still calculate correlations, R-squared, and t-tests, they often will not have the distributions we usually expect them to have. For example, we can calculate a t-test but the statistic we calculate will not have a "t"-distribution when our data set involves integrated time series. In practical terms, while we usually use a t-value of 2 to evaluate statistical significance (difference from zero with 95% significance), the correct critical values will typically be higher, and sometimes far higher (perhaps 5 or 10 instead of 2). See, for example, the critical values provided for tests of "integration" provided by Dickey and Fuller (1979). Other related popular tests for nonstationarity include the "augmented Dickey–Fuller" test and the Phillips–Perron test.

competition authority, or court) will need to make a judgment taking into account all of the various pieces of evidence including price correlation evidence on the correct market definition.

4.3 Natural Experiments

Price correlation analysis is a method we can use to attempt to estimate the degree of substitutability between two products by estimating the extent to which two products' prices move systematically together. On the one hand, price correlations provide rather indirect evidence compared, for example, with attempts to evaluate the cross-price elasticity of demand between two products. On the other hand, the method is simple and in particular far simpler than having to actually estimate a demand function. Natural experiments or "shock analysis," when applied to prices, follow a similar logic but are far more careful at the outset to control the source of the variation in the data that we use to identify substitutability. Rather than evaluating the correlation and then checking explanations for its source, shock analysis looks at the reaction of the price(s) of other goods following an exogenous shock on the price of one good, the one at the center of the investigation. Shock analysis is the simplest way of getting a feel for the magnitude of own- and cross-price elasticities of demand without getting involved in a more complex econometric analysis. Whenever there is a possibility to properly conduct a shock analysis, this method will be helpful since it is both simple to apply and often very informative, making it a powerful technique. Of course, the investigator does nonetheless need to be very careful to ensure that the "shock" causing the initial price shift is genuinely exogenous and not determined by market conditions affecting consumers or competitors.

4.3.1 Informative Exogenous Shocks

To see the logic of natural experiments, assume a sudden unanticipated exogenous decrease in the price of a good A, P^{A}, such as that illustrated in figure 4.7. Such a change may occur, for example, by design, perhaps if a firm conducts a marketing experiment in an attempt to learn about the sensitivity of demand to its price. An exogenous change in the price of good A may feed through into (1) the price of good B, (2) the quantity of good B, and (3) the quantity of good A.

Once the observed exogenous change in P^{A} occurs, we can simply look at the subsequent changes in Q^{A} and Q^{B} to obtain the own- and cross-price elasticities of demand. If the reaction to a decrease of P^{A} is a sharp increase of Q^{A} and a sharp decrease of Q^{B}, then we can confidently assert that A and B are demand substitutes. More closely related to the price-correlation analysis we studied previously, the price decrease in A may lead us to observe a reduction in the price of B. Ideally, an investigation would have data on all the prices and quantities, but the reality is that data sets may frequently be incomplete, with perhaps just the price data available.

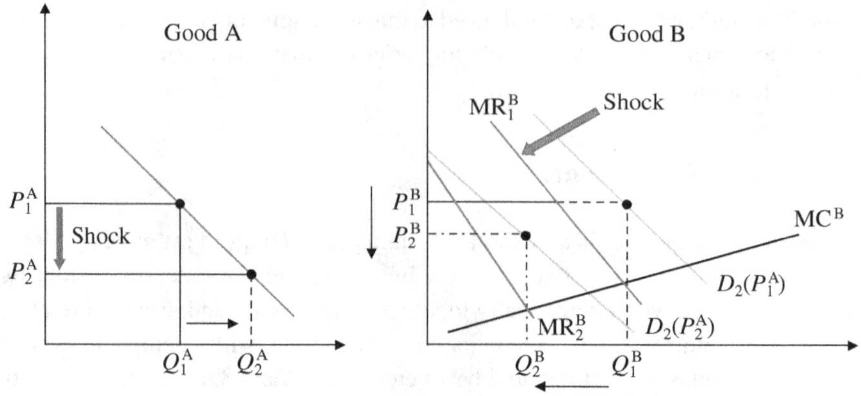

Figure 4.7. Effect of a shock in the price of a good on another good.

A key factor for the success of the methodology is the fact that the original shock on prices is exogenous and not related to the demand of either product A or B, nor related to the cost of inputs for B. It is unfortunately not always easy to find such situations, although opportunities for shock analysis do occur.

A practical example is provided by the decision in 1996 by a cinema in New Haven, Connecticut, to lower the prices of its evening adult admission ticket to newly released films to just \$5 for a three-week period. Such an unusual move was heavily reported by the local newspapers. Given such a move, it enables us to look at the response of the theaters near to the venue which lowered its price.[19] Cinemas are in the same geographical market if moviegoers consider them as alternatives. One can easily imagine someone deciding on a movie by checking the shows in a group of cinemas where she could consider going. If one cinema becomes cheaper, this person might be more likely to attend that cinema, particularly if the movie shown is the same as the ones shown elsewhere. If cinemas compete for customers, then there is an incentive by competing cinemas to also reduce their prices (or show sufficiently unique and attractive movies). Observing the reaction of the cinemas in an area after a unilateral price decrease by one of them can therefore be a good way to determine which cinemas are likely to be competing for the same audience.

There were five cinemas in the New Haven area located around the cinema which cut prices (the Branford 12), as shown in figure 4.8.

The pricing responses of the rival theaters are reported in table 4.5. All the cinemas except for the York Square cinema (number 3) showed first-run, i.e., newly released, films.

Table 4.5 provides useful information about both geographic market definition and also product market definition. First consider geographic market definition. Note that the two closest cinemas showing popular films responded with similar

[19] As we have already noted, exogenous data variation is useful for estimating demand as well. The price and also sales data from this experiment were collected and used in Davis (2002).

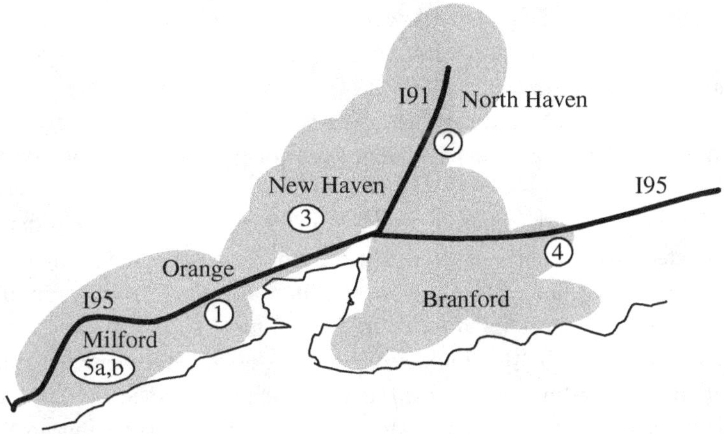

Figure 4.8. Map of locations of cinemas involved in the experiment. The theater labeled "4" was the Branford 12 screen cinema whose price was cut for three weeks.

Table 4.5. Theater pricing responses to the pricing experiment performed by the Branford 12 cinemas.

	Theater	Chain	Pricing strategy/ response
1	Showcase Orange	National Amusements	$4.50 for three weeks
2	Showcase North Haven 8	National Amusements	$4.50 for three weeks
3	York Square (art house)	Independent	No change
4	Branford 12	HOYTS	$5 for three weeks
5a	Showcase Milford 5	National Amusements	No change
5b	Milford Quad	National Amusements	No change

Source: Davis (2002).

price changes while the more distant ones did not. Both the Showcase Orange and the Showcase North Haven responded by decreasing their prices to $4.50, which, as an aside, also provides a nice example that committing to prices provides your rivals with a second mover advantage to undercut you. The two theaters in Milford (denoted as 5a,b in the table and on the map) could have reacted to the change in price initiated by the Branford 12 but they did not and that fact is consistent with those theaters being outside the geographic market appropriate for the Branford 12. On the other hand, it is perhaps more surprising on the face of it that they did not respond to the somewhat closer theater's price, particularly the Showcase Orange, labeled 1 on the map. Since the Showcase Orange theater belongs to the same chain as those in Milford (National Amusements), the incentives to further propagate the price reduction down along the coastline are greatly mitigated. The revenue loss of National Amusements cinemas due the lower price at cinemas 1 and 2 were probably less than the loss of revenue that a lower price for everyone would have generated indicating that for at least some viewers, the Milford cinemas labeled 5a,b was not interchangeable with the other cinemas. These results suggest that a geographic market for the Branford 12 theater involves a radius of approximately five to ten miles around the theater and, in particular, does not extend all the way down toward Milford.

Second, consider product market definition. To see this aspect, note that the "art house" theater in the center of New Haven did not respond even though it was within the distance range of those theaters which did. This could be an indication that commercial and "artistic" movies are in different product markets, and this is indeed consistent with competition case law in the United States, which distinguishes a separate market for "first-run" films. That said, in this instance, since there is only one artistic theater observation one should probably be rather cautious with that conclusion.

4.3.2 A Regression Framework

In the previous section we considered an example where a marketing experiment provided "exogenous" variation in prices—by design. Such marketing experiments benefiting from purely exogenous price movements are fairly rare, but do arise particularly in "local" retail markets. Local markets can mean that the cost of setting prices at potentially the "wrong" experimental level may be small (limited to one area) compared with situations where the market affected is national, EU wide, or even global, while the benefit—information about the most profitable level of prices—can be large if the lesson can be applied across a larger set of markets. Evidence of marketing experiments can arise in company documents.

When direct evidence from marketing experiments about the impact of exogenous price changes is not available, we may nevertheless be able to use evidence from "exogenous" movements in factors which affect demand or supply of one product to infer the extent of substitutability with others. Factors which may move exogenously (i.e., in a fashion unconnected with movements in demand or supply which are due to causes not observed by the investigator) and also affect demand or supply may include entry events, regulatory changes, or indeed more standard instruments such as input cost movements. Movements on either the demand or supply side of either own- or potential rival products can be useful for understanding the extent to which market outcomes are interconnected.

Let us first illustrate the idea and then consider potentially valid critiques of it. Specifically, consider the regression analysis described in Davis (2005), who used a database consisting of a prices and a theater "atlas"—the locations and size of all movie theaters in the 101 largest market areas in the United States.[20] The data were quarterly observations between the first quarter of 1993 and the fourth quarter of

[20] A related paper, which examined revenues instead of prices, is Davis (2006e).

1997, a period when there was a great deal of new cinema building. For a given theater, we attempt to describe the way in which market structure affects its prices. To learn about that, we observe what happens to prices when entry occurs nearby and also what happens when entry occurs in more distant locations. We will use a regression framework to try to pick up the way in which individual theaters are affected by local market structure by using the experience of entry to pick up what happens to prices when local market structure changes. Basically, the idea is that if two theaters are competing for the same customers, i.e., they are potential substitutes, we will expect to see nearby entry affect the price that an incumbent can charge, whereas when entry occurs far enough away from a theater we will not expect to see any pricing reaction. Our aim is to find the distance at which a new entry stopped having an impact on the incumbent.

Consider the following regression for each theater h:

$$p_{hmt} = \alpha_h + \tau_t + \gamma_m + x_{hmt}\beta + \xi_{hmt},$$

where x_{hmt} are counts of own and rivals' screens within a given number of miles at time t in market m. For example, we might measure the number of screens operated by rival theater companies between one and two miles of theater h's location. The coefficient β will then measure the effect of own and rival screens at various distances on the prices of a given theater. We wish to learn about the way market structure affects prices by using the experience of a given theater when faced with changes in its local market structure. In regression analysis, this type of data variation is known as "within" theater data variation. To ensure that we are using this type of data variation, the regression uses theater fixed effects, α_h(see the discussion in chapter 2). The numerical results are presented in graphical form in figure 4.9.

The results suggest that the presence of other movie screens within a range of ten miles have negative effects on the price of a theater. After ten miles, the presence of additional theaters does not seem to impose a constraint on the price. Interestingly, the presence of screens owned by the same chain has an even starker negative effect on price.[21] Such a result looks surprising at first glance; however, this apparent paradox can probably be explained by the nature of contracts between theaters and film distributors. In particular, theaters share the box office revenues collected through the admission price with film distributors while they keep all the revenues from drinks and food sold at the theater. Theaters therefore have a strong incentive to keep admission prices low to attract lots of people to the theater and then charge them for popcorn. One dollar extra from popcorn means a dollar extra in the bank for the theater, whereas one dollar extra from admission prices means only approximately 0.3 cents in the bank for the theater given the form of contractual relationships. A

[21] The exceptions to this general rule are the two estimates in figure 4.9(b) at low distances where estimated effects are insignificantly different from zero. In these two particular distance intervals, 0–0.5 miles and 3–4 miles, there appeared to be a relative paucity of data; there were few cinemas owned by the same chain built at these distances, perhaps because of concerns around cannibalization of revenues.

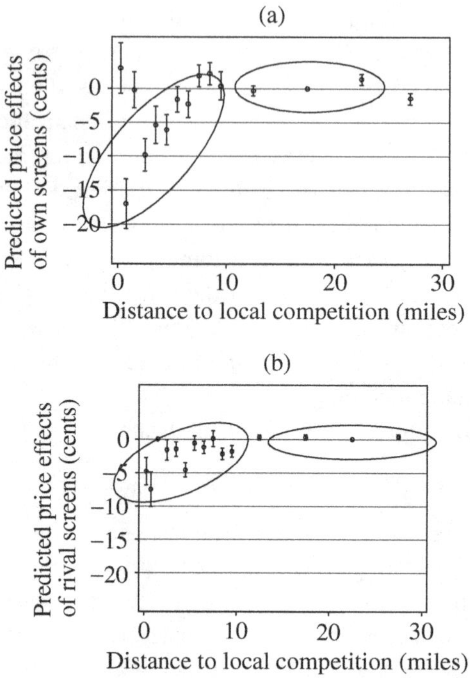

Figure 4.9. Predicted effects of local market structure on pricing. The point represents the numerical predicted effect and the error bars capture the predicted 95% confidence interval around that predicted effect. The ovals indicate the general features of the pattern of results. *Source*: Adapted from figures 3 and 4 of Davis (2005).

chain which owns several theaters locally would then have more bargaining power vis-à-vis the distributors and will use that bargaining power to negotiate low entrance fees. Unfortunately, we do not have the popcorn price data to verify that the popcorn prices in the area are higher. But the economic incentives to lower admission prices turn out to be consistent with the story the data are telling—that there is greater downward pressure on admission prices from the presence of theaters from the same chain than from the presence of theaters from rival chains. The vertical contracts may then explain these otherwise counterintuitive results.[22]

In a study such as the one just described, it is important to argue that entry or in this case the number of theaters in the area is not an endogenous variable in the model. Attempts should usually be made to instrument market structure in a fashion we will describe more in later chapters, particularly chapter 5. Here, for the market structure variables to be exogenous we need to argue that a higher density of cinemas in a given area is not correlated with factors that generate particularly high prices for movies for reasons that we cannot control for. Such factors could be from the demand or cost side since either will also generate high prices. Natural experiments such as the

[22] A related thesis and analysis of popcorn prices is provided by Gil and Hartmann (2007).

one obtained using a genuine marketing experiment generating a sudden unexpected decrease in price by only one theater is rare but an extremely good way to avoid endogeneity issues. Unfortunately, natural experiments are not always available and, where they are, are sometimes one-time events that cannot be replicated. Where they are available, we need to be careful about endogeneity, which can appear in many guises. Consider for example, a pharmaceutical company's response to a new entrant, which may appear after a drug goes off-patent.[23] It is common for the incumbent provider to reposition the branded product so that her unit prices will actually appear to rise following entry. If so, entry causes a movement in the perceived quality of a product (perhaps via increased advertising) and if that element of change is "unobserved" we will suffer from an endogeneity bias when we use entry as a "natural experiment." We discussed econometric strategies for dealing with endogeneity in chapter 2. The central lesson is that when considering the reasonableness of using a given natural experiment to make inferences about market definition, one must not lose sight of the economics of the situation being considered.

4.4 Directly Estimating the Substitution Effect

It is sometimes possible to directly estimate the degree of substitution between a good and its potential substitutes. For this, one either needs to have consumer-level data on the set of possible choices that consumers face and the actual choice that they made or aggregate data on sales of each good. In each case we will also need price data and we may also need other characteristics of the goods being sold. We will discuss the large variety of techniques for directly estimating demand in chapter 9. Here we introduce the topic, discussing several techniques that can be useful when attempting to quantify substitution effects, their link with the theoretical quantities we are attempting to capture, and the issues faced by investigators using these techniques. We begin with a discussion of diversion ratios.

4.4.1 Diversion Ratios

4.4.1.1 Market Shares and Likelihood of Choice

A diversion ratio tries to answer the following question: if the price of good 1 increases, what fraction of lost sales goes to good 2? Some empirical exercises attempt to answer this question by looking directly at the market shares of the competing products and interpreting their share of the total sales as the likelihood of being chosen by the average consumer. However, market shares can be a misleading proxy for what we are actually trying to measure: substitution patterns between goods.

[23] This example was provided by Greg Werden, U.S. Department of Justice (Antitrust Division).

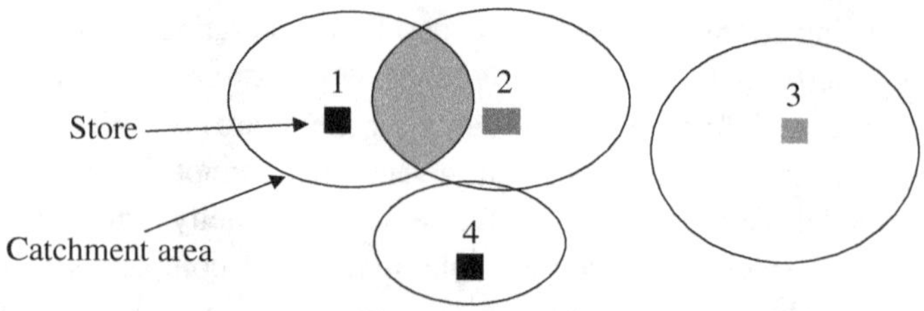

Figure 4.10. Catchment areas. *Source*: Based on the U.K. Competition Commission investigation into the 2005 merger between Somerfield plc and Wm Morrison Supermarkets plc.

Consider an area with different stores that draw customers within a certain distance around them. The area where they can attract customers is called the catchment area. Such a situation could look as in figure 4.10.

We can see that stores 1 and 2 compete for only a subset of their customers. Store 3 on the other hand does not face any constraint from its competitors and does not impose any competitive constraints on them either. Store 4 is only marginally affected by the presence of store 2.

If we only computed market shares for the whole town, we would probably grossly overestimate the constraining effect of stores 3 and 4 on the prices charged at stores 1 and 2. On the other hand, if store 2 has a low market share, we are likely to underestimate the constraining effect of store 2 on the prices that can be charged by store 1. Thus, knowledge beyond town-level market shares will be useful when attempting to understand actual competitive constraints between the stores.

Although this is intuitively clearest in the case of geographic markets, the same situation can occur in product markets where products differ, perhaps in many dimensions, in ways that are valued in different ways by consumers. For a subset of consumers that value one of the characteristics very strongly, two products can be very good substitutes, while for other consumers—those more interested in other aspects of the product—they will not be good substitutes.

4.4.1.2 Diversion Ratios and the Demand Curve

Recall the question that we are trying to answer: if the price of good 1 increases, what fraction of the lost sales will go to good 2? To understand this question, let us look at our workhorse differentiated product demand curves:

$$q_1(p_1, p_2) = a_1 - b_{11}p_1 + b_{12}p_2 \quad \text{and} \quad q_2(p_1, p_2) = a_2 - b_{22}p_2 + b_{21}p_1.$$

The coefficient b_{11} represents the loss of sales of good 1 that will be caused by an increase in p_1 by one unit, say one euro. The coefficient b_{21} represents the increase in sales of good 2 caused by that same price increase. The diversion ratio is then

$$D_{12} = \frac{b_{21}}{b_{11}} = \frac{\partial D_2/\partial p_1}{-\partial D_1/\partial p_1} = \frac{\partial D_2/\partial \ln p_1}{-\partial D_1/\partial \ln p_1}.$$

The last equality only indicates that the question can be also asked in terms of the effect of a percentage increase in prices. After an increase in p_1, some of the sales lost will go to the "outside good," i.e., the consumers will sometimes reduce the total purchases of goods 1 and 2 after an increase in p_1. For this reason, even with only two goods the diversion ratio will most likely not be equal to 1.

Estimating the diversion ratio requires knowledge of how consumers would react to a change in the terms of the goods on offer. The next section discusses how we can obtain the relevant data.

4.4.2 Revealed versus Stated Preferences

There are two ways to find out about consumer preferences. One is to observe their choices and try to explain them given the customers' characteristics and the set of possible choices they had available. In such a case, we are using information about consumers' "revealed" preferences. A second method consists of asking consumers about what they would do if they were to face a specific set of choices. In that case, we would be using information based on stated preferences.

4.4.2.1 Revealed Preferences

A first, very rough, way to look at revealed preferences is to look at market shares. Market shares are simple to obtain and so have the merit of providing information on consumer choices in a very direct form. However, as we have already described, relying on market shares to learn about substitution patterns is at best a crude approximation, although in some cases it may be the best an agency can do in practice.

Ideally, one would use more complete market data than just market shares. Broadly, we could use either market-level data including prices, product characteristics, and market shares to estimate aggregate market demand equations, and hence market elasticities of demand and substitution patterns. Or else we can use individual level data to estimate individual level demand equations and their associated substitution patterns. Given the latter we can then add up across an appropriately weighted collection of individuals to derive market demand curves and hence price elasticities.

For the latter approach, a useful data set for analyzing demand would contain individual level data with actual choices from a list of options that each consumer faced. Ideally, we would have information on all the relevant dimensions of choice: product characteristics, price, and location. Finally, we would want to have the customers' characteristics that may determine preferences such as age or income or indeed consumer's location. With such information, we could attempt to estimate the demand function for a product and retrieve the cross-price elasticity of any two goods of relevance. We refer the reader to chapter 9 for a much more detailed discussion on demand estimation.

4.4.2.2 Stated Preferences

It is not always possible to obtain the necessary data to allow us to reliably predict consumer choices. For instance, we may want to predict the behavior of consumers in a situation that does not yet exist and for which there are no data. One example may be when a firm wants to evaluate the demand for a brand new product, say, television or fourth generation (4G) phones, before such products exist. In such a case, we need to gather information about what consumers would do, under what are, at the time of asking, entirely hypothetical circumstances. The bottom line is that in such a situation where we cannot see what consumers do, we must ask them to "state" what they would do.

Surveys are often used to learn about consumers' or producers' preferences. A representative sample of consumers is chosen and after recording each person's personal characteristics, the surveyor asks each one of them about what they think their choices would be under hypothetical circumstances. Examples of questions would be:

- I notice you have bought brand A. Suppose it cost 50 cents more, would you switch and buy brand B or brand C instead?
- Would you travel to the next big town if tomatoes cost 10 cents per kilo less than here?

The first question would provide information on substitution patterns across products while the second would be relevant for geographical market definition. One can also use surveys to estimate suppliers' responses to an increase in prices by asking questions such as:

- How high would the price of yellow paint have to be in order to induce you to switch your red paint machines to start producing yellow paint?

The European Commission Notice on the Definition of Relevant Market states that such survey evidence conducted in the context of an investigation is only to be taken into account when sufficiently backed by factual evidence.[24] This is sometimes difficult when the questions relate to what would happen under circumstances that have never actually occurred. If investigators want to rely on survey results, they must at least do what they can to ensure the survey is of high quality. Doing so involves making sure that the sample of respondents is sufficiently representative and that the questions asked are clear and well-understood. One needs to be particularly careful to accurately describe the alternative options. An example of a good stated preference survey questionnaire is presented in figure 4.11.

In this questionnaire, the alternatives considered are clear and a description of all the relevant characteristics is provided under all alternative scenarios. There is

[24] Commission Notice on the Definition of the Relevant Market for the purposes of Community Competition Law. OJ C 372 on 9/12/1997.

Eight hypothetical commuting scenarios were constructed for respondents who travel on SR91. Respondents who indicated that their actual commute was less (more) than 45 minutes were given scenarios that involved trips ranging from 20 to 40 (50 to 70) minutes. An illustrative scenario follows:

SCENARIO 1

Free lanes	Express lanes
Usual travel time: 25 minutes	Usual travel time: 15 minutes
Toll: None	Toll: $3.75
Frequency of unexpected delays of 10 minutes or more: 1 day in 5	Frequency of unexpected delays of 10 minutes or more: 1 day in 20
Your choice (check one)	
Free lanes ☐	Toll lanes ☐

Figure 4.11. Stated preferences survey questionnaire. *Source*: Small et al. (2005).

very little room left for subjective interpretation on the part of the respondent. In addition, there is not too much information being asked for. It is therefore possible for respondents to make meaningful comparisons between the options. Note also the careful presentation of "probabilities." Expressing probabilities as frequencies of unexpected delays within a week will be easier for many consumers to understand than a statement along the lines of probability of delay equals 0.2, though the information conveyed to readers of this book, a highly selected sample of the population, may be the same. Survey design is important and being careful about the way in which questions are phrased is central to getting accurate and useable results. Competition authorities that undertake surveys continue to gain experience with the kinds of questions that "work."

An example of a stated preference survey performed in the competition context was the U.K. Competition Commission (CC) study conducted during the 2005 acquisition of 115 Morrisons supermarkets by Somerfield.[25] The study identified 56 stores as presenting potential competition issues. In each store, consumers were asked: "If this store was unavailable today, where would you have shopped?" The CC did not ask customers directly about their reactions to a price increase because they believed that a price increase in a supermarket was too vague to be accurately described to a respondent. There are thousands of goods in a supermarket and asking the question "what would you do if prices went up by 5%" would raise the additional question of which prices? Nevertheless, the results were used by the CC as if they were informative about price-sensitivity parameters in the demand functions and based on this they obtained controversial predicted price effects.[26] In fact, questions about the entry or exit of a product are more akin to asking about reactions to infinite

[25] See www.competition-commission.org.uk/inquiries/ref2005/somerfield/index.htm.

[26] See the RBB presentation at the Association of Competition Economists in Copenhagen, December 2005: www.tcd.ie/iiis/pages/links/3rdannualconferencepres.php. See also the NOP Consumer report prepared for the CC in the context of the investigation, available at www.competition-commission.org.uk/Inquiries/ref2005/somerfield/pdf/consumer_survey_by_nop.pdf.

price variations. The results therefore need to be thought about pretty carefully and should not immediately be assumed to be representative of the effect of small but significant price changes.

To understand exactly what is being measured, consider that the CC we are measuring the proportion of customers that switched from A to B compared with the total number of customers that were shopping at A. In contrast, the diversion ratio (defined in terms of price increases) actually measures the proportion of customers who would switch from A to B if the price at A increased by, say, 5%. By construction, the people who switch following small price increases will tend to be marginal customers—those for whom store A and store B are pretty close substitutes for one another but before the price rise at A there was a small preference for going to A. On the other hand, the CC's survey question is geared toward finding what happens if A goes away entirely. For that reason, the estimated diversion ratio using survey questions of the "if this store were unavailable" kind will tell us about the proportion of A who have B as their "next best option" while the true diversion ratio will tell us about the proportion of A's customers who have B as their "next best option and who are sufficiently close to being indifferent between the two shops." The latter element means that a small price increase at A will convince those customers to switch so they shop at B.

In the Sportech/Vernons merger inquiry a survey undertaken by GfK for the CC suggested that 36% of the (target) customers of Vernons said they would use another football pools operator if Vernons were no longer available, while 19% of Sportech's customers (acquirer) would switch to Vernons (target) if Sportech were no longer available.[27] As an estimate of the diversion ratio, 20–40% of customers switching is probably high enough to cause serious concerns in a merger inquiry (although a proper critical loss analysis is needed to come to a final judgment about the scale of such effects). However, the CC concluded that in this case there were good reasons to consider that the measured diversion ratio overstated the likely true diversion ratio. In particular, there was considerable evidence that lots of customers were both loyal to a particular brand and also dedicated to football pools as an activity. Specifically, the GfK survey found that only 2% of customers had in fact stopped using a football pools company in the previous two years "because another offered better value in terms of entry prices, prizes, or winning changes," while among the GfK survey respondents, 85% had been playing the football pools (mainly weekly) for over ten years and 70% for over twenty years. The Swift 2 survey found that over 50% of customers had played for more than twenty years with the brand they play with now. In short, there appeared to be a clear tension between the GfK survey results using the methodology where a brand went away for an entire customer base, which suggested significant switching, and the other survey and qualitative

[27] A merger of two firms which sell a soft gambling product known as the "Football Pools" (see www.competition-commission.org.uk/inquiries/ref2007/sportech/index.htm). See paragraph 5.38 of the Sportech/Vernons merger final report. And also paragraph 4.9.

Table 4.6. Summary of survey results in the Sportech/Vernons merger inquiry.

Survey	Swift 1	ORC	Swift 2		GfK	
Year	2006	2007	2007		2007	
Respondents	Lapsed Littlewoods players	Lapsed pools players	Current pools players		Current pools players	
Number interviewed	250	300	250[a]		1,100	
Stimulus	None	None	10% price increase	Current operator closed down	10% price increase	Current operator closed down
Would not play with, or would spend less with, current provider (%)	—	—	26		7.5	—
Switched, or would switch, to alternative pools provider (%)	3.5	2[b]	1	36	6.5	24
Switched, or would switch, to other (nonpools) gambling (%)	31	5[c]	4.4	15	1.5[d]	11
Spent, or would spend, the money on nongambling products (%)	65	76	19	49		55

[a]As discussed in paragraph 5.35, around 500 were interviewed, but low weights were applied to around half of these, such that they had very little effect on the results.
[b]The number who stopped/reduced playing one pools game and increased/started another.
[c]Calculated as 7% who had switched to another gambling product minus 2% who had started the pools.
[d]Would not purchase current or alternative provider options. This result is based on customers comparing show-cards with different price offers: when the price offered by their current provider was 10% above current levels, an additional 1.5% said that they would not play the pools.
Source: CC report into Sportech/Vernons anticipated merger (2007, table 1, p. 23).

evidence suggesting inelastic demand but little substitutability, which is consistent with the story that there was already lots of market power over their customer base and therefore little "extra" market power would be generated by the merger.[28]

[28] In the United Kingdom the statutory test under the Enterprise Act (2003) is whether a merger would lead to a "substantial lessening of competition." A potentially important quirk of such a legal test is that two firms that are not competing very hard pre-merger for some reason will be allowed to merge. For example, a market may not be working very well because of high switching costs, perhaps a result of difficulties consumers face in obtaining product comparison information. On some occasions it may be a better outcome for consumers if a competition authority were able to act to reduce switching barriers instead of approving the merger. Such actions would not, however, currently be possible within the context of a merger inquiry.

To help inform the analysis of the large amount of survey evidence considered in that case, a summary of the evidence is presented in table 4.6. In particular, note that the results of four separate surveys are reported. The surveys are called respectively Swift 1, ORC, Swift 2, and GfK after the survey companies which undertook them. The first two surveys were addressed toward customers who had recently stopped playing with a provider ("lapsed" customers) while the second two surveys involved current customers.

In terms of the latter pair of surveys, the Swift 2 survey asked consumers directly how they would respond to a 10% price increase[29] while the GfK survey used show-cards to allow consumers to compare hypothetical product offerings. The CC has found that directly asking consumers about what they would do if prices went up by 10% can sometimes lead to results that are difficult to interpret. Show cards can also sometimes produce surprising results. For example, one part of the GfK survey used show-cards and suggested increasing demand schedules!

Surveys aimed at capturing diversion ratios aim to directly estimate the substitution effect between two products. These methods have the merit that they address directly the issue of interest in market definition and make few theoretical assumptions. But they are heavily reliant on good-quality data obtained through high-quality surveys. Survey design in this area remains under development.

Wherever our information on substitution patterns comes from, surveys or demand estimation, we will of course still need to use that information to evaluate the importance of rival products as constraints on price-setting behavior. In section 4.6, we discuss strategies that can be used both quantitatively, when we have good-quality data, but also sometimes qualitatively when we do not. Before we do so we first turn briefly to one additional technique sometimes useful for geographic market definition.

4.5 Using Shipment Data for Geographic Market Definition

Elzinger and Hogarty (1973, 1978)[30] proposed a two-stage test for geographic market definition. The two stages are known respectively as "little out from inside" (LOFI) and "little in from outside" (LIFOUT). Given a candidate market area, the LIFOUT test considers whether nearly all purchases come from within the region itself or whether there are substantial "imports." Analogously, given a candidate market area, the LOFI test considers whether nearly all shipments go to the region itself or whether there are substantial "exports" from the region. Intuitively, import and export activities suggest competitive interconnectivity. LOFI is also sometimes

[29] The Swift 2 survey asked: "If your pools company increased the cost of playing by 10%, what would you do?"

[30] A nice description of the U.S. judicial history in this (and other) areas is provided by Blumenthal et al. (1985). See also Werden (1981, pp. 82–85).

described as the "supply" element of the test, since it relates particularly to the destination of production coming from a candidate area, while LIFOUT is sometimes considered as the "demand" element of the test since it relates to purchases made by consumers in the candidate market area. The overall idea of the combined test (LIFOUT + LOFI) is to expand the candidate market areas until both "supply" and "demand" sides of the test are satisfied in a market area.

To operationalize this test, we must first define what we mean by "little." Elzinga and Hogarty suggested using benchmarks so that if only 25% (or they later suggested 10%) of production in an area is "exports" or "imports," we would consider there to be respectively LOFI or LIFOUT.

To apply the LOFI test, the authors suggest beginning with the largest firm or plant and finding the area where (say) 25% of that plant's shipments goes to. The LOFI test then asks whether

$$\begin{aligned} \text{LOFI} &= 1 - \frac{\text{Shipments from plants in area to inside}}{\text{Production in candidate area}} \\ &= \frac{\text{Exports}}{\text{Production in candidate area}} \leqslant 0.25. \end{aligned}$$

If so, then the LOFI test is met, since "nearly all" of the sales from plants occur within the area. If the test fails, then area must be expanded to find an appropriate area where the test is indeed satisfied. One option is to find the minimum area needed to account for 75% of output from all plants within the previous candidate area. If the expansion of the area does not involve incorporating any new plants, then such a procedure clearly generates an area that will meet the LOFI test. On the other hand, expanding to capture more sales of the set of plants under consideration may sometimes also place additional plants within the candidate market area and we shall return to this observation in a moment.

The LIFOUT test examines the purchase behavior of consumers within a candidate region, asking whether

$$\text{LOFOUT} = 1 - \frac{\text{Purchases by consumers in area}}{\text{Production in candidate area}} \leqslant 0.25.$$

In some contexts, particularly commodity markets, the Elzinga–Hogarty test has been generally well received by government agencies, the courts, and the competition policy academic community over the last thirty years. However, in the late 1990s the test came under renewed scrutiny after the U.S. agencies and state authorities objected to seven out of a total of 900 hospital mergers between 1994 and 2000 and lost all seven of the cases! A number of these cases were lost because the courts accepted the merging parties' application of the Elzinga–Hogarty test using patient flow data.

A period of reflection and retrenchment followed with the Federal Trade Commission (FTC) and Department of Justice (DOJ) undertaking a major exercise of hearings and consultation, summarized in FTC and DOJ (2004).[31] DOJ and FTC concluded that "the Agencies' experience and research indicate that the Elzinga–Hogarty test is not valid or reliable in defining geographic markets in hospital merger cases" (chapter 4, p. 5).

Proponents of the test would no doubt argue that this is in fact a fairly limited conclusion, in particular perhaps noting that DOJ and FTC do not say that Elzinga–Hogarty is not valid and reliable, only that it is not valid and reliable in hospital mergers. However, at least these comments make the hospital context particularly interesting and so we focus on it. In addition, it is difficult to escape the observation that the primary critiques leveled at Elzinga–Hogarty in that context do appear to apply far more widely.

To see how Elzinga–Hogarty was applied in hospital mergers, note that a patient who lives in a candidate market area but who goes to a hospital outside it for treatment is considered to be "importing" hospital services into the candidate area, and is measured as LIFOUT since she is inside the area and purchasing hospital services outside it. On the other hand, a patient who lives outside the candidate area and who comes into the area to the hospital is considered an "export" of services and so is measured as LOFI.

The first critique of the Elzinga and Hogarty test is that existing "flows" of supply or demand need not be informative about market power. In particular, the fact that some consumers currently use hospitals outside the area does not imply that the level of "imports" would increase dramatically if hospitals within the market area increased prices by a small amount. The FTC and DOJ go on to note that patients travel for a number of reasons, including "perceived and actual variations in quality, insurance coverage, out-of-pocket cost, sophistication of services, and family considerations" (chapter 4, p. 8). If so, then the fact that some consumers travel does not immediately imply that those who are currently not traveling are price-sensitive. Capps et al. (2001) call this logical leap the "fallacy of the silent majority."

The second critique noted that if LIFOUT or LOFI fail with a given candidate region, the algorithm involves expanding the region and considering the wider candidate market. However, doing so changes both the set of customers and the set of production facilities (patients and hospitals), so that the LIFOUT and FIFO tests may fail again in the wider region. In some examples, the resulting geographic market can expand without limit.

The bottom line, as with many techniques we examine in this chapter, is that Elzinga and Hogarty's test can provide a useful piece of evidence when coming to a view on the appropriate market definition. However, as the U.S. hospital experience suggests, it may seriously mislead those who apply the test formulaically and we must be clear that we are finding evidence of interconnectivity which may, in particular, be substantively distinct from a lack of market power.

[31] See, in particular, chapter 4 of FTC and DOJ (2004).

4.6 Measuring Pricing Constraints

One way to think about pricing constraints that restrict a firm's ability to increase prices is that they arise directly from competitors who compete in the same market. Firms without competitors do not face pricing constraints, except to the extent that consumers decide not to purchase at all, and therefore will often have a unilateral incentive to increase prices. Turning these observations around suggests that one way to think about market definition is as a set of products which, if a firm were a monopolist, the constraints arising from weaker substitutes outside the market would be insufficient to restrict the monopolist's incentive to increase prices. An antitrust market is then conceived as a collection of products "worth monopolizing." This is the idea encapsulated in the hypothetical monopolist test (HMT). The focus of such tests is typically prices, but in principle they may equally be applied to relevant nonprice terms. That said, price is often the central dimension of short-run competition and so we will often consider whether a hypothetical monopolist has an incentive to implement a small, nontransitory but significant increase in price (SSNIP). In practice, the HMT is often applied quite informally when data or reliable estimates of relevant elasticities are not available. Informally, the HMT plays an important role in providing a helpful (though certainly imperfect) framework for structuring decision making in market definition. Next we provide a more formal description of the HMT test.

4.6.1 The Hypothetical Monopolist Test

The price-based implementation of the HMT, the SSNIP test, is based on the idea that products within a market as a group do not face significant pricing constraints from products outside of the market.[32] Assume a market that includes all brands of still bottled water. The price of batteries is unlikely to exert a price constraint on the price of bottled water and can therefore be rapidly removed from consideration as a candidate for being in the relevant competition policy market. But what about the price of sparkling water? The SSNIP test calculates whether a monopolist of still bottled water could increase prices without losing profits to sparkling water producers. If so, we would conclude that sparkling water is not in the same competition policy market as still water. If not, we would conclude that sparkling water must also be included in the market definition. A profitable monopolist would have to own both still and sparkling water production plants to be able to exercise market power.

[32] We shall inevitably fall into the traditional activity of equating the HMT and SSNIP tests. However, the SSNIP is actually best considered as one particular implementation of an HMT test—one focused on the profitability of price increase. In some industries, advertising or quality competition may be the dominant form of strategic interaction and if so a narrowly focused SSNIP analysis may entirely miss other opportunities for a hypothetical monopolist to "make a market worth monopolizing."

The logic of a market as a collection of products that is "worth monopolizing" suggests that one approach to defining a market in antitrust investigations is to explicitly abstract from pricing constraints arising from competition within a proposed market, i.e., proposing a hypothetical monopoly over a set of products. A market can then be defined as the smallest set of products such that a hypothetical monopolist would have an incentive to increase prices. If we propose a candidate market which is too small, we will have a monopolist who faces a strong substitute outside the proposed market and so who will have no incentive to raise prices.

Thus the hypothetical monopolist test tries to measure whether there is a significant price constraint on a given set of products that comes not from the intra-candidate market competition but from the availability of other products—outside the proposed market definition—that offer viable alternatives to consumers.[33]

To do this, the HMT assumes that all products within the proposed market definition are owned by one single producer which sets each of their prices in an attempt to maximize the total profits derived from them. If the hypothetical monopolist finds it profitable to increase prices, we will have found that constraints from goods outside the proposed market definition are not a sufficient constraint on producers within the market to render a price rise unprofitable. In other words, prices were kept down by the competition within the market. In practice, to operationalize this idea we must, among other things, be a little more precise about exactly what we mean by a "price rise." To that end most jurisdictions apply the "SSNIP" test, which looks at whether a "small but significant nontransitory increase in prices" would be profitable for the hypothetical monopolist. Usually, "small but significant nontransitory" is assumed to mean 5–10% for a year.[34]

4.6.1.1 Decision Making under the HMT

Decision making when using the HMT can be represented by the algorithm represented in figure 4.12.

We start with the narrowest product or geographic market definition which is usually called the "focal product" and actually usually also the focal product of the investigation. We then need to evaluate whether a monopolist of this product could profitably raise prices by 5–10% for a year. If so, that single product will then

[33] A nice treatment of the SSNIP test is provided in the paper by the previous chairman of the U.K. Competition Commission, Professor Paul Geroski, and his coauthor, Professor Rachel Griffith (see Geroski and Griffith 2003).

[34] This "tradition" in the competition policy world is potentially a dangerous one in the sense that in some markets a 5% price rise would correspond to an absolutely enormous increase in profitability. For example, in markets where volumes are high and margins are thin (e.g., 1%), a 5% increase in prices may correspond to a 500% increase in profitability. Relatedly, the consumer welfare losses associated with a 5% increase in prices may in some circumstances (particularly in very large markets) be huge. In such cases, it may be appropriate to worry about monopolization of markets even where monopolization only leads to an ability to increase prices by say 1% or 2%. As always, the key is for the analyst to think seriously about whether there are sufficient grounds for moving away from the normal practice of using 5–10% price increases for this exercise.

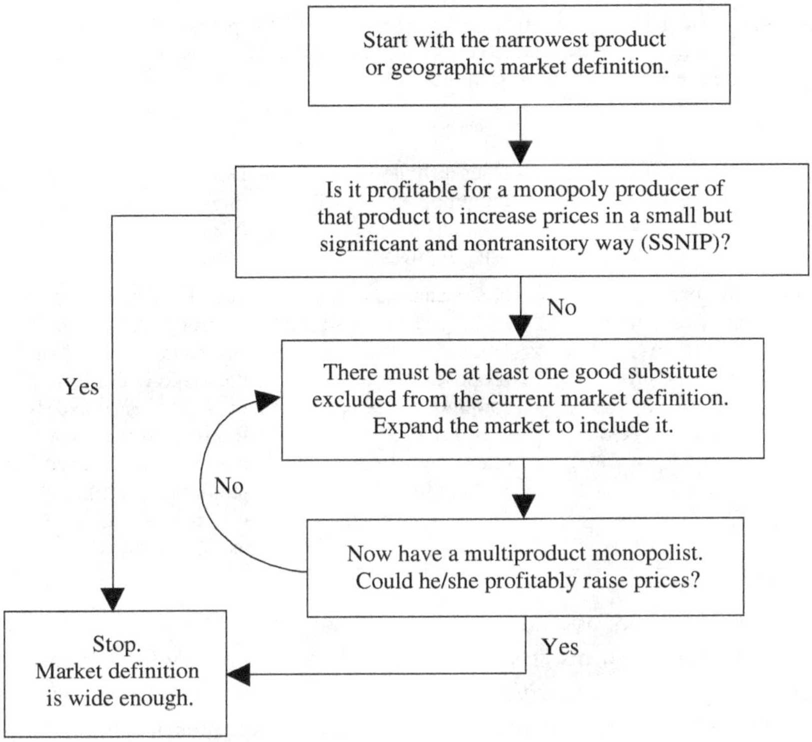

Figure 4.12. The HMT decision tree.

constitute our antitrust market. If not, we must include the "closest" substitute, that product which provides the best alternative to consumers facing the price increase. We then assume again a hypothetical monopolist, this time of each of the products in our newly expanded set of products in our candidate market and we repeat our question, will a 5–10% price increase for a year be profitable? This process continues as long as the answer to the question is "no." A "no" indicates that we are missing at least one good substitute from our current candidate market definition and the omitted product is constraining the profitability of raising prices for our monopolist. We stop the process of adding products when we have a set of products that does indeed allow the hypothetical monopolist to profitably raise prices without losing customers to outside products. We define our antitrust market as the final set of products, the set of products which it is "worth monopolizing."

To illustrate further, suppose we face a situation in which three firms produce three products called, somewhat uninspiringly, products 1, 2, and 3. Each of these products is in fact a very good substitute; for the sake of argument, suppose they are perfect substitutes. Suppose also that there are two other products, products 4 and 5, which are rather poorer substitutes. Product 1 is the focal product. Table 4.7 demonstrates the step-by-step application of the HMT to this case.

Table 4.7. Steps in a hypothetical monopolist test. PMD is proposed market definition.

	Step 1	Step 2	Step 3
PMD	$\{1\}$	$\{1,2\}$	$\{1,2,3\}$
Q	Does monopolization of product 1 give pricing power?	Does a (hypothetical) monopolist of products 1 and 2 have pricing power?	Does a (hypothetical) monopolist of products 1, 2, and 3 have pricing power?
A	No, because there are two perfect substitutes omitted from the proposed market. No ability to raise price of good 1.	No, because there is still a perfect substitute omitted from the proposed market (product 3) that constrains the ability of our hypothetical monopolist of goods 1 and 2 to raise their prices.	Yes, if products 4 and 5 are not good enough substitutes. If so, then the market definition of $\{1,2,3\}$ is accepted. No, if either product 4 or 5 is a good enough substitute to constrain profitability of price increase. In that case, continue the test.

Suppose we did not use the HMT at step 3 but just looked at the pricing power of three independent firms. Those firms would have no pricing power because of constraints that come from *within* the proposed market definition. For example, the firm producing 3 will have no market power because of the presence of producers of goods 1 and 2. Thus the HMT works by explicitly putting the focus on the constraints on pricing power that come from *outside* the proposed market definition.

4.6.1.2 Implementation of the SSNIP Test

The SSNIP test consists of evaluating whether a 5–10% price increase for all the products in the candidate market will produce a profit. Consider the single-product candidate market. Recall that the firm's profits are the total revenues minus the total variable and fixed costs:

$$\Pi(p_t) = (p_t - c)D(p_t) - F,$$

where, for simplicity, we have assumed a constant marginal cost. The change in profits due to an increase in prices from p_0 to p_1 can then be expressed as

$$\Pi(p_1) - \Pi(p_0) = (p_1 - p_0)D(p_1) - (p_0 - c)(D(p_0) - D(p_1)),$$

where the first term of the equality is the gain in revenues from the increase in prices on the sales at p_1 and the second term is the loss of margins due to the decrease in sales after the price hike. The core question is whether the drop in volume of sales at the new price, and consequent loss in variable profit, is big enough to outweigh the increased revenues obtained on goods still sold. This trade-off is shown graphically in figure 4.13.

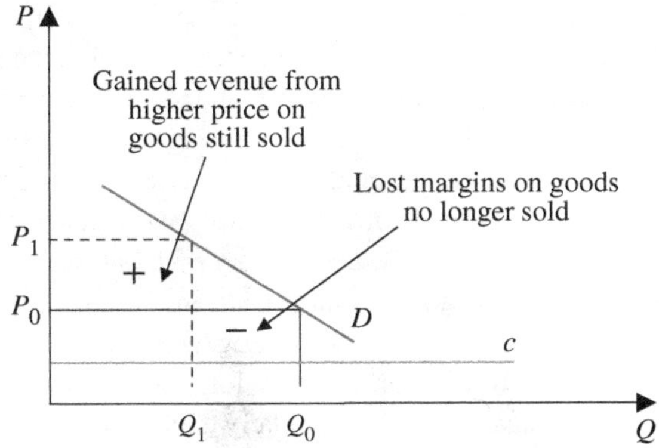

Figure 4.13. The trade-off when evaluating the profitability of a price increase.

Evidently, the crucial assumption of the SSNIP test is that the fall in demand will be large when there are good substitutes available. In fact, we can show that it will be profitable for the monopolist to raise its prices as long as its margin is lower than the inverse of its own-price elasticity of demand.

In our benchmark model, a hypothetical monopolist of a single product in a potentially differentiated product market will solve the profit-maximization problem:

$$\max_{p_1} \Pi(p_1; p_2, \dots, p_J) = \max_{p_1} (p_1 - c) D(p_1, p_2, \dots, p_J).$$

A monopolist of product 1 will increase price as long as it raises their profits, i.e., as long as

$$\begin{aligned}\frac{\partial \Pi(p_1, p_2, \dots, p_J)}{\partial p_1} &= (p_1 - c)\frac{\partial D(p_1, p_2, \dots, p_J)}{\partial p_1} + D(p_1, p_2, \dots, p_J) \\ &\geqslant 0.\end{aligned}$$

We can rearrange the expression to obtain

$$\begin{aligned}\frac{p_1 - c}{p_1} &\leqslant -\frac{D(p_1, p_2, \dots, p_J)}{p_1}\left(\frac{\partial D(p_1, p_2, \dots, p_J)}{\partial p_1}\right)^{-1} \\ &= \frac{1}{\eta_{11}(p_1, p_2, \dots, p_J)}.\end{aligned}$$

We will want to evaluate whether this inequality holds for all prices between p_1^{Comp} and $p_1^{5\%} = 1.05 p_1^{\text{Comp}}$ or $p_1^{10\%} = 1.10 p_1^{\text{Comp}}$ respectively depending on whether we use a 5% or 10% price increase. In this model, the data we need to perform the single-product variant of the SSNIP test are therefore (i) the firms' margin information under competitive conditions and (ii) the product's (candidate market's) own-price elasticity of demand (again in the range $[p_1^{\text{Comp}}, p_1^{5\%}]$ or $[p_1^{\text{Comp}}, p_1^{10\%}]$).[35] For implementation, the important aspect of this single-product variant of the test is that we do not need a full set of cross-price elasticities of demand. The pricing theory analysis of substitutability (usually associated with measuring cross-elasticities) turns into a problem which only involves an evaluation of the own-price elasticity of demand and a comparison of it with variable profit margins. (We will say more shortly.)

A common shortcut for the SSNIP test in geographical market definition is to consider the cost of transporting goods from outside areas into the candidate markets. This relies on the assumption that goods are homogeneous and buyers are indifferent as to the origin of the good. If transport costs are low enough that a price increase by up to 10% by the hypothetical monopolist is likely to be met by an inflow of cheaper product from elsewhere, the candidate market needs to be widened to include the area where the shipped goods are coming from. Evidence on existing shipping activity and transportation costs are therefore often used in practice to determine geographic market definitions.

The purpose of the SSNIP test is to check whether the hypothetical monopolist would find it profitable to increase prices from the competitive level by a material amount (perhaps 5–10%) for a material amount of time (perhaps one year). Note that the reference price for this evaluation is usually described as the "competitive price." This benchmark element of the test is crucial and sometimes it proves problematic as we will illustrate in the next section.

In a formal application of SSNIP we may have an estimate of the marginal cost and also an estimate of a demand curve. This in turn gives us a description of the determinants of profitability so that we can directly evaluate whether

$$\begin{aligned}\Pi(1.05p_1^{\text{Comp}}; p_2, \dots, p_J) - \Pi(p_1^{\text{Comp}}; p_2, \dots, p_J)& \\ = (1.05p_1^{\text{Comp}} - c)D(1.05p_1^{\text{Comp}}, p_2, \dots, p_J)& \\ - (p_1^{\text{Comp}} - c)D(p_1^{\text{Comp}}, p_2, \dots, p_J)& \\ \geqslant 0.&\end{aligned}$$

At this point, we present a brief aside, aiming to note that there is a theoretical underpinning to the observation that the own-price elasticity of demand is informative about substitution opportunities. In fact, we only need for income effects to be small enough to interpret own-price elasticities as the substitution effect. In most fast-moving consumer goods, the income effect will be relatively small, so when we look at the own-price elasticity of demand we are mostly talking about the sum of all the cross-price effects. Looking at own-price elasticity is appropriate when trying to assess the constraint of substitutes as long as we can be confident, as is generally the case, that the income effect is not playing a major role in the decision making.

[35] It will often be very difficult to tell whether the own-price elasticity varies materially in the range, and it is usual to only report a single number estimated using the predicted change in quantity following a 5 or 10% change in prices. Such an elasticity estimated between two given points is also known as an arc-elasticity.

When a function is homogeneous of degree zero, as is the case for an individual's demand function for a product j, we can apply Euler's theorem[36]

$$\sum_{k=1}^{J} p_k \frac{\partial q_j(p,y)}{\partial p_k} + y \frac{\partial q_j(p,y)}{\partial y} = 0.$$

We then obtain

$$\frac{1}{q_j(p,y)}\left[\frac{\partial q_j(p,y)}{\partial \ln p_j} + \sum_{k \neq j} \frac{\partial q_j(p,y)}{\partial \ln p_k} + \frac{\partial q_j(p,y)}{\partial \ln y}\right] = 0,$$

which in turn can be written as

$$\eta_{jj} + \sum_{k \neq j} \eta_{jk} + \eta_{jy} = 0 \quad \text{or} \quad -\eta_{jj} = \sum_{k \neq j} \eta_{jk} + \eta_{jy}.$$

This relationship suggests that the own-price elasticity of demand will be large when either substitution effects are large or the income effect is large. The latter is caused by the fact that the increase in price reduces the customer's real income and their income elasticity is high.

Finally, note that the homogeneity property relies on us doubling the prices of all possible goods in the economy as well as income. In practice, we may treat one good as a composite good consisting of "everything outside the set of goods explicitly considered as potentially within the market," or more simply the "outside good." There will often not be any price data for the outside good, although we could use general price indices as an approximation. Substitution effects can occur to the outside good, so that if we doubled all inside good prices and income we will see that demand for the set of inside goods will fall. If so, then the own-price effects will be larger in magnitude than the sum of the substitution effects (to inside good products) plus the income effect.

More generally, of course, we will want to evaluate whether a price increase for a collection of products is profitable. We discuss this case further in section 4.6.3. First, we consider a particular type of difficulty that often arises—even in a single-product context—when we apply the SSNIP test in practice.

4.6.1.3 *The Cellophane and Reverse-Cellophane Fallacies and Other Difficulties*

The Cellophane Fallacy. In the *U.S. v. DuPont* case in 1956[37] it was crucial to determine whether cellophane ("plastic wrap") represented a market. At that time

---

[36] Assume a function homogeneous of degree r. By definition we have

$$q_j(\lambda p_1, \lambda p_2, \dots, \lambda p_J, \lambda y) = \lambda^r q_j(p_1, p_2, \dots, p_J, y).$$

We obtain Euler's results by differentiating both sides with respect to λ.

[37] *United States v. E. I. DuPont de Nemours & Co.*, 351 US 377 (1956).

DuPont sold 75% of all cellophane paper but only 20% of all "flexible packaging material," a potential alternative market definition. The U.S. Supreme Court ruled in favor of DuPont accepting the appropriate market definition as "flexible packaging material" and clearing the company of attempting to monopolize that market. The reason was that at the prevailing price levels, the court found substantial evidence of demand substitution between cellophane and other packaging materials, such as greaseproof paper.

This case has given rise to the term "cellophane fallacy." The idea is simple. If the Court were looking at evidence from a market which was already monopolized, then the price would already be raised to the point where a number of consumers would already have looked around for imperfect substitutes and indeed switched to them. Furthermore, the remaining customers may substitute away in large numbers if prices were further increased by small amounts since monopolists will always increase prices up to a level where their demand becomes elastic. As long as the demand elasticity is below 1, it is profitable to raise prices and a monopolist would already have done so. This provides a substantive difficulty when defining markets in cartel, monopolization, and sector inquiries using evidence on observed levels of substitution. We will find lots of substitution at monopoly prices and so we will always find markets to be larger than we would if competitive prices were used as the benchmark since prices will have been raised to the point where consumers are considering switching (or quitting). Because this was not understood, the court may have incorrectly determined that greaseproof paper constrained the pricing power of DuPont when selling cellophane (plastic wrap).

The lesson is that it is crucial for the hypothetical monopoly test that we evaluate the profitability of a price increase starting from competitive conditions, i.e., starting with competitive prices and margins. The difficulty is that we may not know what competitive conditions are—and assumptions about the competitive price level will determine the answer for market definition. Specifically, if we determine that actual prices are more than 5% above the unobserved competitive market prices, then we will conclude that our market definition is sufficient and our player is a monopolist. Unfortunately, such an approach would be entirely circular—our assumption would determine our conclusion. There are no easy solutions to this difficulty, but we will describe a range of tools to help determine when observed prices are competitive in chapter 6.

The cellophane fallacy emerges as a central issue only infrequently in merger cases, but nonetheless can arise in at least one guise. Specifically, if in truth the firms are actually monopolists, but there is little substitutability between the products at high prices, then in applying the SSNIP test we may begin the process of looking for other relevant substitutes since raising prices beyond current (monopoly) levels is evaluated to be unprofitable. Fortunately, we will not typically emerge from such a process with a wrong decision even if we end up with a wider market since the competitive effects analysis will usually generate a clearance result—that increasing prices further is unprofitable and hence the merger would be approved under a standard evaluating whether a particular merger will "significantly impede effective competition" (EC (Merger) Regulation no. 139/2004) or result in a "substantial lessening of competition" test (the U.K. Enterprise Act 2003 or Section 7 of the U.S. Clayton Act 1914).[38]

The Reverse Cellophane Fallacy. Froeb and Werden (1992) point out that closely related difficulties can arise when observed prices are below competitive prices. At prices below competitive prices consumers may think the choice between two products is particularly obvious and we may observe little switching between products in response to small variations in relative prices. If so, then we will conclude that markets are narrowly drawn even if, in truth, pricing constraints are severe. Predatory pricing investigations are the most obvious candidates for this difficulty, but it can also arise as an issue in other contexts. For example, observed prices can be "too low" when there are important "menu costs" faced by companies in changing their prices. In the anticipated acquisition of Vernons by Sportech considered by the U.K. Competition Commission in 2007, Sportech had last changed their price in 1999, at which point they had increased their nominal prices by 25%.[39] The evidence suggested that the reason for these infrequent but large price increases was that price changes "disturbed" the customer base and led to consumers switching away from playing the particular gambling product being sold (the football pools). If consumers react to new information by making an explicit evaluation about whether to continue with a particular activity (reoptimizing), whereas in the absence of change they will continue playing, then, as with more traditional menu costs, it may be optimal for the firm to introduce price changes in large discrete amounts infrequently rather than small amounts frequently. The result may be that observed pries are below the competitive level so that firms will appear to have a clear incentive to increase them. The implication for market definition may be that markets are drawn too narrowly in such situations.

The Counterfactual. In merger investigations the central question is often whether the merger will result in an increased ability to raise prices. Often this means we can

---

[38] Note that, more precisely, Section 7 of the Clayton Act 1914 describes that mergers and acquisitions are prohibited where "the effect of such acquisition may be substantially to lessen competition, or tend to create a monopoly." In fact, one of the most important legal words in this sentence is "may," which has meant that the courts have decided that "Section 7 does not require proof that a merger or other acquisition has caused higher prices in the affected market. All that is necessary is that the merger create an appreciable danger of such consequence in the future. A predictive judgement, necessarily probabilistic and judgmental rather than demonstrable, is called for." *Hospital Corp of America v. Federal Trade Commission*, 807 F. 2d 1281, 1389 (7th Cir. 1986). See also *U.S. v. Philadelphia National Bank*, 374 U.S. 321, 362 (1963). In Europe, Article 2(3) of Council Regulation (EC) no. 139/2004 provides that the Commission must assess whether a merger or acquisition "would significantly impede effective competition, in the common market or in a substantial part of it, in particular as a result of the creation or strengthening of a dominant position."

[39] www.mmc.gov.uk/rep_pub/reports/2007/533sportech.htm. See the final report at paragraph 5.6.

use existing pre-merger prices even if some market power is being exercised, since in many jurisdictions the statutory test is whether a merger substantially lessens competition. There are, however, occasions where parties debate the right price to use. For example, in the Sportech/Vernons merger inquiry the parties raised prices by 25% during the inquiry (beginning the process of rolling out the price increases in August 2007) and argued that the SSNIP test should be applied at the new higher price level. Their reasoning was that the price increase was (i) proposed before the acquisition and moreover (ii) was not in any event contingent on the merger being approved. For each reason they argued the relevant benchmark from which to perform the SSNIP test should involve prices after the 25% increase. The first argument implies the relevant pre-merger price includes the 25% increase. The second argument implies that competitive prices should be considered not as pre-merger prices but rather as those prices that would prevail in the future, absent the merger. Obviously, such arguments need to be treated with great caution by competition authorities. In this case documentary evidence traced the proposal to the price increase back to August 2006, but even this was not clearly before the acquisition was under serious contemplation so that the evidence did not clearly support this view. On the second point, in August 2007, Sportech actively began rolling out the 25% price increase to their customers (who may sign up to play the football pools once a week for say eight or ten weeks so that price increases bind only on the renewal of a multiweek contract) potentially indicating that it would go ahead irrespective of the merger. Even so, in this case, the CC did not consider this evidence as entirely convincing as, for example, a price increase could be reversed if the merger were in fact blocked.

To summarize, if competitive conditions are not observed, then competitive prices and margins will sometimes need to be chosen or estimated. In cartel cases or sector/market investigations a simple analysis which, for instance, considered that competitive prices are 5% below the current level would automatically imply a market definition (increasing prices by 5% would be profitable). In chapter 6, we will consider how this problem can be addressed so that we can predict what prices would look like under competition even if the data were generated under a monopoly. Doing so will involve building a model either explicitly or implicitly of price-setting behavior in the industry and in particular how it would change if we changed market structure. Less formally, the tools we discuss in chapter 5 may well also be helpful for this purpose.

4.6.2 Critical Loss Analysis

Critical loss analysis[40] is conceptually closely related to the hypothetical monopolist test. It also uses information about demand and in particular the own-price elastic-

[40]This section draws on Harris and Simons (1989) and also the working papers by O'Brien and Wickelgren (2003) and by Katz and Shapiro (2003).

ity of demand to make inferences about the price constraint exerted by substitute products. The question asked in critical loss analysis is the following: How much do sales need to drop in order to render an $x\%$ price increase unprofitable? In the context of a benchmark homogeneous product model, this question is answered by the following formula:

$$\%\,\text{Critical loss} = 100 \times \frac{\%\Delta\text{Prices}}{\%\Delta\text{Prices} + \%\,\text{Initial margin}}.$$

To derive this critical loss formula, one needs to calculate the demand after the price increase $D(p_1)$ such that given the original demand $D(p_0)$, the original price p_0, and the higher price p_1 we have

$$\Pi(p_1) - \Pi(p_0) = (p_1 - p_0)D(p_1) - (p_0 - c)(D(p_0) - D(p_1)) = 0.$$

Rearranging we obtain

$$\begin{aligned}(p_1 - p_0)[D(p_1) - D(p_0) + D(p_0)] - (p_0 - c)(D(p_0) - D(p_1)) &= 0,\\ (p_1 - p_0 + (p_0 - c))(D(p_1) - D(p_0)) + D(p_0)(p_1 - p_0) &= 0,\\ \frac{D(p_1) - D(p_0)}{D(p_0)} = -\frac{p_1 - p_0}{p_0} \bigg/ \left(\frac{p_1 - p_0}{p_0} + \frac{p_0 - c}{p_0}\right)&.\end{aligned}$$

This is equivalent to

$$\%\,\text{Critical loss} = \frac{100 \times \%\Delta\text{Prices}}{\%\Delta\text{Prices} + \%\,\text{Initial margin}}.$$

To illustrate the use of this formula, consider a 5% increase in prices in a market where the margin at current prices is 60%:

$$\begin{aligned}\%\,\text{Critical loss} &= \frac{100 \times \%\Delta\text{Prices}}{\%\Delta\text{Prices} + \%\,\text{Initial margin}}\\ &= \frac{100 \times 5\%}{5\% + 60\%}\\ &= 7.7\%.\end{aligned}$$

If the quantity demanded falls by more than 7.7% following the 5% price increase, the price increase is not profitable and our candidate market must be expanded.

At least three issues commonly emerge in applying a critical loss test. First, the fact that a 5% price increase is not profitable does not mean that a 50% price increase is not profitable. Yet, we are interested in market power and would clearly wish to draw narrow market boundaries if we found that a hypothetical monopolist could raise prices by 50%.

Second, parties will often argue that the critical loss is likely to be far smaller than the drop in sales that would actually be experienced by a 5% price increase

Table 4.8. Critical loss calculations for various margins using a 5% price increase.

Margin	40%	75%	90%
Critical loss	11.1%	6.3%	5.3%

and therefore a 5% price increase would be unprofitable. When accepting evidence of actual sales declines following price increases, agencies need to be careful about the potential endogeneity of price and sales changes.

Third, when considering critical loss calculations, it is very important to bear in mind that if pre-merger margins are high, i.e., if $(p_0 - c)/p_0$ is big, each unit less of sales is associated with a large fall in profits and so we will get a critical loss in sales that is small. To illustrate, in the case of a 5% price increase we obtain the values for the critical loss shown in table 4.8.

This issue is related to the cellophane fallacy because if the margin is high, it means market power is probably already being exercised and so one must be careful to rely on the effect of price changes on an already supra-competitive price level when drawing conclusions about substitutability and market definition. If the firm has market power, it will increase price up to the point where margins are high and therefore the critical loss appears small.

The "fallacy" in this analysis is to treat the elasticity and the margin as if they were independent from each other. In fact, according to the benchmark model, margins tell us about the own-price elasticity before the price increase. If margins are high, it implies a low price elasticity and that in turn suggests perhaps even strongly there will be low actual losses due to a price increase. Firms sometimes argue that because their critical loss is small, their actual loss is probably bigger and the market should be large. Such arguments should not be accepted uncritically, but rather parties should be pressed to explain why they would have a low elasticity of demand evidenced by the high margins and relatively large actual losses of demand following a price increase.

More generally, this is one example of a tension between the pieces of "data" (the margin and the likely actual loss resulting from a price rise) and the model—which states the Lerner index is inversely related to the own-price elasticity of demand. Whenever a model and our pieces of data are difficult to reconcile, we will want to question each. The apparent tensions may be reconciled by the finding that one or more pieces of data are "wrong," or alternatively that the data are right but the benchmark model is not the correct one for this industry. It is very important to note that the exact form of the critical loss formula depends explicitly on the monopoly model being used to characterize the industry. Thus, table 4.8 captures the results only of one particular type of critical loss exercise.

Finally, we note that it is possible, and sometimes appropriate, to undertake critical loss analysis in terms of product characteristics other than price. For example, in the Sportech/Vernons merger, Sportech's advisors presented a critical loss analysis evaluating whether it would be profitable to reduce the quality of the gambling product being sold, in particular the size of the jackpot paid out to the winner and, relatedly, the fraction of the total "pool" of bets paid out as prizes.[41]

4.6.3 SSNIP Test with Differentiated Products

The SSNIP test discussed above, as well as the critical loss analysis, was presented for a single-product candidate market. In practice, we will often need to undertake, formally or informally, a SSNIP test in a multiproduct context.

To do so we must make a number of decisions. For instance, we must consider whether a hypothetical monopolist of our candidate collection of products has an incentive to materially increase prices, and we usually assume we mean a 5% price increase of all the prices within the candidate market. On the other hand, it may not be appropriate to always increase all the product's prices by 5% since the central element of the SSNIP test is to consider whether material price increases are profitable given a monopoly over a set of candidate products and it will not always, or even usually in fact, be profit maximizing to apply an equal percentage price increase to all products. A merger authority may decide that a material price increase is in fact only 1% when investigating the impact of a particular inquiry or that price increases may occur unevenly.

In a multiproduct context, the simplest approach is to assume that all goods inside the market are effectively perfect substitutes. In that case, there is just one relevant price so that the SSNIP test boils down to evaluating whether or not the candidate market's own-price elasticity is sufficiently high to render a 5% price increase unprofitable. For example, when considering whether the right market for eggs is "free-range" or should be expanded to include "organic," a reasonable approach is to examine the own-price elasticity of (candidate market) demand faced by a hypothetical monopolist for free-range eggs. Doing so would of course be far simpler than worrying about a monopoly price for all the many different variants of free-range eggs, even though there is in fact some modest amount of branding of eggs. If such an approximation is not appropriate in the context being investigated, then SSNIP can be applied more formally in a variety of ways.

Denoting the candidate market demand elasticity as $\eta^{M_1}(p_1; p_2, \dots, p_J)$ we evaluate whether

$$\frac{p_1 - c}{p_1} \leqslant \frac{1}{\eta^{M_1}(p_1, p_2, \dots, p_J)}$$

in the range between p_1^{Comp} and $p_1^{5\%} = 1.05p_1^{\text{Comp}}$ (or, in practice, usually just at $p_1^{5\%}$) holding the prices of all products outside the candidate market $(p_2, \dots, p_J)$

[41] See the U.K. Competition Commission's report Sportech/Vernons (2007) and in particular Appendix F to the final report, paragraphs 32–38 and Annex 1, where the analogous formulas are derived, given a set of assumptions about the ways in which jackpots were related to profits. The report is available at www.competition-commission.org.uk/rep_pub/reports/2007/fulltext/533af.pdf.

as fixed:

$$\frac{p_1 - c}{p_1} \leqslant \frac{1}{\eta^{M_1}(p_1, p_2, \dots, p_J)}.$$

As always, if the elasticity is very low, there will be an incentive to increase prices. In such a case, our approximation assumes that products within the candidate market are homogeneous so that there is a single price and candidate market demand function and corresponding elasticity so that

$$\eta^{M_1}(p_1, p_2, \dots, p_J) = \frac{\partial \ln D^{M_1}(p_1, p_2, \dots, p_J)}{\partial \ln p_1}.$$

In fact, many markets will include differentiated products and given enough data we will perhaps be able to pay attention (formally or informally) to the pattern of substitution within the candidate group of products when determining whether a general price increase for the group is profitable for the hypothetical monopolist.

A formal approach to this problem in a multiproduct context involves more data and takes us some way toward a full merger simulation model. We will show that for market definition purposes we will not normally need to undertake a full merger simulation, but even so it is very useful to understand the deep interconnections between the SSNIP test in a multiproduct context and a full merger simulation model. Merger simulation is a large topic in itself and we discuss it extensively in chapter 8 while this section provides an introduction to that chapter. In section 4.6.4 we outline the full equilibrium relevant market test (FERM) proposed in the 1984 U.S. guidelines and recently implemented by Ivaldi and Lorincz (2009), which is far closer to undertaking a full merger simulation exercise and then "backing out" a market definition. Finally, in section 4.6.5 we discuss the use of "residual" demand functions (following Baker and Bresnahan (1985, 1988)) for market definition in multiproduct contexts.

4.6.3.1 *Multiproduct Profit Maximization*

Consider a candidate market has been proposed which includes several differentiated products. We will consider whether a hypothetical monopolist will have an incentive to increase the prices of all products in the defined market. To begin with we consider the candidate market consisting of the two products and look at the profitability of a price increase in one of the products. We assume our hypothetical monopolist chooses prices to maximize profits holding fixed the prices of those goods outside the candidate market:

$$\max_{(p_1, p_2)} \Pi(p_1, p_2; p_3, \dots, p_J),$$

where

$$\begin{aligned} \Pi(p_1, p_2; p_3, \dots, p_J) \\ &= (p_1 - c_1) D_1(p_1, p_2, p_3, \dots, p_J) \\ &\quad + (p_2 - c_2) D_2(p_1, p_2, p_3, \dots, p_J). \end{aligned}$$

The hypothetical monopolist will find increasing the price of good 1 profitable whenever

$$\frac{\partial \Pi(p_1, p_2; p_3, \dots, p_J)}{\partial p_1} \geqslant 0,$$

i.e.,

$$(p_1 - c_1)\frac{\partial D_1(p_1, p_2, \dots, p_J)}{\partial p_1} + D_1(p_1, p_2, \dots, p_J) + (p_2 - c_2)\frac{\partial D_2(p_1, p_2, \dots, p_J)}{\partial p_1} \geqslant 0.$$

The last term of the inequality represents the reinforcing effect of the increase of the price p_1 on the demand for good 2. While independent producers of products 1 and 2 would ignore these cross-product effects, a multiproduct firm (or here our hypothetical monopolist) would recognize the loss of sales of product 1, but treat those customers that depart completely rather differently from those who were only lost to product 2. In particular, she would take into account the revenue that arises from consumers switching from good 1 to become purchasers of good 2. If goods 1 and 2 are substitutes, the derivative in this last term is positive. For that reason, our hypothetical monopolist will want to increase price p_1 compared with the price that would be set by a firm who only owned product 1.

If goods 1 and 2 are demand substitutes, a hypothetical monopolist will also have an incentive to increase p_2 when p_1 increases.

In chapter 1 we established the general result that the slope of a firm's reaction function (i.e., the profit-maximizing choice of action given the action(s) of rival firm(s)) depends on the sign of the cross-partial derivative of the firm's profit function. Formally, that means the profit-maximizing choice of p_2 will increase as p_1 increases if

$$\frac{\partial^2 \Pi(p_1, p_2; p_3, \dots, p_J)}{\partial p_2 \partial p_1} = \frac{\partial}{\partial p_2}\left(\frac{\partial \Pi(p_1, p_2; p_3, \dots, p_J)}{\partial p_1}\right) \geqslant 0.$$

This in turn will give a boost to the profitability of increasing p_1 if

$$\frac{\partial^2 \Pi(p_1, p_2; p_3, \dots, p_J)}{\partial p_1 \partial p_2} = \frac{\partial}{\partial p_1}\left(\frac{\partial \Pi(p_1, p_2; p_3, \dots, p_J)}{\partial p_2}\right) \geqslant 0.$$

Since the cross derivatives do not depend on the order of differentiation, either both of these derivatives will be positive or neither will be. We showed that in differentiated product pricing games, these cross derivatives depended crucially on whether goods were substitutes or complements. Specifically, when goods 1 and 2 are substitutes, a price increase of good 1 will result in firm 2 having an incentive to increase the price of good 2 and this in turn will generate an incentive for a further price increase for 1. These mutually reinforcing effects continue but in ever smaller amounts until we find the new higher prices for both goods.

In practice, assessing the profitability of an increase in the price of each of the products in the market will require information on the own-price elasticity, the diversion ratios (DRs), relative prices, and the margins on both products. In fact, the first-order conditions for profit maximization suggest that increasing prices will be profitable if

$$\frac{p_1 - c_1}{p_1} \leqslant \frac{1}{\eta_{11}(p_1, p_2, \ldots, p_J)} + \frac{p_2 - c_2}{p_1}\mathrm{DR}_{12}$$

and analogously the price increase for product 2 will be profitable if

$$\frac{p_2 - c_2}{p_2} \leqslant \frac{1}{\eta_{22}(p_1, p_2, \ldots, p_J)} + \frac{p_2 - c_2}{p_1}\mathrm{DR}_{21}.$$

Merger guidance in most jurisdictions suggests it will often be appropriate to apply these formulas using the prices

$$p_1 = p_1^{5\%} \equiv 1.05 p_1^{\mathrm{Comp}} \quad \text{and} \quad p_2 = p_2^{5\%} \equiv 1.05 p_2^{\mathrm{Comp}}$$

in order to examine whether it is profitable to increase p_1 and p_2 by 5% above the competitive levels (or more precisely, since these are first-order conditions, to evaluate whether it is profitable to undertake a further (tiny) price increase when prices are 5% above the competitive level). Note that terms like $(p_2 - c_2)/p_1$ can be written as the product of a margin times relative prices,

$$\frac{p_2 - c_2}{p_1} = \frac{p_2 - c_2}{p_2}\frac{p_2}{p_1}.$$

For completeness we note that above formula is derived as follows. Denote $p = (p_1, \ldots, p_J)$, then the first-order condition for profit maximization when setting the price of good 1 states that p_1 should be increased when

$$(p_1 - c_1)\frac{\partial D_1(p)}{\partial p_1} + D_1(p) + (p_2 - c_2)\frac{\partial D_2(p)}{\partial p_1} \geqslant 0.$$

Rearranging:

$$(p_1 - c_1) + \frac{D_1(p)}{\partial D_1(p)/\partial p_1} + (p_2 - c_2)\frac{\partial D_2(p)/\partial p_1}{\partial D_1(p)/\partial p_1} \leqslant 0,$$

where the inequality changes direction because

$$\frac{\partial D_1(p)}{\partial p_1} < 0.$$

Dividing through by p_1 and using the definition of the diversion ratio gives

$$\frac{p_1 - c_1}{p_1} + \frac{1}{\partial \ln D_1(p)/\partial \ln p_1} - \frac{p_2 - c_2}{p_1}\mathrm{DR}_{12} \leqslant 0,$$

where the analogous formula can easily be written down for good 2.

Table 4.9. Example calculation for multiproduct application of the SSNIP test.

	Product 1	Product 2
Margin	10%	20%
Diversion ratio	0.29	0.5
|Own-price elasticity of demand|	2	4
Ratio of prices p_2/p_1	1	1

Profitability calculation:

$$\frac{p_1 - c_1}{p1} \overset{?}{\leqslant} \frac{1}{\eta_{11}(p_1, p_2, \ldots, p_J)} + \frac{p_2 - c_2}{p_2}\frac{p_2}{p_1}\mathrm{DR}_{12}, \quad 0.1 \leqslant \frac{1}{2} + 0.2 \times 1 \times 0.29 = 0.56$$

$$\frac{p_2 - c_2}{p1} \overset{?}{\leqslant} \frac{1}{\eta_{22}(p_1, p_2, \ldots, p_J)} + \frac{p_1 - c_1}{p_1}\frac{p_1}{p_2}\mathrm{DR}_{21}, \quad 0.2 \leqslant \frac{1}{4} + 0.1 \times 1 \times 0.5 = 0.30$$

Note that this test in a two-product candidate market requires estimates of margins, price elasticities and diversion ratios. While precise estimates of such information are always difficult to obtain, it is not always impossible—so that this formula can actively be applied in practical settings in order to help understand the incentives of multiproduct hypothetical monopolists. An example of such application is given in table 4.9.

4.6.3.2 Implementation of the Test with More than Two Products (Merger Simulation)

The SSNIP can formally be applied in a general multiproduct context.[42] To do so, we wish to evaluate whether monopolistic profits could be derived from goods in a candidate market by a hypothetical monopolist. That is, we must effectively attempt to evaluate profitability under competitive prices and then compare it with the profits that would be generated if prices of all goods in the inside markets were increased by a SSNIP amount, which generally means between 5 and 10% for a period of about a year. If the price increase is profitable, the candidate market is declared a relevant competition policy market.

Formally, suppose we define $(\bar{p}_1, \ldots, \bar{p}_M)$ are the competitive prices of goods in a candidate market, consisting of the set of products, $\Im_M$. A SSNIP test considers whether a price increase to $((1+\kappa)\bar{p}_1, \ldots, (1+\kappa)\bar{p}_M)$, where $(1+\kappa) = 1.05$ or 1.10 would be profitable for a hypothetical monopolist of those goods. Given the

[42] This section draws upon the mathematical formalization of the SSNIP test presented in Ivaldi and Lorincz (2005). A modified version of the paper is found in Ivaldi and Lorincz (2009). We discuss this interesting paper further in a section below. For now we note that not all practitioners would agree that this definition is the right definition of a SSNIP test. For example, as we discuss below, in some circumstances it may be appropriate to allow price increases which are not uniformly all 5% above the competitive price.

profit function for the hypothetical monopolist of that set of products,

$$\pi(\bar{p}_1, \ldots, \bar{p}_J) = \sum_{j \in \Im_J} (\bar{p}_j - c) D(\bar{p}_1, \ldots, \bar{p}_M, \ldots, \bar{p}_J),$$

it is easy to evaluate whether the change in prices is profitable by asking whether

$$\begin{aligned}\Delta\pi &= \pi((1+\kappa)\bar{p}_1, \ldots, (1+\kappa)\bar{p}_M, \bar{p}_{M+1}, \ldots, \bar{p}_J) - \pi(\bar{p}_1, \ldots, \bar{p}_J) \\ &\geqslant 0.\end{aligned}$$

The SSNIP market will be the smallest set of products, $\Im_M$, such that a price increase is profitable.

Analytically, we can evaluate whether the directional derivative is positive, i.e., whether

$$\frac{\partial \pi((1+\kappa)\bar{p}_1, \ldots, (1+\kappa)\bar{p}_M, \bar{p}_{M+1}, \ldots, \bar{p}_J)}{\partial \kappa} \geqslant 0.$$

Implementing the hypothetical monopolist test with multiple products involves having knowledge of pre-merger marginal costs and prices of goods inside and outside the hypothetical monopoly. This exercise can be undertaken using merger simulation models, which will be discussed in chapter 8. A nice example of the kinds of issues which emerge when doing so is provided by Brenkers and Verboven (2005). In that paper, the authors used a multiple-product SSNIP test to define market in the retail automobile industry. They find that the markets that are defined using the SSNIP test do not correspond to those described by the Standard Industry Classification (SIC).

The SSNIP test assumes that the prices of the goods outside of the hypothetical monopoly stay constant following the price increase. In fact, if the goods are related they are likely to react to the change in prices. The next section examines the implications of relaxing this assumption.

4.6.4 The Full Equilibrium Relevant Market Test

The full equilibrium relevant market test (FERM), as proposed by the 1984 U.S. Horizontal Merger Guidelines, is an alternative implementation of the hypothetical monopolist test (HMT) to the traditional SSNIP test. The idea is based on the observation that the SSNIP test is not an equilibrium test in the sense that it does not compare two situations in equilibrium and therefore it does not compare two situations that would actually be found in the real world. To see why, note that the SSNIP test supposes that a monopolist of a candidate market considers the profitability of a unilateral price increase *assuming no reaction to the price increase by producers of goods outside the candidate market.* In contrast, the FERM allows the goods outside the candidate market to respond by changing their prices so we move to a new "equilibrium" set of prices for all products being sold, but where prices inside the candidate market are set by the hypothetical monopolist.[43]

Under FERM there will be a tendency to get narrower markets than under SSNIP because price increases by the hypothetical monopolist will generally be followed by price increases of substitutes outside the candidate market. These in turn will tend to reinforce the profitability of the initial price increase and hence push us toward narrower market definitions. Notice that the question of whether to hold fixed competitive variables, such as price or quantity of those goods which are outside the candidate market, is related to the question of whether to account for supply substitution in market definition. When considering the constraint imposed by supply substitution parties often argue that expansion of output by firms outside the candidate market will defeat an attempted price increase. Parties argue that the implication is that the market definition should be expanded to include other products. In contrast, in a pricing game reactions by firms outside the market will tend to reinforce price increases by the hypothetical monopolist because firms tend to react to price increases by increasing their own prices, i.e., by restricting their supply.

The example below from Ivaldi and Lorincz (2009) illustrates the effect of allowing producers inside and outside the candidate market definition to react to a price increase by the hypothetical monopolist consisting of all products sold inside the candidate market using data from the market for computer servers. The mechanics of applying the test are identical to the tools used in merger simulation, a topic we discuss extensively in chapter 8. Consequently, here, we restrict ourselves to reporting Ivaldi and Lorincz's results.

Table 4.10 reports the results from applying the traditional SSNIP test to a model estimated using data on computer servers from Europe. It applies the test using a 10% price increase. Under the SSNIP test, a market for computer servers in the range of €0–€2,000 is rejected because an attempt to increase prices by 10% in that segment alone is estimated to be unprofitable. On the other hand, the SSNIP applied to all servers priced between €0 and €4,000 does find it profitable to increase all prices by 10%. Hence the SSNIP test suggests that there is a competition policy market for relatively low-end computers, specifically the set of servers priced between €0 and €4,000. In addition the results also suggest there is a mid-range market for computers between €4,000 and €10,000 servers and a high-end market for computers above €10,000.

Table 4.11 reports the analogous results applying the FERM test for market definition. In doing so, Ivaldi and Lorincz obtain the same results for the competition policy market definition for low-end computer servers but the mid range market is

[43] For a detailed description of this method, see Ivaldi and Lorincz (2005) and the revised version Ivaldi and Lorincz (2009). The former paper introduces the nicely descriptive name FERM. The latter drops that name in favor of US84. We adopt the more descriptive term FERM.

Table 4.10. SSNIP test in the market for servers.

Lower price limit ($)	Upper price limit ($)	Number of products	% Change in profits ($\Delta\pi_M^{\text{SSNIP}}$)
0	2,000	27	−1.2
0	3,000	55	−1.5
0	4,000	123	1.7
4,000	5,000	58	−5.6
4,000	6,000	112	−2.1
4,000	7,000	134	−2.0
4,000	8,000	166	−1.2
4,000	9,000	191	−0.3
4,000	10,000	229	2.6
10,000	12,000	21	−24.7
⋮	⋮	⋮	⋮
10,000	1,000,000	272	−10.1

Source: Ivaldi and Lorincz (2009).

split in two. Specifically they obtain one market for the €4,000–€6,000 range and one for the €6,000–€10,000 range.

In a conventional application of the SSNIP test all prices are increased proportionately. In contrast in a FERM test the hypothetical monopolist sets prices of the subset of goods in the candidate market to maximize profits. That means that all prices may increase by differing amounts. The SSNIP test may be applied similarly, but alternatively, to address this concern, the authors propose basing their market definition choice on the average percentage change in prices within the candidate set of products when that set of products switches from competitive (initial equilibrium) to the partially collusive equilibrium in which all prices are reset by the hypothetical monopolist. Their application of the test then defines the set of products as being a market when the average percentage change in prices is above 10%.

4.6.5 The Residual Demand Function Approach (To Market Power)

A related approach is that proposed by Scheffman and Spiller (1987) for homogeneous product markets and Baker and Bresnahan (1985, 1988) for differentiated product markets. The approach is known as the residual demand function approach and can be useful for evaluating the extent of market power or market definition in some particular circumstances. However, these models are explicitly *not* implementing a standard SSNIP test so that the results need not correspond to conclusions that would be drawn from SSNIP tests even if the assumptions on which they rely are correct. On the other hand, since these methods can be useful for evaluating

Table 4.11. FERM test in the market of servers.

Lower price limit (\$)	Upper price limit (\$)	Number of products	% Average price change (Δp_M)
0	2,000	27	4.3
0	3,000	55	7.6
0	4,000	123	2.1
4,000	5,000	58	5.1
4,000	6,000	112	11.0
6,000	7,000	22	0.2
⋮	⋮	⋮	⋮
6,000	300,000	357	9.8
6,000	400,000	365	10.4
400,000	500,000	9	0.004
⋮	⋮	⋮	⋮
400,000	1,000,000	24	0.2

Source: Ivaldi and Lorincz (2009).

the market power of firms, the residual demand approach can be used for market definition in a fashion not unrelated to the FERM test. To see why, we first recall the notion of a residual demand curve.

First, following Landes and Posner (1981) and Scheffman and Spiller (1987) consider the dominant-firm model. In that model, the dominant firm faced a market demand $D^{\text{Market}}(p)$ and also a competitive fringe, acting as price-takers, who are willing to supply an amount based on the price being offered in the market, $S^{\text{Fringe}}(p)$. The residual demand is then that which is left to the dominant firm after the fringe has supplied any units they are willing to supply at that price,

$$D^{\text{Dominant}}(p) = D^{\text{Market}}(p) - S^{\text{Fringe}}(p).$$

We showed in chapter 1, that the dominant firm's price elasticity of demand is

$$\eta_{\text{Demand}}^{\text{Dominant}} = \frac{1}{\text{Share}^{\text{Dom}}}(\eta_{\text{Demand}}^{\text{Market}} - \text{Share}^{\text{Fringe}} \times \eta_{\text{Supply}}^{\text{Fringe}}).$$

This is the residual elasticity of demand, which begins with the market elasticity of demand and then adjusts it to take into account any supply adjustment from the competitive fringe. Note that the residual elasticity of demand typically increases in magnitude with the elasticity of market demand since $\eta_{\text{Demand}}^{\text{Market}} < 0$ and also the elasticity of supply from the fringe since $\eta_{\text{Supply}}^{\text{Fringe}} > 0$.[44] Having subsumed the

[44] Note that when examining residual demand in this way we are incorporating supply substitution from the fringe into our analysis.

supply response of the competitive fringe into a careful definition of the firm's demand function (as distinct from the market demand function), we can then use our standard monopoly pricing formula to conclude that a dominant firm would want to raise price so long as her margins are smaller than the inverse of the elasticity of this "residual" demand elasticity.

The insight of the residual demand function approach is that the residual demand function captures all of the relevant information about the constraint implied by other firms and expresses it in terms of the residual demand elasticity. Specifically, in considering the profitability of price rises for any firm (which for this example and without loss of generality we shall call firm 1) we can substitute the prices $(p_2, \dots, p_J)$ with their equilibrium formula so that the calculation is effectively about the partial residual demand curve elasticity. Firm 1 has an ability to raise prices as long as

$$\frac{p_1 - \text{mc}_1}{p_1} \leqslant \frac{1}{\eta_{11}^{\text{Resid}}}.$$

Notice this is a starkly different calculation from using the SSNIP test for a single-product candidate market definition which would evaluate the candidate market of a single product by considering instead whether

$$\frac{p_1 - \text{mc}_1}{p_1} \leqslant \frac{1}{\eta_{11}}$$

holding the prices of other goods fixed. For a derivation of the residual elasticity and a more technical presentation, see section 4.6.6 below.

Such an analysis clearly provides us with information regarding the actual market power of our dominant firm and, in particular, would suggest that those dominant firms facing a competitive fringe with a high supply elasticity are unlikely to have much pricing power. On the other hand, this analysis does not apply a SSNIP to any candidate market (or at least not one as conventionally applied). To see why, note that a SSNIP applied to the candidate market, "the dominant firm," would ordinarily hold constant the price being charged by rival suppliers, whereas by definition here we have assumed a single price to derive the dominant firm's demand curve and in particular we have assumed that if the dominant firm raises its price, then the competitive suppliers also face a raised price so that the prices of firms "outside" the candidate market (dominant firm) are not held fixed. Similarly, the analysis does not correspond to a SSNIP test on the candidate market consisting of the dominant firm plus the competitive fringe since in that case we would use the (market) demand curve, $D^{\text{Market}}(p)$. On the other hand, the approach is far closer to that suggested by the authors of the FERM approach to market definition. That approach explicitly takes into account reactions by competitors outside the candidate market. One could use the residual demand curve approach for market definition testing a candidate market consisting of a dominant firm alone against the alternative hypothesis of the dominant firm plus the competitive fringe. A high supply elasticity from the fringe would suggest that the competition policy market is wider than the output of only the dominant firm. As we discussed when considering the FERM test, the fact that we allow prices of goods outside the candidate market to rise will tend to reinforce the profitability of price rises within a candidate market. As a result, when applied using differentiated product price competition, this approach appears likely to result in markets which are more narrowly drawn than would typically emerge from a traditional SSNIP analysis.

4.6.6 Residual Demands with Differentiated Products

Baker and Bresnahan (1985) suggest that the residual demand function approach can be used to evaluate market power in markets where differentiated products are produced. Specifically, they consider the following linear-in-parameters differentiated product demand system:

$$\begin{aligned}
\ln q_1 &= \eta_{10} + \eta_{11} \ln p_1 + \eta_{12} \ln p_2 + \eta_{13} \ln p_3 + \cdots \\
&\qquad + \eta_{1J} \ln p_J + x_1' \beta_1 + \xi_1, \\
\ln q_2 &= \eta_{20} + \eta_{21} \ln p_1 + \eta_{22} \ln p_2 + \eta_{23} \ln p_3 + \cdots \\
&\qquad + \eta_{2J} \ln p_J + x_2' \beta_2 + \xi_2, \\
&\vdots \\
\ln q_J &= \eta_{J0} + \eta_{J1} \ln p_1 + \eta_{J2} \ln p_2 + \eta_{J3} \ln p_3 + \cdots \\
&\qquad + \eta_{JJ} \ln p_J + x_J' \beta_J + \xi_J,
\end{aligned}$$

where $x_1', x_2', \dots, x_J'$ are each respectively vectors of demand shifters for each equation, $\beta = (\beta_1, \dots, \beta_J)$, while $p = (p_1, \dots, p_J)$ denote prices and $q = (q_1, \dots, q_J)$ denote quantities of each of the goods indexed $j = 1, \dots, J$. In this isoelastic demand system η is a $J \times J$ matrix of J^2 parameters capturing the own- and cross-price elasticities of demand in this system of equations.

To illustrate the idea, let us suppose that firms produce single products, face a constant (in output) marginal cost and choose price to maximize profit

$$\max_{p_j} (p_j - \text{mc}_j(w_j; \gamma)) D_j(p_1, \dots, p_J, x_j, \xi_j)$$

so that we obtain a pricing (supply) equation for each product which depends on the prices of all products in the market by examining the first-order conditions from the firms' profit-maximization problem:

$$(p_j - \text{mc}_j(w_j; \gamma)) \frac{\partial D_j(p_1, \dots, p_J; x_j, \xi_j, \eta, \beta)}{\partial p_j} + D(p_1, \dots, p_J; x_j, \eta, \beta) = 0$$

for $j = 1, \dots, J$, where w_j are the marginal cost (supply) shifters of product j and γ is the vector of parameters in the marginal cost function. We may solve each equation so that the jth equation is solved for the jth price, giving each firm's reaction function:

$$\ln p_j = g_j(p_1, \dots, p_{j-1}, p_{j+1}, \dots, p_J; x_j, \xi_j, w_j \eta, \beta, \gamma) \quad \text{for } j = 1, \dots, J.$$

These J equations in combination with the J demand equations provide $2J$ equations, which we may potentially solve for the $2J$ unknowns—equilibrium prices and quantities for all of the J goods in the market. We discuss how to solve the full set of $2J$ equations explicitly for an arbitrary ownership structure and general demand systems in our discussion of merger simulation in chapter 8.

The idea of the residual demand function approach is to solve the demand and supply equations for all of the goods except those at the center of the inquiry. Suppose first that we wish to evaluate the market power of firm 1, owner of good 1. Or, more precisely, suppose we wish to test whether a hypothetical monopolist consisting of firm 1 has sufficient market power to raise prices by 5%. The residual demand function approach suggests that we could solve the $2(J-1)$ demand and pricing equations for products $j = 2, \dots, J$. That is, we can solve for

$$\ln p_j = E_j(p_1; x_{[2:J]}, w_{[2:J]}, \xi_{[2:J]}, \eta, \beta, \gamma) \quad \text{for } j = 2, \dots, J,$$

where we denote $x_{[2:J]} = (x_2, \dots, x_J)$ and $w_{[2:J]}$ and $\xi_{[2:J]}$ are defined analogously. These equations provide a description of the equilibrium prices conditional on the price chosen by firm 1.[45] Substituting these equations into the demand function for product 1 gives the "residual demand function" for product 1:

$$\begin{aligned}\ln q_1 = \eta_{10} + \eta_{11} \ln p_1 &+ \sum_{j=2}^{J} \eta_{1j} E_j(p_1; x_{[2:J]}, w_{[2:J]}, \xi_{[2:J]}, \eta, \beta, \gamma) \\ &+ x_1' \beta + \xi_1.\end{aligned}$$

Note that the usual price elasticity of demand η_{11} is adjusted by a factor which captures the responses of rivals to any price change proposed by the firm:

$$\eta_{11}^{\text{Resid}} = \frac{\partial \ln q_1}{\partial \ln p_1} = \eta_{11} + \sum_{j=2}^{J} \eta_{1j} \frac{\partial E_j(p_1; x_{[2:J]}, w_{[2:J]}, \xi_{[2:J]}, \eta, \beta, \gamma)}{\partial \ln p_1}.$$

Firm 1's market power and its ability to raise prices can be evaluated using its first-order conditions. Namely, prices can be raised profitably as long as margins are below (residual) demand elasticities:

$$\frac{p_1 - \text{mc}_1(w_1; \gamma)}{p_1} \leqslant \left(\frac{\partial \ln D_1^{\text{Resid}}(p_1; x_{[2:J]}, w_{[2:J]}, \xi_{[2:J]}, \eta, \beta, \gamma)}{\partial \ln p_j} \right)^{-1}.$$

Note that the central assumption of this approach is that the prices (or quantities if this were a quantity-setting model) of products outside the candidate market adjust

[45] Note that in a Stackleberg equilibrium, where firm 1 is the price leader, we would solve these equations and then allow firm 1 to choose the equilibrium outcome where its profits were maximized.

fully in response to any change in the price of the good in the candidate market. If this were a quantity-setting game, we would be allowing for supply substitutability. Since it is a price-setting game, we are allowing for prices of goods outside the market to adjust and for the firm setting the price of the good in the market to take such adjustments into account when choosing her profit-maximizing strategy.

Suppose now that goods 1 and 2 constitute the candidate market definition. Baker and Bresnahan (1985) extend the residual demand approach described above to this situation, inventing the term "partial residual demand curve." A hypothetical monopolist of products 1 and 2 would solve the profit-maximization problem,

$$\max_{p_1,p_2} (p_1 - \mathrm{mc}_1(w_1;\gamma))D_1(p_1,\dots,p_J;x_j,\xi_j) + (p_2 - \mathrm{mc}_2(w_2;\gamma))D_2(p_1,\dots,p_J;x_j,\xi_j),$$

for which we provided the first-order conditions in section 4.6.3.1, showing that whether a 5% price increase would be profitable depends on the margin for each good, the own-price elasticity of demand at equilibrium prices and the diversion ratios.

Following the logic of the single-product case, Baker and Bresnahan (1985) suggest solving the $2(J-2)$ demand and pricing equations (for products $j = 3,\dots,J$) to provide a description of the equilibrium prices that would result for those products for any given level of prices for goods 1 and 2, the goods in the candidate market. That is, suppose that we solve for the equilibrium prices of goods outside the candidate market for a given set of prices of goods inside the candidate market:

$$\ln p_j = E_j(p_1,p_2;x_{[3:J]},w_{[3:J]},\xi_{[3:J]},\eta,\beta,\gamma) \quad \text{for } j = 3,\dots,J.$$

Substituting these equations into the demand curves for products 1 and 2 gives us the "partial residual demand curves" for the two products:

$$\begin{aligned}\ln q_1 &= \eta_{10} + \eta_{11}\ln p_1 + \eta_{12}\ln p_2 \\ &\quad + \sum_{j=3}^{J} \eta_{1j} E_j(p_1,p_2;x_{[3:J]},w_{[3:J]},\xi_{[3:J]},\eta,\beta,\gamma) + x_1'\beta + \xi_1, \\ \ln q_2 &= \eta_{20} + \eta_{21}\ln p_1 + \eta_{22}\ln p_2 \\ &\quad + \sum_{j=3}^{J} \eta_{2j} E_j(p_1,p_2;x_{[3:J]},w_{[3:J]},\xi_{[3:J]},\eta,\beta,\gamma) + x_2'\beta + \xi_2.\end{aligned}$$

As Baker and Bresnahan (1985) describe (treating the hypothetical monopolist of goods 1 and 2 as if the single-product firms 1 and 2 had undertaken a merger), these "are *residual* demand curves because the actions of firms 3 to J have been taken into account. They are *partial* residual demand curves because, for each firm, the potential merger partner's action remains to be specified." Totally differentiating the partial residual demand curves we can describe the elasticity of partial residual demand as[46]

$$\eta_1^{\text{PR}} = \eta_{11} + \eta_{12} + \sum_{j=3}^{J} \eta_{1j} \frac{\partial E_j(p_1, p_2; x_{[3:J]}, w_{[3:J]}, \xi_{[3:J]}, \eta, \beta, \gamma)}{\partial \ln p_1}$$
$$+ \sum_{j=3}^{J} \eta_{1j} \frac{\partial E_j(p_1, p_2; x_{[3:J]}, w_{[3:J]}, \xi_{[3:J]}, \eta, \beta, \gamma)}{\partial \ln p_2}.$$

In practice, the approach would probably involve approximating the system of partial residual demand equations, perhaps with a log-linear system so that we would estimate

$$\ln q_1 = \eta_{10} + \eta_{11}^{\text{PR}} \ln p_1 + \eta_{12}^{\text{PR}} \ln p_2 + \sum_{j=3}^{J} \lambda_{1j} x_j + \sum_{j=3}^{J} \delta_{1j} w_j + v_{1j},$$

$$\ln q_2 = \eta_{20} + \eta_{21}^{\text{PR}} \ln p_1 + \eta_{22}^{\text{PR}} \ln p_2 + \sum_{j=3}^{J} \lambda_{2j} x_j + \sum_{j=3}^{J} \delta_{2j} w_j + v_{2j},$$

but interpret the estimated parameters as "partial residual" demand elasticities rather than traditional demand elasticities. Given estimates of these demand equations, we have everything we need to calculate whether the hypothetical monopolist's profits will increase prices from competitive prices by say 5%, having allowed the prices of goods outside the candidate market to adjust to those new, higher, prices inside the candidate market.

This approach is certainly feasible, and does remove even the need for data on prices or quantities from goods outside the candidate market. However, the approach is not without problems in practice. To see why, first note that the log-linear demand system will collapse to a form which is linear in logs of prices (or other convenient forms for estimation) only under very strong assumptions. Second, note that all cost and demand shift variables for all products outside the candidate market must in principle be included in each estimating equation. This appears to mean that we must know, for example, the demand shifters of demand equations we have not

[46] Note that generally, the HMT can be implemented by considering the directional derivative of the hypothetical monopolist's profit function. See your favorite undergraduate calculus textbook for the calculation of directional derivatives (e.g., Binmore 1983). Let $p = (1+t)p^0$, where p^0 is given and where $p = (1+t)p^0$ defines a straight line through p^0 and also in the direction of the vector p^0. Consider the bivariate function $f : \mathbb{R}^2 \to \mathbb{R}$ and suppose that $p^0 = (p_1^{\text{Comp}}, p_2^{\text{Comp}})$, then

$$\frac{\mathrm{d} f(p_0 + t p_0)}{\mathrm{d}t} = \frac{\partial f(p)}{\partial p_1}\frac{\partial p_1}{\partial t} + \frac{\partial f(p)}{\partial p_2}\frac{\partial p_2}{\partial t} = \frac{\partial f(p)}{\partial p_1} p_1^{\text{Comp}} + \frac{\partial f(p)}{\partial p_2} p_2^{\text{Comp}}$$

and hence a tiny but proportionate price increase can be evaluated by setting $t = 0$ and hence evaluating

$$\frac{\mathrm{d} f(p_0 + t p_0)}{\mathrm{d}t} = \frac{\partial f(p_0)}{\partial \ln p_1} + \frac{\partial f(p_0)}{\partial \ln p_2}.$$

estimated. Even if we do know which variables to include, there may be a lot of them and this can mean that the partial residual demand functions are estimated imprecisely.[47] Third, note that the prices of goods inside the candidate market are appropriately considered endogenous in these regressions so that an instrumentation strategy is, as usual, required for each included price in the regression, i.e., each price in the candidate market. This approach is further discussed in Scheffman and Spiller (1996) and critically discussed in Froeb and Werden (1991) and Werden and Froeb (1992).

4.7 Conclusions

- Market definition remains an important legal requirement in most competition investigations. However, market definition is not usually an end in itself in a competition investigation. As a result, it is important not to spend a disproportionate amount of time and resources on market definition—the question that "matters" for the substantive evaluation is the effect of the behavior under investigation on the market.
- The hypothetical monopolist test (HMT) provides the standard conceptual framework for analysis of market definition. There is, however, a variety of possible ways to implement the test. Some methods will hold constant everything outside the candidate market while other implementations will not. The results you obtain may depend on which method is adopted in your jurisdiction. A hypothetical monopolist will not have market power if there is a significant degree of demand or supply substitutability to/from products outside a candidate market. Hence, defining a market requires determining the products that have a degree of demand (and sometimes supply) substitution among them such that they impose constraints on each other's ability to exploit market power.
- In theory, when firms compete in prices, the HMT test can be applied by formally evaluating whether a hypothetical monopolist could profitably implement a price increase. The related SSNIP test evaluates whether a small but significant and nontransitory increase in prices (SSNIP) is profitable for the candidate market. In practice, such assessments are generally made "in the round," that is, in light of all of the evidence collected rather than on the basis

[47] Although it would exacerbate the problems of imprecision already alluded to, in principle a nonparametric approach might be taken to the equilibrium functions. For instance, a series estimator would include a polynomial in each demand and cost shifting variable. While such an approach looks theoretically possible, it is important to note that these nonparametric functions would, in general, appear to depend on the unobservables of goods outside the candidate markets as well as all the exogenous observed variables. That observation makes a nonparametric approach to approximating these reduced forms difficult.

of a single formal model's prediction. There are a number of informal tools which are useful.

- Correlation analysis is a simple tool that relies on the substitution among goods determining co-movements in prices. It can be a powerful tool for market definition, but applying it effectively usually requires cross-checks to make sure that prices are indeed being driven together by substitutability and not just by common demand or cost shocks.
- Natural experiments ("shock analysis") provides another useful tool relying on the effect of exogenous shocks on outcome variables such as prices. At its best, a natural experiment provides exogenous variation of a kind that is very helpful econometrically. Unfortunately, natural experiments are not always available and whether it is appropriate to treat events such as entry events as actually econometrically "exogenous" must be carefully evaluated in context.
- In addition it is possible to directly estimate demand substitution effects by analyzing purchase patterns and conducting surveys. Own- and cross-price elasticities can also be estimated econometrically, although doing so sufficiently robustly to withstand judicial scrutiny is by no means an easy task.
- In order to formally evaluate a SSNIP test, it is not sufficient to estimate the own- and cross-price elasticities of demand. Rather we need a standard to evaluate whether those own- and cross-price elasticities are sufficient to make increasing prices above the competitive level profitable. Critical loss analysis provides one method for such an evaluation. Examining the first-order conditions from pricing models provide another, closely related, method.
- Applying SSNIP formally in a differentiated product context is a nontrivial exercise. Ultimately, a judgment must be made about whether a set of products are sufficiently constraining each other to be considered in the same relevant competition policy market. Even when a great deal of quantitative evidence is brought to bear on the various elements of the question of market definition, ultimately in the vast majority of cases a judgment must be made as to what is "in" and what is "out." Both qualitative and quantitative evidence informs judgment, but it will replace it entirely only in a tiny number of cases.
- The FERM test has not been applied in practice widely yet, although the approach is closely related to the residual demand curve approach to the evaluation of market power (which has also been advocated for use in defining markets), which in turn was in the spirit of the 1984 U.S. Horizontal Merger Guidelines. In each case, the central distinction from a conventional application of the SSNIP test is that suppliers outside the candidate market are allowed to adjust their competitive variables. If firms compete in output, we may naturally think of such effects as allowing for supply substitution. When considering supply substitution, it is important to note that when firms

produce substitutes and compete in prices then the profitability of price rises inside the market will tend to lead to, and be reinforced by, price rises outside a candidate market definition.

- We shall see in chapter 8 that simulation models can in principle be used to "miss out" entirely the explicit preliminary consideration of market definition. Instead it suggests we could define broad markets and then proceed to consider competitive effects directly. While potentially theoretically attractive, such an approach is for the moment not consistent with longstanding legal doctrine in a number of significant jurisdictions (including the United States and the European Union).
- In cases where market definition judgments are particularly difficult, when we progress to analyze competition among the set of products in the market we will typically want to keep an eye on what is going on outside our definition of the relevant market. In particular, it may be sensible to evaluate the competitive effects of behavior under more than one potential market definition to come to an informed view of whether (i) market definition is central to the "outcome" of the inquiry and (ii) whether the actual competitive constraints that would be under investigation, as distinct from the competitive constraints faced by a hypothetical monopolist, are sufficient to restrain price increases.

5

The Relationship between Market Structure and Price

Merger investigations usually seek to determine whether the change in market structure caused by a merger will have a significant impact on the market outcomes for consumers. The outcome of most direct concern will be price although quality or choice effects may also be important though typically longer term and usually more difficult to assess. At the core of merger assessment then is the expected relationship between the number and size of firms operating in the market, market structure, and the prices or qualities that result from the competitive process.

Economic theory predicts that market structure affects prices. Under reasonably general conditions, a reduction of the number of players will result in an increase in market prices all else equal. This prediction forms the basis for the "unilateral effect" of a merger, where, post-merger, the new merged firm will usually have a unilateral incentive to raise prices above their pre-merger levels. This unilateral effect in turn may lead others to have an incentive to raise prices and this in turn usually reinforces the original unilateral incentive to increase prices. We term the former effect a "unilateral" effect since it is the incentive a single firm has to unilaterally increase prices. We term the latter effect a "multilateral" incentive since it involves independent actions by multiple parties each of which enjoy an incentive to increase prices following a merger. We will see that such effects are fairly generic in mergers involving firms that produce substitutes for one another.

This chapter explores the frameworks which can help competition agencies when they try to identify this effect in practice. Practically all models of competition predict that a change in market structure will have consequences for market prices. Still, empirically assessing the actual relation between structure and price is by no means always an easy activity. Nonetheless, we will see that several empirical strategies can be used to approximate the extent of an increase in prices that will result when concentration occurs. Understanding the underlying theoretical rationale for the relationship between structure and price will be important in order to design an appropriate way of empirically measuring the effect, so we will spend some time describing the basic underlying theory. We then present examples of methodologies that estimate the effects of market structure on price. Our examples are designed

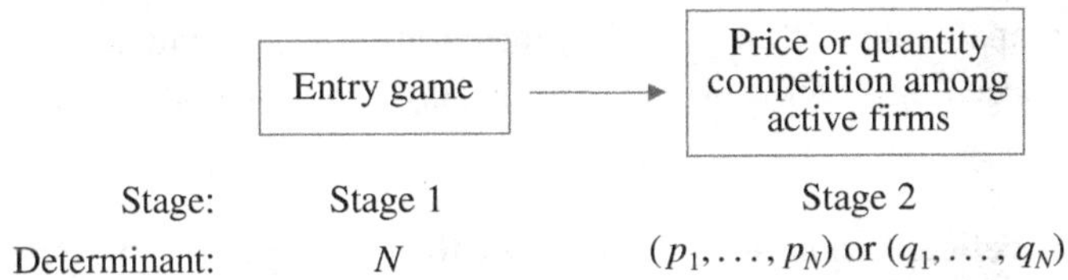

Figure 5.1. A two-stage game.

to provide practical guidance on appropriate data sets and techniques that could be considered for such analysis and also to point to a number of the potential problems previous investigators have faced when trying to identify the way in which price is likely to change with market structure.

Identifying the relationship between price and market structure is hard for a number of reasons. For example, whichever particular methodology we choose, we will need to address the difficult issue of identifying a causal link between market structure and the market outcomes—in particular price. In addition, if we adopt a longer-term perspective, both the number of active firms and the number and type of potential entrants may, on occasion, also constrain pricing power. If so, then in assessing the likely effect of a change of market structure one may also want to evaluate the constraint exerted by potential competitors. These are just two of a large number of potential difficulties analysts in competition agencies often come across. We outline a number of other difficulties below and then go on to describe potential solutions to these problems that the literature has developed.

5.1 Framework for Analyzing the Effect of Market Structure on Prices

We begin our discussion of the relationship between market structure and market outcomes by discussing the effect that the number of active firms has on the ruling equilibrium price or prices in the market under a variety of assumptions about the nature of competition. We then progress to examine methods which can be used to move our model from being purely a theoretical analysis into a framework that is appropriate for undertaking empirical work. Specifically, in the next section, we examine the potential drivers of the decision to enter a market and consider the effect that such entry has on the competitive process and also how we can learn about market power by observing such entry decisions.

We structure our study of the effect of market structure on prices by considering the following two-stage game. At stage one, firms decide whether or not to enter the market. If they enter, they incur a cost which is sunk (irrecoverable) at stage two. We call N the number of firms that decide to enter the market at stage 1. At stage two, the N active firms compete among themselves in prices or quantities. The game is represented in figure 5.1. In what follows, we follow the economics literature in analyzing such a game by starting with the examination of stage two and then proceeding "backward" to discuss stage one, the entry stage in the next section.[1]

5.1.1 Theoretical Predictions about the Effect of Structure on Prices

Many economic models of competition can be embedded into this general two-stage structure and each will predict a relationship between market structure and market prices. We will establish the result for three important cases, namely the models in which firms are (1) price-takers, (2) oligopolists competing in prices, and (3) oligopolists competing in quantities. By examining these three canonical cases we are able to examine the mechanisms by which market structure can affect equilibrium prices. For example, we will see that, generally, a merger between two firms producing substitutes will tend to result in higher prices. Such results form the theoretical backbone of the investigations of the unilateral and multilateral effects of mergers.

5.1.1.1 Market Structure among Price-Taking Firms

The structure of market supply can be important for economic efficiency in a price-taking environment since where production takes place will usually matter for the aggregate costs incurred to produce any given level of output. That is, the number of firms that are producing will usually have an effect on the total costs of production. That in turn matters because the pricing pressures that firms face are determined by the intersection of market demand and market supply, which in a price-taking environment is determined by the industry's marginal costs of production. A reduction in the number of firms will, except in special circumstances, reduce the aggregate supply to the market and hence induce the price to rise. Higher prices in turn induce increases in supply from at least one remaining active firm that, if it suffers from diseconomies of scale, will nonetheless find it profitable to produce extra output despite higher unit costs. Because of the potential diseconomies of scale, a lower number of firms may result in higher prices required to sustain a given level of aggregate output. Generally therefore, assuming a price-sensitive demand and firm-level diseconomies of scale, an equilibrium involving a reduced set of firms will involve lower quantities and higher prices.

A price-taking firm operates in a homogeneous product environment where quantity is usually the firm's decision variable. It solves the following profit-maximization problem,

$$\max_{q_i} p_i q_i - C(q_i),$$

[1] Technically, we examine equilibria of such games using "backward induction" to find the pure-strategy subgame perfect Nash equilibrium of the game; see your favorite game theory textbook.

where C is the total cost function describing the total costs of producing a given level of output q_i such that, for example,

$$C = \begin{cases} cq_i + \frac{1}{2}dq_i^2 + F & \text{if } q_i > 0, \\ 0 & \text{if } q_i = 0. \end{cases}$$

In this model, beyond the first unit of production, marginal costs increase with production and there is a limit to the efficient production scale. Solving the maximization problem describes the optimal quantity that this firm will want to supply at each announced price:

$$q_i^* = \begin{cases} \dfrac{p-c}{d} & \text{if } p_i q_i^* - C(q_i^*) \geqslant 0 \text{ at } q_i^* = \dfrac{p-c}{d}, \\ 0 & \text{otherwise.} \end{cases}$$

Next, suppose there are N symmetric active firms, each of which have produced positive amounts so that their (the firm's) supply function can be summarized as $q_i^* = (p-c)/d$, we may sum to give the market supply function:

$$Q_{\text{Market}}^{\text{Supply}} = N\left(\frac{p^* - c}{d}\right).$$

If we further assume linear individual demands and S identical consumers so that the market demand is $Q_{\text{Market}}^{\text{Demand}} = S(a-bp)$ and that equilibrium price p^* is determined by the intersection of supply and demand, we may write

$$\begin{aligned} Q_{\text{Market}}^{\text{Supply}} &= N\left(\frac{p^* - c}{d}\right) \\ &= S(a - bp^*) \\ &= Q_{\text{Market}}^{\text{Demand}}, \end{aligned}$$

which is an equilibrium relationship that we may solve explicitly to give the equilibrium price:

$$p_i^* = \frac{Nc + Sda}{N + Sbd}.$$

Note, in particular, that the equilibrium price depends on N, that is the market structure, and also on the cost and demand parameters including the size of the market. Note also that with symmetric single-product firms, market structure can be completely described by the number of firms. Richer models will require a more nuanced description.

While the main aim of this section is to note that our various models imply that price is a function of market structure, it would be nice to see an analytical result which fits well with our intuition that prices should fall when the number of competitors goes up. In fact, looking at the equation for the equilibrium price in price-taking environments makes it quite difficult to see immediately that a decrease in N obviously always leads to an increase in price. Fortunately, the result is easier to see if we consider the familiar picture with linear market supply and linear market demand equations (we leave the reader to draw the diagram as an exercise). Reducing N and having firms exit the market shifts the market supply curve leftward, which will clearly generally result in an increase in equilibrium market price. In contrast, entry will shift the aggregate market supply curve rightwards and, in so doing, reduce equilibrium prices. For those who favor algebra, one can easily calculate the derivative of the equilibrium price with respect to the number of firms N to see the negative relation between the two in this example.[2]

5.1.1.2 Market Structure in a Cournot Setting with Quadratic Costs

Consider next an oligopoly in which firms that entered the market compete in quantities of a homogeneous good, the Cournot model. In this market exit does two things. First, it reduces the number of firms so that total market output tends to be reduced. Second, it increases the amount that any incumbent firm will produce due to the shape of each individual firm's equilibrium supply function. The net effect on total output, and hence prices, is therefore potentially ambiguous. It depends on the relative effect of an increase in firm output and a decrease in the number of firms. Usually, we expect the impact of losing a firm not to be compensated for by the expansion in output produced as a result by surviving rivals. In that case, price will rise following the exit of an incumbent firm and fall following entry of a new player.

Let aggregate market demand be

$$Q = S(a - bp),$$

where S is the size of the market, so that the corresponding inverse aggregate demand equation is

$$p(Q) = \frac{a}{b} - \frac{1}{b}\frac{Q}{S}.$$

Assuming again a quadratic cost function,

$$C(q_i) = cq_i + \tfrac{1}{2}dq_i^2 + F,$$

and N profit-maximizing firms that exhibit the following first-order condition for profit maximization:

$$p(Q) + p'(Q)q_i - C'(q_i) = 0,$$

where

$$Q = \sum_{i=1}^{N} q_i.$$

[2] Doing so allows us to check the conditions required on the parameters (a, b, c, d) to ensure that the linear supply and demand curves cross.

Solving this equation for q_i, the firm's reaction function is[3]

$$q_i = \frac{S(a - bc) - \sum_{j \neq i} q_j}{2 + bSd},$$

which in fact is identical for each $i = 1, \dots, N$.

We use the Cournot–Nash equilibrium assumption under symmetry, which allows us to assume that each firm will produce the same amount of output in equilibrium, $q_1 = q_2 = \cdots = q_N = q^*$. The symmetry assumption implies that all N first-order conditions are entirely identical,

$$q^* = \frac{S(a - bc) - (N - 1)q^*}{2 + bSd},$$

and that allows us to solve them all by solving this single equation for q^*. A little more algebra allows us to express the equilibrium quantity supplied by each firm as

$$q^* = \frac{S(a - bc)}{1 + N + bSd}.$$

Plugging the resulting aggregate quantity Nq^* in the demand function, we can retrieve the equilibrium market price:

$$\begin{aligned} p^* &= p(Nq^*) \\ &= p\left(\frac{NS(a - cb)}{1 + N + dbS}\right) \\ &= \frac{a}{b} - \frac{1}{bS}\left(\frac{NS(a - cb)}{1 + N + dbS}\right) \\ &= \frac{a}{b} - \frac{1}{b}\left(\frac{N(a - cb)}{1 + N + dbS}\right). \end{aligned}$$

As with price-taking firms, we see that prices are generally dependent on market structure.

The algebraic relationship between price and the number of firms is not obviously negative. The magnitude of the actual predictions from the model will once again depend on the assumptions about the cost symmetry of firms and the shape of the demand. In the simple case of symmetric firms with decreasing returns to scale and a linear demand, a reduction in the number of firms leads to a reduction in total output and an increase in price.

---

[3] The first-order condition can be expressed as

$$\frac{a}{b} - \frac{\sum_{j \neq i}^{N} q_j}{bS} - \frac{1}{bS} q_i - c - dq_i = 0 \iff aS - \sum_{j \neq i} q_j - 2q_i - bSc - bSdq_i = 0$$

from which the expression in the text immediately follows.

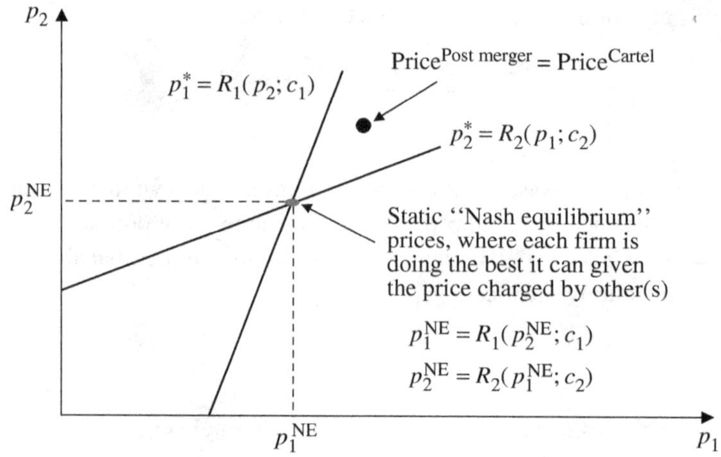

Figure 5.2. Reaction curves and static Nash equilibrium in a two-firm industry and in a single-firm industry.

5.1.1.3 Market Structure in a Differentiated Product Price Competition Setting

As the third of our examples we now consider the case of differentiated products Bertrand competition, in which existing firms in a market produce differentiated products and compete in price for potential customers.

In pricing games where firms produce goods that are substitutes, optimal prices increase in the prices of rivals under fairly weak conditions. That means that if a firm's rival raises its price, the best response of the firm is to also raise its own price. The reaction functions of two firms producing substitute goods and competing in prices are plotted in figure 5.2.

Assuming that firm 1 produces product 1 at marginal cost c_1, the firm's profit-maximization problem can be expressed as

$$\max_{p_1}(p_1 - c_1)D_1(p_1, p_2; \theta),$$

where $D_1(p_1, p_2; \theta)$ is the demand for product 1 and θ is a consumer taste parameter. The first-order condition for this problem can be written

$$\frac{\partial \Pi_1^{\text{Single}}}{\partial p_1} = (p_1 - c_1)\frac{\partial D_1(p_1, p_2)}{\partial p_1} + D_1(p_1, p_2) = 0.$$

Solving this equation allows us to describe firm 1's reaction function,

$$p_1^* = R_1(p_2; c_1, \theta),$$

that is, its optimal choice of price for any given price of firm 2. In a similar way, we could derive the reaction function for firm 2,

$$p_2^* = R_2(p_1; c_2, \theta).$$

This positive relation between the optimal prices of competing firms selling substitutes is the basis for the unilateral effect described above whereby, after a merged firm increases the prices of the substitutes goods it produces, competitors that produce other substitute goods will follow the price increase, turning this price increase into an all-market phenomenon.

We now show analytically why a merging firm combining the production of two substitutes has the incentive to increase both prices post-merger. This result is derived from the fact that the merged firm can appropriate the profits generated by the increase in the demand of the second substitute good if the price of the first good is increased. This ability to get the profits generated by both goods will result in higher equilibrium prices for both goods, all else equal.

Suppose we have one multiproduct firm which produces both the two goods 1 and 2. Such a multiproduct firm will solve the following profit-maximization problem:

$$\max_{p_1,p_2} (p_1 - c)D_1(p_1, p_2) + (p_2 - c)D_2(p_1, p_2).$$

The first-order conditions for this problem are

$$\begin{aligned}\frac{\partial \Pi^{\text{Multiproduct}}}{\partial p_1} &= (p_1 - c)\frac{\partial D_1(p_1, p_2)}{\partial p_1} + D_1(p_1, p_2) + (p_2 - c)\frac{\partial D_2(p_1, p_2)}{\partial p_1}\\ &= 0\end{aligned}$$

and

$$\begin{aligned}\frac{\partial \Pi^{\text{Multiproduct}}}{\partial p_2} &= (p_1 - c)\frac{\partial D_1(p_1, p_2)}{\partial p_2} + D_2(p_1, p_2) + (p_2 - c)\frac{\partial D_2(p_1, p_2)}{\partial p_2}\\ &= 0.\end{aligned}$$

One approach to these equations is to calculate the solution $(p_1^{\text{Multiproduct}}, p_2^{\text{Multiproduct}})$ by solving the two simultaneous equations and then consider how those prices relate to $(p_1^{\text{Single}}, p_2^{\text{Single}})$. We will do that for a very general case in chapter 8. Here, however, we follow a different route. Namely, instead of calculating the equilibrium prices directly, we can instead evaluate the marginal profitability of increasing prices to the multiproduct firm at the prices $(p_1^{\text{Single}}, p_2^{\text{Single}})$ that would have been chosen by two single-product firms. Doing so allows us to evaluate whether the multiproduct firm will have an incentive to raise prices. Note that we can write

$$\frac{\partial \Pi^{\text{Multiproduct}}(p_1^{\text{Single}}, p_2^{\text{Single}})}{\partial p_1} = 0 + (p_2^{\text{Single}} - c)\frac{\partial D_2(p_1^{\text{Single}}, p_2^{\text{Single}})}{\partial p_1}$$

and

$$\frac{\partial \Pi^{\text{Multiproduct}}(p_1^{\text{Single}}, p_2^{\text{Single}})}{\partial p_2} = (p_1^{\text{Single}} - c)\frac{\partial D_1(p_1^{\text{Single}}, p_2^{\text{Single}})}{\partial p_2} + 0$$

since at $p_i = p_i^{\text{Single}}$ profits on the single product are maximized and the first-order condition for single-product maximization holds. So,

$$\operatorname{sign}\left(\frac{\partial \Pi^{\text{Multiproduct}}(p_1^{\text{Single}}, p_2^{\text{Single}})}{\partial p_1}\right) = \operatorname{sign}\left(\frac{\partial D_2(p_1^{\text{Single}}, p_2^{\text{Single}})}{\partial p_1}\right)$$

and

$$\operatorname{sign}\left(\frac{\partial \Pi^{\text{Multiproduct}}(p_1^{\text{Single}}, p_2^{\text{Single}})}{\partial p_2}\right) = \operatorname{sign}\left(\frac{\partial D_1(p_1^{\text{Single}}, p_2^{\text{Single}})}{\partial p_2}\right).$$

These equations give us an important result, namely that if goods are *demand substitutes*, so that

$$\frac{\partial D_1(p_1^{\text{Single}}, p_2^{\text{Single}})}{\partial p_2} > 0 \quad \text{and} \quad \frac{\partial D_2(p_1^{\text{Single}}, p_2^{\text{Single}})}{\partial p_1} > 0,$$

then this "two-to-one" merger will very generally result in higher prices for both goods. For example,

$$\frac{\partial \Pi^{\text{Multiproduct}}(p_1^{\text{Single}}, p_2^{\text{Single}})}{\partial p_1} > 0$$

means that the multiproduct firm will have higher profits if she raises the price of good 1 above the single-product price.

This incentive to raise prices is what is commonly referred to as the "unilateral" effect, or more accurately, the unilateral incentive by merging firms to raise prices after the merger. This incentive is created by the fact that the merged firm would retain revenues on the consumers switching to the alternative product after a price hike. In contrast we can also conclude that if both goods are *demand complements*, then prices will usually fall following a merger.

Graphically, we can represent the unilateral effect of a two-to-one merger of firms producing substitute goods (see figure 5.2).

The prices that result from a joint maximization of profits made on goods 1 and 2 are higher than the prices that are obtained when profits are maximized for each one of the products separately whenever goods are substitutes.

Notice, as explained above, that this result will hold if there were other firms in the market producing other products. If the prices p_1 and p_2 increase, other firms will also increase the prices of their goods as long as they also have upward-sloping reaction functions with respect to p_1 and p_2. This in turn will further cause a further incentive to increase in the prices of p_1 and p_2 and so on until the process settles at higher prices for all substitutable products. How much higher the prices are compared with a situation in which there are single-product firms will depend on the concentration and ownership structure in the market, i.e., on which firm(s) produce(s) which products. Generally, a more concentrated ownership structure will lead to higher prices, everything else constant.

This important prediction will be more closely analyzed in the context of merger simulations and we will formalize this result for a fairly general case in chapter 8. Merger simulation has some disadvantages but it does have the advantage that it allows us to explicitly model the way in which merger effects depend on the shape of demand. By doing so carefully we can reflect both the range of choices that the consumer faces and also the substitution opportunities that exist given the consumer's taste. Chapter 9 discusses the estimation of different models of demand functions that are useful for merger simulation exercises.

In this section, we have illustrated how the most common theoretical frameworks used to characterize competition predict that market structure and in particular the number of players should be expected to affect the level of prices in the market. In particular, in the case of price competition among substitute products, the prediction of the effect of an increased concentration of ownership on the price level of all competing products is unambiguously that price will rise. The European Commission Merger Regulation explicitly mentions the case when a merger will have a negative effect on competition, and therefore on prices, quantity, or quality, because of the reduction in the competitive pressure that firms may face after the merger.[4] In particular, the regulation states that:

> However, under certain circumstances, concentrations involving the elimination of important competitive constraints that the merging parties had exerted on each other, as well as a reduction of competitive pressure on the remaining competitors, may, even in the absence of a likelihood of coordination between the members of the oligopoly, result in a significant impediment to competition.

In practice, the nature and extent of the resulting price change is an empirical question that needs to be addressed using the facts relevant to each case. Not all mergers will be between firms producing particularly close substitutes and some may even involve mergers between firms producing complements. As a result, the magnitude of the likely impact of market structure on prices must be evaluated. In what follows, we describe several methods to empirically determine the relevance of the relationship between market structure and price in specific cases. Although it will not always be possible to perform such detailed quantitative assessments, these techniques highlight the type of evidence that will be relevant for a unilateral effect case and provide guidance on how to assess market evidence even when less quantitative in nature.

5.1.2 Cross-Sectional Evidence on the Effect of Market Structure

One way to look at the possible relation between market structure and prices is to look at the market outcomes (e.g., prices) in situations where the market structure differs. That is, an intuitive approach to evaluating whether a "three-to-two" merger

[4] EC Merger Regulation, Council Regulation on the control of concentrations between undertakings 2004/1.

will affect prices is to examine a market or set of markets where all three firms compete and then look at another market or set of markets where just two firms compete. By comparing prices across the markets we might hope to see the effect of a move from having three active competitors to having just two active competitors. As we will see, such a method while intuitive does need to be applied with great care in practice since it will involve comparing markets that may be intrinsically different. That said, if we do have data on markets with differing numbers of active suppliers, looking at whether there is a negative correlation between the number of firms and the resulting market prices is likely to be a good starting point for analysis.

5.1.2.1 Using Cross-Sectional Information

Using cross-sectional information can be a good starting point for an empirical assessment of the effect of market structure on prices, provided that one can argue that the different markets that are being compared are at least broadly similar in terms of cost structure and demand. Consider a somewhat extreme but illustrative example. Suppose we want to analyze the effect of the number of bicycle shops on the price of bicycles in Beijing. It is pretty unlikely to be very helpful to use data about the price of bicycles in Stockholm, which has fewer bicycle shops, to address the impact of bicycle shop concentration on bicycle prices. Stockholm would have fewer shops and higher prices than Beijing. Even ignoring the likely massive cross-country differences in regulatory environment, the probably huge differences in tastes, market size, and the likely differences in the cost and quality of the bikes involved, the comparison would be effectively meaningless. No matter how concentrated Beijing's market became, there is no obvious reason to believe that equilibrium prices would provide a meaningful comparison with Stockholm's prices for the purposes of evaluating mergers in either Stockholm or Beijing. Even comparing Paris and Amsterdam, where more people favor bicycles as a mean of transportation, may well not be appropriate.

The lesson is that when comparing prices across markets we need to make sure that we are comparing meaningfully similar markets. With that important caveat in mind, there are nonetheless many cases in which cross-market comparisons will be indicative of the actual link between the number of firms competing and the price.

One famous U.S. case in which this method, along with more sophisticated methods, was used involved the proposed merger between Staples and Office Depot.[5] This merger was challenged by the FTC in 1997.[6] The resulting court case was reputedly

[5] The discussion of *FTC v. Staples* in this chapter draws heavily on previous discussion in the literature. See, in particular, those involved in the case (Baker 1999; Dalkir and Warren-Boulton 1999) and also Ashenfelter et al. (2006). There is some debate as to the extent of the reliance of the court on the econometric evidence. See Baker (1999) for the view that econometrics played a central role. Others emphasize that the econometrics was supplementary to more traditional documentary evidence and testimony.

[6] *Federal Trade Commission v. Staples, Inc.*, 970 F. Supp. 1066 (United States District Court for the District of Columbia 1997) (Judge Thomas F. Hogan).

the first in the United States in which a substantial amount of econometric analysis was used by the court as evidence. The merging parties sold office supplies through very large shops (hence they are among the set of retailers known as "big box" retailers) and operated as specialist retailers, at least in comparison with a general department store. Their consumers were mostly small and medium size enterprises which are too small to establish direct relations with the original manufacturers as well as individuals. The FTC proposed that the market should be defined as "consumable office supplies sold through office superstores." Examples of consumable office supplies include paper, staplers, envelopes, and folders. This market definition was somewhat controversial since it (i) excluded durable goods such as computers and printers sold in the same stores since they are "nonconsumable," (ii) excluded consumable office supplies sold in smaller "mom and pop" stores, in supermarkets, and in general mass merchants such as Walmart (not specialized office superstores). To those skeptical about this market definition, the FTC's lawyers suggested gently to the judge that "one visit [to an office superstore] would be worth a thousand affidavits."[7] Since we have considered extensively the process of getting to market definition in an earlier chapter, we will leave the discussion of market definition and instead focus on the empirical evidence that was presented. While some of the empirical evidence is relevant to market definition, its focus was primarily on measuring the competitive pricing effects of a merger. The geographical market was deemed to be at the Metropolitan Statistical Area (MSA) level, which is a relatively local market consisting of a collection of counties.[8]

By 1996, there were only three main players on the market: Staples, with a $4 billion revenue of which $2 billion was in office supplies and 550 stores in 28 states; Office Depot, with a $6.1 billion revenue of which $3 billion was in office supplies and 500 stores in 38 states; Office Max, with a $3.2 billion revenue of which $1.3 billion was in office supplies and 575 stores in 48 states. The merger far exceeded the threshold for scrutiny in the United States in terms of HHI and market shares, at least given the market definition.

The FTC undertook to compare the prices across local markets across the United States at a given point in time to see whether there was a relationship between the number of suppliers present in the market and the prices being charged. They used three different data sources for this exercise. The first data set came from internal documents, particularly Staples's "1996 Strategy Update." The second data set contained prices at the SKU (product) level for all suppliers. The last data set

---

[7] The evidence suggests Judge Hogan did indeed drive around visiting different types of stores such as Walmart, electronics superstores, and other general supplies stores. He concluded that "you certainly know an office superstore when you see one" and accepted the market of office supplies sold in office superstores as a relevant "submarket." See *Staples*, 970 F. Supp. at 1079 also cited in Baker and Pitofsky (2007).

[8] Some MSAs are nonetheless quite large. For example, the Houston Texas MSA is about 150 miles (around 240 km) across.

Table 5.1. Informal internal across-market price comparison.

Benchmark market structure	Comparison: OSS market structure	Price reduction
Staples only	Staples + Office Depot	11.6%
Staples + Office Max	Staples + Office Max + Office Depot	4.9%
Office Depot only	Office Depot + Staples	8.6%
Office Depot + Office Max	Office Depot + Office Max + Staples	2.5%

Source: Dalkir and Warren-Boulton (1999). Primary source: Staples's "1996 Strategy Update."

was a survey with a comparison of average prices for a basket of goods as well as specific comparisons for given products.

The first set of cross-market comparisons came from the parties' internal strategy documents. The advantage of internal strategy documents that predate the merger is that they consist of data produced during the normal course of business and, in particular, not as evidence "developed" to help smooth the process of approval of the merger being considered. If the firm needs the information in a particular document to be reliable because it intends to make decisions involving large amounts of money by using them, then it will usually be appropriate to give such documents considerable evidential weight. In particular, such documents should probably receive far more weight as evidence than protestations given during the course of a merger inquiry, where there can be a clear incentive to present the case in a particular light. In this case, the internal strategy documents provided an informal cross-market comparison of prices by market structure. The results are presented in table 5.1 and suggest that when markets with only Staples in are compared with markets with Staples and Office Depot stores in, then prices are 11.6% lower in the less concentrated market.

In addition to the internal documents, the FTC also examined advertised prices from local newspapers in order to develop price comparisons across markets. In particular, the FTC performed a comparison of Office Depot's advertised prices using the cover page of a January 1997 local Sunday paper supplement. In doing so the FTC tried to choose two markets which provided an appropriate comparison. Ideally, such markets will be identical except for the fact that one market is concentrated while the other is less concentrated. In some regards it is easy to find "similar" markets; for instance, we can fairly easily find markets of similar population to compare. However, at the front of our minds in such an exercise is the concern that if two markets are identical, then why do we see such different market structures? With that caveat firmly in mind, the results are provided in table 5.2 and show considerably higher prices in the market where there is no competition from other office supply superstores.

Table 5.2. Price comparison across markets.

	Orlando, FL (three firms)	Leesburg, FL (Depot only)	Percentage difference
Copy paper	\$17.99	\$24.99	39%
Envelopes	\$2.79	\$4.79	72%
Binders	\$1.72	\$2.99	74%
File folders	\$1.95	\$4.17	114%
Uniball pens	\$5.75	\$7.49	30%

Source: Figure 2 in plaintiff's "Memorandum of points and authorities in support of motions for temporary restraining order and preliminary injunction." Public brief available at www.ftc.gov.os/1997/04/index.shtm.

5.1.2.2 *Comparing Price Levels of Multiple Products across Markets*

Whenever an authority compares prices across multiproduct retailers the investigator immediately runs into the problem of determining which prices should be compared. If there are thousands of products being compared, it is important that parties to the merger evaluation do not have the flexibility to pick the most favorable comparisons and ignore the rest. In this section we consider the element of the studies which explicitly recognized the multiproduct nature of the cross-market pricing comparisons.

The third cross-market study in the Staples case used a Prudential Securities pricing survey which compared prices in Totawa, New Jersey (a market with three players), with prices in Paramus, New Jersey (a market with two players). Since it was difficult to compare prices of 5,000 with 7,000 items, it built a basket of general office supplies that included the most visible items on which superstores usually offer attractive prices. It found that on the "most visible" items, prices were 5.8% lower in the three-player market than in the two-player market.

When comparing price levels across retailers or across multiproduct firms, one is always faced with the problem of trying to measure a price level relating to many products, often thousands of products. Sometimes, the different firms or suppliers will not offer the same products exactly or the same combination of products so that the comparison is not straightforward. A possible solution is indeed to construct a basket of products for which a price index can be calculated. A famous example of a price index is the Stone price index, named after Sir Richard Stone, which can be calculated for a single store s using the formula

$$\ln P_{st} = \sum_{j=1}^{J} w_{jst} \ln p_{jst},$$

where w_{jst} is the expenditure share and p_{jst} is the price of product j in store s at time t. This formula gives a price index for each store and its value will depend on the product mix sold in that particular store. For the purpose of comparing prices across stores, we may therefore prefer to use an index where the weights do not depend on the store-specific product mix, but rather depend on the general share of expenditure within a market, such as

$$\ln P_{st} = \sum_{j=1}^{J} w_{jt} \ln p_{jst},$$

where w_{jt} is the expenditure share of product j in the market rather than at the particular store. Naturally, there is a great deal of scope for arguments with parties about the "right" price index.[9] One could, for instance, reasonably argue for keeping the composition of the basket constant over time as price increases might make people switch to cheaper products. In such a case, the price index would not capture all price increases and would also not necessarily reveal the loss in quality. In the *FTC v. Staples* case, the FTC reportedly solved the choice of index by choosing one which the opposing side's expert witness had himself proposed, thereby making it rather difficult to critique the choice of index too much. Such a strategically motivated choice may not always be available and, even if it were, may not be desirable since there is quite an extensive literature on price indices, not all of which are equally valid in all circumstances.

Discussions about the "right" price index to use can appear esoteric to nonspecialists and therefore a general rule is probably to check that conclusions are robust by exploring the data using a few different indices. Doing so will also have the advantage of helping the investigator understand the patterns in the data if she reflects carefully on any substantive differences that arise.

To construct price indices that are representative, extensive data are needed covering a large range of products and suppliers. Price data can be obtained through a direct survey by the investigators as long as the suppliers are unaware of the action, or the investigatory authority is clear there are no incentives to strategically manipulate observed prices. Alternatively, one could solicit internal company documents that may provide own-price listings of products at different points of time in different stores or markets. Firms do tend to have documents (and databases) with comprehensive list prices. Unfortunately, in some industries, list prices are only weakly related to actual prices once rebates and discounts are taken into account. If such discounts are important in the industry, it is usually advisable to take them into account when calculating the final net price. Allocating rebates to the sales can be a challenging exercise and one should not hesitate to ask companies for the data and clarification as to what rebates apply to which sales. Sometimes, the quality of the data will determine the level of minimum aggregation possible with respect to the products and the time unit used. Finally, one should also inquire about internal

[9] For a review of the price index literature, see, for example, Triplett (1992) and also Konüs (1939), Frisch (1936), and Diewert (1976). For a recent contribution, see Pakes (2003).

documents on market monitoring as very often those will reveal relevant information about competitors' observed behavior.

Unless our price data come from internal computer records generated ultimately from the point of sale, the investigative team is unlikely to have either quantity or expenditure data. Unfortunately, such data are often important for price comparisons—either for computing price indices explicitly or more generally helping to provide the investigators with appropriate weighting to evidence about particular price differences. If a price comparison suggests a problem but the prices involve goods which account for 0.000 01% of store sales, probably not too much weight should be given to that single piece of evidence taken alone. On the other hand, it may be possible to examine the prices associated with a relatively small numbers of goods whose sales are known to account for a large fraction of sales.

In 2000, the U.K. Competition Commission[10] (CC) undertook a study of the supermarket sector.[11] Several data sources were used to compare the prices of specific products and of a basket of products across chains and stores. To construct the basket, the CC asked the twenty-four multiple grocery retailers such as Tesco, Asda, Sainsbury's, Morrisons, Aldi, M&S, and Budgens for details of prices charged for 200 products in 50–60 stores for each company on one particular day before the start of the inquiry: Thursday, January 28, 1999. The basket was constructed using 100 products from the top 1,000 sales lines, picking "well-known" products across each category and 100 products chosen at random from the next 7,000 products "although the choices were then adjusted as necessary to reflect the range of reference product categories."[12] The main difficulty was comparability: finding "similar" products sold across all supermarket chains. The CC also asked for sales revenue data for each product in order to construct sales-weighted price indices.

The inquiry also used internal company documents in which firms monitored the price of competitors. Aldi, for instance, had daily price checks on major competitors as well as weekly, monthly, and quarterly reports on prices of certain goods for selected competitors and across the whole range in discounters. Asda had three different weekly or monthly price surveys of competitors.[13] The aim of collecting all these data was to compare prices across local markets with different market structures. To accomplish this, the CC's economics staff plotted all the stores on a map and visually selected 50–60 stores that faced either "intense," "medium," or "small" amounts of local competition. This appears to be a pragmatic if slightly ad hoc approach with the advantage that the method did generate cross-sectional variation. Recent developments in software for geographic positioning (known as geographic information systems) greatly facilitate characterizing local competition.

---

[10] In its previous guise as the U.K. Monopolies and Mergers Commission.

[11] Available from www.competition-commission.org.uk/rep_pub/reports/2000/446super.htm.

[12] See paragraph 2 in appendix 7.6 of the CC's supermarket final report.

[13] See appendix 7.4 of the CC's supermarket inquiry report.

As always in empirical analysis, getting the right data is a first important step. With very high-quality data on a relevant sample, simple exercises such as the cross-sectional comparisons can be truly revealing. In the *FTC v. Staples* office supplies case, all the results from the cross-sectional comparison pointed to a detrimental effect of concentration on prices. Markets with three suppliers are cheaper than markets with two suppliers, which are in turn cheaper than markets with a single supplier. This was supported by the comparison across market using different data sources. The evidence was enough to indicate that a merger might be problematic in terms of prices to the final consumer.

Still, although local markets in the United States (and particularly neighboring markets such as those used for many of the comparisons) are probably close enough for the comparisons to make sense, the merging parties still claimed that price differences were due to cost differences in the different areas and in particular that price differences were not caused by the lack of additional competitors. The strength of any evidence needs to be evaluated and the "cost difference" critique suggests that the cross-market correlation between market structure and prices may be real but the explanation for the correlation may not be market power. To address this potentially valid critique, the FTC undertook further econometric analysis to take account of possible market differences, and it is to that we now turn.

5.1.2.3 Endogeneity Problems in Cross-Sectional Analysis

Results obtained from a simple cross-sectional comparison across markets with different market structures are informative provided the comparisons involved are sensible. However, such studies will rarely be entirely conclusive by themselves since they are vulnerable to the criticism that, although there might be a link between market structure and price, this link is not causal. For example, if two markets have in truth different costs, then we will tend to see both fewer stores and higher prices in the high cost market. In such a situation an investigator could easily and erroneously conclude that a merger to increase concentration would increase prices. Such a situation is of particular difficulty since costs are often difficult to observe and provides yet another example of an "endogeneity bias."

To summarize the problem consider a regression equation attempting to explain prices as a function of market structure:

$$p_m = \alpha + N_m \gamma + \varepsilon_m,$$

where p_m is the price in market m and N_m is the number of firms in market m. Suppose that the true data-generating process (DGP) is very closely related:

$$p_m = \alpha + N_m \gamma^{\text{True}} + u_m,$$

with the determinants of prices other than "market structure," N_m, captured in the unobserved component, u_m. For instance, costs will affect prices but are not explicitly controlled for, so their effect is a component in the error term. If high costs cause high u_m and therefore high prices as well as low entry (low N_m), then we have $E[u_m N_m] < 0$, i.e., the "random" term in the equation will not be independent of the explanatory variable. This violates a basic condition for getting unbiased estimates of the regression parameters using our standard technique of OLS (see chapter 2). We will find that markets with fewer firms will be associated with higher prices, but the true cause of the high prices is not the market structure but rather the higher costs. One must therefore beware "false positives" when using across-market data variation to identify the relationship between market structure and prices. False positives are possible when there is a factor such as high cost that will positively affect prices and that will also independently negatively affect entry and the number of firms. If this happens, we will find a negative correlation between price and market structure that is due to variation in costs (or other variable) and *not* to differences in pricing power.

False negatives can also occur when using across-market data variation. This happens when there is an omitted factor that increases both prices and the number of firms in the market. For instance, a high demand for reasons we do not see (e.g., demographics, tastes) will result in high prices and also in a large number of firms. In this case, we will tend to find a positive correlation between price and number of suppliers that is due to variation in demands across markets. Again such a positive correlation is *not* down to differences in pricing power, but may act to make pricing power more difficult to identify. Specifically, we may find no correlation at all when there is in fact a negative correlation due to pricing power. This is because the "endogeneity" bias now acts to bias our estimate of γ^{True} upward—toward zero or even above zero.

The endogeneity bias in the cross-sectional comparisons of markets with different structures ultimately occurs when there is a component that we do not account for that affects both prices and the number of firms or in other words it affects both prices and entry.

To illustrate where the endogeneity concern comes from using a theoretical model, consider the equilibrium price in a Cournot model with quadratic costs such as described above:

$$p_m = \frac{a_m}{b} - \frac{1}{b}\left(\frac{N_m(a_m - c_m b)}{1 + N_m + dbS_m}\right),$$

where S is the size of the market, a and b are demand parameters, and c and d are the cost parameters. The demand and costs parameters are unobserved and their effect is therefore included in the error term of the pricing regression. In this model, if we use the free entry assumption to solve for the equilibrium number of firms N, we get

$$N_m^* = \frac{a_m - c_m b}{2}\sqrt{\frac{2S_m(2 + dbS_m)}{bF}} - 1 - dbS_m.$$

And the point to note is that both p and N are correlated with both demand and costs. Thus the unobserved components of both demand and costs will both emerge in the pricing equation's residual and also be a determinant of the number of firms, N.

Sometimes, analysts will be able to convincingly argue that endogeneity is not an issue. Often, it will be advisable to try to control for it. In the following section we illustrate one way of attempting to do so.

5.1.3 Using Changes over Time: Fixed-Effects Techniques

Fixed-effects techniques were introduced in chapter 2 and are closely related to the natural experiment techniques discussed in chapter 4.[14] In both cases, one observes how the outcome of interest (for example price) for similar observations changes over time following changes in the explanatory variable for only some but not all the observations, thereby identifying the effect of that explanatory variable on the outcome of interest. The great advantage of these techniques is that we do not need to control for all the remaining explanatory variables that are assumed to remain constant. Fixed effects are also technically very simple to implement. When used properly, fixed effects are a powerful empirical method that provides solid evidence. But as in many empirical exercises, the ability to produce regression results with easy-to-use software can mean that the technique appears deceptively simple. In reality, the investigator must make sure that the conditions necessary for the validity of the method are satisfied. In this section we discuss fixed effects and highlight when this very appealing technique may be properly used and when, on the contrary, one must be wary of applying it.

5.1.3.1 Fixed Effects as a Solution for Endogeneity Bias

To identify the effect of market structure on the level of prices one must control for each of the determinants of price and obtain the pure effect of the number of competitors on price. The difficulties are both that the number of variables that one needs to control for may be large and that at least some of the variables (particularly cost data) are likely to be difficult to observe. Comprehensive data are therefore unlikely to be available. One way to proceed in the face of this issue is to choose a reasonably homogeneous subset of observations and look at the effect of the change in market structure on that subset. For example, we may look over time at the effect of a change in market structure affecting the price at a particular store. Such an approach uses "within-store" and "across-time" data variation. This kind of data variation is very different from the across-store or across-market data variation used in the previous section to identify the relationship between prices and the number

[14] The econometric analysis of fixed-effects estimators and other techniques for panel data are widely discussed in the literature. For example, readers may wish to consult Greene (2007), Baltagi (2001), or Hsiao (2003).

of stores. If we have just one store, we could use the data variation from that one store and the only data variation would be "within store across time." However, if we have many stores observed over time, then we can combine the cross-sectional information with the time series information that we have for each store. Data that track a particular sample (of firms, individuals, or stores) over time are referred to as panel data. Panel data sometimes offer good opportunities for identification because we can use either cross-sectional or a cross-time data variation to identify the effect of market structure on prices. A panel data regression model for prices can be written

$$p_{st} = \alpha_s + x_{st}\beta + \varepsilon_{st},$$

where s indicates the cross-sectional index (here, the store) and t indicates the time period so that the price p_{st} is store-time specific as are the explanatory variables, x_{st}. Allowing for a store fixed effect α_s in the regression controls for a particular price level to be associated with each store. By introducing this store-specific constant and looking at the effect of a change of structure (i.e., a variable in x_{st}) on that store, we control for all store-specific time-invariant store characteristics. For example, if our data are fairly high frequency and costs change slowly, then the store's cost structure may be sufficiently constant across time for this to be a reasonable approximation. Similarly, the fixed effect may successfully control for the impact of store characteristics such as a particularly good location persistently affecting demand and hence prices. Controlling for these unobserved characteristics by using the store fixed effect will help address the concern we highlighted with the cross-sectional evidence, that, for example, the costs in a particular location are high and this is therefore associated with both high prices and low entry. Thus store fixed effects may help alleviate "endogeneity bias." Such an approach to alleviate endogeneity is often used when the researcher has panel data.[15] Of course, one still needs to account for time-varying effects but permanent structural differences across stores are at least accounted for. To be clear, the fixed-effects technique will only work to the extent that there is not any substantial time-varying change in demand or costs within stores that affect both the number of local stores and prices. If there are, then the fixed-effects approach may not help solve the problems associated with endogeneity bias.

To illustrate this method let us return to our discussion of the *FTC v. Staples/Office Depot* case. In that case, the FTC had product level data from 428 Staples stores in 42 cities for 23 months available. To make the data set manageable, a monthly price index was constructed for each store, based on a basket of goods. The FTC proposed the following fixed-effects regression:

$$p_{smt} = \alpha_s + x_{smt}\beta + \varepsilon_{smt},$$

where as before s indicates store, t indicates the time period, m indicates market or city, p is the price variable, and x, in this instance, is a set of dummy indicators for

[15] For a review of the history of panel data econometrics, see Nerlove (2002). (See, in particular, chapter 1 of that book, entitled "The history of panel data econometrics, 1861–1997.")

the presence of nearby stores such as an Office Depot within five miles ($\text{OD}_{smt}^{5\,\text{miles}}$) or the presence of a local Walmart or other potentially relevant competitor stores. The latter coefficients turned out to be insignificant so we will focus on the effect of the Office Depot store. Note that the regression has a store-specific fixed effect α_s, which means that the changes in the x variables are considered "holding the store effect constant." Specifically, if a single store experiences nearby entry, we will see that either its price drops or it does not. For those stores which experience no change in prices over time, the store fixed effect will absorb all of the variation in prices and so that variation will not be used to help identify the value of the parameters in β. That is, in contrast to the cross-sectional data variation, the store fixed-effects regression uses primarily the "within-store" data variation, albeit using the within-store data variation across the whole sample (see also the discussion on this point in chapter 2).

The fixed-effects regression was meaningful in this case because there was enough informative variation in the data. Prices varied across time and across stores but it is notable that they varied more across stores than across time. Since the store fixed effects will account for all the time-invariant variation across stores, only the relatively small amount of within-store data variation may be left once the fixed effects are allowed for. Fortunately, there was some variation across time within a store in prices and also in the presence of competitors in some of the stores' market. Enough stores experienced entry by nearby rival stores to ensure that it was possible to identify the effect of that change in market structure on prices.

The effect of the presence of a competitor (i.e., an Office Depot store) on Staples's prices can be calculated using the expression:

$$100\frac{\hat{p}_{smt}(\text{OD}_{smt}^{5\,\text{miles}} = 1) - \hat{p}_{smt}(\text{OD}_{smt}^{5\,\text{miles}} = 0)}{\hat{p}_{smt}(\text{OD}_{smt}^{5\,\text{miles}} = 0)} = 100\frac{\hat{\beta}^{\text{OD}}}{\hat{p}_{smt}(\text{OD}_{smt}^{5\,\text{miles}} = 0)},$$

where $\hat{p}_{smt}(\text{OD}_{smt}^{5\,\text{miles}} = 1)$ denotes the predicted price level at store s in market m at time t when the x variable associated with the indicator for whether there is an Office Depot within five miles takes on the value 1 and $\hat{p}_{smt}(\text{OD}_{smt}^{5\,\text{miles}} = 0)$ is defined analogously. This expression provides the predicted percentage decrease in prices at a Staples store which results from having an Office Depot within five miles, all else equal.

The defendants' expert found only a 1% effect of the presence of an office supply superstore on the price and claimed that the difference with the cross-sectional results was due to the endogeneity bias caused by comparing stores in different markets.[16] He argued that the difference between the cross-sectional and fixed-effects estimates arose because the panel data estimates controlled for store-specific costs that were not observed directly and hence not controlled for in either the cross-sectional regression or the panel data regression unless fixed effects were included. However, in the event Baker (1999) argues there were several problems

[16] Specifically, $100 \times \hat{\beta}^{\text{OD}} / \hat{p}_{smt}(\text{OD}_{smt}^{5\,\text{miles}} = 0) = 1\%$.

with the defendant's expert regression. First, the FTC view was that the expert had somewhat arbitrarily drawn circles around stores at 5 miles, 10 miles, and 20 miles and constructed dummies for the presence of stores within that range. The FTC argued that internal documents suggested that companies priced according to pricing zones that were not circles and could sometimes be quite large and as large as the MSA area. While generally an approach of drawing circles around stores would seem a highly plausible way to proceed, the regression aims to capture the data-generating process for prices. Here the documents reveal the nature of competitive interaction and so the specification should be guided by the documentary evidence. Including the count of stores within the MSA tripled the price effect to a range of about 2.5–3.7%. Thus the FTC argued that the merging parties' preferred results were (1) not robust to slight changes in specification and (2) did not reflect the documentary evidence. In addition, Baker (1999) reports that the defendant's expert had dropped from their sample observations from California, Pennsylvania, and a few others for reasons that were not entirely clear. When included back in the data set, the effect was estimated to be three times larger again, between 6.5% and 8.6% depending on the detail of the specification. Thus in sum, the FTC expert concluded that a reasonable estimate was that prices of Staples stores were on average 7.6% lower when an Office Depot store was in the MSA, which was also consistent with their findings using only cross-sectional data variation.

5.1.3.2 *Limitations of Fixed Effects*

Fixed-effect regressions attempt to control for the bias generated by the presence of endogeneity or omitted explanatory variables. These problems can be potentially severe in cross-sectional comparisons and the use of panel data provides an opportunity to at least partially address the endogeneity problem. Fixed-effect regressions control for firm- (or store-) specific characteristics and compute the effect of a change in the variable of interest for a particular firm (or store) only. However, because we force the effect to be measured only within firm (or store), we are, albeit deliberately, no longer fully exploiting the cross-sectional variation.

Suppose, for instance, that there is very little variation in market structure over time, i.e., no entry or exit, and we estimate a specification which includes in x a count of the number of nearby stores. When we estimate

$$p_{st} = \alpha_s + x_{st}\beta + \varepsilon_{st},$$

we will estimate $\beta = 0$ because the store fixed effect will explain all the observed variation in prices and there will be no additional variation in the data allowing us to tell apart the store-specific fixed effect and the effect of local market structure, which did not change for any given store. In an extreme case, when there is literally no time series variation in market structure, our regression package will either fail or else tend to print out estimates of standard errors which involve very large numbers indeed. The reason is that we have tried to estimate a model which is simply not identified unless there is time series variation in the local market structure variables. It is very important to realize that such a finding does not necessarily mean the variation in prices across markets is not at least partly caused by the variation in market structure. In our office supplies example, stores with a competitor nearby may have lower prices and this is just showing up in the difference in the level of the store fixed effect (α_s). Cross-sectional variation may be explained by omitted variables but it might also be due to lack of competition near some stores. Thus, it may be appropriate to consider fixed-effects estimates as low-end estimates when most of the data variation is cross sectional.

In sum, the fixed-effects regression identifies the coefficients in β by using the variation in the data within a group of observations, for example, across time for a given store as well as the across-store variation to the extent that the specification restricts the slope coefficients to be the same across stores (see the extensive discussion in chapter 2). If there is not enough within-store data variation, the regression will be uninformative about slope parameters. In fact, if most of the variation in the data is across groups because little changes within the groups, then by using the fixed effects we effectively lose all the information in the data into the fixed effects. One lesson is that analysts must be aware of the source of information, i.e., the source of the variation in the data set, when choosing the appropriate econometric technique. Fixed-effect estimators will help correct an endogeneity problem but to do so there must be sufficient within-group variation in the data. A second lesson is that fixed-effects estimators can be used to test cross-sectional evidence but the results must be interpreted carefully—a concern raised by a cross-sectional relationship between market structure and price may not be allayed by a finding that the relationship does not survive to the fixed-effects model. A mistaken belief that is the case can mean that a case handler erroneously finds there is no problem with a merger when in fact it is just that there is very little identifying variation in the explanatory variables in her data set.

5.1.4 Using Time and Cross-Sectional Variation

When the variation in the data is mostly cross sectional, fixed-effects techniques that follow a store or a firm over time may not be very informative. Moreover, we have argued that it may be a mistake to take out all of the cross-sectional variation in the data when evaluating the effect of a merger by introducing the fixed effects. We may be controlling for endogeneity but in doing so we might be taking out much of the effect of interest. As a result it will sometimes be useful to revisit cross-sectional data variation. To do so, we can use our panel data set but carefully choose the technique in order to ensure that we use the cross-sectional variation in the data to identify the effect of market structure on prices appropriately.

5.1.4.1 Explaining the Variation in the Data

One approach is to break up the price variance in the sample into a part which varies over time, a part which is firm or store specific, and an idiosyncratic part particular to a time and firm or store. To do this we can run the following regression:

$$p_{st} = \alpha_s + \tau_t + \varepsilon_{st},$$

where α_s is the store-s-specific effect, τ_t is the time-t-specific component, and ε_{st} is the store- and time-specific component for each observation. We can then run the store-specific effect on a set of regressors, including measures of rivalry from competitors:

$$\hat{\alpha}_s = x_s\beta + u_s.$$

This method will have the merit of exploiting all the variation in the data but if we omit variables that are linked with the structure of competition as well as with the price, then we will still have an endogeneity problem just as in the cross-sectional analysis. Specifically, if the covariance between the regressors x_s and the error term u_s is not zero, then OLS estimators will be biased. Assuming we have an endogeneity problem only in one variable, then the sign of the endogeneity bias will be the sign of covariance between the regressor and the error terms. Instrumental variable techniques can help alleviate such biases.

5.1.4.2 Moulton Bias

Regression analysis typically assumes that every observation in the sample is independent and identically distributed (i.i.d.). This means that observations in the sample (Y_i, X_i) are independent draws from the population of possible outcomes. If we use panel data of a cross section over time and there is little change in the variables over time, then the observations are not really independent but are in fact closely related. If so, then we are doing something close to drawing the same observation in each time period. For example, suppose we have monthly data for twenty stores over two years but that during those two years very little changes in terms of the structure of competition and prices. The regression assumes we have $24 \times 20 = 480$ different independent observations but in fact it is closer to the truth to say that we only have twenty independent observations since there is barely any variation over time and the information in the data mostly comes from the cross-sectional variation across the twenty stores. Our 480 pairs (p, N), where p is price and N is the number of competitors, are not i.i.d. The consequence is that the standard errors computed by the standard formula in a regression package will underestimate the true value of uncertainty associated with our estimates, i.e., the precision of the estimated effect will be overstated. As a result, we are more likely to find an effect when there is in reality not enough information to establish one. Correcting this problem involves modeling the error structure to account for the correlation across observations.[17] Alternatively, the technique described above in which we computed the predicted cross-sectional variation in the outcome variable (prices in our example) and related it to possible determinant of prices including the variable of interest (number of competitors in our example) provides a way of ensuring that standard errors are computed based on the relevant number of independent observations.

5.1.5 Summary of Good Practice

The above discussion has we hope provided a focused discussion of the challenges of identifying price-concentration relationships. Along the way the discussion has illustrated some important elements of good practice when attempting to use empirical techniques to identify the effect of one variable on another. Because those good practices are very important to ensure the quality of the results, we proceed to summarize them.

Collect meaningful data. From the beginning of the investigation, it is important to gather data on the relevant variables for a representative sample. One should not hesitate to contrast data from different sources and check whether other evidence such as that coming from company documents does fit the picture that emerges from the empirical analysis.

Check that there is enough variation in the data to identify an effect. Empirical work will only be as good as the data used. If there is not a lot of variation in the variable of interest in the sample that we examine, it will be very difficult to determine the effect of this variable on any outcome. Variation can be cross sectional or across time and it can be explainable or idiosyncratic. Giving considerable thought to the process that is generating the data, i.e., thinking about the determinants of the observed outcome, will be vital both in terms of understanding the data and also in determining the best econometric methodology to use.

Beware of endogeneity. Once it is established that there is enough variation in the data to estimate an effect, one must be able to argue a causal link between the variable of interest and the outcome. In order to do this, it is important to make sure that all other important determinants of the outcome that could bias the coefficient of the variable of interest are controlled for. If they cannot be controlled for, other methods of identification should be tried or else one must explain why endogeneity is not likely to be a problem. Often it will be possible to sign the expected bias emerging from a particular estimation technique. When we change the estimation technique to control for endogeneity, our estimation results should change in the expected direction.

[17] See Kloek (1981) and Moulton (1986, 1990). In practice, statistical packages have options to help correct for Moulton bias. For example, STATA has the option "cluster" to its "regress" command. For a more technical discussion of Moulton bias, see, for example, Cameron and Trevedi (2005).

Perform robustness analysis. Once a regression is run, it is important to make sure that the resulting coefficients are relatively robust to reasonable changes in the specification. For example, results should not be crucially dependent on the exact composition of the sample, except perhaps in deliberate or well-understood ways. They should also not depend on a particular way of measuring the explanatory variables unless we know for sure that it is exactly the correct way to measure them. In general, good results are robust and show up to a higher or lesser extent across many sensible regression specifications.

Use more than one method. One good way to generate confidence in the results of empirical analysis is to use more than one method and show that they all tend toward the same conclusions. If different methods produce divergent results, one should have a convincing explanation of why this happens.

Do not treat econometric evidence as "separate" from the investigation. First, no single source of evidence is likely to be entirely compelling and generally econometric evidence in particular runs the risk of being treated skeptically by judges who are extremely unlikely to be expert econometricians. That risk increases when the results are presented as some form of a mysterious "black box" analysis. Always look for graphs that can be drawn to illustrate the data variation generating the econometric results. Second, when econometric analysis proceeds in a vacuum, disconnected from the rest of the case team and hence the facts of the case, the results are unlikely to capture the core elements of the data-generating process and, as a result, the analysis is fairly unlikely to be either particularly helpful or robust.

In our case study, the FTC's evaluation of the merger of office supplies superstores, the FTC did manage to produce convincing evidence that the number of players and the prices were negatively related. The summary of their findings is presented in table 5.3.

This table presents as convincing a case that the merger between the two superstores will increase prices by more than 5% as is likely to arise in practical case settings. The results are consistent and robust and therefore easy for a nonspecialist judge to accept as credible. In fact, on June 30, 1997, the FTC got a federal district court judge to grant a preliminary injunction blocking the proposed merger between Staples and Office Depot. Subsequently, the parties gave up on their merger plans. That sounds like good news for empirical work in antitrust. However, before coming to that view it is very important for all to realize that such activity probably cannot become the benchmark for the level of evidence required by antitrust authorities in all but the most important cases. The fact that the analysis in Staples took two expert witnesses and about six Ph.D. economists to undertake means it is resource intensive. While the first time will always be harder than the second and third times, the decision

Table 5.3. Estimating merger effects using different sources.

Forecasting method	Estimated price increase from merger
Noneconometric forecast: internal strategy documents	5–10%
Estimate from simple comparisons of average price levels in cities where Staples does/does not compete with Office Depot	9%
Cross-section, controlling for the presence of nonsuperstore retailers	7.1%
Fixed effects, with nonsuperstore retailers in	7.6%
Weighted average of two regional estimates (California and rest of United States)	9.8%

Source: FTC results from a variety of specifications as reported in Baker (1999).

in the more recent Ryanair and Aer Lingus case[18] (which provides a European example of such analysis) runs to more than five hundred pages of careful analysis.

5.2 Entry, Exit, and Pricing Power

In the previous section, we discussed some techniques for determining the impact that market structure has on the level of prices. A great deal of our discussion revolved around the problem of endogeneity, or the fact that the number of firms is potentially not exogenously determined but rather is determined in part by the expected profits that firms think they would make if they enter, and this in turn may be related to prices. Cost and demand factors may simultaneously affect both prices and structure. In simple economic models of the world where entry is assumed relatively unfettered by barriers, high profits will attract entry, which in turn induces higher market output and lower prices. If entry is relatively free, we will expect the process of competition to work, driving prices down to the great benefit of consumers. That said, there is a variety of sources of barriers to entry. Some entry barriers are natural—you cannot enter the gold-mining business unless you have access to gold deposits. Some entry barriers are regulatory—you cannot enter the market for prescribing drugs without the requisite qualifications.[19] On the other hand, oligopolistic firms may strategically

[18] Case no. Comp/M.4439. This decision is available at http://ec.europa.eu/comm/competition/mergers/cases/decisions/m4439_20070627_20610_en.pdf. See, in particular, Annex IV: Regression analysis technical report.

[19] Of course, such regulatory barriers may aim to solve another problem. Free entry into prescription writing may reduce the costs of getting a prescription for a patient, but one might worry both about the suitability of the resulting prescriptions and the total costs of prescribing if the patient's cost of drugs is subsidized by a national health care system.

seek to raise entry barriers and thereby deter entry. For example, firms may try to influence the perceived profits by potential entrants in a way that may deter such entry even if the existing firm is making substantial profits. This section turns to the analysis of entry and potential entry and examines in particular the way in which strategic entry deterrence may take place. In doing so, we hope to illustrate how to inform the sometimes difficult question of whether entry is likely to play the role of an effective disciplinary force.

5.2.1 Entry and Exit Decisions

Entry is the first decision a firm faces. Entering a market involves investment in assets and at least a portion of those investment costs will typically become sunk costs. On the other hand, a firm may choose not to enter and by doing so will save the sunk costs and leave its resources available for other purposes. The simplest model of firm entry behavior therefore posits that a firm will enter a market if the net profits obtained from doing so are at least as large as the best alternative use of its capital. Of course, since sunk costs incurred on entry today will typically generate a stream of profits over some future time horizon, when estimating net profits, we will often want to consider the net present value of the stream of profits it hopes to generate in the future. Such an approach will be familiar to accountants in the form of discounted cash flow (DCF) approaches to evaluating profit opportunities and to financial analysts evaluating whether stocks are appropriately valued. The difference with standard accounting and financial market practice here is that we must typically study such entry opportunities in strategic environments. To that end, in this section we study methods which may help us to analyze such strategic situations.

We begin by studying a practical example for a two-firm game in which each firm must, like an entry game, make a 1 or 0 decision—in this case to exit or stay in the market. Exactly the same methods can apply to the analysis of entry games, although the data required are necessarily more prospective if a firm has not yet decided to enter the market. After this illustrative example, we return to consider the entry game.

For illustration, consider the competition[20] between two air carriers Prime Air and Lean Air considering entering an intercontinental route. Assume initially, Prime Air was awarded the only available slots to link both airports. Having been awarded a monopoly, Prime Air expects to make handsome profit. However, Lean Air announces shortly after that it will also start flying to a sufficiently close airport that has refurbished its facilities for international flights. Prime Air management had thought that the airport in question was too small and remote so that the entry

[20] The observant reader will detect that this is a fictional example, but it is one that has parallels in numerous real-world cases, particularly in the airline industry and local bus markets. For a wonderful and richly historical illustration of these kinds of calculations in a practical setting, see the Harvard Business School case, British Sky Broadcasting versus Sky Television (HBS case number 5-799-078).

Table 5.4. Matrix representation of the strategic situation between the two competitors.

		Prime Air	
		Fight	Exit
Lean Air	Fight	$(V_{\text{Fight}}^{\text{Lean}}, V_{\text{Fight}}^{\text{Prime}})$	$(V_{\text{Fight}}^{\text{Lean}}, V_{\text{Exit}}^{\text{Prime}})$
	Exit	$(V_{\text{Exit}}^{\text{Lean}}, V_{\text{Fight}}^{\text{Prime}})$	$(V_{\text{Exit}}^{\text{Lean}}, V_{\text{Exit}}^{\text{Prime}})$

of a competitor was effectively impossible. However, the smaller airport managed to solve its problems with new infrastructure and thereby was able to facilitate entry by Lean Air.

Suppose, following a frequent reality in such cases that what followed was a massive war of attrition between the incumbent Prime Air, which had previously thought it would be a monopolist and Lean Air as the new, perhaps low-cost, entrant. For example, after the announcement of Lean Air's entry, we might see both Prime and Lean rush to increase their investment in fleets and marketing, spending substantial sums. Alternatively, or in addition at the end of the process, we might see a merger proposal from the two companies. We consider each of these possibilities below, once we have laid out a suitable analytical framework for analysis.

5.2.1.1 Net Present Values

We can study this strategic situation by examining the incentives of Prime Air and Lean Air to continue and to fight one another instead of exiting the market. Specifically, we will use the normal form of the game represented in the (2×2) matrix reported in table 5.4, where $V_j(a_j, a_{-j})$ is the payoff of firm j under a choice of action a_j when its rival chooses action a_{-j}.

Suppose now each firm carefully constructed a financial model detailing its expected net present value of economic profits in each circumstance. As evidence in an investigation such financial forecasts by a firm can be credible evidence, but will probably only be so if they are not prepared for the purposes of the investigation, but rather provided the basis for actual investments, or possibly if they are built using updated data but assumptions that predate an investigation. In such circumstances there is no obvious immediate incentive to "manage" the information provided and also strong incentives to make the forecast as reliable as possible since actual money is at stake.

To illustrate, notice that to put numbers in our 2×2 matrix of payoffs we require a financial model that calculates each firm's payoffs in each strategic situation. For example, the net present value of Lean Air profits at the moment of entry could be calculated for the case where Prime Air remained active but their market share fell to, say, 70% after the entry of Lean Air. If so, that net present value is calculated following the formula:

$$\mathrm{NPV} = \sum_{t=1}^{T} \frac{\Pi_t}{(1+r)^t} - S_0,$$

where Π_t is the economic profit realized at the end of time period t when both firms decide to remain active and fight, S_0 is the initial cost which will be sunk at the start of period 0, and r is the discount rate reflecting the companies' time value of money. For the purposes of this kind of calculation it will often be appropriate to use cash flows since we do not want to have artificial accounting adjustments showing up in economic profits.

Such cash flow numbers can be used to actually put numbers into normal form games of the form that all economists are used to considering as theoretical constructs. Obviously, any net present value forecast provided by a company in, say, a merger case where there was a failing firm, argument would require considerable careful scrutiny.

5.2.1.2 *Nash Equilibrium Strategies in a Static Framework*

Once we calculate net present values of expected profits or payoffs, we can use the numbers to resolve a game such as the one represented in table 5.4. Depending on the Nash equilibrium generated by the values of the payoffs, both firms may choose to stay, or one of them will exit.

Assume Prime Air reacted to the entry by committing to spending large sums of money very quickly, perhaps in marketing or a predation strategy pursued by expanding output. Such a strategy may have been aimed at changing the payoffs of the game by increasing its own expected payoff while at the same time decreasing the returns to Lean Air. One interpretation of such a strategy is that it could be aimed at credibly committing to the (Fight, Fight) outcome. By credibly signaling an intention to fight, Prime Air could in turn convince Lean Air that it faced a strategic reality of almost certainly being forced out of the market. If so, then a merger (takeover) proposal from Prime Air may prove attractive to both parties relative to the cost of progressing down the path of war of attrition.[21]

5.2.1.3 *Multiple Equilibria and Equilibrium Selection*

Following Bresnahan and Reiss (1990, 1991a,b), consider the general form of an entry game, as described in table 5.5.

First we note that throughout the analysis we assume $\Pi^{\mathrm{D}} < \Pi^{\mathrm{M}}$. If $\Pi^{\mathrm{D}} > 0$, the Nash equilibrium is unique and both firms enter the market. If $\Pi^{\mathrm{M}} < 0$, there are no profits to be made in the market and neither firm enters the market. But, for

[21] For example, the U.K. Competition Commission regularly considers such issues in bus merger inquiries. See www.competition-commission.org.uk/inquiries/subjects/bus.htm.

Table 5.5. The entry game.

		Firm 2	
		Enter	Do not enter
Firm 1	Enter	$\Pi^{\mathrm{D}}, \Pi^{\mathrm{D}}$	$\Pi^{\mathrm{M}}, 0$
	Do not enter	$0, \Pi^{\mathrm{M}}$	$0, 0$

instance, if $\Pi^{\mathrm{D}} < 0 < \Pi^{\mathrm{M}}$, there are two possible equilibria in the market, one in which firm 1 enters alone and another in which firm 2 enters alone. In general therefore, for at least some fixed values of payoffs (those where $\Pi^{\mathrm{D}} < 0 < \Pi^{\mathrm{M}}$ in the duopoly game) there will be several possible Nash equilibria in an entry game (N equilibria in an N-firm game, where $\Pi^{\mathrm{D}} < 0 < \Pi^{\mathrm{M}}$). That means this model of firm behavior is, at least for some parameter values, unfortunately generating not one but several possible predictions about what will happen in the world.

One approach to such a situation is to make even stronger assumptions about firm behavior than those required for Nash equilibrium. A Nash equilibrium requires that each firm is playing a best response to its competitors' actions so that no player has an incentive to change its action. In the cases of multiple Nash equilibria, to tie down predicted behavior further we would need to make additional assumptions that remove one outcome as a possibility. That said, sometimes it may not be necessary to determine the exact equilibrium outcome. For example, an antitrust investigator may be content with the prediction that only one firm will survive in the market and there might be no need to know precisely which one will survive.

In reality, many situations will produce multiple Nash equilibria and the payoffs to firms will differ across the different outcomes. For that reason we expect that firms will attempt to influence which outcome does in fact occur. For example, firms will sometimes play quite sophisticated games in which they try to affect the perception of their competitors about what their payoffs are in order to influence their choices and increase the odds of a particularly favorable equilibrium. By playing such games, firms may be able to increase the perceived barriers to entry into their markets and successfully limit rival entry.

An important example of such behavior involves product announcements that are well ahead of their actual launch. For instance, some software firms announce new releases of software, sometimes months or even years in advance. Some commentators have alleged that in doing so they are playing the "FUD" card, that is spreading "fear, uncertainty, and doubt" about whether rivals' products will be successful. Such a strategy would involve sending messages to potential customers that a particular firm will be the eventual "winner" in a market, so, for example, consumers should not risk buying what will ultimately not be a successful product. It is further alleged that an example of such behavior occurred in the mid 1980s when Microsoft's operating system MS-DOS was successful in the operating system market. The price of

MS-DOS increased from $2–5 a copy in 1981 to $25–28 in 1988, even though the allegations suggest relatively few improvements were made to the product. A rival company, Digital, developed an alternative DR-DOS that was released in its 3.31 version in March 1988. In May 1990 as DR-DOS version 5 was being released, it is reported that Microsoft announced that MS-DOS version 5 would be available in the next few months. In fact, MS-DOS 5.0 was not released until June 1991. If, as a result, customers delayed their purchases of a new version of their operating system by waiting for the announced new product, then perhaps the alleged early announcement of the release of MS-DOS 5.0 was effective. It has also been alleged that Microsoft used a similar strategy when it stated that its new Windows 3.1 operating system released in 1991 would not be able to run on DR-DOS. Digital claimed that the beta version of Windows 3.1 released in 1991 contained code that generated error messages when it was running on DR-DOS.[22]

The purpose of strategies such as premature announcements or apparently sinking investments is to change the perception of consumers and/or competitors about the likely final outcome of the competitive process. When there are several possible equilibria, convincing consumers and competitors that a particular outcome is the most likely is often the way to make it actually happen. When performing empirical analysis, one should pay attention to the motives of a firm's choices of action and how those choices affect the competitive process. Actions whose sole purpose and benefit to the firm is the potentially exclusionary effect of other players should be closely scrutinized.

5.2.2 Market Power and Market Structure

In the previous section we saw that there can be several possible equilibrium outcomes in a market. In this section we concentrate on methods that exploit observed entry decisions in markets of different sizes to extract information on the (1) effect of entry on profitability, (2) the magnitude of fixed costs, and (3) the extent of market power.

5.2.2.1 Determinants of Entry

Following the framework laid out in Bresnahan and Reiss (1990, 1991a,b), we can use the two-stage game structure of entry and then competition among the active firms that we outlined at the beginning of this chapter (see figure 5.1). Doing so allows us to consider the outcomes of the second stage of the game to be equilibrium

[22] See accounts of the alleged rivalry on http://en.wikipedia.org/wiki/DR-DOS#Competition_from_Microsoft. See also http://news.bbc.co.uk/2/hi/business/600488.stm and http://news.bbc.co.uk/1/hi/sci/tech/159742.stm and www.nytimes.com/2000/01/11/business/microsoft-and-caldera-settle-antitrust-suit.html. Digital Research was acquired by Novell in 1991 and DR-DOS was subsequently sold to Caldera in 1996 who filed the case. The case was settled only in 2000 and the terms of the settlement are confidential although reported as valued at $275 million in Chissick and Kelman (2002, p. 8, chapter 1).

prices P_N and a level of sales $D(P_N)$ associated with equilibrium of that second stage if N firms decide to enter the market at stage 1. Those in turn allow us to describe the profits for each firm that will result if N firms enter the market. Specifically, define

$$\Pi_N = [P_N - \text{AVC}]D(P_N) - F,$$

where AVC represents average variable cost, $D(P_N)$ firm demand, and F fixed costs. If marginal costs are constant, then AVC is equal to marginal cost and independent of output and hence prices. If we further assume that S is the total market size and that (1) market demand is a scaled version of a representative individual's demand and (2) that the equilibrium of the subgame is symmetric so that total demand is shared equally between active firms, then we can write firm demand as

$$D(P_N) = d(P_N)\frac{S}{N},$$

where $d(P_N)$ represents the units demanded per customer.

Profits as expected depend on the price, which in turn depends on the number of competitors and the costs. But they also crucially depend on market size. We see that as the market size increases, the potential total profits of a firm increase. If firms enter until profits are nonpositive and we ignore the integer constraint so that $\Pi_N = 0$, we can rearrange the expression to describe the minimum market size per firm necessary for entry:

$$s_N = \frac{S}{N} = \frac{F}{[P_N - \text{AVC}]d(P_N)}.$$

The minimum market size is the one that will provide enough customers for N active firms to each make a profit, covering their operating and fixed costs. The higher the fixed costs, the bigger the potential market needs to be, all else equal. Similarly, the higher the margin that the entrant can extract per customer, the smaller the market size for the entrant needs to be everything else constant.

We further describe the role of market size in the entry decision in figure 5.3, where S^{M} is the minimum market size for a single firm to break even and S^{D} is the minimum market size for the operation of two firms in the market. The variable costs per units sold are assumed to be constant, implying that prices and marginal costs do not change with market size. V_N is the variable profit per representative customer with N firms operating in the market so that $V_N = (P_N - \text{AVC})d_N(P_N)/N$.

We have seen earlier in the chapter that a wide class of oligopoly models describing competition in the subgame will predict that additional players will reduce prices and increase output for each given potential market size, S. Intuitively since margins fall on entry of additional players a monopolist may be willing to enter, and charge monopoly prices, at a market size of S^{M}. A second firm, however, would end up only being able to charge duopoly prices so that her margin per customer would be lower. As a result, to recover sufficient monies to cover her fixed costs, the duopolist

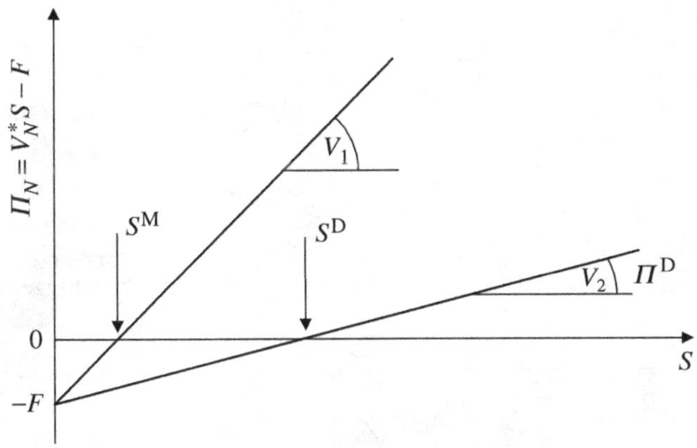

Figure 5.3. Market size and entry decision.
Source: Based on figure 1 in Bresnahan and Reiss (1990).

will not be willing to enter at a market size of $2S^{\mathrm{M}}$ but rather will only enter at some higher market size $S^{\mathrm{D}} > 2S^{\mathrm{M}}$. In terms of figure 5.3, the variable profit per customer will decrease as prices decline and this is reflected in the figure by the slope of the duopolist's profit line being shallower than the slope of the monopolist's profit line. Given the fixed costs, the second entrant will thus require a bigger size of market than the incumbent needed to enter the market. Higher fixed costs for the entrant would further exacerbate this situation since it would shift the duopoly profit line downward. Similarly, if the marginal costs of the entrant were higher it would also reinforce this effect.

Note that this figure also suggests that firms may be able to behave strategically in a number of ways in order to prevent or delay entry. For example, a monopolist may attempt to change the average profit per customer for competitors, increase the required fixed costs F (those costs which will be sunk on entry), or increase the costs of expansion so that the necessary scale of operation for an entrant becomes too large compared with the actual market size. Heavy investments in advertising or in customer-specific infrastructure are potentially ways to achieve this result. What we obtain is a strategic shift downward of the average return per customer that renders monopoly a viable alternative for a given market size. By strategically increasing costs, the incumbent lowers its own profits but prevents or delays entry by a competitor. Even if its own profits are lower, compared with the alternative of a duopoly the monopolist is still better off. Because entry deteriorates the profitability of incumbents, firms in a market may engage in strategic behavior to diminish their own payoffs and that of potential entrants in order to increase the minimum scale they will need to be profitable. Figure 5.4 illustrates in principle how this can be done.

When entry significantly decreases the degree of incumbents' market power, the new firm will need a larger scale of operation than was needed for the first

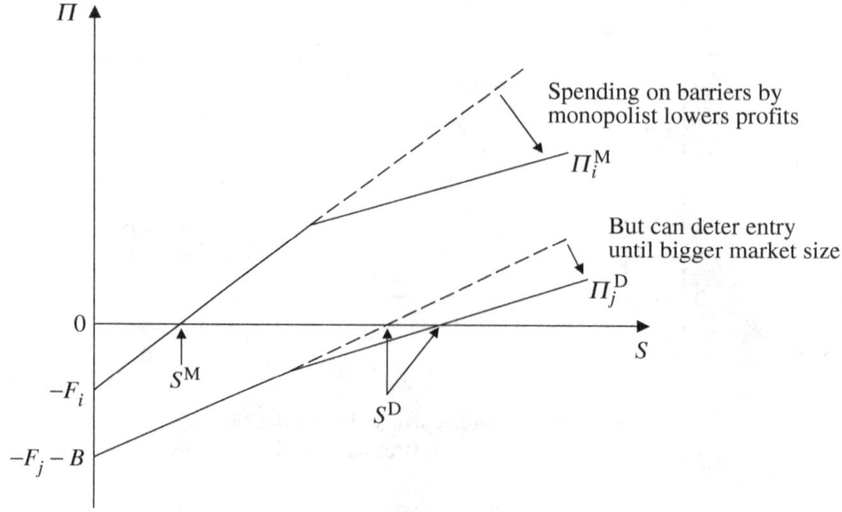

Figure 5.4. Strategic behavior to prevent entry.
Source: Based on figure 2 in Bresnahan and Reiss (1990).

entrant which could benefit from high margins. We explore more formally the relation between the likelihood of entry and market size in different competitive environments.

5.2.2.2 Entry and Market Size

In this section we describe how we can use information on market size and margin behavior to predict the number of firms that will enter a market. We also see that we can alternatively use information on market size and the number of firms to learn about margin behavior, i.e., the extent of market power being exploited.

Theory tells us that a larger number of firms will normally be associated with lower prices, lower margins, and, if market demand is price sensitive, higher quantity demanded. A larger number of firms will then normally be associated with a higher total demand and a lower profitability per customer. This is equivalent to saying that we expect sufficiently large markets to be associated with more firms than smaller markets and, as the number of firms increases, each additional firm will need a bigger increment in market size to cover its fixed costs. Under simple assumptions, a sufficient condition for a larger increment in market size to be associated with entry is that the profitability per customer decreases with the number of firms in the market. If this is so, new firms will only be able to enter if the market is large enough to accommodate them at lower per unit margin levels. In contrast, if per unit margins are constant and independent of the number of players, then we will find that the market size necessary to support N firms is linear in the number of firms and the equilibrium number of firms will increase proportionally with market size. We might expect such a situation where firms are involved in highly competitive markets since then margins will not drop as the number of firms increases. We illustrate this later by considering a game with price-taking firms. If per unit margins decline sufficiently fast with entry of new firms, we will need larger and larger market sizes to sustain one additional firm. This case is illustrated in figure 5.5.

We present the relation between the entry decision and the market size in general terms. Let us define a general function that describes the way in which margins change with the number of firms, $(p_N - \text{AVC}_N) \equiv h(N)$. Since margins typically fall with the number of competitors that enter, let us assume that $\partial h/\partial N < 0$. In that case, if we consider a symmetric equilibrium to the second stage of our game, then we can describe sales by firm i as

$$q_i = d(p_N)\frac{S}{N} = g(N)\frac{S}{N},$$

where $d(p_N)$ is the firm's demand per consumer at price p_N, which in turn depends on N and so we can define a function $g(N) \equiv d(p_N)$. Further, define $f(N) = h(N)g(N)$, which represents the total margin per unit sold times the size of the per firm demand. The zero profit condition, i.e., the breakeven point, is defined as

$$\Pi_N = (p - \text{AVC})q_i - F = f(N)\frac{S}{N} - F = 0,$$

which may be rearranged to solve for the variable we will take as exogenous and may form an important component of a data set, market size:

$$S = \frac{NF}{f(N)} \equiv \phi(N; F).$$

Note that this relationship says that the market size $S = \phi(N; F)$ required to support N active firms increases in the number of firms as we would expect whenever

$$\frac{\partial \phi(N; F)}{\partial N} = F\left(\frac{f(N) - Nf'(N)}{(f(N))^2}\right) > 0.$$

This condition in turn holds provided $f(N) - Nf'(N) > 0$, i.e., assuming positive margins per customer, this will hold whenever $f'(N) < 0$. That is, if markups per customer decline with the number of firms, then, as N increases, the markup per customer $f(N)$ becomes smaller and the necessary market size for sustaining N active firms increases. If $f(N)$ is constant and does not move with N, then the number of firms will increase proportionally with market size. If, on the other hand, the $S = \phi(N; F)$ is convex in N, then inverting the relationship would imply that N will be concave in S, i.e., the number of firms we observe will be a concave function of the potential size of the market. We will get such an outcome when margins per customer $f(N)$ drops sufficiently fast when N increases. We next illustrate these effects within the three formal economic models we examined at the start of this chapter.

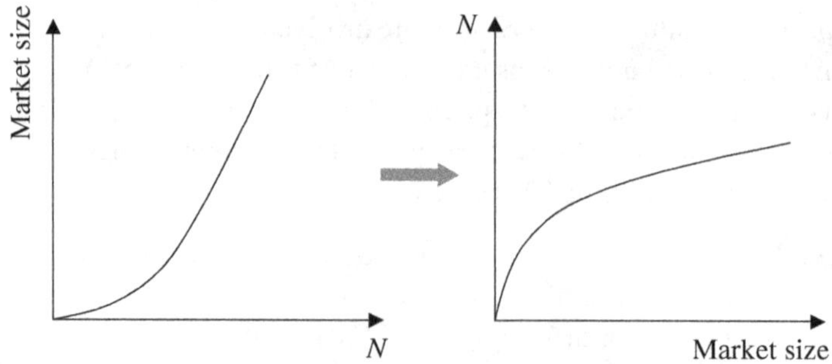

Figure 5.5. The relationship between market structure and market size.

5.2.2.3 *Entry in Price-Taking Competition*

In price-taking environments firms must decide whether to enter given the existing price, knowing that the price will not be affected by its entry in the market. The fact that prices do not decrease following the entry of a single firm actually promotes entry with regards to other competitive environments for a given price level. On the other hand, the lower prices and margins generally present in price-taking markets will discourage the entry of the less efficient firms and encourage only efficient entry.

If we assume an efficient scale for firms, which means that we assume the presence of increasing marginal costs and some fixed costs, then in a price-taking and free-entry environment the theoretical prediction is that the number of firms will increase proportionally with market size. If the market size doubles, the equilibrium number of firms in the market doubles.

To see why, recall that in a price-taking model, firms that enter the market set their quantities to solve the following profit-maximization problem:

$$\max_{q_i} p_i q_i - (cq_i + \tfrac{1}{2}dq_i^2) - F_i \quad \text{so that } q_i^* = \frac{p-c}{d},$$

where we have assumed $C(q_i) = cq_i + \frac{1}{2}dq_i^2 + F$. The equilibrium prices and quantities are, respectively,

$$p_i^* = \frac{Nc + Sda}{N + Sbd} \quad \text{and} \quad q_i^* = \frac{1}{d}\left(\frac{Nc + Sda}{N + Sbd} - c\right),$$

where S is the number of customers in the market. Given this, we can substitute the equilibrium prices and quantities into the profit equation to solve for the equilibrium number of firms in the market:

$$\begin{aligned}\Pi_i &= p_i^* q_i^* - (cq_i^* + \tfrac{1}{2}dq_i^{*2}) - F = (p_i^* - c)\left(\frac{p_i^* - c}{d}\right) - \frac{d}{2}\left(\frac{p_i^* - c}{d}\right)^2 - F \\ &= (p_i^* - c)^2\left(\frac{1}{d} - \frac{1}{2d}\right) - F = \frac{1}{2d}\left(\frac{Nc + Sda}{N + Sbd} - c\right)^2 - F = 0.\end{aligned}$$

So that with a little algebra, the equilibrium number of firms can be described as

$$N^* = Sd\left(\frac{b(c+\sqrt{2dF})-a}{c-(c+\sqrt{2dF})}\right),$$

which is a linear function of the market size S (all else equal) with a slope that is given by demand and technology parameters.

Before turning to study oligopolistic environments, we end this section by noting that this linearity result does not immediately hold in the case of price-taking under constant returns to scale, where, once the fixed costs are covered, there is no further efficiency requirement and hence the cost function does not place a limit on plant or firm size. In that case, the number of firms may increase at a lower pace than market size and we cannot determine *ex ante* how many firms will operate in the market. The basic difficulty is that if firms have constant returns to scale at all levels of output, the size of the firm is fairly fundamentally not determined by the simple theoretical model we have presented. In such a situation it is possible to get predictions which effectively contradict our explicit behavioral assumption, for example, the model may predict a monopoly and yet we have assumed such a monopoly would be a price-taking firm.

5.2.2.4 Entry in Cournot Competition

In Cournot competition, the entry of a firm will cause an increase in output that will lower the equilibrium market price and the expected margins for all firms in the market. As a result, successive potential entrants will need larger and larger additional market sizes to sustain their profitability. In Cournot competition, the margin is partly determined by the number of competing firms in the market. As more firms enter, the price decreases toward the marginal cost and the margin is reduced. Since the profitability per customer decreases with the number of firms, firms need increasingly higher numbers of customers to achieve the breakeven point upon entry. For this reason, the number of firms will increase proportionally less than the market size so that if, for example, we double the size of the market, the number of firms will less than double. This situation is illustrated in figure 5.6.

For a formal derivation, assume the inverse market demand equation

$$p(Q) = \frac{a}{b} - \frac{1}{b}\frac{Q}{S}$$

and a cost function with constant marginal costs, $C(q_i) = cq_i + F$. The firm solves the profit-maximization problem:

$$\max_{q_i} p_i(Q)q_i - cq_i - F_i.$$

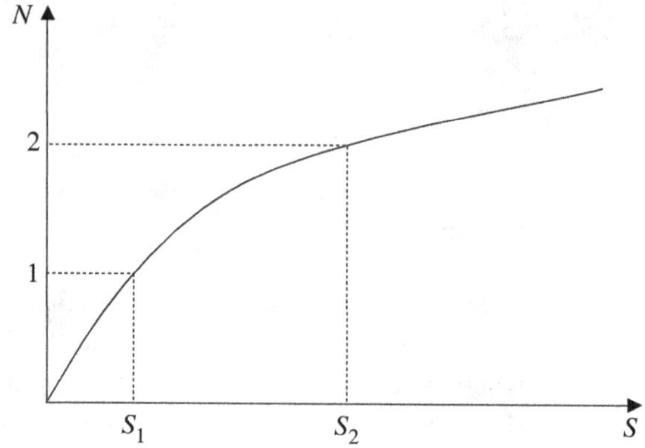

Figure 5.6. The concave relationship between number of firms and market size from a Cournot model.

And in a symmetric equilibrium we can describe equilibrium prices and quantities, respectively, as

$$p_i^* = \frac{a}{b} - \frac{1}{b}\frac{Nq_i^*}{S} \quad \text{and} \quad q_i^* = \frac{S(a - bc)}{N + 1}.$$

As in the previous section, we substitute the optimal quantity back into the profit equation:

$$\begin{aligned} \Pi_i &= p_i^* q_i^* - c q_i^* - F \\ &= \left(\frac{a}{b} - \frac{N}{bS}\left(\frac{S(a - bc)}{N + 1}\right) - c\right)\left(\frac{S(a - bc)}{N + 1}\right) - F \\ &= \left(\frac{a - bc}{N + 1}\right)^2 \frac{S}{b} - F. \end{aligned}$$

For the firm to break even, we need at least $\Pi_i = 0$. If we solve for the corresponding equilibrium number of firms, we obtain

$$N^* = (a - bc)\sqrt{\frac{S}{bF}} - 1.$$

The number of firms is therefore concave in market size S.

The Cournot equilibrium derived above is somewhat special in that, to make the algebra simple, we assumed constant marginal costs. Constant marginal costs are the result of constant returns to scale and, as we noted previously, such a technology effectively imposes no constraint on the scale of the firm. An alternative assumption would be to introduce convex costs, i.e., we could assume that at least eventually decreasing returns to scale set in. In that case, while we will still obtain the same result of concavity for smaller market sizes, we will find that as market size increases the relationship becomes approximately linear. Such a feature emphasizes that in the limit, as market size gets big, the Cournot model becomes approximately competitive and close to the case described for the price-taking firms with decreasing returns. With a large number of firms, the effect of the diseconomies of scale sets in and the size of an individual firm is then mainly determined by technological factors while the number of active firms is determined by the size of the market.

5.2.3 Entry and Market Power

The previous sections explained the basic elements of the entry game and described particularly how market size, demand, technology, and the nature of competitive interaction will determine expected profitability and this in turn will determine the observed number of firms. An interesting consequence of these results is that they suggest we can potentially learn about the intensity of competition by observing how entry decisions occur. Bresnahan and Reiss (1990, 1991a,b) show that for this class of models, if we establish the minimum market size required for the incumbents to operate and the minimum market size for a competitor to enter, we can potentially infer the market power of the incumbents. In other words, we can potentially use the observed relationship between the number of firms and the size of the market to learn about the profitability of firms. Specifically, we can potentially retrieve information on markups or the importance of fixed costs. Consequently, we can learn about the extent to which margins and market power erodes as entry occurs and markets increase in size.

5.2.3.1 Market Power and Entry Thresholds

In this section, we examine the change in the minimum market size needed for the Nth firm s_N as N grows. Particularly, we are interested in the ratio of the minimum market size an entrant needs to the minimum market size the previous firm needed to enter, s_{N+1}/s_N. If entrants face the same fixed and variable costs than incumbents and entry does not change the nature of competition, then the ratio of minimum market sizes a firm needs for profitability is equal to 1. This means the $(N+1)$th firm needs the same scale of operation as the Nth firm to be profitable. If on the other hand entry increases competitiveness and decreases margins, then the ratio s_{N+1}/s_N will be bigger than 1 and will tend to 1 as N increases and margins converge downward to their competitive levels. If fixed or marginal costs are higher for the entrant, then the market size necessary for entry will be even higher for the new entrant. If s_{N+1}/s_N is above 1 and decreasing in N, we can deduce that entry progressively decreases market power.

Given the minimum size s_N required for entry introduced above

$$s_N = \frac{S}{N} = \frac{F}{[P_N - \text{AVC}]d(P_N)}.$$

We have

$$\frac{s_{N+1}}{s_N} = \frac{F_{N+1}}{F_N} \frac{[P_N - \text{AVC}_N]d(P_N)}{[P_{N+1} - \text{AVC}_{N+1}]d(P_{N+1})}.$$

If marginal and fixed costs are constant across entrants, then the relation simplifies to

$$\frac{s_{N+1}}{s_N} = \frac{[P_N - c]d(P_N)}{[P_{N+1} - c]d(P_{N+1})}$$

so that the ratio describes precisely the evolution in relative margins per customer.

5.2.3.2 *Empirical Estimation of Entry Thresholds*

Bresnahan and Reiss (1990, 1991a,b) provide a methodology for estimating successive entry thresholds in an industry using data from a cross-section of local markets. In principle, we could retrieve successive market size thresholds for entry by observing the profitability of firms as the number of competing firms increases. However, profitability is often difficult to observe. Nonetheless, by using data on the observed number of entrants at different market sizes from a cross section of markets we may learn about the relationship.

First, Bresnahan and Reiss specify a reduced-form profit function which represents the net present value of the benefits of entering the market when there are N active firms. The reduced form can be motivated by plugging in the profit function the equilibrium quantities and prices obtained from an equilibrium to a second-stage competitive interaction between a set of N active firms, following the game outlined in figure 5.1, and, say, the price-taking or Cournot examples presented above. The profit available to a firm if N firms decide to enter the market can then be expressed as a function of structural parameters and be modeled as

$$\Pi_N(X, Y, W; \theta_1) = V^N(X; \alpha, \beta)S(Y; \lambda) - F^N(W; \gamma) + \varepsilon = \bar{\Pi}_N + \varepsilon,$$

where X are the variables that shift individual demand and variable costs, W are variables that shift fixed costs, and Y are variables that affect the size of the market. The error term ε captures the component of realized profits that is determined by other unobserved market-specific factors. If we follow Bresnahan and Reiss directly, then we would assume that the εs are normal and i.i.d. across markets, so that profitability of successive entrants is only expected to vary because of changes in the observed variables. Note that this formulation assumes that firms are identical and is primarily appropriate for analyzing market-level data sets. A generalization which is appropriate for firm-level data and also allows firms to be heterogeneous in profitability at the entry stage of this game is provided by Berry (1992).

Bresnahan and Reiss apply their method to several data sets each of which documents both estimates of market size and the number of firms in a cross section of small local markets. Examples include plumbers and dentists. To ensure independence across markets, they restrict their analysis to markets which are distinct geographically and for which data on the potential determinants of market size can be collected. The variables explaining potential market size, Y_m, include the population of a market area, the nearby population, population growth, and number of commuters. The variable used to predict fixed costs for the activities that they consider is the price of land, W_m. Variables included in X_m are those affecting the per customer profitability. For example, the per capita income and factors affecting marginal costs. The specification allows variable and fixed costs to vary with the number of firms in the market so that later entrants may be more efficient or require higher fixed costs.

Denoting market $m = 1, \dots, M$ we may parameterize the model by assuming

$$S(Y_m; \lambda) = \lambda' Y_m,$$

$$V_N = X'_m \beta + \alpha_1 - \left(\sum_{n=2}^{N} \alpha_n \right),$$

$$F_N = W_m \gamma_L + \gamma_1 + \sum_{n=2}^{N} \gamma_n.$$

In order to identify a constant in the variable profit function, at least one element of λ must be normalized, so we set $\lambda_1 = 1$. Note that changes in the intercept, which arise from the gammas in the fixed cost equation, capture the changes in the level of profitability that may occur for successive entrants while changes in the alphas affect the profitability per potential customer in the market. The alphas capture the idea, in particular, that margins may fall as the number of firms increases. Note that all the variables in this model are market-level variables so there is no firm-level heterogeneity in the model. This has the advantage of making the model very simple to estimate and requiring little in the way of data. (And we have already mentioned the generalization to allow for firm heterogeneity provided by Berry (1994).) The parametric model to be estimated is

$$\begin{aligned} \Pi_N(X_m, Y_m, W_m, \varepsilon_m; \theta_1) &= \bar{\Pi}_N + \varepsilon_m \\ &= V^N(X_m; \alpha, \beta) S(Y_m; \lambda) - F^N(W_m; \gamma) + \varepsilon_m \\ &= \left(X'_m \beta + \alpha_1 - \sum_{n=2}^{N_m} \alpha_n \right) (\lambda' Y_m) - W_m \gamma_L - \gamma_1 - \sum_{n=2}^{N_m} \gamma_n + \varepsilon_m, \end{aligned}$$

where ε_m is a market-level unobservable incorporated into the model. A market will have N firms operating in equilibrium if the Nth firm to enter is making profits but the $(N + 1)$th firm would not find entry profitable. Formally, we will observe N firms in a market if

$$\Pi_N(X_m, Y_m, W_m; \theta_1) \geqslant 0 \quad \text{and} \quad \Pi_{N+1}(X_m, Y_m, W_m; \theta_1) < 0.$$

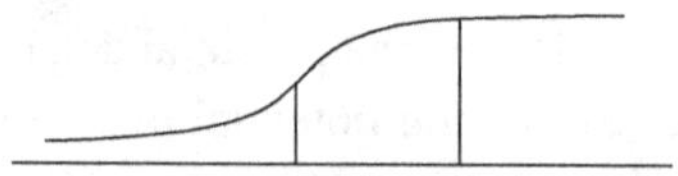

Figure 5.7. The cumulative distribution function $F(\varepsilon)$ and the part of the distribution for which exactly N firms will enter the market.

Given an assumed distribution for ε_m, the probability of fulfilling this condition for any value of N can be calculated:

$$P(\Pi_N(Y, W, Z; \theta_1) \geqslant 0 \text{ and } \Pi_{N+1}(Y, W, Z; \theta_1) < 0 \mid Y, W, Z; \theta_1)$$

$$\Longrightarrow$$

$$\begin{aligned} &P(\bar{\Pi}_N(Y, W, Z; \theta_1) + \varepsilon \geqslant 0 \text{ and } \bar{\Pi}_{N+1}(Y, W, Z; \theta_1) + \varepsilon < 0 \mid Y, W, Z; \theta_1) \\ &\quad = P(-\bar{\Pi}_N(Y, W, Z; \theta_1) \leqslant \varepsilon < -\bar{\Pi}_{N+1}(Y, W, Z; \theta_1) \mid Y, W, Z; \theta_1) \\ &\quad = F_\varepsilon(-\bar{\Pi}_{N+1}; \theta_1) - F_\varepsilon(-\bar{\Pi}_N; \theta_1), \end{aligned}$$

where the final equality follows provided the market-specific profitability shock ε_m is conditionally independent of our market-level data (Y_m, W_m, Z_m). Such a model can be estimated using standard ordered discrete choice models such as the ordered logit or ordered probit models. For example, in the ordered probit model ε will be assumed to follow a mean zero normal distribution. Specifically, the parameters of the model $\theta_1 = (\lambda, \alpha, \beta, \gamma, \gamma_L)$ will be chosen to maximize the likelihood of observing the data (see any textbook description of discrete choice models and maximum likelihood estimation).

If the stochastic element ε has a cumulative density function $F_\varepsilon(\varepsilon_m)$, then the event "observing N firms in the market" corresponds to the probability that ε_m takes certain values. Figure 5.7 describes the model in terms of the cumulative distribution function assumed for ε_m. Note that in this case, if figure 5.7 represents the actual estimated cut-offs from a data set, then it represents a zone where N firms are predicted by the model to be observed, and note in particular that the zone shown is rather large: the value of the cumulative distribution function $F(-\bar{\Pi}_N; \theta_1)$ is reasonably close to zero while $F(-\bar{\Pi}_{N+1}; \theta_1)$ is very close to one. Such a situation might arise, for example, when there are at most three firms in a data set and $N = 2$ in the vast majority of markets.

To summarize, to estimate this model we need data from a cross section of markets indexed as $m = 1, \dots, M$. From each market we will need to observe the data (N_m, Y_m, W_m, Z_m), where N is the number of firms in the market and will play the role of the variable to be explained while (Y, W, X) each play of the role of explanatory variables. Precise estimates will require the number of independent markets we observe, M being sufficiently large; probably at least fifty will be required in most applications. If we assume that ε_m has a standard normal distribution $N(0, 1)$ and

Table 5.6. Estimate of variable profitability from the market for doctors.

Variable	Parameter	Standard errors
$V_1(\alpha_1)$	0.63	(0.46)
$V_2 - V_1 = (\alpha_2)$	**0.34**	**(0.17)**
$V_3 - V_2 = (\alpha_3)$	—	
$V_4 - V_3 = (\alpha_4)$	0.07	(0.05)
$V_5 - V_4 = (\alpha_5)$	—	

Source: Table 4 in Bresnahan and Reiss (1991a).

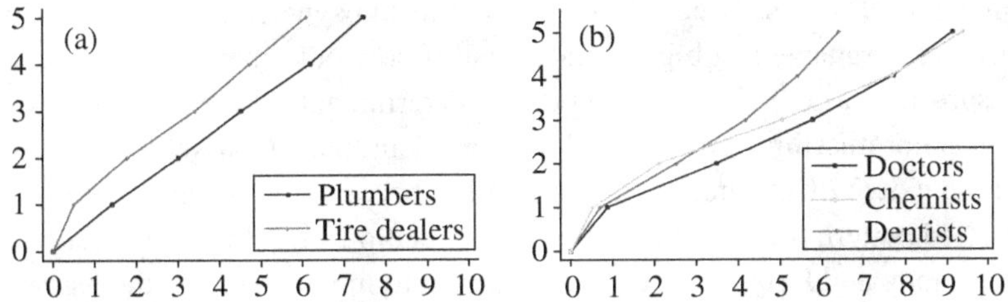

Figure 5.8. Market size and entry. The estimated (N, S) relationships for (a) plumbers and tire dealers and (b) doctors, chemists, and dentists. In each case, the vertical axis represents the predicted number of firms in the market and the horizontal axis represents the market size, measured in thousands of people. Authors' calculations from the results in Bresnahan and Reiss.

independent across observations, we can estimate this model as an ordered probit model using maximum likelihood estimation.[23]

The regression produces the estimated parameters that allow us to estimate the variation of profitability with market size, variable profitability, and fixed profits. Partial results, those capturing the determinants of variable profitability in the market for doctors, are presented for illustration in table 5.6. Note that the results suggest that there is a significant change in profitability between a monopoly and a duopoly market. However, after three firms, further entry does not seem to change the average profitability of firms.

From those results, we can retrieve the market size S_N necessary for entry of successive firms. We present the results in figure 5.8.

Looking first at the results for plumbers and tire dealers, the results suggest first that plumbers never seem to have much market power no matter how many there are. The estimated relationship between N and S is basically linear. In fact, the

[23] For an econometric description of the model, see Maddala (1983). The model is reasonably easy to program in Gauss or Matlab and the original Bresnahan and Reiss data set is available on the web at the Center for the Study of Industrial Organization, www.csio.econ.northwestern.edu/data.html (last verified May 2, 2007).

results suggest that even a monopolist plumber does not have much market power, though it may also be that there were not many markets with just one plumber in. Somewhat in contrast, tire dealers appear to lose their monopoly rent with the second entrant and thereafter the relationship between the number of players and market size appears approximately linear as would be expected in a competitive industry. The results for doctors, chemists, and plumbers and tire dealers appear to fit Bresnahan and Reiss's theory very nicely. Somewhat in contrast, in the dentist's results, while there is concavity until we observe two firms, the line for dentists actually shows convexity after the third entrant, indicating that profitability increases after the third entrant. Such a pattern could just be an artifact resulting from having too little data at the larger market sizes, in which case it can be ignored as statistically insignificant. However, it could also be due to idiosyncracies in the way dentist practices are organized in bigger places and if so would merit further scrutiny to make sure in particular that an important determinant of the entry decision for dentists is not missing from the model. A problem that can arise in larger markets is that the extent of geographic differentiation becomes a relevant factor and if so unexpected patterns can appear in the (N, S) relationship. If in such circumstances the Bresnahan and Reiss model is not sufficient to model the data, then subsequent authors have extended the basic model in a variety of ways: Berry (1992) to allow for firm heterogeneity and Mazzeo (2002) and Seim (2006) extended the analysis and estimation of entry games to allow for product differentiation. Davis (2006c) allowed for some forms of product differentiation and also in particular chain entry so that, for example, each firm can operate more than one store and instead of choosing 0/1 firms choose $0, 1, \dots, N$. Schaumans and Verboven (2008) significantly extend Mazzeo's model into an example of what Davis (2006c) called a "two-index" version of these models. While most of the entry literature uses a pure strategy equilibrium context suitable for a game of perfect information, Seim's paper introduces the idea that imperfect information (e.g., firms have private information about their costs) may introduce realism to the model and also, fortuitously, help reduce the difficulties associated with multiplicity of equilibria. There is little doubt that the class of models developed in this spirit will continue to be extended and provide a useful toolbox for applied work.

A striking general feature of Bresnahan and Reiss's (1990) results is that they find fairly consistently that market power appears to fall away at relatively small market sizes, perhaps due to very relatively low fixed costs and modest barriers to entry in the markets they considered. Although the results are limited to the data they considered their study does provide us with a powerful tool for analyzing when market power is likely to be being exploited and, at least as important, when it is not.

The framework developed by Bresnahan and Reiss (1990) assumes a market where firms are homogeneous and symmetric. This assumption serves to guarantee that there is a unique optimal number of firms for a given market size. The methodology is not, however, able to predict the entry of individual firms or to incorporate the effect of firm-specific sources of profitability such as a higher efficiency in a given firm due to an idiosyncratic cost advantage. But, if we want to model entry for heterogeneous firms, the resulting computational requirements become rather greater and the whole process becomes more complex and therefore challenging on an investigatory timetable. Sometimes such an investment may well be worthwhile, but at present, generally, most applications of more sophisticated methods are at the research and development stage rather than being directly applied in actual cases.

Although agencies have gone further than Bresnahan and Reiss in a relatively small (tiny) number of cases, the subsequent industrial organization literature is important enough to merit at least a brief introduction in this book. For example, if an agency did want to allow for firm heterogeneity, then a useful framework is provided in Berry (1992). In particular, he argues persuasively that there are important elements of both unobserved and observed firm heterogeneity in profitability, for example, in terms of different costs, and therefore any model should account for it appropriately. Many if not all firms, agencies, and practitioners would agree with the principle that firms differ in important ways. Moreover, firm heterogeneity can have important implications for the observed relationship between market size and the number of firms. If the market size increases and efficient firms tend to enter first, then we may observe greater concavity in the relationship between N and S. Berry emphasizes the role of unobserved (to the econometrician) firm heterogeneity. In his model the number of potential entrants plays an important role in telling us about the likely role being played by unobserved firm heterogeneity. Specifically, if firm heterogeneity is important we will actually tend to observe more actual entrants in markets where there are more potential entrants for the same reason that the more times we roll a die the more times we will observe sixes. For a review of some of the subsequent literature see Berry and Reiss (2007).

5.2.4 What Do We Know about Entry?

Industrial organization economists know a great deal about entry and this book is not an appropriate place to attempt to fully summarize what we know. However, some broad themes do arise from the literature and therefore it seems valuable to finish this chapter with a selection of those broad themes. First, entry and exit are extremely important—and in general there is a lot of it. Second, it is sometimes possible to spot characteristics of firms which are likely to make them particularly likely entrants into markets, as any remedies section chief (in a competition agency) will be able to tell you. Third, entry and exit are in reality often, but not exclusively, best thought about as part of a process of growth and expansion, perhaps followed by shrinking and exit rather than one-off events. This section reviews a small number of the important papers on entry in the industrial organization literature. In doing so we aim to emphasize at least one important source of such general observations and also to draw out both the modeling challenge being faced by those authors seeking to generalize the Bresnahan and Reiss article and also to paint a picture of the dynamic market environment in which antitrust investigations often take place.

5.2.4.1 Entry and Exit in U.S. Manufacturing

Dunne, Roberts, and Samuelson (1988) (DRS) present a comprehensive description of entry and exit in U.S. manufacturing by using the U.S. Census of Manufactures between 1963 and 1982. The census is produced every five years and has data from every plant operated by every firm in 387 four-digit SIC manufacturing industries.[24] An example of a four-digit SIC classification is "metal cans," "cutlery," and "hand and edge tools, except machine tools and handsaws," which are all in the "fabricated metal products" three-digit classification. In the early 1980s, a huge effort was undertaken to turn these data into a longitudinal database, the Longitudinal Research Database, that allowed following plants and firms across time. Many other countries have similar databases, for example, the United Kingdom has an equivalent database called the Annual Respondent Database.

The first finding from studying such databases is that there are sometimes very high rates of entry and exit. To examine entry and exit rates empirically, DRS defined the entry rate as the total number of new arrivals in the census in any given survey year divided by the number of active firms in the previous survey year:

$$\text{ENTRY RATE} = \frac{\text{New arrivals this census}}{\text{Active firms}_{t-1}}.$$

Similarly, DRS defined the exit rate as the total number of firms that exited since the last survey year divided by the total number of firms in the last survey year:

$$\text{EXIT RATE} = \frac{\text{Exits since last census}}{\text{Active firms}_{t-1}}.$$

Table 5.7 presents DRS's results from doing so.

First note that the entry rate is very high, at least in the United States, on average in manufacturing. Between 41 and 52% of *all firms* active in any given census year are entrants since the last census, i.e., all those firms have entered in just five years! Similarly, the exit rate is very high, indeed a similar proportion of the total number of firms. Even ignoring entry and exit of smallest firms, the turnover appears to be very substantial. On the other hand, if we examine the market share of entrants and exitors, we see that on average entrants enter at a quarter to a fifth of the average

[24] The Standard Industrial Classification (SIC) codes in the United States have been replaced by the North American Industrial Classification System (NAICS) as part of the NAFTA process. The system is now common across Mexico, the United States, and Canada and provides standard definitions at the six-digit level compared with the four digits of the SIC (www.census.gov/epcd/www/naics.html). The equivalent EU classification system is the NACE (Nomenclature statistique des Activités économiques dans la Communauté Européenne).

Table 5.7. Entry and exit variables for the U.S. manufacturing sector.

	1963–67	1967–72	1972–77	1977–82
Entry rate (ER):				
All firms	0.414	0.516	0.518	0.517
Smallest firms deleted	0.307	0.427	0.401	0.408
Entrant market share (ESH):				
All firms	0.139	0.188	0.146	0.173
Smallest firms deleted	0.136	0.185	0.142	0.169
Entrant relative size (ERS):				
All firms	0.271	0.286	0.205	0.228
Smallest firms deleted	0.369	0.359	0.280	0.324
Exit rate (XR):				
All firms	0.417	0.490	0.450	0.500
Smallest firms deleted	0.308	0.390	0.338	0.372
Exiter market share (XSH):				
All firms	0.148	0.195	0.150	0.178
Smallest firms deleted	0.144	0.191	0.146	0.173
Exiter relative size (XRS):				
All firms	0.247	0.271	0.221	0.226
Smallest firms deleted	0.367	0.367	0.310	0.344

Source: Dunne et al. (1988, table 2). The table reports entry and exit variables for the U.S. manufacturing sector (averages over 387 four-digit SIC industries).

scale of existing firms in their product market and therefore account for only 14–17% share of the total market between the years surveyed. Exiting firms have very similar characteristics. The fact that entering and exiting firms are small gives us our first indication that successful firms grow after entry but unless they maintain that success, then they will shrink before eventually exiting. At the same time other firms will never be particularly successful and they will enter small and exit small having not substantively changed the competitive dynamics in an industry. Small-scale entry will always feature in competition investigations, but claims by incumbents that such small-scale entry proves they cannot have market power are usually not appropriately taken at face value.

The figures in table 5.7 report the average (mean) rates for an individual manufacturing industry and Dunne et al. also report that a large majority of industries have entry rates of between 40 and 50%. Exceptions include the tobacco industry with only 20% of entry and the food-processing industries with only 24%. They found the highest entry rate in the "instruments" industry, which has a 60% entry rate. Finally, we note that DRS find a significant correlation between entry and exit measures, an observation we discuss further below.

5.2.4.2 Identifying Potential Entrants

There are a number of ways to evaluate the set of potential entrants in a market. Business school strategy teachers often propose undertaking a SWOT (strengths, weaknesses, opportunities, and threats) analysis and such analyses do sometimes make their way into company documents. After a company has undertaken such an analysis, identified potential entrants will often be named under "threats," while markets presenting potential entry opportunities may be named in the opportunities category. Thus information on potential entrants may come from company documents or, during an investigation, from surveys and questionnaires of customers or rivals (who may consider backward integration), and/or senior managers (the former may have the experience and skills necessary to consider setting up rival companies). Alternatively, sometimes we can examine the issue empirically and in this section we provide a couple of well-known examples of doing so.

First, let us return to Dunne et al., who found that the average firm produces in more than one four-digit product classification and that single-plant firms account for 93–95% of all firms but only 15–20% of the value of production. The latter figure implies that multiplant firms account for an 80–85% share of total production. Such observations suggest examining entry and exit rates by dividing potential entrants into three types: new firms, diversifying firms entering the market with a new plant, and diversifying firms entering the market using an existing plant.

Table 5.8 shows the entrants by type. Note that in any survey year, most entrants are new firms opening new plants while diversifying firms opening a new plant are a relatively rare event as it is much more common for diversifying firms to enter by diversifying production at their existing plant. On the other hand, when a diversifying firm enters with a new plant, it enters at a much larger scale than the other entrant types, at a whopping 90% or more of the average size of the existing firms in three of the survey years considered. Thus while entry by a multiproduct firm opening a new plant is a relatively rare event, when it happens it will often represent the appearance of a very significant new competitor.

For an example of how this can work, consider the U.K. Competition Commission's analysis of the completed acquisition by Greif Inc. of the "new steel drum and closures" business of Blagden Packaging Group, where new large-scale entry played a very important role.[25] The CC noted that the merger, on its face, was likely to result in a post-merger market share (of new large steel drums and closures in the United Kingdom) of 85%, with the merger increment 32%. On the face of it, since imports were negligible pre-merger, this merger clearly appeared to raise substantial concerns unless there were some mitigating factors such as a very high demand

[25] Closure systems are the mechanism by which the contents of a drum can be poured or pumped out and the drum resealed. The CC found the market in closures was global so that the area of concern was only steel drums. The CC (2007a) "found that, over the past five years, both Greif and Blagden lost more custom to each other than to any other competitor in the world."

Table 5.8. Entry variables by types of firms and method of entry.

Type of firm/ method of entry[a]	1963–67	1967–72	1972–77	1977–82
Entry rate				
Total	0.307	0.427	0.401	0.408
NF/NP	0.154	0.250	0.228	0.228
DF/NP	0.028	0.053	0.026	0.025
DF/PM	0.125	0.123	0.146	0.154
Entrant market share				
Total	0.136	0.185	0.142	0.169
NF/NP	0.060	0.097	0.069	0.093
DF/NP	0.019	0.039	0.015	0.020
DF/PM	0.057	0.050	0.058	0.057
Entrant relative size				
Total	0.369	0.359	0.280	0.324
NF/NP	0.288	0.308	0.227	0.311
DF/NP	0.980	0.919	0.689	0.896
DF/PM	0.406	0.346	0.344	0.298

[a]NF/NP, new firm, new plant; DF/NP, diversifying firm, new plant; DF/PM, diversifying firm, product mix. *Source*: Dunne et al. (1988, table 3). Entry variables by type of firm and method of entry. (Averages over 387 four-digit SIC industries.)

elasticity. However, toward the end of the merger review process, a new entrant building a whole new plant was identified: the Schuetz Group was constructing a new plant at Moerdijk in the Netherlands, including a new steel drum production line "with significant capacity." The company described the facility as consisting of a floorspace of 60,000 m^2 located strategically and ideally located between Rotterdam and Antwerp[26] with a capacity of 1.3 million drums annually per shift.[27] The total U.K. sales of new large steel drums were estimated to be approximately 3.7 million in 2006.[28] This new entrant, whose plant was not operational at the time of the CC's final report, was deemed likely to become an important competitive constraint on the incumbents once it did open at the end of 2007 or early 2008.[29] This appears to be one example of a diversifying firm entering a market by building a new plant of significant scale, although the diversification is relative to the U.K. geographic market rather than the activities of the firm per se.

[26]A press release is available at www.schuetz.net/schuetz/en/company/press/industrial_packaging/english_articles/new_location_in_moerdijk/index.phtml.

[27]See paragraph 8.4 of CC (2007).

[28]See table 2 of CC (2007).

[29]In this case, Schuetz was already involved in some closely related products in the United Kingdom; specifically, it was a U.K. manufacturer of intermediate bulk containers but not new large steel drums. Schuetz was also already active in steel drums and a number of other bulk packaging products elsewhere in the world.

Table 5.9. Number and percentage of markets entered and exited in large cities by airlines.

	Airline	# of markets served	# of markets entered	# of markets exited	% of markets entered	% of markets exited
1	Delta	281	43	28	15.3	10.0
2	Eastern	257	33	36	12.8	14.0
3	United	231	36	10	15.6	4.3
4	American	207	22	12	10.6	5.8
5	USAir	201	20	17	10.0	5.8
6	TWA	174	22	23	12.6	13.2
7	Braniff	112	10	20	8.9	17.9
8	Northwest	75	6	7	8.0	9.3
9	Republic	69	9	6	13.0	8.7
10	Continental	62	9	5	14.5	8.1
11	Piedmont	61	14	2	23.0	3.3
12	Western	51	6	7	11.8	13.7
13	Pan Am	45	1	1	2.2	2.2
14	Ozark	28	18	4	64.3	14.3
15	Texas Int'l	27	3	6	11.1	22.2

Source: Berry (1992, table II). The number and percentage of markets entered and exited in the large city sample by airline.

Interestingly, the fact that entry does not usually happen at the average scale of operation for the industry is at least somewhat at odds with the assumption of U-shaped average cost curves that predict that most firms should have approximately the same efficient scale in the long run, as proposed in the influential Viner (1931) cost structure theory of the size of the firm.[30] Indeed, one could in extremis argue that these data seem to suggest that theory applies to only 2% of the data!

Berry (1992) provides an industry study where it proves possible to provide evidence on the set of people who are likely to be potential entrants. He extensively describes entry activity in the airline sector by using data from the "origin and destination survey," which comprises a random sample of 10% of all passenger tickets issues by U.S. airlines. While Berry's data involve only data from the first and third quarters of 1980, it enables him to construct entry and exit data for that relatively short period of nine months. Specifically, to look at entry and exit over the period he constructs 1,219 "city-pair" markets linking the fifty major cities in the United States. City-pair markets are defined as including tickets issued between the two cities and do not necessarily involve direct flights, but (realistically) assuming that the 10% ticket sample gives us a complete picture of the routes being flown, it enables entry and exit data to be constructed (albeit under an implicitly broad market definition where customers are willing to change planes). The results are provided in table 5.9, which again reveals that there is a lot of entry and exit activity taking place.

[30] See chapter 2 and, in particular, chapter 4 of Viner (1931), reprinted in Stigler and Boulding (1950).

Table 5.10. Joint frequency distribution of entry and exit in airline routes market.

Number of entrants (as %)	Number of exits, as % of total markets in the sample: 0	1	2	3+	Total
0	68.50	10.01	1.07	0.00	79.57
1	15.09	2.63	0.41	0.00	18.13
2	1.96	0.25	0.00	0.00	2.05
3+	0.16	0.08	0.00	0.00	0.24
Total	85.56	12.96	1.48	0.00	100.00

Source: Berry (1992).

Table 5.11. Number of potential entrants by number of cities served within a city pair, with number and percentage entering.

Number of cities served	Total # of potential entrants	# entering	% entering
0	47,600	4	0.01
1	12,650	45	0.36
2	3,590	232	6.46

Source: Berry (1992).

Specifically, if we look at the results by markets, we see that entry and/or exit occurred in more than a third of all markets, which implies significant dynamism in the industry since this entry relates to only a nine-month period. Furthermore, table 5.10 reports that 3.37% of markets, i.e., forty-one city-pair markets, experienced both entry and exit over these nine months. The existence of apparently simultaneous entry and exit indicates that firm heterogeneity probably plays a role in the market outcomes: some firms are better suited to compete in some of the markets.

Berry (1992) examines whether airport presence in one of the cities makes an airline carrier more likely to enter a market linking this city. He finds that this is indeed the case. As illustrated in table 5.11, only rarely is there entry by someone not already operating out of or into at least one of the cities concerned. In this case, if one wants to estimate the likelihood of entry in the short term, potential entrants should be defined as carriers that already operate in at least one of the cities.

To conclude this section, let us say that although the DRS study describes only the manufacturing sector of the U.S. economy of the 1960s to the 1980s, the study remains both important and insightful more generally. In particular, it provides us with a clear picture of the extensive amount of entry and exit that can occur within relatively short time periods. If entry and exit drive competition, and most importantly productivity growth, then protecting that dynamic process will be extremely important for a market economy to function, vital if the new entrants are drivers of innovation. The facts thus outlined suggest in particular that while antitrust authorities can play a very important short-term or even medium-term role in considering whether market concentrations should be allowed to occur, the effect of an increase in concentration which enhances market power may last only a relatively few years provided there are no substantial barriers to entry which act to keep out rivals attracted by the resulting high profits. Making sure that profitable entry opportunities can potentially be exploited by new or diversifying firms, i.e., ensuring efficient entrants face at least a fairly level playing field, thus provides one of the most important functions of competition policy.

5.3 Conclusions

- Most standard models of competition predict an effect of market structure on the level of prices. Generally, all else equal, an increase in concentration or a decrease in the number of firms operating in the market will be expected to raise market prices and decrease output. In the case of firms competing in prices of differentiated products which are demand substitutes, this effect is unambiguously predicted by simple models. Whether such price rises/output falls are in fact material, and whether all else is indeed equal, are therefore central questions in most competition investigations involving changes in market structure.

- One way to examine the quantitative effect of changes in market structure on outcomes such as prices and output is to compare the outcomes of interest across similar markets. The (impossible) ideal is to find markets that differ only in the degree of concentration they exhibit. In reality we look for markets that do not differ "too much" or in the "wrong way." In particular, an analyst must be wary of differing cost or demand characteristics of the different markets and when interpreting such cross-market evidence an analyst must always ask why otherwise similar markets exhibit different supply structures. In the jargon of econometrics, cost and demand differences across markets that are not controlled for in our analysis can result in our estimates suffering from endogeneity problems. If so, then our observed correlation between market structure and price is not indicative of a causal relationship but rather our correlation is caused by an independent third factor.

- When the data allow, econometric techniques for dealing with the endogeneity problem can be very useful in attempting to distinguish correlations from causality. Such techniques include the use of instrumental variables and fixed effects. However, any technique for distinguishing two potential explanations for the same phenomenon relies on assumptions for identifying which of the contenders is in fact the true explanation. For example, when using the fixed-effects technique, there must at a minimum be both (1) within-group variation over time and (2) no other significant time-varying unobserved variables that are not accounted for in our analysis. The latter can be a problem, in particular, when using identifying events over time such as entry by nearby rivals. For example, sometimes prices rise following entry when firms seek to differentiate their product offerings in light of that entry.
- Entry increases the number of firms in the market and, in an oligopoly setting, is generally expected to lower prices and profitability in the market. Factors which will affect whether we observe new entry may include expected profitability for the entrant post entry, which in turn is determined by such factors as the costs of entrants relative to incumbents, the potential size of the market, and the erosion of market power due to the presence of additional firms. Moreover, incumbents can sometimes play strategic games to alter the perceived or actual payoffs of potential entrants in order to deter entry.
- The economics literature emerging from static entry games has suggested that the relationship between market size and the number of firms can be informative about the extent of market power enjoyed by incumbents. To learn about market power in this way, one must, however, make strong assumptions about the static nature of competition. In particular, such analyses largely consider entry as a "one-off" event, whereas entry is often best considered as a "process" as firms enter on a small scale, grow when they are successful, shrink when they are not, and perhaps ultimately exit.
- Relatedly, many markets are dynamic, experiencing a large amount of entry and exit. A considerable amount of the observed entry and exit only involves very small firms on the fringe of a market. However, a large number of markets do exhibit entry and exit over relatively short time horizons on a substantial scale. The existence of substantive entry and exit can alleviate the concerns raised by actual, or, in the case of anticipated mergers, potential market concentration. However, the importance of entry as a disciplining device on incumbent firms also underlines the need for competition authorities to preserve the ability of innovative and efficient new entrants to displace inefficient incumbent firms.

6

Identification of Conduct

In the previous chapter, we discussed two major methods available for assessing the effect of market structure on pricing and market power, the question at the heart of merger investigations. The broader arena of competition policy is also concerned with collusion by existing firms or the abuse of market power by a dominant firm. For example, the U.S. Sherman Act (1890) is concerned with monopolization.[1] In Europe, since the Treaty of Rome (1957) contains a reference to "dominant" firms, collusion is known as the exercise of joint or collective dominance while the latter is known as "single" dominance.[2] Any such case obviously requires a finding of dominance and in order to determine whether a firm (or group of firms) is dominant we need to know the extent of its individual (collective) market power.

In this chapter, we discuss methods for identifying the presence of market power and in particular whether we can use data to discriminate between collusive outcomes, dominant firm outcomes, competing firms acting as oligopolies, or outcomes which sufficiently approximate perfect competition. That is, we ask whether we can tell from market outcomes whether firms are imposing genuine competitive constraints on one another, or instead whether firms possess significant market power and so can individually or collectively reduce output and raise prices to the detriment of consumers.

Abuses of monopoly power (single dominance) are forbidden in European and U.S. competition law. However, the range of abuses that are forbidden differs across jurisdictions. In particular, in the EU both exclusionary (e.g., killing off an entrant) and exploitative abuses (e.g., charging high prices) are in principle covered by competition law while in the United States only exclusionary abuses are forbidden since

[1] For a tour de force of the evolution of U.S. thinking on antitrust, see Shapiro and Kovacic (2000).

[2] The term "dominant" appears in the Treaty of Rome, the founding treaty of the European Common Market signed in 1957 and has played an important role in European competition policy ever since. The term is unwieldy for most economists, as many are more familiar with cartels, monopolies, and oligopolies. Today there are two relevant treaties which have been updated and consolidated into a single document known as the consolidated version of the Treaty on European Union and of the Treaty Establishing the European Community. This document was published in the Official Journal as OJ C. 321 E/1 29/12/2006. The latter treaty is a renamed and updated version of the Treaty of Rome. The contents of Articles 81 and 82 of the treaty are broadly similar to the contents of the first U.S. antitrust act, the Sherman Act (1890) as updated by the Clayton Act (1914). The laws in the European Union and the United States differ, however, in some important areas. In particular, under the Sherman Act charging monopoly prices is not illegal while under EU law, it can be. In addition, jurisprudence has introduced differing legal tests for specific types of violations.

the Sherman Act states that to "monopolize, or attempt to monopolize," constitutes a felony but it does not say that to be a monopolist is a problem. The implication is that a monopolist may, for example, charge whatever prices she likes so long as dominant companies do not subsequently protect their monopolies by excluding others who try to win business. In Europe, a monopolist or an industry collectively charging prices that result in "excessive margins" could in principle be the subject of an investigation.

When discussing collusion (joint dominance) it is important to distinguish between explicit collusion (cartels) and tacit collusion, since the former is a criminal offense in a growing number of jurisdictions. In Australia, Canada, Israel, Japan, Korea, the United Kingdom, and the United States the worst forms of cartel abuses are now criminal offenses so that cartelists may serve time in jail for their actions.[3] Events that increase the likelihood of explicit or tacit coordination are also closely watched by competition authorities due to their negative effect on the competitive process and consumer welfare. For example, a merger can be blocked if it is judged likely to result in a "coordinated effect," i.e., an increased likelihood of the industry engaging in tacit collusion.

We begin our discussion of this important topic by first revisiting the history and tradition of the "structure–conduct–performance" paradigm that dominated industrial organization until the emergence of game theory. While such an approach is currently widely regarded as old fashioned, we do so for two reasons. First it provides a baseline for comparison with more recent work motivated primarily by static game theory. Second, the movement toward analysis of dynamic games where evolution of market shares may sometimes occur slowly over time, and empirical evidence about early mover advantages in mature industries may, in the longer term, restore the flavor of some elements of the structure–conduct–performance paradigm.[4] For example, some influential commentators are currently calling for a return to a "structural presumption," where, for example, more weight is given to market shares in evaluating a merger (see, in particular, Baker and Shapiro 2007).

6.1 The Role of Structural Indicators

The structure–conduct–performance (SCP) framework—which presumes a causal link between the structure of the market, the nature of competition, and market

[3] U.S. cartelists have served jail time for many years since cartelization became a criminal offense (in fact a felony) after the Sherman Act in 1890. Outside the United States, experience of criminal prosecutions in this area is growing. Even where active enforcement by domestic authorities is limited, in a number cases the very fact that legislation has passed criminalizing cartel behavior has enabled U.S. authorities to pursue non-U.S. nationals in U.S. courts. The reason is that bilateral extradition treaties sometimes require that the alleged offense is a criminal one in both jurisdictions.

[4] See, for example, the work by Sutton (1991), Klepper (1996), and Klepper and Simons (2000), and in the strategy literature see Markides and Geroski (2005) and McGahan (2004).

outcomes in terms of prices, output, and profits—has a long history in industrial organization. Indeed, competition policy relies on structural indicators for an initial assessment of the extent of market power exercised by firms in a market. For example, conduct or mergers involving small firms with market shares below a certain threshold will normally not raise competition concerns. Similarly, mergers that do not increase the concentration of a market above a certain threshold are assumed likely to create minimal harm to consumers and for this reason we enshrine "safe harbors" in law.[5] This provides legal certainty, the benefits of which may outweigh any potential competitive damage. Those structural thresholds are useful to provide some discriminating mechanism for competition authorities and allow them to concentrate on cases that are more likely to be harmful. However, "structural indicators" such as market shares are now treated only, as the name emphasizes, as indicators and are not considered conclusive evidence of market power. It is possible that the pendulum will swing back slightly to place more presumptive weight on structure in future years, though it is not clear it will do so at present. However, even if it does, the lessons of static game theory that drive current practice and that we outline below will remain extremely important. Most specifically, in some particular situations, a high market share may provide an incumbent with very little market power.

6.1.1 Structural Proxies for Market Power

Most of the structural indicators that competition authorities consider when establishing grounds for an investigation or to voice concerns are derived from relationships predicted by the Cournot model. For example, the reliance on market shares, concentration ratios, and the importance attributed to the well-known Herfindahl–Hirschman index (HHI) can each be theoretically justified using the static Cournot model.

6.1.1.1 Economic Theory and the Structure–Conduct–Performance Framework

In antitrust, good information on marginal cost is rare, so it is often difficult to directly estimate margins at the industry level to determine the presence of market power. However, if we are prepared to make some assumptions we may have alternative approaches. In particular, we may be able to use structural indicators to infer profitability. For example, under the assumption that a Cournot game captures the nature of competition in an industry, a firm's margin is equal to the individual market share divided by the market demand elasticity:

$$\frac{P(Q) - C_i'(q_i)}{P(Q)} = \frac{s_i}{\eta^{\mathrm{D}}},$$

[5] For a very nice description of the numerous market share thresholds enshrined in EU and U.K. law, see Whish (2003).

where s_i is the market share of the firm and η^{D} the market demand elasticity. Furthermore, under Cournot, the weighted average industry margin is equal to the sum of the squared individual market share divided by the market demand elasticity:

$$\sum_{i=1}^{N} s_i \left(\frac{P(Q) - C_i'(q_i)}{P(Q)} \right) = \frac{1}{\eta^{\mathrm{D}}} \sum_{i=1}^{N} s_i^2.$$

To derive these relationships, recall that in the general Cournot first-order condition for a market with several firms is

$$\frac{\partial \pi_i(q_i, q_{-i})}{\partial q_i} = P\left(\sum_{j=1}^{N} q_j \right) + q_i P'\left(\sum_{j=1}^{N} q_j \right) - C_i'(q_i) = 0.$$

If we denote $Q = \sum_{j=1}^{N} q_j$ and we rearrange the first-order condition, we obtain the firm's markup index, also called the Lerner index, as a function of the firm's market share and the elasticity of the market demand:

$$\frac{P(Q) - C_i'(q_i)}{P(Q)} = q_i \frac{P'(Q)}{P(Q)} \iff \frac{P(Q) - C_i'(q_i)}{P(Q)} = \frac{q_i}{Q} \frac{QP'(Q)}{P(Q)} = \frac{s_i}{\eta^{\mathrm{D}}}.$$

This relationship can be used in a variety of ways. First, note that if we are prepared to rely on the theory, the Cournot–Nash equilibrium allows us to retrieve the markup of the firm using market share data and market demand elasticity. The markup will be higher, the higher the market share of the firm. However, the markup will decrease with the market demand elasticity. That means that a high market share will be associated with a high markup, but that a high market share is not in itself sufficient to ensure high markups. Even a high market share firm can have no market power, no ability to raise price above costs if the market demand is sufficiently elastic. An important fundamental implication is that while high market shares are a legitimate signal of potential market power, high market shares should not in themselves immediately translate into a finding of market power by antitrust authorities. Naturally, measuring the nature of price sensitivity will be helpful in determining if this is, in the particular case under consideration, a factually relevant defense or just a theoretical argument.

There are estimates of average markups in many industries, often constructed using publicly available data. Domowitz et al. (1988), for example, estimate average margins for different industries in the United States using the Census of Manufacturing data and find that the average Lerner index for manufacturing industries in the years 1958–81 is 0.37.

6.1.1.2 The Herfindahl–Hirschman Index and Concentration Ratios

There is a long tradition of inferring the extent of market power from structural indicators of the industry. Firm size and industry concentration are the most commonly

Table 6.1. HHI measures of market concentration: comparison of CR(4) and HHI measures of market concentration.

Market 1			Market 2		
Firm	Share	Share^2	Firm	Share	Share^2
1	20	400	1	50	2,500
2	20	400	2	20	400
3	20	400	3	5	25
4	20	400	4	5	25
5	20	400	5	5	25
—	—	—	6	5	25
CR(4)	80		CR(4)	80	
HHI	2,000		HHI	2,950	

used structural indicators of profitability and both are thought to be positively correlated with market power and margins. The two most common indicators of industry concentration are the K-firm concentration ratio and Herfindahl–Hirschman index (HHI).

The K-firm concentration ratio (CR) involves calculation of the market shares of the largest K firms so that

$$C_K = \sum_{i=1}^{K} s_{(i)},$$

where $s_{(i)}$ is the ith largest firm's market share.

The HHI is calculated using the sums of squares of market shares:

$$\text{HHI} = \sum_{i=1}^{N} s_i^2,$$

where s_i is the ith firm's market share expressed as a percentage so that the HHI will take values between 0 and 10,000 ($= 100^2$). As illustrated above, in the Cournot model, the HHI is proportional to industry profitability and can therefore be related to firms' market power.

The HHI will be higher if the structure of the market is more asymmetric. The examples in table 6.1 show that the HHI is higher for a market in which there are more firms but where one firm is very large compared with its competitors. Also, given symmetry, a larger number of firms will decrease the value of the HHI.

The result that a market with few firms, or a market with one or two very big firms, may be one where firms can exercise market power through high markups is intuitive. As a result the HHI is used as a preliminary benchmark in merger control where the data on a post-merger situation cannot be observed. Both U.S. and EU merger guidelines use the HHI screen for mergers which are unlikely to be of much concern and to flag those that should be scrutinized. This is done by using the pre- and post-merger market shares to compute the pre- and post-merger HHI. Respectively,

$$\mathrm{HHI}^{\mathrm{Pre}} = \sum_{i=1}^{N} (s_i^{\mathrm{Pre}})^2 \quad \text{and} \quad \mathrm{HHI}^{\mathrm{Post}} = \sum_{i=1}^{N} (s_i^{\mathrm{Post}})^2,$$

where, since post-merger market shares are not observed and we need a practical and easy-to-apply rule, post-merger market shares are assumed to simply be the sum of the merging firms' pre-merger market shares. In initial screening of mergers, these values are assumed to be an indicator of the extent of margins before and after the proposed merger and the effect of the merger on such margins. Specifically, in the EU merger guidelines, mergers leading to the creation of a firm with less than 25% market share are presumed to be largely exempt from anticompetitive effects.[6] The regulations use an indicative threshold of 40% as being the point at which a merger is likely to attract closer scrutiny.[7] Mergers that create a HHI index for the market of less than 1,000 are also assumed to be clear of anticompetitive effects. For post-merger HHI levels between 1,000 and 2,000, mergers that increase the HHI level by less than 250 are also presumed to have no negative effect on competition. Changes in the HHI index of less than 150 at HHI levels higher than 2,000 are also declared to cause less concern except in some special circumstances. Similarly, the U.S. Department of Justice Horizontal Merger Guidelines[8] also use a threshold at 1,000, a region of 1,000–1,800 to indicate a moderately concentrated market, and "where the post-merger HHI exceeds 1,800, it will be presumed that mergers producing an increase in the HHI of more than 100 points are likely to create or enhance market power or facilitate its exercise."

To see these calculations in operation, next we present an example of the package tour market using flights from U.K. origins. The first and second firms in the market, Airtours and First Choice with 19.4% and 15% market shares respectively, merged to create the largest firm in the industry with a combined 34.4% market share.[9] The HHI index jumped from approximately 1,982 before the merger to around 2,564 after the merger, an increase of 582. Such a merger would therefore be subject to scrutiny under either the EU or U.S. guidelines. Of course, in using such screens, we can only calculate market shares on the basis of a particular proposed market definition. In practical settings, that often means there is plenty of room for substantial discussion

[6] Guidelines on the assessment of horizontal mergers under the Council Regulation on the control of concentrations between undertakings, 2004/C 31/3, Official Journal of the European Union C31/5 (5-2-2004).

[7] Ibid. In the United Kingdom, the Enterprise Act 2002 empowers the OFT to refer mergers to the CC if they create or enhance a 25% share of supply or where the U.K. turnover of the acquired firm is over £70 million. As an aside, some argue that it is not immediately clear that the term "share of supply" actually does mean the same as "market share."

[8] See the U.S. Horizontal Merger Guidelines available at www.usdoj.gov/atr/public/guidelines/hmg.htm, section 1.5.

[9] *Airtours plc v. Commission of the European Communities*, Case T-342/99 (2002).

Table 6.2. HHI calculations for a merger in the package tour industry.

Company	s_i	s_i^2	Adjustments for merger
Airtours	19.4	376.36	−376.36
First Choice	15.0	225	−225
Combined	34.4	1,183.36	+1,183.36
Thomson	30.7	942.49	
Thomas Cook	20.4	416.16	
Cosmos Avro	2.9	8.41	
Manos	1.7	2.89	
Kosmar	1.7	2.89	
Others (< 1% each)	8.2	$9 \times (8.2/9)^2$	
Total	100	1,982	2,564

Source: Underlying market share data are from Nielsen and quoted in table 1 from the European Commission's 1999 decision on *Airtours v. First Choice*. These calculations treat the market shares of "Others" as being made up of nine equally sized firms, each with a market share of $8.2/9 = 0.83$. The exact assumption made about the number of small firms does not affect the analysis substantively.

over whether a merger meets these threshold tests even though lack of data means it is not always possible to calculate even a precise HHI number so that results near but on opposite sides of the thresholds are not appropriately treated as materially different outcomes.

A practical disadvantage of the HHI is that it requires information on the volume (or value) of sales of all companies, as distinct from a market share which requires estimates of total sales and the sales of the main parties to a merger (the merging companies). Competition agencies with powers to gather information from both main and third parties may usually be able to compute HHI, at least to an acceptable degree of approximation provided they can collect information from all the large and moderately sized players. Very small companies will not usually materially affect the outcome. On the other hand, some significant agencies (e.g., the Office of Fair Trading in the United Kingdom) do not currently have powers to compel information from third parties (while those which do may hesitate to use them) so that even computing a HHI can sometimes face practical difficulties.

It is important to note that it is not the practice to prohibit a merger based on HHI results alone. It is useful to use the HHI as a screening mechanism, but the source of the potential market power should be understood before the measures available to competition authorities are applied. That said, market shares and HHIs will certainly play a role in the weighing up of evidence when deciding whether on balance a merger is likely to substantially lessen competition.

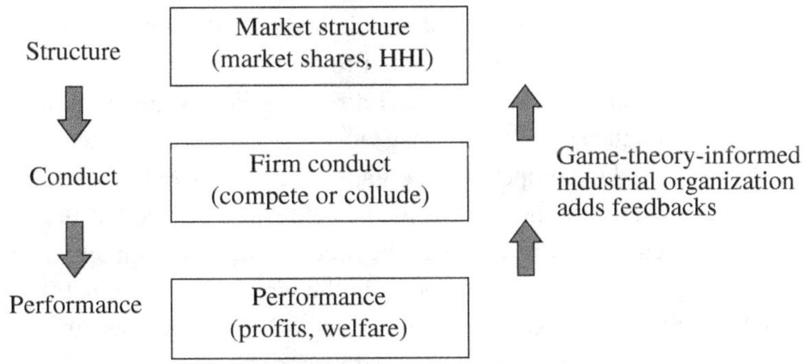

Figure 6.1. SCP versus game theory.

6.1.1.3 Beyond the SCP Framework

Theoretical developments in industrial organization, particularly static game theory, clearly illustrated important limits of the SCP analysis. In particular, static game theory suggests that the relationship between structure, conduct, and performance is not generally best considered to be a causal relationship in a single direction. In particular, the causality between market share and market power is in no way automatically established. Even though the Cournot competition model predicts that markups are linked to the market shares of the firms, it is very important to note that high industry margins are not *caused* by high HHIs, even though they coincide with high HHIs. Rather, in the Cournot model, concentration and price-cost markups are both determined simultaneously in equilibrium. This means that they are ultimately both determined by the strategic choices of the firms regarding prices, quantity, or other variables such as advertising and by the structural parameters of the market, particularly the nature of demand and the nature of technology which affects costs. If the market demand and cost structure are such that optimization by individual firms leads to a concentrated market, high margins may be difficult for even the most powerful and interventionist competition agency to avoid. Under Cournot, for example, firms that are low-cost producers will have high market shares because they are efficient. Their higher markup is a direct result of their higher efficiency.

The pure SCP view of the world that structure actively determines conduct which in turn determines performance has been subjected to a number of serious critiques. In particular, as figure 6.1 illustrates, game theorists have argued that in the standard static (one shot) economic models, market structure, conduct, and market performance typically emerge simultaneously as jointly determined outcomes of a model rather than being causally determined from each other. Such analyses suggest that a useful framework for analysis is one that moves away from the simple SCP analysis, where the link between structure and market power was assumed to be one-way and deterministic, to one in which firms can endogenously choose their conduct and in return affect the market structure.

Although we have stressed the lack of established causality between structure and performance in static models, it is important to note that many dynamic economic models push considerably back in the other direction. For example, in the previous chapter we examined the simplest two-stage models, where firms entered at the first stage and then engaged in competition, perhaps in prices. In that model, structure—in the sense of the set of firms that decided to enter—is decided at the first stage and then does indeed determine prices at the second stage. A complete dismissal of SCP analysis might therefore lead agencies in the wrong direction, but the extreme version of SCP, the view that "structure" is enough to decide whether a merger should be approved, is difficult to square with (at least) a considerable amount of economic theory.

The importance of structural indicators in determining the extent of market power and the anticompetitive effects of a merger has gradually decreased as the authorities increasingly rely on detailed industry analysis for their conclusions. Still, structural indicators remain important among many practitioners and decision makers because of their apparent simplicity and their (sometimes misunderstood) link with economic theory.

6.1.2 Empirical Evidence from Structure–Conduct–Performance

The popularity of the simple SCP framework lies in the fact that it provides a tool for decision making based on data that are usually easily obtained. This has real advantages in competition policy, not least because legal rules based on structural criteria can provide a degree of legal certainty to parties considering how particular transactions would be treated by the competition system. Critics, however, point to disadvantages, particularly that certainty about the application of a simple but inappropriate rule may lead to worse outcomes than accepting the *ex ante* uncertainty that results from relying on a detailed investigation of the facts during a careful investigation.

In considering the debate between the advocates and critics of SCP style analysis, and its implications for the practice of competition policy, it is helpful to understand an outline of the debate that has raged over the last sixty years within industrial organization. We next outline that debate.[10]

6.1.2.1 Structure–Conduct–Performance Regressions

SCP analysis received a substantial boost in the 1950s when the new census data in the United States that provided information at the industry level were made available to researchers. These new data allowed empirical studies based on interindustry

[10] For a classic survey of the profit–market power relationship and other empirical regularities documented by authors writing about the SCP tradition, see Bresnahan (1989).

comparisons to flourish. The influential study by Bain (1951)[11] compared the profitability of firms in different types of industries and attempted to relate industry concentration to industry profitability.

Bain primarily compared group averages of high and low concentration industries, where concentration was measured as the eight-firm concentration ratio, C_8 and each firm's profit rate was measured using accounting data as the ratio of "annual net profit after income taxes to net worth at the beginning of the year." A simple comparison of average industry profit rates between industries with an eight-firm concentration ratio above and below 70% gave a striking difference in average profit rates of between 12.1 and 6.9%, while a test of the difference in means suggested a significant difference with a p-value of less than 0.001.

Subsequent authors, controlling for other potential determinants of profitability, ran the following simple cross-industry regression:[12]

$$y_i = \beta_0 + \beta_2 H_i + \beta' X_i + \varepsilon_i,$$

where y was a measure of profitability (performance) such as the Lerner index $(P - \text{MC})/P$ or the accounting return on assets. The variable H_i denotes a measure of industry concentration, perhaps the HHI index, and X_i denotes a set of variables that measure other factors thought to affect profits such as barriers to entry, the intensity of R&D, the minimum efficient scale, buyer concentration, or product differentiation proxied by the advertising-to-sales ratio. The literature consistently if not entirely universally found[13] $\beta_2 > 0$ and interpreted the positive coefficient as evidence of market power being exploited by firms in more concentrated industries. One potential implication of such a relationship, were it capturing a causal relationship indicating that structure causes high margins and profits, would be that if we broke firms up, reducing concentration, profits but also margins would fall and that would help consumer welfare. Such a policy conclusion relies extremely heavily on the causal nature of the estimated relationship between structure and margins or profitability. We now follow the literature, spurred in particular by Demsetz (1973), in examining whether this relationship is causal.

[11] This paper (with minor corrections reported in the following issue) tests one of the testable hypotheses proposed in Bain (1950). Bain's work was also reported in his classic book on industrial organization (Bain 1956). Specifically, Bain had access to industry concentration data from the 1935 Census of Manufactures on 340 industries of which 149 had profit data available from the Securities and Exchange Commission (SEC) from its publication "Survey of American Listed Corporations 1936–40." To resolve geographic market definition issues, he further selected only those industries classified as both "national" and in which each manufacturer "as a rule" was involved in production of all the products covered by an industry classification, as defined in the U.S. publication "Structure of the American Economy." Doing so left a total of 83 industry-level observations on both profit and concentration. These were further reduced down to a total of 42 industries (355 firms), for example because SEC profit data did not cover a large proportion of industry output.

[12] For a review of the literature from the 1950s to 1970s, see Scherer (1980).

[13] As Pelzman (1977) describes (and cited by Clarke et al. (1984)), "With few exceptions, market concentration and industry profitability are positively correlated."

To establish the kind of concern we might have with such regressions, let us follow Cowling and Waterson (1976) and examine the Cournot competition model in which firms compete by setting their quantities. We showed earlier that in an industry characterized by a Cournot equilibrium, the relationship between an indicator of profitability, the Lerner index, and market share should be positive. Additionally, the estimated coefficient is, according to theory, one over the market price elasticity of demand.

To capture the relationship between margins and market share, we might imagine running a regression reflecting the determinants of profits for the firm along the lines of

$$y_{if} = \beta_0 + \beta_1 s_{if} + \beta X_{if} + \varepsilon_{if},$$

where i is the indicator for the industry and f is the indicator for the firm. Variable s_{if} captures the firm's market share and X_{if} other determinants of firm profitability.

Now Bain and his followers were working primarily with industry-level data rather than firm-level data since only industry-level data were available from the census at that time. We can nonetheless aggregate up to the industry level and consider what we should expect to see in their regression equations. The traditional way to aggregate across firms would be to generate a weighted sum across firms within an industry using market shares as weights. Doing so gives

$$\sum_{f=1}^{F} s_{if} y_{if} = \beta_0 \left(\sum_{f=1}^{F} s_{if} \right) + \beta_2 \sum_{f=1}^{F} s_{if}^2 + \beta \sum_{f=1}^{F} s_{if} X_{if} + \varepsilon_{if},$$

where $\sum_{f=1}^{F} s_{if} y_{if}$ is a measure of industry profitability for industry i and $\sum_{f=1}^{F} s_{if}^2$ is the HHI. Note also that $\sum_{f=1}^{F} s_{if} = 1$.

Strikingly, this is in fact the regression of average industry profits run by Bain and his colleagues using industry-level studies. One interpretation of the literature's regression is therefore that it is exactly what you would expect to see if the world were characterized by a Cournot model. That observation provides the basis for an important critique of the SCP literature since, while the Cournot model suggests that we will observe a positive relationship between market performance (profitability) and market concentration, the relationship is not causal in the sense of running from concentration to profitability. In particular, since the only way in which firms can differ in a Cournot model is by being more efficient, and lower-cost firms will achieve higher market shares, any policy attempting to lower concentration will in fact at best end up moving production from efficient low-cost firms to inefficient high-cost ones. The opponents of SCP conclude that such a policy is highly unlikely to improve welfare and in fact very likely to actively harm consumers and generate higher prices!

For completeness, before moving on be sure to note that the market demand elasticity is also a determinant of industry profitability according to this static economic model. This has the fundamental implication that measures of concentration are not, alone, decisive in determining whether firms in an industry are likely to be able to exploit market power. A high market share in a market where demand is very price sensitive may not endow a firm with market power.

6.1.2.2 *Empirical Caveats of SCP Analysis*

We have noted that the validity of the SCP framework depends heavily on being able to interpret the relationship between structure and profits (i.e., the positive coefficient β_2 in our industry regression estimation) as a causal relationship. If it is causal, then concentration causes the high margins. We have seen that, at least in static models, the number of firms, the degree of concentration, and profitability are simultaneously determined in the market where the underlying primitive factors are the variables determining demand, technology, and the strategic choices made by firms. The advent and application of static game theory naturally lead to such a conclusion.

That said, there are a number of other critiques of SCP that have implications for empirical work. Since this has been such an important force in antitrust and industrial economics history, in the next section we expand on those criticisms, which gave rise to new methodologies to identify and quantify market power.

6.1.3 Criticism of Empirical Estimations of the Effect of Structural Indicators

There are two main sources of criticisms of the studies that relate profitability to structural indicators such as industry concentration. One is an econometric criticism and states that the causality between industry concentration and market power cannot usually be established by simple correlations. The other criticism relates to the difficulty of obtaining economically meaningful measurements of firms' profits. The latter is a topic which all competition agencies that attempt to measure firms' profitability regularly encounter.

6.1.3.1 *Firm Heterogeneity*

The most extreme critique of the SCP framework denies that market structure plays any independent role at all in determining firms' profitability and, as we have described, follows Demsetz (1973) in ascribing the positive relationship solely to efficiency. Demsetz went on to suggest that the competing market power and efficiency explanations of the observed relationship could be examined using within-industry data variation. Specifically, he argued that the efficiency hypothesis should introduce a difference between the rate of return earned respectively by large and small firms. On the other hand, at least in a homogeneous product market, a pure market power story where all firms were equally efficient would find that large and

Table 6.3. Relationship between market share and profitability using firm-level data.

Variable name	Industry data	Firm-level data
Industry concentration	0.0375	−0.0222
	(1.67)	(−1.77)
Firm market share	—	0.1476
		(5.51)

Source: Ravenscraft (1983). t-statistics are reported in parentheses.

small firms alike would earn high returns in concentrated markets. Demsetz (1973) provided results which favored the efficiency hypothesis (and which were critiqued by Bond and Greenberg (1976)).

Ravenscraft (1983) ran the following regression using the FTC's 1975 data on lines of business for a cross-section of individual firms:

$$y_{if} = \beta_0 + \beta_1 H_i + \beta_2 s_{if} + \beta X_{if} + \varepsilon_{if},$$

where H again represents the HHI and where the regression varies from the cross-industry regression in the fact that it uses firm-level data and so is able to allow roles for both market share and also industry concentration.

Putting aside the extremely heroic assumption that all industries can be well approximated by a single Cournot model, with in particular a single price elasticity of demand, this regression may help distinguish the effect of concentration from the indirect effect caused by low-cost firms having high market shares. The reason is that there is no role for the HHI in the firm-level Cournot relationship between the Lerner index and the market share, while the latter controls for firm heterogeneity in the industry-level relationship. This regression involves comparing profits achieved by firms with similar market shares in industries with different degrees of concentration.

The SCP model predicts a positive coefficient for β_1, implying a positive relation between industry concentration and firm profits. There can be many lines of business per firm and the data reveal firms with as many as 47 different lines of business. The average is 8 lines of business per firm. A total of 261 lines of business were considered. A summary of Ravenscraft's results is provided in table 6.3.

First consider the industry-level regression shown on the left in table 6.3. The results indicate a weakly positive effect of industry concentration on the firm's profit. However, once we move to firm-level data and the firm's market share in that line of business is included in the regression, the effect of the level of concentration in the industry seems to disappear. In fact, it has an insignificant but negative coefficient. Critics of the SCP framework suggest that this provides further evidence that profitability may be linked to the firm's market share but not to industry concentration, once we have controlled for important differences in market share which in turn reflect cost differences across firms. Their suggested explanation is that more efficient firms are more profitable and also tend to be larger thereby generating a positive relation between a firm's market share and profitability. The common causal driver of both profitability and market shares is therefore not the industry structure but rather efficiency.

Such a position in its rawest form appears fairly extreme as a critique of the SCP. First, the literature noted that there are a number of potential explanations unrelated to efficiency for the observed within-industry relationship between profitability and market shares. For example, on the demand side product differentiation can endow firms with market power and also drive differentials in market shares, while on the cost side economies of scale may generate market power which is subsequently exploited so that we can benefit from productive efficiency (low costs of production) but suffer the consequences in terms of allocative efficiency (i.e., high-market-share firms may set high markups).[14] In addition, firms that need to incur large fixed costs to enter and operate in an industry will do so only if they can expect large operating profits and a large scale of operations. This will limit the number of entrants and create a link between concentration and operating profitability that is not necessarily linked to a strategic exercise of market power.

Second, as we have seen in chapter 5, many simple dynamic economic theory models do predict that under oligopolistic competition, profits will decrease with the number of firms. In any two-stage game with entry followed by Cournot competition, the theoretical prediction is that concentration is a factor that will tend to increase market power, all else equal (see, in particular, section 1.4 of Sutton (1991)).

The conclusion of this conceptual debate appears to be that the positive relationship between profitability and market structure is robust across industries, but probably has complex causes that may differ significantly across industries. Competition agencies must therefore pay careful attention to market power while also making sure that where evidence of efficiency benefits of concentration via product and process innovation is available it is taken into account. A relevant question is also how much of these efficiencies translate into actual consumer benefit.

[14] For a discussion of these topics see the analysis of the model and U.K. data provided by Clarke et al. (1984), who note, for example, that introducing a U-shaped total variable cost function to the Cournot model suggests that the measured Lerner index (using observed average margins—see below) would be related to both the level and square of market shares so that fitting a linear model in terms of market share alone would result in omitted variable bias. They concluded that, "If anything, the evidence... is more sympathetic to the traditional market power explanation of profitability–concentration correlations at the industry level than to Demsetz. We find no evidence for the U.K. that differences between small and large firm profitability tend to be larger in high concentration industries" (p. 448). They concluded that the relationship between (gross profits to revenues) and the HHI was positive but with a declining slope, $(\Pi/R)_j = (1/\eta_j)\{0.170 + 2.512H_j - 1.682H_j^2\}$, where η_j denotes the market elasticity of demand in industry j.

6.1.3.2 Measuring Profitability

Measuring profitability can be difficult. Margins in an economic sense are rarely very cleanly observed. Margin and profitability figures taken from published accounting documents often include imputations of fixed costs and estimation of depreciation that may well not bear much relation to the economic concepts used to calculate economic costs. Also, accounting profits may be subject to intertemporal or interproduct allocations of revenues and expenses that do not correspond to meaningful economic concepts. (See chapter 3 for a discussion of the differences between accounting and economic profits.)

To take a specific example, the SCP studies generally approximated price-cost margins with $(R-\text{TVC})/R$, where R is revenues and TVC is the total variable cost. If we divide both elements of the ratio by quantity Q, we obtain $(\text{AR}-\text{AVC})/\text{AR}$, where AR is the average revenue per unit and AVC is the average variable cost. This ratio will be similar to the Lerner index if and only if the average variable cost is similar to the marginal cost.

Fixed costs may also play a role in determining the structure of the market, the number of competitors, and the profitability of firms because firms need to recover and make a return on their investments. Ignoring fixed costs will reduce the analysis to short-term comparative statics and may be an inadequate framework for comparing structural equilibria across industries. For example, if we consider pharmaceutical markets we will find both high concentration and high margins but these might (or might not) be driven by very high R&D, drug approval, and marketing costs. Relatedly, Sutton (1991, 1998) challenges the profession to confront his observation that levels of fixed costs will often be choice variables so that market structure and the size of variables often treated as entry barriers (R&D and advertising levels) may be jointly determined.

Many of these points and others were made in the widely cited contribution by Fisher and McGowan (1983), which is sometimes considered to have effectively led industrial organization economists to conclude that efforts at measuring profitability were hopeless and should be abandoned.[15] In coming to a rounded view on such matters it is worth noting that the financial markets do place a great deal of emphasis on financial accounting data while competition authorities can generally also obtain management accounting data, the kind of data often used to at least partially inform investment decisions within organizations. The skepticism of the industrial organization academic community, which has resulted in profit data rarely being used in academic industrial economics, is simply not shared by other professional groups. The response by most other groups has rather been to attempt to adapt financial data to provide evidence on the economic quantities they attempt to measure. For example, in finance, cash flows are often used in firm valuation models rather than data directly from profit and loss statements, while whole organizations have

[15] For a somewhat contrary view, see Geroski (2005) and also OFT (2003).

developed to train analysts in other areas to derive useful information from such accounting evidence. (For example, globally the chartered financial analyst (CFA) qualification is fairly widely recognized as certifying an individual's ability to do so in an investment context.)

6.1.3.3 A Recent Case Example: U.K. Groceries

In its investigation of the supermarket sector, the U.K. Competition Commission ran a regression of store profit margin on local area concentration.[16] The CC ran regressions attempting to relate store (variable) profit margin to local concentration where the latter was measured using a variety of local concentration measures. The CC motivated its regression by reference to two-stage games where entry occurred at the first stage and then competition occurred within the local area, i.e., games of the form studied in chapter 5. Specifically, it constructed a measure of variable profit margin of the form

$$\pi_j = \left(\frac{\text{Store variable profit}}{\text{Store revenues}}\right)_j$$

for a cross section of stores. The margin data relate to the period May 2005 to April 2006 for Tesco, Asda, Morrisons, and Sainsbury's stores with a net sales area of larger than 280 m^2 (and below 6,000 m^2). The CC estimated the regression equations using instrumental variables (particularly local population) in an attempt to control for endogeneity of market structure by using its exogenous correlate population. A selection of the CC's parameter estimates are reported in table 6.4, indicating that the CC found that store profit margins are correlated with local market structure. In particular, the CC considered this evidence that markets were local. The issue of efficiency explanations for the relationship was explicitly considered, although variables relating to local cost conditions were not available and so could not be included.

Slade (2006)[17] provided an expert report evaluating the CC's regressions. She notes that (i) the profitability analysis is difficult to perform because profits and market structure are jointly determined and therefore it is difficult to determine causality; (ii) the regression specifications are free of endogeneity problems under some assumptions, but not others; but that (iii) all the statistical tests they perform indicate that the endogeneity problems has been "overcome or is minor."[18] She concludes, "in spite of potential difficulties, I find the CC regressions to be surprisingly

[16] Competition Commission's Groceries Market Investigation (2007). See, in particular, appendix 4.6 of the CC's provisional findings ("The impact of local competition on grocery store profit margin") available at www.competition-commission.org.uk/inquiries/ref2006/grocery/provisional_findings.htm.

[17] Available from www.competition-commission.org.uk/inquiries/ref2006/grocery/pdf/expert_report_margaret_slade.pdf.

[18] In particular, local market population measures may potentially be correlated with store profitability. If so, local population would not be a valid instrument.

Table 6.4. Profit margins and local market structure in U.K. supermarkets.

	Number of competing fascias over 280 m^2 within 10 min	Number of competitor stores within 10 min	Combined net sales area (thousands) of competitors within 10 min	Share of competitors' net sales area in total net sales area within 10 min
Effect on store profit margin	−0.0096[a]	−0.0034[a]	−0.0026[a]	−0.1545[a]
t-statistics	(−3.05)	(−2.93)	(−3.06)	(−2.99)

[a] $p < 0.01$.
Source: Table 1, appendix 4.6, CC's Groceries Market Investigation (2007).

robust to changes in market structure, the functional form of the equation, and the choice of instruments. The evidence is thus supportive of the hypothesis that very local market conditions are important determinants of grocery store profits."

Margaret Slade's observations fit a common theme that emerges regularly when considering the appropriate treatment of econometric evidence: we either need robustness of results or else we need to have clearly established that one set of regression evidence is materially better than alternative specifications. Panel data were not available in the supermarket case. However, it is important to note that where panel data are available we can use the identification strategies we previously discussed extensively in chapter 5 when examining regressions of price on market structure.

In the next section we discuss new methodologies that have been developed that try to identify the extent of market power within an industry by looking at the firms' behavior within an industry. Such analyses use predictions of economic theory regarding firms' behavior in different competitive environments to identify the nature of competition, firms costs, and also the resulting profitability using firms' observed behavior.

6.2 Directly Identifying the Nature of Competition

Cross-industry regression analysis relied on the assumption that all industries are characterized by similar empirical relationships.[19] However, game theory quickly brought home to researchers that apparently small details in industry characteristics such as institutional or technological characteristics can, at least in the theory, be of great significance in the determination of industry equilibrium outcomes. For instance, how much market information is accessible to firms can play an important

[19] For a nice review of identification methodologies by one of the key innovators, see Bresnahan (1989).

role in the likelihood or at least nature of a collusive outcome (see, for example, Stigler 1964; Green and Porter 1984). If so, then cross-industry comparisons used in the Bain-style regression analysis will have a hard time identifying the links between observed market characteristics and outcomes since they compare environments that are in fact not easily comparable. On reflection it seems highly plausible that computers, pharmaceuticals, aircraft manufacturers, and shampoo manufacturers are incredibly different industries and therefore empirical work which captures all of their differences in a single equation is probably a rather optimistic exercise.[20]

As a result, since the late 1970s the majority of empirical research in industrial organization has evolved to focus mainly on industry-specific studies. There are a few exceptions, notably Sutton (1991, 1998), but they remain a fairly rare activity, if one that is probably growing. Our interest in the relationships between structure, conduct, and performance remains, but the dominant methodology in industrial organization now involves examining particular industries in substantial detail.[21]

To do so, industrial organization economists have developed specific methodologies that use observed data on cost drivers, prices, and quantities in order to infer the nature of competition in the market. An empirical model which nests a number of possible theoretical models can be used to discriminate among these potential competitive environments, given a suitable identification strategy. The starting point of any such analysis is careful examination of institutional structure, market history, and also the basic patterns revealed in the data. Once a researcher is ready to begin to model the process which has generated the data, the approach is to specify a structural model based on the potential behavioral assumptions that we would like to discriminate between. For example, we might want to consider a model of competition where firms individually profit maximize and then choose the firms' strategic variables (price or quantities) that will explicitly characterize the competitive outcome in a Nash equilibrium. On the other hand, we might suspect collusion between the firms and thus our alternative model for the process which has generated the data would be a collusive model where firms might choose quantities in an attempt to maximize industry profitability. Whenever we want to distinguish

[20] That said, and in recognition of the substantial contributions made by the authors writing in the SCP tradition, it is important to note that such illustrative characterizations are in truth caricatures of at least the best empirical work that was undertaken in this area.

[21] This progression to detail is sometimes noted with amusement or even on occasion with frustration by academic colleagues from other fields within economics who in private will remark that prominent industrial organization researchers, whom they refer to as "the [radio/TV/movie/breakfast cereal/cement guy/woman]," are doing very detailed work which looks on the face of it to be rather like toying at the margins of an economy. Such observations are striking to many economists when we compare industrial organization papers to those studying "the knowledge economy" or trade economists studying "world trade flows." On the other hand, local studies can sometimes illustrate very big ideas. For example, the study of the general topic of the diffusion of technology is often traced back to work on hybrid corn by Griliches (1957).

two models that might have generated the same data, some feature of the data must allow us to tell them apart. We will call this our "identification strategy." (See also chapter 2.)

In the next section, we first review the key concept of identification by examining the classic case of identification of demand and supply equations in multi-equation structural systems. We then progress to explain the extension of the methodology that has been developed for some classic models from industrial economics. For example, when we want to tell apart standard competitive models from collusive models. We will examine some classic cases, but many of the lessons of identification are important ones far more generally since the analysis of identification is exactly what allows us to test between competing economic models.

6.2.1 Structural Models of Supply and Demand

The study of identification is fundamental to distinguishing between economic models. We saw in chapter 2 that the identification of supply and demand is the canonical example which demonstrates the difficulties typically faced when developing an identification strategy. We begin this section by revisiting the identification of supply and demand in structural models. Doing so provides an important stepping stone toward the analysis of the problem of using data to identify firm conduct.

6.2.1.1 Formalizing a Structural Models of Supply and Demand

The basic components for any structural model of an industry are the demand function and the supply function, where the reader will recall that in oligopoly settings the "supply" function is best thought about as a "pricing equation" since it represents the price at which a firm is willing to supply a given quantity of output.[22] In a homogeneous product industry we will face a single market demand curve and similarly we can derive a single market supply curve. We observe the equilibrium market outcome, the price–quantity combination that equates aggregate firm supply with aggregate consumer demand. This market outcome is the result of factors affecting both the demand and the supply functions.

The theoretical analysis (whose prestigious origins we describe in our discussion of identification in chapter 2)[23] will show that when a variable affects both supply and demand, we will only be able to separately identify the magnitude of the effect on price–quantity outcomes that occurred through movement of demand and the effect which occurred through movement of supply curve in particular circumstances. In

[22] See chapter 1 for a review of the determinants of market outcome. In oligopolistic competition the supply function is referred to as the pricing function to distinguish it from the perfect competition supply function which is given by the marginal cost curve. In oligopolistic markets, the supply function does not trace the marginal cost curve since profit maximization implies pricing above marginal cost at each quantity.

[23] For a more formal treatment of identification in linear systems, see, for example, Johnston and Dinardo (1997).

contrast, we will usually be able to observe the so-called "reduced-form" effect, that is, the aggregate effect of the movement of the exogenous variables on the equilibrium market outcomes (price, quantity). The reduced-form effects will tell us how exogenous changes in demand and cost determinants affect market equilibrium outcomes, but we will only be able to trace back the actual parameters of the demand and supply functions in particular circumstances.

Let us assume the following demand and supply equations, where a_t^{D} and a_t^{S} are the set of shifters of the demand and supply curve respectively at time t:

$$\begin{aligned}\text{Demand:} \qquad Q_t &= a_t^{\mathrm{D}} - a_{12} P_t, \\ \text{Supply:} \qquad Q_t &= a_t^{\mathrm{S}} + a_{22} P_t.\end{aligned}$$

Further, let us assume that there is one demand shifter X_t and one supply shifter W_t so that

$$a_t^{\mathrm{D}} = c_{11} X_t + u_t^{\mathrm{D}} \quad \text{and} \quad a_t^{\mathrm{S}} = c_{22} W_t + u_t^{\mathrm{S}}.$$

The supply-and-demand system can then be written in the following matrix form:

$$\begin{bmatrix} 1 & a_{12} \\ 1 & -a_{22} \end{bmatrix} \begin{bmatrix} Q_t \\ P_t \end{bmatrix} = \begin{bmatrix} c_{11} & 0 \\ 0 & c_{22} \end{bmatrix} \begin{bmatrix} X_t \\ W_t \end{bmatrix} + \begin{bmatrix} u_t^{\mathrm{D}} \\ u_t^{\mathrm{S}} \end{bmatrix}.$$

Let $y_t = [Q_t, P_t]'$ be the vector of endogenous variables and $Z_t = [X_t, W_t]'$ the vector of exogenous variables in the form of demand and cost shifters which are not determined by the system. We can write the *structural system* in the form $A y_t = C Z_t + u_t$, where

$$A = \begin{bmatrix} 1 & a_{12} \\ 1 & -a_{22} \end{bmatrix} \quad \text{and} \quad C = \begin{bmatrix} c_{11} & 0 \\ 0 & c_{22} \end{bmatrix},$$

and u_t is a vector of shocks

$$u_t = \begin{bmatrix} u_t^{\mathrm{D}} \\ u_t^{\mathrm{S}} \end{bmatrix}.$$

The "*reduced-form*" equations relate the vector of endogenous variables to the exogenous variables and these can be obtained by inverting the (2×2) matrix A and performing some basic matrix algebra:

$$y_t = A^{-1} C Z_t + A^{-1} u_t.$$

Let us define $\Pi \equiv A^{-1} C$ and $v_t \equiv A^{-1} u_t$ so that we can write the reduced form as

$$y_t = \Pi Z_t + v_t.$$

Doing so gives an equation for each of the endogenous variables on the left-hand side on exogenous variables on the right-hand side. Given enough data we can learn about the parameters in Π. In particular, we can learn about the parameters using changes in Z_t, the exogenous variables affecting either supply or demand.

6.2.1.2 Conditions for Identification of Pricing Equations

The important question for identification is whether we can learn about the underlying structural parameters in the structural equations of this model, namely the supply and demand equations. This is the same as saying that we want to know if, given enough data, we can in principle recover demand and supply functions from the data. We examine the conditions necessary for this to be possible and then, in the next section, we go on to examine when and how we can retrieve information about firm conduct based on the pricing equations (supply) and the demand functions thus uncovered.

Structural parameters of demand and supply functions are useful because we will often want to understand the effect of one or more variables on either demand or supply, or both. For instance, to understand whether a "fat tax" will be effective in reducing chocolate consumption, we would want to know the effect of a change in price on the quantity demanded. But we would also want to understand the extent to which any tax would be absorbed by suppliers. To do so, and hence understand the incidence and effects of the tax we must be able to separately identify demand and supply.

As we saw in chapter 2, the traditional conditions to identify both demand and supply equations are that in our structural equations there must be a shifter of demand that does not affect supply and a shifter in supply that does not affect demand. Formally, the number of excluded exogenous variables in the equation must be at least as high as the number of included endogenous variables in the right-hand side of the equation. Usually, exclusion restrictions are derived from economic theory. For example, in a traditional analysis cost shifters will generally affect supply but not demand. Identification also requires a normalization restriction that just rescales the parameters to be normalized to the scale of the explained variable on the left-hand side of the equation.

Returning to our example with the supply-and-demand system:

$$Ay_t = CZ_t + u_t.$$

The reduced-form estimation would produce a matrix Π such that

$$\Pi = A^{-1}C = \begin{bmatrix} 1 & a_{12} \\ 1 & -a_{22} \end{bmatrix}^{-1} \begin{bmatrix} c_{11} & 0 \\ 0 & c_{22} \end{bmatrix} = \frac{1}{-a_{22} - a_{12}} \begin{bmatrix} -a_{22}c_{11} & -a_{12}c_{22} \\ -c_{11} & c_{22} \end{bmatrix}$$

so that our reduced-form estimation produces

$$Q_t = \frac{-a_{22}c_{11}}{-a_{22} - a_{12}} X_t - \frac{a_{12}c_{22}}{-a_{22} - a_{12}} W_t + v_{1t},$$
$$P_t = \frac{-c_{11}}{-a_{22} - a_{12}} X_t - \frac{c_{22}}{-a_{22} - a_{12}} W_t + v_{2t}.$$

The identification question is whether we can retrieve the parametric elements of the matrices A and C from estimates of the reduced-form parameters. In this example there are four parameters in Π which we can estimate and a maximum of eight parameters potentially in A and C. For identification our sufficient conditions will be

- the normalization restrictions which in our example require that $a_{11} = a_{21} = 1$;
- the exclusion restrictions which in our example implies $c_{12} = c_{21} = 0$.

For example, we know that only cost shifters should be in the supply function and hence are excluded from the demand equation while demand shifters should only be in the demand equation and are therefore excluded from the supply equation.

In our example the normalization and exclusion restrictions apply so that we can recover the structural parameters. For instance, given estimates of the reduced-form parameters, $(\pi_{11}, \pi_{21}, \pi_{12}, \pi_{22})$, we can calculate

$$\frac{\pi_{11}}{\pi_{21}} = \left(\frac{-a_{22}c_{11}}{-a_{22} - a_{12}}\right) \bigg/ \left(\frac{-c_{11}}{-a_{22} - a_{12}}\right) = a_{22}$$

and similarly π_{21}/π_{22} will give us a_{12}. We can then easily retrieve c_{11} and c_{22}.

Intuitively, the exclusion restriction is the equivalent of the requirement that we have exogenous demand or supply shifts in order to trace or identify supply or demand functions respectively (see also the discussion in chapter 2 on identification). By including variables in the regression that are present in one of the structural equations but not in the other, we allow one of the structural functions to shift while holding the other one fixed.

6.2.2 Conduct Parameters

Bresnahan (1982)[24] elegantly provides the conditions under which conduct can be identified using a structural supply-and-demand system (where by the former we mean a pricing function). More precisely, he shows the conditions under which we can use data to tell apart three classic economic models of firm conduct, namely Bertrand price competition, Cournot quantity competition, and collusion. We begin by following Bresnahan's classic paper to illustrate the technique.[25] We will see that successful estimation of a structural demand-and-supply system is typically not enough to identify the nature of the conduct of firms in the market.

[24] The technical conditions are presented in Lau (1982).

[25] We do so while noting that Perloff and Shen (2001) argue that the model has better properties if we use a log-linear demand curve instead of the linear model we use for clarity of exposition here. The extension to the log-linear model only involves some easy algebra. Those authors attribute the original model to Just and Chern (1980). In their article, Just and Chern use an exogenous shock to supply (mechanization of tomato harvesting) to test the competitiveness of demand.

In all three of the competitive settings that Bresnahan (1982) considers, firms that maximize static profits do so by equating marginal revenue to marginal costs. However, under each of the three different models, the firms' marginal revenue functions are different. As a result, firms are predicted to respond to a change in market conditions that affect prices in a manner that is specific to each model. Under certain conditions, Bresnahan shows these different responses can distinguish the models and thus identify the nature of firm conduct in an industry.

To illustrate, consider, for example, perfect competition with zero fixed costs. In that case, a firm's pricing equation is simply its marginal cost curve and hence movements or rotations of demand will not affect the shape of the supply (pricing) curve since it is entirely determined by costs. In contrast, under oligopolistic or collusive conduct, the markup over costs—and hence the pricing equation—will depend on the character of the demand curve.

6.2.2.1 *Marginal Revenue by Market Structure*

Following Bresnahan (1982), we first establish that in the homogeneous product context we can nest the competitive, Cournot oligopoly and the monopoly models into one general structure with the marginal revenue function expressed in the general form:

$$\text{MR}(Q) = \lambda Q P'(Q) + P(Q),$$

where the parameter λ takes different values under different competitive regimes. Particularly,

$$\lambda = \begin{cases} 0 & \text{under price-taking competition,} \\ 1/N & \text{under symmetric Cournot,} \\ 1 & \text{under monopoly or cartel.} \end{cases}$$

Consider the following market demand function:

$$Q_t = \alpha_0 - \alpha_1 P_t + \alpha_2 X_t + u_{1t}^{\text{D}},$$

where X_t is a set of exogenous variables determining demand. The inverse demand function can be written as

$$P_t = \frac{\alpha_0}{\alpha_1} - \frac{1}{\alpha_1} Q_t + \frac{\alpha_2}{\alpha_1} X_t + \frac{1}{\alpha_1} u_{1t}^{\text{D}}.$$

The firms' total revenue TR will be the price times its own sales. This will be equal to

(i) $\text{TR} = q_i P(Q(q_i))$ for the Cournot case,

(ii) $\text{TR} = QP(Q)$ for the monopoly or cartel case,

(iii) $\text{TR} = q_i P(Q)$ for the price-taking competition case, where Q is total market production and q_i is the firm's production with $q_i = Q/N$ in the symmetric Cournot model. Given these revenue functions marginal revenues can respectively be calculated as

(i) $\text{MR} = q_i P'(Q) + P(Q)$ for the Cournot case,

(ii) $\text{MR} = QP'(Q) + P(Q)$ for the monopoly or cartel case,

(iii) $\text{MR} = P(Q)$ for the price-taking competition case.

All these expressions are nested in the following form:

$$\text{MR} = \lambda QP'(Q) + P(Q).$$

6.2.2.2 Pricing Equations

Profit maximization implies firms will equate marginal revenue to marginal costs. Using the marginal revenue expression we obtain the first-order condition characterizing profit maximization in each of the three models:

$$\lambda QP'(Q) + P(Q) = \text{MC}(Q).$$

Under one interpretation, the parameter λ provides an indicator of the extent to which firms can increase prices by restricting output. If so then the parameter λ might be interpreted as an indication of how close the price is to the perceived marginal revenue of the firm (see Bresnahan 1981). If so, then λ is an indicator of the market power of the firm and a higher λ would indicate a higher degree of market power while $\lambda = 0$ would indicate that firms operate in a price-taking environment where the marginal revenue is equal to the market price. This interpretation was popular in the early 1980s but has disadvantages that has led the field to view such an interpretation skeptically (see Makowski 1987; Bresnahan 1989). More conventionally, provided we can identify the parameter λ, we will see that we can consider the problem of distinguishing conduct as an entirely standard statistical testing problem of distinguishing between three nested models.

The pricing equation or supply relation indicates the price at which the firms will sell a given quantity of output and it is determined in each of these three models by the condition that firms will expand output until the relevant variant of marginal revenues equals the marginal costs of production. The pricing equation encompassing these three models will depend on both the quantity and the cost variables. Its parameters are determined by the parameters of the demand function $(\alpha_0, \alpha_1, \alpha_2)$, the parameters of the cost function, and the conduct parameter, λ.

Assuming a linear inverse demand function and marginal cost curve, the (supply) pricing equation can be written in the form:

$$P(Q_t) = \beta_0 + \gamma Q_t + \beta_2 W_t + u^{\text{S}}_{2t},$$

where γ is a function of the cost parameters, the demand parameters, and the conduct parameter, and W are the determinants of costs.

Given the inverse linear demand function,

$$P_t = \frac{\alpha_0}{\alpha_1} - \frac{1}{\alpha_1}Q_t + \frac{\alpha_2}{\alpha_1}X_t + \frac{1}{\alpha_1}u_{1t}^{\mathrm{D}}$$

and the following linear marginal costs curve:

$$\mathrm{MC}(Q) = \beta_0 + \beta_1 Q + \beta_2 W_t + u_{2t}^{\mathrm{S}},$$

where W are the determinants of costs, then the first-order condition that encompasses all three models, $\lambda Q P'(Q) + P(Q) = \mathrm{MC}(Q)$, can be written as

$$\frac{\lambda}{\alpha_1}Q_t + P(Q_t) = \beta_0 + \beta_1 Q_t + \beta_2 W_t + u_{2t}^{\mathrm{S}}.$$

By rearranging we obtain the firm's pricing equation:

$$P(Q_t) = \beta_0 - \frac{\lambda}{\alpha_1}Q_t + \beta_1 Q_t + \beta_2 W_t + u_{2t}^{\mathrm{S}},$$

which can be written in the form that will be estimated:

$$P(Q_t) = \beta_0 + \gamma Q_t + \beta_2 W_t + u_{2t}^{\mathrm{S}},$$

where $\gamma = \beta_1 - \lambda/\alpha_1$.

We wish to examine the system of two linear equations consisting of (i) the inverse demand function and (ii) the pricing (supply) equation. We have seen in chapter 2 and the earlier discussion in this chapter that we can identify the parameters in the pricing equation provided we have a demand shifter which is excluded from it. Similarly, we can identify the demand curve provided we have a cost shifter which moves the pricing equation without moving the demand equation. In that case, we can identify the parameter γ from the pricing equation and also the parameter α_1 from the demand curve. Unfortunately, but importantly, this is not enough to learn about the conduct parameter, λ, the parameter which allows us to distinguish these three standard models of firm conduct. Given (γ, α_1) we cannot identify β_1 and λ individually.

In the next section we examine the conditions which *will* allow us to identify conduct, λ.

6.2.2.3 *Identifying Conduct when Cost Information Is Available*

There are cases in which the analyst will be able to make assumptions about costs that will allow identification of the conduct parameter. First note that if marginal costs are constant in quantity (so that we know the true value of β_1, in this example $\beta_1 = 0$), then if we can estimate the demand parameter α_1 and the regression parameter γ, we can then identify the conduct parameter, λ since $\gamma = \beta_1 - \lambda/\alpha_1 = -\lambda/\alpha_1$. Then we can statistically check whether λ is close to 0 indicating a price-taking environment or closer to 1 indicating a monopoly or a cartelized industry. In that special case, the conditions for identification of both the pricing and demand equations and the conduct parameter remains that we can find (i) a supply shifter that allows us to identify the demand curve, the parameter α_1, and (ii) a demand shifter that identifies the pricing curve and hence γ.

Alternatively, if we are confident of our cost data, then we could estimate a cost function, perhaps using the techniques described in chapter 3, or a marginal cost function and then we could equally potentially estimate β_1 directly. This together with estimates of α_1 and γ will again allow us to recover the conduct parameter, λ.

6.2.2.4 *Identifying Conduct when Cost Information Is Not Available: Demand Shifts*

There are many cases in which there will not be satisfactory cost information available to estimate or make assumptions about the form of firm-level marginal cost functions. An important question is whether it remains possible to identify conduct. Without information about costs, the only market events that one could use for identification are changes in demand. In this section and the next we consider respectively demand shifts and demand rotations and in particular whether such data variation will allow us to recover both estimates of the marginal cost function and also estimates of the demand function. Demand shifts arise, for instance, because of an increase in disposable income available to consumers for consumption. Demand rotations on the other hand must be factors which affect the price sensitivity of consumers. There are many examples, including, for example, the price sensitivity of the demand for umbrellas, which probably falls when it is raining, while the demand for electricity to run air conditioners will be highly price insensitive when the weather is very hot.

First consider demand shifts. We have already established that demand shifters provide useful data variation, helping to identify the supply (pricing) equation. We have also algebraically already shown that such demand shifters are not generally useful for identifying the nature of conduct in the market. In this section our first aim is to build intuition first for the reason demand shifters do not generally suffice to identify conduct. We will go on to argue in the next section that demand rotators will usually suffice.

Suppose that we observe variation in market demand because of changes in disposable income. Such variation in demand will trace out the pricing curve, i.e., the optimal prices of suppliers at different quantity levels. The situation is illustrated in figure 6.2, which shows the changes in price and quantity in a market following a shift in demand from D_1 to D_2. Notice in particular that demand shifts trace out the pricing equation to give data points such as (Q_1, P_1) and (Q_2, P_2), but that such a pricing equation is consistent with different forms of competition in the market. First it is consistent with the firm setting $P = \text{MC}$ in a case where marginal costs are increasing in quantity, in which case the "pricing equation" is simply a marginal cost

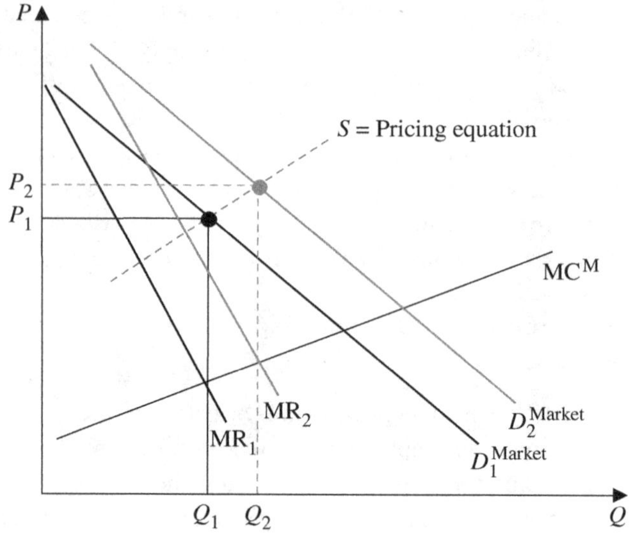

Figure 6.2. Demand shifts do not identify conduct.
Source: Authors' rendition of figure 1 in Bresnahan (1982).

curve. Second, the same pricing curve could be generated by a more efficient firm that exercises market power by restricting output so that marginal revenue is equal to marginal cost but where marginal revenue is not equal to price. If the pricing curve is the marginal cost curve, then we are in a price-taking environment. If the firm faces a lower marginal cost curve and is setting MR = MC and then charging a markup, the firm has market power. The two ways of rationalizing the same observed price and quantity data are shown in figure 6.2. The aim of the figure is to demonstrate that the demand shift provides no power to tell the two potential underlying models apart (unless we have additional information on the level of costs) even though demand shifts do successfully trace out the pricing equation for us.

6.2.2.5 *Identifying Conduct when Cost Information Is Not Available: Demand Rotations*

The underlying behavioral assumption in each of the three models considered is that firms maximize profits and to do so they equate marginal revenue and marginal costs. Each of the three models (competitive, Cournot, and monopoly) differs only because they suggest a different calculation of marginal revenue and this has direct implications for the determinants of the pricing curve. Each model places a differential importance on the slope of (inverse) demand for the pricing equation. This can be seen directly from the first term in the first-order condition which describes the pricing equation, $\lambda QP'(Q)+P(Q) = \mathrm{MC}(Q)$. Alternatively, we can rearrange this equation to emphasize that prices are marginal cost plus a markup which depends

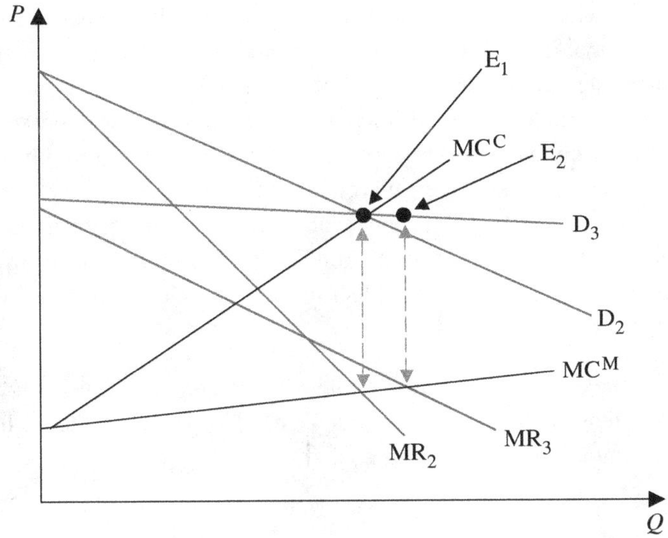

Figure 6.3. Reactions of competitive firm and monopolist to a demand rotation.
Source: Authors' rendition of figure 2 in Bresnahan (1982).

on the slope of demand, $P(Q) = \text{MC}(Q) + \lambda Q|P'(Q)|$, differentially across the models.

This equation suggests a route toward achieving identification. Specifically, if a variable affects the slope of demand, then each of the three models will make very different predictions for what should happen to prices at any given marginal cost. For the clearest example, note that in the competitive case absolutely nothing should happen to markups while a monopolist will take advantage of any decrease in demand elasticity to increase prices. Given this intuition, we next consider whether conduct can be identified when the demand curve rotates.

Rotation of the demand curve changes the marginal revenue of oligopolistic firms. Flatter demand and marginal revenue curves will cause firms with market power to lower their prices. On the other hand, price-taking firms will keep the price unchanged since lowering the price would cause them to price below marginal cost and make losses. Figure 6.3 illustrates this point graphically by considering a demand rotation around the initial equilibrium point, E_1. In particular the figure allows us to compare the lack of reaction of a price-taking firm, which starts and finishes with prices and quantities described by E_1, with the response of the monopolist who begins at E_1 but finishes with different price and quantities, those at E_2, after the demand rotation.

Intuitively, demand rotations allow us to identify conduct even when we have no information about costs because such changes should not cause any response in a perfectly competitive environment, there should be some response in a Cournot market and a much larger response in a fully collusive environment. If demand becomes more elastic, prices will decrease and quantity will increase in a market with a high degree of market power. If, on the other hand, demand becomes more inelastic and consumers are less willing to adjust their quantities consumed in response to changes in prices, then prices will increase in oligopolistic or cartelized markets. Prices will remain unchanged in both scenarios if the market is perfectly competitive and firms are pricing close to their marginal costs.

While intuitive, a simple graph cannot show that given an arbitrarily large amount of data a demand rotator is sufficient to tell apart the three models, which is the statement that we would like to establish for identification. We therefore examine the algebra of demand rotations.

Let us look at the algebra of identification using the demand rotation. Formally, we can specify a demand function to include a set of variables Z that will affect the slope (and potentially the level) of demand:

$$Q_t = \alpha_0 + \alpha_1 P_t + \alpha_2 X_t + \alpha_3 P_t Z_t + \alpha_4 Z_t + u^{\text{D}}_{1t}.$$

For our three models the encompassing pricing equation becomes

$$P_t = \left(\frac{-\lambda}{\alpha_1 + \alpha_3 Z_t}\right) Q_t + \beta_0 + \beta_1 Q_t + \beta_2 W_t + u^{\text{S}}_{2t}.$$

To consider identification note that if we can estimate demand and retrieve the true parameters α_1 and α_3, then we can construct the variable $Q^* = -Q/(\alpha_1 + \alpha_3 Z)$. In that case, the conduct parameter will be the coefficient of Q^* when estimating the following equation:

$$P_t = \beta_0 + \lambda Q^*_t + \beta_1 Q_t + \beta_2 W_t + u^{\text{S}}_{2t}.$$

An important challenge in the demand rotation methodology is to identify a situation where we can be confident that we have a variable which resulted in a change in the sensitivity of demand to prices. On the other hand, a nice feature of the demand estimation method is that when estimating the demand curve we can test whether a variable actually does rotate the demand curve or whether it merely shifts the curve. Events that may change the price elasticity of a product at a particular price include the appearance of a new substitute for a good or a change in the price of the main substitutes. For instance, the popularization of the downloading of music through the internet may have increased the elasticity of the demand for physical CD players because consumers may have become more price sensitive and more willing to decrease their purchases of music CDs in the case of a price increase. In the case of digital music, one might expect that there has been both a demand rotation and a demand shift so that at given prices, the demand for physical CDs has dropped. Only the demand rotation will help us identify conduct. Similarly, weather may affect both the level of demand for umbrellas and also demand may be less elastic when it is raining. While there is no theoretical difficulty if the same variable affects both the level and the slope of demand, we may run into the practical difficulties associated with multicollinearity, which may make telling apart the demand shift and the demand rotation rather hard empirically. Empirical work is challenging and also requires creativity.

A second important practical issue is the difficulty of explaining a somewhat technical issue to a nontechnical legal audience. However, this can be overcome by understanding the principles and explaining them correctly in plain language. By using demand rotators, we are trying to use the fact that firms with market power will adjust to changes in the level of their market power while firms with no market power will price close to marginal cost and will not react to changes in the level of demand elasticities. Firms pricing close to marginal cost will not react to changes in the price sensitivity of demand while firms with some degree of market power will adjust their prices to such changes, according to these models.

A third issue is whether to estimate λ or test models with particular values against one another. If we estimate λ, we will rarely (or never) get values of 0 or 1 but most likely something between the two. In practice, we would get an estimate of, say, $\lambda = 0.234\,352$ and we could then test the hypotheses that $\lambda = 0$ or $\lambda = 1$ or $\lambda = 1/N$, where N is the number of firms, since we know that these correspond to competition, perfect collusion, and the Cournot model. For example, we could test whether the data suggest that the parameter value is more likely to be one or another value of the parameters using, for example, a likelihood ratio test (see, in particular, Vuong 1989). Such an approach allows us to tell whether the data are consistent with one of the three models given enough data.

The reason to prefer the specific values of λ is that we are usually really trying to test which of the three specific models best fit the data since it can be difficult to draw a specific conclusion on a value of λ between 0 and 1 that does not equal any of the values predicted by the theory models we have outlined. Specifically, we do not usually have a model which corresponds directly to an estimated value of a number like $\lambda = 0.234\,352$. For that reason most researchers prefer to test between the perfect competition, the perfect cartel model, and the symmetric Cournot model rather than over-interpreting intermediate values of λ. That said, in a challenge to that practice, Kalai and Stanford (1985) do present a model which may rationalize a continuum of equilibrium solutions between the competitive and monopoly outcomes.

Finally, we note the difficulties researchers face when identifying marginal costs using first-order conditions derived from theoretical models, particularly when the theoretical model involves some level of market power. The estimation approach we described implies that a researcher is able to identify both demand and supply equations, and subsequently marginal costs. There are some mixed assessments of our ability to identify marginal costs using first-order conditions derived from theory. Genovese and Mullin (1998) test this methodology by comparing costs implied by the estimated conduct and demand structure with the actual cost data in the cane sugar refining industry in the late nineteenth century and early twentieth century in the United States. They first find that the estimated conduct parameter using no cost data is not too different from the one derived using actual cost information. The estimated costs will nevertheless be very sensitive to the imposition of a particular static model of competition. The authors defend the usefulness of defining a "loose" conduct parameter in the specification of the pricing equation. Corts (1999) and Kim and Knittel (2006) have less enthusiastic assessments of the accuracy of the estimated costs when a particular competitive setting is imposed. The estimated marginal costs, those consistent with the estimated demand elasticities and price levels, will sometimes be negative. The reason is clear: if demand is estimated to be inelastic but observed prices are actually fairly low, then margins can be predicted to be so high that the only marginal costs that can rationalize the high margins would be negative. In a recent paper Kim and Knittel (2006) find that the conduct parameter technique poorly estimates markups and markup adjustments to cost shocks in the California electricity market.

Corts argues that the estimation of conduct parameters in the above methodology will often fail to measure market power accurately not least because the model of perfect collusion Bresnahan emphasizes is not motivated from a specific dynamic pricing model of collusion and moreover it is only one of many potential models of collusion (other models of collusion may have features such as price rigidity making such exercises likely to be problematic). Salvo (2007) argues that unobserved constraints faced by firms can limit their pricing levels resulting in an underestimation of their ability to react to price changes following changes in demand conditions. Concretely, he shows that threat of entry kept the prices of a cement industry cartel in Brazil lower than would have been predicted by its documented market power. The conduct parameter technique miscalculates the costs and underestimates the degree of market power in that particular case. On the other hand, Salvo provides a potential solution to the threat of entry difficulty while Puller (2006) and Kim (2005) each suggest a solution to at least one element of the Corts critique.

In summary, the objective of this branch of the industrial organization literature is to facilitate our ability to test between the various models of firm behavior to see which best matches the data. In order to test one model against the other we must have some appropriate sources of identifying data variation. In the case we examined the sources of the required data variation were isolated as (1) demand shifters, (2) cost shifters, and (3) demand rotator(s). In all but very special circumstances all three were required.

More generally, the main theoretical and practical challenge to such an approach is to understand the kind of data variation that will help distinguish one economic model from another and then find an actual variable or set of variables which provide that source of data variation in the particular case at hand. While the homogeneous product Bertrand, Cournot, and perfect collusion cases studied by Bresnahan are now well-understood, the challenge to develop a raft of identification results for standard industrial organization models has not been widely taken up by the industrial organization academic community and there are numerous important examples of identification results which remain to be explored and tested. For example, one case that regulators and competition authorities should certainly like to understand would involve identification results for the difference between Ramsey and monopoly prices. Identification results exist for only a relatively small subset of standard industrial organization models.[26] For that reason a major and important topic for future research in industrial organization involves the study of identification.

6.2.3 Identifying Tacit Collusion

Collusion occurs when firms in an industry coordinate to maximize (or at least increase) joint industry profits as opposed to individual profits. In standard models of oligopolistic competition, firms maximize their own profits and ignore the consequence of their actions on competitor's profitability. As a result of this fundamental horizontal externality, whereby a firm takes actions (e.g., increases output or cuts prices) without any consideration of the negative impact on its competitors' profits, total industry profits are not maximized and firms will end up producing more and at lower prices than if they were acting together in a concerted fashion. Thus economic theory argues that selfish actions by individual firms are (i) ultimately self-defeating and (ii) ultimately generate great benefits for consumers in the form of lower prices and higher output.

In any discussion of collusion, it is useful to distinguish between a cartel or explicit collusion and tacit collusion. In an explicit cartel, firms will directly communicate with each other about their expected behavior and reactions and will jointly decide on the market outcome.[27] In contrast, under tacit collusion, there will be no explicit communication, but firms will nonetheless understand their rivals' likely reactions when setting output and prices. If a sufficiently large fraction of the players in an industry understand that selfish behavior will ultimately be self-defeating and they also understand that their rivals understand that, we may find that coordinated behavior emerges even without the need for explicit communication. Under such tacit collusion, the expected reaction of competitors to moves in prices or output

[26] One area where this line of research—the development of identification results—has been more active is the auction literature (see, for example, Athey and Haile 2002).

[27] For an extensive discussion of the determinants of the success of cartels, see the edited volume by Grossman (2004). For a detailed discussion of three prominent U.S. cases during the 1990s (the lysine, vitamins, and citric acid cartels), see the account by Connor (2001). The title comes from an infamous quote by James Randall, President of Archer-Daniels-Midland of the United States during a meeting with fellow lysine cartel members Anjinimoto Co. of Japan in 1993. Mr. Randall was captured secretly on tape by another ADM employee (who had signed an agreement with the FBI to be an informant in their investigation). A fuller version reads (see Eichenwald 1997, 1998): "We have a saying at this company," said Mr. Randall. "Our competitors are our friends and our customers are our enemies."

will be to follow these moves. Firms may succeed in tacitly coordinating using signaling of strategies through media, suppliers, or customers and perhaps also engage in occasional punishments so that, without needing explicit communication, firms end up pricing in ways that increases margins and total industry profits. Informal evidence of both tacit and explicit collusion can emerge from company pricing or strategy documents.

Legally, the treatment of the two forms of collusion is radically different as cartels are per se illegal and even criminalized in many jurisdictions (including the United States, the United Kingdom, Israel, Korea, and Australia) while tacit collusion is not typically criminalized and yet would, at least in principle, be subject to antitrust enforcement. For example, in the European Union, some forms of tacit collusion could be covered by Article 81, which prohibits "concerted practices." In addition, tacit collusion would be included in the concept of "collective dominance," which has been interpreted by the courts as a particular form of "dominance" and abuse of dominance is, for example, prohibited under Article 82.[28] In addition, mergers that are thought to result in an increase of "collective dominance" are forbidden in EU law. Furthermore, sector inquiries (in the EU) and in particular market inquiries (in the United Kingdom) can be used to target industries where such behavior is suspected.

The legal distinctions between tacit and explicit collusion may reflect economic reality since explicit and tacit collusion differ in the sense that the form and nature of collusion are typically explicitly agreed between the players in a cartel, so that it may be more effective at raising prices or restricting output than a collection of firms that are only tacitly colluding. Specifically, tacit colluders must find ways to convey sufficient information to each other indirectly, and they must overcome uncertainty about the extent to which rivals are "playing along" since the kind of direct—perhaps face-to-face or even evidenced with independent accounting reviews—reassurance possible in a cartel will not generally be possible for tacit colluders. Such communication difficulties may diminish either the effectiveness of the collusive arrangement or its longevity. The lack of direct communication may in particular reduce a tacitly colluding set of firms' ability to react optimally to changes in market conditions.

Both cartels and tacitly collusive accommodations can be unstable. Successful coordinated behavior will generate high prices, high margins, and low output and

[28] See, in particular, *Laurent Piau v. Commission* T-193/02, which confirms that collective dominance can be a form of dominance for Article 82, a view already existent in the EC merger regime following Airtours. On the other hand, a tacit collusion case has not arisen yet and indeed it would be an unusually difficult case since it would simultaneously be both a (i) "collective dominance" case and (ii) an "exploitative abuse" case (i.e., prices are high). Each form of case is rare. Specifically, *Laurent Piau v. Commission* involved a football industry association, FIFA, which introduced structural links between companies, whereas a tacit collusion case would not involve direct linkages. Furthermore, exploitative abuse cases against (single) dominant firms are rare in comparison to "exclusionary abuse" cases such as those involving predatory pricing. Thus it seems a pure tacit collusion case could in principle now be developed, but would need to overcome two potentially very difficult hurdles.

as a result every firm will have a private short-run incentive to increase its sales to take advantage of the higher margin. But it must do so undetected so that there are no reactions by competitors to eliminate the benefits of the deviation. If competitors respond by increasing their own output and causing prices to drop to competitive levels, the benefits of the deviation and thereby the incentives to deviate disappear. The potential lack of stability of a collusive agreement is therefore related to the likelihood that firms can carry out deviations that are both significant and undetected or a detectable deviation that brings enough profits to more than compensate for the losses of the cartel benefits. On the other hand, game theorists since the 1970s have demonstrated that there do exist credible punishment mechanisms that can eliminate incentives to deviate from a collusive agreement and result in stable tacitly collusive equilibria.[29] Furthermore, some "stable" agreements are of rather complex appearance. For example, some will involve recurrent periods of apparent "price wars" but in fact these are just one part of the stable agreement designed to deal with episodic periods of low demand resulting in low prices (Green and Porter 1984).

Either form of collusion in an industry harms consumers because it drives market prices up (and output down) toward monopoly outcomes where firms can extract much of the value generated by market activity to the detriment of consumers. It is, however, difficult to detect collusion when evidence of explicit collusion is missing or does not exist. How do we identify cartelized behavior from price competition? How do we distinguish tacit collusion from legitimate oligopolistic competition?

6.2.3.1 Difficulties in Directly Identifying Tacit Collusion

Identifying tacit collusion or the likelihood of tacit collusion is notoriously difficult. One direct approach to showing the existence of collective dominance is to attempt to establish the extent to which any firm's price is based on market demand sensitivity to price changes as distinct from the firm's own demand sensitivity to price changes.

To understand the logic of this direct approach, consider first that an indication from company documents that a firm's prices are being set with the reaction of consumers in mind is an indication of market power (although every firm has some degree of market power and not every firm is involved in pricing behavior of concern to competition authorities). If the prices of an individual firm are found to be set taking into account the anticipated full extent of the reaction of market demand as distinct from their own firm's demand, then we may have an indication of a collusive industry. Indeed, on the face of it, if the firm monitors and takes into account the effect of its actions on other market participants profitability, then we potentially have direct evidence for tacit or explicit collusion. In practice, such evidence must be interpreted carefully as many firms will engage in monitoring of rivals' behavior and this may be normal strategic behavior as distinct from the kind of dynamic strategic behavior that results in collusive outcomes. Evidence of

[29] This is formalized in Friedman (1971) and Abreu (1986).

monitoring rivals is certainly not in itself evidence of tacit collusion. Rather we must find evidence that the firm is taking, or attempting to take, decisions which actively accommodate its rivals' needs and in particular their likely profitability. Such direct evidence may be available from company documents or testimony, but even apparently direct documentary evidence can appear ambiguous given the intervention of skilled legal professionals. Evidence may also be available from econometric analysis (following the approach to identifying collusion outlined in the first part of this chapter which emphasized the power of "demand rotators" for identification in simple models) but again such evidence is rarely unambiguous. The difficulty in making these distinctions in practice should not be understated.

To further understand the difficulties in establishing tacit collusion directly, note that firms may tacitly collude with varying degrees of success. First, if firms are heterogeneous, they may not gain much directly from the optimal tacitly collusive action. For example, consider that a two-plant monopolist may sometimes minimize costs by using only its most efficient plant and not its inefficient plant. A tacitly collusive arrangement between two single-plant firms in which one firm produced nothing would probably be difficult to sell to the owner of the unused plant, at least without some form of (possibly indirect) side-payments between players, perhaps through industry associations, shared industry-level advertising, or commercial activities in other markets. Second, the world changes and tacitly colluding firms must have a strategy for dealing with change. For example, demand or costs may be high or low and, in a standard model of firm behavior, collusive prices would change with costs and demand conditions. If so, then tacitly colluding firms may need to re-establish a new tacit agreement about the level of collusive prices fairly frequently. However, if change threatens stability, then collusive arrangements may well involve only very infrequent changes in pricing or market territories. For each of these reasons the outcomes of a tacitly collusive arrangement can be somewhat or greatly distinct from either competitive or perfectly collusive outcomes.

We have already mentioned the critique of the econometric attempts to measure market power provided in Corts (1999). However, the critique in large part also applies to noneconometric evidence. Fundamentally, the problem is that dynamic game theory has only succeeded in showing that tacit collusion may be a sustainable market outcome and then provided us with a wide variety of examples of (potentially complex) pricing strategies that could result. The theory has not then yet provided a comprehensive "identification" strategy for distinguishing general classes of models of collusion from models of competition. Numerous market histories appear consistent with collusion and yet also appear consistent with other competitive environments. For example, collusion can produce stable prices or a succession of price wars depending on the level of uncertainty or the nature of the punishments. Collusion may also produce procyclical or countercyclical prices depending on, for example, capacity utilization levels or whether we are at turning points of business cycles or not.[30] Some consensus has emerged on the conditions that are more likely to promote collusion: small numbers of players, stability of demand, and firm symmetry.[31] But these characteristics are mostly indicative as collusion is still possible when these characteristics are absent. For example, symmetry will rarely be the case in differentiated product markets and, we shall see, firm asymmetry makes collusion harder in at least one important sense, but on the other hand does not typically rule out situations arising when collusion can nonetheless be sustained.

Because of the apparently weak predictive power of economic theory with regards to the exact manifestation of collusion, most empirical casework to detect collusion has centered on showing that the very basic conditions that are necessary for collusion to exist can be found in a given market. The presumption is that if these necessary conditions exist (so that firms have both the ability and incentive to collude), then collusion is likely. The analysis of coordination in antitrust settings currently tends to consist of analysis of the three essential points introduced by Stigler (1964) nearly fifty years ago, which we present below.

6.2.3.2 Assessing the Conditions for Agreement, Monitoring, and Enforcement

Stigler (1964) provided a general framework for evaluating the features of a market which are likely to facilitate the movement toward coordination. Subsequently this framework has largely been adopted in most jurisdictions, although the exact terminology varies from guidance to guidance.[32] It relies on the conclusion that for collusion to be viable, it must be feasible for participants to reach an *agreement* on the terms of coordination; it must also be possible to *monitor* that this agreement is being respected by the colluding firms; and deviating firms must be punished and, in the case of tacit collusion, it is the credibility of this punishment mechanism that holds the collusive agreement together, i.e., *enforces* it. The framework is equally applicable for explicit or tacit collusion, but the form of each element can differ. In the case of cartels for example, agreement may be arrived at by discussion, monitoring may occur by exchange of information, perhaps even independent reports by accounting firms and/or trade associations, while enforcement may in some cases remain via similar mechanisms to those emerging from tacit collusion.[33] In others the mechanism may be quite different. For example, in the extreme case of legal cartels, enforcement may result from contract enforcement via the courts. It is worth noting that export cartels remain legal in a number of jurisdictions. We next discuss each element of Stigler's framework in turn.

---

[30] See, in particular, Rotemberg and Saloner (1986) and Haltiwanger and Harrington (1991). See also Garcés et al. (2009) for a brief review of the subsequent collusion literature.

[31] For a summary of the literature, see Ivaldi et al. (2003).

[32] For example, the categories Agreement, Monitoring, and Enforcement are sometimes replaced with the terms Consensus, Detection, and Punishment.

[33] For example, in the lysine case, sales were reported to a trade association and each year a firm of accountants audited the sales numbers in both London and Decatur, IL.

Agreement. Colluders must reach some form of understanding about what exactly it means to coordinate. This means that there must be an understanding of the dimensions on which coordination is taking place as well as an indication of the expected behavior. In tacit collusion the agreement will not be explicit but will have to be inferred by market players from the information available to them. Firms can publicize their price lists and make public announcements to provide the market with an indication of a potential focal point around which behavior will be coordinated. These signaling practices are normally frowned upon by market authorities when they suspect collusive behavior, but on the other hand publishing price information is not uncommon and in other circumstances is actively encouraged by competition authorities, for example, to facilitate consumer search. Focal points may also be inferred from past behavior or historical prices and in such cases markets may tend to exhibit stronger degrees of price rigidity. A market with complex transactions or with customized transactions will be less susceptible to firms being able to find a mutually acceptable understanding of what it means to tacitly collude. Similarly, a market with very diverse products such as different brands and different versions of a particular product will be more difficult to coordinate. Since complexity makes agreements about what it would mean to collude difficult to achieve, sometimes we see firms adopting practices that "simplify their prices for consumers" or harmonize the conditions for a transaction. For an example of a pricing structure which might be considered by some authorities to potentially facilitate collusion, recall that at one stage some U.S. airlines proposed using per-mile pricing so that every route between every city would be easy to price by all parties.[34] Such initiatives may have the ultimate purpose of facilitating a collusive outcome since coordination largely reduces to tacitly agreeing on a single number, the per-mile price. Finally, when firms have very different incentives, perhaps because of differences in scale or efficiency, it will be harder to get everyone to agree to a particular market outcome. It may be easier to evolve toward agreements in industries where change occurs only slowly as it is not always obvious for firms to understand or agree on a coordinated response to change.

In a coordinated effects merger case it is desirable but probably should not be necessary to say exactly what the form of a coordinated agreement might look like, since it is unlikely that a competition authority will put the same effort into finding an ingenious solution to a difficult problem as the companies involved, should they have a sufficiently strong incentive to cooperate. For this reason, most competition authorities do not give quite the same weight to the agreement element of Stigler's framework in their guidelines as they do to the monitoring and enforcement areas. Even explicit agreements can be incredibly difficult to uncover. In the famous "phases of the moon" cartel case, twenty-nine colluding firms in the market

[34] See, for example, O'Brian (1992). To see that such proposals may not succeed, see, for example, McDowell (1992).

for electrical equipment led by the two giants General Electric and Westinghouse literally devised a codebook of lists of numbers which determined how much each company in the cartel would bid on a particular contract. The price spread was geared toward giving an impression of competition and the fact that the price spreads across companies were cyclical led to the cartel being known as the "phases of the moon" cartel. That particular cartel lasted seven years and rigged bids estimated to be worth a total of $7 billion.[35]

Monitoring. Dynamic oligopoly theory suggests that for coordination firms must be aware of the behavior of their competitors. They must be able to observe it or at least to infer it with certain degree of confidence. In particular they must be able to spot deviations from prevailing behavior in order that "cheaters" from the coordinated prices can be spotted. Monitoring will be harder in markets where prices and/or quantity choices are difficult to observe, demand or cost shocks are large, or when orders are lumpy and as a result both prices and quantities tend to be volatile. But it has been argued in the economics literature that tacit collusion can certainly occur without full transparency. Specifically, the literature emanating from Green and Porter (1984) has shown that tacit collusion is possible even without full monitoring of firms' prices and quantities. For example, a strategy that would temporarily revert to a price war every time market prices fell below a threshold can sustain tacit collusion.[36] In this case, tacit collusion would take the form of alternating phases of price stability and price wars.

In spite of these contributions, the issues of transparency, complexity, and the ability to monitor competitors' actions and prices are usually considered very important for a finding of collusion or coordinated effects. It is possible to look at the extent of monitoring and the extent of both complexity and transparency of information both through interview evidence and documentary evidence. Price lists, price announcements, and industry association publications are clear ways of announcing one's behavior but more may be needed to detect small-scale deviations. List prices or "price books" can sometimes facilitate coordination because they can dramatically improve the amount of information available to rivals. If customers mainly pay list prices, or list prices are highly correlated with transaction prices (in the extreme, transaction prices may be some fixed discount from list prices), then such price lists may help firms find their way toward coordination. Price lists need not be paper price lists and in some famous examples the price lists have been electronic. For example, in the U.S. Airline Tariff Pricing case, participating U.S. airlines could post nonbinding ticket prices for particular routes that were for an initial period unavailable to customers. In fact, they used features of the electronic fare system

[35] For a wonderful description of what has become known as the great electrical conspiracy, see "The great conspiracy," *Time Magazine*, February 17, 1961.

[36] For the first test of the Green and Porter model, see Porter (1983).

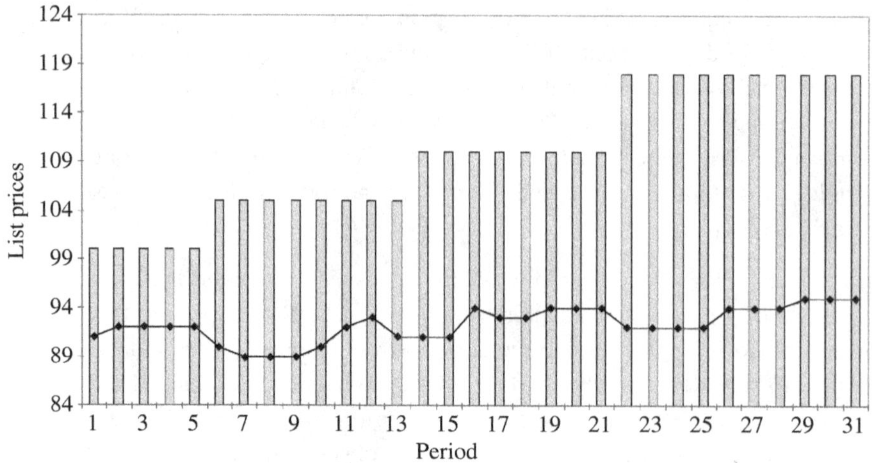

Figure 6.4. List prices versus actual prices.
Source: Scheffman and Coleman (2003, figure 4).

as signaling devices.[37] Baker (1996) provides an interesting commentary on information exchange in cyberspace. However, before condemning price lists, one must keep in mind that, at their best, price lists can hugely improve the information available to consumers which in turn can save consumer search costs, increase the price sensitivity of demand, and encourage firms to charge lower prices than their rivals.

Information flows between customers and suppliers in the case of stable customer–supplier relationships can be an important way of getting exact market information particularly when customers shop from different suppliers. The visibility of contracts and of changes in market shares is useful to detect potential deviations. Investigators should certainly invest in assessing the level of transparency and monitoring mechanisms that may imply that a coordinated outcome is viable.

Scheffman and Coleman (2003) provide a nice summary of the kinds of empirical work that may be undertaken to assess coordination. Those authors emphasize that coordination can happen in a number of ways and may involve coordination on prices, quantities, capacities, or some form of market division, say, by territory or type of customer. As a result many of the following remarks while phrased in terms of prices are equally relevant to other potential dimensions of coordination. Scheffman and Coleman suggest, for example, that we may wish to look empirically at the following:

1. Differences or patterns in the relationship between list and transaction prices. Figure 6.4 provides an example where list prices have little predictive power for actual transaction prices. In this case, list prices do not carry enough information about actual market prices and cannot be used as a monitoring device.

[37] *United Stated v. Airline Tariff Publishing Co.* (D.D.C., August 10, 1994) (final consent decree).

Table 6.5. Example of a company's estimates of competitor activity

	Competitor Y	Competitor Z
Number of customers that company X		
identifies as supplying	55	46
identifies as supplying when did not	22	12
does not identify as supplying when did	12	8
Percentage of customers for whom company X's		
volume estimate was off by more than 20%	75%	82%
volume estimate was off by more than 60%	39%	47%

Source: Scheffman and Coleman (2003, figure 5).

2. Variation in prices across consumers, controlling for observable differences in the type of customer or order behavior in terms of volume or location. We can look at the coefficient of variation and range of prices paid by various customer types. To that end a transaction-level regression of price on volume, location, and customer characteristics may be run in order to understand and evaluate the extent of variation in prices across customers or customer groups.
3. Variation in transaction prices within customer for the same product across different suppliers. We may also want to look at the percentage of instances where prices to the same customer by different suppliers differ by, say, more than 5%. We might, for example, want to break that down by customer type.
4. Variation in changes in transaction prices across customers again controlling for observable differences.

As with all such studies it is vital to bear in mind that the mere existence of co-movement in, say, list and transaction prices does not prove coordination since we would expect co-movement to result for innocent reasons such as cost variation. However, the basic intuition that such analysis relies on is that if significant variation in a firm's price changes is found, we might expect that coordinated interaction is likely to be more difficult. We examine this approach further (see section 6.2.3.4) by looking at the European Commission's empirical evidence in the Sony–BMG merger case.

We may also want to look at transparency directly by comparing one company's estimates of competitors' volumes versus their competitors' actual volumes. Such an analysis is provided in table 6.5, which shows that competitor X's estimates were quite considerably different from the truth.

Enforcement. In the theory of tacit collusion, enforcement action involving members of the cartel (internal enforcement) takes the form of the threat of a credible punishment directed at either a deviating firm or in a nontargeted fashion at all firms if they move away from the tacitly collusive outcome when a deviation is detected.

A successful punishment regime will eliminate the potential gains from cheating on other participants. When cheating on a collusive agreement is easily detected and a credible punishment exists for such behavior, tacitly collusive environments are predicted to be stable. Moreover, in some (at least theoretical) environments, no actual punishments need ever be observed which may make detection by competition authorities rather difficult.

On the other hand, while many theoretical models generate tacit collusion rather easily, it does seem that even explicit cartels, where direct communication is possible, do certainly break down. In a review of a large set of known cartels, Suslow and Levenstein (1997) find that the average longevity of an explicit cartel is about five years but that the distribution is bimodal: while some cartels last for decades, many others last for less than a year.

In addition to a mechanism that enforces internal stability of a collusive arrangement, there must be some form of mechanism for enforcing "external" stability. In particular, all else equal, high profits will soon attract new entrants so that it will be necessary to have either actual barriers to entry or an ability to punish entrants so as to deny them returns (in the sense of profit) following entry. For example, in the lysine case, a cartel member, Archer-Daniels-Midland, quickly built a new plant as part of strategy to deter a new entrant (Connor 2001). For tacit collusion to be an antitrust problem an industry must be able to benefit from both internal and externality stability.

In addition to suggesting that a credible punishment mechanism is important, economic theory does make some suggestions regarding the nature of such punishments. One particularly simple punishment involves the reversion to static competition. The theory suggests that the threat of a permanent or even temporary price war can be an effective punishment provided cartel participants are sufficiently patient and such punishments may sometimes involve "harsher" punishments than reversion to the competitive price.[38] Such theoretical results suggest that a key variable linked to the effectiveness of punishment is the ability of the punishing firms to rapidly expand output so that prices fall sharply enough to generate the losses that will deter opportunistic deviation. As a result there is an important literature on the role of excess capacity both on the incentives to cheat and the ability to punish. Excess capacity is generally considered to facilitate tacit coordination (see, for instance, Brock and Scheinkman 1985; Davidson and Deneckere 1990). Highly asymmetric holdings of capacity on the other hand probably, but not necessarily, hinder collusion (Compte et al. 2002; Vasconcelos 2005).

Other forms of punishment can exist particularly in multiproduct markets, although Bernheim and Whinston (1990) suggest that multimarket contact is actively helpful to sustaining collusion in the presence of firm or market asymmetry (Bernheim and Whinston 1990). Such asymmetry seems likely to arise fairly generically in

[38] See Abreu et al. (1990). Harsher punishments can involve prices below the competitive levels and stability can sometimes be maintained by using harsh but fairly short punishments.

real world markets making multimarket contact potentially a relevant consideration. Intuitively, under perfect firm and market symmetry, the incentive to collude and the incentive to cheat for all firms in all markets will be identical so that multimarket contact adds little. However, with firm and/or market asymmetry, the incentives for collusion and cheating will generally differ across firms in multimarket contexts. Within market, firm asymmetry means that different firms must each find collusion attractive. Multimarket contact means that incentive constraints will be evaluated in total across markets rather than within any individual market. As a result, punishments, for example, might be targeted to greatest effect.

Punishment mechanisms should be effective not only at deterring participating firms in an industry from cheating (internal stability) but also at deterring potential entrants in the market (external stability). Because it is difficult to discipline a very large number of firms that could enter at any time in an industry, tacit collusion will be more effective in markets that exhibit some barriers to entry. Indeed, in their review of the case history, Suslow and Levenstein (1997) find that, while cartels do sometimes break up occasionally because of cheating by incumbents, entry and an ability to react to changes in market positions pose a greater problem. Relatedly, not all firms in an industry will necessarily be involved in a particular cartel and if customers of those which are in a cartel can react by switching to nonparticipating suppliers, then that will help destabilize a collusive equilibrium.

While Stigler (1964) introduces the agreement, monitoring, and enforcement framework we have described, there is an important question as to the extent of analysis necessary about the form of the likely agreement. In particular, the summary of the European Court of First Instance judgment in the Airtours case reads:[39]

> Three conditions are necessary for the creation of a collective dominant position significantly impeding effective competition in the common market or a substantial part of it:
>
> - first, each member of the dominant oligopoly must have the ability to know how the other members are behaving in order to monitor whether or not they are adopting the common policy. In that regard, it is not enough for each member of the dominant oligopoly to be aware that interdependent market conduct is profitable for all of them but each member must also have a means of knowing whether the other operators are adopting the same strategy and whether they are maintaining it. There must, therefore, be sufficient market transparency for all members of the dominant oligopoly to be aware, sufficiently precisely and quickly, of the way in which the other members' market conduct is evolving;
> - second, the situation of tacit coordination must be sustainable over time, that is to say, there must be an incentive not to depart from the common policy on the market. It is only if all the members of the dominant oligopoly maintain the parallel conduct that all can benefit. The notion of retaliation in respect of conduct deviating from the common policy is thus inherent in this condition.

[39] *Airtours plc v. Commission of the European Communities*, Case T-342/99.

> In that context, the Commission must not necessarily prove that there is a specific retaliation mechanism involving a degree of severity, but it must none the less establish that deterrents exist, which are such that it is not worth the while of any member of the dominant oligopoly to depart from the common course of conduct to the detriment of the other oligopolists. For a situation of collective dominance to be viable, there must be adequate deterrents to ensure that there is a long-term incentive in not departing from the common policy, which means that each member of the dominant oligopoly must be aware that highly competitive action on its part designed to increase its market share would provoke identical action by the others, so that it would derive no benefit from its initiative;
>
> – third, it must also be established that the foreseeable reaction of current and future competitors, as well as of consumers, would not jeopardise the results expected from the common policy.

Broadly, the first condition relates directly to monitoring, while the second and third relate directly to internal and external enforcement. Thus, the agreement element of Stigler's framework is played down in the current EU legal environment presumably for reasons we have discussed earlier in this section.

In establishing these conditions, the competition case handler will need to examine carefully the specific facts about an industry, understanding the nature of multimarket contact, the extent of asymmetry, the lumpiness or orders, and so forth. An analyst would also go on to attempt to understand at least qualitatively the incentives of firms in an industry to sustain collusion and hence their ability to do so before she is able to conclude whether tacit collusion is likely or unlikely to be viable.

6.2.3.3 Other Evidence Potentially Relevant to an Inference of the Presence of Tacit Coordination

The issue of whether mergers are likely to increase the likelihood of tacit collusion will most certainly consist of an assessment of the evidence regarding the three elements discussed above, in particular in Europe as determined by the Court of First Instance's Airtours decision of 2002. Regarding the assessment of existing tacit collusion, the Court for First Instance in its Impala judgment said that:

> ...in the context of the assessment of the existence of a collective dominance position, although the three conditions defined by the CFI in *Airtours v. Commission* ...are indeed also necessary, they may, however, in the appropriate circumstances, be established indirectly on the basis of what may be a series of indicia and items of evidence relating to the signs and manifestations and phenomena inherent in the presence of a collective dominant position. (§251 *Impala v. Commission*)[40]

The European Court of Justice, in its annulment of the CFI decision, upheld the right of the court to freely assess different items of evidence. It also argued against the mechanical application of the so-called Airtours conditions detailed above but

[40] *Impala v. Commission of the European Communities*, Case T-464/04 (2006).

rather asked for these criteria to be related to an "overall economic mechanism of a hypothetical tacit coordination."[41] So that any evidence pointing to tacit collusion is admissible but a realistic mechanism of collusion consistent with the economic theory of collusion must also be laid out.

This can be understood as an invitation to use available evidence to directly identify a collusive outcome as distinct from the outcome generated by a competitive oligopoly. We have already seen that this is very difficult to do due in part to the lack of a wide variety of predictions that emerge from the theoretical framework for tacit collusion. It is particularly important to keep two factors in mind. First, coordination need not be complete in the sense of implementing the perfectly collusive outcome in a market. Second, information need not be perfect to sustain collusion. Most realistic scenarios of tacit collusion assume some degree of incomplete information which may then be reflected in some inefficiency in the reaction of the coordinated firms.

Still, one can certainly pay attention and give proper weight to such things as the existence of facilitating practices: observed industry practices which seem to have no other purpose than to allow information to flow or to facilitate an agreement. For instance, Kühn (2001) proposes that, given the intrinsic difficulty in inferring whether prices are the result of competitive oligopoly or of tacit collusion, it is more desirable to focus on suppressing certain forms of communication between firms, which do not bring efficiency and are likely to sustain a collusive equilibrium. His paper contains a review of the experimental evidence of the positive role of communication in collusion. See also the more recent experimental evidence reported in Cooper and Kühn (2009).

The extent of price rigidity may be relevant to such an evaluation of tacit collusion, and/or the presence of unexplained price wars in a market, where legitimate explanations for such outcomes can potentially be excluded. If prices sometime oscillate widely when there are no obvious demand or cost causes, competition authorities will want to consider alternative potential explanations, one of which is tacit collusion.

Since all actual instances of tacit collusion are likely to occur in a world of imperfect information, it is likely that agreements will not always work smoothly all the time. Firms will also rarely be completely symmetric and agreements, once reached, may not satisfy the ambitions of all players robustly. Some firms will probably have more incentives than others to cheat and to do so they will be more likely to take advantage of sudden fluctuations in demand or costs to lower prices and sell more than their agreed share. Competitors, unable to distinguish between the consequences of demand changes and cheating may retaliate and all this instability may become apparent in the data. It is possible that an examination of price series

[41] ECJ ruling of 10/07/08 in case C-413/06P in particular paragraphs 117–34.

shows periods of price stability alternating with periods of price drops and output expansion. If such sequences of price stability and price fluctuations cannot be explained by exogenous changes in demand, costs, or institutional environment, one may consider the possibility of a change in the competition regime in the industry with collusion alternating with competition. For example, Suslow and Levenstein (2006) find that problems in resolving the bargaining game played by cartel participants following changes in market conditions have frequently played an important role in cartel breakdowns.

Porter (1983), Bresnahan (1987), and Baker (1989) each suggest that examination of the way conduct varies over time can provide a useful source of information about the likelihood of tacit collusion. For example, Baker (1989) empirically identifies changes in competition regime that occur after unpredicted negative demand shocks trigger cheating from a cartel and causes temporary reversion to competition in the U.S. cartelized steel industry between 1933 and 1939.

In general, a tacitly collusive arrangement that is working well will sometimes, perhaps even often, tend to stabilize prices and/or quantities particularly when the terms of the agreement are complex and the transaction costs of renegotiating the targeted outcome are high. Also, when there is a lot of uncertainty about the evolution of the market, communicating and agreeing on new collective behavior can be difficult. For this reason, colluding industries can sometimes be less reactive to observed changes in costs or demand compared with a competitive market as they may tend to keep doing what they know until they succeed (or not) in collectively adjusting to change. Excessive price rigidity in the face of changing market conditions can therefore also be the sign of a colluding industry, especially if no particular efficiency gains can be attributed to the high stability of prices.

Abrantes-Metz et al. (2006) examine the effect of the collapse of a bid-rigging conspiracy in the frozen seafood industry on price levels and dispersion. The collapse of the cartel caused a decrease in price by 16% while the price variance more than doubled. Based on these results, Abrantes-Metz et al. designed a test that they applied to the market for retail gasoline in Louisville, Kentucky, between 1996 and 2002, and did not find a pattern of particularly low variance in the data. Connor (2005) provides a review of the empirical evidence and the theory underlying the relation between collusion and price dispersion. In principle, a reduction in price dispersion will sometimes be expected in a collusive setting for reasons including: production may be allocated more efficiently; shocks may provoke a coordinated response; the effect of differences in buyer's search costs on the price they ultimately get is diminished. In practice, most of the few studies that have analyzed price dispersion during collusion periods have found a reduction of the variance during the coordination. Bolotova et al. (2008) fail to detect this reduction in price variance during the citric acid cartel although those authors do find it in the lysine cartel. Such findings, however, relate mostly to explicit cartels where communication is likely to be better than in a tacitly collusive environment.

An alternative and significantly more involved approach to assessing the likelihood of tacit collusion involves empirically estimating the incentives and ability to collude in a way that is explicitly motivated by theoretical models. Kovacic et al. (2006) explicitly propose calculating the payoff to collusion between various subsets of firms in order to evaluate the incentive to collude. They propose empirically evaluating the profits that would be available from various firms getting together to collude with the Coasian view that firms are good at solving coordination problems when there are sufficient incentives in place. This approach requires only an application of the framework used for unilateral effects merger simulation, which we cover in detail in chapter 8.

Davis and Sabbatini (2009) go further.[42] Those authors propose building on the contributions of Friedman (1971) and the unilateral effects mergers simulation literature (see chapter 8). Specifically, they propose calculating not only the incentive to collude should collusion be successful but also (i) evaluate the other potentially relevant incentives such as the incentive to "cheat" and (ii) evaluate the ability of a given group of firms to sustain coordination. To do so they note that a standard dynamic oligopoly game suggests that firm f will only be able to sustain collusion if the net present value of payoffs to collusion are greater than the net present value of the payoff to cheating (defecting) subtracting the consequences of whatever punishments rivals impose.

Following Friedman (1971), let the one-period payoff to collusion, defection, and competition be respectively $\pi_f^{\text{Collusion}}$, $\pi_f^{\text{Defection}}$, and π_f^{NE}. The net present value (NPV) incentive compatibility constraint can be written:

$$V_f^{\text{Collusion}}(\delta_f) > V_f^{\text{Defection}}(\delta_f) \quad \Longleftrightarrow \quad \frac{\pi_f^{\text{Collusion}}}{1-\delta_f} > \pi_f^{\text{Defection}} + \frac{\delta_f \pi_f^{\text{NE}}}{1-\delta_f},$$

where δ_f represents firm f's discount factor and the punishment is assumed to be a reversion to Nash competition.

Davis and Sabbatini (2009) follow Friedman's (1971) model of tacit collusion while allowing for firm heterogeneity and differentiated products. Primarily, their modest contribution is to propose actually empirically implementing that model in differentiated product (and multimarket) contexts where previously authorities have only used a checklist of factors likely to facilitate collusion to arrive at a view where collusion is more or less likely. Given the development of the theory described in the technical box, they show (and we will see in chapter 8) that $\pi_f^{\text{Collusion}}$ and π_f^{NE} are available from unilateral effects merger simulation models while the theory suggests we can also fairly trivially calculate $\pi_f^{\text{Defection}}$ as the payoff to cheating against cooperating rival firms that are choosing the cooperative price and this can

[42] The joint paper combines and extends two earlier discussion papers, one from each author: the first was by Sabbatini (2006) and the second by Davis (2006f).

also be calculated using the techniques developed by the unilateral effects merger simulation literature. Davis and Huse (2009) implement the approach using data from the network computer server market and evaluate the incentives to coordinate in the HP–Compaq merger (see chapter 8).

6.2.3.4 Empirical Assessment of Collective Dominance: The Sony–BMG Merger

The Sony–BMG merger provides an important recent example of an empirical assessment of the likelihood of collective dominance in a market. The assessment was undertaken by the European Commission following a notified joint venture between SONY Music and BMG that would bring together the worldwide recording businesses of both music majors. The merger was cleared by the Commission in 2004 but that decision was subsequently annulled in July 2006 by the Court of First Instance, which decided that the Commission had made manifest errors of assessment when considering the case. The merger was renotified in 2007 and subsequently cleared a second time by the European Commission that same year after an in-depth investigation. The European Court of Justice eventually overturned the Court of First Instance decision in 2008, validating the first decision.[43]

Before the merger the industry was dominated by five music majors: Universal, Sony, BMG, EMI, and Warner Music. There were also significant "independent" labels but there was a concern that these labels were not in a position or did not have the incentives to challenge a potential coordination on recorded music CD prices by the majors. The assessment of the merger therefore centered on establishing whether conditions in the market were sufficiently conducive to tacit coordination. Stigler's three conditions (and hence the three Airtours conditions)—agreement, monitoring, and enforcement—were examined but the core of the assessment centered on whether there was sufficient transparency in the market for recorded music for an agreement to be monitored and therefore enforced. To analyze this question, the European Commission gathered the most extensive database it had ever collected. Specifically, it requested from merging parties and third parties transaction-level data that indicated what CD title was sold to what customer at what price on a particular day or week between January 2002 and June 2006.[44] In addition, titles were categorized according to whether they were in the charts at the time of the transaction and how long they had been released on the market. The data provided information on both the list price and the net price of the transactions. This extensive data set allowed the Commission to perform a comprehensive data analysis of the stability and therefore the predictability of the discounts.

---

[43] ECJ of 10/07/08 C-413/06P.

[44] Customers are retailers of various kinds (specialized music stores, nonspecialized stores like electronics chains, mass merchants, and supermarkets) or intermediate distributors such as rack jobbers.

Table 6.6. Methodology used by the European Commission in the assessment of the SONY–BMG merger.

Customer	No. of CDs	Published price to dealers (PPD)	Chart	First week?	Average total discount	Weighted average standard deviation	Low dispersion?
A	500	€12.5	Yes	Yes	15%	1 pp	Yes
A	100	€12.5	Yes	No	10%	3 pp	No
A	200	€12.5	No	No	15%	5 pp	No
A	200	€10.0	Yes	No	8%	1 pp	Yes

Source: European Commission.

At any point in time there are thousands of CDs actively sold in the market representing a large variety of artists, styles, and degrees of popularity. Still, as they are sold in a similar format and distributed in similar ways, the Commission acknowledged the possibility that one might think of a CD as a fairly generic item. It also considered the fact that most sales in the music business are actually generated by a very limited number of charted CDs so that collusion could be profitable by only coordinating the prices of these "few" high sales CDs. Moreover, because most of the sales of an album are generated in the first few weeks after its release, the Commission focused on whether there was coordination on prices at and shortly after the release date.

The fundamental question that the Commission asked to evaluate the extent of price transparency was: can a knowledgeable market participant infer the net price of a transaction from observable transaction characteristics? The observable characteristics of a transaction were the title, the customer, the time, whether the title was in the chart, whether the title was in its first week of release, and the list price of the title. What was not observed was the discount granted by the major to the retailer (customer) and the question was whether these discounts were sufficiently systematic to be sufficiently predictable.

To answer this question the Commission separated titles of each major into groups according to the observable characteristics mentioned above: list price (published price to dealers), whether it is the first week of release, whether charted, and customer identity. For every such group, the average discount and weighted within-group average standard deviation of the discount level was calculated. Groups of titles were then separated in two categories: those for which the discount variation is deemed respectively to be large and small. Specifically, large (small) was defined as those that exhibit a weighted standard deviation of more than (less than) two percentage points (pp). A summary of the results for a particular combination of major and customer for four groups of titles might look like table 6.6.

The total number of units in groups with low dispersion is then related to the total units sold by that major. In our example, and assuming there was only this customer, the number of units sold by that major under a "regime" of low dispersion of discounts would represent 70% of the sales.[45]

Commission results showed that before the merger, sales under a regime of "discount stability" represented less than 60% of all sales for most majors. This was sufficient evidence for the Commission to decide that it was highly improbable that there was coordination on the prices of CDs based on whether they were charted or newly released. A higher degree of complexity in the segmentation of products for the purpose of coordination was also deemed unlikely, since it would have involved a more complex definition of CD groupings.

6.2.3.5 *Bid-Rigging: Collective Dominance in Auctions*

Bidding markets are often the subject of coordination investigations. When a market is such that contracts are awarded by customers through auctions or bids from suppliers, procurement auctions, suppliers may agree to coordinate in order to keep prices high. In such cases, firms decide in advance who will win which auction and those not selected commit to offer higher prices on that particular auction, usually in exchange for winning in other auction processes. In such collusion, competitors' prices or bids are sometimes not directly observable by competitors but the outcome usually is.[46] A firm can then monitor whether any competitor cheated by lowering its particular bid when it was not supposed to.

It can be difficult to detect collusion in such markets because transactions are sometimes less frequent and the goods involved may even be unique, making it difficult to compare prices or even establish a market price. Consider, for example, how many aircraft carriers governments buy: very few. Nonetheless, several strategies have been proposed to detect coordination in auction markets. For fairly recent surveys, see Bajari and Summers (2002), Porter (2005), or Harrington (2008).

Efforts to identify collusion using empirical applications of auctions now have a long and distinguished history, though the techniques are generally not for the technicality shy. Authors in this empirical tradition include Porter and Zona (1993, 1999), Baldwin et al. (1997), and, more recently, Bajari and Ye (2001). The latter, for example, argue that identification is best achieved noting that bids should fulfill two conditions, which, if violated, would exclude competitive behavior.[47] First, that

---

[45] (Sales in rows 1 and 4)/(Total sales in rows 1 to 4) = $(500 + 200)/(500 + 100 + 200 + 200) = 700/1{,}000 = 0.7$, i.e., 70% of sales are low dispersion.

[46] Sometimes, particularly in procurement auctions by government agencies, there is a tendency to tell all participants all of the bids in an auction. While good practice in terms of transparency of government, on balance such a practice can lead to serious problems breaking coordination and as a result procurement will only occur at sometimes very high prices. Governments can be very inelastic demanders in some procurement areas, e.g., military equipment.

[47] For a nontechnical exposition, see Bajari and Summers (2002).

once we take into account all publicly observable cost information that determines a conditional expected value of the bid amount, the deviations from that expected value of the bid should not be correlated among bidders. That is, we should not see many firms bidding particularly highly at any time.[48] Their second condition is exchangeability: the bid of a firm should not be affected by the identity of the firm with the next lower costs. A competing firm will always bid such as to cover its costs and beat firms with the next highest cost and it should not matter who their closest competitor is beyond the rival's cost when there is competition. In contrast, when the closest competitor is a member of a cartel, then the firm will be able to price above this competitor's costs and still win the bid. In this case, the identity of the closest competitors, whether it is a cartel member or not, will affect the amount of the firm's bid. Bajari and Ye propose statistical ways to test these conditions which each form the basis of a method of identifying whether data are generated by one model or another. In particular, they argue that violations of these conditions are not consistent with a competitive market. If markets are such that bids seem uncorrelated and there is "exchangeability" of competitors, there is no proof that competition is taking place but competition cannot be rejected. We leave the reader with this highly incomplete introduction and a route to those authors' papers for further information but note that their proponents suggest that the power of these kinds of tests are demonstrable since, for example, both Porter and Zona (1993, 1999) and Pesendorfer (2000) analyze data sets where collusion is known to have taken place and they find that (1) cartel members tend to bid less aggressively than noncartel members and (2) the bids of cartel members tend to be more correlated with each other than with the bids of noncartel members.

6.2.4 Single Dominance: Market Power with Differentiated Products

Collusion often arises in markets where the products are relatively homogeneous so that, under competitive conduct, firms impose a significant competitive constraint on each other. Because firms can exploit little market power individually, they have an incentive to coordinate to extract rent collectively. With differentiated products, firms have some degree of market power due to the fact that consumers have preferences for particular goods offered by the different firms and are often willing to pay more for the specific product they like compared with other similar products. Firms do exert pricing constraints on each other because customers will eventually switch if their preferred product becomes relatively too expensive, but the degree of the constraint can vary greatly. The exercise of market power obtained through product differentiation is not the subject of competition policy scrutiny in itself in many jurisdictions, most notably the United States, but such exploitative abuses by

[48] Such an identification strategy appears to rely heavily on the bidding firms knowing no more "public" knowledge than the investigator.

dominant firms are potentially actionable in other jurisdictions, including Europe, so that sufficient differentiation could generate concerns. In addition, actions undertaken by a firm for the purpose of eliminating significant competitive constraints and thereby maintaining or increasing its own market power are not allowed when they seriously harm consumers (exclusionary abuses). While the appropriate extent of activity to combat exploitative abuses is a matter of debate, many jurisdictions examine the consequences of firms' decisions to acquire or merge with rivals because such actions have the potential to generate substantial increases in market power that would be detrimental to consumers. In this section we begin our analysis of the pricing power of firms in a market for differentiated products in which firms compete on prices. The framework we describe is discussed in further detail in chapter 8, where we present a general analysis of merger simulation models testing for unilateral effects. We then discuss the conditions for the identification of coordination in a differentiated product pricing setting. Doing so allows us to examine how to extend Bresnahan's (1982) identification results for the homogeneous goods context (described above) to a differentiated product context. Nevo (1998) provides a numerical example while we follow the more formal identification results provided in Davis (2006d). We then illustrate with an empirical example drawing on Bresnahan (1987).

6.2.4.1 Pricing Equations

In order to identify the competitive behavior of firms in differentiated product markets, we must understand the pricing decisions made by the different market players and also how they interact. We will see that (static) economic theory suggests that firms will react to the presence of close substitutes owned by rivals by pricing more aggressively. Identifying the pricing equations of firms can help us measure the level of market power faced by an individual firm in a particular market.

Consider a simple theoretical example involving two differentiated but substitute products whose prices must be determined. We contrast the incentives to set the prices of (i) two firms competing in prices in a standard differentiated products' Bertrand model with (ii) a single firm owning both products. (For background, see the introductory discussion in chapters 1 and 5.) When comparing the two sets of first-order conditions generated by these two different models, the firm maximizing joint profits takes into account the effect of the change in price of good j on the quantity of all goods and not only on the quantity of good j. If an increase of the price of good 1 causes the demand for good 2 to increase, this increase in the revenues coming from the sales of good 2 will mitigate the impact of the lower sales of good 1. Therefore, the firms maximizing joint profits will have more of an incentive to increase prices compared with the single-product firm.

Generally, we can write down first-order conditions which encompass both models as follows:

$$\text{for good 1:}\qquad (p_1 - c_1)\frac{\partial Q_1(\underline{p})}{\partial p_1} + Q_1(\underline{p}) + \Delta_{12}(p_2 - c_2)\frac{\partial Q_2(\underline{p})}{\partial p_1} = 0,$$

$$\text{for good 2:}\qquad \Delta_{21}(p_1 - c_1)\frac{\partial Q_1(\underline{p})}{\partial p_2} + Q_2(\underline{p}) + (p_2 - c_2)\frac{\partial Q_2(\underline{p})}{\partial p_2} = 0,$$

where Δ_{ij} indicates whether changes in the quantity demanded of product j will affect the pricing of product i (see box). In the single-product firm's case, $\Delta_{12} = \Delta_{21} = 0$. In the case where one firm produced both products, we set $\Delta_{12} = \Delta_{21} = 1$. In an industry with several firms producing different ranges of products we would have a pricing equation for each product and a Δ matrix indicating the ownership structure of the industry. We will consider the general version of this game in chapter 8.

Suppose the demand function for each of the firms are linear in parameters and prices, so that the demand for product j is given by

$$Q_j = \alpha_{j0} + \alpha_{j1} p_1 + \alpha_{j2} p_2.$$

If two single-product firms play a Bertrand–Nash pricing game, they will maximize profits with respect to prices

$$\max_{p_j} \pi_j(p_1, p_2) = \max_{p_j}(p_j - c_j)Q_j(\underline{p}),$$

where $\underline{p} = (p_1, p_2)$ denotes the vector of prices and this will result in a set of optimal pricing equations:

$$\text{for firm 1:}\qquad (p_1 - c_1)\frac{\partial Q_1(\underline{p})}{\partial p_1} + Q_1(\underline{p}) = 0,$$

$$\text{for firm 2:}\qquad (p_2 - c_2)\frac{\partial Q_2(\underline{p})}{\partial p_2} + Q_2(\underline{p}) = 0.$$

Next let us assume that one firm now produces both of the two goods. It will maximize the joint profits from both goods:

$$\max_{p_1, p_2} \pi_1(p_1, p_2) + \pi_2(p_1, p_2) = \max_{p_1, p_2}(p_1 - c_1)Q_1(p) + (p_2 - c_2)Q_2(p).$$

The resulting optimal pricing equations become

$$\text{for good 1:}\qquad (p_1 - c_1)\frac{\partial Q_1(\underline{p})}{\partial p_1} + Q_1(\underline{p}) + (p_2 - c_2)\frac{\partial Q_2(\underline{p})}{\partial p_1} = 0,$$

$$\text{for good 2:}\qquad (p_1 - c_1)\frac{\partial Q_1(\underline{p})}{\partial p_2} + Q_2(\underline{p}) + (p_2 - c_2)\frac{\partial Q_2(\underline{p})}{\partial p_2} = 0.$$

In the case of linear demands, each of the derivative terms will be parameter values, α_{j1}, α_{j2}.

Note that different ownership structures or different competition models will have different implications for the equilibrium prices. In this constant marginal cost example, shocks to cost and demand will affect prices differently depending on the value of Δ_{ij}, which indicates the products that enter a given firm's profit-maximization function.

If we can estimate the demand equations, then we will have estimates of the demand parameters, α. From a traditional analysis of estimation of linear equations, we know we can do this for a demand equation if we have as many excluded cost variables (or, more generally, supply (pricing) equation shifters) as we have endogenous variables in the demand equation. In the case where marginal costs are constant in quantity we can therefore retrieve the conduct parameters Δ_{ij} in much the same way as was done in the homogeneous product case. Demand and cost shifters will be needed for identification and given enough of them will also be sufficient to test our model of collusion against the analogous model of competition. In this case, instead of a single demand and a single pricing equation, we will have a system of J demand and J pricing equations. Much like in the homogeneous goods example, we can substitute the demand function for the quantities in the pricing equation and reduce the system to one which involves "only" J equations. The estimated parameters capturing the effect of demand and cost shifters on other products will provide us with information about the extent to which these products are constraining the price of the product being analyzed.

We illustrate with a very simple example using our equation for equilibrium prices. Assuming the products' linear demand functions,

$$Q_j = \alpha_{j0} + \alpha_{j1} p_1 + \alpha_{j2} p_2,$$

the pricing equations become

$$(p_1 - c_1)\alpha_{11} + (p_2 - c_2)\Delta_{12}\alpha_{21} + Q_1(\underline{p}) = 0,$$
$$(p_1 - c_1)\Delta_{21}\alpha_{12} + (p_2 - c_2)\alpha_{22} + Q_2(\underline{p}) = 0,$$

which can be written in matrix form as

$$\begin{bmatrix} \alpha_{11} & \Delta_{12}\alpha_{21} \\ \Delta_{21}\alpha_{12} & \alpha_{22} \end{bmatrix} \begin{bmatrix} p_1 - c_1 \\ p_2 - c_2 \end{bmatrix} + \begin{bmatrix} Q_1(\underline{p}) \\ Q_2(\underline{p}) \end{bmatrix} = 0.$$

The differentiated product setting moves us from our usual demand and supply (pricing) equations in a homogeneous product setting, where we analyze two simultaneous equations, to a situation with a total of J demand and J supply curves, where J is the number of products being sold. In this case, such an approach would leave us with four equations to solve. The $2J$ equations form the "structural form" of the differentiated product model. Alternatively, we need solve only a two-equation system if we substitute in the demand system

$$\begin{bmatrix} Q_1(\underline{p}) \\ Q_2(\underline{p}) \end{bmatrix} = \begin{bmatrix} \alpha_{11} & \alpha_{12} \\ \alpha_{21} & \alpha_{22} \end{bmatrix} \begin{bmatrix} p_1 \\ p_2 \end{bmatrix} + \begin{bmatrix} \alpha_{01} \\ \alpha_{02} \end{bmatrix}$$

to give

$$\begin{bmatrix} \alpha_{11} & \Delta_{12}\alpha_{21} \\ \Delta_{21}\alpha_{12} & \alpha_{22} \end{bmatrix} \begin{bmatrix} p_1 - c_1 \\ p_2 - c_2 \end{bmatrix} + \begin{bmatrix} \alpha_{11} & \alpha_{12} \\ \alpha_{21} & \alpha_{22} \end{bmatrix} \begin{bmatrix} p_1 \\ p_2 \end{bmatrix} + \begin{bmatrix} \alpha_{01} \\ \alpha_{02} \end{bmatrix} = 0.$$

A small amount of matrix algebra allows us to solve for equilibrium prices:

$$\begin{bmatrix} p_1 \\ p_2 \end{bmatrix} = -\begin{bmatrix} 2\alpha_{11} & \Delta_{12}\alpha_{21} + \alpha_{12} \\ \Delta_{21}\alpha_{12} + \alpha_{21} & 2\alpha_{22} \end{bmatrix}^{-1} \begin{bmatrix} \alpha_{01} \\ \alpha_{02} \end{bmatrix}$$
$$+ \begin{bmatrix} 2\alpha_{11} & \Delta_{12}\alpha_{21} + \alpha_{12} \\ \Delta_{21}\alpha_{12} + \alpha_{21} & 2\alpha_{22} \end{bmatrix}^{-1} \begin{bmatrix} \alpha_{11} & \Delta_{12}\alpha_{21} \\ \Delta_{21}\alpha_{12} & \alpha_{22} \end{bmatrix} \begin{bmatrix} c_1 \\ c_2 \end{bmatrix}.$$

A numerical example may be useful. Suppose, for example, that $\alpha_{11} = \alpha_{22} = -2$, $\alpha_{12} = 2$, and $\alpha_{21} = 1$. Then two single-product firms in a competitive scenario would produce the following prices:

$$\begin{bmatrix} p_{1t} \\ p_{2t} \end{bmatrix} = \frac{-1}{14} \begin{bmatrix} -4 & -2 \\ -1 & -4 \end{bmatrix} \begin{bmatrix} \alpha_{01t} \\ \alpha_{02t} \end{bmatrix} + \frac{1}{14} \begin{bmatrix} 8 & 4 \\ 2 & 8 \end{bmatrix} \begin{bmatrix} c_{1t} \\ c_{2t} \end{bmatrix}.$$

While under collusion the prices will be determined by

$$\begin{bmatrix} p_{1t} \\ p_{2t} \end{bmatrix} = \frac{-1}{7} \begin{bmatrix} -4 & -3 \\ -3 & -4 \end{bmatrix} \begin{bmatrix} \alpha_{01t} \\ \alpha_{02t} \end{bmatrix} + \frac{1}{7} \begin{bmatrix} 2 & 2 \\ -2 & 5 \end{bmatrix} \begin{bmatrix} c_{1t} \\ c_{2t} \end{bmatrix}.$$

Note that under collusion the firms have a weight of $\frac{3}{7}$ on the impact of other products' demand shifters when setting the price for good 1. Under perfect competition, however, the firms only put a weight of $\frac{2}{14} = \frac{1}{7}$ on product 2's demand shifter.

As our numerical example illustrates, in this model common ownership or coordinated behavior puts greater weight on what happens to the demand of the other product setting its price. As a result, the differentiated products Bertrand model suggests that movements in the rival product's demand will affect a product's price far more under collusion than under perfect competition. Such a result is perhaps intuitive since collusive arrangements "internalize" effects across products. Given demand estimates and an ownership structure, we can measure how these transmissions occur. In doing so we can compare how much weight is genuinely given to rivals' demand or cost shifters. This difference in transmission reactions to demand or cost shifts can be enough to identify whether firms are setting the prices of products independently or not. This can be considered intuition for identification in an econometric model, but it can also be helpful when collecting other evidence in a given case (e.g., documentary evidence). On the other hand, such an observation may concern us since we noted earlier that on occasion cartels have often resulted in relatively less variation in prices, perhaps because of stability concerns. As Corts (1999) noted, a different model of collusion would have different implications for observed collusive prices.

6.2.4.2 *Identification of Pricing and Demand Equations in Differentiated Markets*

In a fashion entirely analogous to the homogeneous products case, the identification of conduct generally requires that the parameters of the demand and pricing equations are identified. Even if demand rotation can also be used to identify conduct in differentiated industries in the same way as is done for homogeneous products, demand does need to be estimated to confirm or validate assumptions. This presents a challenge because a differentiated product industry has one demand curve and one pricing function for each of the products being sold. In contrast, in the homogeneous product case, there is only one market demand and one market supply curve that need to be estimated. Now we will need to estimate as many demand functions as there are products and also as many pricing equations as there are products. Identification naturally becomes more difficult in this case and some restrictions will have to be imposed in order to make the analysis tractable. We discuss differentiated product demand estimation extensively in chapter 9.

A general principle for identification of any linear system of equations is that the number of parameter restrictions on each equation should be equal to, or greater than, the number of endogenous variables included in the equation. A normalization restriction is always imposed in the specification of any equation so in practice the number of additional restrictions must equal or be more than the number of endogenous variables less one.[49] This is equivalent to saying that the restrictions must be equal to or more than the number of endogenous variables on the "right-hand side" of any given equation. The total number of endogenous variables is also the number of equations in the structural model. This general principle is known as the "order condition" and is a necessary condition for identification in systems of linear equations. It may, however, not be sufficient in some cases. Previously, we encountered the basic supply-and-demand two-equation system, where we had two structural equations with two endogenous variables: price and quantity. In that case we needed the normalization restrictions and then at least one parameter restriction for each equation for identification. We obtained the parameter restrictions from theory: variables that shifted supply but not demand were needed in the equations to identify the demand equation and vice versa (these exclusion restrictions are imposed by restricting values of the parameters to zero). A more technical discussion

[49] The normalization restriction is usually imposed implicitly by not placing a parameter on whichever one of the endogenous variables is placed on the left-hand side of an equation.

Table 6.7. Nature of competition in the U.S. car market.

Year	Auto production (units)	Real auto price/CPI	% in quality-adjusted prices	Sales revenues ($)	Quantity index
1953	6.13	1.01	—	14.5	86.8
1954	5.51	0.99	—	13.9	84.9
1955	7.94	0.95	−2.5	18.4	117.2
1956	5.80	0.97	6.3	15.7	97.9
1957	6.12	0.98	6.1	16.2	100.0

Source: Bresnahan (1987).

of identification of demand and pricing equations in markets with differentiated products is provided in the annex to this chapter (section 6.4), which follows Davis (2006d).

6.2.4.3 *Identification of Conduct: An Empirical Example*

When conduct is unknown, we will want to assess the extent to which firms take into account the consequences of pricing decisions on other products when they price one particular good. In this case, one strategy is to estimate the reduced form of the structural equations and retrieve the unknown structural parameters by using the correspondence between reduced-form and structural parameters derived from the general structural specification. Assuming that the demand parameters are identified and marginal costs are constant, we will need enough demand shifters excluded from a pricing equation to be able to identify the conduct parameters (see Nevo 1998). In particular, we will need as many exogenous demand shifters in the demand equation as there are products produced by the firm. Although identification of conduct is therefore technically possible, in practice it may well be difficult to come up with a sufficient number of exogenous demand and cost shifters.

An early and important example of an attempt to identify empirically the nature of competition in a differentiated product market is provided by Bresnahan's (1987) study of the U.S. car industry in the years 1953–57. Bresnahan considers the prices and number of cars sold in the United States during those years and attempts to explain why in 1955 prices dropped significantly and sales rose sharply. In particular, he tests whether this episode marks a temporary change of conduct by the firms from a coordinated industry to a competitive one. The data that Bresnahan (1987) is trying to explain are presented in table 6.7. The important feature of the data to notice is that it is apparent that 1955 was an atypical year with low prices and high quantities. Real prices fell by 5%, quantity increased by 38%, and revenues increased by 32%.

To begin to build a model we must specify demand. Bresnahan specifies demand functions where each product's demand depends on the two neighboring products in terms of quality: the immediately lower-quality and the immediately higher-quality product. He motivates his demand equation using a particular underlying discrete choice model of demand but ultimately his demand function takes the form,

$$q_i = \delta\left[\frac{P_j - P_i}{x_j - x_i} - \frac{P_i - P_h}{x_i - x_h}\right],$$

where P and x stand for price and quality of the product and h, i, and j are indicators for products of increasing quality. Quality is one dimensional in the model, but captures effects such as horsepower, number of cylinders, and weight. Note that, all else equal, demand is linear in the prices of the goods h, i, and j and that given a price differential the cross-price slopes will increase with a decrease in the difference in quality, x. In this rather restrictive demand model there is only a single parameter to estimate, δ.

To build the pricing equations, he assumes a cost function where marginal costs are constant in quantity produced but increasing in the quality of the products so that $x_j \geqslant x_i \geqslant x_h$ for products j, i, and h. These assumptions imply that the whole structure can be considered as a particular example of a model where demand is linear in price and marginal costs are constant in output. By writing a linear-in-parameters demand equation, where $q_i = \alpha_{i0} + \alpha_{ii} p_i + \alpha_{ij} p_j + \alpha_{ih} p_h$, we can see that for fixed values of the quality indices, x_i, x_j, and x_h, the analysis of a pricing game using Bresnahan's demand model can be incorporated into the theoretical structure we developed above for the linear demand model where the parameters in the equation are in fact functions of data and a single underlying parameter. (More precisely, we studied the linear demand model with two products above and we will study the general model in chapter 8.) Specifically, the linear demand parameters are of the form,

$$\alpha_{ii} = -\delta\left(\frac{1}{x_j - x_i} + \frac{1}{x_i - x_h}\right),$$

$$\alpha_{ij} = \delta\left(\frac{1}{x_j - x_i}\right),$$

$$\alpha_{ih} = \delta\left(\frac{1}{x_i - x_h}\right).$$

Bresnahan estimates the system of equations by assuming first that there is Nash competition so that the matrix Δ describes the actual ownership structure of products (i.e., there is no collusion). Subsequently, he estimates the same model for a cartel by setting all the elements of the Δ matrix to 1 so that profits are maximized for the entire industry. He can then use a well-known model comparison test called the Cox test to test the relative explanatory power of the two specifications.[50] Bresnahan

[50] We have shown that the two models Bresnahan writes down are nested within a single family of models so that we can follow standard testing approaches to distinguish between the models. In Bresnahan's case he chooses to use the Cox test, but in general economic models can be tested between formally irrespective of whether the models are nested or nonnested (see, for example, Vuong 1989).

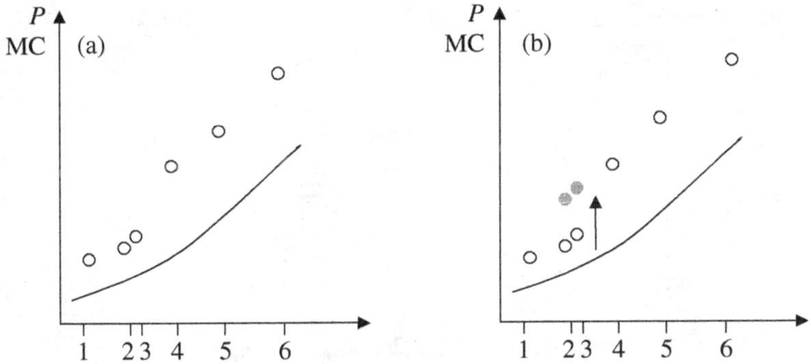

Figure 6.5. Expected outcomes under (a) competition and (b) collusion. *Source*: Authors' rendition of figure 2 in Bresnahan (1987). (a) Under competition, products with close substitutes produced by rivals get very low markups over MC. (b) Under collusion, close substitutes produced by rivals get much higher markups over MC.

concludes that the cartel specification explains the years 1954 and 1956 while Nash competition model explains the data from 1955 best. From this, he concludes that 1955 amounted to a temporary breakdown of coordination in the industry.

Intuitively, Bresnahan is testing the extent to which close substitutes are constraining each other. If the firm maximizes profits of the two products jointly, there will be less competitive pressure than in the case where the firm wants to maximize profits on one of the products only and therefore ignores the negative consequences of lower prices on the sales of the close substitute product. Thus, in figure 6.5, if close substitute products 2 and 3 are owned by rivals, then they will have a low markup under competition but far higher markups under collusion.

Given his assumptions about costs and the nature of demand, Bresnahan finds that the explanation for the drop in price during 1955 is the increase in the level of competition of close substitutes in the car market.

The demand shifters that helped identify the parameter estimates are presented in table 6.8 as well as the accounting profits of the industry. The accounting profits, however, are not consistent with Bresnahan's theory, as he notes. If firms are coordinating in the years 1954 and 1956, industry profits should be higher than in 1955 when they revert to competition. Bresnahan's response is that accounting profits are not representative of economic profits and are not to be relied upon. We must therefore make a decision in this case about whether to believe the accounting measures of profitability or the econometric analysis. In other cases, one might hope each type of evidence allows us to build toward a coherent single story.

6.3 Conclusions

- Structural indicators such as market shares and concentration levels are still commonly used for a first assessment of industry conduct and performance,

Table 6.8. Demand and cost shifters of the car market in the United States 1953–57.

Year	Per capita disposable income: Level	Per capita disposable income: Growth	Interest rates	Durable expenditures (nonauto)	Accounting profits ($)
1953	1,623	—	1.9	14.5	2.58
1954	1,609	−0.9%	0.9	14.5	2.25
1955	1,659	3.0%	1.7	16.1	3.91
1956	1,717	3.5%	2.6	17.1	2.21
1957	1,732	0.9%	3.2	17.0	2.38

Source: Bresnahan (1987).

although they are not usually determinative in a regime applying an effects-based analysis of a competition question. The fact that they are not determinative does not mean market shares are irrelevant, however, for a competition assessment and many authors consider they should carry some evidential weight.

- Developments in static economic theory and the availability of data have shown that causality between market concentration and industry profitability cannot be easily inferred. However, economic theories built on dynamic models do frequently have a flavor of considerable commonality with the older SCP literature. For example, Sutton (1991, 1998) emphasizes that prices are indeed expected to be a function of market structure in two-stage games where entry decisions are made at the first stage and then active firms compete in some way (on prices or quantities) or collude at a second stage.

- The broad lesson of game theory is that quite detailed elements of the competitive environment can matter for a substantial competition analysis. The general approach of undertaking a detailed market analysis aims at directly identifying the nature of competition on the ground and therefore the likely effects of any merger or alleged anticompetitive behavior.

- Technically, the question of identification involves asking the question of whether two models of behavior can be told apart from one another on the basis of data. The hard question in identification is to establish exactly which data variation will be helpful in moving us to a position where we are able to tell apart some of our various models. The academic analysis of identification tends to take place within the context of econometric models, but the lessons of such exercises typically move directly across to inform the kinds of evidence that competition authorities should look for more generally such as evidence from company documents.

- The degree to which firms are reactive to changes in demand conditions in the market can provide direct evidence of the extent of a firm's market power. Formal econometric models can use the methods involving the estimation of conduct parameters in structural models to determine whether the reactions of firms to changes in prices are consistent with competitive, competing oligopoly, or collusive settings. However, the more general lesson is that changes in the demand elasticity can provide useful data variation to identify conduct. For example, we might (at least conceivably) find documentary evidence suggesting that firms' pricing reactions accommodate prices in a fashion consistent with a firm's internal estimates of market demand sensitivities (rather than firm demand sensitivities).

- We examined identification results for both homogeneous product markets and also subsequently differentiated products markets. Analysis of identification in the former case suggests that demand rotators are the key to identification. In the differentiated product case, the results suggest that (i) examining the markups of close-substitute but competing products may be useful and (ii) examining the intensity with which demand and cost shocks to neighboring products are accommodated may sometimes be helpful when understanding the extent of coordination in a market.

- In examining the likelihood of collusion, one must assess whether the necessary conditions for collusion exist. Following Stigler (1964), those are agreement, monitoring, and enforcement. The assessment of each of these conditions will typically involve a considerable amount of qualitative evidence although a considerable amount of quantitative evidence can be brought to bear to answer subquestions within each of the three conditions. For example, the European Commission examined the extent to which transaction prices were predictable given list prices to examine market transparency in the Sony–BMG case.

- In addition to qualitative analysis of the factors which can affect the likelihood of collusion, it is sometimes possible and certainly desirable to develop an understanding of the incentives to compete, collude, and also to defect from collusive environments.

6.4 Annex: Identification of Conduct in Differentiated Markets

In this annex we follow Davis (2006d), who provides a technical discussion of identification of (i) pricing and demand equations in differentiated product markets and (ii) firm conduct in such markets. In particular, we specify in more detail our example of a market with two firms and two differentiated products. Define the marginal costs of production which depend on variables w such as input costs to be independent of output so that

$$\begin{bmatrix} c_{1t} \\ c_{2t} \end{bmatrix} = \begin{bmatrix} \gamma_1' & 0 \\ 0 & \gamma_2' \end{bmatrix} \begin{bmatrix} w_t^1 \\ w_t^2 \end{bmatrix} + \begin{bmatrix} u_{1t} \\ u_{2t} \end{bmatrix}.$$

Similarly, suppose that demand shifters depend on some variables x such as income or population size which affect the level of demand for each of the products:

$$\begin{bmatrix} \alpha_{01t} \\ \alpha_{02t} \end{bmatrix} = \begin{bmatrix} \beta_1' & 0 \\ 0 & \beta_2' \end{bmatrix} \begin{bmatrix} x_t^1 \\ x_t^2 \end{bmatrix} + \begin{bmatrix} \varepsilon_{1t} \\ \varepsilon_{2t} \end{bmatrix}.$$

Then linear demand functions for the two products can be written as

$$\begin{bmatrix} q_1 \\ q_2 \end{bmatrix} = \begin{bmatrix} \alpha_{01} \\ \alpha_{02} \end{bmatrix} + \begin{bmatrix} \alpha_{11} & \alpha_{12} \\ \alpha_{21} & \alpha_{22} \end{bmatrix} \begin{bmatrix} p_1 \\ p_2 \end{bmatrix},$$

while the pricing equations derived from the first-order conditions are

$$\begin{bmatrix} \alpha_{11} & \Delta_{12}\alpha_{21} \\ \Delta_{21}\alpha_{12} & \alpha_{22} \end{bmatrix} \begin{bmatrix} p_1 - c_1 \\ p_2 - c_2 \end{bmatrix} + \begin{bmatrix} q_1 \\ q_2 \end{bmatrix} = 0.$$

The full structural form of the system of equations is

$$\begin{bmatrix} \alpha_{11} & \Delta_{12}\alpha_{21} & 1 & 0 \\ \Delta_{21}\alpha_{12} & \alpha_{22} & 0 & 1 \\ -\alpha_{11} & -\alpha_{12} & 1 & 0 \\ -\alpha_{21} & -\alpha_{22} & 0 & 1 \end{bmatrix} \begin{bmatrix} p_1 \\ p_2 \\ q_1 \\ q_2 \end{bmatrix} - \begin{bmatrix} \alpha_{11}\gamma_1' & \Delta_{12}\alpha_{21}\gamma_2' & 0 & 0 \\ \Delta_{21}\alpha_{12}\gamma_1' & \alpha_{22}\gamma_2' & 0 & 0 \\ 0 & 0 & \beta_1' & 0 \\ 0 & 0 & 0 & \beta_2' \end{bmatrix} \begin{bmatrix} w_t^1 \\ w_t^2 \\ x_t^1 \\ x_t^2 \end{bmatrix} = \begin{bmatrix} v_{1t} \\ v_{2t} \\ v_{3t} \\ v_{4t} \end{bmatrix}$$

or, more compactly in matrix form,

$$Ay_t + Cx_t = v_t,$$

where the vector of error terms is in fact a combination of the cost and demand shocks of the different products,

$$\begin{bmatrix} v_{1t} \\ v_{2t} \\ v_{3t} \\ v_{4t} \end{bmatrix} = \begin{bmatrix} \alpha_{11} & \Delta_{12}\alpha_{21} & 0 & 0 \\ \Delta_{21}\alpha_{12} & \alpha_{22} & 0 & 0 \\ 0 & 0 & 1 & 0 \\ 0 & 0 & 0 & 1 \end{bmatrix} \begin{bmatrix} u_{1t} \\ u_{2t} \\ \varepsilon_{1t} \\ \varepsilon_{2t} \end{bmatrix}.$$

Following our usual approach, this structural model can also be written as a reduced-form model:

$$y_t = -A^{-1}Cx_t + v_t = \Pi x_t + v_t.$$

The normalization restrictions are reflected in the fact that every equation has a 1 for one of the endogenous variables. This sets the scale of the parameters in the reduced form so that the solution is unique. If we did not have any normalization restrictions, the parameter matrix Π could be equal to $-A^{-1}C$ or equivalently (in terms of observables) equal to $-(2A)^{-1}2C$.

In our structural system we have four equations and four endogenous variables. Our necessary condition for identification is therefore that we have at least three parameter restrictions per equation besides the normalization restriction. In general, in a system of demand and pricing equations with J products, we have $2J$ endogenous variables. This means that we will need least $2J-1$ restrictions in each equation besides the normalization restriction imposed by design.

There are exclusion restrictions that are imposed on the parameters that come from the specification of the model. First, we have exclusions in the matrix A which are derived from the first-order conditions. Any row of matrix A will have $2J$ elements, where J is the total number of goods. There will be an element for each price and one for each quantity of all goods. But each pricing equation will have at most one quantity variable in, so that for every equation we get $J-1$ exclusion restrictions immediately from setting the coefficients on other good's quantities to 0.

Second, the ownership structure will provide exclusion restrictions for many models. Specifically, in the pricing equations, there will only be J_i parameters in the row, where $J_i = \sum_{j=1}^{J} \Delta_{ij}$ is the total number of products owned by firm i (or, under the collusive model, the total number of products taken into account in firm i's profit-maximization decision). The implication is that we will have $J - J_i$ restrictions.

Third, in each of the demand equations in matrix A, we also have $J-1$ exclusion restrictions as only one quantity enters each demand equation (together with all J prices); the parameters for the other $J-1$ quantities can be set to 0.

Fourth, we have exclusion restrictions in matrix C which come from the existence of demand and cost shifters. Demand shifters only affect prices through a change in the quantities demanded and do not independently affect the pricing equation. Similarly, cost shifters play no direct role in determining a consumer's demand for a product; they would only affect quantity demanded through their effect on prices. Those cost and demand restrictions are represented by the zeros in the C matrix. Define k^{D} as the total number of demand shifters and k^{C} as the total number of cost shifters. For each of the pricing equations in C we have k^{D} exclusion restrictions because none of the demand shifters affect the pricing equation directly. Similarly, for each of the demand equations we have k^{C} exclusion restrictions since none of the cost shifters enter the demand equations.

Additionally, even though any row in matrix C will have as many elements as there are exogenous cost variables and demand shifters, there will only be as many new parameters in a pricing equation as there are cost shifters in that product's pricing equation. Similarly, there will only be as many new parameters in the demand equation as there are demand shifters in that product's demand equation.

In addition to the exclusion restrictions we have just described, there are also cross-equation restrictions that could be imposed on the model. Cross-equation restrictions arise, for example, when we have several products produced by a firm. In that case, since prices are set to maximize joint profits for the firm, their pricing equations will be interdependent for that reason. Theory predicts that the way the demand of product j affects product i's pricing equation is not independent of the way the demand of product i affects product j's pricing equation. This gives rise to potential cross-equation restrictions. For example, the matrix A we wrote down has a total of sixteen elements but in fact it has only four structural parameters. We could impose that the reduced-form parameters satisfy some of the underlying structural (theoretical) relations. For instance, the first elements of rows 1 and 3 are the same parameter with opposite signs. This could be imposed when determining whether the structural parameters are in fact identified from estimates of the reduced-form parameters. The more concentrated the ownership of the products in the market the more cross-equation restrictions we will have, but the fewer exclusion restrictions we will have since we will have fewer zero elements of Δ. In addition, we will need more exclusion restrictions in each pricing equation to identify all the demand parameters that will be included.

7
Damage Estimation

The estimation of damages has been one field within antitrust economics where quantitative analysis has been used profusely. Most of the work has been done in countries where courts set fines or award compensation payments that are based on the estimated damages caused by infringing firms. Effective deterrence using fines, as distinct from, say, criminal conviction of individuals, requires that imposed fines be at least as high as the expected additional profits of firms that would emanate from the behavior to be deterred. Expected profits can be difficult to measure and in cartel cases they are currently often approximated by the damages caused to affected customers. This chapter describes the issues investigators confront in estimating the damages caused by the exercise of market power by cartels. We also briefly discuss damage calculations from abuses by a single firm.

7.1 Quantifying Damages of a Cartel

A presumption of antitrust law is that cartels are bad for consumers. Both antitrust agencies and customers see that cartels increase prices and reduce the supply available on the market. For this reason, cartels are illegal in most jurisdictions. For example, the Sherman Act in the United States, Article 81 in the EU and Chapter 1 of the Competition Act (1998) in the United Kingdom each prohibit firms from coordinating in order to reduce competition. Nonetheless, because cartels that work can be very profitable there is a temptation to collude when the conditions in the market make it possible. Illegality per se is not enough of a deterrent when it is not accompanied by at least the potential for a punishment that will hopefully wipe out the expected benefits of participating in a cartel. Cartels are increasingly punished with substantial fines and in some jurisdictions including the United States and the United Kingdom some cartel behavior is a criminal offense.[1] For a fine to

[1] Section 188 of the U.K. Enterprise Act 2002 introduced a criminal offense for collusion in the United Kingdom. It says, for example, that an individual is guilty of an offense if he "dishonestly agrees with one or more other persons" to, in particular, directly or indirectly fix prices. Note that the word "dishonestly" qualifies the word "agrees" so that not all agreements to fix prices are immediately dishonest and hence not all cartel offenses are criminal offenses. The term dishonest is frequently used under other parts of criminal law and so has clear legal status relating both to whether a person's actions were honest

be an effective deterrent, its expected value should be linked to the expected gains extracted by the cartel. Private enforcement, which is common in the United States and which is developing in Europe, comes with compensation payments for the affected customers.[2] In the United States those payments are normally linked to the damages suffered by these customers. It becomes necessary in those cases to assess and quantify the impact of a cartel and to calculate the profit it generated for the firms and the harm it caused to customers downstream. The next section discusses the effect of a cartel and the following section proceeds to explain the different techniques used to quantify damages. The pass-on defense is discussed and finally the issue of determining the duration of the cartel is presented in more detail.[3]

7.1.1 Effect of Cartels

According to the economic theory traditionally relied upon as an underlying rationale to impose sanctions against cartel members, cartels have two effects on welfare: first they decrease the total welfare generated by the market and second they redistribute rent from consumers to the firms. The damages caused by a cartel are in principle the total welfare loss experienced by the customers due to the combination of those two factors. In fact, damages are in practice defined in a more restricted way and usually refer to the overcharge that the customers must pay for their purchases, which is only part of the loss suffered by consumers.

7.1.1.1 Welfare Effects of a Cartel

When firms form a cartel, they coordinate to increase, perhaps even maximize, joint profits. If firms successfully maximize joint profits, then a cartel price can be approximated by that of a monopolist setting total production at the level where aggregate marginal revenue equals cartel marginal cost. Compared with a competitive market where prices are set close to marginal costs, this reduces the quantity and raises the price. Because prices are higher in a cartel, firms are able to appropriate some of the consumer surplus that would go to consumers in competitive markets. In addition

---

according to the standards of most people but also whether the individuals believed such actions were honest. The latter might be informed, for example, by evidence of, say, secretly held meetings or seeking to hide collusive behavior so these may distinguish criminal from civil cartel behavior. In the United States there have been criminal sanctions for cartel behavior since 1890. The United Kingdom's first criminal sanctions were handed down in June 2008 in the "marine hose" cartel. Marine hoses are a type of flexible pipe used to transport oil from storage to tankers. Three individuals received between two and three years each out of a maximum sentence of five years' imprisonment. In jurisdictions with both criminal and civil penalties, enforcement will generally proceed in parallel as criminal and civil sanctions are not a substitute for each other.

[2] For example, the United Kingdom has some scope for limited private actions and the EU is currently consulting on the appropriate scale of private actions.

[3] A nontechnical discussion of issues relevant to the estimation of damages can be found in Ashurst (2004).

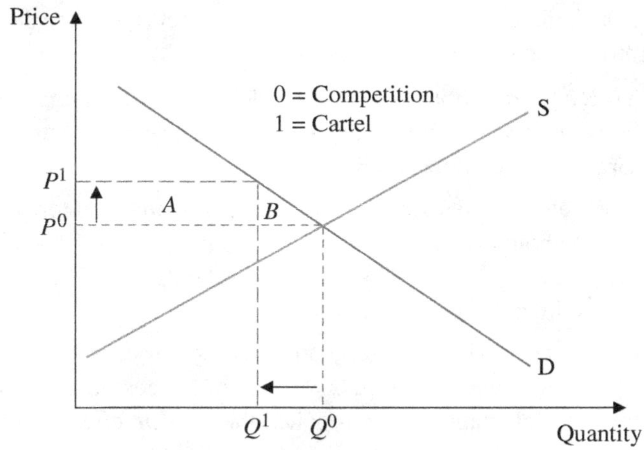

Figure 7.1. Welfare effect of a cartel.

the decrease in the aggregate quantity produced causes total welfare to decrease and generates deadweight loss. The consequences of a cartel on an otherwise competitive market are illustrated in figure 7.1. The area indicated by A represents the rent transfer from consumers to producers. Consumers pay P^1 instead of P^0 and they purchase only Q^1 compared with a higher Q^0 under competition. Area B represents the net welfare loss, known as deadweight loss. This is consumer welfare that is eliminated due to the restriction in output and not captured by the cartel.

The total welfare loss generated by the cartel is represented by area B. The total damage to the consumer is represented by areas $A + B$. The benefit of the cartel to the firm is represented by A. Although the total consumer loss is represented by $A + B$, the loss of area B is generally ignored when calculating damages to consumers. Although in principle we would like to estimate both, damages are generally defined as the illegal appropriation of profits by the firms represented by the area A. For practical purposes we assume that the firm's illicit profit and the damages to consumers are equivalent and this amount is commonly called the overcharge. The overcharge on a given unit is the difference between P_1 and P_0. The total overcharge is $Q^1(P^1 - P^0)$. Such an approximation will often not be too bad if the deadweight loss effects associated with area B are small relative to the size of the transfer from consumers to firms associated with area A. (But see the discussion of Harberger triangles in chapter 1.)

7.1.1.2 Direct and Indirect Damages

Many cartels are among firms that provide inputs to firms downstream, which then sell on to final customers. To understand the consequences of such a situation, consider the case of a downstream firm being the customer of the cartelized industry, so that the cartel's price is (or affects) the marginal cost of the downstream firms.

Following Van Dijk and Verboven (2007), we show below that the damage for the downstream firm can be decomposed into three terms:[4]

- The first element describes the decline in downstream profits due to the higher costs associated with buying the input from the cartel. This is the direct overcharge on the cartelized input.
- The second element describes the lost margin on units no longer sold under the cartel. Without the cartel we would have sold an extra $(q^0 - q^1)$ units and earned a margin $(p^0 - c^{\text{Comp}})$ on them. This "output" effect is seldom taken into account in damages calculations.
- The third element is the increase in profits earned by charging a higher downstream price and captures the pass-through of the cost increase by the cartel to downstream customers. This is called the *pass-on* effect and it attenuates the damage suffered by the downstream firm. It is also called the indirect effect on the final consumers because it measures the overcharge or damages suffered by those final consumers rather than the actual customer of the cartel, which is the downstream firm. The treatment of the indirect effect both in the calculation of damages to the intermediate firms or in calculation of potential damages to the final consumer is determined by the legal framework.

Formally, this downstream firm's profits under the cartel can be expressed as follows:

$$\pi^1 = (p^1 - c^{\text{Cartel}})q^1,$$

where the superscript "1" indicates prices, quantities, and profits of the downstream firm under a cartel regime. Under competition in the upstream market, the downstream firm's profits will be

$$\pi^0 = (p^0 - c^{\text{Comp}})q^0,$$

where the superscript "0" indicates prices, quantities, and profits of the intermediate firm under competition. The difference between the two downstream profits is

$$\pi^0 - \pi^1 = (p^0 - c^{\text{Comp}})q^0 - (p^1 - c^{\text{Cartel}})q^1.$$

With some algebra manipulation we get an expression for the difference in profits involving three terms corresponding to the bullet points above:

$$\begin{aligned}\Delta\pi &\equiv \pi^0 - \pi^1 \\ &= (p^0 - c^{\text{Comp}})q^0 - (p^1 - c^{\text{Cartel}})q^1 + (q^1(c^{\text{Comp}} - c^{\text{Comp}}) + q^1(p^0 - p^0)) \\ &= -q^1(c^{\text{Comp}} - c^{\text{Cartel}}) + (q^0 - q^1)p^0 - (q^0 - q^1)c^{\text{Comp}} + q^1(p^0 - p^1) \\ &= -q^1\Delta c + (\Delta q)(p^0 - c^{\text{Comp}}) + q^1(\Delta p).\end{aligned}$$

[4] Van Dijk and Verboven's paper also provides a very helpful discussion on the legal framework applying in Europe and the United States regarding the legal standings of individual and firms directly or indirectly affected by price fixing.

7.1.1.3 Empirical Issues

Calculating the damages of a cartel could be important to establish the appropriate level of compensation to give to the victims of the cartel or to estimate the illegal profits of the cartelized industry, the gains from colluding, for the purpose of imposing an appropriate fine. In either case, quantifying damages presents some important conceptual and empirical challenges.

To start with, one must define the concept being quantified. In many cases, damages are defined to be the overcharge to the direct customer of the cartelized firms. That damage will be a lower bound to the true damage of the cartel at any point in time since the reduction in quantities and consequent deadweight loss is ignored.

Second, damage calculations can become subject to some very complex issues if we take into account the potential dynamic effects. Dynamic effects might increase damages if competition would have had positive consequences for quality or innovation. On the other hand, if high profits would have involved increased spending on product quality or R&D, then, at least in principle, damages might be reduced although one may find it appropriate to consider the incentives to innovate in a cartelized environment. Due to the complexity of incorporating dynamic effects and their usually speculative nature, such effects are generally ignored in damage calculations although one obviously can debate the merits and disadvantages of doing so. Generally, the policy stance in most jurisdictions reflects an expectation that cartels will harm consumers in the longer term. One should keep in mind that such dynamic negative effects can occur and in those industries where they are likely to be very important they should serve to aggravate the harm estimated to be caused by the cartel.

The treatment of the pass-on effect on the quantification of total damages or of the potential damage to claimants is generally defined by the legal framework. Is the pass-on effect allowed to attenuate the potential damage claims of the intermediate firm? Can final consumers claim damages? The answers to these questions help define the appropriate theoretical framework in which the damage calculation takes place and clearly these answers need to be understood by the economic analyst before a quantification exercise is undertaken.

The most important and difficult part of damage estimation is the actual quantification of the overcharge. Calculating the amount of the price increase due to the cartel requires the analyst to estimate what the price would have been in the event of a competitive market upstream. Several techniques are available to construct what is referred to as the "but for" prices—the prices that would have prevailed had the cartel had not existed. Unfortunately, the "but for" prices posit a counterfactual world since the world without the cartel simply did not happen. Such a situation is not unfamiliar in the competition policy world—mergers must similarly be evaluated before they have happened—but counterfactual situations always involve both estimation and also forecasting either statistically or using a model. Each of these steps must be undertaken carefully and must rest on reasonable assumptions.

Finally, in order to define the illegal profits and the damages of the cartel, one must define the duration of the cartel. Cartel damages should be calculated for the entire duration of a cartel since customers will be harmed and colluding firms will profit as soon as the prices rise and for as long as the prices stay artificially high. Timing the cartel precisely may be a very difficult task. Often, one will see sharp unexplained increases in prices at the beginning of a cartel and a gradual collapse of those prices at the end of it, sometimes a sudden collapse. However, sometimes the price pattern is not so conveniently obvious. Cartels may take time to form, there may be episodes of cheating and temporary reversion to competition, and the cartel may take time to unwind because firms take time to realize the cartel cannot be sustained any longer. Also, structural shifts of supply and demand conditions may interfere with the effect of the cartel generating a price pattern that is not easily interpreted without careful analysis.

Because damages may occur over an extended period of time, the calculation will have to be translated into real terms so that the penalty is equivalent in value to the damage inflicted. Whether claimants are allowed to recover interest in the event of a private claim is also a legal issue that needs to be clarified by the analyst.

Each of the issues mentioned above will typically need to be addressed by the economist in a damage estimation exercise. In the next section we discuss the quantification of the direct damage.

7.1.2 Quantifying Direct Damages

Quantifying damages involves estimating the price that would have occurred absent the cartel during the period of the cartel. Clearly, the price we need is not and never will be observable so that the exercise will always rely on assumptions and a certain degree of speculation. Such is the nature of forecasting. Different methods will rely on different assumptions and it is important that the investigator is not only aware of the assumptions but also explicitly states what they are. The reasonableness of particular assumptions, and hence the best method, may well depend on the particular circumstances of the case. However, when a cartel clearly succeeded in raising prices, the effect of the cartel should be apparent using more than just one method as long as those methods are correctly applied. In practice, conscientious economic experts will sometimes need to build an estimation framework that combines elements of the different methodologies. Doing so will sometimes help to ensure that all the available data that are informative for the estimation of the "but for" prices are used. As with any econometric exercise, it will be important to test the robustness of the result to small changes in specification and, as with any other kind of evidence, no econometric exercise will be completely robust.

The exercise of quantifying damages must be supported by an in-depth qualitative analysis of the industry, which should help provide the justification for the methodology and specification chosen. To carry weight, any econometric results will need to be plausible given the known facts about the industry.

7.1.2.1 Using a Model of Competition

Given an economic model relating pricing to industry structure, it will be possible to analytically derive the effect of moving from competition to a cartel on prices. For example, under perfect competition with no fixed costs the price will be equal or close to marginal cost. The overcharge of a cartel forming in that market would then be the difference between the price observed during the cartel and the marginal cost of the industry. The cartel price is observed and the competitive price can theoretically be calculated if we have information on costs. Note that if costs change during the cartel period, the prices that would have prevailed under competition during the time of the cartel also change.

To make these observations concrete, let us review our simplest pricing equations under conditions of competition and also under a cartel. If we assume marginal costs are c_t and the following linear inverse demand equation, $p_t = a_t - bQ_t$, then profit maximization by a cartel will involve setting marginal revenue equal to marginal cost:

$$\mathrm{MR}_t(Q) = c_t \iff a_t - 2bQ_t = c_t \iff Q_t = \frac{a_t - c_t}{2b}.$$

Substituting this cartel output choice into the demand function, we obtain the prices under a cartel:

$$p_t = a_t - bQ_t = a_t - b\left(\frac{a_t - c_t}{2b}\right) = \tfrac{1}{2}a_t + \tfrac{1}{2}c_t.$$

Under perfect competition the price will be $p_t = c_t$ and the equilibrium quantity will be such that $p_t = a_t - bQ_t$. The overcharge per unit in this case will be the difference between the prices and the marginal cost:

$$\begin{aligned}\text{Overcharge per unit} &= p^{\text{Cartel}} - p^{\text{Comp}}\\ &= \tfrac{1}{2}a_t + \tfrac{1}{2}c_t - c_t.\end{aligned}$$

In many cases, oligopolistic competition such as Cournot may provide a more realistic "but for" scenario instead of perfect competition. Obviously, the "but for" prices for Cournot or for other oligopolistic models can each be analytically derived and doing so provides the specification of the pricing equation. However, the model is further complicated by the fact that the quantity produced by both the colluding firms and also the equilibrium price that would prevail absent the cartel will each be sensitive to changes in demand since firms explicitly take into account demand conditions when setting their prices or quantities both under Cournot and under the cartel. Prices in competitive oligopolistic markets may be less stable than under perfect competition, all else equal.

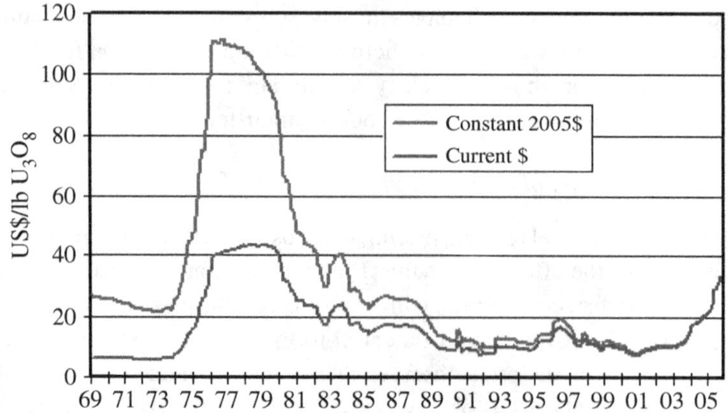

Figure 7.2. Price time series in suspected cartel. *Source*: uxc.com. The price of uranium 308. The reader may wish to speculate when the period of the cartel was.

7.1.2.2 *Before and After*

The "before-and-after" methodology uses the historical time series of the prices of the cartelized goods as the main source of information. It looks at the prices before and after the cartel and compares them with the prices that prevailed during the cartel. The damages are then calculated as the difference between the cartel prices and the prices under competition multiplied by the amount of sales during the cartel:

$$\text{Damages}_t = (P_t^{\text{Cartel}} - P_t^{\text{Comp}})Q_t^{\text{Cartel}}.$$

This is an extremely simple method, perhaps even simplistic, but may provide a sufficiently good approximation in cases in which the cartel is stable and the basic conditions of demand and supply do not change too much. In such cases, a time series of the prices may look as shown in figure 7.2.

The before-and-after method just links with a straight line the price levels occurring before and after the cartel. In cases where there is an underlying trend in the data one can take into account the trend to determine the hypothetical prices under perfect competition. In the example of the uranium cartel presented, there seems to be a declining trend in the price of uranium 308 right before the cartel (measured in constant 2005 dollars). When competition is re-established, prices settle at a level slightly lower in real terms than that which predates the cartel. In this case, a simple before-and-after calculation of the damages in real terms could resemble the area above a line drawn between a competitive price of say $21 per pound in 1974 and a competitive price of say $18 in 1989. It is important to note, however, that there is a very important caveat to this calculation: namely that the cartel is alleged to have lasted between 1972 and 1975 although the high prices clearly lasted for far longer. Thus an important question is whether those higher prices persisted because coordination arrangements had been settled during a period of explicit collusion and

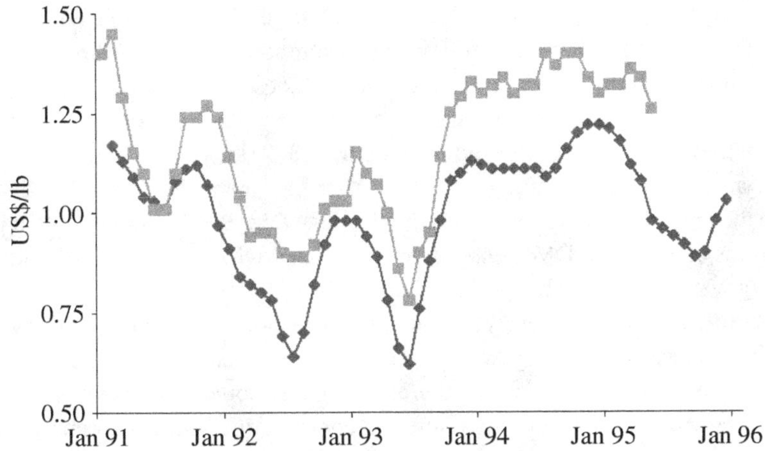

Figure 7.3. Lysine transaction prices in the U.S. and EU markets 1991–95. *Source*: Connor (2008).

so could be followed by tacit arrangements or, perhaps more innocently, competitive costs went up considerably during those years for other reasons. One thing is clear, depending on the court's view of the end date for collusive prices, the damages calculation clearly looks materially different. (For a detailed description of the case, see Taylor and Yokell (1979).)

Some price series will be even less obvious to interpret.[5] Figure 7.3, for example, shows the transaction prices of lysine, a farm feed additive, in the United States and European Union markets between 1991 and 1996. The figure shows successive periods of sharp price drops followed by sharp price increases. In itself the time series of prices does not present an obvious picture of what the "but for" prices should be or even of the exact period of the cartel. One must know some of the facts of the case to start making sense of the picture.

In 1991, ADM entered the lysine market by building a very large new plant for lysine production that doubled the world's production capacity.[6] After starting sales at very low prices, ADM started communicating that it was willing to coordinate its entry to the market with competitors. ADM used the threat of its large capacity to convince competitors that they would be better off in a coordinated agreement than in a world of competition. ADM even offered its competitors tours of their large new plant to emphasize the point. The cartel worked quite well but eventually attracted the attention of authorities. The spectacular investigation in the United States, which involved the FBI's undercover agents, moles, and secret recordings, was made public in 1995.

[5] This discussion draws on Connor (2008).

[6] European Commission Decision 2001/418/EC, 7/6/2000, L 152/24.

Knowing these facts perhaps makes figure 7.3 more understandable. There is a first attempt at raising prices in 1992 followed by a temporary collapse of the conspiracy and resumption in mid 1993. The cartel happily goes on until early 1995 when the investigation is made public. Of course, even if we can establish a clear understanding of the patterns in the price data shown in figure 7.3, it does not immediately provide a clear answer to the question of what the "but for" price should be. For example, before the first known attempt at coordination by ADM, there is a sharp fall in prices, which was caused by ADM's entry. However, was ADM entering at artificially low prices or was the massive but perhaps ultimately temporary excess capacity keeping prices artificially low post entry? In the other direction, one might wonder whether the 1991 prices before entry were competitive or whether price fixing activities were already taking place. In fact, there is allegedly some evidence to suggest that the main suppliers of lysine were already coordinating and had orchestrated the sharp increase in prices in 1991. It is not clear that there is a particular moment when the market would have been clearly in competitive equilibrium in these data and, as a result, the before-and-after method should probably only be used after an appropriately careful and rigorous analysis. At trial, the plaintiffs used the periods May–June 1992 and April–July 1993 as the "but for" price, claiming that there has been a reversion to competition during these periods. The defendants, on the other hand, claimed that aggressive competition was not the most likely equilibrium "but for" scenario in this concentrated oligopolistic industry.[7]

There is relatively little economic theory in the "before-and-after" methodology although in some special cases the results are very intuitive and may even be fairly accurate. In other contexts, there are cases where a purely statistical approach to forecasting can sometimes perform better than building an economic model and basing the forecast on that. Either approach requires assumptions. For example, the raw form of the before-and-after methodology implicitly assumes that market conditions are unchanged since if demand and supply conditions vary during the cartel period or between the competition and cartel periods, the methodology is bound to be incorrect to at least some extent. Naturally, if the cartel has a long duration, then it is more likely that conditions in the market changed materially during the period. If a cartel has been around for a long time, the level of prices outside of the period of the illegal conduct will be probably less indicative of what would have happened during the cartel period if competition had prevailed.

7.1.2.3 *Multivariate Approach*

One can attempt to overcome the criticisms of the simplest version of the "before-and-after" method by taking into account changes in demand and supply conditions. By running a reduced-form regression of the price level on demand and cost factors

[7] For a good discussion of the overcharge estimation in lysine cartel case, see Connor (2004).

that affect the price but are not controlled by the cartel and then also including a dummy variable for the time of the cartel. The dummy variable will, we hope, then capture the magnitude the unexplained increase in prices that occurs during the cartel. The regression run is as follows:

$$p_t = \alpha + \gamma D_t + x_t \beta + \varepsilon_t,$$

where D_t is a dummy variable taking on the value 1 if the cartel is active in period t and 0 otherwise and x_t is a vector of demand and cost factors that affect the price but are not controlled by the cartel. The coefficient γ will give the amount of the overcharge per period.

Economic experts working for the defendant will typically want to include a lot of variables in x in an attempt to reduce the size and significance of the coefficient γ and thereby show no or few damages are due. It is important that no irrelevant variables are included in the regression, particularly those which might be spuriously correlated with the cartel dummy D_t. Also results from a reduced-form regression should be robust to small changes in the specification of the regression. We discussed regression analysis in more detail in chapter 2.

Such an approach, of course, raises the question of whether the impact of the cartel can be well captured by a discrete upward shift of the price during the cartel. The coefficient γ on the dummy variable will measure the average price increase during the entire selected duration of the cartel, independently of movements in market conditions that may have occurred during that time. But it is likely that changes in demand and supply will affect the impact of the cartel on the prices and that a richer specification would capture a more complex effect. Also, cartels may unwind slowly so that in the last months or even years of a cartel the overcharge is gradually decreasing. A dummy specification assigns the same magnitude of the cartel effect to all years and will return only an average for the entire period. Although it is still relatively uncommon to perform more elaborate regressions, it is important that the results of the reduced form be at least compared with alternative specifications to check for robustness.

A second multivariate approach is to forecast the "but for" price that would have prevailed during the cartel period absent the conspiracy. Using pre-cartel and post-cartel data the effect of the determinants of demand and cost shifters on price can be estimated. Those values of the parameters can be used to predict the "but for" price during the cartel. The difference between the actual price and the predicted price provides a prediction of the overcharge. As opposed to the simple before-and-after method, forecasting the price by running multivariate regression can allow for changes in the demand and supply conditions. However, it assumes that the structural relation between the variables remains unchanged. In particular, it supposes that the conduct of the firms and that the way demand and costs affect prices would each have remained stable. Such an assumption would clearly be violated if there was a big technological change or a substantial shift in the tastes of consumers.

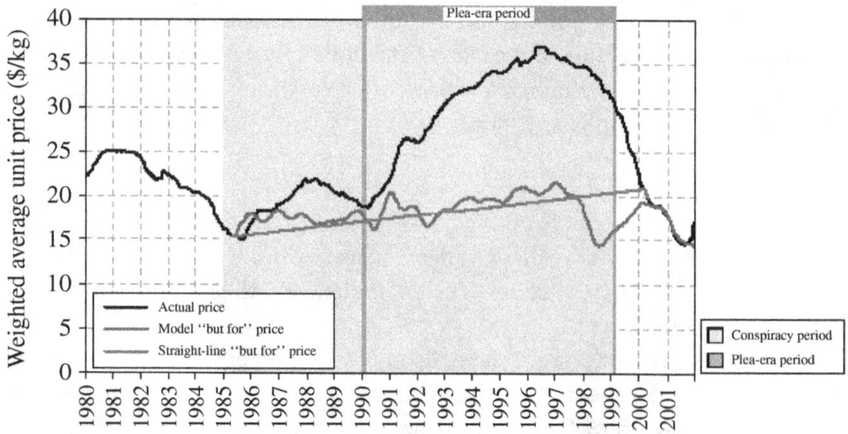

Figure 7.4. Vitamin E acetate oil USP price and "but for" price. *Source*: Figure 14.2 of Bernheim (2002), also cited in Connor (2008).

A "but for" estimation was performed in the context of the vitamin cartel in the 1990s. In his expert report for the Vitamin Antitrust Litigation, Professor Bernheim (2002) estimated the prices that would have prevailed absent the conspiracy using reduced-form regressions. The price regression was specified as follows:

$$P_t = \alpha P_{t-1} + \beta x_{t-1} + \varepsilon_t,$$

where P_t is the price of the vitamin product in month t and x_t are exogenous supply and demand variables. Exogenous determinants of supply are the price of traded raw materials needed to manufacture the vitamins, the wage index for the industry, the interest rate, and exchange rates with currencies where manufacturers are located. Many potential determinants of demand are also considered: population size, income per capita, pounds of different slaughtered animals that feed on those vitamins, quantity produced of pharmaceuticals, and quantity produced of products that use vitamins as an input such as toiletries, cheese, and milk. The price of substitute products are also included such as wheat, corn, soybean, a series of vegetables and fruit, as well as other food products.

A new element of this specification compared with our earlier specifications is the lagged price variable. Introducing a lagged endogenous variable introduces some dynamics into the model and means, for example, that shocks to prices will persist. In fact, the lagged price term not only included the lagged price of the product in question but also the lagged prices of all the vitamin products within the same family of vitamins. To estimate the model Bernheim used the data from before the cartel and also the data available twelve months after the end of the cartel for those products where there are more than two manufacturers and post-cartel tacit coordination is assumed to have been ineffective. The predicted prices for a type of vitamin E during the cartel period using the Bernheim model are shown in figure 7.4.

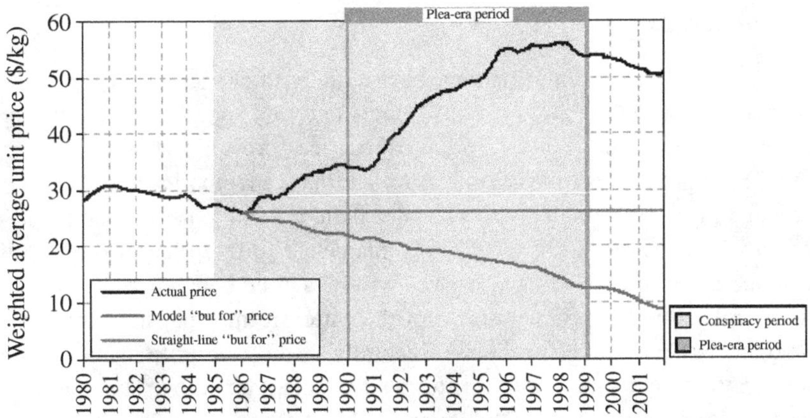

Figure 7.5. Vitamin A acetate 500 USP price and "but for" price. *Source*: Figure 14.6 of Bernheim (2002), also cited in Connor (2008).

The specification in the Bernheim report includes quite a number of explanatory variables, although the actual results of the regression are not reported in the publicly available testimony. The sharp upward shift of the "but for" price before the actual price is actually raised, for example, must be due to one or more variables in the model. In any exercise like this, it would be very interesting to see how well the model can predict actual prices in the period prior to the cartel. The methodology appears on the face of it to produce reasonable results, though as observers not steeped in the detail we probably conclude the results are reasonable at least partly because the resulting "but for" world is in fact not so different from the one estimated through a simple "before-and-after" analysis using a straight-line "but for" price.

The same cannot be said immediately of the "but for" prices predicted for the vitamin A acetate 500 USP, which is presented in figure 7.5. The predicted prices appear to extrapolate the trend in pre-cartel prices throughout the period of the cartel. In this case, post-cartel prices were not used to estimate the model since only two manufacturers produced it and therefore there was no presumption of reversion to a competitive scenario at the end of the cartel. Of course, in order to believe the results emerging from this model we really need to believe that whichever variable is driving the predicted "but for" prices to trend down captures a real driving force for competitive prices.

These examples help illustrate that the estimation of a "but for" price using multivariate regression leaves plenty of room for reasonable people to hold a debate about the right measure of damage. That said, it can be a very effective tool when applied correctly. As with any powerful tool, it needs to be used with a great deal of care and in particular a very good understanding of the data, institutions, and facts of the case.

7.1.2.4 Yardsticks

When the cartel does not appear to have been equally stable during all years or when the demand and supply conditions have fluctuated in a significant way during the cartel, extrapolating the "but for" price from prices prevailing before or after the cartel will not produce the right answer. An alternative method is to choose a price of a related product, a product that was not included in the cartel, and use it as a benchmark to construct what would have happened to the price of the cartelized good in the event of competition. A price will be a good benchmark if the product is closely related to the product object of the cartel. It must be similar in terms of demand, costs, and market structure. Generally, it must be in the same region or country so that main shocks and institutional factors are similar. The market must be expected to have behaved in a manner similar to the cartelized market had it not been cartelized.

Let us consider an example based on the steel cartel.[8] There was allegedly a series of meetings in the steel industry in the 1990s during which sensitive information was exchanged between competitors. Volume information and price targets of some steel products in the European Union were discussed. The economic experts ran a linear regression as follows:

$$\begin{aligned}\text{Price}_{ijklt} = {} & \alpha + \beta\,\text{Costs}_{ijklt} + \gamma\,\text{Demand}_{ijklt} + \delta\,\text{Bargaining power}_{ijklt} \\ & + \lambda\,\text{Discussions}_{ijklt} + \theta_k \text{Trend}_t + \rho_i + \eta_j + \mu_k + \tau_t + \varepsilon_{ijklt},\end{aligned}$$

where i indicates the product, j the subsidiary, k the country, l the client, and t is the time period. The data vary both across time and across products so the regression can use a combination of the data variation used for both the "before-and-after" method and also the benchmark approach. In addition, the data vary across subsidiaries, countries, and clients (customers). The coefficient λ captures the effect of a meeting on the price level of the good. In this specification, the effect is taken to be contemporaneous so that discussions during time period t are assumed to affect prices during time period t. The direct effect of the cartel will be given by the magnitude of the coefficient λ, which one would hope would be statistically significant if there are enough data to pick up the effects. Such a specification is certainly open for debate and indeed econometric specification testing. For example, the analyst may wish to explore whether the effect of the cartel on prices captured in this specification as an indicator variable which takes the value 1 when cartel members held discussions or whether the effects of discussions are likely to be something closer to an investment which accumulates over time, but perhaps also depreciates at some rate. Such questions regarding the appropriate "modeling" of the effects of cartel discussions on cartel outcomes is difficult to evaluate in the abstract but must be considered during a case, upon whose facts the correct answer

[8] This example is based on LECG's presentation by David Sevy at the Association of Competition Economists Conference in Copenhagen in 2005.

will depend. We put "modeling" deliberately in quotes because we always have to bear in mind that this is a reduced-form regression equation, not a structural price equation. In principle a structural model of prices could also be built and that provides another route to damage calculation which we study below (see section 7.1.2.6).

Note that the regression has separate fixed effects for products, subsidiaries, clients, and country as opposed to fixed effects for a given product in a given subsidiary delivered for a given customer, which would involve an awful lot more fixed effects. This specification puts more structure on the nature of data variation and allows different sources of data variation to identify the coefficient λ. It would probably be helpful to try specifications with various types of fixed effects in order to isolate the source of the data variation that is helping to identify λ. Doing so helps us, for example, understand whether we are using primarily time-series variation as in the "before-and-after" method or else cross-sectional variation, which is more akin to the yardstick approach. A good way to understand what drives the results we find is to run the regression without any dummies and add the dummies sequentially taking the data variation one dimension at a time. First, we can control for products, then for countries, then for subsidiary, and finally for customer. Naturally, the less sensitive the estimate of λ is to changes in the specifications, the more the data variation in all directions agrees and hence we can be confident that we have identified the correct effect. However, if the estimate of λ does change according to the types of fixed effects included, as it will on many occasions, it helps us understand where the data variation suggesting "bad" effects of the cartel is coming from and this may in turn help us evaluate whether we believe the results are truly capturing the effect of the cartelists' discussions on the price.

To calculate damages, we need to estimate the price for each product, subsidiary, country, and customer using the estimated coefficients but setting the coefficient λ to 0. In this example, the predicted "but for" price was calculated using the formula:

$$\begin{aligned}\text{Price}^{\text{Comp}}_{ijklt} &= \hat{\alpha} + \hat{\beta}\,\text{Costs}_{ijklt} + \hat{\gamma}\,\text{Demand}_{ijklt} + \hat{\delta}\,\text{Bargaining power}_{ijklt} \\ &\quad + 0\,\text{Discussions}_{ijklt} + \hat{\theta}_k \text{Trend}_t + \hat{\rho}_i + \hat{\eta}_j + \hat{\mu}_k + \hat{\tau}_t.\end{aligned}$$

And so the damages for each particular product and customer at a specific time will be calculated as

$$\text{Damages}_{ijklt} = (\text{Price}^{\text{Cartel}}_{ijklt} - \text{Price}^{\text{Comp}}_{ijklt})Q^{\text{Cartel}}_{ijklt}.$$

Equivalently, of course, since with our definitions, $\lambda = (\text{Price}^{\text{Cartel}}_{ijklt} - \text{Price}^{\text{Comp}}_{ijklt})$, one can just multiply λ by the quantity sold during the cartel period to get an aggregate damage figure for the cartel.

7.1.2.5 Cost Plus Method

Another method for constructing a "but for" price adds an estimated margin to the costs of the firm. This method presupposes that the expert can (1) estimate costs of the firm and (2) estimate the profitability of the firm absent the conspiracy since the method usually involves using cost data and then adding to it a "reasonable" rate of return. In general, neither costs nor an appropriate margin are by any means easy to measure.

Margins are not only dependent on the market structure but given a particular form of oligopolistic competition they also vary with supply and demand conditions. Periods of high demand may tend to increase margins.[9] Fixed costs arising from lumpy investments will typically also be relevant and difficult to take into account because they transcend a nice clean time period for analysis. For example, the economics are pretty clear in ensuring that industries such as pharmaceuticals will tend to have high margins but also incur a great deal of expenditure undertaking often highly speculative research and development for which a "reasonable" rate of return will need to be allowed (see, for example, Ashurst 2004). Of course, a cartel in one submarket might argue that the returns are needed to finance research across their product line. Portfolio effects of this form and lumpy investment expenditure make damage estimation in such contexts extremely difficult, although some companies' internal systems may help address these kinds of issues. For example, some companies use activity-based costing (ABC) methods in accounting to systematically allocate costs, including fixed costs, to each of their activities. Other contexts may introduce other difficulties. For example, the rate of return that companies would obtain in a world without a cartel will depend on the type of competition the firms would face. If the alternative to cartel is perfect competition, "reasonable" returns should be lower than if the firms had found themselves playing a Cournot game or some other form of oligopolistic competition. The economic expert will need to clearly justify any choice of "reasonable rate of return" but such judgments may be difficult even if the aim is realistically to determine an order of magnitude.

While "reasonable" rates of return may be difficult in practice, even conceptually the right choice of the cost measure may be difficult. One could, on the basis of economic theory, argue that the right costs for damage calculations are marginal costs or perhaps long-run incremental costs. Alternatively, one might reasonably decide that the average cost is the best measure since firms that will survive in the market cannot make losses for a long time.[10] As a general rule, one should not include costs that are irrecoverable given movements in, say, technology, i.e., those costs which are sunk and would not be recovered under competition should be excluded from the cost calculation since well-functioning markets are forward

[9] In fact, the observation that margins tend to vary with the business cycle has also motivated some of the literature on collusion (see, for example, Rotemberg and Saloner 1986).

[10] The usual prediction that competitive firms price at marginal cost ignores the requirement that profits be positive. For example, if marginal costs are constant and a firm sets prices by maximizing profit subject to profits being at least zero, then with fixed costs the familiar prediction that $p = c$ will never cover fixed costs and so will not be optimal. Deciding when to take into account the "profits must be nonnegative" constraint is important since it fundamentally changes the theory's prediction for pricing whenever there are fixed costs of production.

looking and unlikely to reimburse these types of sunk costs. Some sunk costs are, however, legitimately recoverable. To see why, consider, for example, a two-stage game where firms decide whether to sink an entry cost at the first stage and then compete on prices. The second stage prices will, for a given number of active players, not depend on the level of sunk costs. However, firms would not sink the investment without an expectation of an appropriate return including a risk premium. Thus, it is reasonable to expect that an industry with large sunk costs will be associated with a certain degree of market power so as to allow firms to recover the value of their initial investments.

The bottom line is that if excessive profits overall are competed away during the entry stage, then firms may simply be making an overall fair return on their investments, including their sunk investments. On the other hand, if on a forward-looking basis the sunk costs of entry have reduced, perhaps because technological progress has reduced the cost of building a new plant, then a competitive market would, in fact, not reward the full extent of the sunk costs. For these reasons, it is probably fair to say that most competition and regulatory agencies do consider that it can be appropriate to allow recovery of some sunk costs, but it is probably not appropriate to allow recovery of all sunk costs. How much a firm should be allowed to recover will depend on the facts of the case.

Conceptual difficulties aside, finding cost data and cost measures that are economically meaningful is by no means an easy exercise. Cost information will often be obtained from accounting documents and accounting costs can dramatically diverge from economic costs. Chapter 1 discusses some of the discrepancies between economic and accounting costs and at least some of the adjustments that may need to be made to retrieve economically meaningful cost figures.

Even with all of those difficulties overcome we may face additional conceptual and practical hurdles. For example, except in the rare case of perfect competition with homogeneous firms, where the price is equal to the marginal cost of all active firms and the margin is zero, the relation of prices to costs in competitive models is not straightforward. For instance, more efficient firms will have higher margins and earn higher returns, indeed efficient firms earn supranormal profits even under perfect competition. The reason—that prices will tend to be "set" by the marginal costs of the least efficient active firm in the industry—can be simply illustrated by considering a Bertrand game with two firms each with different marginal costs. In that case, in equilibrium, the efficient firm will price at or just below the marginal cost of their less efficient rival. Thus reasonable margins could only be determined by considering both own costs and those of rivals.

One could argue that when the "cost plus" method is applied one should use the costs of the most efficient firm in order to prevent overestimating the competitive prices. However, given our previous observation that prices, even in very competitive settings, will tend to be determined by rival's costs, such a recommendation is not obviously right. For example, if we used the most efficient firms' costs to measure the

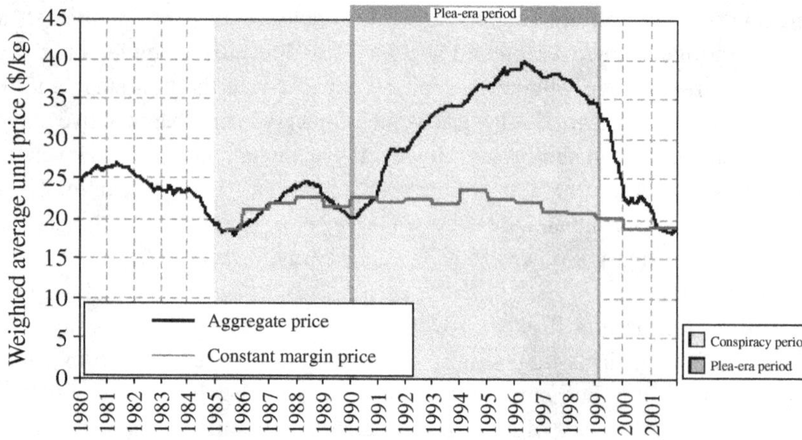

Figure 7.6. Vitamin E aggregate 100% basis price with constant margin price. *Source*: Figure 14.4 of Bernheim (2002), also cited in Connor (2008).

costs of production and then added a "reasonable" margin, we may generate a price below the actual competitive price which would be determined by less efficient firms costs. Similarly, if we overestimate the margin or add a reasonable rate of return to an inefficient firm, we will overestimate the competitive price and hence underestimate the damage caused by the cartel. No general rule will escape all such difficulties but it will be true that the recommendation of using the most efficient firms may indeed prevent overestimating (but not underestimating) the competitive price. The same logic could presumably be used to argue that using data from the least efficient firm in the industry could help in avoiding underestimating the competitive price.

Returning to the vitamin industry cartel as an example, the plaintiff's expert assumed a constant percentage difference between the price of the product and the variable cost. The predicted competitive price using a constant margin method for a vitamin E product is shown in figure 7.6.

7.1.2.6 Simulations

The most sophisticated way of calculating damages is to build a structural model and simulate the difference between competitive and collusive prices. A simulation model will require us to fully specify a model of the industry and so this method relies on structural assumptions about the nature of competition which are explicitly stated and imposed on the data. As a part of this approach the investigator will also need to specify, perhaps after estimation, a demand function and a cost function. The nature of competition is described by a behavioral rule such as a static Nash game where the strategic variable is either price or quantity. Once the model is laid out, the equilibrium prices can be calculated in the case of competition and compared with the equilibrium price obtained with a coordinating behavior. Such an exercise sounds complex but with a little practice is relatively straightforward to apply for a professional economist with appropriate training in such methods—at least provided the economist is willing to go with a commonly applied class of models rather than build one from scratch.

For example, simulating the effect of a cartel in an industry that normally competes like a typical Cournot game is in principle fairly simple. Let us assume a homogeneous good in an industry where firms choose the quantity they will produce taking into account the production of rivals. Calculating the equilibrium prices only requires that we have information on market shares, the market demand elasticity and marginal cost. Alternatively, we may observe the demand elasticity and the HHI and industry marginal costs (defined as the weighted average of the marginal costs of the different firms with weights given by their market shares). To see why, recall that in chapter 1 we saw that equilibrium in a Cournot game implied that:

$$\text{Firm's markup equation:} \quad \frac{P - \text{MC}_i}{P} = \frac{s_i}{\eta},$$

$$\text{Share-weighted industry markup equation:} \quad \frac{P - \text{MC}}{P} = \frac{\text{HHI}}{\eta},$$

where η is the market demand elasticity, s_i is the market share of sales from firm i, and in the latter equation we have defined $\text{MC} \equiv \sum_{i=1}^{N} s_i \text{MC}_i$. With sufficient information on demand and market shares, the "but for" margin can be easily constructed using either equation while with an estimate of marginal cost so can the firm's "but for" price. This can be done at the firm level, in which case all differences in margins will directly result from differences in observed market shares, which may or may not be reasonable. Or it can be done at the industry level but then we will need an appropriate approximation for the weighted average marginal cost in the industry in order to calculate "but for" prices.

When applying this method an important feature of the world to be acutely aware of is the fact that cartels may allocate production and therefore the market share of firms may be determined by the cartel. If so, then for such a simulation to be correct, one should either therefore use pre- or post-cartel market shares or argue why the cartel market shares are a good approximation of the relative sizes of the firms that would be observed in a competitive environment.

Information on costs and demand parameters allow us to undertake simulations under other simple competitive frameworks. Consider, for example, an industry with two differentiated products produced by firms competing in prices and facing linear differentiated product demands and constant (in quantity) marginal costs of production. The structural form of the "supply" (i.e., pricing) and demand equations can be expressed in the following matrix form (see chapter 6 for a derivation of the structural form matrices):

$$\begin{bmatrix} \alpha_{11} & \Delta_{12}\alpha_{21} & 1 & 0 \\ \Delta_{21}\alpha_{12} & \alpha_{22} & 0 & 1 \\ -\alpha_{11} & -\alpha_{12} & 1 & 0 \\ -\alpha_{21} & -\alpha_{22} & 0 & 1 \end{bmatrix} \begin{bmatrix} p_1 \\ p_2 \\ q_1 \\ q_2 \end{bmatrix} - \begin{bmatrix} \alpha_{11}\gamma_1' & \Delta_{12}\alpha_{21}\gamma_1' & 0 & 0 \\ \Delta_{21}\alpha_{12}\gamma_2' & \alpha_{22}\gamma_2' & 0 & 0 \\ 0 & 0 & \beta_1' & 0 \\ 0 & 0 & 0 & \beta_2' \end{bmatrix} \begin{bmatrix} w_t^1 \\ w_t^2 \\ x_t^1 \\ x_t^2 \end{bmatrix} = \begin{bmatrix} v_{1t} \\ v_{2t} \\ v_{3t} \\ v_{4t} \end{bmatrix}.$$

The reduced form of the expected values (with the random element set to zero) is

$$\begin{bmatrix} p_1 \\ p_2 \\ q_1 \\ q_2 \end{bmatrix} = \begin{bmatrix} \alpha_{11} & \Delta_{12}\alpha_{21} & 1 & 0 \\ \Delta_{21}\alpha_{12} & \alpha_{22} & 0 & 1 \\ -\alpha_{11} & -\alpha_{12} & 1 & 0 \\ -\alpha_{21} & -\alpha_{22} & 0 & 1 \end{bmatrix}^{-1} \times \begin{bmatrix} \alpha_{11}\gamma_1' & \Delta_{12}\alpha_{21}\gamma_1' & 0 & 0 \\ \Delta_{21}\alpha_{12}\gamma_2' & \alpha_{22}\gamma_2' & 0 & 0 \\ 0 & 0 & \beta_1' & 0 \\ 0 & 0 & 0 & \beta_2' \end{bmatrix} \begin{bmatrix} w_t^1 \\ w_t^2 \\ x_t^1 \\ x_t^2 \end{bmatrix}.$$

Given parameter estimates (α, γ, β), calculating the price in the case of a cartel will involve the estimation of this equation system by using these equations with Δ_{12} set to 1 to give us the cartel's optimal prices and quantities. Calculating the "but for" price for the case of competition will require calculating the prices using the same estimated structural parameters but setting Δ_{12} to 0. Alternatively, one can estimate the structural model for the competitive period and use the estimated coefficients to calculate the "but for" prices during the conspiracy period.

Simulations put a great deal of structure in the model and in this respect they are very different from trying to identify the outcome of a cartel using a dummy variable in a reduced-form regression. The results from simulation models will be sensitive to the assumptions made. In particular, the results will depend on the treatment given to the cost and demand parameters and the way cost and demand are allowed to affect prices. In addition, the results will be sensitive to the assumptions made regarding the success of the cartel in raising prices and the competitive environment in the "but for" world. In the example presented above, for example, the cartel is assumed to work perfectly for its entire duration. This may not always be the case and indeed bargaining problems and cartel breakdowns suggest it is not. In addition, one should also be fairly confident that the competitive framework chosen for the industry absent the cartel is broadly realistic. The flexibility in the "but for" model may also provide some options for the defense. For instance, in the lysine cartel case (Connor 2000):

> [The defendants] presented data that demonstrated that the lysine market was highly concentrated (HHI = 3,500), with high barriers to entry, no product differentiation, and large numbers of dispersed buyers. ... The defendants then go on to assert that, given such a market configuration, "conditions are conducive to the implicit oligopolistic coordination that would keep prices substantially above the long run [competitive] price."

This quote appears to suggest that the defendants argued that even without explicit collusion prices would end up somewhere close to the level that we would expect under "legal" tacit coordination. Assuming for the moment that tacit collusion were in fact legal (which is not obvious in many cases), such a position would in extremis mean absolutely no damages were due since explicit and tacit collusion might lead to exactly the same pricing outcomes. Such an argument would, shall we say, appear somewhat optimistic even if theoretically a possibility.

The defendants also argue that the "but for" prices should be based on a Cournot model rather than the homogeneous product Bertrand model. There is obviously an incentive for defendants to generally do so since the Cournot model will suggest "but for" prices above those that emerge from the Bertrand model with the consequence that the estimated damages will be lower.

Since the alternative world of competitive prices is not observed, we must inevitably rely on assumptions about the way markets would have behaved absent the cartel. Steps must be taken to check that the models chosen are relevant for the markets that are the subject of the analysis. Generally, standard models such as Cournot or Bertrand games are used for simulation exercises and this exposes simulation to the criticism that it relies on simplistic static models which are an overly simplified version of reality. Those models may be a very good approximation of reality in some cases but sometimes they will not fit the facts of the industry. It is important that the analyst uses good judgment to decide when a particular theoretical framework is an appropriate representation of the reality of the price determination process in an industry. Generically, the explicit nature of the assumptions somewhat ironically tend to make the structural models more vulnerable to legal challenge since they require their proponents to defend what will inevitably be substantial approximations embodied in the model's assumptions. A scientific ideal of stating assumptions can easily become a handicap unless one is prepared to actively defend your model's assumptions on the grounds that they are reasonable ones given the context and given the state of economic knowledge. In doing so, it will usually be helpful for the proposed model not be explicitly rejected by the data before, during, or after the cartel period.

The bottom line is that all methodologies, including those which seem very flexible at first glance rely on assumptions, and usually strong and often arguably implausible assumptions at that. Some methods impose lots of structure and can identify the effect of a cartel but only so long as the structure is correct. Other methods allow for more flexibility and do not impose a single structural form on the data. However, when using such an approach the economist must be able to explain very clearly exactly what pattern in the data is identifying the effect of the cartel on prices and how, for example, they can be sure that they are not capturing the effect of other variables in their measurement of the cartel's impact on prices. At the same time, judges and other case decision makers should recognize that assumptions always have to be made to estimate damages, even if the assumptions are not explicitly stated. Thus they should carefully evaluate the merits of model-based approaches with clearly stated assumptions relative to approaches that are less clear about their assumptions. Ultimately, assumptions are both always wrong and always required. That fact makes economic analysis interesting but difficult for both analysts in competition agencies and subsequently judges.

7.1.3 The Pass-On Defense

When the customers of a cartel are downstream firms, they may be in a position to pass on some of the increase in the price of the inputs to their final customers. Customers in this situation do not suffer the whole of the price increase generated by the cartel because of this pass-on effect. In the event of private damages claims, the defendants could in principle use a "pass-on defense" and argue a pass-on effect should reduce the amount of the plaintiff's claim. There appears little reason beyond perhaps deterrence for an intermediate firm to have the right to recoup the full damages caused by a cartel. In fact, whether the pass-on defense is allowed or not depends on the legal jurisdiction.

7.1.3.1 The Pass-On Effect

Measuring the pass-on effect is equivalent to measuring the increase in the price of the good sold by the downstream firm to the final consumer. For the downstream firm, the price increase caused by the cartel upstream is equivalent to an increase in its marginal cost.[11] Earlier in the chapter, we saw that the magnitude of the pass-on can be expressed as

$$\text{Pass-on} = q^1 \Delta p = q^1(p^1 - p^0),$$

where q^1 is the quantity of the good sold by the downstream firm during the cartel and Δp is the increase in the price of the downstream good sold to the final consumers during the cartel period. We followed Van Dijk and Verboven (2007) and showed that this is one of three elements of the change in profits of a downstream firm associated

[11] Richer vertical contracts than those involving simple uniform pricing will bring into question this equivalence. We discuss this issue further in chapter 10.

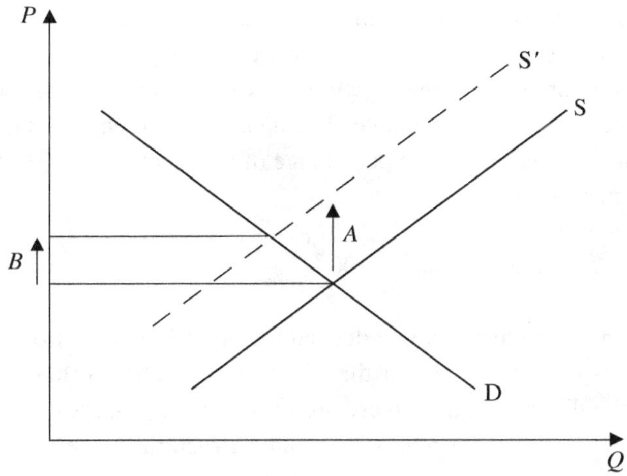

Figure 7.7. The pass-on rate under perfect competition downstream.

with a movement from a competitive to a cartelized upstream market. Specifically, we showed that

$$\Delta\pi = -q^1 \Delta c + (\Delta q)(p^0 - c^{\text{Comp}}) + q^1(\Delta p).$$

We describe the pass-on effect as complete if $\Delta p = (p^1 - p^0) = (c^{\text{Cartel}} - c^{\text{Comp}})$, where c^{Cartel} represents the marginal cost of the downstream firm when the input is cartelized and c^{Comp} is its marginal cost when it benefits from competition upstream. If the downstream firm can increase the price of the good by the same amount as the increase in the marginal cost, we will have a pass-on of 100% and the firm will only have suffered from the cartel to the extent that it has lost margins on some products no longer sold. In this case, the first and third terms cancel so that the downstream firms change in profits is

$$\Delta\pi = -(\Delta q)(p^0 - c^{\text{Comp}}).$$

A complete pass-through of cartel prices will happen only under very specific supply or demand conditions in the downstream market. More often, the firm will only be able to pass on a fraction of the input price increase and will suffer some reduction in margin on its continuing sales. Firms with market power will be able to pass on the effect of the cost increase more easily. Although the remaining effect, the loss of margin on sales not made under the cartel, is often not counted if the pass-on defense is allowed, and if the output effect is large, one may want to include it in the calculation of the damages as otherwise the defendant may largely escape punishment by using the pass-on defense (see Van Dijk and Verboven 2007).

The pass-on effect in the case of a perfectly competitive market downstream can be represented as shown in figure 7.7. Assume the cartel increases the price of the input by an amount A. If the downstream firm uses one unit of input per unit of output, this results in an increase in the marginal cost of the same magnitude which causes a contraction of the supply and an increase in the price. Final customers react to the increase in prices by reducing purchases which mitigates the actual amount of the price increase that is profitable. The final price increase by the downstream firm is B. The pass-on rate or the percentage of the increase in costs that is passed on to the consumers is:

$$\text{Pass-on rate} = 100\frac{q^{\text{Cartel}}(\Delta p)}{-q^{\text{Cartel}}\Delta c} = 100\frac{B}{A}.$$

The ability to pass on the effect will depend on the ability of the firm to raise prices to its customers to compensate for the effect of the higher costs on profits. As in the case for the direct damages, there are two basic approaches to estimating the pass-on effect: a reduced-form approach and a structural model approach and we discuss each in turn.

7.1.3.2 Reduced-Form Approach for Calculating the Pass-On

The reduced-form approach measures the effect of an increase in the cost of an input on the prices of the intermediate firm during the cartel period. As before, a reduced-form specification will control for all other exogenous factors affecting demand and supply and will try to identify the effect of the increase in input prices caused by the cartel on the price of the claimant's product.[12] One way is to use the actual cartel price to directly measure the "pass-on" effect:

$$p_t^{\text{Claimant}} = x_t'\beta + \alpha_1 p_t^{\text{Cartelized input}} + \varepsilon_t.$$

In this specification, we are assuming that the price of the cartelized input is exogenously determined by the cartelized industry and that it is not, for example, dependent on the quantity bought by the claimant. That restriction would, for example, suggest this approach may not work well in markets where countervailing buyer power is present. Note that the quantity variable is not included in the specification so that the coefficient α_1 is assumed to capture not only the direct effect of the increase in cost on the price but also the effect of the quantity adjustments that follow. In a reduced form such as this one with no underlying structural model, we cannot identify the nature of the adjustment. We are in effect only evaluating the impact of an exogenous change in cartel price on the equilibrium downstream price.

If the reduced-form specifications are sound, the coefficient of the dummy or the price of the cartelized input can be interpreted as the magnitude of the pass-on effect, to be potentially deducted from the per unit direct damages.

[12] The reduced form does not control for endogenous variables such as quantity since those would only enter a structural form if prices and quantities are determined in equilibrium.

7.1.3.3 Structural Approach for Calculating the Pass-On

The structural approach specifies a model of competition in the downstream market. It must specify a demand function and a pricing equation. An example of this approach is provided by Verboven and Bettendorf (2001), who examine an alleged cartel in the coffee bean market and wanted to know how much of the price increase in coffee beans was passed on to the final purchasers of coffee.

Following their model, suppose a linear model of demand for coffee,

$$Q_t = \alpha_{0t} - \alpha_1 p_t,$$

and a constant-in-output-marginal-cost equation,

$$\text{mc}_t = \beta_0 w_t^{\text{Other inputs}} + \beta_1 w_t^{\text{Beans}} + \beta_2 w_t^{\text{Labor}},$$

where the ws represent various input prices. Following the approach developed in chapter 6 for nesting the pricing equation from cartel, Cournot, and perfectly competitive models, we can write the pricing equation encompassing all three models as

$$\begin{aligned} P_t &= \left(\frac{\lambda}{\alpha_1}\right) Q_t + \text{mc}_t \\ &= \left(\frac{\lambda}{\alpha_1}\right) Q_t + \beta_0 w_t^{\text{Other inputs}} + \beta_1 w_t^{\text{Beans}} + \beta_2 w_t^{\text{Labor}}, \end{aligned}$$

where λ is the conduct parameter in the coffee market. Note that $\beta_1 = \partial \text{mc}_t / \partial w_t^{\text{Beans}}$ so that the coefficient β_1 tells us how much the marginal cost of coffee changes as the result of an increase in the price of beans. The effect of the increase in marginal cost on equilibrium prices cannot be calculated from this equation alone since it represents only the supply (pricing) side of the market. Any change in marginal cost will feed through into a movement of the supply curve but we are not interested just in finding the price that must be charged for the firm(s) to be willing to sell the old output level given the new costs. Rather we want to calculate the new equilibrium price. Thus, to calculate the full impact of a change in the price of beans on the price of coffee we need to estimate both the demand and supply (pricing) equations described above.

Formally, the structural demand-and-supply system described above can be expressed as follows:

$$\begin{bmatrix} 1 & \lambda/a_1 \\ \alpha_1 & 1 \end{bmatrix} \begin{bmatrix} P_t \\ Q_t \end{bmatrix} = \begin{bmatrix} 0 & \beta_0 & \beta_1 & \beta_2 \\ \alpha_0' & 0 & 0 & 0 \end{bmatrix} \begin{bmatrix} x_t \\ w_t^{\text{Other inputs}} \\ w_t^{\text{Beans}} \\ w_t^{\text{Labor}} \end{bmatrix} + \begin{bmatrix} u_t^{\text{S}} \\ u_t^{\text{D}} \end{bmatrix},$$

which gives the reduced-form equations for the equilibrium outcomes (price, quantity):

$$\begin{bmatrix} P_t \\ Q_t \end{bmatrix} = \begin{bmatrix} 1 & \lambda/a_1 \\ \alpha_1 & 1 \end{bmatrix}^{-1} \begin{bmatrix} 0 & \beta_0 & \beta_1 & \beta_2 \\ \alpha_0' & 0 & 0 & 0 \end{bmatrix} \begin{bmatrix} x_t \\ w_t^{\text{Other inputs}} \\ w_t^{\text{Beans}} \\ w_t^{\text{Labor}} \end{bmatrix} + \begin{bmatrix} 1 & \lambda/a_1 \\ \alpha_1 & 1 \end{bmatrix}^{-1} \begin{bmatrix} u_t^{\text{S}} \\ u_t^{\text{D}} \end{bmatrix}.$$

Note that in this case the specification is derived from a structural model so that parameters can be interpreted. Note also that estimating this two-equation system allows us to calculate the impact of an increase of the price of beans on equilibrium coffee prices. This effect will be given by the derivative $\partial P_t/\partial w_t^{\text{Beans}}$, which, for clarity, will not be the same as the estimated coefficient of w_t^{Beans} in the pricing equation β_1. $\partial P_t/\partial w_t^{\text{Beans}}$ tells us the effect of changing input prices on equilibrium coffee prices while β_1 tells us the effect of changing input prices on the output pricing equation, i.e., holding quantity fixed.

The advantage of this choice of structural system is that it allows us to calculate the pass-on for three popular alternative competitive models downstream: perfect competition, symmetric Cournot, or (trivially) monopoly.

7.1.3.4 Determinants of the Pass-On Effect

Another alternative to structural estimation is to estimate the elements that determine the likelihood of a greater pass-on. We have seen that the extent of the pass-on depends on the direct effect of an increase in costs on the supply function and on the price elasticities of both demand and supply. In particular, for any given increase in costs and shift in the supply curve, the pass-on will be larger when the supply curve is more elastic and when the demand curve is more inelastic.

Figure 7.8 compares the pass-on rate for a competitive market with an elastic demand to that with a competitive market with an inelastic demand. We do so by rotating the demand curve at the point where supply and demand intersect and in each case seeing what happens when supply shifts. The graph shows that when demand is inelastic, the quantity effect is smaller and so the increase in marginal cost will be passed on to consumers to a larger extent than when demand is elastic, all else equal. An elastic demand makes price increases less profitable for the producer and therefore less of the cost increase will be passed on to consumers in the form of higher prices.

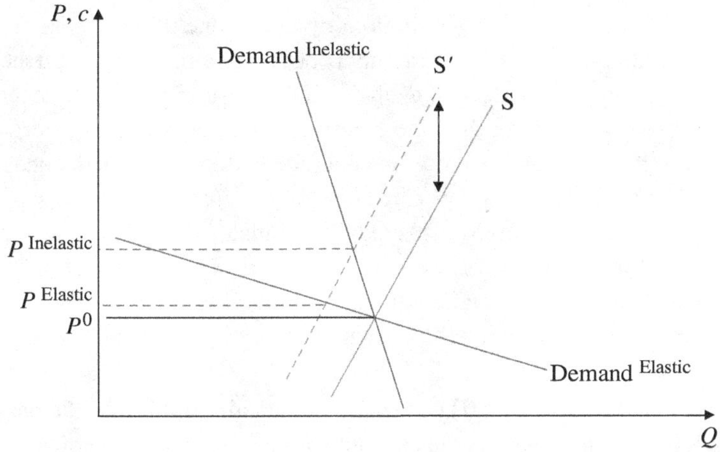

Figure 7.8. Pass-on with elastic and inelastic demand.

For a formal demonstration, consider a price-taking firm, solving

$$\max_q pq - C(q; c),$$

where $C(q; c)$ represents the total cost function and c represents a cost driver. From this problem we derive the firm supply function $q = s(p, c)$ and from that in turn, given N identical firms, we derive an industry supply curve $S(p; c)$, increasing in p and decreasing in c. We may now define a function

$$F(p; c) \equiv D(p) - S(p; c) = 0,$$

which implicitly defines the equilibrium price as a function of our cost driver, c. We can then apply the Implicit Function Theorem to get an expression for the pass-through $\partial p/\partial c$. Specifically, totally differentiating gives

$$\frac{\partial D(p)}{\partial p} = \frac{\partial S(p; c)}{\partial p} + \frac{\partial S(p; c)}{\partial c}\frac{\partial c}{\partial p},$$

which in turn suggests that when the downstream market is perfectly competitive the pass-on effect can be expressed as

$$\begin{aligned}\frac{\partial p}{\partial c} &= \frac{\partial S(p; c)}{\partial c}\bigg/\bigg(\frac{\partial D(p)}{\partial p} - \frac{\partial S(p; c)}{\partial p}\bigg)\\ &= \bigg(-\frac{\partial \ln S(p; c)}{\partial c}\bigg)\bigg/\bigg(-\frac{\partial \ln D(p)}{\partial p} + \frac{\partial \ln S(p; c)}{\partial p}\bigg),\end{aligned}$$

where the latter equality follows by noting first that $D(p) = S(p; c)$, second that for any nonzero differentiable function $f(p)$ we can write

$$\frac{\partial \ln f(p)}{\partial p} = \frac{1}{f(p)}\frac{\partial f(p)}{\partial p}$$

and thirdly by multiplying top and bottom by minus one. Finally, note that (i) the demand elasticity is negative while the supply elasticity is positive so that the denominator will be positive and (ii) supply will decline as costs increase so that the numerator is also positive, making the ratio positive so that equilibrium prices increase with cost, $\partial p/\partial c > 0$. Furthermore, we conclude that the pass-on depends on both the demand and supply elasticities as well as on the cost elasticity of supply. Both elastic demand or elastic supply make the denominator large and hence reduce the pass-through down toward zero. Similarly, and intuitively, when the cost elasticity of supply is small so that costs tend not to impact on ability to supply the downstream good, the rate of pass-through will be small.

Verboven and Van Dijk (2007) derive the analytical formulas for the pass-on rate under perfectly competitive markets and under markets with oligopolistic competition. Furthermore, they evaluate the relative importance of the pass-on and output effects for a variety of settings. They note that the pass-on effect should be applied and the amount of the overcharge discounted by this effect when the claimant operates in a fully competitive setting. But when the claimant's industry—the downstream industry—is less competitive, the output effect and the loss of sales volume by the claimant starts mitigating the effect of the pass-on on the claimants profits. The output effect should in such cases limit the discount in the damages granted by a pass-on defense. Their paper provides analytical expressions for the total discount to be applied to the overcharge of the cartel, taking into account both the pass-on and the output effects.

Cournot competition in quantities the pricing function has the form

$$P(Q) + P'(Q)q = \text{mc},$$

which under firm symmetry implies

$$P(Q) + P'(Q)\frac{Q}{N} = \text{mc}$$

or

$$1 + \frac{1}{N\eta(Q)} = \frac{\text{mc}}{P(Q)},$$

where η is the price elasticity of demand,

$$\eta(Q) \equiv \frac{\partial \ln P(Q)}{\partial Q} = \frac{1}{P(Q)}\frac{\partial P(Q)}{\partial Q}.$$

This equation defines implicitly our equilibrium output

$$F(Q, \text{mc}) \equiv 1 + \frac{1}{N\eta(Q)} - \frac{\text{mc}}{P(Q)} = 0,$$

which in turn means, given the demand equation, we can calculate the implied level of prices since the inverse demand curve describes $p = P(Q)$. First, recall that if $p = P(Q(\text{mc}))$, then

$$\frac{\partial p}{\partial \text{mc}} = \frac{\partial P(Q)}{\partial Q}\frac{\partial Q(\text{mc})}{\partial \text{mc}},$$

where the former is just a property of the inverse demand equation and the latter we can calculate by applying the implicit function theorem to the Cournot equilibrium equation:

$$F(Q, \text{mc}) = 0.$$

Noting that[13]

$$\frac{\partial F(Q,\text{mc})}{\partial Q} \equiv -\frac{1}{N(\eta(Q))^2}\frac{\partial \eta(Q)}{\partial Q} + \frac{\text{mc}}{P(Q)^2}\frac{\partial P(Q)}{\partial Q}$$

and

$$\frac{\partial F(Q,\text{mc})}{\partial \text{mc}} \equiv -\frac{1}{P(Q)},$$

we can apply the implicit function theorem by noting that

$$\frac{\partial Q(\text{mc})}{\partial \text{mc}} = -\left(\frac{\partial F(Q,\text{mc})}{\partial \text{mc}}\right)\left(\frac{\partial F(Q,\text{mc})}{\partial Q}\right)^{-1}$$

and hence, given the results above, that

$$\begin{aligned}\frac{\partial p}{\partial \text{mc}} &= \frac{\partial P(Q)}{\partial Q}\frac{\partial Q(\text{mc})}{\partial \text{mc}} \\ &= \frac{\partial P(Q)}{\partial Q}\left(\frac{-1}{P(Q)}\right)\Big/\left(-\frac{1}{N(\eta(Q))^2}\frac{\partial \eta(Q)}{\partial Q} + \frac{\text{mc}}{(P(Q))^2}\frac{\partial P(Q)}{\partial Q}\right).\end{aligned}$$

Rearranging gives

$$\begin{aligned}\frac{\partial p}{\partial \text{mc}} &= \frac{\partial P(Q)}{\partial Q}\frac{\partial Q(\text{mc})}{\partial \text{mc}} \\ &= \frac{\partial \ln P(Q)}{\partial Q}\left(\frac{1}{N(\eta(Q))}\frac{\partial \ln \eta(Q)}{\partial Q} - \frac{\text{mc}}{P(Q)}\frac{\partial \ln P(Q)}{\partial Q}\right)^{-1} \quad \Longleftrightarrow\end{aligned}$$

so that canceling terms gives

$$\frac{\partial p}{\partial \text{mc}} = \left(\frac{Q}{N}\frac{\partial \ln \eta(Q)}{\partial Q} - \frac{\text{mc}}{P(Q)}\frac{1}{Q}\right)^{-1},$$

where η is the price elasticity of demand. Note that in the Cournot model the sensitivity of the price elasticity of demand to the output level affects the pass-through. The expression does not allow us to predict whether the pass-on under Cournot will be lower or higher than under perfect competition.

7.1.4 Timing the Cartel

An area we have not yet considered is the timing of the cartel. We need to understand the time when the cartel was active since damages will accrue over that period. In fact, getting the period sufficiently approximately correct may be at least as important for the final damages number as pinning down exactly what the difference between collusive and competitive prices would have been in any given time period. In addition, most methodologies rely at least to some extent on pre-cartel or post-cartel data to extract information about the competitive scenario and it is therefore rather important that the data deemed to be the result of competition are in fact genuinely the result of competition, or something very close to it.

Most commonly investigators use direct data from company executives to time the cartel: notes from diaries, records of meetings, emails referring to meetings or exchange of information, and memos describing pricing schemes. All these are the best sources for timing the cartel, as well as proving it existed in the first place. Because they are generally simple and less controversial pieces of evidence, it is by far the preferred source of information. Such information may be obtained from raiding company offices or executives' home addresses. Alternatively, it may emerge from the now widespread use of leniency programs, where leniency (particularly for second and subsequent leniency applications in a given case) can sometimes be conditional on providing evidence about the workings of a cartel.

However, if there is not enough hard documentary evidence to time the cartel precisely, investigators may want to consider looking for a structural break in the data. The idea is to look for a change in the competition regime prevailing in the industry and the intuition is that we expect changes in conduct to be associated with otherwise unexplained changes in the levels of prices and/or quantities being sold. One way to do this is to specify dummy variables that allow for multiple possible starting and finishing dates. For instance, one might run the following regression:

$$p_t = x_t'\beta + \alpha_1 D_t^{\text{April 06 to May 06}} + \alpha_2 D_t^{\text{June 06 to July 06}} + \varepsilon_t.$$

This specification nests two timing options with two different starting dates. If $\alpha_1 = 0$ and $\alpha_2 > 0$, then the starting date of the cartel is June 2006. If $\alpha_1 = \alpha_2 > 0$, then the starting date of the cartel is April 2006.

One can undertake a similar exercise for the end dates of the cartel but end dates are often trickier to pin down than start dates. Reversion to competition can be a gradual process and is not always marked by a discrete event such as a meeting among executives. Cartels often collapse little by little due to cheating, entry, a diversion of interests, or due to scrutiny by a competition authority. One may observe prices falling with several attempts to re-establish coordination having some limited success. Documenting and incorporating these data into the analysis may not be straightforward.

Additionally, there are reasons to think that the cartel may be replaced by a competition regime that is not necessarily genuine competition. The fact that a cartel had explicitly solved the problem of agreeing what it meant to be colluding meant that the first of Stigler's conditions for tacit collusion may be satisfied, namely agreement (see the discussion in chapter 6). There are numerous indications that tacit collusion may be more likely after periods of explicit collusion and examples that are widely cited include those which followed the breakdown of the electrical cartels in the late 1950s.[14] Alternatively, firms in the previously cartelized industry which are being exposed to damage claims may sometimes have an incentive to price above the noncollusive level in the post-cartel period in order to minimize the size of their penalty (Harrington 2003).

Finally, it is worth noting that the focus on claims made by downstream firms in the discussion of cartel damages reflects, in part, a legal reality, at least in Europe. The fact is that groups of final consumers often find it very difficult to coordinate together to generate a successful damages claim. Legal fees in a damages case can be substantial, even if a regulator has already put together a civil case establishing there was a cartel, while each consumer's damage may be small. For example, in the football shirt case in the United Kingdom (JJB Sports) that consumer organization *Which?* took to the Competition Appeals Tribunal on behalf of consumers, each consumer was awarded £20 in damages from the company. However, since in the United Kingdom this kind of private action requires consumers to opt into the group of consumers that were represented by *Which?*, only approximately 1,000 consumers were expected to receive £20 each in compensation while almost one million shirts were estimated to have been affected by the cartel.[15] The possibility for a limited form of U.S.-style class-action suits, where groups of consumers would need to opt out of an action rather than opt into it, is under consideration in a number of European jurisdictions.[16]

7.2 Quantifying Damages in Abuse of Dominant Position Cases

Damages are mostly explicitly calculated for cartel infringements. However, monopolization cases (or in EU language abuse of a dominant position cases) may also harm the process of competition and ultimately consumers. Because the tradition of

---

[14] Specifically, the General Electric–Westinghouse case provides an example where it was subsequently alleged that tacit collusion replaced the explicit collusion of the late 1950s (see Porter 1980).

[15] See, for example, "Thousands of football fans win 'rip-off' replica shirt refunds" (http://business.timesonline.co.uk/tol/business/law/article3159958.ece). The other aspect of the incentive to take such cases on behalf of consumers is the allocation of costs. If a case is won by a consumer organization, it can seek its costs; however, this "loser-pays" principle puts a considerable risk of a large downside on consumer organizations if the court decides that a claim for damages is without merit.

[16] See www.oft.gov.uk/news/press/2007/63-07 for the United Kingdom and http://ec.europa.eu/comm/competition/antitrust/actionsdamages/index.html for the European Commission's consultation on private actions.

private litigation is not yet fully developed in Europe, there are not many examples of calculated damages for individual misconduct unrelated to price fixing. This section only briefly introduces the topic and draws from Hall and Lazear (1994) and the Ashurst (2004) study for the European Commission.

7.2.1 Lost Profits

Abuses of dominant position hurt consumers directly through exploitative abuses (high prices) but additional harm to consumers often also occurs because competition has been impaired in some way. For example, rivals have been prevented from operating in the market either entirely or perhaps their scale of operation has been reduced. In either case, we will say they have suffered from an exclusionary abuse. Who, if anybody at all, is entitled to claim damages is a matter of law and differs by jurisdiction.

The calculation of damages arising from an abuse of dominant position is a fairly uncommon activity for competition authorities, far rarer than damage calculations are for cartels. One reason may be that the damage inflicted by a dominant firm on customers and the extra profits generated by the abusive conduct can be very difficult to calculate whenever there is a significant element of exclusionary abuse. Indeed, there are few well-understood methodologies for evaluating the damage caused by exclusionary abuses, although a simulation model could be used in principle. By its very nature estimating what competition would have been like with additional firms active is a very difficult exercise. The quantification of the additional profits generated by the abuse, on the other hand, may be of interest if the authority wants to assess the incentives that firms face for engaging in abusive behavior of some kind. The methods presented here could also be used for such a purpose.

When the injured party is a rival and not a customer, the damage calculation is even less straightforward. Typically, damages will be expressed as the additional profits that would have been obtained if the abuse had never taken place. The counterfactual is more difficult to establish than the effect on consumers since it will involve the performance of a particular firm if it had faced different conditions on the market. While our current generation of simulation models might be used to incorporate individual abusive conduct and to produce comparative static results of outcomes with and without the conduct, the data required to undertake such an exercise robustly would quite possibly rarely be available.

The design of a counterfactual and the quantification of the profit differential with and without the conduct is the most essential and also the trickiest part of such a damage estimation exercise. There are, however, other empirical issues that will also be relevant. For example, if plaintiffs can recover interest from their past losses, there will have to be a calculation of the present value of past damages. Similarly, future losses due to irreparable damage will have to be divided by a suitable discount rate in order to be expressed in net present value. The choice of the interest rate and the discount factor theoretically appropriate will take into account the characteristics of the firm and the risk of the investment. While such general statements are widely acknowledged to be standard practice, they are not the same as stating the right number for any given context. Doing so with any confidence would require a substantial endeavor. Finally, the timing of injury may not coincide with timing of the infringement since injury can extend beyond the infringement and the claimant may not have been directly affected by the abuse since it took place.

7.2.2 Valuation of Lost Profits

The quantification of lost profits due to an abuse of dominant position by another firm may well mostly involve using accounting data and accounting concepts to construct the profitability that would have occurred in the counterfactual world where no abuse took place. One approach is to base the damage calculations on the claimant company's earnings: the damages will be the discounted estimated change in the cash flow. The cash flow is defined as the firm's earnings actually received minus the costs actually incurred. The calculation of cash flow would exclude depreciation since the cost of depreciation is not actually paid. Assumptions must be made about how costs would have changed with different output and revenues. The calculation of "but for" cash flow will have to be carefully based on information about the company situation before the injury and its likely prospects on the market. The latter, in particular, means that a sufficiently deep knowledge of the firm and industry is required for such an exercise, and/or at least a willingness to make reasonable assumptions.

A second approach to evaluating lost profits is to use a market-based approach. Damages could be estimated by calculating the loss of sales due to injury and multiplying that by the stock market valuation of a similar company as a multiple of its sales. If a similar company's stock price implies a valuation of double the sales revenues, the damage to lost sales will be double. This approach eliminates the need to discount the loss in profits over time but the calculation of the loss in sales raises the same issues as the calculation of the "but for" cash-flow or the "but for" scenario in general. A related assets-based approach would calculate the damages as the change in the book value of assets before and after the infringement. Of course, for such an approach to be a sensible one, the analyst must be confident that the change in asset valuation is a consequence of the abuse and reflects the value of damage.

Each of these techniques has advantages and disadvantages and they all raise the challenge of constructing a credible "but for" world. Case handlers may have to draw on the knowledge and industry expertise of an array of professionals such as industry experts, accountants, and strategy managers in order to construct a reasonable estimate of such damages.

7.3 Conclusions

- Cartels increase prices and diminish output causing both a loss in total welfare and also a transfer of welfare from customers to producers. Profits go up and consumer surplus will generally go down under a cartel relative to a competitive market.
- The total harm caused by a cartel to its customers consists of a direct effect on the customers who buy from the cartel in the form of an increase in prices and also an indirect effect due to the restriction in output on those customers who decide not to buy from a cartel given its high prices. If the cartel sells an input to downstream firms who then sell on to final consumers, damages to the downstream firm may be mitigated by the downstream firm's ability to pass on the increase in its costs to final consumers.
- In practice, cartel damages are often approximated by the direct damage or the total amount of the overcharge to the customers. This is the increase in price times the actual quantity sold during the cartel period.
- Quantifying the damages will require estimating the price that would have prevailed absent the cartel. When market conditions do not vary greatly, this can be done by looking at historical time series and taking the price of the competitive periods as the benchmark competitive price during the cartel period. If market conditions do vary over time, one may nonetheless be able to use a regression framework to predict the "but for" prices during the cartel period. Structural simulations of the market are also possible but require reasonable assumptions on the nature of demand and the type of competition that would prevail absent the cartel.
- Using the trend in the prices of a similar product to infer the price in the cartelized market is also possible, assuming such a benchmark is available. Applying a "reasonable" margin to the cost of the cartelized industry during the cartel can also provide a "but for" price when such "reasonable" margin can be inferred from the industry history or other benchmark markets.
- Timing the cartel is a necessary part of damage estimation. It is best done using documentary evidence but evidence of unexplained structural breaks in the pricing patterns can sometimes also provide useful guidance.
- The treatment of the pass-on effect in the calculation of damages depends on the legal framework. The extent of the pass-on will depend on the sensitivity of the firm's supply function to the change in costs and also on the demand and supply elasticities that it faces. When the output effect is very large, so that a downstream firm's profits suffer as they lose the margins that would have been earned on competitive volumes, the ability to pass on cost increases may not successfully mitigate the damage suffered by the downstream firm.

- In addition to the difficulties in cartel cases, the exercise of quantifying damages in cases of abuse of dominant position (attempted monopolization) is further complicated by the difficulty in defining the "but for" world. Dynamic and strategic elements which are difficult to incorporate might be particularly relevant in such settings. For example, suppose a claim for damages were made following the EU's case against Microsoft for abuse of dominance. To evaluate the damages suffered by rival firms, we may need to take a view on the counterfactual evolution of the computer industry—by any measure a nontrivial task.

8
Merger Simulation

Simulating markets in order to predict the unilateral effect of mergers on prices has seen considerable growth in popularity since the method was refined during the 1990s in a series of papers including the famous papers by Farrell and Shapiro (1990), Werden and Froeb (1993b), and Hausman et al. (1994). Such exercises, called merger simulations, are used for two purposes. First, they can serve as a screening device. In that case a standard model is usually taken as an admittedly very rough approximation to the world with the expectation that the merger simulated with that model provides at least as good a screen as the use of market shares or concentration indices alone and hence is a complementary assessment tool to these simple methods. The second purpose of merger simulation involves building a more substantial model with the explicit aim of providing a realistic basis for a "best guess" prediction of the likely effects of a merger.

Although merger simulation is now familiar to most antitrust economists and has been applied in a number of investigated cases, authorities remain cautious in the use of the results of these simulations as evidence. One important reason is that most authorities' decisions are subject to review by judges and the courts have not universally embraced merger simulation as solid probative material. In turn, the reason for judicial concern is that merger simulation models are based on important structural assumptions regarding the nature of consumer demand, the nature of firm behavior, and the structure of costs. Evaluating whether a simulation model is likely to be accurate therefore implies determining the appropriateness of those assumptions. Unfortunately, there is usually considerable uncertainty regarding the price-setting mechanism in the market, the nature of demand, and the nature of costs. Yet a model builder must make explicit assumptions about each of these important elements of a merger simulation model.

The alternative empirical approach is to try to use "natural experiments." In some cases natural experiments will allow an empirical evaluation with fewer explicit assumptions. We discussed this important approach in detail in chapter 4. Such an approach is, however, not always either available or convincing. As a result, many investigations use a mixture of theoretical arguments, quantitative indicators, and qualitative descriptions of industry features to decide whether a merger will lead to a substantial lessening of competition (SLC) causing prices to rise. Such an approach, as the proponents of simulation models point out, will usually not involve stating explicitly the structural and modeling assumptions on which an SLC decision is based. Not stating assumptions is clearly not a satisfactory approach scientifically but it does appear unfortunately to have the legal tactical advantage that it makes the analysis less prone to challenge. At least, this seems to be the current state of affairs. At the same time, the appropriate standard of proof for an investigation should probably not include the requirement to produce a simulation model of the industry with absolutely realistic assumptions. On many occasions either peculiar static or dynamic features of a market would make detailed custom-built simulation modeling extremely difficult. Indeed, such a process may often be unrealistic on merger inquiry timescales and budgets, particularly when an authority is investigating relatively small mergers.

Most moderate observers think the bottom line is that a well-designed simulation model can potentially be very informative and can even in some cases provide a satisfactory approximation of a merger effect. By integrating the results in a broader analysis of the qualitative aspects of the industry, merger simulation can provide further evidence of the effect of mergers on competition. Qualitative and descriptive analysis can be used to go through the vital task of subjecting any output from a simulation model, such as predicted prices, to careful scrutiny and "reality checks," or at least "sanity checks."

The uncertainty over exactly the appropriate modeling assumptions has a number of implications. First, it will mean that one can never claim to have pinned down with certainty the effect of a merger. Second, it means that measures of uncertainty calculated under the assumption that the class of models considered includes the "truth" should probably be treated with appropriate caution. And third, consequently, it will usually be necessary to at least explore the robustness of the prediction to deviations in the assumptions made. With these important caveats in mind we turn to a detailed consideration of simulation models. We present first the general rationale for merger simulation exercises and a simple illustrative example. We then provide a more involved discussion going into delving further into the technical complexities. Finally, we discuss the potential use of merger simulation techniques to assess the impact of a merger on the incentives to coordinate.

8.1 Best Practice in Merger Simulation

A merger simulation exercise will produce credible results if certain best practices are followed.[1] Those practices relate to the choice of assumptions, to the data used, and to the framing of the results within a broader analysis.

Practitioners need to justify their choice of modeling assumptions. It is not enough to use one of the "standard models" and claim that its widespread use justifies its

[1] For a discussion on the assessment of merger simulations, see Werden et al. (2004).

applicability. Instead, one should be able to argue why the theoretical assumptions are a reasonable approximation of the facts of the case. For example, if firms appear to compete primarily in advertising rather than prices, then the differentiated product Bertrand model may not be a good fit for the industry. Such a situation may be the case in the music industry, where huge amounts of money are spent promoting some artists and songs. It would presumably be unwise to focus all of our modeling attention on the price of the CD or MP3 file, as we would essentially be doing if we chose a Bertrand pricing model as a description of the way prices are determined in the industry. Similarly, in industries where we have important technological diffusion effects, static pricing models may well miss important dynamic dimensions of competition. For example, firms may want to manage diffusion in order to price discriminate, charging the high-value "first adopters" high prices before moving price down to service the mass market. Or they may want to accelerate the spread of the technology by subsidizing the first users. In each case, a simple Bertrand model would miss the primary economic factors driving economic outcomes in the industry.

Analogously, in industries where customers really care about the identity of the producer, be it for quality or institutional reasons, the Cournot model would probably provide a poor approximation to reality. Other factors that may be important for the choice of model are the nature of contractual relationships, the identity of the buyers, the extent of innovation, and the nature of competition either upstream or downstream. In his commentary on merger simulation models, Walker (2005) notes how, in defending their Volvo–Scania merger simulation, the expert economists pointed out that their predicted margins may have been overestimates of the actual margins because firms may have sold under the equilibrium price to recoup the lower profits with increased aftermarket sales. Walker argues that if this argument is correct, then perhaps this pricing behavior should have been captured by the pricing equation in the model (see also Crooke et al. 1999). And indeed, in building a merger simulation model investigators need to constantly remind themselves that they are trying to capture what would actually happen if the proposed change in industry structure is allowed. The best model may well not be a "standard" one. That said, there is obviously a limit to the time and resources available to any investigator and every model anyone has ever built is only an approximation of reality. If the likely bias in predicted prices can be signed, a simulation model may nonetheless be informative.

Each of these examples suggests that some simulation exercises, perhaps many, will require bespoke industry-specific models. If building such models with sufficiently good explanatory power proves intractable within the time available for a merger inquiry, then it may be that the analysis should rely on careful and informed, broader, qualitative assessment. Some of the time, however, given enough resources, it will be possible to construct a model that fits the market sufficiently.

If a merger simulation model is built, then the investigator will have to show that it predicts the facts of the industry reasonably well. In particular, predicted prices, costs, and margin behavior must be consistent with the reality of the industry. It is therefore vital to take the time to refine and check the model sufficiently before proceeding to the merger forecasting exercise. Methods to check the validity of simulation models include both the use of "in-sample" and "out-of-sample" predictions. Consider, for example, a differentiated products Bertrand model. On the one hand, checking the fit of the model in terms of predicted prices within sample will be useful. We may also check "out-of-sample" predictions by estimating the model on a subset of the data and then using the model to predict prices during the rest of the sample. However, such direct checks are not usually the end of the matter. For example, if estimates of price elasticities are wrong, then a Bertrand model will often produce negative estimates of marginal costs, which obviously cannot be right. Checking such predictions can provide additional important sanity or possibly even reality checks.

When the theoretical framework is chosen, parameters need to be estimated or calibrated. If there are sufficient market data available, econometric estimation may be possible and good practice for econometric and regression analysis applies. If there are insufficient data or indeed insufficient time available for estimation and the model is being used solely as a rough-and-ready screening device, then underlying parameters may be calibrated using the predicted structural relationships between observed variables. A poor model will not successfully predict the relationship between observed variables and, with sufficient attention to validity and checking, this will usually become very apparent. Of course, the other side of cross checking is making sure that the data used are representative and correctly measured. In particular, data on margins, marginal costs, or demand elasticities, which may be retrieved from industry information, must be checked for consistency and plausibility.

Finally, one should keep in mind that most merger simulations currently involve static models and do not incorporate dynamic effects. Firms may respond to a merger by issuing new products, repositioning their current products, or by innovating (see, for example, Gandhi et al. 2005). Each of these reactions will not be captured by a merger simulation. If there is a lot of evidence that the market in question has behaved in the past in a very dynamic fashion and that the competitive environment is subject to constant change, the merger simulation exercise will certainly lose relevance for the medium-term prediction of industry outcomes. In those cases, appropriate weight needs to be given to evidence indicating potential dynamic responses of the market, although these may well be beyond the usual time horizon of a merger inquiry since often we expect entry or other competitive responses to at least mitigate the problems generated by mergers within a few years.

In summary, merger simulation results will usually only be one part of the total evidence base when evaluating the effects of a merger. Qualitative analysis of the elements that determine pricing behavior and particularly qualitative analysis of the aspects of competition not captured by any merger simulation exercise must be properly incorporated. Only when the model used in the merger simulation fits the facts on the ground and the prediction of the effects is consistent with the rest of the evidence, should a merger simulation be used as part of the evidence. Ultimately, the analyst will want to be solidly aware that judges, rightly, do not like "black boxes" generating evidence, so every effort must be made to make the analysis clear and transparent.

The remaining sections in this chapter explain the rationale of merger simulation using simple and popular models. The purpose is both to outline these popular options but also to concentrate on the underlying principles that allow investigators to undertake customized modeling as well as undertake simulations using these popular modeling choices. There is little doubt that in the future better models will emerge for a variety of particular circumstances. In addition, better demand systems and better approaches to cost estimation will be used to generate genuinely data-driven answers in unilateral effects merger simulation. Experience and a good understanding of the underlying economics will help the investigating economist discriminate among the various options and select the appropriate models.

8.2 Introduction to Unilateral Effects

This section will use a simple framework to introduce the economic rationale of merger simulation and the basic methodological foundations of the exercise. To ease exposition we will use a familiar framework. Indeed, a major aim of this section is to put simulation models, which tend to be numerical, into the standard economic frameworks that are entirely familiar to all professional economists and ubiquitous tools for analysis. Empirical merger simulation primarily puts those models on a computer and makes estimates/guesses or "guesstimates" of the parameters of the models. Along the way we hope to make clear the contribution, assumptions, and limitations of this approach for analyzing unilateral effects of a merger.

8.2.1 An Introductory Model: Homogeneous Product Cournot

In industries where the product supplied by the firms is homogeneous, firms compete in quantities with the aim of maximizing profits, and customers do not differentiate between suppliers, competition can be modeled as a Cournot game. In this setting, firms choose the quantity of the good that they will produce given the quantity already supplied by competitors and then offer it at the price determined by aggregate demand and supply. Firms can affect prices with their output decisions and are able to raise prices by restricting output or lower them by increasing production. A merger of undertakings in such a market will have effects that can be easily described. Farrell and Shapiro (1990) provide a nice discussion of merger analysis in a Cournot setting. Below, we describe a merger simulation for the very simple case of a duopoly merging to monopoly in a homogeneous product market. The simplicity of this scenario will help illustrate the concepts involved in an empirical merger simulation exercise.

8.2.1.1 Mergers in Cournot Industries

In any game theoretic context including Cournot, economists characterize firm behavior by their best response functions. Consequently, simulating the effect of a merger involves calculating the best response functions for both the pre-merger and post-merger scenarios and solving for the corresponding equilibrium prices and quantities. In the Cournot model, if firms are symmetric in costs, the only difference between the pre- and post-merger scenarios will be the total number of firms operating in the market and so this is the variable that will need to be adjusted in the reaction functions. Symmetry assumptions simplify analysis because, with N players, N reaction functions arising from a Cournot model become just one equation to actually solve since all reaction functions are identical. If firms are heterogeneous, we will, in general, need to solve for equilibrium quantities by solving all N reaction functions. We will see this process in action a number of times during this introductory section.

Whether firms are assumed symmetric or not, we will need an estimate of marginal cost(s) as well as parameters of the market demand. Once these parameters are estimated, we can compute the pre-merger quantities and profits using the reaction functions of a market corresponding to the number of firms existing in the pre-merger world. We then compute the post-merger quantities and profits. To illustrate, consider the case of a merger in an industry with only two firms, we would just compare the output and prices emerging from a Cournot duopoly, the pre-merger situation, with the output and prices of the monopoly that would exist post-merger.

We develop the analytical model for a two-to-one merger in a homogeneous product market where the strategic variable involves quantities.

The pre-merger model. Let us consider the case of a duopoly. Profit maximization involves choosing the optimal quantity given the demand function, the rival's output, and the costs facing the firm:

$$\max_{q_j} \Pi_j(q_1, q_2) = \max_{q_j}(P(q_1 + q_2) - \text{mc}_j)q_j,$$

where the subscript j represents either firm 1 or firm 2 and where we assume constant marginal costs. The first-order condition for maximization is

$$P(q_1 + q_2) - \text{mc}_j + \frac{\partial P(q_1 + q_2)}{\partial q_j} q_j = 0.$$

Assume a linear inverse market demand function of the form,

$$P(q_1 + q_2) = a - b(q_1 + q_2),$$

which implies

$$\frac{\partial P(q_1 + q_2)}{\partial q_j} = -b.$$

Plugging the inverse demand function and its derivative in the first-order condition, the best response functions simplify to

$$q_1 = \frac{a - bq_2 - \text{mc}_1}{2b} \quad \text{and} \quad q_2 = \frac{a - bq_1 - \text{mc}_2}{2b}.$$

Solving these two equations would give us Cournot–Nash equilibrium quantities,

$$q_i = \frac{a + \text{mc}_j - 2\text{mc}_i}{3b}.$$

Summing across firms we can calculate the total industry output:

$$Q = \frac{2a - \text{mc}_1 - \text{mc}_2}{3b}.$$

And substituting total output into the inverse demand function implies that the market price will be

$$P = \frac{a + \text{mc}_1 + \text{mc}_2}{3}.$$

Thus the quantities produced by each firm in equilibrium are determined by the demand parameters and also the firm's own-marginal cost and its rivals' marginal costs. Note that more-efficient firms will produce higher quantities and have larger market shares.

The post-merger model. Suppose now that the two firms merge to form a monopoly with two plants. Profit maximization by the new firm now takes into account the profits of both plants. In assessing the profitability of a price increase, the change in revenues from the sales at the second plant will now also be taken into account:

$$\begin{aligned} &\max_{q_1, q_2} \Pi_1(q_1, q_2) + \Pi_2(q_1, q_2) \\ &\qquad = \max_{q_1, q_2} (P(q_1 + q_2) - \text{mc}_1)q_1 + (P(q_1 + q_2) - \text{mc}_2)q_2. \end{aligned}$$

In modeling the post-merger world we must always decide what happens to differences across firms when they merge. Here each plant has a different constant marginal cost and a monopolist would profitably choose to shut down one plant, the inefficient (high marginal cost) one. For simplicity, but also perhaps for realism, in this first example we therefore set marginal costs to be the same for both plants and equal to the lower of the two, suppose mc_1. This would, for example, be the case if best practice is transferred across to the second plant or, in this constant marginal cost example, if the second plant were entirely shut down and all production used the more efficient plant. (We will see that this is not necessarily true when marginal costs are eventually increasing in output at a plant. More generally, if each plant faces an increasing marginal cost function, then a monopolist will allocate production efficiently across the plants to minimize total costs of any given level of production. Since Cournot is a homogeneous product model there is no demand-side return to keeping both plants open but there may be a cost advantage in the presence of dis-economies of scale at the plant level.) In that case, the firm's profit-maximization problem simplifies to

$$\max_{q_1,q_2}(P(q_1+q_2)-\text{mc}_1)(q_1+q_2)=\max_{Q}(P(Q)-\text{mc}_1)Q,$$

where the equality follows since the former optimization program only depends on the total output, $Q = q_1 + q_2$. The first-order condition for profit maximization is

$$P(Q)+P'(Q)Q=\text{mc}_1.$$

Replacing the demand function and its derivative, we obtain the optimal monopoly quantity which will also depend on the demand parameters and the firm's costs

$$a-bQ-bQ=\text{mc}_1$$

so that post-merger market output is

$$Q=\frac{a-\text{mc}_1}{2b}\quad\text{and}\quad P=\frac{a+\text{mc}_1}{2}.$$

Comparison. Comparing pre- and post-merger quantities,

$$\begin{aligned}Q^{\text{Pre}}=\frac{2a-\text{mc}_1-\text{mc}_2}{3b}&\geqslant\frac{a-\text{mc}_1}{2b}=Q^{\text{Post}}\\ \iff\quad 4a-2\text{mc}_1-2\text{mc}_2&\geqslant 3a-3\text{mc}_1\\ &\iff\quad a\geqslant 2\text{mc}_2-\text{mc}_1,\end{aligned}$$

so that if firms are also equally efficient pre-merger, $\text{mc}_1 = \text{mc}_2$, this condition becomes $a \geqslant \text{mc}_1$, which simply requires that the marginal value placed on the first unit of output a is greater than its marginal cost of production, a condition that will generically be satisfied in active markets.

This result suggests that post-merger quantities will be lower than pre-merger quantities and prices will be correspondingly higher post-merger.

If firms are not equally efficient pre-merger, the situation is slightly more complex, and quantities will reduce post-merger if $a \geqslant 2\text{mc}_2 - \text{mc}_1 = \text{mc}_2 + (\text{mc}_2 - \text{mc}_1)$. That is, if the consumer's valuation of the first unit of demand is larger than the marginal cost of producing it at plant 2 plus the efficiency gain from producing it at plant 1 post-merger. This particular result is obviously dependent on the linear form of demand assumed, but it is indicative of the general result that cost reductions arising from a merger can reverse the general result that mergers result in higher prices and reduced output. We explore the effect of this "efficiency defense" below. We also examine the situation where marginal costs increase in output below. In that

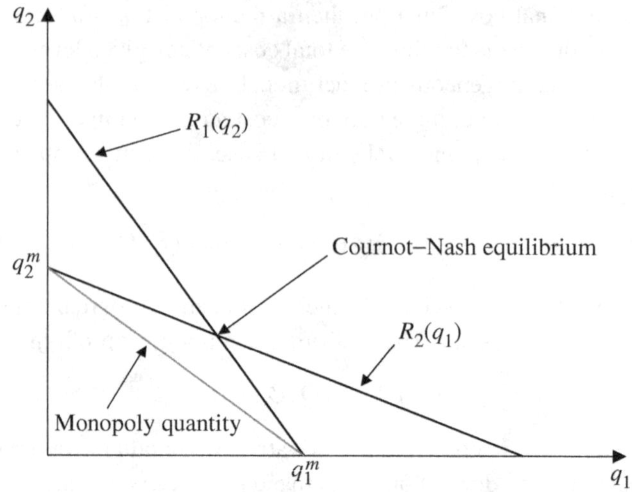

Figure 8.1. Merger simulation from two to one in Cournot setting: effect on quantities.

case, the monopolist may choose to operate both plants post-merger and so we may cleanly decompose the effect of a merger on prices into the effect that arises from quantity restriction and also a cost-reduction effect.

Comparing the aggregate quantity in both the Cournot duopoly and the monopoly scenarios under firm symmetry shows that output under monopoly, i.e., after the merger, is lower and thus, in the usual circumstance that demand slopes down, market price will be higher and consumers will be worse off.

In Cournot, increases in the production of a firm decrease the optimal output of competitors. The monopoly optimal quantity is what a pre-merger duopoly firm would choose if the competitor chose to produce nothing. As soon as the second firm starts producing a positive output, the preexisting firm cuts down on its own output but the total output in the industry increases because the reduction is less than the new production. Figure 8.1 illustrates the best response functions for a symmetric duopoly as well as the line of possibilities between q_1^m and q_2^m for the monopoly outcome which, under symmetry depends only on the total amount produced and, in particular, not where it is produced. The monopoly has a single total equilibrium level of output which it can produce in different ways across plants with symmetric costs, at the same total cost.

As the algebra suggests, figure 8.2 shows the impact of the two-to-one merger on prices and makes it clear that the merger results in a decrease in total output and will therefore raise prices to consumers. Under monopoly, the markup over the marginal cost will be higher than under a duopoly.

The symmetric Cournot model can be easily extended to allow for oligopoly markets with an arbitrary number of firms.

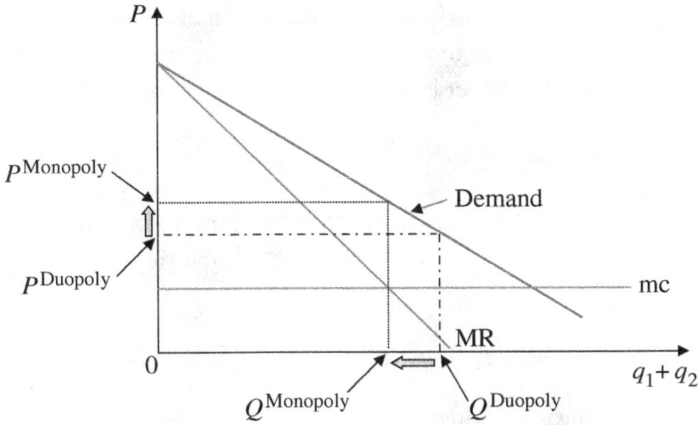

Figure 8.2. Merger simulation from two to one in Cournot setting: effect on prices.

The reaction functions of firms in a market with N symmetric firms are

$$q_i = \frac{a - \text{mc}}{b(N + 1)}$$

and the market price will be

$$P = \frac{a + N\text{mc}}{N + 1}.$$

Differentiating this equilibrium price function with respect to N shows that a merger in a Cournot type of competition will always cause equilibrium quantities to fall and equilibrium prices to go up unless the merger produces cost savings that are large enough to offset the effect. The increase in price is due to the fact that, by merging, firms maximize profits jointly across plants and incorporate in their calculation the loss of profits in all production centers associated with the decrease in prices that results from a higher output in any of the plants. That said, Cournot as a merger simulation model can have some odd properties. For example, Salant et al. (1983) show that if we assume that the change in market structure is exogenous, many mergers in Cournot games will actively reduce the joint profits of the merging firms.[2] Such a situation challenges directly the plausibility of the model, since it questions the profit motivation to complete such a merger. In extremis, one might argue that such a result ultimately means that the model is either wrong or only consistent with a merger whose motivation is efficiency gain. This issue will not arise in pricing games where all mergers will be potentially profitable and, depending on your point of view, this is either a problem (firms are judged guilty by the authority's choice of model) or a virtue (the authority can examine how much efficiency gain is needed

[2] In fact, they show that in the Cournot model (and in the absence of efficiencies), a merger between two firms is always bad for the merging firm unless the merger is a two-to-one merger creating a monopoly. The reason is that parties to the merger always restrict output post merger but their nonmerging rivals respond to their abstinence by increasing output since quantity games are games of strategic substitutes.

to offset the price increases likely to arise when producers of substitute products merge). We discuss the "endogenous merger" constraint, that mergers should be expected to be profitable, further below.

8.2.1.2 Numerical Example

A simple practical example is useful to illustrate how to operationalize a merger simulation. Let us assume an industry with three symmetric firms and the following demand function:

$$P = a - b(q_1 + q_2 + q_3) = 1 - (q_1 + q_2 + q_3).$$

In this example we have assumed for simplicity that $a = b = 1$. In practice, the demand function will have to be estimated or calibrated prior to a merger simulation.[3] This is generally the trickiest and most crucial part of the exercise. We assume throughout this chapter that demand is known and refer the reader to chapter 9 for a discussion of issues the investigator faces when attempting to estimate demand. We also assume, purely for simplicity, that marginal costs are zero so that $\text{mc} = 0$.

In a market with N symmetric firms ($Q = Nq_i$) the Nash equilibrium of firm i will be

$$q_i = \frac{a - \text{mc}}{b(N+1)}$$

so that, in our case,

$$q_i = \frac{1-0}{1(3+1)} = \frac{1}{4}.$$

Since the firms have symmetric costs, the total quantity produced in the market before the merger is

$$Q^{\text{Pre}} = 3 \times \tfrac{1}{4} = \tfrac{3}{4}.$$

The corresponding price is

$$P^{\text{Pre}} = 1 - \tfrac{3}{4} = \tfrac{1}{4}.$$

Each firm has a market share of $\frac{1}{3}$.

The HHI before the merger is

$$\text{HHI}^{\text{Pre}} = 10{,}000 \sum_{i=1}^{N} s_i^2 = 10{,}000((\tfrac{1}{3})^2 + (\tfrac{1}{3})^2 + (\tfrac{1}{3})^2) = 3{,}333.$$

---

[3] One simple approach to calibrating the demand function, if an estimate of the own-price elasticity of demand is available, perhaps from an earlier econometric study, is to take an observation on price and quantity and then note that $\eta = (P/Q) \times (\partial Q/\partial P)$ so that with the linear demand function $b = [(Q/P) \times (-\eta)]$ and then $a = bQ + P$. This is to say that if (η, P, Q) are treated as known, we can construct both a and b.

Now let us consider the merger of two firms. The new HHI index as calculated for screening purposes is

$$\text{HHI}^{\text{Post}}_{\text{Noneq}} = 10{,}000 \sum_{i=1}^{N} s_i^2 = 10{,}000((\tfrac{1}{3})^2 + (\tfrac{2}{3})^2) = 5{,}555.$$

The increase or "delta" in the HHI is 2,222. Both the HHI level and the change in the HHI would make this hypothetical merger come under the scrutiny of competition authorities under either the European Commission or the U.S. Horizontal Merger Guidelines.

Next let us calculate the post-merger equilibrium prices and quantities. Using the Cournot equilibrium formula and taking into account the fact that there are now two firms ($N = 2$), we obtain the production level for each firm

$$q_i^{\text{Post}} = \tfrac{1}{3},$$

the total market output

$$Q^{\text{Post}} = \tfrac{2}{3}$$

and the market price

$$P^{\text{Post}} = 1 - (\tfrac{1}{3} + \tfrac{1}{3}) = \tfrac{1}{3}.$$

As predicted by the theory, the total production of the two production units (firms pre-merger, plants post-merger) that merged is now lower since it goes from $\frac{1}{2}$ to $\frac{1}{3}$. The higher prices induce the nonmerging firm to expand output as a reaction and its production increases from $\frac{1}{4}$ to $\frac{1}{3}$. Note that the HHI calculated on the new equilibrium output and market shares is considerably lower than the raw calculation of HHI commonly used to screen mergers:

$$\text{HHI}^{\text{Post}}_{\text{Equ}} = 10{,}000((\tfrac{1}{2})^2 + (\tfrac{1}{2})^2) = 5{,}000.$$

The simulation of mergers using the Cournot model was proposed and discussed in Farrell and Shapiro (1990).[4] In that paper the authors discuss asymmetries in costs and size and cost functions with economies of scale. They show that mergers in a Cournot industry will always result in higher prices unless there are efficiency gains. With efficiencies, a merger may reduce prices if concentration increases the output produced by the larger more efficient firm. However, Farrell and Shapiro argue that the efficiencies or economies of scale necessary to produce that result must be rather large.

8.2.1.3 Static versus Dynamic models

Merger analysis is based on comparative statics of equilibrium outcomes meaning that two equilibrium outcomes are compared: the pre-merger equilibrium outcome

[4] The article also discusses total welfare effect of mergers in Cournot industries.

and the post-merger equilibrium outcome with one firm less operating in the market. Such an approach implicitly assumes that the merger decision is exogenous and not, for example, caused as a dynamic response to market conditions. The baseline counterfactual assumes that absent the merger the world would not change.[5] In fact, mergers may occur precisely because the market is not in equilibrium and one optimal way of reacting to prevailing conditions may be to purchase a competitor. In this case, taking the pre-merger situation as the situation that would prevail absent the merger is potentially problematic since the pre-merger situation was not stable. Similarly, competitors may react to the merger, perhaps by merging.[6]

The version of the HHI calculation that is typically used by competition agencies to screen mergers is an extreme example of ignoring the dynamic aspects of competition because they assume that the post-merger market shares of those outside the merger are unchanged while those inside the merger are simply the total of the pre-merger market shares. In Cournot models, a merger is predicted to cause merging firms to decrease their output and competitors to increase their production as a response. Market shares will change analogously and so the typically calculated HHI therefore tends to systematically overestimate the level of concentration in the market after the merger. Still, this does not invalidate the use of HHI as a useful screening device since even exact HHI calculations will still only be a rough indicator of whether a merger is likely to be problematic. The greater the "stickiness" in market shares perhaps because switching by consumers only takes place over long periods the better the approximation will be, at least in the short term.

Taking into account the dynamics of the market is extremely difficult since numeric dynamic games, while actively under development by the academic community, remain in their infancy. In addition, dynamic models generally involve multiple equilibrium solutions. Most numeric dynamic models in industrial organization build on the framework introduced by Maskin and Tirole (1988a), Ericson and Pakes (1995), and Pakes and McGuire (2001). Gowrisankaran (1999) builds on their framework but also introduces a model where horizontal mergers are endogenously determined according to a particular auction process. His paper has the merit of illustrating the interrelation of merger decisions with decisions regarding entry, exit, and investment. The model is consistent with the fact that by internalizing some of the externalities generated by an investment, a merger may promote such investment. Mergers may prevent exit of failing firms with the subsequent loss of

[5] The counterfactual is a favorite term among merger investigators and merging parties' advisors alike. It is used to indicate the situation that would be the case absent the merger, perhaps because the merger were prohibited. To evaluate the merger the right benchmark may be the status quo, or it may be a more appropriate benchmark dependent on the particular facts of the case. For example, if a firm is failing, then the right counterfactual is not two competing firms absent the merger, but rather one failed firm and one active firm. Sometimes by verifying that a firm truly is failing competition agencies will allow a merger that would otherwise have been blocked.

[6] We know empirically that mergers appear to come in "waves." In addition, theoretical research suggests that mergers are best considered as strategic complements, suggesting that one merger may make another merger more likely. See Nocke and Whinston (2007).

capital from the industry. Mergers may also generate more industry profits and induce entry. Still, the analytical solution of such a model is not straightforward if not outright impossible and the particular auction specification he used is just one of many possible ways of endogenizing the merger process. Such activities provide a serious avenue for research but do not appear likely to provide a practical toolbox for merger authorities in the immediate future.

The general practice in the near term is therefore likely to remain for us to keep on using static models with exogenous mergers and in many cases this will provide a satisfactory approximation of the short-run effects of a merger. The next steps are likely to be exogenous mergers evaluated using dynamic frameworks such as that provided by Ericson and Pakes (1995) and also static models with an endogenous merger decision, or at least a merger decision which satisfies the endogenous merger constraint that post-merger profits should be expected to be higher. For now such activities remain largely in the realm of research, although practitioners should both be aware of such emerging developments and also wary of applying static frameworks in markets where dynamic factors are particularly important in the kinds of time horizons (a few years) that authorities often have in mind.[7]

8.2.2 Merger Efficiencies

In most standard oligopoly models, a merger among competitors will result in a drop in the quantity produced by the merging parties and an increase in prices charged to consumers. Such a perspective on mergers provides at best only a very narrow view of the potential motivations of mergers. Mergers can be strategic in nature, perhaps bringing together a company great at marketing with another whose skills lie in product design or engineering. Perhaps companies may simply realize that by joining production efforts, they can produce output more efficiently than they could as separate companies. Joint production can create synergies, allow the exploitation of economies of scale, and facilitate the better use of expertise. For each of these reasons, mergers may create production efficiencies and actively reduce costs. When those cost reductions are passed on to consumers, they may offset the negative effect of the loss of a competitor on market prices and output.

8.2.2.1 Rationale for Efficiencies in Merger Simulation

It is only relatively recently that efficiency considerations were introduced into merger appraisals. While making the case for efficiency arguments in merger analysis, Williamson (1977) acknowledged that noneconomists and particular the legal community would be reticent to include the analysis of a complex trade-off into their assessment but, in the event, Williamson was right to be hopeful about the future of

[7] Most authorities make consumer welfare claims from intervention against proposed mergers only over two or three years.

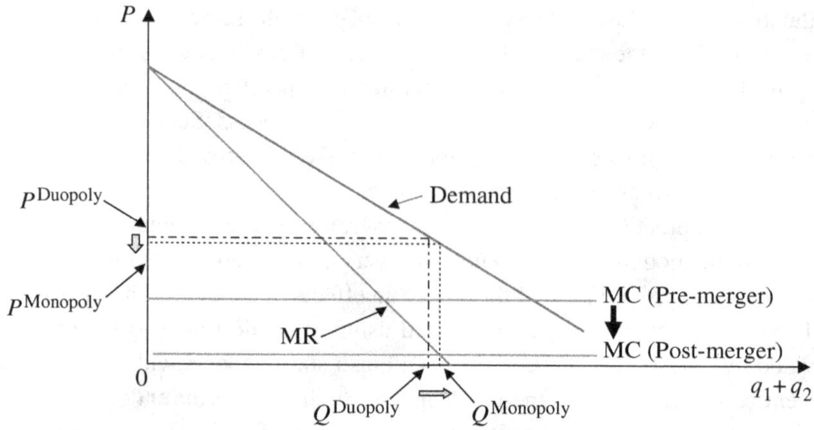

Figure 8.3. A two-to-one merger with substantial efficiencies. In this example, the reduction in marginal costs means post-merger prices are actually below the pre-merger prices despite the increase in market power generated by the merger.

the efficiency defense. Although the parties of mergers still have the burden to prove that efficiency gains exist and are relevant, it is now widely accepted that efficiencies may have a potential countervailing positive effect in the post-merger world.

In a nutshell, the basic efficiency defense goes as follows. When mergers lead to reduction in the costs of production it is no longer obvious that the merger will have a detrimental effect for the consumer even if the merger generates additional market power. Lower marginal costs will tend to lower prices and increase output. The relative magnitude of this effect compared with the negative impact of the merger due to the elimination of a competitor will depend on the magnitude of the cost savings, the elasticity of demand, and the extent of competition pre- and post-merger. Although the rationale is very simple, the case-by-case analysis may be quite complex.[8]

To illustrate the effect of cost efficiencies, let us consider a merger from a duopoly to a monopoly that reduces production marginal costs.

Figure 8.3 illustrates how the increase in prices due to monopoly pricing can be more than offset by the fall in marginal costs. The initial duopoly price is chosen to be lower than the monopoly price but higher than the marginal cost, a prediction common to all oligopolistic forms of competition. The post-merger price is the monopoly price which can be calculated by equating marginal cost to marginal revenue, as would be suggested by a monopolist maximizes her profits.

This example can be generalized to any merger where the elimination of a player will increase the margins that the remaining firms can obtain but where the merger

[8] A less common but equally valid efficiency defense involves the quality of the product. If a merger will result in a higher-quality product, demand may shift out as a result of the merger. Although prices may not decrease, even if the costs of production increase, total consumer welfare may be higher post-merger than before the merger.

generates cost efficiencies. In those cases, the final outcome on prices to consumers is uncertain but it is generically possible that cost reductions can be large enough for the merger to actually induce decreases in prices compared with the pre-merger situation.

The empirical assessment of the impact of the efficiencies on prices and quantities requires an estimate of the marginal costs of the post-merger firm. Unless the post-merger market is perfectly competitive, in which case one wonders what an authority is investigating, the analyst who wishes to quantify efficiency effects using a merger simulation model will need to model the competition and recompute market equilibrium prices in order to calculate the level of pass-on of the cost savings to the final consumer. In the symmetric Cournot setting, doing so will require adjusting for the number of firms and using the new lower-cost figure to estimate the new equilibrium prices. In the differentiated product industries discussed later in this chapter, the pricing equations of multiproduct firms can be constructed under the new ownership structure and at the new marginal costs. But before we discuss that popular model we first discuss the multiplant production model since it lies at the heart of many a stated efficiency defense.

8.2.2.2 *Marginal Costs in Multiplant Production*

One very straightforward source of potential cost efficiencies is the rationalization that involves allocating production efficiently across plants.[9] We first outline the argument and then comment on whether such an argument is likely to lead to efficiencies that are likely to be achieved absent the merger. Consider a merger that involves two firms and results in one firm with two plants. Let us assume a plant H with a cost function $C_{\mathrm{H}}(q_{\mathrm{H}})$ and a plant L with cost function $C_{\mathrm{L}}(q_{\mathrm{L}})$. The plants produce q_{H} and q_{L} respectively. The combined revenue from production is $R(q_{\mathrm{H}}+q_{\mathrm{L}})$. Note that the combined revenue depends on the total production and it does not depend on where the goods are produced. This is because the price obtained for each product will not depend on the plant where it originated. Profits on the other hand will depend on the allocation of production across plants since this allocation will influence total costs. The firm profit maximization is represented by

$$\max_{q_{\mathrm{H}},q_{\mathrm{L}}} \Pi = R(q_{\mathrm{H}}+q_{\mathrm{L}}) - C_{\mathrm{H}}(q_{\mathrm{H}}) - C_{\mathrm{L}}(q_{\mathrm{L}}),$$

which gives the first-order condition result in the following equivalence:

$$\mathrm{MC_H}(q_{\mathrm{H}}) = \mathrm{MC_L}(q_{\mathrm{L}}) = \mathrm{MR}(q_{\mathrm{H}}+q_{\mathrm{L}}).$$

For profit maximization, the marginal costs of production in both plants must be the same and equal to marginal revenue. The tendency to equate marginal costs is intuitive. If marginal costs are lower in a particular plant, the firms will get more

[9] This section follows closely elements of a lecture the author originally taught with Tom Stoker at MIT and who originally constructed the numerical example we use in this section.

profits by producing the next units in that lower-cost plant. Production will be allocated to the most efficient plant until the efficiency advantage is exhausted and producing at that plant is no longer cheaper.

Let us assume the following marginal cost functions for plants H and L respectively:

$$\mathrm{MC_H}(q_\mathrm{H}) = 5 + \frac{q_\mathrm{H}}{10} \quad \text{and} \quad \mathrm{MC_L}(q_\mathrm{L}) = 4 + \frac{q_\mathrm{L}}{20}.$$

Each plant's marginal cost is linear and increases in quantity so that there are diseconomies of scale. The firm will produce only in the low-cost plant until an extra unit becomes as costly to produce as in the high-cost plant. In this example, it will produce in plant L until $q_\mathrm{L} = 21$. The 22nd unit costs the same whether it is produced in plant L or in plant H:

$$\mathrm{MC_H}(1) = 5 + \frac{1}{10} = 5.1 \quad \text{and} \quad \mathrm{MC_L}(22) = 4 + \frac{22}{20} = 5 + \frac{2}{20} = 5.1.$$

For an output larger than 21 units, the firm will allocate production across the two plants so that the marginal costs stay equal. To formalize the marginal cost function of the firm for an output larger than 21, we take the horizontal sum of the marginal cost curves. Performing a horizontal sum requires defining the total production at each level of marginal costs. The marginal cost curve of each plant can be expressed in the following way:

$$q_\mathrm{H} = -50 + 10\mathrm{MC} \quad \text{and} \quad q_\mathrm{L} = -80 + 20\mathrm{MC}.$$

Then,

$$q_\mathrm{T} = q_\mathrm{H}(\mathrm{MC}) + q_\mathrm{L}(\mathrm{MC}) = -130 + 30\mathrm{MC}.$$

Rearranging that expression we can write the marginal cost curve for the firm:

$$\mathrm{MC_T}(q_\mathrm{T}) = \begin{cases} 4 + \dfrac{q_\mathrm{T}}{20} & \text{if } q_\mathrm{T} \leqslant 21, \\[2ex] \dfrac{130}{30} + \dfrac{q_\mathrm{T}}{30} & \text{if } q_\mathrm{T} > 21. \end{cases}$$

Figure 8.4 illustrates the marginal costs function of the firm owning both plants, $\mathrm{MC_T}(q_\mathrm{T})$.

The optimal choice of production fulfilling the requirement that marginal revenue equals marginal cost is represented by figure 8.5.

This simple example illustrates the fact that profit maximization is associated with a very specific allocation of production across plants with different costs. A merger will pool plants and put them under a single management with the potential effect that production efficiency will increase due to a more efficient use of capacity. This type of efficiency will appear when there are cost asymmetries across merged plants and there is no post-merger capacity constraint at the more efficient centers of

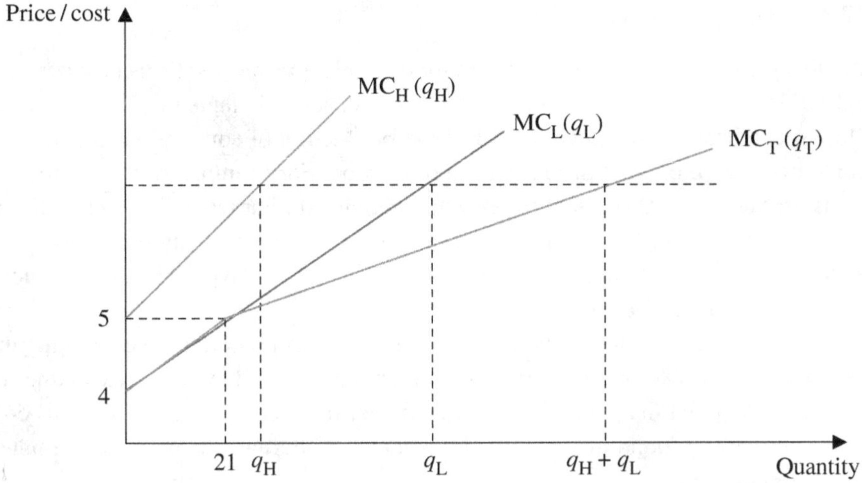

Figure 8.4. Derivation of a multiplant firm's marginal cost curve.

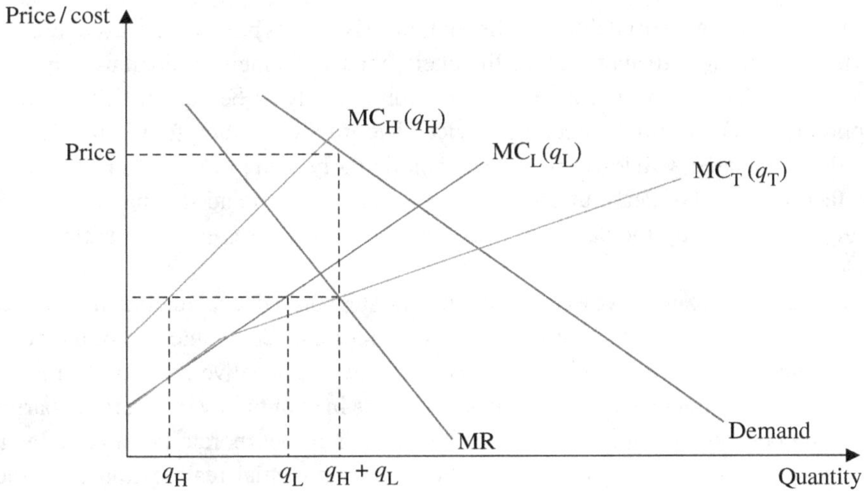

Figure 8.5. Pricing with a multiplant monopoly firm.

production. Notice, however, that such efficiencies are, in and of themselves, unlikely to generate efficiencies for merger evaluation since they will usually be generated by prices even with multiple single-plant firms. Specifically, any two firms producing homogeneous products so that they face the same market demand, and hence the same marginal revenue curve, will also tend to act to equalize marginal costs across active plants since each will expand production until their marginal cost equals the common marginal revenue associated with producing one more unit of the good. In most jurisdictions, efficiencies must be "merger specific" to count.

8.2.2.3 Multiproduct Firms

Efficiency gains can be obtained when, for example, pre-merger firms produce several different products in the same plant. Merging several plants might for instance allow specialization by allocating all of the production of some good to one plant and letting the other plant produce a different good. For example, if two competing plants produce several types of paper which require similar technologies but different pressing plates, a merger may allow the firm to save costs by eliminating the downtime needed to change plates if the number of different types of paper produced in each plant can be reduced.

Estimating the marginal costs for the new merged firm will require estimating the cost savings. One needs to have information on the costs of having the extra lines of product in the plant that could be eliminated after the merger. Estimates of this cost can sometimes be found in company documents or, alternatively, may be estimated by plant managers.

8.2.3 The HHI and the Welfare Effect of Mergers

Traditionally, the Herfindahl–Hirschman Index (HHI) has been widely used by competition authorities to approximate the likely impact of a merger, albeit usually with the acknowledgement that the approximation is likely to be very rough and only appropriate as an initial screening device. The implicit assumption is that a high HHI is associated with lower welfare and particularly with lower consumer welfare. In fact, there is no clear-cut correlation between the two and this has been gradually recognized by the decreasing reliance of merger assessment on simple HHI calculations.

Earlier in the chapter we established that the standard HHI calculation undertaken by merger authorities is an imperfect prediction of the actual outcome of a merger. Even under the Cournot model, it will overestimate the negative effect of the merger because it does not take into account adjustments in quantity by the merging parties and competitors. In addition, the HHI also does not incorporate possible gains in efficiency from the merger and in particular any potential reallocation of output across plants or the existence of other sources of synergies brought about by the merger are not considered, even though they may lead to real industry-wide gains in productive efficiency. We saw that Williamson's analysis suggests that a merger that increases output at currently large firms and reduces it at small firms will result in a higher HHI but may potentially increase welfare if the reallocation of production generated cost savings that are large enough.

In a Cournot world, efficient firms tend to be large and their less efficient brethren are smaller. There is no product differentiation and there are no dynamics. In markets with high degree of product differentiation, the concentration of the market may not capture either the extent of market power or more generally the extent and nature of competitive constraints faced by firms. Similarly, as is the case for merger simulations, in dynamic markets with entrants, technological change, or structural shifts of demand, the HHI is at best a highly imperfect instrument to capture the likely impact of a merger.

For all these reasons, the use of HHI is typically limited to contributing to determining the degree of scrutiny that a merger deserves and is certainly not necessarily indicative of the outcome of a more in-depth assessment.

8.3 General Model for Merger Simulation

Merger simulation is easily applied in homogeneous product markets that fit the type of competition characterized by a Cournot game. This is particularly true because in homogeneous markets there is only one single demand function to estimate and if estimation proves too difficult there are few parameters to "guess," infer, or approximate from industry information. However, merger simulation can be used in any competitive interaction framework and many, probably most, merger simulations are performed in industries where there is product differentiation and firms are assumed to compete on prices as in the Bertrand game. That said, the methodology of merger simulation is entirely general and conceptually relatively simple so that in general its application is primarily limited by the ability of economists to estimate suitable demand and cost models and embed those into a suitable framework describing both firms' individual motivations and the nature of their interaction. There is usually also a computation problem, since we must solve for best responses and then equilibrium. For example, in a pricing game, we must solve for the firms' pricing equations under the different models of oligopolistic competition being used by the investigator.

8.3.1 The General Framework

All merger simulations require that one writes down a structural model involving the following equations: (1) a demand equation or a system of demand equations (one for each product in the market); (2) a cost function or a marginal cost function for each product; (3) a description of the firms' strategic variables (e.g., prices, advertising, or quantities) and their objectives (e.g., to maximize profits); and (4) a description of the way in which all the firms' competing objectives fit together, usually via an equilibrium assumption. We will follow the literature in emphasizing pricing as the strategic variable in differentiated product contexts, but there is no conceptual difficulty in considering, for example, advertising. Indeed, in most merger inquiries the fundamental question is whether there will be a substantial lessening of competition as a result of the merger. We discuss each of the above-mentioned elements in turn.

Demand. To write down a demand function one may want to make well-motivated assumptions about consumers' preferences and build up from that level of detail to firms' or market demand curves. That is the approach taken by most microeconomics texts, but doing so is not always necessary since, for example, we do not need to go into incredible depth about whether consumers really are utility-maximizing consumers if, at the end of the day, all that will matter for price setting is the extent to which a firm's demand curve slopes down.[10] However, in other cases we will want to consider carefully questions such as the following. What is the set of options that are actually considered by consumers? Is there a sequence in the way consumers make decisions? Are consumers largely choosing a market segment and then comparing prices of similar options or are they comparing combinations of characteristics across products, perhaps trading off quality of the product against its cost across a wider set of products? We will also sometimes need to understand the ways in which consumers differ. The reality of merger simulations is that the nature of consumer demand may have very important impacts on the result of the merger simulations and it is therefore not surprising that in confrontational judicial or regulatory settings, arguments will often revolve around the adequacy of the demand specification. There are several standard demand functions that are commonly used to describe consumer preferences and each of them will have implications for the prediction of the effect of a merger. For an in-depth discussion of the main techniques, we refer the reader to chapter 9, where demand estimation is discussed in more detail.

Costs. Cost functions can also be explicitly laid out taking into account the technological characteristics of the production process. Are there diseconomies of scale? Do we have constant marginal costs? For the determination of equilibrium prices, only marginal costs will typically be relevant, although that is subject to the very important caveat that pricing on that basis nonetheless allows firms to recover their fixed costs so that their economic profits in such an equilibrium are positive. One option is to estimate marginal cost curves directly from industry cost information if this is possible. However, sometimes, given the pricing equations, the market prices and demand parameters, marginal costs can be inferred. In those cases, the accuracy of the cost estimate will be hugely dependent on both the demand estimates and the model of competition being the "right" model. It is vital then to perform appropriate reality checks to see whether the marginal cost estimates make any sense at all. It is not at all unusual in such an exercise to get negative marginal cost estimates at the first attempt. This is usually an indication that either the competition assumption is wrong or else the demand estimates are. The question that needs to be addressed is why. Tracking down the source of apparently crazy predictions is a very valuable part of the process of developing a sensible model.

---

[10] This is the case, for example, in a normal monopoly setting where a profit-maximizing firm will set margins equal to the inverse of the price elasticity of demand. All that matters then for market power is the price elasticity of demand, not whether the demand function comes from rational carefully optimizing consumers or indeed fairly hopelessly optimizing ones. All that matters to the firm when setting prices is how sensitive consumer demand is to prices.

Strategic Variables and Firm Objectives. The strategic variables are those variables which firms choose in a way that takes into account decisions being taken by rivals. The key strategic variables can usually be inferred from company documents since, for example, those who compete on prices may well actively study their rivals' prices and analyze whether they in turn are pricing at the right level in light of that analysis. Alternatively, the appropriate strategic variables could be quantities, advertising, and/or indeed product quality although in many cases decisions around product quality are considered as longer-term strategic decisions. For example, American Airlines famously decided to expand the space allocated for each economy class seat but it is probably fair to say that changing the configuration of a large number of aircraft is more complex and harder to reverse than reversing a price change. Moving on to firm objectives, generically we will follow traditional economic analysis in assuming that firms maximize profits, although we do pause to note that in principle one could certainly build and indeed empirically test simulation models based around other behavioral assumptions.[11]

The Nature of Competition. The last explicit assumption that is needed for merger simulation is a description of the nature of the competition taking place in the industry. When describing firms' strategic variables and their objectives, we have outlined a world in which firms attempt to pursue objectives that are rarely mutually reinforcing. Indeed, the essence of competition is that firms act independently, ignoring the impact on rivals' profits that follows, say, a decision to decrease price. As a result we must explicitly describe the way in which firms' disparate objectives fit together. Simulation models follow the traditional economic approach of defining a notion of "equilibrium" as the way of fitting those various competing objectives together. Of course, since there are potentially many ways of resolving conflicting objectives, economics has developed many potential equilibrium assumptions. That said, there is a core traditional set of equilibrium assumptions based around Nash equilibrium for models involving perfect information, and Bayesian Nash equilibrium for models involving imperfect information.[12]

---

[11] Note that in a particular sense "behavioral economics" is misnamed. All economics is behavioral but most neoclassical economics makes the behavioral assumption that consumers maximize utility and that firms maximize profits. As an aside, it is striking that when talking to competition agencies, some who favor behavioral approaches infer that it will lead to much more intervention while others infer exactly the opposite. If firms do not profit maximize, perhaps they, at least in part, act altruistically and with an eye to corporate responsibility and caring about their customers. If so, one side of the debate argues that we should not worry so much about market power. Similarly, if firms behaviorally maximize market share rather than profits, then again the appropriate policy might involve far less worry about market power. On the other side, if consumers do not take information seriously, choice confuses them, or consumers are not able to make rational choices at all, then there is considerably more of a case for intervention to protect them. The appeal to behavioral economics is common, though the stories told are of quite different character and unsurprisingly therefore lead proponents of each view to very different conclusions from each other about the appropriate policy stance.

[12] In addition, the concept of Markov perfect equilibrium has received a great deal of attention by the numeric dynamic industry model builders (see, for example, Ericson and Pakes 1995).

There are two main models used in practical merger simulation. First, the Cournot model, where the product is homogeneous and firms' strategic variables are output levels, which they choose to maximize profits. The equilibrium assumption is a pure strategy Nash equilibrium. The second most popular model is the differentiated product Bertrand model, where firms compete in prices and produce differentiated products. In that case the strategic variables are prices, the firms' objectives are again profit maximization, and the equilibrium assumption is again Nash. We have already developed merger simulation within a simple Cournot model and we will go on next to develop merger simulation for the differentiated products Bertrand model. But any well-specified competition game that would produce sufficiently analytically or numerically tractable pricing, advertising, or quantity equations could in principle be used for merger simulation. Unfortunately, not many complex models will produce easily characterized equilibrium conditions and for this reason these two relatively simple models remain popular for merger simulation exercises. That said the practicing economists' potential toolkit is clearly far richer than Cournot and differentiated product Bertrand models.

When estimating merger simulation models one can either proceed by estimating the demand and cost sides of the model and then inputting them into the pricing/quantity/advertising equations, or one can attempt to estimate the demand, cost, and pricing/quantity/advertising equation parameters together. The right approach may depend on the data and in particular on the reliability of the supply side of the model and the equilibrium assumption since these provide a great deal of information potentially about demand-side parameters, if the model is correct. If it is not correct, then imposing the supply side of the model and the equilibrium concept being used will bias the estimates of the demand-side parameters. This observation can also potentially form the basis of a Durbin–Wu–Hausman style test of the pricing equations. For example, in the Bertrand model we can estimate the pricing and demand models simultaneously, which gives us an efficient and consistent estimate of both under the null hypothesis that the pricing model is correct and we can then estimate the demand parameters alone, which gives us consistent estimates of the demand-side parameters even if the pricing equations are incorrect. Such a comparison is the basic mechanism of the Hausman test.[13]

Given estimated demand and cost parameters of the model, we will see in the next section that the investigator can easily consider changes in ownership structure by modifying the pricing equations appropriately, as well as the cost equations if needed, and then computing the new equilibrium solution. Comparing the pre- and post-merger equilibrium prices and quantities will give an estimate of the (static) effects of the merger. At the end of the day, the simulation model is just a theoretical model to which we give particular values to the parameters via estimation or calibration

[13] See, for example, the discussion in chapter 2 or Maddala (1989), in particular pp. 435–36, or Hausman (1978).

that we hope are either right or sufficiently close to being right to be helpful. The model can then be used to predict changes in prices but also the change in profits and consumer welfare following the merger. Once a model is in hand, we will see that performing merger simulations becomes extremely simple. Of course, getting to the point where the model's predictions are reasonable is usually not a matter of simply estimating demand and costs and then running the simulation. Usually, a battery of robustness checks and sensitivity analyses will need to be performed. Often the first few attempts at estimation will fail at least some of those tests and this should result in an improvement of the model. Typically, the experience will also leave the analyst with either a better understanding of the market being investigated or at least good questions about the economics of the market being studied. Often the model will not fit in one or more directions and that, together with the facts of the industry, may point the investigator to the need to enrich the model in a particular direction.

8.3.2 Implementation of a Merger Simulation in Price-Setting Competition

In the rest of this section we present a more technical discussion of merger simulation under different competitive settings. We introduce mergers under price-setting competition and illustrate the steps required to practically implement a merger simulation in an industry with differentiated products. Basic knowledge of matrix algebra is assumed in most of what follows. The reader who is only interested in a nontechnical discussion of merger simulation may want to read the nontechnical introductions to the different topics and jump directly to the discussion of the concrete examples of simulations performed in the context of actual investigations.

8.3.2.1 Single-Product Firms

When the merger occurs in a market where every firm produces only one product, the pre-merger pricing equations result from a simple profit maximization exercise on the sale of only one product for every firm. For each firm, only one demand function and one cost function is relevant. There will be one pricing equation for each product in the market. To find the equilibrium prices of the J goods sold in the market given the demand parameters and a vector of marginal costs for each good we need "only" to solve analytically or numerically the set of J (potentially nonlinear) pricing equations, one for each product (here firm). This is just like solving any other J-dimensional set of nonlinear equations and computer programs can generally be used to tackle the task. In many cases it is possible to fairly easily solve for the equilibrium prices for up to a few hundred prices.[14]

[14] In fact, a nice property of pricing games is that they appear to have very nice convergence properties meaning that often simple algorithms such as iterated best responses will in fact often converge to equilibrium prices. See, for example, the work on pricing games in Milgrom and Roberts (1990) and the discussion below.

Let us assume J single-product firms engage in a Bertrand pricing game in a differentiated product market. That is, we suppose that each firm solves the following profit-maximization problem:

$$\max_{p_j} \Pi_j(p_j, p_{-j}) = \max_{p_j}(p_j - \text{mc}_j(w_j; \theta_1))D_j(\underline{p}; \theta_2),$$

where j indicates the product of the firm and $-j$ indicates the other products in the market with $j = 1, \dots, J$ while w_j are marginal cost shifters. The first-order condition (FOC) is

$$D_j(\underline{p}; \theta_2) + (p_j - \text{mc}_j(w_j; \theta_1))\frac{\partial D_j(\underline{p}; \theta_2)}{\partial p_j} = 0,$$

where $\underline{p} = (p_j, p_{-j}) = (p_1, \dots, p_J)$ is the just vector of prices of all the goods in the market written in three different ways. Rearranging the FOC produces the standard Bertrand pricing equation:

$$\frac{p_j - \text{mc}_j(w_j; \theta_1)}{p_j} = \frac{1}{\eta_j(p_1, \dots, p_J; \theta_2)},$$

where

$$\eta_j(\underline{p}; \theta_2) \equiv -\frac{\partial \ln D_j(\underline{p}; \theta_2)}{\partial \ln p_j}$$

is the own-price elasticity of demand of product j. We have one of these equations for each $j = 1, \dots, J$ products giving a total of J nonlinear equations to solve for the J equilibrium prices, $\underline{p}$.

Pre-merger actual prices are observed. What needs to be estimated are the demand and cost parameters in the equations, (θ_1, θ_2). We use pre-merger market prices and quantities to estimate the parameters of the demand systems using one of the demand estimation methods outlined in chapters 2 and 9. In addition, when possible estimates of costs are directly retrieved from company or industry information, the parameters of the cost function can be estimated. Alternatively, if we have a good estimate of the demand system the marginal costs can potentially be retrieved from the equilibrium price equation. That is, instead of solving the J first-order conditions for equilibrium prices given demand functions and marginal cost functions, instead we may solve the J first-order conditions for the J marginal costs, one for each product. We do so by assuming that we know about the shape of the demand system and that the observed prices in the market are exactly equilibrium prices. Doing so means we can plug the equilibrium (observed) prices into the J equations as known values, and then solve for the J remaining unknowns, namely the marginal costs, mc_j, $j = 1, \dots, J$. (For an algebraic description of this process using linear demand curves, see section 8.3.2.4.)

Typically, we will therefore use the pricing equations in two ways. First, using pre-merger data on prices and the model of demand we will solve the pricing equations for the J marginal costs. Then, once the parameters of the demand and cost components of the model are obtained, the post-merger equilibrium prices can be obtained by plugging the demand and cost functions into the pricing equation that corresponds to the new post-merger ownership structure. Our second use of the pricing equation then involves taking demand system estimates together with estimates of marginal costs, possibly obtained from the pre-merger period, and solving for predicted equilibrium prices using post-merger market structure. The latter approach ensures that pre-merger prices will match the data exactly and then post-merger prices, quantities, and profits can be computed using the model and compared with their pre-merger values to assess the effect of the merger.

The post-merger firm will produce more than one product. In contrast with what happens in the homogeneous product market, the new firm does not combine the capacities of the merged firms to produce a unique product. Instead, it considers the optimal pricing (and output) decision for both differentiated products previously produced by the independent single-product firms. In doing so, the new firm will internalize the effect of the price increase of one of its goods on the demand and sales of the remaining goods that it produces. If the goods the firm produces are substitutes, the effect of the merger will generally involve an increase in the equilibrium prices of all goods.

To see this process in the context of our model, let us suppose the market has two products: i and j (or 1 and 2). Suppose also that the two firms producing one product each merge to form a monopoly. The pricing equations for the new firm are the result of the following maximization problem:

$$\max_{\underline{p}} \Pi(p_i, p_j) = \max_{\underline{p}} (p_i - \text{mc}_i) D_i(\underline{p}) + (p_j - \text{mc}_j) D_j(\underline{p}).$$

The first-order conditions are

$$\frac{\partial \Pi(p_i, p_j)}{\partial p_i} = D_i(\underline{p}) + (p_i - \text{mc}_i) \frac{\partial D_i(\underline{p})}{\partial p_i} + (p_j - \text{mc}_j) \frac{\partial D_j(\underline{p})}{\partial p_i} = 0,$$

$$\frac{\partial \Pi(p_i, p_j)}{\partial p_j} = D_j(\underline{p}) + (p_j - \text{mc}_j) \frac{\partial D_j(\underline{p})}{\partial p_j} + (p_i - \text{mc}_i) \frac{\partial D_i(\underline{p})}{\partial p_j} = 0.$$

The pricing equations can be directly derived from the first-order conditions by solving for $\underline{p}$. We can then compute the post-merger prices by plugging the previously estimated demand and cost parameters into the new pricing equations. In this case, the only extra information that we need in order to simulate the merger compared with the case of a homogeneous product is an estimate of the cross-price elasticities of demand. Potentially, there are two cross-price effects,

$$\frac{\partial D_1(\underline{p})}{\partial p_2} \quad \text{and} \quad \frac{\partial D_2(\underline{p})}{\partial p_1},$$

which may in general be different from one another. In a simple parametric demand function, these cross-price effects will be determined by additional parameters in

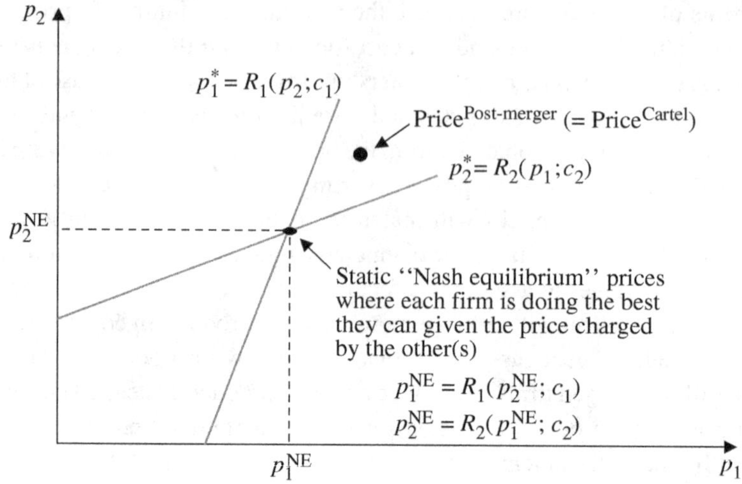

Figure 8.6. A two-to-one merger in a differentiated product pricing game.

the demand model. For example, the linear model could involve $D_2(\underline{p}) = a_2 + b_{21}p_1 + b_{22}p_{22}$ so that $\partial D_2(\underline{p})/\partial p_1 = b_{21}$ and, analogously, $\partial D_1(\underline{p})/\partial p_2 = b_{12}$.

Note that if the two products are substitutes and $\partial D_i(\underline{p})/\partial p_j > 0$, then the equilibrium price for a firm maximizing joint profits will be higher, absent countervailing efficiencies. This is because the monopolist, unlike the single-product firm in the duopoly, gains the profits from the customers who switch to the competing product after a price increase. We illustrated this fact for the two-product game in chapter 2.

The effect of a merger in a two-to-one merger in a market with two differentiated single-product firms is illustrated in figure 8.6. Because Bertrand price competition with differentiated products is a model where products are strategic complements, the reaction functions are increasing in the price of the other good. The intersection of the two pricing functions gives the optimal price for the Bertrand duopoly. After the merger, the firm will price differently since it internalizes the effect of changing the price of a product on the other product's profits. This will result in higher prices for both products. In this case, the post-merger price is also that which would be associated with a perfect cartel's prices.

8.3.2.2 *Multiproduct Firms*

Let us now consider the case of a firm producing several products pre-merger. If a market is initially composed of firms producing several products, this means that firms' profit maximization already involves optimization across many products. The pricing equation of given goods will also depend on the demand and cost parameters of other goods which are produced by the same firm. A merger will result in a change in the pricing equation of certain goods as the parameters of the cost and demand of the products newly acquired by the firm will now enter the pricing equations of all previously produced goods. This is because the number of products over which the post-merger firm is maximizing profits has changed relative to the pre-merger situation.

Suppose firm f produces a set of products which we denote $\Im_f \subseteq \Im = \{1, \dots, J\}$ and which is unique to this firm. The set of products produced by the firm does not typically include all J products in the market but only a subset of those. The profit-maximization problem for this firm involves maximization of the profits on all the goods produced by the firm:

$$\max_{\underline{p}_f} \sum_{j \in \Im_f} \Pi_j(\underline{p}_f, \underline{p}_{-f}) = \max_{\underline{p}_f} \sum_{j \in \Im_f} (p_j - \text{mc}_j) D_j(\underline{p}).$$

Solving for the profit-maximizing prices will result in a set of first-order conditions. For firm f, the system of first-order conditions is represented as follows:

$$D_k(\underline{p}) + \sum_{j \in \Im_f} (p_j - \text{mc}_j) \frac{\partial D_j(\underline{p})}{\partial p_k} = 0 \quad \text{for all } k \in \Im_f.$$

To these equations, we must add the first-order conditions of the remaining firms so that in the end we will, as before in the single-product-firms case, end up with a total of J first-order conditions, one for each product being sold. Solving these J equations for the $J \times 1$ vector of unknown prices p^* will provide us with the Nash equilibrium in prices for the game.

In comparison with the case where firms produced only a single product, the first-order conditions for multiproduct firms have extra terms. This reflects the fact that the firms internalize the effect of a change in prices on the revenues of the substitute goods that they also produce. Because of differences in ownership, first-order conditions may well not have the same number of terms across firms.

To simplify analysis of this game, we follow the literature and introduce a $J \times J$ ownership matrix Δ with the jkth element (i.e., jth row, kth column) defined by

$$\Delta_{jk} = \begin{cases} 1 & \text{if same firm produces } j \text{ and } k, \\ 0 & \text{otherwise.} \end{cases}$$

We can rewrite the first-order conditions for each firm $f = 1, \dots, F$ as

$$D_k(\underline{p}) + \sum_{j=1}^{J} \Delta_{jk} (p_j - \text{mc}_j) \frac{\partial D_j(\underline{p})}{\partial p_k} = 0 \quad \text{for all } k \in \Im_f,$$

where the Δ_{jk} terms allow the summation to be across all products in the market in all first-order conditions for all firms. The matrix Δ acts to select the terms that involve the products produced by firm f and changes with the ownership pattern of products in the market. At the end of the day, performing the actual merger simulations will only involve changing elements of this matrix from zero to one and tracing through the effects of this change on equilibrium prices. Once again, we will have a set of equations for every firm resulting in a total of J pricing equations, one first-order condition for each product being sold.

In order to estimate demand parameters, we need to specify demand equations. For simplicity, let us assume a system of linear demands of the form,

$$q_k = D_k(p_1, p_2, \ldots, p_J) = a_k + \sum_{j=1}^{J} b_{kj} p_j \quad \text{for } k = 1, \ldots, J.$$

This specification conveniently produces

$$\frac{\partial D_k(p)}{\partial p_j} = b_{kj}.$$

So that the first-order conditions become

$$a_k + \sum_{j=1}^{J} b_{kj} p_j + \sum_{k=1}^{J} \Delta_{jk}(p_j - \text{mc}_j) b_{jk} = 0$$
$$\text{for all } k \in \Im_f \text{ and for all } f = 1, \ldots, F.$$

This will sometimes be written as

$$q_k + \sum_{k=1}^{J} \Delta_{jk}(p_j - \text{mc}_j) b_{jk} = 0 \quad \text{for all } j, k = 1, \ldots, J$$

but one must then remember that the vector of quantities is endogenous and dependent on prices. Writing the system of equations this way and adding it together with the demand system provide the $2J$ equations which we could solve for the $2J$ endogenous variables: J prices and J quantities. Doing so provides the direct analogue to the standard supply-and-demand system estimation that is familiar for the homogeneous product case. Sometimes we will find it easier to work with only J equations and to do so we need only substitute the demand function for each product into the corresponding first-order condition. Doing so allows us to write a J-dimensional system of equations which can be solved for the J unknown prices.

Large systems of equations are more tractable if expressed in matrix form. Following the treatment in Davis (2006d) to express the demand system in matrix form, we need to define the matrix of demand parameters B' as

$$B' = \begin{bmatrix} b_{11} & \cdots & b_{1j} & \cdots & b_{1J} \\ \vdots & & \vdots & & \vdots \\ b_{k1} & \cdots & b_{kj} & \cdots & b_{kJ} \\ \vdots & & \vdots & & \vdots \\ b_{J1} & \cdots & b_{Jj} & \cdots & b_{JJ} \end{bmatrix},$$

where $b_{kj} = \partial D_k(p)/\partial p_j$, and also define

$$a = \begin{bmatrix} a_1 \\ \vdots \\ a_k \\ \vdots \\ a_J \end{bmatrix},$$

which is the vector of demand intercepts and where the prime on B indicates a transpose. The system of demand equations can then be written as

$$\begin{bmatrix} q_1 \\ \vdots \\ q_k \\ \vdots \\ q_J \end{bmatrix} = \begin{bmatrix} a_1 \\ \vdots \\ a_k \\ \vdots \\ a_J \end{bmatrix} + \begin{bmatrix} b_{11} & \cdots & b_{1j} & \cdots & b_{1J} \\ \vdots & & \vdots & & \vdots \\ b_{k1} & \cdots & b_{kj} & \cdots & b_{kJ} \\ \vdots & & \vdots & & \vdots \\ b_{J1} & \cdots & b_{Jj} & \cdots & b_{JJ} \end{bmatrix} \begin{bmatrix} p_1 \\ \vdots \\ p_j \\ \vdots \\ p_J \end{bmatrix},$$

or, far more compactly in matrix form, as $q = a + B'p$.

In order to express the system of pricing equations in matrix format, we need to specify the $J \times J$ matrix $\Delta \cdot B$, which is the element-by-element product of Δ and B, sometimes called the Hadamard product.[15] Note that B is the transpose of B'. Specifically, define

$$\Delta \cdot B = \begin{bmatrix} \Delta_{11}b_{11} & \cdots & \Delta_{j1}b_{j1} & \cdots & \Delta_{J1}b_{J1} \\ \vdots & & \vdots & & \vdots \\ \Delta_{1k}b_{1k} & & \Delta_{jk}b_{jk} & & \Delta_{Jk}b_{Jk} \\ \vdots & & \vdots & & \vdots \\ \Delta_{1J}b_{1J} & \cdots & \Delta_{jJ}b_{jJ} & \cdots & \Delta_{JJ}b_{JJ} \end{bmatrix},$$

where $b_{jk} = \partial D_j(p)/\partial p_k$. The rows will include the parameters of the pricing equation of a given product k. The term Δ_{jk} will take the value of either 1 or 0 depending on whether the firm produces goods j and k or not and $\Delta_{jj} = 1$ for all j since the producer of good j produces good j.

Recall the analytic expression for the pricing equations:

$$D_k(\underline{p}) + \sum_{j=1}^{J} \Delta_{jk}(p_j - \text{mc}_j)\frac{\partial D_j(\underline{p})}{\partial p_k} = 0 \quad \text{for all } k \in \Im_f \text{ and for all } \Im_f.$$

The vector of all J first-order conditions can now be expressed in matrix terms as

$$a + B'p + (\Delta \cdot B)(p - c) = 0,$$

[15] Such matrix products are easily programmed in most computer programs. For example, in Gauss define $A = B * C$ to define the Hadamard element-by-element product so that $a_{jk} = b_{jk}c_{jk}$ for $j = 1, \dots, J$ and $k = 1, \dots, J$.

where

$$c = \begin{bmatrix} \text{mc}_1 \\ \vdots \\ \text{mc}_J \end{bmatrix} \quad \text{and} \quad a = \begin{bmatrix} a_1 \\ \vdots \\ a_J \end{bmatrix}.$$

Alternatively, as we have already mentioned we may sometimes choose to work with the J pricing equations without substituting the demand equations: $q + (\Delta \cdot B)(p - c) = 0$. We will then need to work with a system of equations comprising these J equations and also the J demand equations.

Written in matrix form, the equations that we need to solve simultaneously can then compactly be written as

$$q + (\Delta \cdot B)(p - c) = 0 \quad \text{and} \quad q = a + B'p.$$

Using a structural form specification with all endogenous variables on the left side of the equations and the exogenous ones on the right side we have

$$\begin{bmatrix} (\Delta \cdot B) & I \\ -B' & I \end{bmatrix} \begin{bmatrix} p \\ q \end{bmatrix} = \begin{bmatrix} (\Delta \cdot B) & 0_{(J \times J)} \\ 0_{(J \times J)} & I_{(J \times J)} \end{bmatrix} \begin{bmatrix} c \\ a \end{bmatrix},$$

which is equivalent to

$$\begin{bmatrix} p \\ q \end{bmatrix} = \begin{bmatrix} (\Delta \cdot B) & I \\ -B' & I \end{bmatrix}^{-1} \begin{bmatrix} (\Delta \cdot B) & 0_{(J \times J)} \\ 0_{(J \times J)} & I_{(J \times J)} \end{bmatrix} \begin{bmatrix} c \\ a \end{bmatrix}.$$

This expression gives an analytic solution for all prices and all quantities for any ownership structure that can be represented in Δ since we may arbitrarily change the values of Δ_{jk} from 0s to 1s to change the ownership structure provided only that we always respect the symmetry condition that $\Delta_{jk} = \Delta_{kj}$.

With this system in place, once the parameters in B, c, and a are known, we can calculate equilibrium prices after a merger by setting the corresponding elements of Δ_{jk} to 1. Indeed, we can calculate the equilibrium prices and quantities (and hence profits) for any ownership structure.

8.3.2.3 Example of Merger Simulation

To illustrate the method, consider the example presented in Davis (2006f), a market consisting of six products that are initially produced by six different firms. Suppose the demand for product 1 is approximated by a linear demand and its parameters have been estimated as follows:

$$q_1 = 10 - 2p_1 + 0.3p_2 + 0.3p_3 + 0.3p_4 + 0.3p_5 + 0.3p_6.$$

By a remarkably happy coincidence, the demands for other products have also been estimated and conveniently turned out to have a similar form so that we can write the full system of demand equations in the form

$$q_j = 10 - 2p_j + 0.3 \sum_{k \neq j} p_k \quad \text{for } j = 1, 2, \ldots, 6.$$

Let us assume marginal costs of all products are equal to 1 and that the merger will generate no efficiencies so that $c_j^{\text{Pre}} = c_j^{\text{Post}} = 1$ for $j = 1, 2, \ldots, 6$.

The pricing equation for the single-product firm is derived from the profit maximization first-order condition and takes the form

$$\frac{\partial \Pi(p_j)}{\partial p_j} = D_j(\underline{p}) + (p_j - c_j)\frac{\partial D_j(\underline{p})}{\partial p_j} = 0.$$

In our example this simplifies to

$$q_j = (p_j - c_j)(2).$$

The system of pricing and demand equations in the case of six firms producing one product each is then written as a total of twelve equations:

$$\begin{bmatrix} (\Delta^{\text{Pre}} \cdot B) & I \\ -B' & I \end{bmatrix} \begin{bmatrix} p \\ q \end{bmatrix} = \begin{bmatrix} (\Delta^{\text{Pre}} \cdot B) & 0_{(J \times J)} \\ 0_{(J \times J)} & I_{(J \times J)} \end{bmatrix} \begin{bmatrix} c \\ a \end{bmatrix},$$

where Δ^{Pre} takes the form of the identity matrix and

$$B' = \begin{bmatrix} -2 & 0.3 & 0.3 & 0.3 & 0.3 & 0.3 \\ 0.3 & -2 & 0.3 & 0.3 & 0.3 & 0.3 \\ 0.3 & 0.3 & -2 & 0.3 & 0.3 & 0.3 \\ 0.3 & 0.3 & 0.3 & -2 & 0.3 & 0.3 \\ 0.3 & 0.3 & 0.3 & 0.3 & -2 & 0.3 \\ 0.3 & 0.3 & 0.3 & 0.3 & 0.3 & -2 \end{bmatrix},$$

$$(\Delta^{\text{Pre}} \cdot B) = \begin{bmatrix} -2 & 0 & 0 & 0 & 0 & 0 \\ 0 & -2 & 0 & 0 & 0 & 0 \\ 0 & 0 & -2 & 0 & 0 & 0 \\ 0 & 0 & 0 & -2 & 0 & 0 \\ 0 & 0 & 0 & 0 & -2 & 0 \\ 0 & 0 & 0 & 0 & 0 & -2 \end{bmatrix},$$

$$c = \begin{bmatrix} 1 \\ 1 \\ 1 \\ 1 \\ 1 \\ 1 \end{bmatrix}, \qquad a = \begin{bmatrix} 10 \\ 10 \\ 10 \\ 10 \\ 10 \\ 10 \end{bmatrix}.$$

We can solve for prices and quantities:

$$\begin{bmatrix} p \\ q \end{bmatrix} = \begin{bmatrix} (\Delta^{\text{Pre}} \cdot B) & I \\ -B' & I \end{bmatrix}^{-1} \begin{bmatrix} (\Delta^{\text{Pre}} \cdot B) & 0_{(J\times J)} \\ 0_{(J\times J)} & I_{(J\times J)} \end{bmatrix} \begin{bmatrix} c \\ a \end{bmatrix}.$$

If the firm that produced product 1 merges with the firm that produced product 5 the ownership matrix will change so that

$$(\Delta^{\text{Post-merger}} \cdot B) = \begin{bmatrix} -2 & 0 & 0 & 0 & 0.3 & 0 \\ 0 & -2 & 0 & 0 & 0 & 0 \\ 0 & 0 & -2 & 0 & 0 & 0 \\ 0 & 0 & 0 & -2 & 0 & 0 \\ 0.3 & 0 & 0 & 0 & -2 & 0 \\ 0 & 0 & 0 & 0 & 0 & -2 \end{bmatrix}.$$

This is because the new pricing equation for product 1 will be derived from the following first-order condition:

$$\frac{\partial \Pi(p)}{\partial p_1} = D_1(\underline{p}) + (p_1 - c_1)\frac{\partial D_1(\underline{p})}{\partial p_1} + (p_5 - c_5)\frac{\partial D_5(\underline{p})}{\partial p_1} = 0,$$

which in our example results in

$$q_1 = (p_1 - c_1)(2) - (p_5 - c_5)(0.3).$$

New equilibrium prices and quantities can then be easily calculated using the new system of equations:

$$\begin{bmatrix} p \\ q \end{bmatrix} = \begin{bmatrix} (\Delta^{\text{Post-merger}} \cdot B) & I \\ -B' & I \end{bmatrix}^{-1} \begin{bmatrix} (\Delta^{\text{Post-merger}} \cdot B) & 0_{(J\times J)} \\ 0_{(J\times J)} & I_{(J\times J)} \end{bmatrix} \begin{bmatrix} c \\ a \end{bmatrix}.$$

These kinds of matrix equations are trivial to compute in programs such as Matlab or Gauss. They may also be programmed easily into Microsoft Excel, making merger simulation using the linear model a readily available method. The predicted equilibrium prices for each product under different ownership structure are represented in table 8.1. The market structure is represented by $(n_1, \dots, n_F)$, where the length of the vector F indicates the total number of active firms in the market and each of the values of n_f represents the number of products produced by the fth firm in the market. The largest firm is represented by n_1. Tables 8.1 and 8.2 show equilibrium prices and profits respectively for a variety of ownership structures. The results show, for example, that a merger between a firm that produces five products and one firm that produces one product, i.e., we move from market structure (5, 1) to the market structure with one firm producing six products (6), increases the prices by more than 33%. Table 8.2 shows that the merger is profitable.

Table 8.1. Prices under different ownership structures.

Product	Market structure $(n_1, \dots, n_F)$					
	(1, 1, 1, 1, 1, 1)	(2, 2, 2)	(3, 3)	(4, 2)	(5, 1)	6 (Cartel)
1	4.8	5.3	5.9	6.62	7.87	10.5
2	4.8	5.3	5.9	6.62	7.87	10.5
3	4.8	5.3	5.9	6.62	7.87	10.5
4	4.8	5.3	5.9	6.62	7.87	10.5
5	4.8	5.3	5.9	5.77	7.87	10.5
6	4.8	5.3	5.9	5.77	5.95	10.5

Table 8.2. Profits under different ownership structures.

Firms	Market structure $(n_1, \dots, n_F)$					
	(1, 1, 1, 1, 1, 1)	(2, 2, 2)	(3, 3)	(4, 2)	(5, 1)	6 (Cartel)
1	28.88	63.39	105	139	188.54	270.8
2	28.88	63.39	105	77.6	48.99	
3	28.88	63.39				
4	28.88					
5	28.88					
6	28.88					
Industry profits	173	190	210	217	238	270.8

8.3.2.4 *Inferring Marginal Costs*

In cases where estimates of marginal costs cannot be obtained from industry information, appropriate company documents, or management accounts, there is an alternative approach available. Specifically, it is possible to infer the whole vector of marginal costs directly from the pricing equations provided we are willing to assume that observed prices are equilibrium prices. Recall the expression for the pricing equation in our linear demand example:

$$a + B'p + (\Delta \cdot B)(p - c) = 0.$$

In merger simulations, we usually use this equation to solve for the vector of prices p. However, the pricing equation can also be used to solve for the marginal costs c in the pre-merger market, where prices are known. Rearranging the pricing equation we have

$$c = p + (\Delta \cdot B)^{-1}(a + B'p).$$

More specifically, if we assumer pre-merger prices are equilibrium prices, then given the demand parameters in (a, B) and the pre-merger ownership structure embodied in Δ^{Pre}, we can infer pre-merger marginal cost products for every product using the equation:

$$c^{\text{Pre}} = p^{\text{Pre}} + (\Delta^{\text{Pre}} \cdot B)^{-1}(a + B' p^{\text{Pre}}).$$

One needs to be very careful with this calculation since its accuracy greatly depends on having estimated the correct demand parameters and also having assumed the correct firm behavior. Remember that the assumptions made about the nature of competition determine the form of the pricing equation. What we will obtain when we solve for the marginal costs are the marginal costs implied by the existing prices, the demand parameters which have been estimated and also the assumption about the nature of competition taking place, in this case differentiated product Bertrand price competition.

Given the strong reliance on the assumptions, it is necessary to be appropriately confident that the assumptions are at least a reasonable approximation to reality. To that end, it is vital to proceed to undertake appropriate reality checks of the results, including at least checking that estimated marginal costs are actually positive and ideally are within a reasonable distance of whatever accounting or approximate measures of marginal cost are available. This kind of inference involving marginal costs can be a useful method to check for the plausibility of the demand estimates and the pricing equation. If the demand parameters are wrong, you may well find that the inferred marginal costs come out either negative or implausibly large at the observed prices. If the marginal costs inferred using the estimated demand parameters are unrealistic, then this is a signal that there is often a problem with our estimates of the price elasticities. Alternatively, there could also be problems with the way we have assumed price setting works in that particular market.

8.3.3 General Linear Quantity Games

In this section we suppose that the model that best fits the market involves competition in quantities. Further, suppose that firm f chooses the quantities of the products it produces to maximize profits and marginal costs are constant, then the firm's problem can be written as

$$\max_{\underline{q}_f} \sum_{j \in \Im_f} \pi_j(q_1, q_2, \dots, q_J) = \max_{\underline{q}_f} \sum_{j \in \Im_f} (P_j(q_1, q_2, \dots, q_J) - c_j) q_j,$$

where $P_j(q_1, q_2, \dots, q_J)$ is the inverse demand curve for product j. The representative first-order condition (FOC) for product k is

$$\sum_{j=1}^{J} \Delta_{kj} \frac{\partial P_j(q)}{\partial q_k} q_j + (P_k(q) - c_k) = 0.$$

We can estimate a linear demand function of the form $q = a + B'p$ and obtain the inverse demand functions

$$p = (B')^{-1} q - (B')^{-1} a.$$

In that case, the quantity setting equations become

$$(\Delta \cdot (B')^{-1})q + p - c = 0.$$

And we can write the full structural form of the game in the following matrix expression:

$$\begin{bmatrix} I & \Delta \cdot (B')^{-1} \\ -B' & I \end{bmatrix} \begin{bmatrix} \underline{p} \\ \underline{q} \end{bmatrix} = \begin{bmatrix} I & 0 \\ 0 & I \end{bmatrix} \begin{bmatrix} c \\ a \end{bmatrix}.$$

As usual, the expression that will allow us to calculate equilibrium quantities and prices for an arbitrary ownership structure will then be

$$\begin{bmatrix} \underline{p} \\ \underline{q} \end{bmatrix} = \begin{bmatrix} I & \Delta \cdot (B')^{-1} \\ -B' & I \end{bmatrix}^{-1} \begin{bmatrix} c \\ a \end{bmatrix}.$$

8.3.4 Nonlinear Demand Functions

In each of the examples discussed above, the demand system of equations had a convenient linear form. In some cases, more complex preferences may require the specification of nonlinear demand functions. The process for merger simulation in this case is essentially unaltered. One needs to calibrate or estimate the demand functions, solve for the pre-merger marginal costs if needed and then solve for the post-merger predicted equilibrium prices. That said, solving for the post-merger equilibrium prices is harder with nonlinear demands because it may involve solving a $J \times 1$ system of nonlinear equations. Generally, and fortunately, simple iterative methods such as the method of iterated best responses seem to converge fairly robustly to equilibrium prices (see, for example, Milgrom and Roberts 1990).

Iterated best responses is a method whereby given a starting set of prices, the best responses of firms are calculated in sequence. One continues to recalculate best responses until they converge to a stable set of prices, the prices at which all first-order conditions are satisfied. At that point, provided second-order conditions are also satisfied, we will know we will have found a Nash equilibrium set of prices. The process is familiar to most students used to working with reaction curves as the method is often used to indicate convergence to Nash equilibrium in simple two-product pricing games that can be graphed.

In practice, iterated best responses work as follows:

1. Define the best response for firm f given the rival's prices as the price that maximizes its profits under those market conditions:

$$R_f(\underline{p}_{-f}) = \underset{\underline{p}_f}{\operatorname{argmax}} \sum_{j \in \Im_f} (p_j - \text{mc}_j) D_j(\underline{p}).$$

2. Create the following algorithm (following steps 3–5) in a mathematical or statistical package.

3. Pick a starting firm $f=1$ and a starting value for the prices of all products
$$\underline{p}^0 = (\underline{p}_f^0, \underline{p}_{-f}^0).$$
Set $k = 0$.
4. For firm f, solve $\underline{p}_f^{k+1} = R_f(\underline{p}_{-f}^k)$ and set $p^{k+1} = (\underline{p}_f^{k+1}, \underline{p}_{-f}^k)$.
5. Iterate:
   - if $|\underline{p}^{k+1} - \underline{p}^k| < \varepsilon$, then stop;
   - else set $k = k + 1$ and $f = \begin{cases} f+1 & \text{if } f < F, \\ 1 & \text{otherwise;} \end{cases}$
   - go to step 4.

If the process converges, then all firms are setting $p_f^k = R_f(\underline{p}_{-f}^k)$ and we have by construction found a solution to the first-order conditions. Provided the second-order conditions are also satisfied (careful analysts will need to check), we have also found a Nash equilibrium.

In pricing games we do not need to use iterated best responses and typically a large range of updating equations will result in convergence of prices to an equilibrium price vector. In the empirical literature, it has been common to use a simply rearranged version of the pricing equation to find equilibrium prices. To ease presentation of this result we will change notation slightly. Specifically, we denote demand curves as $q(p)$ in order for $D_p q(p)$ to denote the differential operator with respect to p applied to $q(p)$. Specifically, denote the $J \times J$ matrix of slopes of the demand curves as $D_p q(p)$ which has (j,k)th element, $\partial q_j(p)/\partial p_k$. Using the general form of the first-order conditions for nonlinear demand curves, we can write our pricing equations as
$$q(p) + [\Delta \cdot D_p q(p)](p - c) = 0,$$
where as before the "dot" denotes the Hadamard product. As a result the empirical literature has often used the iteration
$$p^{k+1} = c - [\Delta \cdot D_p q(p^k)]^{-1} q(p^k)$$
to define a sequence of prices beginning from some initial value p^0, often set equal to c. In practice, for most demand systems used for empirical work, this iteration appears to converge to a Nash equilibrium in prices. The closely related equation
$$c = p - [\Delta \cdot D_p q(p)]^{-1} q(p)$$
can be used to define the value of marginal costs that are consistent with Nash prices for a given ownership structure in a manner analogous to that used for the linear demand curves case in section 8.3.2.4.

Iterated best responses do not generally work for quantity-setting games because convergence is not always achieved due to the form of the reaction functions. There are other methods of solving systems of nonlinear equations, but in general there are good reasons to expect iterated best responses to work and converge to equilibrium when best response functions are increasing.[16]

As in most games, one should in theory check for multiple equilibria. Once we have more than two products with nonlinear demands, the possible existence of multiple equilibria may become a problem and, depending on the starting values of prices, it is possible that we may converge to different equilibrium solutions. That said, if there are multiple equilibria, supermodular game theory tells us that in general pricing games among substitutes we will have "square" equilibrium sets. One equilibrium will be the bottom corner, another will be the top corner, and if we take the values of the other corners they will also be equilibria. This result is referred to as the fact that equilibria in pricing games are "complete lattices" (i.e., squares).[17] If we think firms are good at coordinating, one may argue that the high price equilibrium will be more likely. In that case, it may make sense to start the process of iterating on best responses from a particularly high prices levels since such sequences will tend to converge down to the high price and therefore high profit equilibrium.

Even though it is good practice, it is by no means common practice to report in great detail on the issue of multiple equilibria beyond trying the convergence to equilibrium prices from a few initial prices and verifying that each time the algorithm finds the same equilibrium.[18]

8.3.5 Merger Simulation Applied

In this section, we describe two merger exercises that were executed in the context of merger investigations by the European Commission. The discussion of these merger simulations includes a brief description of the demand estimation that underlies the simulation model, but we also refer the reader to chapter 9 for a more detailed exploration of the myriad of interesting issues that may need to be addressed in that important step of a merger simulation. The examples we present below illustrate

[16] The reason is to do with the properties of supermodular games. See, for example, the literature cited in Topkis (1998). In general, in any setting where we can construct a sequence of monotonically increasing prices with prices constrained within a finite range, we will achieve convergence of equilibrium. For those who remember graduate school real analysis, the underlying mathematical reason is that monotonic sequences in compact spaces converge. Although, in general, quantity games cannot be solved in this way, many such games can be (see Amir 1996).

[17] See Topkis (1998) and, in particular, the results due to Vives (1990) and Zhou (1994).

[18] Industrial economists are by no means unique in such an approach since the same potential for multiplicity was, for example, present in most computational general equilibrium models and various authors subsequently warned of the dangers of ignoring multiplicity in policy analysis. The computation of general equilibrium models became commonplace following the important contribution by Scarf (1973). The issue of multiplicity has arisen in applications. See, for example, the discussion in Mercenier (1995) and Kehoe (1985).

what actual merger simulations look like and also provide examples of the type of scrutiny and criticisms that such a simulation will face and hence the analyst needs to address.

8.3.5.1 The Volvo–Scania Case

The European Commission used a merger simulation model for the first time in the investigation of its Volvo–Scania merger during 1999 and 2000. Although the Commission did not base its prohibition decision on the merger simulation, it mentioned the fact that the results of the simulation confirmed the conclusions of the more qualitative investigation.[19] The merger involved two truck manufacturers and the investigation centered on five markets where the merger seemed to create a dominant firm with a market share of more than or close to 50% in Sweden, Norway, Finland, Denmark, and Ireland. Ivaldi and Verboven (2005) details the simulation model developed for the case. The focus of the analysis was on heavy trucks, which can be of two types known as "rigid" and "tractor," the latter carrying a detachable container.

The demand for heavy trucks was modeled as a sequence of choices by the consumer, who in this case was a freight transportation company. Those companies chose the category of truck they wanted and then the specific model within the chosen category.

A model commonly used to represent this kind of nested choice behavior is the nested logit model. In this case, because the data available were aggregate data, a simple nested logit model was estimated using the three-stage least-squares (3SLS) estimation technique (a description of this method can be found in general econometric books such as, for example, Greene (2007), but see also the remarks below). The nested logit model is worthy of discussion in and of itself and, while we introduce the model briefly below for completeness, the reader is directed to chapter 9 and in particular section 9.2.6 for a more extensive discussion. Here, we will just illustrate how assumptions about customer choices underpin the demand specifications we choose to estimate.

The nested logit model supposes that the payoff to individual i from choosing product j is given by the "conditional indirect utility" function:[20]

$$u_{ij} = \delta_j + \zeta_{ig} + (1 - \sigma)\varepsilon_{ij},$$

where δ_j is the mean valuation for product j which is assumed to be in nest, or group, g. We denote the set of products in group g as G_g. A diagram describing

[19] Commission Decision of 14.03.2000 declaring a concentration to be incompatible with the common market and the functioning of the EEA Agreement (Case no. COMP/M. 1672 Volvo/Scania) Council Regulation (EEC) no. 4064/89.

[20] This is termed the conditional indirect utility model because it is "conditional" on product j, while it depends on prices (through $\delta_j = -\alpha p_j + \beta x_j + \xi_j$ as explained further below). Direct utility functions depend only on consumption bundles.

the nesting structure in this example is provided in figure 9.5. Note that ε_{ij} is product-specific while ζ_{ig} is common to all products within group g for a given individual. The individual's total idiosyncratic taste for product j is given by the sum, $\zeta_{ig} + (1-\sigma)\varepsilon_{ij}$. The parameter σ takes a value between 0 and 1 and note that it controls the extent to which a consumer's idiosyncratic tastes are product- or group-specific. If $\sigma = 1$, the individual consumer's idiosyncratic valuations for all the products in a group are exactly the same and their preferences for each good in the group g are perfectly correlated. That means, for example, that a consumer who buys a good from group g will tend to be a consumer with a high idiosyncratic taste for all products in group g. In the face of a price rise by the currently preferred good j, such a consumer will tend to substitute toward another product in the same group since she tends to prefer goods in that group. In Volvo–Scania the purchasers of trucks were freight companies and if σ is close to 1 it captures the taste that some freight companies will prefer trucks to be rigid while others will prefer tractors, and in each case freight companies will not easily shop outside their preferred group of products. In contrast, if $\sigma = 0$ and we make a judicious choice for the assumed distribution of ζ_{ig}, then the valuation of products within a group is not correlated and consumers who buy a truck in a particular group will not have any systematic tendency to switch to another product in that group.[21] They will compare models across all product groups without exhibiting a particular preference for a particular group.

The average valuation δ_j is assumed to depend on the price of the product p, the observed characteristics of the product x_j, and the unobserved characteristics of the products ξ_j that will play the role of product specific demand shocks. In particular, a common assumption is that

$$\delta_j = -\alpha p_j + \beta x_j + \xi_j.$$

In this case, the observed product characteristics are horsepower, a dummy for "nationally produced," as well as country- and firm-specific dummies.

Normalizing the average utility of the outside good to 0, $\delta_0 = 0$, and making usual convenient assumptions about the distribution of the random terms, in particular, that they are type 1 extreme value (see, for example, chapter 9, Berry (1994), or, for the technically minded, the important contribution by McFadden (1981)), the nested logit model produces the following expression for market shares, or more precisely the probability s_j that a potential consumer chooses the product j:

$$s_j = \frac{\exp(\delta_j/(1-\sigma))D_g^{1-\sigma}}{D_g(1+\sum_{g=1}^{G} D_g^{1-\sigma})},$$

[21] This is by no means obvious. We have omitted some admittedly technical details in the formulation of this model and this footnote is designed to provide at least an indication of them. As noted in the text, for this group-specific effect formulation to correspond to the nested logit model, we must assume a particular distribution for ζ_{ig} and moreover one that depends on the value of σ so that it is more accurate to write $\zeta_{ig}(\sigma)$. In fact, Cardell (1997) shows that there is a unique choice of distribution for ζ_{ig} such that if ε_{ij} is an independent type I extreme value random variable, then $\zeta_{ig}(\sigma) + (1-\sigma)\varepsilon_{ij}$ is also an extreme value random variable provided $0 \leqslant \sigma < 1$.

where

$$D_g = \sum_{k \in G_g} \exp\left(\frac{\delta_k}{1-\sigma}\right)$$

and the expression for δ_j is provided above. The demand parameters to be estimated are α, β, and σ. To be consistent with the underlying theoretical assumptions of the model it turns out that we need some parameters to satisfy some restrictions. In particular, we need $\alpha > 0$ and $0 \leqslant \sigma \leqslant 1$. We discuss this model at greater length in chapter 9. For now we note one potentially problematic feature of the nested logit model: the resulting product demand functions satisfy the assumption of "independence of irrelevant alternatives" (IIA) within a nest. IIA means that if an alternative is added or subtracted in a group, the relative probability of choosing between two other choices in the group is unchanged. This assumption was heavily criticized by the opposing experts in the case.

The data needed for the estimation are the prices for all products, the characteristics of the products, and the probability that a particular good is chosen. This probability is approximated by the product market share so that

$$s_j = \frac{q_j}{M},$$

where q_j is the quantity sold of good j and M is the total number of potential consumers. The market share needs to be computed taking into account the outside good, which is why the total number of potential consumers and not the total number of actual buyers is in the denominator. Ivaldi and Verboven assume that the potential market is either 50% or 300% larger than the actual sales. A potential market that is 50% larger than market sales can be described as $M = 1.5(\sum_{j=1}^{J} q_j)$.

Ivaldi and Verboven (2005) linearize the demand equations using a transformation procedure proposed by Berry (1994). We refer the reader to the detailed discussion of that transformation procedure in chapter 9, for now noting that this procedure means that estimating the model boils down to estimation of a linear model using instrumental variables. In addition, the authors assume a marginal cost function which is constant in quantity and which depends on a vector of observed cost shifters w_j and an error term. The observed cost shifters included horsepower, a dummy variable for "tractor truck," a set of country-specific fixed effects, and a set of firm-specific fixed effects. The marginal cost function is assumed to be of the form,

$$c_j = \exp(w_j \gamma + \omega_j),$$

where γ is a vector of parameters to be estimated, w_j denotes a vector of observed cost shifters and ω_j represents a determinant of marginal cost that is unobserved by the econometrician and which will play the role of error terms in the pricing (supply) equations (one for each product). As we have described numerous times in this chapter, the profit of each firm f can be written as

$$\pi_f = \sum_{j \in \Im_f} (p_j - c_j) q_j(p) - F,$$

where $\Im_f$ is the subset of product produced by firm f, c_j is the marginal cost of product j, which is assumed to be constant, and F are the fixed costs. The Nash equilibrium for a multiproduct firm in a price competition game is represented by the set of j pricing equations:

$$q_j + \sum_{k \in \Im_f} (p_k - c_k) \frac{\partial q_k}{\partial p_j} = 0.$$

Replacing the marginal cost function results in the pricing equation:

$$q_j + \sum_{k \in \Im_f} (p_k - \exp(w_j \gamma + \omega_j)) \frac{\partial q_k}{\partial p_j} = 0 \quad \text{for } j \in \Im_f \text{ and also for each firm } f.$$

These J equations, together with the J demand equations, provide us with the structural form for this model. Note that the structural model involves a demand curve and a "supply" or pricing equation for each product available in the market, a total of $2J$ equations. The only substantive difference between the linear and this nonlinear demand curve case is that these supply (pricing) and demand equations must be solved numerically in order to calculate equilibrium prices for given values of the demand- and cost-side parameters and data.

The data used to estimate the model covered two years of sales from truck companies in sixteen European countries. To estimate the model, we use identification conditions based on the two error terms of the model. Specifically, we assume that at the true parameter values, $E[\xi_j(\beta^*, \gamma^*) \mid z_{1j}] = 0$ and $E[\omega_j(\beta^*, \gamma^*) \mid z_{2j}] = 0$ (where z_{1j} and z_{2j} are sets of instrumental variables) in order to identify the demand and supply equations. These moment conditions are exactly analogous to the moment conditions imposed on demand and supply shocks in the homogeneous product context.[22] Ivaldi and Verboven undertake a simultaneous estimation of the demand and pricing equations using a nonlinear 3SLS procedure. While in principle at least the demand side could be estimated separately, the authors use the structure to impose all the cross-equation parameter restrictions during estimation. The sum of horsepower of all competing products in a country per year and the sum of horsepower of all competing products in a group per year are used as instruments to account for the endogeneity of prices and quantities in both the demand and pricing equation following the approach suggested initially by Berry et al. (1995). The technique they use, 3SLS, is a well-known technique for estimation of simultaneous equation

[22] The analyst may on occasion find it appropriate to estimate such a model using $2J$ moment conditions, one for each supply (pricing) and demand equation. Doing so requires us to have multiple observations on each product's demand and pricing intersection, perhaps using data variation over time from each product (demand and supply equation intersection). Alternatively, it may be appropriate to estimate the model using only these two moment conditions and use the cross-product data variation directly in estimation. This approach may be appropriate when unobserved product and cost shocks are largely independent across products or else the covariance structure can be appropriately approximated.

Table 8.3. Estimates of the parameters of interest.

	Potential market factor			
	$r = 0.5$		$r = 3.0$	
	Estimates	Standard error	Estimates	Standard error
α	0.312	0.092	0.280	0.094
σ	0.341	0.240	0.304	0.240

Source: Table 2 from Ivaldi and Verboven (2005).

models. The first two stages of 3SLS are very similar to 2SLS while in the Ivaldi–Verboven formulation the third stage attempts to account for the possible correlation between the random terms across demand and pricing equations.

Estimation produces results consistent with the theory such as the fact that firm-specific effects that are associated with higher marginal costs produce higher valuations for consumers. Horsepower also increases costs. On the other hand, the authors find that horsepower has a negative albeit insignificant effect on customer valuation. The authors explain this by arguing that the higher maintenance costs associated with higher horsepower may lower the demand but the result is nevertheless somewhat troubling. The authors also report that they obtain positive and reasonable estimates for marginal costs and mean product valuations. The estimated marginal costs imply margins which were higher than those obtained in reality, although this observation was a criticism rejected by the authors on the grounds that accounting data do not necessarily reflect economic costs.

Table 8.3 shows the results for a subset of the demand parameters, namely α and σ, for two scenarios regarding the size of the total potential market. Specifically, $r = 0.5$ corresponds to $M = 1.5(\sum_{j=1}^{J} q_j)$ while $r = 3.0$ describes a potential market size 300% greater than the actual market size. The parameter σ is positive and less than 1 but insignificantly different from 0, which means that the hypothesis that rigid and tractor trucks form a single group of products cannot be rejected. Since the hypothesis that $\sigma = 1$ can be rejected, the hypothesis of perfect correlations in idiosyncratic consumer tastes across the various trucks within a group can be rejected.

Ivaldi and Verboven (2005) calculate the implied market demand elasticities for the two different potential market size scenarios. The larger the potential market size, the larger is the estimated share of the outside good and the higher is the implied elasticity. The reason is that the outside option has a higher likelihood—by construction. Estimating a large outside option produces a large market demand elasticity and therefore a smaller estimate of the effect of the merger. The higher elasticity was therefore chosen to predict the merger effect. Analysts using merger simulation models, or evaluating merger simulation models presented by the parties' expert economists, must be wary of apparently reasonable assumptions that are driving the results to be those desired for the approval of a merger.

Once the parameters for the demand, cost, and pricing equations are estimated for the pre-merger situation, post-merger equilibrium prices are computed using a specification of the pricing equations that takes into account the new ownership structure. That is, as before we change the definition of the ownership matrix, Δ. The new system of demand function and pricing equations, for which estimates of all the parameters are now known, needs to be solved numerically to obtain equilibrium prices and quantities. Equilibrium prices and quantities were also computed assuming a 5% reduction in marginal costs to simulate the potential effect of merger synergies on the resulting prices. The resulting estimated price increases are not duplicated here. Since the model is built on an explicit model of consumer utilities, we may use the model to calculate estimates of consumer surplus with and without the merger. The study finds that two countries—Sweden and Norway—would experience decreases in consumer welfare higher than 10% and three additional countries—Denmark, Finland, and Ireland—would each have consumer surplus declines larger than 5%. Finland, Norway, and Sweden were predicted to have consumer welfare decreases of more than 5% even in the event of a 5% reduction in marginal costs.

8.3.5.2 The Lagardère–VUP Case

A similar model was used in the context of the Lagardère–VUP case investigated by the European Commission in 2003, and this time the results of the simulation were cited in the arguments supporting the decision.[23] The merger was subsequently approved under some divestment conditions. The case involved the proposed acquisition by French group Lagardère, owner of the second largest publisher in the market, Hachette, of Vivendi Universal Publishing (now Editis), the largest publisher in the market. Foncel and Ivaldi performed the merger simulation for the Commission.[24] In this simulation, consumer preferences were also modeled using the nested logit model. The nesting structure involved consumers first choosing the genre of the book they wanted to buy (novel, thriller, romance, etc.) and then choosing a particular title.

The data used were from a survey of sales of the 5,000 pocket books and the 1,500 large books with the highest sales. The data included sales by type of retailer, prices, format, pages, editor, and title and author information. Only the general literature

[23] Commission Decision of 7.01.2004 declaring a concentration compatible with the common market and the functioning of the EEA Agreement (Case COMP/M.2978 Lagardère/Natexis/Vivendi Universal Publishing) Council Regulation (EEC) no. 4064/89. See paragraphs 700–707.

[24] "Evaluation Econométrique des Effets de la Concentration Lagardère/VUP sur le Marché du Livre de Littérature Générale," Jérôme Foncel et Marc Ivaldi, revised and expanded final version, September 2003.

titles were considered for the study. The total potential size of the market, M in the notation above, was defined as the number of people in the country that do not buy a book in the year plus the number of books sold during that year. The explanatory variables for both the demand and the cost function were the format of the book, the pages in the book, the purchase place, and measures of the authors' and editors' reputations.

The instruments chosen were versions of the observed variables such as the format of other books in the same category and the number of competing products, again following the approach suggested by Berry et al. (1995). Instruments are supposed to affect either the supply (pricing) equation or the demand but not both. To correctly identify the demand parameters, one must have at least one instrumental variable per demand parameter to be estimated on an endogenous variable that affects the supply of that product but not the demand. With the particular demand structure used in this case, if only price is treated as an endogenous variable and instrumented in the demand model and moreover price enters linearly in the conditional indirect utility model, then we need only one instrument to estimate the demand side in addition to the variables which explain demand and which are treated as exogenous (e.g., in this case the book characteristics). As in the previous case, the experts worked with aggregate data and estimated the parameters of the model using 3SLS. Based on the estimates obtained, they computed the matrix of own- and cross-price elasticities, the marginal costs, and therefore obtained the predicted margins.

To simulate the effect of the merger, the pricing equations were recalculated given the new ownership structure and the predicted equilibrium prices were calculated. The merger simulation estimated price increases of more than 5% for a market size smaller than 100 million. The merger simulation was also conducted assuming an ownership structure that incorporated remedies in the form of disinvestments by the new merged entity.

In addition to calculating the predicted price increase, the authors built a confidence interval for the estimated price increase using a standard bootstrap methodology. To do so, they sampled 1,000 possible values of parameters using their estimated distribution and calculated the corresponding price increases. Doing so allowed them to calculate an estimate of the variance of the predicted price increase.

8.4 Merger Simulation: Coordinated Effects

The use of merger simulation has been generally accepted in the analysis of unilateral effects of mergers. In principle, we can use similar techniques to evaluate the effect of mergers on coordinated effects. Kovacic et al. (2007) propose using the output from unilateral effects models to evaluate both competitive profits and also collusive profits and thereby determine the incentive to collude. The authors argue that such analyses can be helpful in understanding when coordination is likely to take place since firms can be innovative when finding solutions to difficult coordination problems if the incentives to do so are large enough (Coase 1988). Davis (2005) and Sabbatini (2006) each independently also argue that the same methods used to analyze unilateral effects in mergers can be informative about the way a change in market structure affects the incentives to coordinate.[25] However, they take a broader view of the incentives to collude and propose evaluating each of the elements of the incentive to collude that economic theory has isolated, following the classic analysis in Friedman (1971).[26] Staying close to the economic theory allows them to use simulation models to help inform investigators about firms' ability to sustain coordination, and in particular how that may change pre- and post-merger. In Europe, the legal environment also favors such an approach since the Airtours decision explicitly linked the analysis of coordinated effects to the economic theory of coordination.[27] We follow their discussion in the rest of this section and refer the reader to Davis and Huse (2008) for an empirical example applying these methods in the network server market.

8.4.1 Theoretical Setting

The current generation of simulation models that can be used to estimate the effect of mergers on coordinated effects rests on the same principles as the use of merger simulation in a unilateral effect setting. Each type of simulation model uses the estimates of the parameters in the structural model to calculate equilibrium prices and profits under different scenarios. Whereas in the simulation of unilateral effect, one need only calculate equilibrium under different ownership scenarios, in a coordinated effect setting, one must also calculate equilibrium prices and profits under different competition regimes, in a sense we make precise below.

8.4.1.1 Three Profit Measures from the Static Game

Firms face strong incentives to coordinate to achieve a higher prices, but when the higher prices prevail each firm usually finds it has an incentive to cheat to get a higher share of the profits generated by the higher price. This incentive to cheat may therefore undermine the strong incentive to collude.

Friedman (1971) suggested that to analyze the sustainability and therefore the likelihood of collusion one must evaluate the ability to sustain collusion and that is related to the incentives of each firm to do so. That in turn suggests that we need

---

[25] These authors have now combined working papers into a joint paper (Davis and Sabbatini 2009).

[26] Important theoretical contributions are currently being made. For the differentiated product context, see, most recently, Kühn (2004).

[27] *Airtours Plc v. Commission of the European Communities*, Case no. T342-99. The Commission's decision to block the Airtours merger with First Choice in 1999 was annulled by the European Court of First Instance (CFI) in June 2002. In the judgment the CFI outlined what have become known as the "Airtours" conditions building largely on the conventional economic theory of collusion.

to attempt to estimate, or at least evaluate, each of the three different measures of profit outlined above and which we now describe further:

(i) Own competitive profits π_f^{Comp} are easily calculated for all firms using the prices derived from the Nash equilibrium formula derived in our study of unilateral effects merger simulation.

(ii) Own fully collusive profits π_f^{Coll} may also be calculated using the results from unilateral effects merger simulation for the case where all products are owned by a single firm. Having used that method to calculate collusive prices, each firm's achieved share of collusive profits can be computed. Doing so means that firms will obtain profits from all the products in their product line but not those produced by rival firms. Because firms' product lines are asymmetric, the individual firm's collusive profits will not generally correspond to simply total industry profits divided by the number of firms.

(iii) Economic theory suggests that a firm's own defection profits π_f^{Def} should be calculated by setting all rival firms' prices to their collusive levels and then determining the cheater's own best price by finding the prices that maximize the profit the firm can achieve by undercutting rivals and boosting sales given their rivals' collusive prices and before their rivals discover that a firm is cheating. Capacity constraints may be an important issue and, as we show below, can be taken into account as a constraint in the profit-maximization exercise.

Specifically, consider a collusive market where rivals behave so as to maximize total industry profits and set prices at the cartel level. A defector firm f will choose its price to maximize its own profits from the goods it sells and will therefore fulfill the following first-order condition for maximization:

$$\max_{\{p_j \mid j \in \Im_f\}} \sum_{j \in \Im_f} (p_j - c_j) D_j(\underline{p}_f, \underline{p}_{-f}^{\text{Coll}}),$$

where j is a product in the set $\Im_f$ of products produced by firm f. Firm f chooses the set of prices $\underline{p}_f$ for all the goods $j \in \Im_f$ it produces at its profit-maximizing levels. The prices of all products from all firms except those of firm f are set at collusive levels.

If capacity utilization is high and firms face limits on the extent to which they can expand their output, we can include a capacity constraint restriction of the form $D_j(\underline{p}_f, \underline{p}_{-f}^{\text{Coll}}) \leqslant \overline{\text{Capacity}}_j$.

The competitive Nash equilibrium price, the collusive price, and the defection price are each represented in figure 8.7 for the case of a two-player game. The prices for defection are selected to fulfill $p_2^{\text{Def}} = R_2(p_1^{\text{Coll}}; c_2)$ and $p_1^{\text{Def}} = R_1(p_2^{\text{Coll}}; c_1)$.

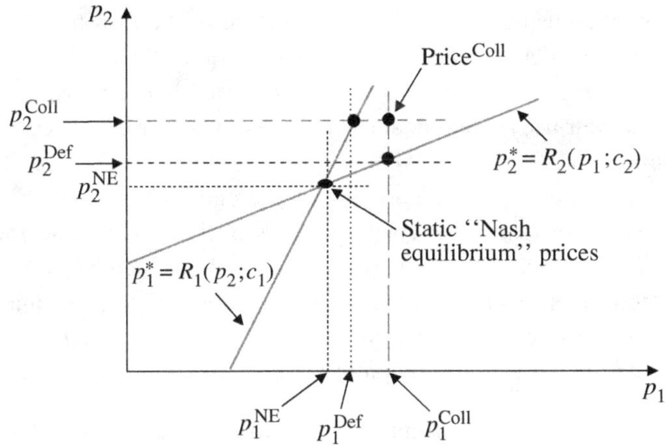

Figure 8.7. Depiction of the competitive Nash equilibrium price, the collusive price, and the defection price for a two-player pricing game. *Source*: Davis (2006f).

8.4.1.2 *Comparing Payoffs*

Now that we have defined the static payoffs under the different firm behaviors, we will need to construct the dynamic payoffs for a multiperiod game given the strategies being played. The economics of collusion rely on dynamic oligopoly models. To solve for equilibrium strategies in a dynamic game, we must specify the way in which firms will react if they catch their competitors cheating on a collusive arrangement. In such models, equilibrium strategies will be dynamic. One standard dynamic strategy that can sustain equilibria of the dynamic game is known as "grim strategies." Davis and Sabbatini (2009) use that approach and so assume that if a firm defects from a cartel, the market will revert to competition in all future successive periods.

If firms follow "grim strategies," then the cartel will be sustainable if there are no incentives to defect, which requires that the expected benefits from collusion be higher than the expected benefits from defection.

Formally, following Friedman (1971), the firm's incentive compatibility constraint can be written as

$$V_f^{\text{Coll}} = \frac{\pi_f^{\text{Coll}}}{1-\delta} > \pi_f^{\text{Def}} + \frac{\delta \pi_f^{\text{Comp}}}{1-\delta} = V_f^{\text{Cheat}},$$

where δ is the discount factor for future revenue streams (and which may be firm-specific and if so should be indexed by f). This inequality follows from subgame perfection, which requires that in collusive equilibrium firms must prefer to coordinate whenever they have the choice not to. Davis and Huse (2008) estimate each firm's discount factor δ using the working average cost of capital (WACC), which in turn is computed using the debt-equity structure of the firm together with estimates of the cost of debt finance and the cost of equity finance. The cost of debt can be observed from listed firms using their reported interest costs together with information on their use of debt finance. The cost of equity can be estimated using an asset pricing model such as CAPM which uses stock market data. To illustrate the potential importance of this, note that they found Dell to have an appreciably lower discount factor than other rivals, perhaps in light of the uncertainties during the data period arising from investor concern about the chance of success of its direct-to-consumer business strategy. Factors such as the rate of market growth and the chance of discovery by competition authorities may well be important to incorporate into these incentive compatibility constraints.

In multiperiod games, the incentives to tacitly coordinate will depend on the discount factor. The exact shape of the inequality will also depend on the strategies being used to support collusion. For instance, there may be a possibility to return to coordination after a period of punishment or there may not. If there is a punishment period, then we will also wish to calculate the net present value of the returns to the firm during the punishment period since that will enter the incentive compatibility constraint. (We will have another incentive compatibility constraint arising from the need for strategies followed during the punishment periods to be subgame perfect, although we know these incentive constraints are automatically satisfied under a punishment regime involving Nash reversion such as occurs when firms follow grim strategies.)

Next we further consider the example we looked at earlier in the chapter (see section 8.3.2.3 and in particular tables 8.1 and 8.2, which reported prices and profits in Nash equilibrium for a variety of market structures for the example) in which six single-product firms face a linear symmetric demand system. An example of the payoffs to defection under different ownership structures in the one-period game is presented in table 8.4. In our example, firms are assumed to have the same costs and demand and are therefore symmetric in all but product ownership structure. As we described above, the profits when a firm defects is calculated using the defection prices for the defecting firms and the cartel prices for the remaining firms. Without loss of generality, the table reports the results when firm 1 is the defector and the other firms set their prices at collusive levels.

Table 8.5 presents the net present value payoffs under both collusion and defection when defection is followed by a reversion to competition. Results are shown for different assumptions for the value of the discount factor and for two different market structures. With a zero discount factor, the firms completely discount the future and so the model is effectively a unilateral effects model. As the discount factor increases, future profits become more valuable and collusion becomes relatively more attractive. In the example with market structure = $(1, 1, 1, 1, 1, 1)$ so that there are six single-product firms, the critical discount factor is about 0.61. Collusion is

Table 8.4. One-period payoffs to defection and collusion.

Market structure/ firm	(1, 1, 1, 1, 1, 1)	(2, 2, 2)	(3, 3)	(4, 2)	(5, 1)	6 (Cartel)	Collusive payoffs under cartel
1	70.50	128.47	174.50	210.00	238.30	270.75	45.12
2	34.97	52.03	57.05	31.17	19.74		45.12
3	34.97	52.03					45.12
4	34.97						45.12
5	34.97						45.12
6	34.97						45.12

Firm 1: one-period defection payoffs after defection π_f^{Def}.
Source: Davis (2006f).

Table 8.5. The value of collusion and cheating under the two market structures.

	Market structure = (1, 1, 1, 1, 1, 1)		Market structure = (2, 2, 2)	
δ	V^{Coll}	V^{Cheat}	V^{Coll}	V^{Cheat}
0	45.1	70.5	90	128
0.1	50.1	73.7	100	136
0.2	56.4	77.7	113	144
0.3	64.4	82.9	129	156
0.4	75.2	89.8	150	171
0.5	90.2	99.4	180	192
0.6	112.8	113.8	226*	224
0.7	150.4*	137.8	301*	276
0.8	225.6*	186.0	451*	382
0.9	451.2*	330.4	902*	699
0.99	4,512.4*	2,929.0	9,025*	6,405

Source: Davis (2006f). *Denotes IC constraint satisfied.

sustainable for all discount factors higher than this value. Unsurprisingly, this is consistent with the general theoretical result that cartels are more sustainable with high discount factors, i.e., when income in the future is assigned a higher value.

We can calculate the critical discount factor for different market structures. To do so, the second set of figures correspond to a post-merger market structure where a total of three symmetric mergers have occurred, producing three firms each producing two products. Considering such a case, while a little unorthodox, is useful as a presentational device because it ensures that firms are symmetric post-merger as well as pre-merger, thus ensuring that every firm faces an identical incentive compatibility constraint before the merger and also afterward. This helps to present the results more compactly. The before-and-after incentives to collude are, of course, different from one another and, in fact, the critical discount factor after which collusion is sustainable with the new more concentrated market structure is reduced to just below 0.6, compared with 0.61 before the mergers.

For collusion to be an equilibrium, the incentive compatibility constraint must hold *for every single active firm*. In the example discussed, the firms are symmetric so all will fulfill this condition at the same time. For merger to generate a strengthening of coordinated effects, the inequality must hold in some sense "more easily" for all or some firms after the merger than it did before the merger. One way to think about "more easily" is to say coordination is easier post-merger if the inequality holds for a broader range of credible discount factors. On the other hand, Davis and Huse (2009) show that for a given set of discount factors, mergers will generically (1) not change perfectly collusive profits, (2) increase Nash profits, and (3) either leave unchanged defection profits (nonmerging firms) or increase them (merging firms). Since perfectly collusive profits are unchanged while (2) and (3) mean that the defection payoffs generally increase, the result suggests that mergers will generally make the incentive compatibility constraint for coordination harder to satisfy.

8.4.2 Merger Simulation Results for Coordinated Effects

The next two tables show numerical examples of the effect of mergers on the incentives to tacitly coordinate. We first note that the results confirm that asymmetric market structures can be bad for sustaining collusion. Table 8.6, for instance, shows that if the market has one large firm producing five products and one small firm producing one product, collusion will never be an outcome unless there is a system of side payments to compensate the smaller firm. In the table, stars denote situations where the incentive compatibility constraint (ICC) suggests that tacit coordination is preferable for that firm. This result from Davis (2006f) establishes that a "folk" theorem—which, for example, suggests that in homogeneous product models of collusion there will always exist a discount factor at which collusion can be sustained—do not universally hold in differentiated product models under asymmetry.

Table 8.7 presents two examples of merger simulation from three to two firms. Suppose the pre-merger market structure involves one firm producing four products and two firms producing one product each, denoted by the market structure (4, 1, 1). The ICCs for the four-product firm and the (two) one-product firms are shown in the last four columns of table 8.7. Tacit coordination appears sustainable if both firms ICCs are satisfied, which occurs if discount factors are above 0.8. First suppose that the larger firm acquires a smaller firm making the post-merger market structure (5, 1) and second suppose that in the other case the two smaller firms merge making the

Table 8.6. Example showing that folk theorems need not hold in differentiated product models.

Market structure	δ_f	Firm with five products IC constraint: Collude	Firm with five products IC constraint: Cheat	Firm with one product IC constraint: Collude	Firm with one product IC constraint: Cheat
(5,1)	0	226	238	45	71
(5,1)	0.1	251	259	50	76
(5,1)	0.2	282	285	56	83
(5,1)	0.3	322*	319	64	92
(5,1)	0.4	376*	364	75	103
(5,1)	0.5	451*	427	90	120
(5,1)	0.6	564*	521	113	144
(5,1)	0.7	752*	678	150	185
(5,1)	0.8	1,128*	992	226	266
(5,1)	0.9	2,256*	1,935	451	511
(5,1)	0.99	22,562*	18,904	4,512	4,921

Source: Davis (2006f). *Denotes IC constraint satisfied.
In this example, the small firm can never be induced to collude fully. It simply does too well from undercutting its larger rival under competition.

post-merger market structure $(4, 2)$. As before, stars show the scenarios in which collusion is sustainable according to an individual firm's ICC. If the two small firms merge, there is effectively no change in the incentives to collude and thus there will not be any change in the incentives for coordination. However, if the big firm buys one of the smaller firms, the likelihood of collusion actually diminishes! Indeed, in this example the presence of one small firm in a market playing against a far larger rival effectively makes coordination entirely unsustainable without side payments. Of course, it is important to note that such a result only establishes that perfect collusion is harder to sustain with asymmetric market structures, not that no collusion is possible.

Generally, the results from these kinds of models suggest that collusion is surprisingly easy to sustain. The results are surprising because we know empirically that cartels break down and often have an average lifespan measured in years rather than decades. (See the discussion on the duration of cartels in chapter 7 as well as Levenstein and Suslow (2006).) Reasons may include the difficulties of bargaining without communication, in particular, in a world with considerable uncertainty over prices, costs, outside options, and imperfect monitoring. In the theoretical literature, these issues have been tackled, for example, by Green and Porter (1984) and Rotemberg and Saloner (1986) and some empirical support for the patterns suggested by that literature are, for example, provided in Porter (1983) and Borenstein

Table 8.7. Results from a coordinated effects merger simulation model.

	(5, 1)				(4, 2)				(4, 1, 1)			
	Firm with 5 products		Firm with 1 product		Firm with 4 products		Firm with 2 products		Firm with 4 products*		Firm with 1 product	
δ	Co.	Ch.	Co.	Ch.	Co.	Ch.	Co.	Ch.	Co.	Ch.	Co.	Ch.
0.0	226	238	45	71	181	210	90	128	181	210	45	71
0.1	251	259	50	76	201	225	100	137	201	225	50	75
0.2	282	285	56	83	226	245	113	148	226	243	56	80
0.3	322*	319	64	92	258	270	129	162	258	267	64	87
0.4	376*	364	75	103	301	303	150	180	301*	299	75	96
0.5	451*	427	90	120	361*	349	181	206	361*	343	90	108
0.6	564*	521	113	144	451*	419	226	245	451*	410	113	127
0.7	752*	678	150	185	602*	534	301	310	602*	521	150	159
0.8	1,128*	992	226	266	902*	766	451*	439	903*	743	226*	222
0.9	2,256*	1,935	451	511	1,805*	1,461	902*	827	1,805*	1,410	451*	412

Source: Davis (2006f). *Denotes IC constraint satisfied.

and Shephard (1986). While Davis and Huse (2009) provide a fully fledged merger simulation model for the complete information case, there are not yet any empirical coordinated effects merger simulation models under imperfect information. In addition, an important role may be played by the presence of antitrust authorities, fines, leniency programs, and criminal sanctions for cartels, which may, at least in principle, sometimes be triggered even by firms attempting to coordinate only tacitly.

8.5 Conclusions

- Merger simulation can be a useful tool in the assessment of the effects of a merger. Currently, it is rarely used as determinative evidence but it can provide good supporting evidence to a sound qualitative assessment of the merger.
- Compared with just using the HHI, merger simulation makes more realistic assumptions as it allows for post-merger adjustments in production by merging firms. Merger simulation can also incorporate the effect of potential efficiencies through an adjustment of the value of the post-merger marginal costs.
- Merger simulation exercises rely heavily on structural assumptions about the nature of consumer demand, the nature of costs, firms' objectives and behavior, and the nature of equilibrium—the latter in the sense that differing firm

objectives must be reconciled. Ensuring that these assumptions are sufficiently consistent with reality is an essential component of a well-done piece of simulation work. In particular, the choice of strategic variables and the importance of static versus dynamic effects must be evaluated so that the model incorporates the actual drivers of market outcomes. The promise of merger simulation models is not easy to deliver on within statutory time limits.

- The stages in merger simulation are the same in most instances. One must estimate the parameters of the components of the model and use the model to forecast the likely change in outcomes of interest arising from the change in ownership structure. For example, the differentiated product Bertrand model establishes a link between market structure and prices. Having estimated its components the actual merger simulation involves only changing the ownership structure and observing how prices are forecast to change. The analyst may subsequently want to undertake an analysis of the impact of any efficiencies arising from the merger.
- The quality of the results from a merger simulation will depend crucially on the quality of the model and in particular how well it captures the realities of the process generating the data that we are modeling. Robustness and sensitivity checks are important stages of the process of developing such a model. In addition, reality checks must also be undertaken. For instance, the analyst could check that the margins implied by the model, or marginal costs when those have been inferred, have realistic values and are consistent with the available qualitative and quantitative information.
- In the main, merger simulation has so far only been used to assess the likely unilateral effects of a merger. However, in principle, merger simulation can also be used to assess the likely coordinated effects of a merger. To do so we want to evaluate firms' incentives to coordinate both before and after the merger and establish whether such incentives are materially changed as a result of the merger.

9
Demand System Estimation

The previous chapters in this book have provided numerous illustrations of the importance of firm and market demand for understanding competition. For example, we have seen that demand is important in determining firm behavior such as pricing decisions and we have also seen that demand is a central determinant of the effect of changes in market structure—such as those that occur from merger and acquisition activity—on market outcomes such as prices. Relatedly, we have seen that demand elasticities are a fundamental element of the tools of competition policy such as the hypothetical monopolist test for market definition. Company revenues depend on the preferences of consumers and so necessarily demand is a fundamental element in shaping market outcomes.

In this chapter, we turn to the estimation of demand functions. In general, though not exclusively, competition policy has a focus on price competition and as a result estimates of the own- and cross-price elasticities of demand are often important. However, as in the rest of the book, much of the analysis can equally be applied should a nonprice variable such as advertising provide the main dimension of competition. We begin the chapter by describing models of "continuous choice" demand and then proceed to discuss "discrete choice" demand models. We shall see that the distinction arises from the nature of the choices that consumers make. Specifically, continuous choice demand models capture the situation in which an individual consumer decides "how much" of a good to consume, whereas "discrete choice" models consider the situation where an individual consumer decides only whether or not to purchase an individual good. Examples might be an individual deciding how much electricity to use or deciding whether to buy a particular type of car, say a Toyota Rav4.[1]

[1] Hybrid models also exist, for example, if consumers decide both whether to use electricity (or, say, gas) and also how much to use, or perhaps whether to have an air conditioner and how much to use it (see, for example, Dubin and McFadden 1984). In addition, a "discrete choice" might involve deciding how many goods to purchase as well as which ones (see, for example, Hendel 1999).

9.1 Demand System Estimation: Models of Continuous Choice

In this section, we introduce the simplest model of all, the demand for a single homogeneous good, and we progress to describe one of the most popular demand models for differentiated product markets, the almost ideal demand system (AIDS[2]).

9.1.1 Single-Product Demand

Estimating the market demand in a market with a single homogeneous product is, in principle, relatively straightforward, not least because there is only one market demand equation to be estimated. The proposition that markets are homogeneous may usefully be considered by looking at actual firm-specific demands since we will either observe no cross-firm variation in prices or else small price differences across firms driving large variations in sales for that firm. However, in this section we focus on the estimation of market demand in homogeneous product markets, leaving the estimation of firm-level demand curves to the section on differentiated product markets. Note that homogeneous product markets can be considered a limiting case of differentiated product markets, where goods provided by rival firms are very close substitutes.

In this section we present a practical example of estimation of a homogeneous product demand model and in the process we discuss practical difficulties that arise when estimating demand equations. In particular, we will try to draw out the enormous difficulties that emerge when "econometrics" is separated off from an investigation as a piece of work that is unconnected to the process of understanding the industry at the focus of an investigation.

Novice econometricians often sit in front of their computers attempting to come up with the "best" econometric model and usually get very frustrated after having put in a lot of work and generated few useful results. A few days or weeks later they announce to the other staff helping the investigation that the econometrics "aren't working out" and that, in this caricature, would be an end to the econometric analysis in that case. At no point during the process of running hundreds of regressions, perhaps staying late into the night, would our novice econometrician feel the need to talk to the rest of an inquiry team about the industry, the patterns in the data that are generating her results, and the puzzles that she faces. Our view is that such an approach is worse than useless: if the results are given weight as evidence, they may well be positively dangerous.

In contrast, experienced econometricians realize that looking at data usually forces them to ask often very difficult questions about the nature of consumer behavior, the industry, and its institutions. The reason is that collectively these forces (together with the actual process of collecting the data) are generating the data that we are

[2] An unfortunate acronym, which has led some authors to describe the model as the nearly ideal demand system (NIDS).

observing and that our model is attempting to explain. Only by a process of moving back and forth from data and regression results to industry documents and expertise can the econometrician typically successfully use her incredibly powerful toolkit to estimate informative econometric models. In this section, we examine that process in the context of attempting to understand the nature and determinants of demand.

9.1.1.1 Estimating the Demand for a Homogeneous Product

In some markets customers do not care about the brand of the product, so long as it fulfills certain standard specifications, at least to a reasonable approximation. Examples might include commodities such as sugar, oil, corn, or steel. If so then suppliers' products are interchangeable in the eyes of consumers. In this section we suppose the market we are studying is, to a reasonable approximation, such a market so that we can consider it as effectively composed of one homogeneous product.

Consider the popular log-linear demand function:

$$Q_t = D(P_t) = \mathrm{e}^{a+\xi_t} P_t^{-b},$$

where P denotes market price and ξ represents the component of demand which is unexplained by the model. This component of the model represents a part of the process which is unknown to the investigator and therefore stochastic in the eyes of the econometrician. Econometric techniques make assumptions about the nature of ξ in order to allow the estimation of the model's parameters (a, b). As a result, we shall see, we must be careful about the assumptions we make about it. For example, what is unknown to a researcher may be known to the firms in the industry and, if so, P and ξ may be correlated. Note that in a homogeneous product market, the market demand function will depend on the price of the product but will not depend on the prices of any other potential substitute products.[3]

The log-linear demand function is so named because if we take natural logarithms, the specification produces the following demand model which is linear in parameters (a, b) to be estimated:

$$\ln Q_t = a - b \ln P_t + \xi_t.$$

In such a market, the parameter of greatest interest will typically be the magnitude of the own-price elasticity of demand. To evaluate it, we need to estimate the market demand function and observe that

$$\eta^{\mathrm{PED}} = \frac{\partial \ln Q}{\partial \ln P} = -b.$$

In principle, to estimate this simple demand model in a homogeneous product market, one only need have data on the market prices and quantities sold as well as data on a potential instrument to address the likely endogeneity of the price variable.

[3] Naturally, if we wish to test whether an alternative product B imposes a constraint on the ability of a monopolist of product A to raise her prices, then we may need to at least consider specifications which allow the price of product B to matter in the demand for product A in order that we do not suffer from "omitted variable" bias in estimating of the parameters in the demand equation for product A.

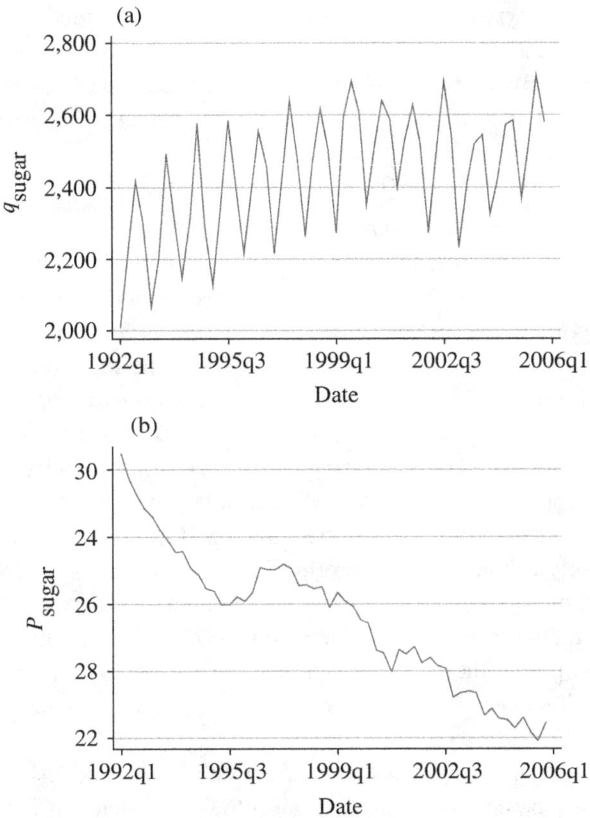

Figure 9.1. Quantity and retail price of sugar in the United States 1992–2006. *Source*: Sugar and sweetener yearbook tables, Economic Research Service, USDA. The data are available at www.ers.usda.gov/Briefing/Sugar/data.htm (accessed September 2007).

Suppose, by way of example, we aim to estimate the demand for sugar and for that purpose we have collected data on the quantity of sugar sold in millions of pounds and the price at which they were sold in cents per pounds. The first step for analysis is to plot the available data. Figure 9.1 shows the quantities and prices of sugar sold: (a) and (b) show respectively the quantity (deliveries) and (retail) price of sugar for the period 1992–2006.

It becomes immediately apparent that there is a strong seasonality in the deliveries of sugar with peaks in the third quarter of each year. Overall deliveries are increasing over time during the years 1992–2006 with a cyclical downturn around 2002. If we look at the price of sugar, there is a clear downward trend during that same period, which is particularly sharp in the years 1992–95 but also continues during 1997–2006.

There is a negative correlation of prices and quantities during this period, but does this correlation represent a causal effect from lower prices to higher demand?

Demand certainly typically slopes down, but the simple fact is that we cannot, or at least should not, look at these data and assume that all of the systematic increase in demand we observe is *caused* by the decrease in prices. Yet implicitly that is effectively what estimating the log-linear demand system assumes. Since the specified model is

$$\ln Q_t = a - b \ln P_t + \xi_t,$$

only prices drive systematic variation in demand.

In this case we have a fairly clearly misspecified model since the data tell us there are substantial quarterly variations in the level of deliveries, even though there are no corresponding variations in the level of prices. Similarly, demand may be shifting for other nonprice reasons during this time period—reasons which from this data set are not so immediately obvious. For example, consumers may have become far more health conscious during the period and as a result the demand of sugar may have decreased (shifted downward). On the other hand, demand may have increased perhaps as consumers got wealthier or busier. If any of these effects are at work, then our model as currently written down will incorrectly ascribe the increase in demand solely to the decrease in prices and as a result incorrectly estimate the effect of price on the demand for sugar. Fundamentally, the job for the analyst is to investigate the factors that are understood to affect demand under the period of study and incorporate the substantial factors into the analysis. An analyst simply cannot do that if she is only looking at regression results—she needs to look at the data and study the industry.

Of course, supply factors may also affect deliveries, not just demand factors, and we can only be confident that we can retrieve the demand function (quantity demanded as a function of price) from these data if we know that our model is correctly specified in the sense that it satisfies the assumptions required to justify our estimation technique. For instance, we know that for OLS to be justified we will need our unobserved component of demand to be uncorrelated with our included regressors:

$$E[\xi_t(\theta^*) \mid P_t] = 0$$

at the true parameter values, $\theta^* = (a^*, b^*)$.[4] This condition suggests that one method for examining its validity is to plot the estimated residuals against (each of) the regressors and look to see if we can spot patterns. It is also useful to plot the residuals over time and, in this example, we would see a seasonal pattern in the residuals plotted over time which suggests a first potential avenue for improving on our initial specification.

Since the data present clear seasonality, we introduce quarterly indicator variables, omitting the fourth quarter (since otherwise the four quarterly indicators and the constant would be collinear). Our model of demand becomes

$$\ln Q_t = a - b \ln P_t + \gamma_1 q_1 + \gamma_2 q_2 + \gamma_3 q_3 + \xi_t,$$

[4] See the discussion in chapters 2 and 6 on the identification of supply and demand curves.

Table 9.1. OLS estimation results based on fifty-six observations.

Regressors	Coefficient	Robust std. err.	t	$P > \|t\|$	[95% Conf. Interval]	
$\ln(P_{\text{Sugar}})$	−0.38	0.05	−7.46	0.00	[−0.48	−0.28]
Quarter 1	−0.10	0.01	−8.09	0.00	[−0.12	−0.07]
Quarter 2	−0.01	0.01	−1.60	0.12	[−0.02	0.00]
Quarter 3	0.02	0.00	4.43	0.00	[0.01	0.03]
Constant	9.05	0.16	55.35	0.00	[8.72	9.38]

$R^2 = 0.803$. The dependent variable in this regression is $\ln(Q_{\text{Sugar}})$.

where q_1, q_2, and q_3 are indicator variables taking on the value 1 in the respective quarter and 0 otherwise. The regression results are represented in table 9.1.

We see that demand is significantly higher in the third quarter of each year during summer months and is lowest in the first quarter of the year. The own-price elasticity of demand, which is directly estimated by the parameter on the log of price, is

$$\eta = \frac{\partial \ln Q}{\partial \ln P} = -0.38.$$

The market demand for sugar resulting from our model appears to be fairly inelastic.

On the one hand the coefficient is, reassuringly, negative as we would expect in a demand curve. On the other hand, we face the question of whether we should genuinely base policy on this estimate. For instance, if we were applying a hypothetical monopolist test for market definition, we would conclude on the basis of this estimate that such a monopolist of the market for sugar could indeed profitably increase its price by 5% above the competitive market price and so we should consider a market which is no wider than sugar for the purposes of antitrust. Indeed, an estimate of the elasticity of demand of −0.38 suggests an optimal gross margin for a monopolist of 268%.[5] Of course, even a monopolist would in reality need to be able to cover her fixed costs from that margin.

9.1.1.2 *Instrumental Variable Estimation*

The OLS identification condition, which requires that at the true parameter values $E[\xi_t(\theta^*) \mid (1, q_1, q_2, q_3, \ln(P_t))] = 0$, can fail for numerous reasons. First, non-price drivers of the unobserved component causing demand variation may also cause market prices to rise. If so, then the "demand shocks" will cause variation in prices and therefore demand shocks and prices will be correlated. The implication of such movement is most easily seen by considering what happens when the demand curve moves. In an extreme case where supply is stable, such variation will trace out the

[5] Using the Lerner index formula from profit maximization, $\dfrac{p-c}{p} = \dfrac{1}{-\eta} = \dfrac{1}{0.38} = 2.68$.

supply curve rather than the demand curve. Second, the model can be misspecified perhaps because of omitted variables that are correlated with prices so that the misspecified model introduces a correlation between the model's error term and prices thereby introducing a bias in the estimated parameter.

Each case results in an "endogeneity problem" that the analyst must address. In each case, the unobserved component of the demand model and the price data will be correlated and, as a result, the OLS estimate of the price coefficient is likely to be biased. To address these concerns, at some point during a demand estimation exercise an economist will almost always want to consider using instrumental variable (IV) techniques in an attempt to control for endogeneity.

We refer the reader to chapter 2 for a more detailed discussion of the econometric theory underlying IV techniques. Here, we recall that the basic requirements for an instrumental variable is that it be (1) correlated with the potentially endogenous regressor and (2) uncorrelated with the unobserved component of demand. One popular estimator which addresses the endogeneity concern is the "two-stage least-squares" (2SLS) estimator.[6] If price is the endogenous variable then the two stages are (1) run a regression of ln(prices) on the exogenous variables in the demand curve plus the instrument and (2) use predicted ln(prices) instead of the actual ln(price) data to estimate the demand curve. In fact, the 2SLS technique gets its name from the fact that the estimator can be obtained by using the predicted explanatory variable from the first-stage regression in the estimation of the model instead of the original variable.

The 2SLS estimator itself can also be obtained in one step, but it is usually helpful to look at the output from both steps for reasons we now explain. Specifically, note that the first necessary condition for an instrument to be valid can be tested by running a regression of the endogenous explanatory variable (here prices) on the other variables included in the demand model and treated as exogenous plus the instrument. This is known as the "first-stage" regression because it is exactly the regression used as the first step in constructing the 2SLS estimator. If the instrument appears to be statistically significant in the first-stage regression, we conclude that it is conditionally correlated with prices in a way which is potentially helpful for solving the endogeneity problem. The second condition for an instrument to be valid is that it is not correlated with the demand shock. Usually, the assessment of this second condition is harder, but one albeit imperfect approach is to plot the error term against the instrument to check for correlation.[7]

To illustrate, recall our example estimating the demand of sugar and suppose we consider using quarterly farm wages as a potential instrument for prices. Farm wages

---

[6] In addition to the discussion provided in chapter 2, see, for example, Greene (2000). 2SLS can be shown to be a GMM estimator (see Hansen 1982).

[7] A plot of the error against the instrument in an IV regression is analogous to that illustrated for OLS in chapter 3, where the residual was plotted against the x variable. Although the model will construct estimates $\hat{\theta}$ to ensure that $(1/T)\sum_{t=1}^{T}\xi_t(\hat{\theta})z_t = 0$, the graph may nonetheless demonstrate correlations such as cycles in a plot of the data points: $\{\xi_t(\hat{\theta}), z_t\}_{t=1}^{T}$.

Table 9.2. IV estimation results based on forty-four observations.

Regressors	Coefficient	Robust std. err.	t	$P > \|t\|$	[95% Conf.	interval]
$\ln(P_{\text{Sugar}})$	−0.27	0.08	−3.41	0.00	[−0.43	−0.11]
Quarter 1	−0.10	0.01	−9.23	0.00	[−0.12	−0.08]
Quarter 2	−0.01	0.01	−1.99	0.05	[−0.02	0.00]
Quarter 3	0.01	0.00	3.71	0.00	[0.01	0.02]
Constant	8.69	0.25	34.71	0.00	[8.19	9.20]

$R^2 = 0.80$. The dependent variable in this regression is $\ln(Q_{\text{Sugar}})$.

are a cost of producing sugar and will therefore ordinarily affect observed prices according to economic theory (and also farmers!). On the other hand, given that farmers are a small minority of the population and that the increase in their wages is not likely to translate into material increases in sugar consumption, farm wages are unlikely to materially affect the aggregate demand for sugar.

The 2SLS estimation proceeds in two stages:

$$\text{1st-stage regression:} \quad \ln P_t = a - b \ln W_t + \gamma_1 q_{1t} + \gamma_2 q_{2t} + \gamma_3 q_{3t} + \varepsilon_t,$$

$$\text{2nd-stage regression:} \quad \ln Q_t = a - b \widehat{\ln P_t} + \gamma_1 q_{1t} + \gamma_2 q_{2t} + \gamma_3 q_{3t} + v_t,$$

where W_t is the farm wage at time t and $\widehat{\ln P_t}$ is the estimated log of price obtained from the first-stage regression. Most statistical computer packages are able to perform this procedure and in doing so provide the output from both regressions.[8]

The quarterly dummies are also included in the first-stage regression since the requirement for an instrument to be valid is that it is correlated with an endogenous variable conditional on the included exogenous variables. Demand is itself seasonal, so that the quarterly dummies are not correlated with prices conditional on the included exogenous variables and hence are not valid instruments for prices, even if they are valid instruments for themselves, i.e., can be treated as exogenous.

The results of the instrumental variable estimation are presented in table 9.2.

The results show a lower coefficient for the price variable. The elasticity of demand is now −0.27 and is below the previous OLS estimate. Because of data availability on farm wages some observations had to be dropped so that the data for the two regressions are not exactly the same. Nonetheless, formally a Durbin–Wu–Hausman test could be used to test between the OLS and IV regression specifications (see Greene 2000; Nakamura and Nakamura 1981). The central question is whether the instruments are in fact successfully addressing the endogeneity bias problem that motivated our use of them. Often inexperienced researchers use IV regression results even if the resulting estimate moves the coefficient in the direction opposite to that expected as a result of endogeneity bias.

[8] STATA, for example, provides the "ivreg" command.

Results in IV estimations should be carefully scrutinized because they will only be reliable if the instrument chosen for the first-stage regression is a good instrument. We know that for an instrument to be valid it must satisfy the two conditions:

$$\text{(i) } E[\xi_t \mid (X_t, W_t)] = 0 \quad \text{and} \quad \text{(ii) } E[\ln(P_t) \mid (X_t, W_t)] \neq 0,$$

where in our case $X_t = (1, q_1, q_2, q_3)$ are the exogenous regressors in the demand equation and W_t is the instrument, farm wages. As we described earlier, the first of these conditions is difficult to test; however, one way to evaluate whether it holds is to examine a picture of the estimated residuals against the regressors. We should see no systematic patterns in the graphs—whatever the value of X_t or W_t the error term on average around those values should be mean zero. Such tests can be formalized (see, for example, the specification tests due to Ramsey (1969)). But there are limits to the extent to which this assumption can be tested since the model will, to a considerable extent, actively impose this assumption on the data in order to best derive the IV estimates obtained. A variety of potential IV results can certainly be tested against each other and against specifications which use more instruments than strictly necessary to achieve identification. But the reality is that the first of these assumptions is ultimately quite difficult to test entirely convincingly and one is likely to ultimately mainly rely on economic theory—at least to the extent that the theory robustly tells us that, for example, a cost driver will generally not affect consumer demand behavior and so will have no reason to be correlated with the unobserved component of demand.

The second condition is easier to evaluate and the most popular method is to run a regression of the potentially endogenous variable (here $\ln(P_t)$) on all the exogenous explanatory variables in the demand equation and also the instruments, here $\ln(W_t)$. To see whether the second condition holds, we examine the results of the following "first-stage" regression:

$$P_t = a - b \ln W_t + q_1 + q_2 + q_3 + \varepsilon_t.$$

For the variable farm wage to be a good instrument, we want the coefficient b to be robustly and significantly different from zero in this equation. If the instrument does not have explanatory power in predicting the price, the predicted price used in the second-stage regression will be poorly correlated with the actual price given the other variables already included in the demand equation. In that case, the estimated coefficient of the price variable in the second-stage regression will be imprecisely estimated and indeed may not be distinguishable from zero. Even with "good instruments" in the sense that they are conditionally correlated with the variable being instrumented, we will expect the coefficient of an instrumented variable in an IV regression to be less precisely estimated (have a higher standard error) than the analogous coefficient estimated using OLS (with the latter a meaningful comparison only if in fact the OLS estimate is a valid one). IV estimation relaxes the assumptions

Table 9.3. First-stage regression results.

ln(Price)	Coefficient	Std. err.	t	$P > \|t\|$	[95% conf.	interval]
Quarter 1	0.05	0.02	2.93	0.01	[0.01	0.08]
Quarter 2	0.00	0.01	0.53	0.60	[−0.01	0.02]
Quarter 3	−0.01	0.01	−1.43	0.16	[−0.02	0.00]
ln(Farm wage)	−1.13	0.12	−9.71	0.00	[1.36	−0.89]
Constant	4.94	0.18	27.47	0.00	[4.58	5.30]

required to get valid estimates but one must always remember it does so at a price: lower precision. There will, as a result, be cases where the OLS estimates cannot be rejected when compared with the IV estimates and may as a result be preferred.

Results for the first-stage regression for our example are shown in table 9.3.

First note that, as one would hope, the coefficient for the ln(Farm wage) variable is significant and has a high t-statistic, indicating that it is precisely estimated. However, note that the coefficient reported is rather surprising: its sign is negative! The economic theory motivating our choice of instrument tells us that an increase in costs should translate into higher prices as the supply curve shifts leftward. Indeed, our aim in selecting an instrument is intuitively to use that instrument to allow us to use only the variation in observed prices which we know is due to the variation in the supply curve.

When conundrums such as this one arise, one should address them. While for econometric theory purposes "conditional correlation" is all that is required to support the use of the instrument, one should not proceed further without understanding why the data are behaving in an unexpected way. In this case, one may want to investigate, for example, whether farm wages have a trend that negatively correlates with prices and for which we did not control. Figure 9.2 graphs farm wage data over time. In particular, note that there is an upward trend in wages between 1995 and 2006 during the time that sugar prices fell. Clearly, while farm wages may still be an important determinant of sugar prices, they are not likely to be a major factor driving the price of sugar down. We must look elsewhere for an instrument that helps explain the major source of variation in prices conditional on the exogenous variables in the demand equation.

To search for a good instrument we must attempt to better understand the factors that are driving sugar prices down over time. One possibility is that other costs in the industry are falling dramatically. Alternatively, there may be an institutional reason such as changes in the amount of subsidy offered to farmers or in the tariff or quota system that governs the supply from imports. There may have been substantial entry during the period. Another possibility is that the price change may be driven by important demand factors that we have omitted thus far from our model. Perhaps the taste for sugary products changed over time? Or perhaps substitutes (e.g., high-fructose corn syrup) appeared and drove down prices?

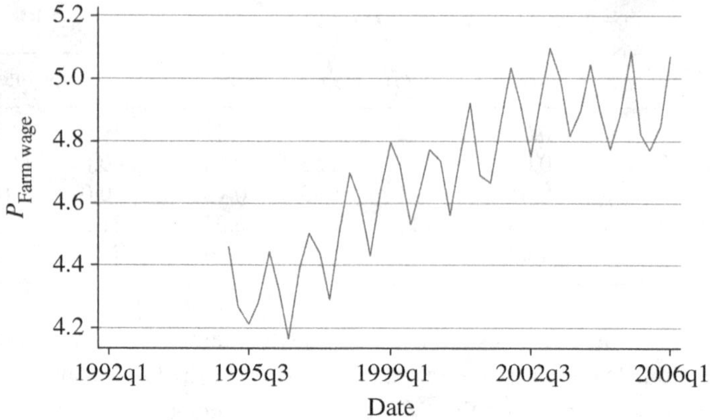

Figure 9.2. Farm wages plotted over time.

At this point we need to go back to our industry experts and descriptive analyses of the industry to attempt to find possible explanations for the major variation in prices and in particular the price decline. The data and regression results have provided us with a puzzle which we need to solve by using industry expertise. Only once we have thought hard about what in the industry is generating our data will we generally be able to move forward to generating econometric results we can believe. It is for this reason that we described in the introduction to this section that it is very rare for an econometrician to be able to work in isolation late into the night with her existing data set and generate sensible regression results without going back to think about the nature and drivers of competition in an industry.

That said, we generally do not need to understand everything about the price-setting process to obtain reliable demand estimates. In particular, in a demand estimation exercise we are not trying to estimate the pricing equations that explain how firms optimally choose their prices. Although the first-stage regression in a 2SLS estimation may closely resemble the reduced form of the pricing equation in a structural model of prices and quantities (see chapter 6), it is not quite the same. We saw in the previous chapters that factors affecting demand are included in the pricing equation and so are cost data. However, the first-stage equation of the 2SLS regression is materially different from a reduced-form pricing equation in that we do not need to have all the cost data: we really only need one good supply-side instrument to identify the price coefficient in a homogeneous product demand equation.

9.1.2 Differentiated Products Demand Systems

Most markets do not consist of a single homogeneous product but are rather composed of similar but differentiated goods that compete for customers. For instance, in the market for shampoos there is not a single type of generic shampoo. Rather there is a variety of brands and types of shampoo which consumers do not consider absolutely equivalent. We must take such demand characteristics into account when attempting to estimate demand in differentiated product markets. In particular, we need to take account of the fact that consumers are choosing among different products for which they have different relative preferences and which will usually have different prices. Differentiated product demand systems are therefore estimated as a system of individual product demand equations, where the demand for a product depends on its own price but also on the price of the other products in the market.

9.1.2.1 Log-Linear Demand Models

One popular differentiated product demand system is the log-linear demand system, which is simply a set of log-linear demand functions, one for each product available in the market. We label the products in the market $j = 1, \dots, J$. In each case, the quantity of the good purchased potentially depends on the prices of all the goods in the market and also income y (Deaton and Muellbauer 1980b). Formally, we have the following system of J equations:

$$\begin{aligned}
\ln Q_{1t} &= a_1 - b_{11} \ln P_{1t} + b_{12} \ln P_{2t} + \dots + b_{1J} \ln P_{1J} + \gamma_1 \ln y_t + \xi_{1t}, \\
\ln Q_{2t} &= a_2 - b_{21} \ln P_{1t} + b_{22} \ln P_{2t} + \cdots + b_{2J} \ln P_{Jt} + \gamma_2 \ln y_t + \xi_{2t}, \\
&\vdots \\
\ln Q_{Jt} &= a_2 - b_{J1} \ln P_{1t} + b_{J2} \ln P_{2t} + \cdots + b_{JJ} \ln P_{Jt} + \gamma_J \ln y_t + \xi_{Jt}.
\end{aligned}$$

Maximizing utility subject to a budget constraint will generically provide demand equations which depend on the set of all prices and income (see, for example, Pollak and Wales 1992). Clearly, with aggregate data we might use aggregate income as the relevant variable for the demand equations (e.g., GDP). However, since many studies focus on a particular sector of the economy, the consumer's problem is often recast and considered as a two-stage problem. At the first stage, we posit that consumers decide how much money to spend on a category of goods—for example, beer—and at the second stage we posit that the chosen level of expenditure is allocated across the various products that the consumer must choose between, perhaps the different brands of beer. Under particular assumptions on the shape of the utility function, this two-stage process can be shown to be equivalent to solving a single one-stage utility-maximization problem (see Deaton and Muellbauer 1980b; Gorman 1959; Hausman et al. 1994). Using the two-stage interpretation, "expenditure" may be used instead of income in the demand equations but the demand equations will then be termed "conditional" demand equations as we are conditioning on a given level of expenditure.

A well-known example of an such an exercise is Hausman et al. (1994). In fact, those authors estimate a three-level choice model where consumers choose (1) the level of expenditure on beer, (2) how to allocate that expenditure between three broad categories of beer (respectively termed premium beer, popular beer, and light

Table 9.4. Market segment conditional demand in the market for beer.

	Premium	Popular	Light
Constant	0.501	−4.021	−1.183
	(0.283)	(0.560)	(0.377)
log(Beer exp)	0.978	0.943	1.067
	(0.011)	(0.022)	(0.015)
$\log(P_{\text{Premium}})$	−2.671	2.704	0.424
	(0.123)	(0.244)	(0.166)
$\log(P_{\text{Popular}})$	0.510	−2.707	0.747
	(0.097)	(0.193)	(0.127)
$\log(P_{\text{Light}})$	0.701	0.518	−2.424
	(0.070)	(0.140)	(0.092)
Time	−0.001	−0.000	0.002
	(0.000)	(0.001)	(0.000)
log(# of stores)	−0.035	0.253	−0.176
	(0.016)	(0.034)	(0.023)

Number of observations = 101.

Source: Table 1, Hausman et al. (1994).

beer) which marketing studies had identified as market segments, and (3) how to allocate expenditure between the various brands of beer within each of the segments.

At level (3), we could use the observed product level price and quantity data to estimate our differentiated product demand system. However, in fact, since level (3) is modeled as a choice of brands (e.g., Coors, Budweiser, Molsen, etc.), at levels (1), (2), and (3) we would need to use price and quantity indices constructed from underlying product-level data to give measures of price and quantity for each of the brands or segments of the beer industry. For example, we might use a price index with expenditure share weights for the underlying prices within each segment s to produce a segment-level price index, $P_{st} = \sum_j w_{jt} p_{jt}$.[9] Similarly, we might choose to use volumes of liquid to help aggregate over the brands to give segment-level quantity indices.[10]

Estimates of the second level of their demand system using price and quantity indices are shown in table 9.4. At the second level of the choice tree, the demand system is a conditional demand system because the amount of money to be spent on beer has already been chosen at stage 1.

[9] Expenditure shares can be defined as $w_{jt} = p_{jt}q_{jt} / \sum_j p_{jt}q_{jt}$, where p represents prices and q quantities.

[10] Formally, Deaton and Muellbauer (1980b) show that there are "correct" price and quantity indices which can be constructed for this process to preserve the multilevel models' equivalence to a single utility-maximization problem (under strong assumptions). In practice, the authors do not seem to have settled on a universally best choice of price and quantity indices.

Since we are dealing with a log-linear model, the b_{jj} coefficients provide estimates of the own-price elasticity of demand while the b_{jk} $(j \neq k)$ parameters provide estimates of the cross-price elasticities of demand. If we are using segment-level data, we must be careful to place the correct interpretation on the elasticities. For example, the results from table 9.4 suggest that the own-price elasticity of *segment* demand is −2.6 for premium beer, −2.7 for popular beer, and −2.4 for light beer.

These price elasticities could be used as important evidence toward a formal test of the hypothesis that each beer segment is a market in itself by performing a SSNIP test. That said, generally, the price elasticity relevant for such a test would include the indirect effect of prices through their effect on the total amount of expenditure on beer. If the price of premium beer goes up, some consumption will be reallocated to other beer segments but the total consumption of beer might also fall as people either switch to other products such as wine or reduce consumption altogether. The elasticities we can read off from the equation in this instance are conditional elasticity estimates—they are conditional on the level of expenditure on beer. Thus for market definition, if we use expenditure levels and price indices to perform market definition tests, we must be careful to trace through the effect of a price change back through its effect on total expenditure on beer. To do so, Hausman et al. (1994) also estimates a single top-level equation so that the demand for beer in total is expressed as a function of prices and income. In this case, the equation estimated depended on income (GDP) and also a price index constructed to capture the general price of beer as well as demographics, Z_t:

$$\ln Q_t^{\text{Beer}} = \beta_0 + \beta_1 \ln y_t^{\text{GDP}} + \beta_2 \ln P_t^{\text{Beer}} + Z_t\delta + \varepsilon_t.$$

The choice of instruments in differentiated product demand systems is generically difficult. First, we may need a lot of them. In particular, we need at least one instrument for every product whose price is considered potentially endogenous in a demand function (although sometimes a given instrument may in fact be used to estimate more than one equation). Second, a natural source of instruments involves cost data. However, since products are often produced in a very similar way, and cost data are often recorded less frequently than prices are set, at least in financial or management accounts, we are often unable to find cost variables that are genuinely sufficiently helpful for identification of each of the demand curves. Data such as exchange rates and wages are often useful in homogeneous product demand estimation, but fundamentally such data are not product (or here segment) specific and so will face difficulties as instruments in the differentiated product context.

The reality is that there are no entirely persuasive solutions to this problem. One potential solution, that Hausman et al. (1994) suggest, is to use prices in other cities as instruments for the prices in a given city. The logic is that if, and it is often a very big "if," (1) demand shocks are city specific and independent across cities and (2) cost shocks are correlated across markets, then any correlation between the price in this market and the prices in other markets will be due to cost movements. In that case, the prices in other cities will be valid instruments for the price in this city. Obviously, these are strong assumptions. For example, there must not be any effect of, say, national advertising campaigns in the demand shocks since then they would not be independent across cities. Alternatively, another potentially satisfactory instrument would be the price of a good that shares the costs but which is not a substitute or complement. For example, if a product under study had costs that were each heavily influenced by the oil price, then the price of another good also subject to a similar sensitivity might be used. Of course, in such a situation it would be easier to use the oil price so examples where this approach would genuinely be useful are perhaps hard to think of.

We will explore another option for constructing instruments once we have discussed models based on product characteristics in a later section.

9.1.2.2 Indirect Utility and Expenditure Shares Models

A log-linear demand system is easy to estimate because all the equations are linear in the parameters. However, they also impose considerable assumptions on the nature of consumer preferences. For example, they impose constant own- and cross-price elasticities of demand. In addition, there is a potentially serious internal consistency issue that we face when estimating log-linear demand functions using aggregate data. Namely, the aggregate demand function may well depend on more than aggregate income. If we only include an aggregate income variable, estimates may suffer from "aggregation bias."[11]

Misspecification and aggregation bias is easily demonstrated by taking the log-linear demand equation for an individual,

$$\ln Q_{it} = a - b \ln P_t + \gamma \ln y_{it} + \xi_t,$$

transforming it to the level of quantities

$$Q_{it} = \exp(a_i + \xi_t)(P_t)^b (y_{it})^\gamma$$

and adding up across individuals, which gives

$$\sum_i Q_{it} = \exp(a + \xi_t)(P_t)^b \sum_i (y_{it})^\gamma$$

so that if we take logs again we get

$$\ln\left(\sum_i Q_{it}\right) = a + \xi_t + b \ln(P_t) + \ln\left(\sum_i (y_{it})^\gamma\right).$$

Thus even with this special case, where there is no heterogeneity across individuals other than in their income, estimating a log-linear demand equation using aggregate data will involve estimating a misspecified model.

[11] This debate was particularly important for macroeconomists, where it was common practice to estimate a representative agent model using aggregate data.

The economics profession searched for models which were internally consistent in the sense that they either only depended on exactly the aggregate analogous data, say $\sum_i y_{it}$, or in a weaker sense that they only depended on aggregate data—perhaps the aggregate income but also the variance of income in the population. Doing so was called the study of "aggregability conditions." The reason to mention this fact is that the study of aggregability provided the motivation for many of the most popular demand system models that are in use today—they satisfy these "aggregability" conditions. One such example is the almost ideal demand system (AIDS) due to Deaton and Muellbauer (1980a). We discuss that model below.[12]

Before we do so, however, let us briefly recall the amazingly useful contribution of choice theory to the practical exercise of specifying demand systems. In particular, recall that an indirect utility function $V(p, y; \vartheta)$ is defined as

$$V(p, y; \vartheta) = \max_q u(q; \vartheta) \quad \text{subject to} \quad pq \leqslant y,$$

so that $V(p, y; \vartheta)$ represents the maximum utility $u(q; \vartheta)$ that can be achieved at a given set of prices and income (p, y), where p and q may be vectors of prices and quantities, respectively. Choice theory tells us that specifying $V(p, y; \vartheta)$ is entirely equivalent to specifying preferences, provided $V(p, y; \vartheta)$ satisfies some properties.[13]

In an amazing contribution, choice theory also tells us that the solution to this constrained optimization problem is described by Roy's identity:[14]

$$q_j(p, y; \vartheta) = -\frac{\partial V(p, y; \vartheta)}{\partial p_j} \bigg/ \frac{\partial V(p, y; \vartheta)}{\partial y}.$$

On the one hand, this is interesting as a piece of theory. However, it is not just theory—it has an extremely practical implication for anyone who wants to estimate a demand curve. Namely, that we can easily derive parametric demand systems—all we need to do is to write down an indirect utility function and differentiate it. In particular, Roy's identity allows us to avoid solving the constrained multivariate maximization problem entirely and moreover gives us a very simple method for generating a whole array of differentiated product demand systems.

There is a version of Roy's identity which uses expenditure shares and we shall use this version below. Recall the expenditure share for good 1 is defined as the expenditure on good 1 divided by total expenditure y, $w_1 \equiv p_1 q_1 / y$.

---

[12] Historically, there was great focus in the literature on being able to estimate flexible Engle curves from aggregate data. Fairly recently, this tradition has resulted in a number of contributions including the "QuAIDS" model (see Banks et al. 1997; Ryan and Wales 1999).

[13] In particular, it must be increasing in y, homogeneous in degree 0 in income and prices, and quasi-concave in income and prices. See your favorite microeconomics textbook, for example, chapter 3 of Varian (1992).

[14] This identity is derived by applying the envelope theorem to the Lagrangian expression in the utility-maximization exercise.

In that case, Roy's identity can be equivalently stated:

$$\begin{aligned} w_j(p, y; \vartheta) &\equiv \frac{p_j q_j(p, y; \vartheta)}{y} \\ &= \left(- p_j \frac{\partial V(p, y; \vartheta)}{\partial p_j} \right) \Big/ \left(y \frac{\partial V(p, y; \vartheta)}{\partial y} \right) \\ &= \left(- \frac{\partial V(p, y; \vartheta)}{\partial \ln p_j} \right) \Big/ \left(\frac{\partial V(p, y; \vartheta)}{\partial \ln y} \right). \end{aligned}$$

Estimating a model using the expenditure share on a good provides exactly the same information as a model of the demand for the good. We can compute own- and cross-price elasticities of demand directly from the expenditure share equation. If the indirect utility function is linear in parameters but involves terms such as $\ln p_j$ and $\ln y$, then this formulation will tend to provide an algebraically more convenient model for us to work with, as we shall see in the next section.

9.1.2.3 *Almost Ideal Demand System*

AIDS is perhaps the most commonly used differentiated product demand system (Deaton and Muellbauer 1980a). AIDS satisfies a nice aggregability condition. Specifically, if we take a lot of consumers behaving as predicted by an AIDS model and aggregate their demand systems, the result is itself an AIDS demand system. The relevant parameters of an AIDS specification are also quite easy to estimate and the estimation process requires data that are normally available to the analyst, namely prices and expenditure shares.

In AIDS, the indirect utility function $V(p, y; \vartheta)$ is assumed to be

$$V(p, y; \vartheta) = \frac{\ln y - \ln a(p)}{\ln b(p) - \ln a(p)},$$

where the functions $a(p)$ and $b(p)$ are sometimes described as "price indices" since they are (parametric) functions of underlying price data:

$$\ln a(p) = \alpha_0 + \sum_{k=1}^{J} \alpha_k \ln p_k + \sum_{k=1}^{J} \sum_{j=1}^{J} \gamma_{jk} \ln p_k \ln p_j$$

and

$$\ln b(p) = \ln a(p) + \beta_0 \prod_{k=1}^{J} p_k^{\beta_k}.$$

Applying Roy's identity for the expenditure share for product j gives

$$w_j = \left(- \frac{\partial V(p, y; \vartheta)}{\partial \ln p_j} \right) \Big/ \left(\frac{\partial V(p, y; \vartheta)}{\partial \ln y} \right) = \alpha_j + \sum_{k=1}^{J} \gamma_{jk} \ln p_k + \beta_j \ln \left(\frac{y}{P} \right),$$

where P can be thought of as the price index that "deflates" income:

$$\ln P = \alpha_0 + \sum_{k=1}^{J} \alpha_k \ln p_k + \frac{1}{2} \sum_{k=1}^{J} \sum_{j=1}^{J} \gamma_{jk} \ln p_k \ln p_j .$$

In practice, this price index is often replaced by a "Stone" price index (named after Sir Richard Stone, who won the Nobel Memorial Prize in economics in 1984 and was responsible for the first estimation of the linear expenditure system (Stone 1954)[15]), which does not depend on the parameters of the model:

$$\ln P = \sum_{k=1}^{J} w_j \ln p_j .$$

One advantage of using a Stone price index is that it makes the AIDS expenditure shares linear in the parameters to be estimated $(\alpha_j, \gamma_{j1}, \dots, \gamma_{jJ}, \beta_j)$. Models that are linear in their parameters are easy to estimate using standard regression packages and also allow us to easily use IV techniques to address the potential endogeneity problems that arise in demand estimation. Also, because the Stone index does not depend on all of the model's parameters and prices, one does not need to estimate the full system but rather even a single equation can be estimated. Sometimes, the Stone index is used first to get initial starting values and then the full nonlinear AIDS system model is estimated.

In practice, an AIDS system can be implemented in the following way.

1. Calculate w_{jt}, the expenditure share of a good j at time t, using the price of j at time t, p_{jt}, the quantity demanded of j at time t, q_{jt}, and total expenditure defined as $y_t = \sum_{j=1}^{J} p_{jt} q_{jt}$.
2. Calculate the Stone price index: $\ln P_t = \sum_{j=1}^{J} w_{jt} p_{jt}$.
3. Run the following linear regression:

$$w_{jt} = \alpha_j + \sum_{k=1}^{J} \gamma_{jk} \ln p_{kt} + \beta_j \ln \left(\frac{y_t}{P_t} \right) + \xi_{jt},$$

   where p_{kt} is the own price and the price of the goods that are substitutes and ξ_{jt} is the error term.
4. Retrieve the $J + 2$ parameters of interest $(\alpha_j, \gamma_{j1}, \dots, \gamma_{jJ}, \beta_j)$.

The own- and cross-price elasticities can be retrieved from the AIDS parameters by noting that

$$\ln w_j = \ln p_j + \ln q_j - \ln y \quad \Longleftrightarrow \quad \ln q_j = \ln w_j - \ln p_j + \ln y,$$

[15] Stone used the linear expenditure system (LSE) model, which had previously been developed theoretically by Lawrence Klein and Herman Rubin.

so that the demand elasticities can be computed as

$$\eta_{jk} = \begin{cases} \dfrac{\partial \ln q_j}{\partial \ln p_k} = \dfrac{\partial \ln w_j}{\partial \ln p_k} - 1 & \text{if } j = k, \\ \dfrac{\partial \ln q_j}{\partial \ln p_k} = \dfrac{\partial \ln w_j}{\partial \ln p_k} & \text{if } j \neq k. \end{cases}$$

Differentiating the AIDS expenditure share equation yields

$$\frac{\partial \ln w_j}{\partial \ln p_k} = \frac{\gamma_{jk} - w_k \beta_j}{w_j}$$

and therefore we can see that the own- and cross-price elasticities of demand depend on both the model parameters and the expenditure shares

$$\eta_{jk} = \begin{cases} \dfrac{\gamma_{jk} - w_k \beta_j}{w_j} - 1 = \dfrac{\gamma_{jk}}{w_k} - \beta_j - 1 & \text{if } j = k, \\ \dfrac{\gamma_{jk} - w_k \beta_j}{w_j} = \dfrac{\gamma_{jk}}{w_j} - \dfrac{w_k}{w_j} \beta_j & \text{if } j \neq k. \end{cases}$$

Note that there is a slightly dangerous character to these formulas. Namely, if there is very little information available in the data and as a result all the relevant parameters are estimated to be close to zero, perhaps due to lack of variation in the data, the own-price elasticities will be computed as -1 and the cross-elasticities will appear to be close to 0. In practice, this is a dangerous feature of the AIDS model because these numbers do not appear immediately implausible—unlike finding an own-price elasticity of say 0, which is what would result from a log-linear demand system if the coefficients are estimated to be 0. The result of -1 is imposed by the model and not by the data, so one must be very careful not to draw erroneous conclusions. For instance, when estimating the reaction of a hypothetical monopolist to a potential increase in its own prices, if we find an own elasticity of -1, this means that the monopolist will find it profitable to increase its prices above competitive levels. The resulting conclusion would be that this product constitutes a market and the zero cross-elasticity estimates would appear to confirm that conclusion. However, those results could also be entirely due to imprecision in our demand estimates and in truth be indicative only that there is no meaningful information in your data set!

Although one can estimate all the equations in an AIDS model separately one by one, it will be more efficient to estimate all the equations together provided that all the equations are correctly specified. Of course, the assumption that all the equations are correctly specified is a much stronger assumption than the assumption that a single demand equation is correctly specified. Thus before attempting the simultaneous estimation, good practice suggests looking at single equation estimates (although there are limits to the practicality of doing so if you have many demand equations to study).

In addition, in many applications we will care more about the nature of one or a small number of demand equations than the whole system. Keeping that fact in the forefront of your mind can considerably ease the econometric problems that must be solved.

9.1.3 Parameter Restrictions on Demand Systems

Demand system estimation requires the estimation of many more parameters than those involved in single equation estimation. The number of parameters that must be estimated can easily render the estimation intractable and restrictions are often imposed on the parameters in order to reduce the number to be estimated. We detail below the most common restrictions. Although widely applied, one still needs to be very cautious when imposing such restrictions and the analyst must always check whether they are supported by the data.

Let us assume that we are interested in the demands of two differentiated but related products. We estimate a differentiated product demand system with two simultaneous demand equations:

$$Q_1 = a_1 - b_{11}p_1 + b_{12}p_2 + c_1 y \quad \text{and} \quad Q_2 = a_2 - b_{21}p_1 + b_{22}p_2 + c_2 y.$$

If good 2 is a demand substitute to good 1, we will observe $\partial Q_2/\partial p_1 = b_{21} > 0$ since an increase in the price of good 1 will induce our consumer to switch some of her consumption to good 2. Alternatively, if good 2 is a demand complement to good 1, $\partial Q_2/\partial p_1 = b_{21} < 0$ since an increase in the price of good 1 will induce our consumer to reduce her demand for good 2.

9.1.3.1 *Slutsky Symmetry*

Choice theory suggests that when individual consumers maximize utility they choose their levels of demand for each product by carefully trading off the utility provided by each unit of each good. In fact, they are predicted to do it so carefully that there will be a relationship between demands for each good.

The so-called Slutsky symmetry equation establishes the following equivalence, which is derived from the rational individual utility-maximization conditions:

$$\frac{\partial Q_1}{\partial p_2} + Q_2 \frac{\partial Q_1}{\partial y} = \frac{\partial Q_2}{\partial p_1} + Q_1 \frac{\partial Q_2}{\partial y}.$$

This is equivalent to saying that the total substitution effect, including the income effect that results from a change in prices, is symmetric across any pair of goods.

If true, Slutsky symmetry is a very useful restriction from economic theory because it decreases the number of parameters that we need to estimate. For instance, in our linear model, Slutsky symmetry can only hold if $b_{12} + Q_2 c_1 = b_{21} + Q_1 c_2$. Since Q_1 and Q_2 will take on many different values depending on relative prices, this relation will only hold if $b_{21} = b_{12}$ and $c_1 = c_2 = 0$. In fact, in general, one set of sufficient (but not necessary) conditions for Slutsky symmetry condition to be fulfilled are

$$\frac{\partial Q_1}{\partial y} = \frac{\partial Q_2}{\partial y} = 0 \quad \text{and} \quad \frac{\partial Q_1}{\partial p_2} = \frac{\partial Q_2}{\partial p_1}.$$

These restrictions respectively impose the restrictions that (1) the income effects for both products are negligible and (2) there is symmetry in the cross-price demand derivative across products. It is sometimes reasonable to assume income effects are small. For example, if the price of a packet of sweets increases, then it is true that my real income falls, but the magnitude of the effect is reasonably assumed to be negligible.

The great advantage of imposing Slutsky symmetry on our demand system—if the restriction is indeed satisfied by the DGP—is that it implies we have fewer parameters to estimate. In our example, our restriction implies $b_{12} = b_{21}$ and we can retrieve b_{12} from either one of the two equations. If we have data on p_1, p_2, and Q_1, we can estimate the first demand equation and retrieve b_{12} directly. If on the other hand we have no data on Q_1 but we do have data on Q_2, Slutsky symmetry would say that we could nonetheless retrieve b_{12} by estimating $b_{21} = b_{12}$ in the second equation. Thus Slutsky symmetry is indeed a powerful restriction, if a restrictive one.

Sadly, aggregate demand systems will not in general satisfy Slutsky symmetry.[16] To see why, suppose Coke currently sells 100 million units to 1 million customers per year, whereas Virgin Cola sells 100,000 units per year to 10,000 customers. When Coke puts up its price by €0.10, then 1 million individuals will think about whether to switch some of their demand to Virgin Cola. On the other hand, if Virgin Cola puts its prices up by the same amount, then just 10,000 customers will think about whether they should switch to Coke. In each case, the people considering whether to switch are different and, moreover, there can be very different numbers of them. For each of these reasons, we do not expect to find symmetry in general aggregate demand equations and therefore generally we will have

$$\frac{\partial Q_{\text{Virgin}}}{\partial p_{\text{Coke}}} \neq \frac{\partial Q_{\text{Coke}}}{\partial p_{\text{Virgin}}}$$

and we may need to estimate both b_{12} and b_{21}. If we impose this restriction on our estimates, we must be reasonably confident that there are good reasons to believe we are not imposing such strong patterns in our data set. The restriction imposed should always be tested.

[16] The fact that the rationality restrictions of classical choice theory do not survive aggregation is established by the Debreu–Mantel–Sonnenschein theorem, which integrates the results of three papers (Debreu 1974; Mantel 1974; Sonnenschein 1973). In contrast to Slutsky symmetry, aggregate demand systems do inherit properties of continuity (sums of continuous functions are continuous) and homogeneity of degree zero in prices and income (although see below).

The aggregate cross-price elasticities of two products will not generally be symmetric even if Slutsky symmetry is satisfied:

$$\eta_{12} = \frac{\partial \ln Q_1}{\partial \ln P_2} = \frac{\partial Q_1}{\partial P_2}\frac{P_2}{Q_1} = \frac{P_2}{Q_1}b_{12},$$

$$\eta_{21} = \frac{\partial \ln Q_2}{\partial \ln P_1} = \frac{\partial Q_2}{\partial P_1}\frac{P_1}{Q_2} = \frac{P_1}{Q_2}b_{21},$$

so that $\eta_{12} \neq \eta_{12}$.[17]

Note that an important implication of these results is that we should not, in general, expect symmetry in substitution patterns. That means, for example, that small shops may be materially constrained by larger ones but not vice versa (market definitions may well be asymmetric).[18] Another example arises from complementarity—left and right shoes may be obviously symmetric demand complements in the sense that most people will genuinely only care about a pair of shoes so that the price of left shoes increasing will reduce demand for right shoes and vice versa. However, other very different situations can easily arise. For instance, in after-market (or secondary product market) cases, complementarity tends to operate in only one direction. To see why consider a specific example involving loans and insurance on loans known as Payment Protection Insurance (PPI). The U.K. Competition Commission argued that consumers largely choose their loan provider on the basis of the interest rate available, their relationship with their bank, and more generally the brand available.[19] Many consumers will go on to buy PPI, but most do not seriously consider whether to purchase PPI until they reach the point of sale of credit, for example, actually sitting in a bank branch having filled out a loan application.[20] That means consumer demand for credit probably does not depend greatly on the price of the PPI, while, in contrast, the demand for PPI depends heavily on the price of credit since that directly affects the number of consumers who arrive at the branch to buy the credit and hence the PPI. We called this a situation of asymmetric complementarity and noted that such asymmetric complementarities underlies all of the antitrust cases involving after-market goods.[21]

---

[17] For completeness, the own-price elasticities in the linear demand system we study in this section are

$$\eta_{11} = \frac{\partial Q_1}{\partial P_1}\frac{P_1}{Q_1} = \frac{P_1}{Q_1}(-b_{11}) \quad \text{and} \quad \eta_{22} = \frac{\partial Q_2}{\partial P_2}\frac{P_2}{Q_2} = \frac{P_2}{Q_2}(-b_{22}).$$

[18] See, for example, the CC report on Groceries available at www.competition-commission.org.uk/inquiries/ref2006/grocery/index.htm.

[19] See the CC report on PPI available at www.competition-commission.org.uk/Inquiries/ref2007/ppi/index.htm.

[20] Survey results suggested that only 11% of personal loan customers who went on to buy PPI and 21% of mortgage customers who went on to buy mortgage PPI shopped around for the bundle of credit and PPI, i.e., a protected loan.

[21] Probably the most famous recent after-market case involved after-sales parts and servicing for photocopiers and went to the U.S. Supreme Court: *Kodak v. Image Technical Services*, 504 U.S. 451 (1992). Not

9.1.3.2 Homogeneity

Choice theory suggests that individual demand functions will be homogeneous of degree 0 in prices and income. That restriction implies that if we multiply all prices and income by a constant multiple, the consumer's demand will not change. For instance, if we double all prices and we double the income, the individual demand for all goods remains the same. In general, for any $\lambda > 0$, we will have

$$q_i(\lambda p_1, \dots, \lambda p_J, \lambda y) = q_i(p_1, \dots, p_J, y).$$

This restriction follows immediately from the budget constraint in a utility-maximization problem. To see why, note that the two problems,

$$\max_q u(q) \text{ subject to } \sum_j p_j q_j = y \quad \text{and} \quad \max_q u(q) \text{ subject to } \sum_j \lambda p_j q_j = \lambda y,$$

are entirely equivalent since the λs in the latter problem simply cancel out. Thus the demand obtained from the two problems should be identical.

Furthermore, this assumption survives aggregation (by the Debreu–Mantel–Sonnenschein theorem) provided it is interpreted in the right way. Namely, that when prices increase by a factor λ, *all* consumers' incomes need to increase by the same factor. In that eventuality, the aggregate demand will similarly be unchanged. Since no individuals demand changes, neither can the aggregate. On the other hand, if prices double and aggregate income doubles but only because a few people increased their income by a very large amount, then aggregate demand may change. The people who experienced the income increase will be able to afford more goods than before because their income more than doubled while prices only doubled. On the other hand, the rest of the population would be able to afford fewer goods because their income growth did not match the price rise. Consequently, aggregate income will be spent differently than before—the richer members of the population will not typically buy what the poorer people can no longer afford. For example, if all prices double and the income also doubles but the extra income is earned by the richer individuals, consumption will change toward a pattern of more luxury goods and fewer basic products. One therefore needs to be very careful in applying homogeneity restrictions to aggregate demand and this example illustrates in particular that aggregate demand may depend on far more than aggregate income—demand will often also depend on, at least, the important features of the distribution of income.

9.1.3.3 Homogeneity in Expenditure Share Equations

Theory suggests that individual expenditure share functions are homogeneous of degree zero in income and prices. An alternative way to put the argument above that homogeneity survives aggregation is that the sum of homogeneous degree zero

---

all junior courts in the United States appear to agree with the logic of that decision and so, subsequently, the judgment has been interpreted narrowly (see Goldfine and Vorrasi 2004).

functions is homogeneous of degree zero. For that reason, it is sometimes reasonable to impose homogeneity of degree zero restrictions on aggregate expenditure share functions. Homogeneity of degree zero implies that

$$w_j(\lambda p_1, \dots, \lambda p_J, \lambda y) = w_j(p_1, \dots, p_J, y) \quad \text{for } \lambda > 0.$$

Recall the AIDS model expenditure share function is

$$w_{jt}(p, y) = \alpha_j + \sum_{k=1}^{J} \gamma_{jk} \ln p_{kt} + \beta_j \ln\left(\frac{y_t}{P_t}\right) + \xi_{jt},$$

so that the homogeneity restriction requires that

$$w_{jt}(\lambda p, \lambda y) = \alpha_j + \sum_{k=1}^{J} \gamma_{jk} \ln \lambda p_{kt} + \beta_j \ln\left(\frac{\lambda y_t}{P_t(\lambda)}\right) + \xi_{jt} = w_{jt}(p, y)$$

and this in turn implies that the following parameters restrictions must hold:

$$\sum_{j=1}^{J} \alpha_j = 1, \qquad \sum_{j=1}^{J} \gamma_{jk} = 0, \qquad \sum_{k=1}^{J} \gamma_{jk} = 0,$$

where the sum over j indicates a restriction across equations and the sum over k a restriction within an equation. To illustrate where these restrictions come from, note that

$$\begin{aligned} \sum_{k=1}^{J} \gamma_{jk} \ln \lambda p_{kt} &= \sum_{k=1}^{J} \gamma_{jk} (\ln \lambda + \ln p_{kt}) \\ &= (\ln \lambda)\left(\sum_{k=1}^{J} \gamma_{jk}\right) + \sum_{k=1}^{J} \gamma_{jk} \ln p_{kt} = \sum_{k=1}^{J} \gamma_{jk} \ln p_{kt}, \end{aligned}$$

where the latter equality only holds if $\sum_{k=1}^{J} \gamma_{jk} = 0$. The other parameter restrictions can be derived by noting that we require $P_t(\lambda) = \lambda P_t(1)$, where

$$\ln P(\lambda) = \alpha_0 + \sum_{k=1}^{J} \alpha_k \ln \lambda p_k + \frac{1}{2} \sum_{k=1}^{J} \sum_{j=1}^{J} \gamma_{jk} (\ln \lambda p_k)(\ln \lambda p_j).$$

9.1.3.4 Additivity

Another restriction that can be imposed on individual demand systems is the additivity restriction—the requirement that the demands must satisfy the budget constraint:

$$\sum_{j=1}^{J} p_j q_j = y, \quad \text{where } q_j = q_j(p, y),$$

where q_j is the quantity purchased of good j. This provides cross-equation restriction(s) on our model. In an expenditure share model this restriction is typically imposed as

$$\sum_{j=1}^{J} \frac{p_j q_j}{y} = \frac{y}{y} \quad \text{or} \quad \sum_{j=1}^{J} w_j(p, y) = 1,$$

i.e., that the expenditure shares add to one.

In the almost ideal demand system, the additivity restrictions emerge from the requirement that we can impose on the model that

$$\begin{aligned}\sum_{j=1}^{J} w_{jt}(p, y) &= \sum_{j=1}^{J} \left(\alpha_j + \sum_{k=1}^{J} \gamma_{jk} \ln p_{kt} + \beta_j \ln \left(\frac{y_t}{P_t} \right) + \xi_{jt} \right) \\ &= \sum_{j=1}^{J} \alpha_j + \sum_{k=1}^{J} \ln p_{kt} \left(\sum_{j=1}^{J} \gamma_{jk} \right) + \ln \left(\frac{y_t}{P_t} \right) \sum_{j=1}^{J} \beta_j + \sum_{j=1}^{J} \xi_{jt} \\ &= 1,\end{aligned}$$

whatever the values of prices and income. Necessary conditions for our expenditure share system to always satisfy this condition therefore gives us the "additivity" cross-equation restrictions on the parameters:

$$\sum_{j=1}^{J} \alpha_j = 1, \qquad \sum_{j=1}^{J} \gamma_{jk} = 0, \qquad \sum_{j=1}^{J} \beta_j = 0.$$

In addition, additivity requires the restriction $\sum_{j=1}^{J} \xi_{jt} = 0$, which means that the variance–covariance of the errors from the full collection of expenditure share equations will be singular. First note that the parameters of the Jth equation are entirely determined by estimates of the $J - 1$ equations using the additivity restrictions. The fact that the system variance–covariance matrix is nonsingular will mean that it will not be possible to estimate all the equations together, one must be dropped. It does not usually matter which one in terms of the econometric estimates obtained under the assumption of additivity but it will obviously be easier to drop an equation relating to a product which is not the focus of the study (see Barten 1969; Berndt and Savin 1975; see also Barton 1977 and the references therein).

9.1.4 An Example of AIDS Estimation

An application using AIDS is provided by Hausman et al. (1994). We examined earlier in this chapter the first and second levels of their three-level demand system. At the first stage they modeled demand for beer. At the second stage they modeled the allocation of expenditure on beer between different market segments, estimating a log-linear differentiated product demand system, conditional on a level of beer expenditure. We now turn to their third-level model, where they apply the AIDS methodology to model consumer allocation of expenditure within a segment of the beer market. We focus on their model of consumer behavior within the market segment for premium beer, where they considered a system of five expenditure share equations at the brand level ($j = 1, \dots, 5$), one for each Budweiser, Molson, Miller, Labatts, and Coors. They used panel data with sales volumes and prices for each brand in a cross section of markets ($m = 1, \dots, M$) over time ($t = 1, \dots, T$).

Specifically, they estimate

$$w_{jmt} = \alpha_j + \sum_{k=1}^{5} \gamma_{jk} \ln p_{kmt} + \beta_j \ln\left(\frac{y_{mt}}{P_{mt}}\right) + \lambda_j t + \delta_j \ln(n_{\text{Stores}}) + \xi_{jmt},$$

where y_{mt} is the total expenditure on the goods in the market segment (here premium beer), P_{mt} is the Stone price index in the premium beer segment, t is a time trend, and n_{Stores} is the number of stores in the market where the brand is present. Adding such characteristics in the equation is acceptable, indeed may be desirable if they control for important elements of data variation. Doing so, however, must be recognized as a pragmatic fix to control for particular variation in the data while allowing an approximation to the DGP rather than an attempt to model the structural DGP itself. Such reduced-form "fixes" to simple static models are common and a necessary fact of life in applied work. The fully structural alternative in this case would probably involve developing a model in which consumers choose which shop to go to as well as which products to buy. Aggregate product-level demand would add up across shops and hence would depend explicitly on the set of shops that carry the product. On the one hand, building a model of shop choice will add a great deal of complexity—consider that supermarket choice may depend on far more than the price of a particular category of goods, say, tissue paper—and we may have no data about that. On the other hand, the analyst must also be aware that reduced-form fixes to simplify the modeling process do nonetheless raise important questions about whether the rest of the model can in fact be treated as "structural" when there are important dimensions of data variation captured only as reduced forms. Such is the sometimes theoretically messy nature of real-world demand modeling. The reality is that even the most ardent modeler cannot model everything and frankly there is not much point in trying to unless the data are rich in the dimensions that will facilitate estimation of the model.

Hausman et al. (1994) impose all of the symmetry, homogeneity, and additivity restrictions discussed above on their model. Since the additivity of the budget constraint is also assumed to hold, they omit the equation specifying the expenditure share of Coors.

As we have discussed, the restrictions that impose homogeneity on this system are

$$\sum_{j=1}^{J} \alpha_j = 1, \qquad \sum_{j=1}^{J} \gamma_{jk} = 0, \qquad \sum_{k=1}^{J} \gamma_{jk} = 0,$$

while the first two restrictions are also needed for additivity to hold.

Symmetry imposes the restrictions, $\gamma_{jk} = \gamma_{kj}$ for all $j \neq k$.

The results of their estimation are shown in table 2.1 and illustrate that the cross-equation symmetry restrictions are imposed. See, for example, that the coefficient on the price of Budweiser in the Molson regression is 0.372, which is identical to the price coefficient on Molson in the Budweiser equation.

The parameters for the Coors price coefficient are not reported. However, we can retrieve the implied coefficient for the price of Coors using the additivity restriction that $\sum_{j=1}^{J} \gamma_{jk} = 0$. Since symmetry is imposed, we can equivalently derive the coefficient using the equation for the determinants of Budweiser purchases, since $\sum_{k=1}^{J} \gamma_{jk} = 0$, that is,

$$\sum_{k=1}^{J} \hat{\gamma}_{jk} = -0.936 + 0.372 + 0.243 + 0.15 + \hat{\gamma}_{\text{Bud,Coors}} = 0$$

$$\Longrightarrow \quad \hat{\gamma}_{\text{Bud,Coors}} = 0.171.$$

9.2 Demand System Estimation: Discrete Choice Models

Discrete choice demand models attempt to represent choice situations in which consumers choose from a list of options. Typically, the models focus on the case where consumers choose just one option from the choices available. For example, a consumer may choose which type of car to buy but would never choose "how much" of a car to buy; optional extras aside, a car is usually a discrete purchase.[22] The main advantage of the available discrete choice models is that they impose considerable structure on consumers' preferences and doing so greatly reduces the number of parameters we need to estimate in markets with a multitude of products.

For example, in the AIDS model developed earlier in the chapter, before the restrictions of choice theory are imposed there are a total of J^2 parameters on prices (J per equation) to estimate. To be clear, a demand system with 200 products such as that needed for a product-level demand system of a market like the car market would generate a base model with 40,000 parameters on prices that we would need to estimate. Analogously, there are 40,000 own- and cross-price elasticities to be estimated. This is clearly impossible with the kinds of data sets we usually have and so it became clear that some structure would need to be placed on those 40,000 own- and cross-price elasticities. The multilevel model used by Hausman et al. (1994) is one way to impose structure on the set of elasticities. An alternative is to use

[22] There are discrete choice models which allow the menu of choices to include a choice of "how many" cars to buy (see, for example, Hendel 1999).

"characteristics" based models.[23] Historically, the discrete choice demand literature followed the characteristics approach while the continuous choice demand literature followed the "product"-level approach, although there are some recent exceptions, most notably Slade et al. (2002). There is no obvious practical reason why we cannot have "characteristics" and "product"-level models of both continuous choice and discrete choice varieties. In the future, therefore, the main distinguishing feature of these classes of models may revert to the only real source of difference: the nature of consumer choice. For the moment, however, most of the discrete choice literature is characteristics based while the continuous choice models are product-level models. In this section we discuss the most popular discrete choice models currently in use.[24]

9.2.1 Discrete Choice Demand Systems

The foundation of discrete choice demand functions is not fundamentally different from our usual utility maximization framework with the exception that in this context our consumer faces constraints on her choice set: discrete goods can only be consumed as 0,1 choices. For each of these discrete goods, consumers either buy one or they do not buy one. Below, we follow the literature in building such models by first considering an individual's choice problem and then deriving a model of aggregate demand by aggregating over individuals.

9.2.1.1 Individual Discrete Choice Problem

Consider the familiar utility-maximization problem:

$$V(\underline{p}, y; \theta_i) = \max_{\underline{x} \in X} u(\underline{x}; \theta_i) \quad \text{subject to } \underline{p}\underline{x} \leqslant y,$$

where θ_i represents the parameters specific to individual i. The parameter θ_i is customer specific and can be interpreted as indicating a certain customer "type." Different consumer "types" have different preferences and will therefore make different choices. The difference from our usual context is that discrete choice models put constraints on the choice set so that the individual must choose whether to buy or not a certain product within a group of products or to spend all of her resources on some alternative "outside" good(s). The outside good is so-called because it constitutes the rest of the consumers' choice problem outside the focus of study. Usually, we include just one composite commodity as an outside good and in fact it is often useful to think of it as the good money. We will normalize the price of the outside

[23] See Lancaster (1966) and Gorman (1956). There are also, of course, classic individual studies of demand which predate both Lancaster and even Gorman and which use characteristics of products to control for quality differentials. For example, Hotelling (1929) uses store location as a product characteristic in a model of consumers' choice of store.

[24] A discrete choice model with potentially large numbers of parameters akin to the AIDS and Translog style models is provided in Davis (2006b). For a very good introduction, see Pudney (1989). See also a number of classic contributions to the literature in Manski and McFadden (1981).

good to 1, $p_0 = 1$, which we can do without loss of generality since we have the freedom to choose the units of the outside good.

Formally, for a standard discrete choice model the choice set X can be represented as the set of combinations between a given choice of product and an amount of outside goods:

$$X = \{x \mid x_0 \in [0, M] \text{ and } x_j \in \{0, 1\} \text{ for all } j = 1, \dots, J, \text{ where } M < \infty\},$$

where x_0 is the quantity of the outside good. Note that it is a continuous choice variable in the sense that we can choose any amount of it from zero to a very large finite number M (perhaps all the money in the world). The other choice variables x_j, $j = 1, \dots, J$, take on the value 1 if product j, belonging to the set of potential choices or "inside goods," is chosen and 0 otherwise.

An example of a choice set is the choice between types of car as the inside good choices while the outside good represents the amount of money you keep for other things. We will usually want to assume that only one inside good can be chosen and to do so we further impose the restriction that no two inside good quantities can be positive,

$$x_j x_k = 0 \quad \text{for all } j \neq k \text{ and } j, k > 0.$$

The budget constraint in discrete choice frameworks includes the quantity of the outside good consumed for each choice and also reflects the option of only buying the outside good. Thus the budget constraint reduces to

$$\begin{aligned} p_0 x_0 + p_j x_j &= y \quad \text{if } x_j = 1 \text{ and } j > 0, \\ p_0 x_0 &= y \quad \text{if } x_j = 0 \text{ for all } j > 0, \end{aligned}$$

so that, if $I(j > 0)$ is an indicator variable taking the value one if $j > 0$, the amount of outside good consumed can be written as

$$x_0 = \frac{y - p_j I(j > 0)}{p_0} = y - p_j I(j > 0).$$

If I buy a car, then I have my income less the price paid. If I do not buy a car, then I have all of my income to "spend" consuming alternative goods and services,

$$x_0 = \frac{y}{p_0} = y.$$

Thus our consumer's choice problem can be written as the maximization of utility over the set of choices among the inside goods together with the additional possibility of allocating all the budget to the outside good. The conditional indirect utility function represents the maximum utility that can be achieved given the prices, income, and customer type. This maximum utility will be the utility generated by the preferred good among those in the set of options, including the outside good, for every level of prices and income.

Formally,

$$V(\underline{p}, y, \theta_i) = \max_{\substack{\underline{x} \in \{[0,\infty) x \{0,1\}^J | x_j x_k = 0 \\ \text{for all } j,k>0 \text{ subject to } j \neq k\}}} u(\underline{x}; \theta_i) \quad \text{subject to } \underline{px} \leqslant y,$$

which reduces to

$$V_i(\underline{p}, y, \theta_i) = \max_{j=0,\dots,J} v_j(y - p_j I(j > 0); \theta_i),$$

where $v_j(y - p_j I(j > 0); \theta_i)$ is the utility provided by the choice regarding good j and where the option 0 captures the option of not purchasing any of the inside goods. Specifically,

$$v_j(y - p_j I(j > 0); \theta_i) \equiv \begin{cases} u(y - p_j I(j > 0), 0, \dots, 0, x_j = 1, 0, \dots, 0; \theta_i) & \text{if } j > 0, \\ u(y, 0, \dots, 0; \theta_i) & \text{if } j = 0, \end{cases}$$

which is formally known as the "conditional indirect utility function" for option j and consumer i.[25]

By using the structure of the choice set we have simplified the consumer's problem to be a choice over $J+1$ discrete options. A consumer will choose a particular option if the value of the indirect utility function for that option at given prices and income is the highest. As usual, the solution to the maximization problem provides us with an individual demand function for each product. However, the inside good demands are discrete so the demand for inside good $j > 0$ is

$$x_j(y, p; \theta_i) = \begin{cases} 1 & \text{if } v_{ij} = \max_{k=0,\dots,J} v_{ik}, \\ 0 & \text{otherwise,} \end{cases}$$

where the maximization over k covers the whole range of options.

9.2.1.2 Introducing Product Characteristics

Gorman (1956) and Lancaster (1966) suggested that consumers choose products based on their intrinsic product characteristics rather than the products themselves. Assume the vector $\underline{w}$ represents a set of characteristics which are "produced" by consuming the products x, according to the "production" relation $\underline{w} = f(\underline{x})$. The consumer's problem can then be rewritten as maximizing the utility derived from characteristics subject to both the budget constraint and the "production" relation describing the way in which a purchase of products provides consumers with their characteristics:

$$V(\underline{p}, y, \theta_i) = \max_{\underline{x} \in X} u(\underline{w}; \theta_i) \quad \text{subject to } \underline{px} \leqslant y \text{ and } \underline{w} = f(\underline{x}).$$

[25] It is an indirect utility function because it has had the quantities and budget constraint substituted in and hence depends on prices. It is conditional because it is only the indirect utility function should choice j turn out to be optimal.

Typically, purchasing one good will provide a bundle of product characteristics. For instance, one car will provide horsepower, size, a number of coffee cup holders, and so on. The vector of characteristics will have elements that take on different values depending on the product chosen.

Following the same process of substituting in the budget constraint as above, we can derive the conditional indirect utility function incorporating product characteristics. The result is that the conditional indirect utility function now depends on product characteristics as well as income, prices and consumer tastes:

$$v_j(y - p_j I(j > 0), w_j; \theta_i) = \begin{cases} u(y - p_j I(j > 0), \underline{w}_j; \theta_i) & \text{if } j > 0, \\ u(y, 0, \dots, 0; \theta_i) & \text{if } j = 0. \end{cases}$$

If each good has a characteristic that is unique to that good, then we get back to the product-level utility model. Thus although the characteristics model is usually used to "simplify" product-level models, at a conceptual level the model is a strictly more general framework than the standard utility model, one that allows products to supply customers with a combination of features individually valued by the consumer.

9.2.1.3 *When Income Drops Out*

So far we have derived a form for conditional indirect utility that depends on a consumer's income, price for any inside good, and also the product characteristics of that good. Suppose further that we have a form of additive separability between income and prices in all of the conditional indirect utilities. Formally, this means that

$$v_j(y - p_j I(j > 0), w_j; \theta_i) = \alpha y + \bar{v}_j(p_j I(j > 0), w_j; \theta_i) \quad \text{for } j = 0, 1, \dots, J.$$

If so, since $\max_{k=0,\dots,J} v_{ik} = \alpha y + \max_{k=0,\dots,J} \bar{v}_{ik}$, the resulting demand functions for any given individual will be identical whether we solve the problem on the right-hand side or the maximization problem on the left-hand side. In each case, the resulting demand functions will be independent of the consumer's level of income. This assumption underlies many models where conditional indirect utility functions are written simply as a function of prices and product characteristics which do not include income:

$$\bar{v}_j(p_j, w_j; \theta_i) \equiv \bar{\bar{v}}_j(w_j; \theta_i) - \alpha p_j.$$

Note that in order to be consistent with an underlying utility structure, conditional indirect utility specifications which "ignore" income must be additively separable in prices with a coefficient that does not depend on the option chosen, or else the income term would not have dropped out in the first place. For example, the specification,

$$v_j(y - p_j I(j > 0), w_j; \theta_i) = \alpha_j (y - p_j I(j > 0)) + \bar{\bar{v}}_j(w_j; \theta_i),$$

does not fulfill this condition and so would not allow us to take the income term through the maximization.

This assumption requires that the marginal utility of income is independent (i) of the option chosen and (ii) of the other determinants of the utility of choosing a given option. If an individual's demand depends on their level of income, then this assumption must be violated since that is telling you that income should not drop out and you will probably prefer to work with an alternative functional form. For example, Berry et al. (1995) believe that the demand for a type of car will depend on a consumer's level of income and work with the natural logarithm formulation,

$$v_j(y - p_j I(j > 0), w_j; \theta_i) = \alpha \ln(y - p_j I(j > 0)) + \overline{\overline{v}}_j(w_j; \theta_i),$$

so that the marginal utility of income depends on the level of income.

9.2.1.4 Aggregating Demand

The market (aggregate) demand for product j will simply add up the demands of all the individuals who purchase the product. If we have a total mass of S consumers and the density of each unit mass of consumers types is characterized by the perhaps multivariate density function, $f_{\underline{\theta}}(\underline{\theta})$, we can write

$$\begin{aligned} D_j(\underline{p}, w_j) &= S \int_{\theta} x_j(\underline{p}, w_j, \underline{\theta}) f_{\underline{\theta}}(\underline{\theta})\, \mathrm{d}\underline{\theta} \\ &= S \int_{\{\underline{\theta} \mid v_j(\theta_j .) > v_k(\theta_k .) \text{ for all } k \neq j\}} f_{\underline{\theta}}(\underline{\theta})\, \mathrm{d}\underline{\theta}. \end{aligned}$$

Note that if there is only one dimension of consumer heterogeneity, this will be a univariate integral. On the other hand, there may be many dimensions of consumer heterogeneity, in which case computing aggregate demand will involve solving a multidimensional integral with one dimension for each of the dimensions of θ defining the consumer type. For each individual of type $\underline{\theta}$ who buys the product j, x_j takes the value 1 so the second equality indicates that the demand for inside good j is just the set of consumers who choose that option over the alternatives. The integral will be easy to calculate if we make enough appropriate assumptions regarding the distribution of the types in the population and/or assuming independence of the distribution of the different types. In other words, making the different elements of $\underline{\theta}$ independent and choosing f conveniently, we can facilitate the computation of the aggregate demand. On the other hand, like all assumptions the convenient ones may not be the ones which most closely capture reality. The nature of consumer heterogeneity will depend on the market being studied, but will often include income levels y_i.

In models of product differentiation we distinguish between "horizontal" dimensions of product differentiation and dimensions of "vertical" product differentiation. The basic distinction is that consumers disagree about product quality rankings along "horizontal" dimensions while consumers agree about product quality rankings along "vertical" quality dimensions. For example, two consumers may disagree about which of two otherwise identical supermarkets to shop in if they live in different places. In contrast, consumers would agree that all else equal a faster computer CPU clock speed is better than a slower computer CPU clock speed. If so, then we might think of "location" as a horizontal dimension of product differentiation while CPU clock speed is a "vertical" dimension of product differentiation. Naturally, a quality ranking is not the same as a preference ranking—different consumers will choose different options even in the case of vertical product differentiation since they will trade off quality and price in different ways. Thus we can all agree perhaps that a Rolls Royce is a better car than a Citroen 2CV, but not all consumers would (or could) choose to buy the Rolls Royce. We discuss each of these models in more detail in the sections that follow. In doing so, our primary aim is to allow the reader to relate the econometric discrete choice models to the perhaps more familiar economic theory presentation of discrete choice models and vice versa. Doing so allows both a fairly direct application of all the reader knows about theory models to econometric model building and, furthermore, allows us to generalize the theory models we work with by working with them on the computer. Doing so in turn allows us to build more realistic demand models.

9.2.2 Horizontal Product Differentiation

In models with horizontal product differentiation, products differ in a way that means that at equal prices consumers will disagree which product they prefer to buy. Consider for example choosing a film to watch. Some people like action films while others prefer romantic comedies. People's preferences are different and therefore they disagree about which is "best" even if both films were available at equal prices. There are many possible examples, however, the term "horizontal" comes from the study of consumer's choice of shop among those available in a city and more specifically from Hotelling's classic paper on retail demand, published in 1929. Recent empirical discrete choice models of retail demand build directly on Hotelling's discrete choice model and it is perhaps the nicest framework within which to see the profound links between the empirical and theoretical discrete choice models.

9.2.2.1 The Hotelling Model

Hotelling (1929) developed his demand model and used it to examine the equilibrium outcomes when stores strategically interact while choosing location and perhaps also prices. We know that one solution to Bertrand's paradox, that price is driven down to marginal cost even in a duopoly situation, is to introduce product differentiation. Firms have an incentive to differentiate their products because it softens price competition and therefore allows higher margins.

In this chapter, we are only interested in the demand side of the Hotelling model. We study the minor variant of Hotelling's demand model introduced in an important

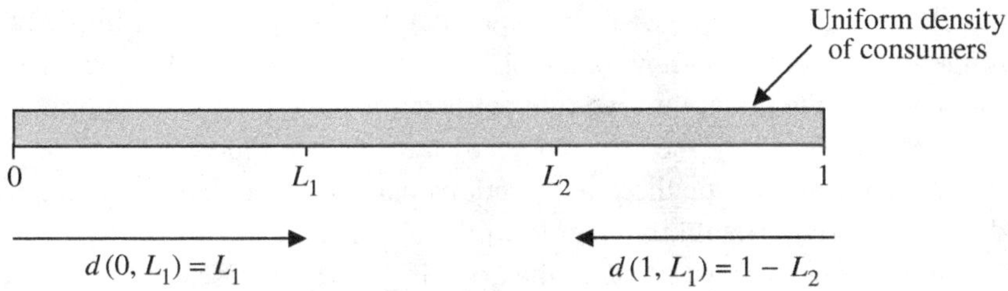

Figure 9.3. Hotelling's linear city model with a uniform density of consumers shown as the shaded area above the line.

paper by d'Aspremont et al. (1979).[26] It is well worth noting that Hotelling went on to embed his demand model in a two-stage game, where firms choose location (at stage one) and prices (at stage two). Demand, as ever, forms one of the fundamental building blocks of the rich structure that allows us to go on to study firm behavior, in this case in both location and pricing decisions. The fundamental driver of the demand model is that firms differentiate from rivals by using their location and are more attractive to nearby customers all else equal, which in this model means at the same prices.

For simplicity, the space over which individuals are spread is assumed to be one dimensional and represented by a line between [0, 1], known as Hotelling's "linear city." Let us assume that customers are distributed evenly over that line with a total mass of S consumers so that

$$f(L_i; S) = \begin{cases} S & \text{if } L_i \in [0, 1], \\ 0 & \text{otherwise.} \end{cases}$$

Often the presentation of this model puts the parameter $S = 1$ so that consumers have a proper uniform density with total mass one and then authors multiply the resulting demand function by S. The two approaches are entirely equivalent. While density functions are familiar, and the analysis fundamentally identical, it is clearly closer to reality to have a total mass of S consumers and so we follow that approach in this section.

Let us assume there are two firms or "shops" that are respectively located at L_1 and L_2 and that the firms' locations and their prices are each for the moment fixed. Without loss of generality we assume that $L_1 \leqslant L_2$. The situation can be represented in figure 9.3.

Consumers "live" in different locations and are therefore differentiated by their closeness to locations L_1 and L_2. For the purposes of simplicity, we assume that each consumer will buy from only one shop (they make a discrete choice) and we also assume that they must buy from one of the shops. Not buying is not an option

[26] Those authors famously showed that Hotelling's original paper, while profound in many ways, including implicitly using the subgame perfect Nash equilibrium concept as later defined by Selten, the characterization of the equilibrium was incorrect and shown not to always exist.

so that there is no "outside good" in this model. We assume that the utility of the consumer only depends on how far she is from the shop and on the price that she needs to pay for the good; thus we rule out heterogeneity in product offerings and also in the "retail services" being provided by the different shops. We shall see later in the chapter that each of these assumptions can easily be relaxed in empirical models that build on Hotelling's classic work.

Denote the consumer valuation of the good if there is no distance to be traveled and the price is zero as "s." This is the valuation of the good by the consumer if there were zero cost to obtaining it. We assume the happiness that consumer i gets from consumption depends on this surplus s, the distance between the location of the consumer L_i and location of the shop L_j, and the price at the shop p_j. A higher distance to the shop decreases the valuation for the product and so does a high price:

$$v_{ij} = s - td(L_i, L_j)^2 - p_j, \quad j = 1, 2,$$

where $d(L_i, L_j)$ is the distance between the customer and the store and t is a transport cost parameter. In terms of the general framework laid out in the introduction to this section, this is the "conditional indirect utility function" for the Hotelling model, where in this model there is just one dimension of consumer heterogeneity: the consumer's (unidimensional) location $L_i \in [0, 1]$.

Along a line, Euclidean distance between two points is measured as

$$d(L_i, L_j) = |L_i - L_j| = \sqrt{(L_i - L_j)^2} \quad \text{so that } d(L_i, L_j)^2 = (L_i - L_j)^2.$$

In our example, the cost of transport is quadratic in distance so that utility decreases more rapidly as distance increases. In principle, travel costs could be any function of distance and we could have costs that increase proportionally with distance. However, quadratic costs avoid bothersome issues with the existence of an equilibrium price and in that sense present a technical advantage.[27]

Consumers buy from the store that gives them the highest utility so that to compute the demand function we must solve the discrete choice problem: $\max\{v_{i1}, v_{i2}\}$. It follows immediately that people (the set of consumer types) who choose good 1 will be

$$\{L_i \mid v_{i1} \geqslant v_{i2}\} = \{L_i \mid s - td(L_i, L_1)^2 - p_1 \geqslant s - td(L_i, L_2)^2 - p_2\},$$

[27] For an empirical model, this question is important. D'Aspremont et al. (1979) show that Hotelling's model based on a linear distance cost did not always have an equilibrium and they also show that his proposed "minimum differentiation" in locations equilibrium was not, in fact, an equilibrium when examining the two-stage location then prices game. D'Aspremont et al. (1979) solve the difficulty by introducing a quadratic distance cost to the model. They show that in their model—the one outlined here—the equilibrium is characterized by "maximum differentiation." Each case is clearly special and therefore restrictive and in general an empirical model would need to face a reality that firms do not always locate either next to one another or as far away from one another as possible. On the other hand, an empirical model would also need to know that an equilibrium of the game exists and can be computed robustly—otherwise researchers and their computers may spend a lot of time looking for equilibria that do not exist.

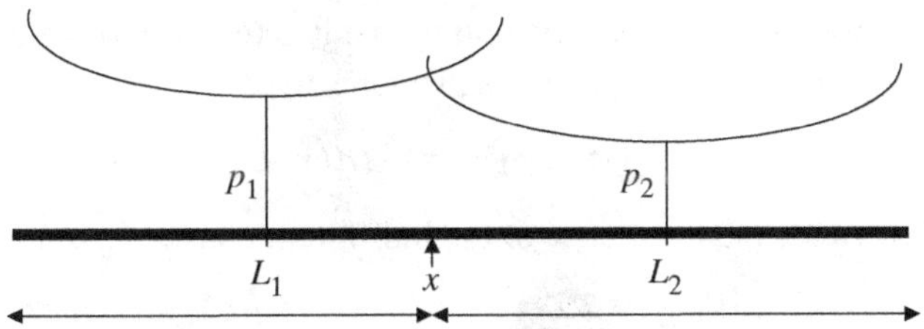

Figure 9.4. Hotelling and the indifferent consumer with quadratic transport costs.

or, more succinctly,

$$\{L_i \mid d(L_i, L_1)^2 - d(L_i, L_2)^2 \leqslant (p_2 - p_1)/t\},$$

so that formally we may write aggregate demand as[28]

$$D_1(p_1, p_2; L_1, L_2, t, S) = \int_{\{L_i \mid d(L_i, L_1)^2 - d(L_i, L_2)^2 \leqslant (p_2 - p_1)/t\}} f(L_i; S)\, \mathrm{d}L_i.$$

Solving this integral is very easy on a computer—it is a simple univariate integral—for given values of $(p_1, p_2, L_1, L_2, t, S)$. In principle, we might want to use data from such a market to estimate the parameters, (t, S). In practice two-dimensional models will typically be more appropriate to take to retail data and we discuss the generalization below.

Figure 9.4 demonstrates the situation graphically using an "umbrella" picture.[29] The vertical bar captures the price associated with that option while the "fabric" part of the (inverted) "umbrella" captures the way in which quadratic transport costs increase for consumers who live further away from the firms' locations. Thus the umbrella captures the total cost associated with each good. Since the gross surplus is identical across firms, consumers will choose the option which can be obtained at minimum cost, as shown in the diagram. The picture illustrates a case where prices and locations are such that both goods are purchased and there is an indifferent consumer located between the firms at a point labeled "x." If we shorten the vertical bar associated with product 2, which corresponds to a lowering of p_2, we can use the picture to trace through the implications for demand for each product.[30]

---

[28] Similarly,

$$D_2(p_1, p_2; L_1, L_2) = \int_{\{L_i \mid d(L_i, L_1)^2 - d(L_i, L_2)^2 \geqslant (p_2 - p_1)/t\}} f(L_i)\, \mathrm{d}L_i.$$

[29] The origin of this picture is unknown to the authors, but it is an extraordinarily useful tool for the Hotelling model and can easily be adapted, for example, to facilitate consideration of the linear transport cost case.

[30] In particular, doing so makes clear that for some prices and locations the result will be all of the demand arising at firm 1 or at firm 2. Such cases are important for a full analysis, but for ease of exposition we assume interior solutions. Since our two firms can always make positive profits in this model by differentiating themselves and serving some customers, the assumption is not restrictive.

Analytically, we can solve for x by noting that it is the location of the indifferent consumer, that is, the value of location x, which solves[31]

$$s - td(x, L_1)^2 - p_1 = s - td(x, L_2)^2 - p_2.$$

A little algebra yields the location x of the indifferent consumer,

$$x = \frac{p_2 - p_1}{2t(L_2 - L_1)} + \frac{L_1 + L_2}{2}.$$

Anyone to the right of the indifferent consumer will prefer shop 2. Anyone to the left will prefer store 1. Thus, given the uniform density of the consumers, the demand functions for shops 1 and 2 respectively take the form:[32]

$$\begin{aligned} D_1(p_1, p_2; L_1, L_2) &= \int_0^x f(L_i)\,\mathrm{d}L_i = Sx \\ &= \frac{S(p_2 - p_1)}{2t(L_2 - L_1)} + S\left(\frac{L_1 + L_2}{2}\right), \\ D_2(p_1, p_2; L_1, L_2) &= \int_x^1 f(L_i)\,\mathrm{d}L_i = S(1 - x) \\ &= S\left(1 - \frac{p_2 - p_1}{2t(L_2 - L_1)} - \frac{L_1 + L_2}{2}\right). \end{aligned}$$

The demands depend on the prices of both shops and on the location of both shops. For equal prices, firm 1 will sell to everyone to the left of its location and to exactly the midway point between the firms. Charging $p_2 \geqslant p_1$ means that demand at location 1 is higher than demand at location 2 since the indifference point moves closer to L_2 compared with the equal prices case. For fixed locations, this is a demand model which is linear in prices and where parameters are functions of the other product's characteristics, in this case the locations of the two products.[33]

---

[31] Simplifying gives $t(x - L_1)^2 + p_1 = t(x - L_2)^2 + p_2$ and rearranging yields

$$(x - L_1)^2 - (x - L_2)^2 = \frac{p_2 - p_1}{t},$$

which can be expanded and simplified to give

$$\not{x}^2 - 2xL_1 + L_1^2 - (\not{x}^2 - 2xL_2 + L_2^2) = \frac{p_2 - p_1}{t},$$

and hence

$$2x(L_2 - L_1) = \frac{p_2 - p_1}{t} + L_2^2 - L_1^2$$

since

$$\frac{L_2^2 - L_1^2}{L_2 - L_1} = \frac{(L_2 - L_1)(L_2 + L_1)}{L_2 - L_1} = L_2 + L_1.$$

[32] Provided prices and locations are such that the indifferent consumer is between the two firms.

[33] This provides one familiar example of a case where the potentially large number of parameters in a linear demand model are restricted to a smaller number of more primitive parameters—here (S, t)—by making the parameters of a linear demand system functions of the product characteristics which govern substitution patterns between goods.

9.2.2.2 Richer Models of Horizontal Product Differentiation

Hotelling's linear city is extremely useful as a theoretical tool, but not very useful for studying most markets empirically at least in the sense that few markets are actually "lines."[34] Similarly, Salop's (1979) model of a circular city has advantages—particularly given some road systems—but ultimately most cities are two dimensional and most retail markets therefore best considered in that context. Fortunately, richer demand structures suitable for real retail markets are no more complicated conceptually than the simple Hotelling model and easily put on a computer.

Specifically, recall the conditional indirect utility function for Hotelling:

$$v_{ij}(p_j, L_j; L_i) = s - tg(d(L_i, L_j)) - p_j,$$

where L_i is the parameter indicating the consumer type, in this case her location, and L_j is the characteristic of product j that denotes location. In two-dimensional models all we need do is describe location of consumers and products appropriately. Specifically, along a line we described above that Euclidean distance can be defined as $d(L_i, L_j) = |L_i - L_j| = \sqrt[2]{(L_i - L_j)^2}$ while in a two-dimensional setting location will be defined by two coordinates. In cases of geographical distance, we could simply use the coordinates $L_i \equiv (\text{Lat}_i, \text{Long}_i)$ for consumer locations and similarly $L_j \equiv (\text{Lat}_j, \text{Long}_j)$ for the shop characteristics. The Euclidean distance between two points can then be expressed as

$$d(L_i, L_j) = \sqrt{(\text{Lat}_i - \text{Lat}_j)^2 + (\text{Long}_i - \text{Long}_j)^2}.$$

Alternatively, we might want to use the "drive time" between two locations in a city given the road system which will similarly depend on the start and finish locations. Various models can provide such time data. For instance, in the U.K. Competition Commission's recent supermarket inquiry, estimates of "drive time" between stores were calculated using a geographic information system.[35]

In a fashion identical to our analysis of the Hotelling model, in order to calculate aggregate demand we need only sum up the individual choices over all types of individuals, which in this case would give us a two-dimensional integral to compute:

$$D_j(\underline{p}, w) = \int_{\{\underline{\theta} \equiv (\text{Lat}_i, \text{Long}_i) | v_j(\theta_j .) > v_k(\theta_k .) \text{ for all } k \neq j\}} f_{\underline{\theta}}(\underline{\theta}) \, \mathrm{d}\underline{\theta}.$$

For further details, see Davis (2000, 2006) and the references therein.

[34] The closest example we have found is Madison, WI, in the United States, where the city center is squeezed on a fairly narrow strip of land between two lakes and so has some geographic similarity with Hotelling's line. Beaches and perhaps the location of petrol stations on motorways might provide other instances where the model is directly applicable.

[35] See the CC report available at www.competition-commission.org.uk/inquiries/ref2006/grocery/index.htm and in particular appendix 3.2 of the final report.

9.2.3 Vertical Product Differentiation

Vertical dimensions of product differentiation are those which arise when consumers can agree on which products are better along a given qualitative or quantitative dimension. For instance, all customers will tend to agree that more memory is better than less in a computer, all else equal. Similarly, when choosing among cars it is clearly the case that, all else equal, lower fuel consumption is more desirable. Vertical characteristics do not mean that all customers will buy one product since consumers will have individual preferences which encapsulate their own personal trade-off between price and quality. Thus, some customers will buy the expensive high-quality products and others will choose the cheaper low-quality products. Some people may gain very little extra utility from having designer shoes and as a result will be unwilling to pay the difference in price even if they perceive "designer" to be a desirable trait all else equal so that at the same price, they would choose the designer shoes.

The simplest models of vertical preferences use the following form for the conditional indirect utility function:

$$v_{ij} = \begin{cases} \vartheta_i z_j - p_j & \text{if individual } i \text{ buys good } j, \\ 0 & \text{if she chooses outside option,} \end{cases}$$

where as usual θ_i is the parameter reflecting the type of customer i, z_j denotes the vertical quality characteristic, and p_j is the price. We can define the maximum utility achieved by individual i as

$$V(z, p, \theta_i) = \max\{0, \theta_i z_1 - p_1, \dots, \theta_i z_J - p_J\}.$$

Tastes differ in the population and therefore we assume that θ has a density $f(\theta)$ and a cumulative distribution function $F(\theta)$. The aggregate demand for any given product then takes the form:

$$D_j(\underline{p}, w) = S \int_{\{\theta_i \mid v_j(\theta_j.) > v_k(\theta_k.) \text{ for all } k \neq j\}} f_{\underline{\theta}}(\underline{\theta})\,\mathrm{d}\underline{\theta},$$

where S is the total mass of consumers. To derive this integral, at least in special cases, suppose the goods are indexed in order of quality so that $z_1 \leqslant \cdots \leqslant z_J$. Consider the choice between two options j and $j+1$, a consumer of type θ_i will prefer to buy $j+1$ if

$$\theta_i z_{j+1} - p_{j+1} \geqslant \theta_i z_j - p_j \quad \text{or} \quad \theta_i \geqslant \frac{p_{j+1} - p_j}{z_{j+1} - z_j} \equiv \Delta_j,$$

while the choice between any good and the outside option provides the inequalities $\theta_i \geqslant p_j/z_j$ so that only consumer types below the cutoff Δ_0 will not buy any good, i.e., they will buy nothing if $\theta_i \leqslant \min\{p_1/z_1, \dots, p_J/z_J\} \equiv \Delta_0$.

For some combinations of prices and quantities, specifically those for which the ratios of price differences to quality differences increase so that we are able to rank the inside good cutoffs as $\Delta_0 \leqslant \Delta_1 \leqslant \cdots \leqslant \Delta_J$, we can derive the demand curve exactly for any cumulative distribution function describing consumer types, $F(\theta)$. For this reason, this is often the case presented in textbooks.[36] If so, then we can write that piece of the demand function for any product j as

$$\begin{aligned} D_j(\underline{p}, z) &= S \int_{\{\theta_i \mid v_j(\theta_j \cdot) > v_k(\theta_k \cdot) \text{ for all } k \neq j\}} f_{\underline{\theta}}(\underline{\theta})\,\mathrm{d}\underline{\theta} = S \int_{\Delta_j}^{\Delta_{j+1}} f_{\underline{\theta}}(\underline{\theta})\,\mathrm{d}\underline{\theta} \\ &= S(F(\Delta_{j+1}) - F(\Delta_j)). \end{aligned}$$

9.2.4 The Multinomial Logit Model

Probably the most famous discrete choice model that analysts take to data is the multinomial logit (MNL) model developed by McFadden (1978, 1981) and subsequently applied by literally thousands of researchers. In this section we show how this model fits into our general framework, providing an example of a model where there can be a large number of dimensions of consumer types.[37] The beauty of the model is that despite this potentially large number of dimensions of consumer "types" (i.e., the presence of lots of consumer heterogeneity), the resulting demand functions are entirely analytic, making analysis and estimation relatively straightforward. That said, below we also discuss some important disadvantages of the MNL model and some extensions to it.

9.2.4.1 The Multinomial Logit Framework

Suppose an individual i's preferences (more formally, their conditional indirect utility) can be expressed as

$$v_j(p_j, w_j; \theta_i) = \bar{v}_j(p_j, w_j) + \varepsilon_{ij} \quad \text{for } j = 0, 1, \ldots, J,$$

where, as before, p_j and w_j respectively denote prices and product characteristics of good j and the consumer type is given by the vector $\theta_i = \varepsilon_i \equiv (\varepsilon_{i0}, \varepsilon_{i1}, \ldots, \varepsilon_{iJ})$, which has a dimension of $J + 1$. Note that consumers only differ in their tastes by additive terms which are individual and product-specific. According to this specification some consumers will have a particular liking for product j. Substituting this form gives our familiar discrete choice problem:

$$\max_{j=0,1,\ldots,J} \bar{v}_j(p_j, w_j) + \varepsilon_{ij}.$$

Note that this yields exactly the same demand equations as the analogous maximization problem, where we have added or subtracted an arbitrary constant from the payoff to each option. That means all such models are observationally equivalent and we can impose a normalization on the model (or, more precisely, we must

[36] See, for example, the canonical graduate textbook on industrial organization by Tirole (1993).

[37] For a discussion of this and other demand forms in the context of merger simulation, see Werden and Froeb (2005).

impose a normalization if we wish to identify the parameters of such a model).[38] Generally, authors choose to normalize the utility of the outside good to zero $\bar{v}_0 = 0$ so that the normalized conditional indirect utility for the outside good is

$$v_{i0} = \bar{v}_0 + \varepsilon_{i0} = 0 + \varepsilon_{i0}.$$

The MNL model makes a particularly tractable assumption about the distribution of consumer types in the population. In particular, MNL assumes that $\theta_i = \varepsilon_i \equiv (\varepsilon_{i0}, \varepsilon_{i1}, \dots, \varepsilon_{iJ})$ is i.i.d. across products (and as usual individuals) and has a standard type I extreme value density function:[39]

$$f_{\varepsilon_J}(\varepsilon_j) = \exp\{-\exp(-\varepsilon_j) - \varepsilon_j\}.$$

The resulting aggregate demand for product j takes the form:

$$\begin{aligned} D_j(\underline{p}, w) &= S \int_{-\infty}^{+\infty} \cdots \int_{-\infty}^{+\infty} x_{ij}(\underline{p}, w, \underline{\varepsilon}) f_{\varepsilon}(\underline{\varepsilon}) \, \mathrm{d}\varepsilon_0 \cdots \mathrm{d}\varepsilon_J \\ &= S \frac{\exp\{\bar{v}_j(p_j, w_j)\}}{\sum_{k=0}^{K} \exp\{\bar{v}_k(p_k, w_k)\}}, \end{aligned}$$

where S is the total mass of potential consumers and the denominator in the ratio is the sum of the exponential across all products including the outside good but where $\exp\{\bar{v}_0(p_0, w_0)\} = \exp\{0\} = 1$ because of the normalization. Note the key advantage of the MNL model: that the careful choice of the type I extreme value density function produces a nice analytical expression for all the demand functions. (For a proof of this result, see McFadden (1981).)

Often this model is written down in terms of market shares, the proportion of individuals that choose a particular product. In this model, this is the same as the likelihood that an individual chooses a particular product. This likelihood multiplied by the total mass of consumers will give the size of the demand. Hence, demand and market shares are simply related according to the formula:

$$D_j(\underline{p}, w) = S s_j(\underline{p}, w),$$

where

$$s_j(\underline{p}, w) = \frac{\exp\{\bar{v}_j(p_j, w_j)\}}{\sum_{k=0}^{K} \exp\{\bar{v}_k(p_k, w_k)\}}.$$

Market shares add to one, so $\sum_{j=0}^{J} s_j(\underline{p}, w) = 1$.

---

[38] $$\operatorname*{argmax}_{j=0,1,\dots,J} \ \bar{v}_j + \varepsilon_{ij} \iff \operatorname*{argmax}_{j=0,1,\dots,J} \ \bar{v}_j - \bar{v}_0 + \varepsilon_{ij}.$$

[39] The type I extreme value distribution is

$$f_{\varepsilon_J}(\varepsilon_j) = \frac{1}{\varphi_1} \exp\left\{-\exp\left\{\frac{-(\varepsilon_j - \varphi_2)}{\varphi_1}\right\} - \frac{\varepsilon_j - \varphi_2}{\varphi_1}\right\}$$

and its standard version sets $\varphi_1 = 1$ and $\varphi_2 = 0$. A probit model would assume that $\underline{\varepsilon}_i$ has a normal distribution.

9.2.4.2 Independence of Irrelevant Alternatives

In the MNL model, the formula for market shares implies that they only depend on the utilities provided by each product that are common across individuals, or more precisely their exponents. More specifically, note that two identical products will have equal market shares by construction and similarly market shares do not depend on how close the goods are in terms of utility but rather only on the exponent of the level of utility $\exp\{\bar{v}_j(p_j, w_j)\}$ relative to an index of the level of utility provided by all goods in the market (the denominator $\sum_{k=0}^{K} \exp\{\bar{v}_k(p_k, w_k)\}$).

Consider intuitively what should happen to market shares when we introduce a new product into the market which is an "irrelevant alternative," one which is entirely identical to an existing product in terms of both its product characteristics and its price. Intuitively, we might expect such a new product to potentially seriously cannibalize the existing perfect substitute (somehow splitting demand between them) but to have very little if any impact on other differentiated products, since consumers already had the option of buying the identical good on identical terms before the irrelevant alternative was introduced. There appears no good reason to switch following its introduction. Unfortunately, the MNL model does not make predictions that fit with that rather strong intuition. In fact, many people would say that that MNL generates obviously implausible substitution patterns following new product introduction.

In fact, an irrelevant alternative in this model will get an equal weight in the denominator to the existent good and also an equal weight in the numerator. Thus, it would receive a market share identical to its existent perfect substitute good, while acting to reduce the market shares of other differentiated products in the market. Thus the formula arising from the MNL model does not immediately appear to generate obviously plausible substitution patterns following new product entry.

Moreover, note that the exact mix of characteristics for each option simply does not matter in this model—all that matters is the level of common utility associated with each option—albeit transformed according to a monotonic transformation, the exponent. For example, suppose $\bar{v}_0 = 0$ and $\bar{v}_1 = \ln 2$ so that $\exp\{\bar{v}_0\} = 1$ and $\exp\{\bar{v}_1\} = 2$ so that MNL market shares are

$$s_0 = \frac{1}{1+2} = \frac{1}{3} \quad \text{and} \quad s_2 = \frac{2}{1+2} = \frac{2}{3}.$$

If we introduce a new option with the same utility as good 1, $\bar{v}_2 = \ln 2$, we will get the new market shares

$$s_0 = \frac{1}{1+2+2} = \frac{1}{5} \quad \text{and} \quad s_1 = s_2 = \frac{2}{1+2+2} = \frac{2}{5}.$$

Our irrelevant alternative impacts all goods' market shares, not just its identical twin.

Unsurprisingly, since effectively all that matters in this model is the relative level of utility, as we shall see below the MNL model imposes severe limitations on own-

and cross-price elasticities. In practice, therefore, MNL models are quite good for learning about the characteristics which tend to be associated with high or low levels of market shares, but we recommend strongly against using MNL models in situations where we must learn about substitution patterns (e.g., for merger simulation). There have been a number of responses to the problems the literature has identified with MNL and we explore some of those responses in the rest of this section. The important lesson from MNL and the property of independence of irrelevant alternatives (IIA) is not that the MNL is a hopeless model (though that is probably true), but rather that we can use the IIA property to our advantage; since the MNL makes unreasonable predictions about what will happen to market shares following entry, if we observe what happens to market shares following entry, we will be able to use data to reject MNL models and identify parameters in richer discrete choice models. Furthermore, the literature has grown from MNL models and many of its tools are most simply explained in that context. For example, in the next section we explore the introduction of unobserved product characteristics in the context of the MNL models but we shall see later that the basic techniques for analyzing models with unobserved product characteristics can be used in far richer discrete choice models.

9.2.4.3 *Introducing Unobserved Product Characteristics in MNL Models*

A famous, possibly true, marketing story is that the first car which introduced a cupholder experienced dramatically high sales—customers thought it was a great novel idea. Economists working with data from the time period, however, probably would not have had a variable in their data set called "cupholder"—it would have been a product characteristic driving sales, differentiating the product, which would be observed by customers but unobserved by our analyst. Such a situation must be common. As a result Bultez and Naert (1975), Nakanishi and Cooper (1974), Berry (1994), and Berry et al. (1995) have each argued that we should introduce an unobserved product characteristic into our econometric demand models. Following Berry (1994), denote the unobserved product characteristic ξ_j so that the conditional indirect utility function that an individual gets from a given product j is

$$v_{ij} = \bar{v}_j + \varepsilon_{ij} = x_j'\beta - \alpha p_j + \xi_j + \varepsilon_{ij},$$

where x_j is a vector of the observed product characteristics, ξ_j is the unobserved product characteristic (known to the consumer but not to the economist), and consumer types are represented by $\underline{\varepsilon}_i = (\varepsilon_{i0}, \varepsilon_{i1}, \dots, \varepsilon_{iJ})$. In general, there may be many elements comprising ξ_j but the class of models which have been developed all aggregate unobserved product characteristics into one.

The parameters of the model which we must estimate are α and β. The basic MNL model attempts to force observed product characteristics to explain all of the variation in observed market shares, which they generally cannot. Instead of estimating a model

$$s_j = s_j(\underline{p}, x; \alpha, \beta) + \text{Error}_j, \quad j = 0, \dots, J,$$

where an error term is "tagged on" to each equation in the demand system, the new model gives an explicit interpretation to the error term and integrates it fully into the consumer's behavioral model, $s_j = s_j(\underline{p}, \underline{x}, \underline{\xi}; \alpha, \beta)$.

Of course, just introducing an unobserved product characteristic does not get you very far. In particular, there is a clear potential problem with introducing unobserved product characteristics in that the term enters in a nonlinear way—it is not obvious how to run a regression in such cases. Fortunately, Nakanishi and Cooper (1974) and Berry (1994) have shown that we can recover the unobserved product characteristics from every product in the MNL model. Berry et al. (1995) then extend the "we can recover the error terms" result to a far wider set of models.

To see how, define the vector of common (across individuals) utilities with the common utility of the outside good normalized to zero $\bar{v} = (0, \bar{v}_1, \dots, \bar{v}_J)$. Suppose we choose $\bar{v}$ to make the MNL model's predicted market shares exactly match the actual market shares so that

$$s_j(\underline{p}, \bar{v}) = s_j \quad \text{for } j = 1, \dots, J.$$

Since $\bar{v} = (0, \bar{v}_1, \dots, \bar{v}_J)$, we have J equations like the one specified above with J unknowns. If the J equations match the predicted and actual market share of all markets, then the market share of the outside good will also match $s_0(\underline{p}, y, \bar{v}) = s_0$ since the actual and predicted market shares must add to one.[40] Taking logs of the market share equations gives us an equivalent system with J equations of the form:

$$\ln s_j(\underline{p}, \bar{v}) = \ln s_j \quad \text{for } j = 1, \dots, J,$$

where at a solution we will also have $\ln s_0(\underline{p}, \bar{v}) = \ln s_0$. Recalling the normalization condition $\bar{v}_0 = 0$ so that $\exp\{\bar{v}_0\} = 1$, we can write

$$s_j(\underline{p}, \bar{v}) = \frac{\exp\{\bar{v}_j\}}{1 + \sum_{k=1}^{K} \exp\{\bar{v}_k\}} = s_0(\underline{p}, \bar{v}) \exp\{\bar{v}_j\},$$

so that

$$\ln s_j(\underline{p}, \bar{v}) = \ln s_0(\underline{p}, \bar{v}) + \bar{v}_j \quad \text{for } j = 1, \dots, J.$$

[40] In the continuous choice demand model context, we studied the constraint imposed by "adding up": that total expenditure shares must add to one. In a differentiated product demand system, we get a similar "adding up" condition which enforces the condition that market shares add to one

$$\sum_{j=0}^{J} s_j = \sum_{j=0}^{J} s_j(\underline{p}, \underline{x}, \underline{\xi}; \alpha, \beta) = 1.$$

As a result of this condition we will, as before, be able to drop one equation from our analysis and study the system of J equations. Generally, in the differentiated product context, the equation for the outside good is dropped from the system of equations to be estimated. We impose the normalization that $\overline{v}_0 = 0$, which in turn can be generated in part by the assumption that $\xi_0 = 0$.

So that our J equations become

$$\ln s_j = \ln s_0(\underline{p}, \bar{v}) + \bar{v}_j \quad \text{for } j = 1, \dots, J.$$

At a solution we know that $\ln s_0(\underline{p}, \bar{v}) = \ln s_0$ so that we know a solution must have the form

$$\bar{v}_j = \ln s_j - \ln s_0,$$

where the shares on the right-hand side are observed data. Thus the mean utilities $\bar{v} = (0, \bar{v}_1, \dots, \bar{v}_J)$ that exactly solve the market share equations $s_j(\underline{p}, \bar{v}) = s_j$ are just

$$\bar{v}_j = \ln s_j - \ln s_0 \quad \text{for } j = 1, \dots, J,$$

where $s_0 = 1 - \sum_{k=1}^{J} s_k$. This formula states that, for the MNL model, we only need information about the levels of market shares to figure out what the utility levels of the models must be in order to rationalize those market shares. The mean utility vector $\bar{v}$ is uniquely determined by the observed market shares. This allows us to write and estimate the linear equation with now "observed" level of utility as the dependent variable:

$$\ln s_j - \ln s_0 = x_j\beta - \alpha p_j + \xi_j.$$

Note that this formulation of the model provides a simple linear-in-the-parameters regression model to estimate, a familiar activity. The prices p_j and product characteristics x_j are observed, the parameters to be estimated are α and β and the error term is the unobserved product characteristic ξ_j. Since this is a simple linear equation we can use all of our familiar techniques upon it, including instrumental variable techniques.

For the avoidance of doubt, note that the market shares in this equation are volume market shares (or equivalently here number of purchasers, since in this model only one inside good can be chosen per person). In addition, the market shares must be calculated as a proportion of the total potential market S including the set of people who choose the outside good. The appropriate way to calculate the total potential market can be a matter of controversy, depending on the setting. In the new car market it may be reasonable to assume that the largest potential market is for each person of driving age to buy a new car. In breakfast cereals it may be reasonable to assume that at most all people in the country will eat one portion of cereal a day, so, for example, no one eats bacon and eggs for breakfast if the price of cereal is sufficiently low and the quality sufficiently high. Obviously, such propositions are not uncontroversial: some people own two cars and some people eat two bowls of cereal a day. It may sometimes be possible to estimate the market size S, though few academic articles have managed to. More frequently, it is a very good idea to test the sensitivity of estimation results to whatever assumption has been made.

Table 9.5 presents results from Berry et al. (1995). Specifically, in the first column they report an OLS estimation of the logit demand specification and in the second

Table 9.5. Estimation of the demand for cars.

Variable	OLS logit demand	IV logit demand	OLS ln(price) on w
Constant	−10.068	−9.273	1.882
	(0.253)	(0.493)	(0.119)
HP/weight[a]	−0.121	1.965	0.520
	(0.277)	(0.909)	(0.035)
Air	−0.035	1.289	0.680
	(0.073)	(0.248)	(0.019)
MP$[a]	0.263	0.052	—
	(0.043)	(0.086)	—
MPG[a]	—	—	0.471
	—	—	(0.049)
Size	2.431	2.355	0.125
	(0.125)	(0.247)	(0.063)
Trend	—	—	0.013
	—	—	(0.002)
Price	−0.089	−0.216	—
	(0.004)	(0.123)	
Number of inelastic demands (±2 SEs)	1,494 (1,429–1,617)	22 (7–101)	n.a.
R^2	0.387	n.a.	0.656

Notes: The standard errors are reported in parentheses.
[a]The continuous product characteristics—horsepower/weight, size, and fuel efficiency (miles per dollar or miles per gallon)—enter the demand equations in levels but enter the column 3 price regression in natural logs.
Source: Table III from Berry et al. (1995).
Columns 1 and 2 report MNL demand estimates obtained using (1) OLS and (2) IV. Column 3 reports a regression of the price of car j on the characteristics of car j, sometimes called a "hedonic" pricing regression. *If* a market were perfectly competitive, then price would equal marginal cost and the final regression would tell us about the determinants of cost in this market.

column the instrumental variable (IV) estimation. Note in particular that the move from OLS to IV estimation moves the price coefficient downward. This is exactly as we would expect if price were "endogenous"—if it is positively correlated with the error term in the regression. Such a situation will arise when firms know more about their product than we have data about and price the product accordingly. In terms of our opening example, a car which introduces the feature of cupholder will see high sales and the firm selling it may wish to increase its price to take advantage of high or inelastic demand. If so, then the unobserved product characteristic (our error term) and price will be correlated.

We have mentioned previously that the multinomial logit model, even with the introduction of an unobserved product characteristic, imposes severe and undesirable structure on own- and cross-price elasticities. To see that result, recall that

$$\begin{aligned}\ln s_j(\underline{p}, \underline{x}, \underline{\xi}) &= \bar{v}_j(\underline{p}, \underline{x}, \underline{\xi}) - \ln(s_0(\underline{p}, \underline{x}, \underline{\xi})) \\ &= \bar{v}_j(p_j, x_j, \xi_j) - \ln\left(1 + \sum_{k=1}^{J} \exp\{\overline{v}_k(p_k, x_k, \xi_k)\}\right),\end{aligned}$$

where $\bar{v}_j = x_j\beta - \alpha p_j + \xi_j$. Differentiating, it follows that

$$\begin{aligned}\frac{\partial \ln s_j(\underline{p}, \underline{x}, \underline{\xi})}{\partial \ln p_k} &= -\alpha p_k s_k(\underline{p}, \underline{x}, \underline{\xi}) = -\alpha p_k s_k \quad \text{for } j \neq k, \\ \frac{\partial \ln s_j(\underline{p}, \underline{x}, \underline{\xi})}{\partial \ln p_j} &= -\alpha p_j(1 - s_j(\underline{p}, \underline{x}, \underline{\xi})) = -\alpha p_j(1 - s_j),\end{aligned}$$

where the latter equalities follow when we evaluate the elasticities at a point where predicted and actual market shares match.

This means that all own- and cross-price elasticities between any pair of products j and k are entirely determined by one parameter α, the market share of the good whose price changed and also the price of that good. Most strikingly, substitution patterns do not depend on how good substitutes goods j and k really are, for example, whether they have similar product characteristics. Because of the inflexible and unrealistic structure that the MNL model imposes on the preferences, they probably should never be used in merger simulation exercises or in any other exercise where the pattern of substitution plays a central role in informing decision makers about appropriate policy.

Despite all of the comments above, the MNL model does remain tremendously useful in allowing analysts a simple way of exploring which product characteristics play an important role in determining the levels of market shares. However, it is often the departures from the simple MNL model that are most informative. For example, it can be informative to include rival characteristics in product j's payoff since that may inform us when close rival products drive down each individual product's market share because each product cannibalizes the demand for the other. Indeed, it is precisely such patterns in the data that richer models will use to generate more realistic substitution patterns than those implied by models such as MNL with IIA. The observation is useful generally, but it also provides the basis of the formal specification tests for the MNL proposed by Hausman and McFadden (1984).

9.2.5 Extending the Multinomial Logit Model

In this section we follow the literature in extending the MNL model to allow for additional dimensions of consumer heterogeneity. To illustrate the process, we bring together the MNL model with the Hotelling model and also the vertical product differentiation model.

Specifically, suppose that the conditional indirect utility function can be defined as

$$v_j(z_j, L_j, p_j, \xi_j, \gamma_i, L_i, \varepsilon_{ij}) = \gamma_i z_j - tg(d(L_i, L_j)) - \alpha p_j + \xi_j + \varepsilon_{ij},$$

where the term z_j is a quality characteristic where all consumers agree that all else equal more is better than less—a vertical source of product differentiation. Additionally, products are available in different locations L_j and depending on the consumer's location L_i the travel cost may be small or large—a horizontal source of product differentiation. Finally, we suppose that consumers have an intrinsic preference for particular products as in the multinomial logit. The consumer type in this model is $\theta = (\varepsilon_{i0}, \varepsilon_{i1}, \dots, \varepsilon_{iJ}, L_i, \gamma_i)$, where ε_{ik} represents the idiosyncratic preference of consumer i for product k, L_i indicates the individual's taste for the horizontal product characteristic, and γ_i represents his or her willingness to pay for the vertical product characteristic.

As usual, aggregate demand is simply the sum of individual demands,

$$x_j(\underline{z}, \underline{L}, \underline{p}, \underline{\xi}; \gamma_i, L_i, \varepsilon_{i0}, \dots, \varepsilon_{iJ}),$$

over the set of all consumer types. In the first instance, that sum involves a $(J+3)$-dimensional integral involving $(J+1)$ dimensions for the epsilons plus 1 each for the location and vertical tastes L_i, γ_i. Thus aggregate demand is

$$\begin{aligned} D_j(\underline{s}, \underline{L}, \underline{p}, \underline{\xi}) &= \iiint_{\underline{\varepsilon}, L, \gamma} x_j(\underline{z}, \underline{L}, \underline{p}, \underline{\xi}; \gamma_i, L_i, \varepsilon_{i0}, \dots, \varepsilon_{iJ}) f_{\underline{\varepsilon}, L, \gamma}(\underline{\varepsilon}, L_i, \gamma; \theta)\, \mathrm{d}\underline{\varepsilon}\, \mathrm{d}L_i \mathrm{d}\gamma \\ &= \int_\gamma \int_L \frac{\exp\{\gamma z_k - tg(d(L_j, L_i)) - \alpha p_j\}}{\sum_{k=1}^K \exp\{\gamma z_k - tg(d(L_k, L_i)) - \alpha p_k\}} f_{L,\gamma}(L_i, \gamma)\, \mathrm{d}L_i \mathrm{d}\gamma. \end{aligned}$$

For any given L_i, γ_i, the model is exactly an MNL model. Thus we can use the MNL formula to perform the integration over the $(J+1)$ dimensions of consumer heterogeneity arising from the epsilons. Doing so means that the resulting integration problem becomes in this instance just two dimensional, which is a relatively straightforward activity that can be accomplished using numerical integration techniques such as simulation.[41]

Berry et al. (1995) show that even in this kind of context we can follow an approach similar to that taken to analyze the MNL model. We discuss their model below, but before doing so we describe the nested logit specification, which is a less flexible but more tractable alternative popular among some antitrust practitioners.

[41] For an introductory discussion in this context, see Davis (2000). For computer programs and a good technical discussion, see Press et al. (2007). For a classic text, see Silverman (1989). For the econometric theory underlying estimation when using simulation estimators, see Pakes and Pollard (1989), McFadden (1989), and Andrews (1994).

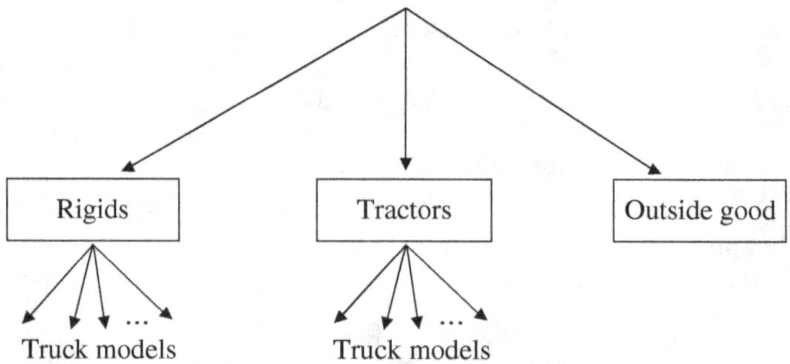

Figure 9.5. A model for the demand for trucks. *Source*: Ivaldi and Verboven (2005).

9.2.6 The Nested Multinomial Logit Model

The nested multinomial logit (NMNL) model is a somewhat more flexible structure than the MNL model and yet retains its tractability.[42] It is based on the assumption that consumers each choose a product in stages. The concept is very similar to the nested model we studied by Hausman et al. (1994) for the demand for beer. In each case, consumers first choose a broad category of products and then a specific product within that category. Hausman et al. estimated their model using different regressions for each stage. In contrast, the NMNL model allows us to estimate the demand for the final products in a single estimation. Ivaldi and Verboven (2005) apply this methodology in their analysis of a case from the European merger jurisdiction, the proposed Volvo–Scania merger.[43] The product overlap of concern involved the sale of trucks generally and heavy trucks in particular since the commission found that heavy trucks constituted a relevant market. The authors suggest that the heavy trucks market can be segmented into two groups involving (1) rigid trucks ("integrated" trucks, from which no semi-trailer can be detached) and (2) tractor trucks, which are detachable. A third group is specified for the outside good. Figure 9.5 describes the nesting structure they adopt.

The NMNL model itself can be motivated in a number of ways.

Motivation method 1. McFadden (1978) initially motivated the NMNL model by assuming that consumers undertook a two-stage decision-making process. At the first stage he suggested they decide which broad category (group) of goods $g = 1, \dots, G$ to buy from and then, at the second stage, they choose between goods within that group. Each of the groups consists of a set of products and all products are in only one group. The groups are mutually exclusive and exhaustive collections of products.

[42] The link between consumer theory and discrete choice models is discussed in McFadden (1981) and for the NMNL model, in particular, see also Verboven (1996).

[43] Case no. COMP/M. 1672. Their exercise is described in chapter 8.

Motivation method 2. Cardell (1997) (see also Berry 1994) provide an alternative way to motivate the NMNL model as a random coefficient model with a conditional indirect utility function defined as

$$v_{ij} = \sum_{l=1}^{K} x_{jl}\beta_{il} + \xi_j + \varsigma_{ig} + (1-\sigma)\varepsilon_{ij} \quad \text{for product } j \text{ in group } g,$$

$$v_{i0} = \varsigma_{i0} + (1-\sigma)\varepsilon_{i0} \quad \text{for the outside good,}$$

where x_{jl} is the lth observed product characteristics of product j, ξ_j are the unobserved product characteristics, ς_{ig} is the consumer preference for product group g, and ε_{ij} is the idiosyncratic preference of the individual for product j. For reasons we describe below, since for every individual any products in group g get the same value of ς_{ig}, which in turn depends on σ, the parameter σ introduces a correlation in all consumers' tastes across products within a group. Consumers with a high taste for group g, a large ς_{ig}, will tend to substitute for other products in that group when the price of a good in group g goes up. The consumer type in a model with G pre-specified groups is

$$\theta_i = (\varsigma_{i1}, \dots, \varsigma_{iG}, \varepsilon_{i0}, \varepsilon_{i1}, \dots, \varepsilon_{iJ}).$$

Cardell (1997) showed that for given σ, if ς_{ig} are independent with ε_{ij} having a type I extreme value distribution, then the expression $\varsigma_{ig} + (1-\sigma)\varepsilon_{ij}$ will also have a type I extreme value distribution if and only if ς_{ig} has a particular type I extreme value distribution.[44] Cardell (1997) also showed that the required distribution of ς_{ig} depends on the parameter σ so that some authors prefer to write $\varsigma_{ig}(\sigma)$ and $\varsigma_{ig}(\sigma) + (1-\sigma)\varepsilon_{ij}$. The parameter σ is restricted to be between zero and one. As σ approaches zero the model approaches the usual MNL model and the correlation between goods in a given group becomes zero. On the other hand, as σ increases to one, so does the relative weight on ς_{ig} and hence correlation between tastes for goods within a group.

Motivation method 3: the MEV class of models. A third way to motivate the NMNL model is to consider it a special case of McFadden's (1978) generalized extreme-value (GEV) class of models (which is probably more appropriately called the multivariate extreme-value (MEV) class of models since the statistics community use GEV to mean a generalization of the univariate extreme value distribution). That model effectively relaxes the independence assumptions across the tastes $(\varepsilon_{i0}, \dots, \varepsilon_{iJ})$ embodied in the MNL model. The basic bottom line is that the MEV class of models assumes that the joint distribution of consumer types can be expressed as

$$F(\varepsilon_{i0}, \dots, \varepsilon_{iJ}; \phi) = \exp(-H(\mathrm{e}^{-\varepsilon_{i0}}, \dots, \mathrm{e}^{-\varepsilon_{iJ}}; \phi)),$$

[44] As Cardell describes, his result is analogous to the more familiar result that if $\varepsilon \sim N(0, \sigma_1^2)$ and ε and v are independent, then $\varepsilon + v \sim N(0, \sigma_1^2 + \sigma_2^2)$ if and only if $v \sim N(0, \sigma_2^2)$.

where $H(r_0, \ldots, r_J; \phi)$ is a possibly parametric function (hence the inclusion of parameters ϕ) with some well-defined properties (e.g., homogeneity of some positive degree in the vector of arguments). We have already mentioned that the standard MNL model has distribution function $F(\varepsilon_{ij}) = \exp(\mathrm{e}^{-\varepsilon_{ij}})$ so that under independence the multivariate distribution of consumer types is

$$\begin{aligned} F(\varepsilon_{i0}, \ldots, \varepsilon_{iJ}; \phi) &= F(\varepsilon_{i0}) F(\varepsilon_{i1}) \cdots F(\varepsilon_{iJ}) \\ &= \exp\biggl(-\sum_{j=0}^{J} \mathrm{e}^{-\varepsilon_{ij}}\biggr). \end{aligned}$$

In that case the MNL corresponds to the simple summation function

$$H(r_0, \ldots, r_J; \phi) = \sum_{j=0}^{J} r_j.$$

The "one-level" NMNL model developed by McFadden (1978) corresponds to a choice of function

$$H(r_1, \ldots, r_J; \phi) = \sum_{g=1}^{G} \biggl(\sum_{j \in \Im_g}^{J} r_j^{1/(1-\sigma)}\biggr)^{1-\sigma},$$

where $\Im_g$ denotes the set of products placed into group g, $\phi = \sigma$, and the distribution function is evaluated at $r_j = \mathrm{e}^{-\varepsilon_{ij}}$. The outside good will often be put into its own group. Davis (2006b) discusses this approach to understanding the discrete choice literature and also proposes a new member of the MEV class of discrete choice models which can be used to estimate discrete choice models which have far less restrictive substitution patterns.

Whichever method is used to motivate the NMNL model, specifying the groups appropriately is absolutely vital for the results one will obtain. The groups must be specified before proceeding to estimate the model, and the choice of groups will have implications for which goods the model predicts will be better substitutes for one another. Recall that the parameter σ controls the correlation in tastes between goods within a group. Company information on market segments or consumer surveys may be helpful in establishing which products are likely to be "closer" substitutes and therefore form distinct market segments that can be associated with a particular group.

Following the earlier literature, Berry (1994) shows that in a manner very similar to that used for the MNL model the NMNL model can also be estimated using a regression equation linear in the parameters that can be estimated with instrumental variables (see Bultez and Naert 1975; Nakanishi and Cooper 1974). In particular, we have

$$\ln s_j - \ln s_0 = \sum_{l=1}^{K} x_{jl} \beta_l + \sigma \ln s_{j|g} + \xi_j,$$

where $s_{j|g}$ is the market share of product j among those purchased in group g. If q_j denotes the volume of sales of product j, then $s_{j|g} = q_j / \sum_{j \in \Im_g} q_j$. The use of instrumental variables is likely to be essential when using this regression equation since there will be a clear correlation between the error term ξ_j and the conditional market shares $s_{j|g}$. Verboven and Brenkers (2006) suggest allowing the parameter of the model controlling the within-group taste correlation to be group-specific so that

$$H(r_1, \dots, r_J; \phi) = \sum_{g=1}^{G} \left(\sum_{j \in \Im_g}^{J} r_j^{1/(1-\sigma_g)} \right)^{1-\sigma_g}.$$

In that case, they show that Berry's regression can be estimated similarly by estimating G group-specific taste parameters,

$$\ln s_j - \ln s_0 = \sum_{l=1}^{K} x_{jl} \beta_l + \sigma_g \ln s_{j|g} + \xi_j.$$

The additional taste parameters will help free-up substitution patterns across goods within each group since they are no longer constrained to be the same across groups. However, even this model will suffer from similar problems as MNL when examining substitution across groups.

9.2.7 Random Coefficient Models

Economists studying discrete choice demand systems have used consumer heterogeneity to generate models with better properties than either pure MNL or even NMNL models. These approaches have been taken with both aggregate data and also consumer-level data. We focus primarily on approaches with aggregate-level data but note that the models are identical, although their method of estimation typically is not.[45] In the aggregate demand literature, the first random coefficient models were estimated by Boyd and Mellman (1980) and Cardell and Dunbar (1980) using data from the U.S. car industry. Those authors did not incorporate an unobserved product characteristic into their model. The modern variant of the random coefficient model for aggregate data was developed in Berry et al. (1995) and through their initials (Berry, Levinsohn, and Pakes) is often referred to as the "BLP" model. In principle, random coefficients can provide us with very flexible models that put few constraints on the substitution patterns in demand. If the models place few constraints on substitution patterns, then in an ideal world with enough data we will be able to use that data to learn about the true substitution patterns.

Because the utility is expressed in terms of product characteristics and not in terms of products, the number of parameters to be estimated does not increase exponentially with the number of products in the market as in the case of the AIDS

[45] See Davis (2000) and the references therein for more on the connections between the two types of discrete choice models.

model. It is richer but also substantially harder to program and compute than either the AIDS or the nested logit models.

The model allows for individual tastes for product characteristics. Following BLP, suppose the individuals' conditional indirect utility functions are expressed as follows:

$$v_{ij} = \sum_{l=1}^{K} x_{jl}\beta_{il} + \alpha \ln(y_i - p_j) + \xi_j + \varepsilon_{ij}, \qquad v_{i0} = \varepsilon_{i0},$$

where as before the variable x_{jl} represents the characteristic l of product j. For example, a product characteristic might be horsepower in the case of a car. The coefficient β_{il} is the taste parameter of individual i for characteristic l. There is a product-specific unobserved product characteristic ξ_j and there is the usual MNL random component ε_{ij} capturing an individual's idiosyncratic taste for a given product. As in previous cases, the valuation of the outside good is assumed to consist only of an individual random component.

In this model, the consumer's type can be summarized by the vector of individual specific taste parameters and the individual's income:

$$(y_i, \beta_{i1}, \dots, \beta_{iK}, \varepsilon_{i0}, \varepsilon_{i1}, \dots, \varepsilon_{iJ}).$$

As always, in an aggregate data discrete choice demand model we have to make an assumption about how these types are distributed across the population, and we assume the MNL elements are independent of the other tastes:

$$\begin{aligned} f(y_i, \beta_{i1}, \dots, \beta_{iK}, \varepsilon_{i0}, \varepsilon_{i1}, \dots, \varepsilon_{iJ}) \\ = f(\beta_{i1}, \dots, \beta_{iK} \mid y_i) f(y_i) f(\varepsilon_{i0}, \varepsilon_{i1}, \dots, \varepsilon_{iJ}). \end{aligned}$$

Furthermore, BLP assume the distribution of the individual idiosyncratic terms $f(\varepsilon_{i0}, \varepsilon_{i1}, \dots, \varepsilon_{iJ})$ is made up of independent standard type I extreme value terms (i.e., the multinomial logit assumption). For $f(y_i)$, one can use the empirical distribution of income, perhaps observed from survey data. One needs only to assume a distribution for the random taste coefficients. The taste parameters may or may not be independent of income, $f(\beta_{i1}, \dots, \beta_{iK} \mid y_i)$. BLP assume they are while Nevo (2000) allows the taste parameters to vary with consumer characteristics including income.

As always, the market demands are just the aggregated individual demands. Let

$$\underline{\theta} = (y, \beta_1, \dots, \beta_K, \varepsilon_0, \varepsilon_1, \dots, \varepsilon_J),$$

the vector of $1 + K + J + 1$ elements determining the consumer type. The demand for product j will be

$$
\begin{aligned}
&D_j(\underline{p}, \underline{x}, \underline{\xi}) \\
&= S \int_{\{\underline{\theta} \mid v_j(\theta.) > v_k(\theta.) \text{ for all } k \neq j\}} f_{\underline{\theta}}(\underline{\theta})\, \mathrm{d}\underline{\theta} \\
&= S \int_{\{\underline{\theta} \mid v_j(\theta.) > v_k(\theta.) \text{ for all } k \neq j\}} f_{\underline{\varepsilon}}(\underline{\varepsilon}) f_{(y,\beta_1,\dots,\beta_K)}(y, \beta_1, \dots, \beta_K)\, \mathrm{d}\underline{\varepsilon}\, \mathrm{d}y\, \mathrm{d}\beta_1 \cdots \mathrm{d}\beta_K \\
&= S \int_{y,\beta} s_{ij}^{\mathrm{MNL}}(\underline{p}, \underline{x}, \underline{\xi}; y_i, \beta_{1i}, \dots, \beta_{iK}) f_{\beta|y}(\beta_1, \dots, \beta_K \mid y) f_y(y)\, \mathrm{d}\beta_1 \cdots \mathrm{d}\beta_K,
\end{aligned}
$$

where we have imposed the independence assumption between the individual-product taste random vector ε and the individual's income and tastes for characteristics. We also assume the multinomial logit distribution for ε allows us to express the individual demand for product j given the individual's tastes for characteristics and income, which we have denoted $s_{ij}^{\mathrm{MNL}}(\underline{p}, \underline{x}, \underline{\xi}; y_i, \beta_{1i}, \dots, \beta_{iK})$. Computing aggregate demand then "only" requires the $(K+1)$-dimensional integral to be calculated numerically. This is typically performed using simulation techniques.[46]

In their paper, BLP assume that the tastes for characteristics $f(\beta_{i1}, \dots, \beta_{iK})$ are normally distributed in the population and independent of income. Let $(\omega_{i1}, \dots, \omega_{iK})$ be a set of standard normal $N(0,1)$ random variables. Define $\bar{\beta}_1, \dots, \bar{\beta}_K$ to be the mean consumer's taste parameters. And define $(\sigma_1, \dots, \sigma_K)$ as variance parameters in the distribution of tastes. Then we can write

$$\beta_{il} = \bar{\beta}_l + \sigma_l \omega_{il} \quad \text{for } l = 1, \dots, K,$$

which implies that the distribution of tastes in the population is normal:

$$\begin{pmatrix} \beta_1 \\ \vdots \\ \beta_K \end{pmatrix} \sim N\left(\begin{pmatrix} \bar{\beta}_1 \\ \vdots \\ \bar{\beta}_K \end{pmatrix}, \begin{pmatrix} \sigma_1^2 & 0 & 0 \\ 0 & \ddots & 0 \\ 0 & 0 & \sigma_K^2 \end{pmatrix}\right).$$

Given these distributional assumptions for tastes, we can equivalently write the random coefficient conditional indirect utilities by decomposing the individual taste for a given characteristic into a component which depends on the individual taste and one which does not. We get

$$v_{ij} = \sum_{l=1}^{K} x_{jl} \bar{\beta}_l + \xi_j + \sum_{l=1}^{K} \sigma_l x_{jl} \omega_{il} + \alpha \ln(y_i - p_j) + \varepsilon_{ij},$$

where the first two terms do not contain individual-specific elements (they are constant across individuals) while the last three terms do contain individual-specific elements. For example, the third term involves expressions $\sigma_l x_{jl} \omega_{il}$ which puts a

[46] See Nevo (2000) and also, in particular, the appendix of Davis (2006a), which provides practical notes on the econometrics including how to calculate standard errors.

parameter from the distribution of tastes in the population (which is to be estimated) σ_l on an interaction between product characteristic x_{jl} and consumer taste for that characteristic, ω_{il}.

The individual conditional indirect utility function can be rewritten as

$$v_{ij} = \bar{v}_j + \mu_{ij},$$

where

$$\bar{v}_j \equiv \sum_{j=1}^{J} x_{jl}\bar{\beta}_l + \xi_j \quad \text{and} \quad \mu_{ij} \equiv \sum_{l=1}^{K} x_{jl}\sigma_l\omega_{il} + \alpha \ln(y_i - p_j) + \varepsilon_{ij}.$$

As always, market demands are just the aggregate of individual demands which is, in this case, an integral. In terms of market shares,

$$s_j(\underline{p}, \underline{x}, \bar{v}) = \int_{y,\beta} s_{ij}(\bar{v}_j, y_i, \beta_{1i}, \dots, \beta_{iK}, \dots) f(y, \beta)\, \mathrm{d}y\, \mathrm{d}\beta_1 \cdots \mathrm{d}\beta_K,$$

where $\bar{v}_j \equiv \sum_{j=1}^{J} x_{jl}\bar{\beta}_l + \xi_j$ is common across individuals. The BLP paper shows that for given values of the prices $\underline{p}$, observed product characteristics $\underline{x}$, and parameters $(\sigma_1, \dots, \sigma_K, \alpha)$, the J nonlinear equations

$$s_j(\bar{v}, \underline{p}, \underline{x}; \sigma_1, \dots, \sigma_K, \alpha) = s_j, \quad j = 1, \dots, J,$$

can be considered as J equations in the J unknowns $\bar{v}_j$ and furthermore that there is a unique solution to these equations under fairly general conditions. Furthermore, BLP provide a remarkably useful technique for calculating the solution to these nonlinear equations rapidly. Specifically, they show that all we need to do is to pick an initial guess, perhaps a vector of zeros, and then use the following very simple iteration:

$$\bar{v}_j^{\text{New guess}} = \bar{v}_j^{\text{Old guess}} + \ln s_j^{\text{o}} - \ln s_j(\underline{p}, \underline{x}, \bar{v}^{\text{Old guess}}) \quad \text{for } j = 1, \dots, J,$$

where s_j^{o} is the observed market share and $s_j(\underline{p}, \underline{x}, \bar{v}^{\text{Old guess}})$ is the predicted market share at this iteration's values of the variables.

The BLP technique means that for fixed values of a subset of the models' parameters, namely $(\sigma_1, \dots, \sigma_K, \alpha)$, we can solve for the J common components of the conditional indirect utilities $(\bar{v}_1, \dots, \bar{v}_J)$ and so we can run the instrumental variable linear regression exactly as we did in the MNL case

$$\bar{v}_j = \sum_{l=1}^{K} x_{jl}\bar{\beta}_l + \xi_j$$

in order to estimate the remaining taste parameters $\bar{\beta}_1, \dots, \bar{\beta}_K$ and also evaluate the error term ξ_j. We will get different residuals from this regression for each value of the taste distribution parameters $(\sigma_1, \dots, \sigma_K, \alpha)$. Hence, we will write $\xi_j(\sigma_1, \dots, \sigma_K, \alpha)$. These taste distribution parameters need to be estimated. BLP

Table 9.6. BLP model: estimated parameters of demand equations.

Demand-side parameters	Variable	Parameter estimate	Standard error	Parameter estimate	Standard error
Means ($\bar{\beta}$)	Constant	−7.061	0.941	−7.304	0.746
	HP/weight	2.883	2.019	2.185	0.896
	Air	1.521	0.891	0.579	0.632
	MP$	−0.122	0.320	−0.049	0.164
	Size	3.460	0.610	2.604	0.285
Standard deviations (σ_β)					
	Constant	3.612	1.485	2.009	1.017
	HP/weight	4.628	1.885	1.586	1.186
	Air	1.818	1.695	1.215	1.149
	MP$	1.050	0.272	0.670	0.168
	Size	2.056	0.585	1.510	0.297
Term on price (α)	$\ln(\gamma - \rho)$	43.501	6.427	23.710	4.079

Source: Table IV in Berry et al. (1995).

use the general method of moments (GMM), but one might initially simply choose them by minimizing the sum of squared errors in the model:[47]

$$\min_{(\sigma_1,\dots,\sigma_K,\alpha)} \sum_{l=1}^{K} \xi_j(\sigma_1,\dots,\sigma_K,\alpha)^2.$$

BLP apply their method to estimate the demand for cars. Their estimation results are shown in table 9.6 while the resulting own-characteristic elasticities of demand are shown in table 9.7.

Their results[48] show the own-price elasticity of a Mazda 323 to be 6.4 at a price of $5,049 while the own-price elasticity of a BMW 735i is 3.5 evaluated at the price of $37,490. Overall, the results predict that markups will be much higher for high-end BMWs and Lexuses than for low-end Mazdas and Fords.

9.3 Demand Estimation in Merger Analysis

The above introduction to the common models used for demand system estimation has hopefully served at least to illustrate that estimating demands, although an essential part of many quantification exercises, is quite a complex and even optimistic task. An analyst is faced with a trade-off between imposing structure from the model that may not fully reflect reality and developing a model that is flexible

[47] For technical details on the econometrics, see also Berry et al. (2004).

[48] Note that table 9.7 describes the value of the attribute for that car as the first entry in each cell in the table and the elasticity with respect to the characteristic as the second entry in each cell in the table.

Table 9.7. The own-characteristic elasticity of demand.

Model	Value of attribute/price Elasticity of demand with respect to: HP/weight	Air	MP$	Size	Price
Mazda323	0.366	0.000	3.645	1.075	5.049
	0.458	0.000	1.010	1.338	6.358
Sentra	0.391	0.000	3.645	1.092	5.661
	0.440	0.000	0.905	1.194	6.528
Escort	0.401	0.000	4.022	1.116	5.663
	0.449	0.000	1.132	1.176	6.031
Cavalier	0.385	0.000	3.142	1.179	5.797
	0.423	0.000	0.524	1.360	6.433
Accord	0.457	0.000	3.016	1.255	9.292
	0.282	0.000	0.126	0.873	4.798
Taurus	0.304	0.000	2.262	1.334	9.671
	0.180	0.000	−0.139	1.304	4.220
Century	0.387	1.000	2.890	1.312	10.138
	0.326	0.701	0.077	1.123	6.755
Maxima	0.518	1.000	2.513	1.300	13.695
	0.322	0.396	−0.136	0.932	4.845
Legend	0.510	1.000	2.388	1.292	18.944
	0.167	0.237	−0.070	0.596	4.134
TownCar	0.373	1.000	2.136	1.720	21.412
	0.089	0.211	−0.122	0.883	4.320
Seville	0.517	1.000	2.011	1.374	24.353
	0.092	0.116	−0.053	0.416	3.973
LS400	0.665	1.000	2.262	1.410	27.544
	0.073	0.037	−0.007	0.149	3.085
BMW 735i	0.542	1.000	1.885	1.403	37.490
	0.061	0.011	−0.016	0.174	3.515

Notes: The value of the attribute or, in the case of the last column, price, is the top number and the number below it is the elasticity of demand with respect to the attribute (or, in the last column, price). *Source*: Table V in Berry et al. (1995).

but computationally complex (or at least difficult). If the simpler option is chosen, perhaps because of lack of resources one must be extremely cautious and probably treat the answers obtained as at most indicative. Using models which impose the answer is not learning about the world, it is learning only about the property of your model, and obviously we should not, for example, be making merger decisions because of properties of econometric models. Although the use of the simpler models such as NMNL and its variants may be appropriate in many cases, in some instances estimating such an "off-the-shelf" model can be useless at best and in fact actively misleading. As in any quantitative exercise, demand estimation must be undertaken by knowledgeable economists and the assumptions and results must be confronted with the facts of the case. As a rule of thumb, if all the documents and the industry and consumer testimony in a case points in one direction while the econometric results point in another, then treat the econometric results with extreme caution. It may be that the econometrics is right and able to tell you more than the anecdotes but it may also be that the econometric analysis is based on invalid assumptions, a poor model specification, or the data are not good enough. In this section we point out some practical issues relating to model specification and the data needed for estimation.[49]

9.3.1 Specification Issues

The purpose of demand estimation is often to retrieve price elasticities and to calculate their effect on optimal pricing. In the merger context, for example, we usually want to evaluate the impact of a change in ownership on pricing and we saw in chapter 8 that the impact depends on the own- and cross-price elasticities at least between the merging parties' products. Demand estimation can be very useful, particularly if other more straightforward sources such as company estimates are unavailable. For example, sometimes companies choose to measure price sensitivity and run experiments to evaluate particularly their own-price elasticity of demand. We discussed one such marketing experiment in chapter 4, where we also discussed approaches to measuring diversion ratios using survey data. Demand estimation is another tool in the economists' toolbox—but one that is sometimes easy to physically implement and yet difficult to use well.

If demand estimation produces unrealistic demand elasticities, one must revise the specification of the demand model. Assuming that the demand estimation is correctly specified and that proper instruments are being used, one must check for other sources of error. It could be that the time frame used is incorrect so that quantity variation is not being correctly matched to the appropriate price variation; contracts, for example, can mean price variation occurs annually while you might have quarterly data. It could also be that other factors explaining variation in sales such as promotions, advertising campaigns, rival product entry, or changes in tastes are not being appropriately accounted for. Those simple checks should be undertaken first. Ultimately, it may be that the model is misspecified, particularly if a lot of structural assumptions on the shape of preferences have been imposed. In this case, other more flexible demand specifications may be more appropriate. Always remember that our aim is to write down an approximation to the data-generating process (DGP) and that the DGP will incorporate both the underlying economic process and the sampling process being used to physically generate the data that end up on your computer.

[49] The discussion draws partly on Hosken et al. (2002).

9.3.1.1 The Functional Specification of the Demand System

Merger simulation results are sensitive to the assumed demand specification and this has been elegantly demonstrated in Crooke et al. (1999). In simulation exercises evaluating mergers in differentiated markets with price competition, they found that simulations based on a log-linear specification predicted price increases three times larger than simulations using linear demands. Using AIDS models produced price increases twice as big as the linear demand model and the logit model showed an increase in price 50% higher than the linear demand model. These results reflect the fact that the greater the curvature of the demand curve, the lower the price elasticity of demand as prices increase (think about moving upward and leftward along an inverse demand curve that is either steeply or shallowly curved) and the greater the incentives to increase prices after a merger.

On the one hand, such sensitivity is theoretically a highly admirable feature of merger simulation models: the predicted price increases for a given merger will depend on the form of the demand curve, an important input to the model. On the other hand, it can often be difficult to have an a priori idea of which demand specification is more adequate, particularly if there have not been large historical variations in prices. With enough data we will be able to tell which type of demand curve best fits the data, but we do not always (or even often) have large enough data sets to be able to perform such checking systematically.[50]

One response is to consider running merger simulations using several demand specifications in order to assess the robustness and sensitivity of the estimates. Crooke et al.'s experience suggests that estimation using a log-linear or an AIDS model is likely to produce higher-end estimates of price effects while linear specification will produce lower-end estimates. It is not uninteresting to examine the bracket of outcomes generated by the different models. If the sensitivity to the model specification is very large, the merger simulation exercise may not be informative.

9.3.1.2 Accuracy of the Estimate of Demand Elasticity

Using evidence presented in court in merger proceedings, Walker (2005) also illustrates that small changes in the demand elasticity estimates at current prices can have significant effects on the results of merger simulations. Even variation within the confidence interval of very precisely estimated coefficients can significantly alter predicted price increases from mergers. One should therefore be wary when slight changes within realistic ranges of the elasticity estimate produce sharp changes in

[50] On some occasions it would be possible to nest the models and use statistical tests to examine which is preferred by the data; for example, linear and log-linear models can be tested using the Box–Cox test. On the other hand, models such as linear demands and AIDS may need to be tested against each other using nonnested model tests.

predicted price increases. Best practice is to calculate measures of uncertainty for the price increases, not just for the parameters of the model that generates them.[51]

9.3.2 Data Issues

One of the factors that has contributed to the development of demand estimation is the increase in the availability of data. In particular, access to scanner data at the retail level has provided economists with invaluable databases to estimate the demand for consumer goods. Nonetheless, case workers often face considerable difficulties and in this section we discuss some of the issues that practitioners commonly face with respect to data.

9.3.2.1 Availability

Obviously, in order to successfully estimate demand curves one must have suitable data available. Before undertaking an involved econometric exercise, one must be as sure as possible that the data necessary to construct a meaningful model are available. The data available may determine the choice of specification since different models have different data requirements, but this discretion in choosing demand functional forms because of data constraints should not be abused. The models make different assumptions which may or may not be valid. Rather, it makes more sense to choose an appropriate class of models that are realistically feasible in the time-frame likely to be available for analysis and to try to gather the necessary data early in the investigation. This can be done by obtaining public data, by purchasing data from third party suppliers, or in a competition agency by issuing data requests to the firms. In some sectors such as consumer goods retail data are available through specialized firms such as TNS, IRI, or AC Nielsen. In other sectors data will be more difficult to obtain but authorities should not hesitate to press firms to provide their transaction data, which are typically available in some form.[52]

Ideally, the data collected—though not necessarily from the firm—must include a set of instruments that will make possible the identification of the demand function. These instruments can be cost shifters for single demand estimation or variables

[51] This can be done simply by drawing values of the models' estimated parameters from their estimated distribution; we typically have estimated some parameters $\hat{\beta}$ and $\text{Var}[\hat{\beta}]$. If we draw an appropriately large number, say 1,000, of values of the parameters from the normal distribution $N(\hat{\beta}, \text{Var}[\hat{\beta}])$ and for each value of those parameters calculate the predicted price from the merger coming from a merger simulation model, then we will get a distribution of predicted prices. Taking the 2.5th and 97.5th percentiles of that distribution will give us a 95% confidence interval for the price increase arising from the merger.

[52] This need not be burdensome on the firms if the agency is willing to clean the data. Indeed, it may even provide free data-cleaning services to the firm involved if the cleaned data is subsequently returned. On the other hand, if extracting appropriate data is a major task which will distract the entire computer expertise of a firm, then obviously it would be appropriate to carefully consider whether it was necessary to proceed on this basis. Firms will sometimes have an incentive to keep data away from competition agencies so such "it's impossible" claims should not be taken at face value. It is often appropriate to send a member of staff to talk to the "data person" at a company, although often an "offer" to do so will overcome apparently significant hurdles.

that determine each of the prices to be estimated without affecting the demand of that product in the case of markets with several differentiated products. Hausman, for example, suggested using prices from other markets while BLP suggested using product characteristics of rival products. In some contexts firms appear to run price promotions in a way that is unrelated to the level of demand and in those cases we can use price variation from such experiments to identify the slope of demand curves—we will be able to estimate downward-sloping demand curves. For example, demand curves estimated using supermarket scanner data are usually found to slope downward and display what appear to be sensible substitution patterns, albeit ones that need to be very carefully considered in light of dynamic effects.[53] The reason is that demand in a given store is often unrelated to the decision to run a price promotion which may be a regional or national decision. Cost data are sometimes available from firms, but are often burdensome on firms to collect in a form that can be used, and moreover are often not available at a frequency which would be genuinely useful; many attempts to obtain cost data from firms will generate data sets where costs appear not to vary over time. On the other hand, in some instances high-quality cost data are available and then they can be used as instruments.

9.3.2.2 *Aggregation*

An observation in an econometric estimation is often an aggregate of many individual transactions. For instance, one may aggregate purchases of a given good over a day, a week, or a month. Also one may aggregate over stores, chains, or distribution channels. Aggregation typically works better when it is done over homogeneous elements. Aggregating over distribution channels will make sense if the purchases in all channels are similar in that they are done by similar customers at similar prices. If this is not the case, aggregating transactions in a supermarket with transactions in a specialty store may produce a demand elasticity which does not reflect any customer group's actual elasticity. That said, if it is the aggregate elasticity that is required, then it may make sense to work with aggregate data.

Aggregation over time may involve taking into account the periodicity at which prices change since we are attempting to model the data-generating process. If we aggregate to a greater length of time, then doing so can sometimes remove a considerable amount of the useful price variation in a data set. On the other hand, aggregation can sometimes reduce the effect of measurement error.[54] The possibility

[53] Short-run elasticities of demand can be far greater than long-run elasticities of demand (or vice versa) depending on the context. For the recent literature, see the overview by Hendel and Nevo (2004). For a more technical dynamic model of consumer choice with inventories, see Hendel and Nevo (2006a,b). For the earlier literature see an older applied econometrics textbook using partial adjustment models such as Berndt (1991). The latter are often more informative as practical tools within a merger context.

[54] Adding together two independent random measurement error terms will not reduce variance—aggregation will add up the noise. On the other hand, averaging will reduce variance so that, for example, aggregate market shares calculated using large numbers of individual demands will suffer from very little sampling error.

of intertemporal allocation such as inventory accumulation may also be considered in order to avoid overestimating the demand elasticity when there are temporary reductions in prices such as sales or promotions. That said, in a practical context it may be possible to simply avoid modeling complex detailed dynamics that are irrelevant for the issues at hand by choosing the right time period for analysis.

Aggregating over different varieties of products or types of packaging can also impact the results since a "generic" price is constructed for a "generic" bundle of product. One could test the sensitivity of different price and quantity specifications on the results to make sure that the latter are sufficiently robust to be meaningful, though doing so is often a time-consuming exercise.

While there are many theoretical and real dangers in aggregation in practice, if you are interested in an aggregate quantity you will at some point have to aggregate. Thus the choice is often not whether to aggregate, but rather whether to model the disaggregate data and then aggregate or alternatively to model the aggregate data directly. Theoretically, the former is likely to be preferred, but in practice the latter will often produce more reliable results at lower cost. The reason is simple, namely that the analyst is focusing directly on the quantity of interest. Suppose, for example, one is interested in understanding the aggregate demand for computers. An analyst must decide whether it truly makes sense to attempt to model the dynamics for all individual brands, or not. A disaggregated approach would involve modeling perhaps hundreds of demand equations, necessarily imperfectly. In contrast, looking at the aggregate data involves looking at one time series and hiding a lot of the variation across brands. Working with aggregate data will involve imperfect price, volume, and quality measures. However, the dominant features of the aggregate data will be clear, and in the computer industry are likely to involve prices going down while volumes and quality go up.

9.3.3 Retail and Wholesale Elasticities

Retail transaction data are more likely to be publicly available than wholesale data so the demand elasticity at the retail level may be easier to calculate than the derived demand elasticity faced by manufacturers. There are intrinsic differences between retail and manufacturer level elasticities. In cases where we are interested in the upstream market, the retail demand elasticity can be useful to know, since, for example, highly elastic downstream customers will tend to make the retailer a highly elastic demander of manufacturers products. However, an estimated retail demand elasticity should not "replace" a serious consideration of the actual demand elasticity faced by the manufacturer, if that ultimately is the object of interest.

At the end of the day the retailer and manufacturer are participants in a different market from the one involving transactions between retailer and end-consumer. Prices in upstream markets are often more complex than prices at retail. Long-term relationships between manufacturers and retailers are not uncommon and contracts may simultaneously cover a broad range of goods. The resulting pricing schemes are often nonlinear and may also incorporate rebates, de facto bundling, contracting of shelf space, or promotional co-payments. Retailer's demand can be stickier than consumers' demand because of those contractual agreements for a given price range. It can also be stickier because individuals who work with one another for a period of time may simply like each other. On the other hand, manufacturers may face very high demand elasticities, and such elasticities may be evidenced by experience of large retailers deciding to drop the manufacturer's products altogether from its shelves after modest price increases. Service levels are often important to retailers and so in upstream retail markets it may be appropriate to obtain data on service levels (e.g., percentage of orders of the manufacturers product actually delivered by week) as well as data on prices.

In the simplest theoretical context, the elasticity of the derived demand at the wholesale level can be expressed in term of the demand elasticity faced by retailers. To see how, consider a retailer who sets a pure uniform linear price by solving

$$\max_{p}(p - w)D^{\mathrm{R}}(p),$$

where p is the retail price, w the wholesale price of the good and therefore the cost to the retailer, and R is the index indicating the demand is that faced by the retailer. The solution to this problem will be a retail (downstream) pricing function $p^*(w)$ so that, assuming a one-to-one technology, where one unit of the manufacturer's product is sold downstream as one unit of the retailer's product, the manufacturer's demand can be written as $D^{\mathrm{M}}(w) = D^{\mathrm{R}}(p^*(w))$.

Following, for example, Verboven and Brenkers (2006), we may write

$$\frac{\partial \ln D^{\mathrm{M}}(w)}{\partial \ln w} = w\frac{\partial \ln D^{\mathrm{R}}(p^*(w))}{\partial w} = w\frac{p}{p}\frac{\partial \ln D^{\mathrm{R}}(p)}{\partial p}\frac{\partial p^*(w)}{\partial w}$$

or

$$\varepsilon_w = \frac{w}{p} \times \varepsilon_r \times (\text{pass-through rate}) = \varepsilon_r \times \varepsilon_{wr},$$

where w/p is the ratio of the wholesale price over the retail price,

$$\varepsilon_w = \frac{\partial \ln D^{\mathrm{M}}(w)}{\partial \ln w}$$

is the demand elasticity faced by the manufacturer,

$$\varepsilon_r = \frac{\partial \ln D^{\mathrm{R}}(p)}{\partial \ln p}$$

is the demand elasticity faced by the retailer, and

$$\varepsilon_{wr} = \frac{\partial \ln p^*(w)}{\partial \ln w}$$

is the retailer's *price* elasticity with respect to the wholesale price. Since the elasticity of the retail price with respect to the wholesale price is likely to be less than one, this equivalence implies that the elasticity of the derived demand for the manufacturer will generally be lower in absolute terms than the retailer demand elasticity.

Some considerable progress has been made recently on modeling vertical chains using both uniform and nonlinear pricing structures to describe the contracts between retailers and manufacturers. See, in particular, the recent contributions by Verboven and Brenkers (2006), Villas-Boas (2007a,b), and Bonnet et al. (2006). That said, those of us working in competition agencies still face important challenges in modeling using the kinds of data sets we do sometimes have, namely data from both manufacturer and retailer. One important characteristic of such data is that it sometimes demonstrates surprisingly little variation over time, in particular, in prices while volumes vary enormously over time. (We discuss vertical relationship further in chapter 10.)

9.4 Conclusions

- Demand estimation is central to the empirical analysis of competition issues. The reason is simply that a model of demand allows us to characterize the revenues that firms will obtain from their products. In turn, revenue plays an important role in determining firm profitability, firm conduct, and market outcomes.
- In principle, estimating market demand functions for homogeneous products is the easiest activity for an applied economist as there is only one demand equation to estimate and it depends on only one price variable (and any demand shifters such as income). Still, one must be careful to understand the drivers of variation in the observed data and doing so will involve understanding consumer behavior in that market as well as any significant factors that affect it.
- In addition to industry understanding, even in a homogeneous product market, particular attention must be paid to the specification of the model and the data variation that is allowing the demand curve to be identified. Most demand estimation exercises will require us to use instrumental variable techniques in order to achieve identification. Good instruments must explain variation in price given the variation already explained by the included exogenous variables and also be uncorrelated with unobserved determinants of demand. In demand estimation, suitable instruments will typically involve a determinant of supply that has no role on the demand side. The reason is that shifts in the supply (pricing) side of the market will identify (trace out) the demand curve.
- Linear or log-linear demand models provide simple specifications to take to data since the models are each linear in the parameters to be estimated. Naturally, either assumption involves placing strong restrictions on the way

in which price elasticities of demand vary (or do not vary in the log-linear case) along the demand curve.

- There are various ways of categorizing demand models. One is according to the number of products, homogeneous or differentiated product. Another is by the nature of the choice consumers make—either continuous quantity choices or discrete (0,1) quantity choices. A third categorization is to consider those models which specify preferences over products and those which specify preferences in terms of product characteristics.

- Almost ideal demand systems (AIDS) provide one important example of a continuous choice differentiated product demand model that provides a specification of preferences over products. The AIDS model is easy to estimate and has some attractive properties as an aggregate demand model.

- When there are many products in the market, further restrictions on the parameters are often necessary to make the model estimable given the kinds of databases usually available. One source of parameter restrictions is choice theory. Restrictions that can be imposed include the Slutsky symmetry, homogeneity in prices and income, and additivity, whereby expenditure shares must add to one. In doing so the analyst must keep in mind that Slutsky symmetry does not necessarily hold in aggregate demand systems, even if the underlying consumer demands are generated strictly by consumers satisfying the axioms of choice theory. A second approach to reducing the number of parameters to be estimated is to model demand as generated by a multistage budgeting process where first consumers choose which market segment to buy from and then choose the specific brand to buy within that market segment. Such models impose structure on the matrix of own- and cross-price elasticities and in doing so reduces the number of parameters to be estimated. These two approaches are not mutually exclusive.

- A third approach to reducing the number of parameters is to assume that consumers care about product characteristics rather than products themselves. In product-characteristic models we typically distinguish between horizontal and vertical sources of product differentiation. Horizontal differentiation refers to situations in which customers' ranking of options are different. The Hotelling model produces demand functions dependent on prices and the product characteristics. The distribution of individual consumer types is either observed (when it is based on location, for instance, and the decision is the choice of store) or must be assumed. Vertical differentiation refers to situations where consumers rank options equally (all agree that one is better than the other) although they vary in how they value quality and hence trade-off quality and price.

- Consumer preferences are commonly defined over product characteristics in discrete choice demand models. The multinomial logit (MNL) model is a simple example of a discrete choice model. However, MNL is not directly useful in many modeling exercises as its structure places unrealistic restrictions on substitution patterns. For this reason it is not a recommended model when we are trying to understand actual substitution patterns, although it can be useful for understanding what data variation drives variation in the levels of market shares.
- The nested multinomial logit (NMNL) model provides a discrete choice model which allows subsets of goods to be "closer" substitutes within a group than with those in other groups. In such models, following a price rise of a particular product, individuals will tend to substitute to goods in the same group, by which we will mean a market segment or category. This model provides greater flexibility in preferences than MNL and is useful when the market segments can be clearly identified, although it is important to note that the substitution patterns remain highly restrictive.
- The random coefficient MNL model allows the model to predict a greater variety of substitution patterns but at the same time is harder and hence more costly to estimate than the NMNL or AIDS models. The BLP version of this model has now been estimated on quite a large variety of occasions. The richer model allows the data to drive predicted substitution patterns rather than the model, but it is important to note that, in practice, some researchers have found the model's parameters quite difficult to identify on limited data sets. In addition, more popular implementations of the model often inadvertently impose some quite important restrictions on demand systems, in particular, Slutsky symmetry. Nonetheless this class of random coefficient models is an important step forward for many applications—at least compared with NMNL and MNL models.
- We end this chapter with a plea to the practitioner. When estimating demand systems with the aim of retrieving elasticities and predicting price increases, perhaps following a merger, one must be confident that the specification and data used are both adequate. Reality checks and sensitivity tests are very important during the process of model specification and in casework it is generally important that where at all possible econometrics and model predictions should be supported by other evidence in the investigation, particularly qualitative information, before decision makers are encouraged to draw strong policy conclusions.

10

Quantitative Assessment of Vertical Restraints and Integration

In previous chapters we have discussed estimation and identification of the main determinants of market outcomes, in particular demand estimation, cost estimation, and estimation of strategic choice equations such as pricing equations. We also discussed the effects of changes in market structure or in the form of competition on firms' prices and output, both using reduced- and structural-form equations. In this chapter, we examine firms' decisions relating to issues beyond just their own prices and output. In particular, we look at the restraints that firms may sometimes impose on their commercial customers downstream. We discuss when we can empirically determine the motives and effects of such behavior on market outcomes and, specifically, final consumers. Our intention is not to define what constitutes anticompetitive behavior, as that will vary by jurisdiction, but rather to discuss potential techniques that may help evaluate types of conducts that are often subject to antitrust scrutiny.

Before beginning any analyst should be aware that the empirical assessment of vertical restraints is generally considerably more difficult than analysis of at least a straightforward single horizontal merger for at least three reasons. First, in order to understand vertical restraints it is usually necessary to understand at least two markets, the market upstream and the market downstream. Second, the economic theoretical framework is less fully developed than models such as Bertrand pricing. And third, the empirical analysis of such markets is not very accessible to basic (i.e., academic) researchers since we are often seeking to understand the contractual relationships between firms which, while often observed by competition authorities, are often unobserved by the academic community. The consequence has been less empirical research on these topics overall.

A formal quantitative analysis of the effect(s) of vertical restraints or integration is therefore both a complex task and one where the set of tools available for empirical analysis is modest. For that reason, vertical restraints are often tackled using qualitative arguments about the likelihood of foreclosure and consumer harm rather than detailed quantitative analysis. There have, however, been some interesting attempts at empirical estimation of the effect of vertical practices and vertical integration and we explore many of them in this chapter. Moreover, since the trend in the legal standard for evaluation is toward a case-by-case "effects-based" analysis of such practices, the need for sound empirical analysis is becoming ever more immediate.

Before we critically discuss the empirical techniques that have proved useful in determining the effects of vertical restraints in the academic and case literature, for comprehensiveness we briefly present the main elements of the theoretical literature evaluating these practices. One important reason to do so is that it will illustrate the complexity of the factors involved and the difficulty of even predicting the direction of potential effects.

10.1 Rationales for Vertical Restraints and Integration

Vertical restraints can take on many forms.[1] Some take the form of price restraints and impose conditions on the price that the downstream firm can charge for the good that is purchased from the upstream firm while others take the form of nonprice restraints. Examples of price restraints include minimum resale price maintenance (RPM), where the producer sets a floor for the price that a retailer can charge for its product. This was at one stage the most common form of vertical restraint. There can also be instances of price ceilings, known as maximum RPM. Nonprice restraints can be divided in four main categories: (i) territorial restrictions, (ii) exclusive dealing, (iii) tying and bundling, and (iv) refusal to deal, or more generally "raising rivals' costs."

On the one hand, each of these vertical restraints can potentially arise normally in the course of business and with the exception of refusal to deal may well ultimately be welfare enhancing for consumers. On the other hand, and probably in a minority of cases, each of these restraints can potentially result in some foreclosure effects either downstream, which we may call "customer foreclosure," or upstream, which we will call "input foreclosure." Territorial restrictions cause the division of a downstream market in a set of distinct geographical areas that prevent resellers from operating in any another area than their own. Exclusive dealing, also called single branding, induces retailers (or more generally distributors) to sell only the manufacturer's brand and none of the competing products. An example occurred when Anheuser-Busch, the beer manufacturer, began a campaign called "100% share of mind" and offered beer distributors extended credit, increased marketing support and other incentives for becoming exclusive.[2] Outright refusals to deal occur when a firm refuses to supply another firm downstream. This would be the case if, for example, a phone network operator denied access to its network to one or all competing phone service providers. Another example might arise if a patent holder refused to license

[1] An excellent recent survey of theoretical results is provided by Rey and Tirole (2005). See also the special edition of the *Journal of Industrial Economics*, September 1991, edited by John Vickers and Mike Waterson (see Vickers and Waterson (1991) and, of course, Church (2004)). Finally, the interested reader may like to refer to Dobson and Waterson (1996).

[2] For the source of this example and a detailed examination of it, see Asker (2005).

their patent thereby restricting the use of a given technology. The different categories of vertical restraints can group several types of conducts. For instance, exclusive dealing can be contractual or can be the result of a rebate scheme or a tying practice. The common characteristic is that companies take measures to restrict the activities of firms with which they have vertical relationships.

We begin the discussion by presenting some of the potential motivations for imposing vertical restraints or perhaps even vertically integrating. As we shall see, many of the possible motivations for vertical restraints are likely to fit well with the market generating good outcomes for consumers. On the other hand, vertical restraints and integration can generate harm to consumers and therefore form a legitimate focus of attention for a competition authority.

10.1.1 Incentives for Vertical Control

Vertical restraints are, as the name suggests, restrictions that are imposed contractually by an upstream firm on the behavior of a distinct downstream firm, or vice versa. The ultimate vertical restraint, of course, is to take the control of both the upstream and downstream firms which is what will happen if the firms vertically integrate. The motivations for vertical restraints are therefore often related to the incentive to vertically integrate and so we have grouped the two topics for this chapter. That fact means many of the tools we discuss in this chapter will be directly useful for the evaluation of vertical mergers. In this section we review some of the reasons for control over vertical relationships. Most of those reasons relate to attempts by the either upstream or downstream firm to achieve an efficient price and output level. However, there are various potential reasons for vertical restraints to be a matter of concern for antitrust authorities, most directly are the concerns that vertical restraints may provide a mechanism by which firms can attempt to foreclose either downstream or upstream markets.

10.1.1.1 Transaction Costs and Contractual Incompleteness

Following the work of Williamson (1975, 1979, 1985),[3] one clear potential motivation for vertical integration is the existence of transaction costs. Even simple negotiations can become costly if they are frequent enough and case-specific enough. Having to constantly negotiate the terms of a transaction such as the terms of the delivery, the complementary services involved, and the degree of flexibility in the face of unexpected events can quickly become burdensome. One solution to such transaction costs is to vertically integrate. Another is to negotiate long-term contracts. Long-term contracts may make vertical integration unnecessary even if relationship-specific investments must be made (see, for example, Eccles 1981; Joskow 1985). For example, a coal mine and a power station located next to each other would

[3] See also Klein et al. (1978), Klein (1988), and Riordan and Williamson (1985).

each respectively require their owners to sink investments that are, potentially, subject to attempts at *ex post* appropriation by the other. Long-term contracts may avoid those dangers and thus enable investments to be made. However, even when contract renegotiations are infrequent, negotiating "complete" contracts, contracts which cover every potential contingency that may arise, can be difficult to write and the risk of substantial incompleteness, particularly in dynamic environments, is inevitably high. Industries that are highly dependent on an essential input, or on access to a given distribution channel, will tend to establish long-term contractual arrangements or might integrate in order to avoid constant renegotiation and reduce contractual uncertainty. Similarly, firms that produce outputs that require significant sunk investments may want to secure the output allocation before incurring the sunk costs in order to minimize the risk of having to aggressively search for potential buyers later on. The market for individual firms is not always a particularly liquid one.[4] Full vertical integration is one of a plethora of potential vertical structures with a pure spot market between manufacturer and retailer at the other end of the spectrum. In between is a rich variety of contractual forms acting to endow a potentially large variety of control rights (for either a long or short time) across firms in a supply chain. There is a large literature discussing such choices. (See, in particular, Grossman and Hart (1986), Hart and Moore (1990), the summary provided by Hart (1995), but also the empirical evidence discussed in Whinston (2003).[5])

10.1.1.2 Double Marginalization and Other Vertical Externalities

The existence of double marginalization is the most widely cited motivation for vertical relationships and has become a core concept in this area of economic theory. It is therefore worth explaining it in detail. Double marginalization was introduced by Cournot (1838) and more recently by Spengler (1950) and can be understood as a vertical pricing externality. The principle of double marginalization states that an independent retailer will have an incentive to raise prices compared with the retail price charged by a vertically integrated firm. Thus the price charged by the independent retailer is not the one that maximizes profits for the vertically integrated firm. The result is higher prices and lower quantities at the retail level when the firm is not vertically integrated.

To illustrate the concept, assume a vertically integrated firm which maximizes total profits. If c^{Up} and c^{Down} are the marginal costs of the product upstream and

[4] Competition agencies with a "remedies" department oversee the process of selling companies and so often contain individuals with considerable insight into the market for companies. Competition agencies may, for example, need to oversee the sale of a company if a completed merger must be reversed following a decision that it caused a substantial lessening of competition and that the suitable remedy is a structural one. One lesson that comes from such agency experience is that the market for companies is sometimes illiquid.

[5] Whinston discusses the empirical evidence available regarding the property rights/incomplete contracts theory of integration and, in particular, its limitations.

downstream respectively, an integrated firm maximizes the following profit function:

$$\max_p \Pi_f = \max_p (p - c^{\text{Up}} - c^{\text{Down}}) D(p),$$

which results in the following first-order condition:

$$\frac{\partial \Pi_f}{\partial p} = (p - c^{\text{Up}} - c^{\text{Down}}) D'(p) + D(p) = 0,$$

which in turn determines the optimal price for the vertically integrated firm, p^{VI}, which is the price that solves this equation. We assume that demand slopes down, $D'(p) < 0$.

Assume now that we have a manufacturer and a retailer. Their respective profit functions are

$$\max_{p^{\text{w}}} \Pi^{\text{Manufacturer}} = \max_{p^{\text{w}}} (p^{\text{w}} - c^{\text{Up}}) D(p^{\text{w}}),$$

$$\max_p \Pi^{\text{Retailer}} = \max_p (p - p^{\text{w}} - c^{\text{Down}}) D(p).$$

If the relationship between manufacturer and retailer involves only the specification of a single per unit wholesale price p^{w}, then that will also be a contributor to marginal cost for the retailer. The first-order condition for the retailer is

$$\frac{\partial \Pi^{\text{Retailer}}}{\partial p} = (p - p^{\text{w}} - c^{\text{Down}}) D'(p) + D(p).$$

Adding and subtracting c^{Up} and rearranging we obtain the following expression:

$$\frac{\partial \Pi^{\text{Retailer}}}{\partial p} = (p - c^{\text{Up}} - c^{\text{Down}}) D'(p) + D(p) - (p^{\text{w}} - c^{\text{Up}}) D'(p).$$

Note that at the optimal price for the vertically integrated firm p^{VI} the first two terms of the expression add to zero so that at that price we have

$$\frac{\partial \Pi^{\text{Retailer}}(p^{\text{VI}})}{\partial p} = -(p^{\text{w}} - c^{\text{Up}}) D'(p^{\text{VI}}) > 0.$$

The derivative is positive meaning that if retail price is increased then retailer profits will go up. This means that the optimal retail price for the vertically integrated firm is not the optimal price for the independent retailer. Specifically, the inequality implies that a retailer will increase profits by increasing the retail price above the price that is optimal for the vertically integrated firm.

Note that the resulting prices are even higher than we would obtain with a single monopoly!

Double marginalization, the fact that retailers increase their margins in a way that is detrimental to the total industry profits, is considered a vertical price externality. In the double marginalization case, the downstream firm does not take into account the effect that their price setting has on the profits of the upstream firm. This analysis provides an important example of the perhaps general statement that it may be better to have a monopoly than a string of monopolies.[6] Of course, it remains even better to have competitive markets!

Double marginalization is not the only externality that can occur in a vertical relationship. There may, for example, also be vertical service externalities in a manufacturer–retailer relationship. We define services as being everything the firms can do to facilitate customers' purchases in terms of information, convenience, or quality. The vertical service externality can arise because the benefits of retailers' services or sales effort accrue not only to the retailer itself but also to the manufacturer whenever the manufacturer makes a positive margin. Its products will experience an increase in sales if the retailer's sales increase, while the costs of service may be borne solely by the retailer. Naturally, the retailer will only take into account its own benefits when choosing the optimal amount of service effort and therefore the theory suggests that independent retailers may choose a service level which is lower than the optimal one for the manufacturer, the vertical chain as a whole, and often also consumers. Manufacturers therefore have an incentive to elicit higher service levels from retailers and they sometimes can do so by imposing some restrictions on retailers' operations.

10.1.1.3 Horizontal Externalities

Winter (1993) also identifies what can be called horizontal pricing and service externalities. These occur because of actions taken at a given stage in the vertical chain, i.e., either upstream or downstream, but their effects can be felt by all players. An example arises when the manufacturer sells to several firms that compete downstream, as is the case in most manufacturer/retailer settings. In such instances, the prices and services delivered by retailers may not be optimal in terms of either profits or welfare. For example, if investments in services by one retailer also benefit its rival competing retailers, which in turn decreases the incentives to provide those services for any one retailer.[7] Such a situation may arise if, say, a bookstore promotes a book only to see customers buy it online once they have been convinced to purchase it. Although the manufacturer may be indifferent to where the purchase takes place, the retailer might be discouraged from investing in promotional activities and that can hurt both the manufacturer and also consumer welfare. On the other hand, retailers may benefit more than the manufacturer from unilateral retailer price decreases if they increase their store profits by attracting customers from competing retailers, a move that does not increase the manufacturer profits. This business-stealing effect provides an example of a negative horizontal externality. Putting these factors together, Winter argues that in competitive retail environments, retailers may have a tendency to attract an extra customer away from another retailer by lowering its price

[6] For an analysis of double marginalization under incomplete information, see Gal-Or (1991).

[7] The problem of retailers free riding on services was introduced in Telser (1960).

instead of by increasing promotional services, a decision that increases its profits but potentially lowers the profits of the manufacturer and may hurt consumer welfare.

In summary, the effect of horizontal externalities on retailer pricing and service provision suggests that both retailer pricing and retailer service may be too low relative to that which a manufacturer would prefer. In terms of the vertical externalities, double marginalization and positive margins may respectively mean that retail prices are too high and retail service may be too low. The net effect of the horizontal and vertical externalities generated by the provision of services appears to unambiguously result in insufficient services, at least relative to the level of services the manufacturer would prefer. With respect to prices, the horizontal and vertical externalities may counterbalance each other and the net result is, in general, ambiguous for the manufacturer. In terms of ultimate consumer welfare, in many cases consumers will end up paying higher prices but benefit from greater service under either vertical integration or vertical restraints. Later in the chapter we explore methods to help competition agencies determine whether this change in outcomes benefits consumers in a given case under investigation.

10.1.1.4 Softening of Competition and Foreclosure

Although there is a debate as to the frequency with which vertical restraints are used for purely anticompetitive purposes, with some influential commentators taking the position that such activities are fairly rare (see, in particular, Lafontaine and Slade 2005), the fact is that vertical restrictions can, albeit perhaps infrequently, result in behavioral restrictions on firms downstream or upstream that may potentially have anticompetitive effects. Vertical restraints can be useful to foreclose rival suppliers in a market by raising their operating costs or, alternatively, facilitate foreclosure of rivals' access to consumers downstream.[8] A substantial body of economic literature has developed which analyzes exactly the conditions under which exclusive vertical arrangements may result in anticompetitive foreclosure (see, for example, Mathewson and Winter 1987; Bernheim and Whinston 1998; Rey 2003). Many competition authorities structure analyses of such potential effects by considering first whether a vertical restriction (or merger) would enhance a firm's ability to foreclose, second whether a firm would in fact have an incentive to foreclose, and third whether a firm would harm final consumers. Such a structure can be useful, but in practice analysis in a specific instance can be hard to cleanly divide up under these three headings. Sometimes vertical restraints will not result in complete foreclosure but can instead create conditions in which rival producers soften the intensity of their price competition. This can be achieved, for instance, through partial foreclosure, resale price maintenance, exclusive territories, and even in some circumstances with exclusive

[8] Salop and Scheffman (1983). For a brief discussion of the incentives to agree to exclusive arrangements and the anticompetitive effects of vertical restraints, see Verouden (2005) as well as the cited bibliography.

dealing contracts (see, for example, Rey and Stiglitz 1995; Jullien and Rey 2008). We discuss each of these issues in the sections that follow.

10.1.2 Solving Double Marginalization

Firms facing externalities resulting in divergent incentives do not always need to integrate to resolve those issues. Contractual arrangements can be agreed that affect firms' behavior downstream or upstream and secure more favorable outcomes. In this section, we briefly review the most common ways in which vertical restraints can be used by firms to induce behavior by either parties at other stages of the vertical chain (e.g., upstream and downstream) or by parties at a particular stage of the vertical chain (e.g., service provision across retailers.) As we progress the reader will also note that several different vertical contracting practices can sometimes be used for addressing any one difficulty in vertical relationships, indeed this is why some authors consider it odd that resale price maintenance is treated differently from other forms of vertical restraints in some jurisdictions.[9]

10.1.2.1 Resale Price Maintenance: Ceiling

Resale price maintenance in the form of a price ceiling is a straightforward way by which firms can solve the double marginalization problem. By setting a maximum price, they can successfully stop retailers increasing prices further from the optimal integrated firm price. In such cases, resale price maintenance works to the benefit of consumers since they put a cap on the prices to consumers. This example provides a central illustration of a general proposition that vertical restraints can sometimes be good for both profits and also consumer welfare.

10.1.2.2 Two-Part Tariffs

Two-part tariffs are another contractual way in which firms can realign incentives of firms downstream to match their own incentives. The theoretical formalization of two-part tariffs is due to Oi (1971), who discusses potential payment systems in Disneyland, where there is an entrance fee and one can potentially set additional payments per ride. Two-part tariffs are pricing systems whereby the upstream firm[10] sets a fixed payment and an additional price per unit purchased. By setting the per unit payment equal to the marginal cost of the firm upstream and the fixed payment equal to, or rather slightly lower than, the downstream firm's gross profit, this payment structure allows the upstream firm to maximize total industry profits and recover most of the generated rent with the fixed fee to the downstream firm.

[9] Others note that RPM can help facilitate collusive outcomes and so consider a separate treatment entirely justified.

[10] This structure endows the manufacturer with all the bargaining power through a first-mover advantage. The alternative move order wherein the retailer moved first would give the retailer all the bargaining power.

In a two-part-tariffs pricing system, the manufacturer announces a tariff $T(q)$ composed of a fixed fee A^{w} and a fee that varies with quantity $p^{\mathrm{w}}q$:

$$T(q) = A^{\mathrm{w}} + p^{\mathrm{w}}q.$$

Let us formalize the decision process of the firms. Given the tariff, the downstream firm chooses its optimal quantity q that maximizes its profits. Note that purchasing nothing is an available alternative and so, formally, the retailer solves

$$\max\left\{\max_{p}(p - c^{\mathrm{Down}} - p^{\mathrm{w}})D(p) - A^{\mathrm{w}}, 0\right\},$$

where p is the price charged by the downstream firm and c^{Down} is the marginal cost of the downstream firm. The upstream firm chooses $(A^{\mathrm{w}}, p^{\mathrm{w}})$ to maximize its own profits subject to the constraint that the downstream firm is willing to buy a positive quantity. Formally,

$$\max_{p^{\mathrm{w}},A^{\mathrm{w}}} T(D(p)) - c^{\mathrm{Up}}D(p) \quad \text{subject to } \max_{p}(p - c^{\mathrm{Down}} - p^{\mathrm{w}})D(p) - A^{\mathrm{w}} \geqslant 0,$$

where c^{Up} is the marginal cost for the upstream firm. Substituting in $T(q)$,

$$\max_{p^{\mathrm{w}},A^{\mathrm{w}}} A^{\mathrm{w}} + (p^{\mathrm{w}} - c^{\mathrm{Up}})D(p) \quad \text{subject to } \max_{p}(p - c^{\mathrm{Down}} - p^{\mathrm{w}})D(p) - A^{\mathrm{w}} \geqslant 0.$$

Analytically, such a framework is rather similar to a principal–agent type of problem in which the upstream firm plays the role of principle since she is effectively given all the bargaining power. Let us examine the solution to such a problem. Consider the potential solution which involves first maximizing the total surplus by setting the variable part of the tariff to the upstream firm's marginal cost, that is, to set $p^{\mathrm{w}} = c^{\mathrm{Up}}$. And second, allowing the upstream firm to extract as much surplus from the downstream firm as is possible with a fixed tariff, leaving the downstream firm with only enough profits to make it marginally willing to participate (and no more). Formally, the upstream firm sets A^{w} equal to the profits of the downstream firm when the marginal price faced by the retailer is set equal to the marginal cost of production by the upstream firm:

$$A^{\mathrm{w}} = \max_{p}(p - c^{\mathrm{Down}} - c^{\mathrm{Up}})D(p).$$

Instead of extracting monopoly profits at the upstream level, such a "nonlinear" pricing contract allows the upstream firm to (1) set the wholesale price at the marginal cost of production, effectively allowing the downstream firm to price like an integrated firm, and (2) then appropriates the monopoly profits through the fixed fee. Note that if the fixed fee $A^{\mathrm{w}} = 0$, the downstream firm gets all the profits while setting the fixed tariff A^{w} equal to the downstream firm's profits gives the upstream firm all the profits. The exact quantity of A^{w} will in all likelihood depend on the relative bargaining power of both firms. If the fixed component of the tariff is high, the downstream firm bears a lot of risk and, in uncertain environments, two-part tariffs may not provide an optimal pricing scheme to maximize total profits and redistribute the resulting rent. In predictable environments, this price structure solves the double marginalization problem and can maximize profits for the upstream firm by achieving a profit level comparable with the one that would result from vertical integration. Finally, note that in practical settings we may see negotiation over the appropriate division of A^{w} between the upstream and downstream firms. The important aspect of the two-part-tariff solution is that profits from the vertical chain are maximized by making the retailer's marginal cost of an input equal to the input's marginal cost of production. How the resulting spoils are divided between upstream and downstream firms may then be a matter of negotiation between the players. Only if competition authorities were concerned for some reason about the division of profits in the vertical chain, perhaps because of incentives for investment, would the vertical restraint be an immediate focus for concern. Market power either upstream or downstream, on the other hand, may well be of interest.

10.1.2.3 Quantity Forcing

An alternative way to elicit the appropriate downstream price from the intermediate firm would be to set a wholesale price equal to the target retail price minus the distributors' competitive return while at the same time imposing a stipulated quantity to trade. This quantity forcing does not need to be explicit but can alternatively be induced by a system of rebates that result in the intermediate firm buying from the producer the latter's optimal quantity.

Quantity forcing can be an issue when the upstream firm induces downstream firms to purchase a volume that is large enough to foreclose the entry of other firms in the market. Such an issue was raised in the European Commission investigation against Coca Cola. In 2005 Coca Cola provided the European Commission with commitments that included, among other things, a prohibition on rebate schemes that were linked to growth targets. Similarly, it prohibited rebates conditional on buying less popular products of the brand. Competitors had complained that the incentives and rebate practices of Coca Cola left them with little shelf space at retailers.[11]

10.1.2.4 Intrabrand Competition Downstream

If there is strong intrabrand competition downstream, there will be no need to solve the double marginalization problem since the individual firms downstream cannot extract a supra-competitive margin by exercising market power to increase downstream prices and therefore reduce the manufacturers' sales.

Assuming for simplicity that each unit downstream requires one unit of the upstream input, the price downstream will be set at the level of the total marginal

[11] COMP/39.116-Coca Cola, OJ L 253, 29.09.2005, p. 21.

cost of production so that

$$p = p^{\text{w}} + c^{\text{Down}}.$$

In this case, the upstream firm gets the integrated firm's monopoly profit by setting the wholesale price to be

$$p^{\text{w}} = p^{\text{VI}} - c^{\text{Down}},$$

where p^{VI} is the retail price set by a hypothetical vertically integrated firm. Doing so ensures that the upstream firm can get the downstream price to be just at the level that the vertically integrated firm would optimally choose

$$p = p^{\text{w}} + c^{\text{Down}} = (p^{\text{VI}} - c^{\text{Down}}) + c^{\text{Down}} = p^{\text{VI}}.$$

This scenario illustrates that, when the downstream market is highly competitive, the Chicago critique applies. This critique states that it is not possible to extract more than one monopoly profit along the vertical chain. It was a response to previously prevailing anticompetitive interpretations of vertical restraints and, in its extreme form, implies that the purpose of vertical restraints can *only* be to elicit pro-competitive behavior downstream since there could be no rational motive by an upstream monopoly to restrict competition downstream. Attempting to monopolize a market downstream by a monopoly upstream is not profitable since all rents can be extracted at any one level as illustrated above. Such logic applies when downstream markets are competitive and vertical contracts are appropriately flexible. However, such unambiguously general statements are not supported by current economic research (see, for example, Ordover et al. 1990; Riordan 1998; Church 2008).

10.1.3 Addressing Other Externalities

Firms also use contractual means to address other types of misalignment in incentives that result from individual profit maximization by firms in a vertical chain. We have already mentioned that when price is not the only determinant of the demand, a producer will want to elicit the right level of services, such as promotional services by downstream firm(s). In setting the right level of services, the manufacturer needs to take into account the vertical externalities between the manufacturer and the retailers *and* the horizontal externalities across retailers or even suppliers. If retailers do not capture all the benefits from providing promotions and/or retail services and some go to the manufacturer, the level of promotions and/or service provided by retailers will tend to be lower than optimal for the vertical chain as a whole. Retailers will also be able to free ride on each other's promotional activities or service efforts on a given product and therefore the incentives to promote or indeed inform consumers about products will be further reduced.

In this section we discuss certain relatively common practices that can address these problems. Because these practices also have a potential anticompetitive effect, they have often been the object of scrutiny by antitrust authorities.

10.1.3.1 Territorial Restrictions

Territorial restrictions are normally used to reduce intrabrand competition downstream. When sales and service efforts by the retailer are important to the manufacturer, they will want to ensure that retailers reap the rewards of their investments in service quality. By granting exclusive rights of sale in a given territory to a single retailer or a group of retailers, the manufacturer can ensure that retailers in different areas do not free ride on each other's investment. By eliminating the capacity to attract shoppers from other territories, the horizontal pricing externality, whereby retailers hurt the manufacturer by lowering prices to steal customers from each other, is also removed. It is, of course, essential for this practice to have the desired effect that arbitrage opportunities are eliminated. That said, exclusive territories actively prevent competition between retailers and therefore may clearly potentially have important anticompetitive consequences. Indeed, it is exactly the "horizontal pricing externality" which competition authorities usually fight very hard to protect precisely because it results in low prices for consumers. In an extreme case, with a monopoly manufacturer and a set of retailers who, absent the territorial restrictions, would otherwise compete, territorial restrictions could enforce a market division arrangement entirely equivalent to explicit collusion between the retailers. To evaluate such a policy we may need to evaluate the way in which consumers trade off potentially higher prices for goods against any higher quality of service provided.

Territorial restrictions as described above have been a tradition in the car sales sector in Europe, where markets were traditionally defined as national, with a distribution system characterized by exclusive dealing and geographic restrictions, including a restriction by manufactures of cross-border sales. In 2002, the European Commission concluded that exclusive dealing agreements between car manufacturers and car dealers as well as the exclusive sales territories granted by the manufacturers to the dealers were not justified on grounds of efficiency as the consumers were "not getting a fair share of the resulting benefits."[12] The European Commission issued new conditions for the sale of cars in the European Union notably imposing the right of exclusive dealers to sell to operators outside of the manufacturer's official network.[13]

10.1.3.2 Resale Price Maintenance: Minimum Price

An alternative way to induce retailers to provide the level of services, sales effort, or advertisement that is optimal for the manufacturer is to establish a minimum sales price thereby restricting price competition. Firms could, for example, simply refuse

[12] "Commission adopts comprehensive reform of competition rules for car sales and servicing" IP/02/1073 of 17/07/2002 available at http://europa.eu/rapid/pressReleasesAction.do?reference=IP/02/1073&format=HTML&aged=0&language=EN&guiLanguage=en.

[13] Commission Regulation (EC) no. 1400/2002 of July 31, 2002 on the application of Article 81(3) of the Treaty to categories of vertical agreements and concerted practices in the motor vehicle sector.

to sell to retailers who charge a retail price below an established minimum. For instance, in the second half of the 1990s, music recording companies in the United States allegedly notified music retailers that, if they advertised music CDs at a price less than a stipulated amount, the recording companies would withdraw the financial support for advertisement and sales that they usually granted to those retailers. Those advertisement and promotion payments were an important source of revenue for retailers and the rule was alleged as a de facto establishment of a price floor, triggering a multidistrict class action by purchasers of prerecorded music against the music majors.[14] Because resale price maintenance can also facilitate collusive agreements and was, until the Leegin[15] decision, a per se offense in the United States, the recording companies allegedly tried to circumvent the antitrust statutes by penalizing advertised prices as opposed to sales prices. Recording companies claimed that some electronic and mass merchant stores were setting low prices of popular CDs to attract customers into their stores, thereby undercutting specialized music stores that provided services such as listening stations, in store advice, and promotional events. Those services resulted in an increase of music sales that was allegedly essential to the music business. The case was finally settled in 2003 for $143 million and the practice of establishing a minimum advertised price was terminated.[16] It remains a useful illustration of an alleged attempt by manufacturers to prevent aggressive price competition at the retail level that appears to have been dramatically decreasing the provision of services and sales effort. Of course, the per se status of RPM during that case meant that it was not necessary to show that consumers suffered harm as a result of the practice. Following Leegin, that will no longer be the case in the United States and as a result such cases will probably be far harder to prosecute in either public or private antitrust spheres.

In Europe, in general the attitude to RPM is less permissive than the new legal regime in the United States. Specifically, in the EU, RPM is currently treated as a hardcore pricing restriction that is illegal unless the parties bring forward substantiated claims of efficiencies, that is, there is a "rebuttable presumption of illegality."[17] One stated reason is that RPM is often associated with increasing prices. RPM can also be used as a facilitating device to cartelize retailers' prices because it effectively sets final retailer prices across retailers by way of a contract. What may look like a vertical contract may on occasion be a device for horizontal price fixing with negative consequences for final consumers. The challenge for antitrust agencies under

[14] *In re Compact Disc Minimum Advertised Price Antitrust Litigation*, M.D.L. no. 1361 (U.S.D.C. Me).

[15] *Leegin Creative Products Inc. v. PSKS Inc.*, Supreme Court of the United States, June 28, 2007.

[16] District of Maine, *In re Compact Disc Minimum Advertised Price Antitrust Litigation*, M.D.L. Docket no. 1361 Litigation Decision and Order on Notice, Settlement Proposals, Class Certifications, and Attorney Fees.

[17] RPM is considered an "object" restriction under Article 81 of the EC treaty (and its U.K. embodiment, the Competition Act, 1998). As a result RPM is viewed as harmful by object—that is, very likely to be anticompetitive so that a harmful effect may be presumed.

a rule-of-reason approach is to tell apart the efficient use of RPM from its potential far less benign use.

10.1.3.3 Exclusive Dealing

Exclusive dealing, also called single branding, occurs when the upstream firm requires or induces the retailer to only sell its brand. There can be an explicit requirement for exclusive dealing or alternatively such an outcome can be generated via a carefully designed pricing structure. For example, we may de facto see exclusive dealing if advantageous rebates are granted only to those retailers who purchase all their products from a single provider, the result will effectively enforce an exclusive dealing arrangement. There are, of course, many entirely valid substantial reasons that an upstream firm may want this type of contractual arrangement. One clear motivation may be a desire to protect their own investment in advertisement and quality by preventing retailers from steering consumers who arrive in the store to lower-priced, less well-known rival products once the consumer is in the store. Retailers might have an incentive to do so if rival products were able to provide retailers with higher margins despite lower sales prices, for example, because few advertising costs were incurred. Thus exclusive dealing may solve a horizontal externality across producers within the retailer. A related example may arise if a manufacturer invests in its distribution channels to increase the level of service and promotional activity. It is possible that a retailer might choose to use these skills or resources to promote products from other producers. The contract in that case provides a mechanism for the retailer to credibly commit not to engage in such activity and thereby provide the manufacturer with incentives for promotion to the potential benefit of both firms and also quite probably consumers. On the other hand, exclusive dealing may also provide a mechanism for foreclosure.[18]

10.1.3.4 Tying and Bundling

Tying and bundling are also ways in which manufacturers can condition the decisions of retailers downstream. These practices consist of conditioning the sale of a good on the sale of another, usually complementary, good. This can be done, for example, through a contractual obligation or because the pricing structure renders it unprofitable to purchase the two goods separately. An example might be aircraft engines and aircraft instrumentation.

There is a large body of literature analyzing the reasons for tying and bundling. The explanations range from quality concerns to price discrimination and of course simple transaction cost advantages. Bundling can also be motivated by potential economies of scale and scope in production or distribution that allows the firm to

[18] See, in particular, the foreclosure models discussed by Salop and Scheffman (1983), Comanor and Frech (1985), Schwartz (1987), Mathewson and Winter (1987), Rasmusen et al. (1991), Bernheim and Whinston (1998), Segal and Whinston (2000), and Simpson and Wickelgren (2007).

lower prices and increase sales by bundling the sales of several products. In theory, tying complementary goods can increase the incentives to lower prices since the firm will benefit from the increase in the demand of the initial product and also the tied product. In the case of metering and price discrimination, the outcome is less clear and will vary across customers.

Although tying can have many nonexclusionary motivations, it can nevertheless also lead to intended or unintended foreclosure on the market. Whinston (1990) and Nalebuff (1999) among others analyze the incentives to tie and present conclusions for stylized examples involving assumptions about the consumer valuation of the tying product, the link between the valuations of the tied and tying products, and the nature of competition in the tied market (see also Bakos and Brynjolfsson 1998; Carlton and Waldman 2002). Whinston (1990) illustrates that a monopolist can, under some circumstances, profitably foreclose a market by tying and thereby commit to a low price for the bundle. His results also show that even though tying complementary products is less "costly" for the firm, the incentives to tie are also less obvious unless some particular conditions are fulfilled. Nalebuff (1999) shows that with heterogeneous preferences, bundling for complementary products can be profitable and foreclosure can be achieved. In a dynamic market characterized by innovation tying can also be used to weaken or foreclose potential competitors (Choi 2004; Carlton and Waldman 2002).

This literature contrasts sharply with the position taken by the Chicago school, who heavily critiqued what they called "leverage theory." Proponents of that view argued that if a firm had a monopoly in one good but faced competition in a second complementary product and consumers desired the goods in fixed proportions, then a "one-monopoly-profit" argument holds. Specifically, the monopolist in the first product need not monopolize the second market to extract monopoly profits. Two recent empirical papers consider variants of this debate. Chevalier and Scott Morton (2008) consider a horizontal version of the one-monopoly-profit argument arising from tying casket sales and funeral services together and their results favor the one-monopoly-profit argument. However, Genakos et al. (2006) find evidence that incentives for foreclosure exist empirically, looking at Microsoft's incentive to leverage its monopoly in the "client operating system market" (aka regular Windows) to the "server operating system market" (aka Windows for network servers). In particular, they find that an incentive to leverage market power can exist provided perfect price discrimination is not possible for a monopolist. If so, then leverage can become a method that can help a monopolist to extract more rents from the monopoly market.[19]

[19] In support of their theory the authors report that in 1997 Microsoft's Chairman Bill Gates wrote in an internal memo: "What we're trying to do is to use our server control to do new protocols and lock out Sun and Oracle specifically... the symmetry that we have between the client operating system and the server operating system is a huge advantage for us."

10.1.3.5 Refusals to Deal

There exist cases of straight refusal to deal whereby a firm upstream simply refuses to supply a firm downstream that wants its output as an input. The legal treatment of this type of conduct varies under different jurisdictions. Increasingly, the goal of protecting the incentives for innovation and large upfront investments is balanced against the benefits that an access to the input would generate through a more intense competition downstream. In general, refusal to deal is unlikely to be regarded as a problematic action unless the upstream firm has some degree of market power. One important source of upstream market power may arise from the fact that a firm operates an essential facility. A deepwater port is an example of something that may be considered to be essential facility. A country may, for instance, have only one or two deepwater ports suitable for handling large cargo vessels. Entry, building a new port, is fairly obviously costly and may be impossible depending on geography, while transport costs for goods within a country may mean a given port owner has substantial market power. The difficulty for antitrust authorities is that there will also be cases in which the firm stops supplying a downstream firm with which it was previously trading for perfectly legitimate reasons. The termination of a relationship with a firm downstream may occur because the supplier thinks the intermediate firm is not keeping up with quality standards or otherwise not fulfilling aspects of an explicit or implicit contract. It may also be the result of changes in market conditions that affect the incentives of the firm upstream, for instance, changes in costs meaning that marginal units become loss-making. Clearly, even a dominant firm should not be forced to sell goods at a loss if economic efficiency is our aim. Thus, an antitrust authority must attempt to distinguish "legitimate" refusals to deal from illegitimate ones. Quantification of the effect of refusals to deal are generally quite difficult and involve comparing the outcome of a world where a business exists with one where the business does not exist. Perhaps as a result, to date, the assessment of refusal to deal cases has therefore been primarily qualitative in nature.

10.1.4 Effects of Vertical Restraints on Market Outcomes

To summarize this first section of the chapter, the theoretical effect of vertical restraints on consumer welfare is, in many cases, ambiguous. On the one hand there are numerous potential motivations for vertical restraints that are entirely innocent and unlikely to cause legitimate concern to antitrust authorities. On the other hand vertical restraints may also facilitate outcomes that should be of concern to agencies seeking to make markets work well for consumers. Vertical restraints can sometimes be used as mechanisms to soften competition. In extreme cases the incentive to compete on prices can be entirely eliminated by the existence of such restraints. In other cases, vertical restraints may result in foreclosure of either inputs or customers. The bottom line is that economic theory does not allow general conclusions about whether vertical restrains are "good" or "bad" for welfare. In any given instance the question is an empirical one, which means the competition authorities must first attempt to determine the circumstances in which a vertical practice may be cause for concern and should therefore be the object of scrutiny. Second, they must attempt to evaluate whether or not the vertical restraint should be banned or restricted for the benefit of consumers.

Because theoretical predictions are not always, or even usually, clear about the net effect of vertical contractual arrangements on either total or consumer welfare, there have been a limited but perhaps increasing number of attempts to empirically assess the effect of vertical practices in both the case and academic literatures. In the next section, we present a number of different methodologies that have been used to try to assess the effect of vertical restraints. In looking at each example we will strive to illustrate both the benefits and limitations of such exercises.

10.2 Measuring the Effect of Vertical Restraints

In the first section of this chapter we established that the motivations for vertical restraints are many and also that the theoretical predictions regarding the effect of these practices on welfare are often ambiguous. Sometimes a vertical restraint will solve an important externality problem to the benefit of both firms and consumers. On other occasions, it is exactly the externalities that drive good outcomes for consumers and so removing them via a vertical restraint generates poor outcomes for consumers. An example is when a vertical restraint acts to remove the horizontal pricing externality between firms, the one that usually means that competition leads to low prices and high-quality goods.

Sometimes the ultimate goal of the practice is outright foreclosure and the result may be higher prices and lower output with no concomitant efficiency gains. On other occasions, the two effects will cumulate. Empirical analysis is a way to try to determine the effects of vertical restraints on consumer welfare in a particular case. Unfortunately, precisely because many of the effects we are trying to isolate are difficult to measure, it is particularly difficult to undertake an effects-based analysis of vertical restraints. Empirical strategies that have been used to determine the effects of vertical arrangements include regression analysis, particularly fixed-effects regressions, natural experiments, and event studies. Each is familiar from elsewhere in the book. However, it is important to note that such methods can only potentially help solve identification issues when there are data available on the situation with and without the practice. *Ex ante* analysis requires the construction and estimation of a structural model, which is very difficult to do without making stringent and quite possibly unrealistic assumptions about firm behavior. We discuss each of the available strategies in the rest of this chapter. Before doing so we briefly discuss informal and semiformal quantitative methods for evaluating the incentive for foreclosure.

10.2.1 Informal and Semiformal Analysis of Incentives

Informal quantitative analysis can sometimes be insightful for evaluating the incentive for foreclosure. An example of such an analysis was provided involving a merger between English, Welsh and Scottish Railway Holdings (EWS) and Marcroft Engineering (Marcroft). EWS is a freight haulier on the railways, whereas Marcroft was a provider of railway maintenance services mainly serving the rail freight industry. The United Kingdom's Office of Fair Trading (OFT) in its phase I investigation considered whether EWS would have an incentive to foreclose access to the Marcroft maintenance depots since by doing so it could potentially harm its competitors in the downstream rail haulage market. To evaluate this option the OFT considered (1) the potential returns in the downstream market to foreclosure and also (2) the cost of foreclosing access to the Marcroft maintenance facilities. The OFT decision document notes from company accounts and information provided by third parties that both volume and profit margin are lower in the upstream maintenance market than they are in the downstream freight haulage market.[20] Assuming the margins do not change, a rough calculation of the incentive to foreclose would involve an evaluation of loss in upstream profits from maintenance

$$\Delta\text{Profit}_{\text{Maintenance}} = \text{Margin}_{\text{M}}\Delta\text{Volume}_{\text{M}}$$

against the gain from higher downstream profits from haulage

$$\Delta\text{Profit}_{\text{Haulage}} = \text{Margin}_{\text{H}}\Delta\text{Volume}_{\text{H}}.$$

Obviously, even these simplified expressions involve changes in volume rather than the levels of volume, but the OFT may have believed that the expected changes in volume would be reflective of the overall levels of each activity. Thus, since $\text{Margin}_{\text{H}} > \text{Margin}_{\text{M}}$ and if

$$\text{Volume}_{\text{H}} > \text{Volume}_{\text{M}} \quad \Longrightarrow \quad \Delta\text{Volume}_{\text{H}} > \Delta\text{Volume}_{\text{M}}.$$

Then

$$\begin{aligned}\Delta\text{Profit}_{\text{Haulage}} &= \text{Margin}_{\text{H}}\Delta\text{Volume}_{\text{H}} > \Delta\text{Profit}_{\text{Maintenance}} \\ &= \text{Margin}_{\text{M}}\Delta\text{Volume}_{\text{M}}.\end{aligned}$$

Obviously, such a rough calculation involves some very strong assumptions as are appropriate for an authority exploring whether there is the potential justification for further investigation. In the end the OFT decided to refer the merger to the U.K. Phase II merger body, the Competition Commission, but decided that since it had also found potential horizontal problems with the merger, it did not need to come to a final view on the potential vertical concerns. In the end the CC accepted

[20] See, in particular, paragraph 43, OFT decision document available at www.oft.gov.uk/shared_oft/mergers_ea02/2006/railway.pdf.

undertakings from the company involving the divestment of part of the Marcroft maintenance business.[21]

In 2008, the European Commission investigated a vertical merger involving the upstream market for the databases that allow the construction of navigable digital maps (NDMs) and the downstream market involving various electronic navigation devices.[22] Specifically, TomTom, a producer of personal navigation devices (PNDs), proposed a merger with the navigable digital map database provider TeleAtlas.[23] Public documents do not allow a complete reconstruction of the calculations performed to evaluate the total foreclosure story considered by the Commission, but nonetheless exploring the example is instructive.

The vertical arithmetic approach suggests that to evaluate the plausibility of either a total or partial foreclosure theory of harm, the competition agency should evaluate the loss of profit upstream and the potential gain in profit downstream. Doing so allows an evaluation of the incentive to engage in foreclosure. Under a total foreclosure strategy, the vertically integrated firm will lose profits upstream because it stops selling to the "merchant market"—those firms competing with its downstream subsidiary. That means those rivals will face higher costs because, according to the theory of harm, they will have to buy from rival upstream suppliers who no longer face competition in supply and so will raise prices. In the TomTom–TeleAtlas case this total foreclosure theory of harm amounts to TeleAtlas deciding to stop competing for the custom of rival PND companies that need navigable maps to build their navigation devices. As a result, TeleAtlas's rival Navteq would face a reduction of competition and be able to increase prices (or more generally follow some other strategy such as reduce quality).

---

[21] See www.competition-commission.org.uk/inquiries/ref2006/marcroft/index.htm for further details.

[22] We will not divert our discussion with a detailed evaluation of the various market definitions. However, we do pause to note there that the Commission came to the view that: (1) Upstream there was demand-side substitution between the navigable digital maps provided by TeleAtlas and Navteq. However, there was no demand-side substitution between navigable maps and more "basic" digital maps which could not be used for real-time navigation while driving your car. Moreover, the Commission received estimates that it would take something like 1,000–2,000 people five to ten years to upgrade a basic map to the quality of a navigable map. Thus there was neither demand nor supply substitution. Geographic markets upstream were left ambiguous as they were judged not to affect the conclusion of the analysis. (2) Downstream, the Commission noted that there were various forms of navigation devices: personal navigation devices (in the form of a handheld device that you could put in your car), maps on personal digital assistants, "in-dash" navigation devices (navigation devices built into car dashboards), and GPS enabled mobile phones. The Commission after looking at the evidence decided that PNDs constituted a downstream market in itself.

[23] See Case no. COMP/M.4854 TomTom/TeleAtlas. At around the same time Nokia (the mobile phone producing company) merged with TeleAtlas's main rival navigable map producer, Navteq. (See Case no. COMP/M.4942 Nokia/Navteq.) Both mergers were ultimately cleared. The analysis undertaken in these mergers was widely seen as testing the European Commission's latest vertical (nonhorizontal) merger guidelines, which were adopted in November 2007. The new set of guidelines was developed partly in response to criticisms from the Court of First Instance following the European Commission's controversial decision to block the proposed merger between GE and Honeywell. (See Case no. COMP/M.2220 General Electric/Honeywell.)

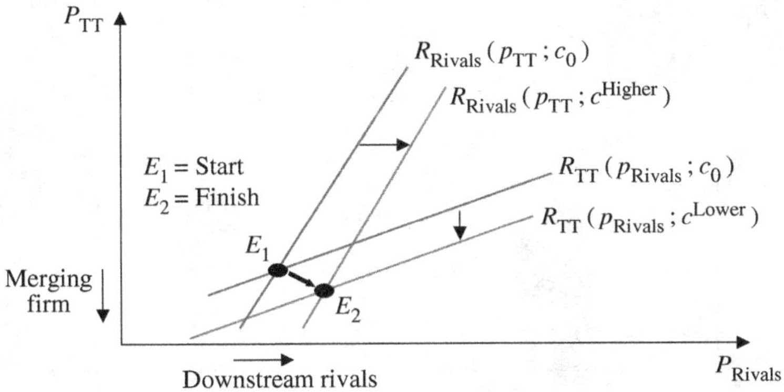

Figure 10.1. The impact of a vertical merger on own and rivals' costs.

In effect, a vertical merger followed by input foreclosure by the vertically integrated firm would mean that (1) TomTom's competitors in the downstream market would face higher input costs following the merger while (2) TomTom itself, as the downstream division of a vertically integrated firm, would be able to reduce its costs if vertical integration has aided the reduction or avoidance of double marginalization. In the case of TomTom–TeleAtlas we know from the Commission's decision document that pre-merger upstream gross margins were high, approximately 85%. The reason is that developing a digital map involves a great deal of essentially fixed-cost investment while the resulting database can subsequently be duplicated at low marginal cost. That means that if pre-merger vertical contracting was not able to solve the double marginalization problem, then TomTom's (TT's) marginal costs could decline considerably post-merger. At the same time, rival downstream firms would, according to the theory of harm, face higher input costs as they would now suffer from a lack of competition upstream.

Figure 10.1 presents the impact of vertical integration when it (1) reduces double marginalization for the merged firm and (2) increases marginal costs for rivals because the merged firm follows a foreclosure strategy. The former effect shifts TT's reaction function downward while the latter effect shifts the rival's reaction function rightward to reflect an increase in input costs (for any given price of TT, rivals will now choose to charge a higher price).

Figure 10.1 shows that the impact of such a change on downstream competitive outcomes can involve lower prices for the vertically integrating firm as well as potentially higher prices from its downstream rival(s). Naturally, the aggregate welfare impact of such a change will depend on the relative magnitudes of the consequent profit and consumer surplus gains and losses. It is this observation that induces many agencies to choose a framework for vertical merger analysis which includes an analysis of ability, incentive, *and* consumer harm. That said, those competition agencies whose statutory framework do not immediately "net-off" consumer surplus gains and losses will note that some customers have lost out under a merger

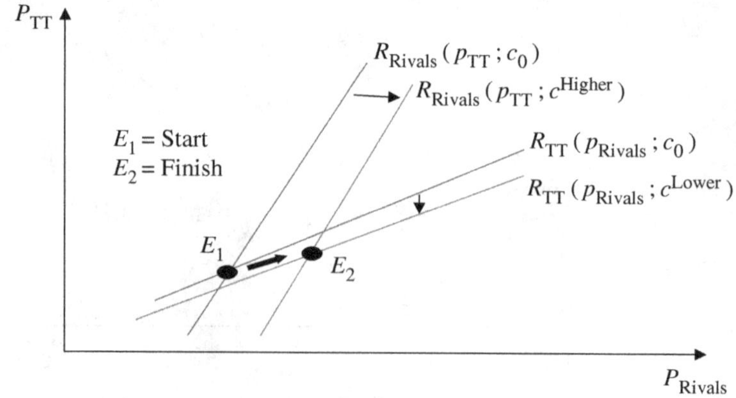

Figure 10.2. The impact of a vertical merger on own and rivals' costs (2).

that led to this outcome, even if ultimately overall consumer welfare is higher, perhaps because the vertically integrating firm has a far larger share of the market who benefit from lower prices post-merger.

Figure 10.2 shows that when the integrating firm benefits from removing double marginalization are small relative to the magnitude of the effect of increased costs suffered by rivals in the downstream market, the outcome will tend to involve the prices charged by all firms increasing. Such an outcome would clearly be unambiguously bad for consumers, all else equal.

Taking some data from the TomTom–TeleAtlas case, according to the case documents, there were unit sales of 10.8 million NDMs for PNDs with an average selling price of €14.6. Moreover, pre-merger TeleAtlas sold their database to TomTom and also to other downstream producers, who accounted for between 10 and 30% of the downstream market,[24] that is, between $10.8 \times 0.1 = 1.1$ and $10.8 \times 0.3 = 3.2$ million units. TomTom's downstream rivals include Garmin, Mio-Tech & Navman, Medion, and My Guide. Since the case tells us that gross margins were 85%, a foreclosure strategy would involve sacrificing profits (or at least a "contribution" to upstream fixed costs) of between €$14.6 \times 1.1 \times 0.85 =$ €13.7 million and €$14.6 \times 3.2 \times 0.85 =$ €39.7 million.

To simulate the potential gain downstream, in principle we could analyze the static downstream game and then make reasonable assumptions about the changes in costs that TomTom and also rivals were likely to experience following a merger and a decision by the vertically integrated firm to pursue a foreclosure strategy. This was the type of calculation undertaken by the European Commission. Unfortunately, there is not sufficient information in the public domain to repeat the Commission's simulation exercise, but the reader familiar with the analysis of the differentiated product Bertrand pricing game presented in chapter 8 will be able to see exactly how

[24] Only a range is available in the public decision document.

such an exercise could be performed, given the analysis presented in figures 10.1 and 10.2. Rather than present the full calculations, we present a rough back-of-an-envelope calculation, looking directly at the change in profits associated with a potential change in market shares and margins.

First note that if subscript "0" denotes pre-merger and subscript "1" denotes post-merger prices, quantities, and costs, then we can write the impact on downstream profits as

$$\begin{aligned}\Delta\pi^{\text{TomTom}} &\approx (p_1 - c_1)q_1 - (p_0 - c_0)q_0 \\ &\approx p_1\frac{p_1 - c_1}{p_1}q_1 - p_0\frac{p_0 - c_0}{p_0}q_0.\end{aligned}$$

Now suppose, in particular, that TomTom's pre-merger market share was 40% and it were to grow to 45% if TeleAtlas–TomTom followed a foreclosure strategy. Doing so would mean its sales would grow from $q_0 = 0.4 \times 10.8 = 4.31$ million to $q_1 = 0.45 \times 10.8 = 4.85$ million, a growth of 0.53 million customers per year. In the downstream market, gross margins were reported to be between 0 and 50%, so suppose 25% while average final price pre-merger was $p_0 = €200$. For simplicity, suppose that downstream gross margins did not change pre- and post-merger while prices did fall by some amount because some of the reduction in database input costs was passed through to final consumers. With a gross margin of 85% upstream and a pre-merger average selling price upstream of €14.6 per unit, the reduction in TomTom's marginal cost may be as large as $0.85 \times 14.6 = €12.4$. Thus final prices would be between €200 and €187.6, depending on the extent of the pass-through of the cost reduction to final customers. Supposing pass-though were 50%, then we would have $p_1 = €193.8$ and hence the increase in downstream profits would be

$$\begin{aligned}\Delta\pi^{\text{TomTom}} &\approx p_1\frac{p_1 - c_1}{p_1}q_1 - p_0\frac{p_0 - c_0}{p_0}q_0 \\ &= 193.8 \times 0.25 \times 4.85 - 200 \times 0.25 \times 4.31 \\ &\approx 235 - 215.5 \\ &= 19.5 \text{ m.}\end{aligned}$$

This figure is within the range of estimated lost profits upstream of between €13.7 million and €39.7 million, so that the calculation does not make a clear case either for or against the incentive for total foreclosure. However, in most jurisdictions, the burden of proof is on the competition agency to establish the harm likely to be caused by a merger and, if so, this calculation would suggest that burden of proof would not be discharged.

Obviously, we have made a lot of assumptions in this rough calculation and a more careful calculation would get closer to real numbers for the potential upstream losses and downstream gains from foreclosure. For now we note that while our back-of-the-envelope calculation does not make a clear case for or against the incentive for total foreclosure, such a calculation can help us to explore which alternate assumptions (e.g., about captured market share, downstream margins and how they are likely to change, and pass-through rates) that would provide grounds for either concern or reassurance. Naturally, in such an evaluation it will be important to think about the realities of the market place. For example, one downstream PND producer, Garmin, had signed a fairly long-term contract with Navteq in 2007, due to expire in 2015, although even then there was an option to extend until 2019. Such a contract meant that for at least seven years Navteq would not be able to increase prices for its database to a major downstream producer. Such a fact is clearly important in evaluating the likely profitability of a downstream foreclosure strategy premised on the idea that Navteq would have the incentive and ability to be able to raise the price of its database to TomTom's downstream rivals.

Before closing this discussion of foreclosure strategies, we make three further comments. First, we note the important contribution from Hart and Tirole (1990). Their paper suggests that a total foreclosure strategy may not ultimately be an equilibrium in a static game since a firm attempting to foreclose downstream competitors may actually be better off (given the strategies of rivals) by deviating from the foreclosure strategy by selling into the merchant market. Thus, Hart and Tirole suggest that the commitment not to sell to the merchant market is not a credible one. Ordover et al. (1992) disagreed and, more generally, the role of reputation and credibility of commitments may be best studied within a repeated game context. Whatever the appropriate scope of these theoretical concerns, the experimental evidence appears to suggests that the commitment problem may not always be overwhelming (Normann et al. 2001; Normann 2007).

Second, we note that within the context of a static model, partial foreclosure models, where the firm may find it optimal to raise prices to the merchant market and thus partially foreclose it, are not subject to the credibility concerns. They may, however, result in fewer occasions where the actual economic effects of foreclosure are harmful to consumers.

And, finally, we note that in the TomTom–TeleAtlas case there were potentially important efficiency benefits from the merger, namely that cars driving around with TomTom PNDs could actually send information back to TeleAtlas about where drivers could and could not drive. The parties argued that, in the future, allowing such information transfer from cars back to the database will reduce the cost of collecting the detailed up-to-date information required for generating navigable maps.

10.2.2 Regression Analysis of Vertical Integration

In this section we illustrate the use of regression analysis in the vertical merger context. We begin by looking at the kind of data set that may be available from a "natural experiment."

10.2.2.1 Estimating the Effects of Vertical Integration in the Retail Gasoline Market

An empirical attempt to determine the impact of vertical arrangements on consumer retail prices in the gasoline market in the United States can be found in Hastings (2004). That paper looks at the sale in California of Thrifty, a chain of independent gas stations, to ARCO, a large U.S. oil company which is vertically integrated. The sale occurred in March 1997 after the 75-year-old owner of the Thrifty gas stations decided to retire. There was a 60-day waiting period after which all Thrifty stations fell under the control of ARCO. Thrifty stations were just branded as ARCO and placed under new contracts. Some of the gas stations became company operated and others were leased to dealers who operated them under the ARCO brand. There was no remodeling, expansion, or other investment in the gas stations. The rebranding process was completed in September 1997.

Hastings uses panel data of retail prices at the station level for four months in the Los Angeles and San Diego Metropolitan Statistical Areas (MSAs). The data cover the months of February, June, October, and December 1997 so that the data provide information on a range of markets before and after the sale. Hastings (2004) assumes that the geographic market definition is one mile along a surface street or freeway around the petrol station. The sale of Thrifty to ARCO was arguably an event that was largely independent of market conditions given the owner's desire to retire, and it generated an increase in vertical integration in some local retail gasoline markets while in other markets the ownership structure remained unchanged. Specifically, there were 669 stations in the price sample and 99 of them had a Thrifty within one mile and therefore saw the structure of vertical ownership in the market as a result of the acquisition change with an increase in the level of vertical integration of the retail gas market. The data set appears therefore to provide a nice exogenous movement in the extent of vertical integration in some markets whose effects on prices we should be able to trace. Moreover, the fact that some markets were unaffected means that we also have a "control" sample of markets which may allow us to control for any other factors changing over the time period of the study. Doing so mean Hastings can use a difference-in-differences approach to identification, comparing the change in prices (before and after) the merger in markets which were affected with the change in markets which were not.

The data show that the average retail prices at gas stations that competed with Thrifty increased after the sale relative to the retail prices at gas stations that were not affected by the sale. This is shown in figure 10.3. Gas stations which have a Thrifty station within one mile had prices 3 cents lower than the rest of the gas stations before the sale. After the acquisition was completed in September 1997, the average price for those same gas stations was 2 cents higher than the average price of the gas stations unaffected by the sale. Hastings reports that a similar result was obtained for the San Diego area and that she found no price difference among the

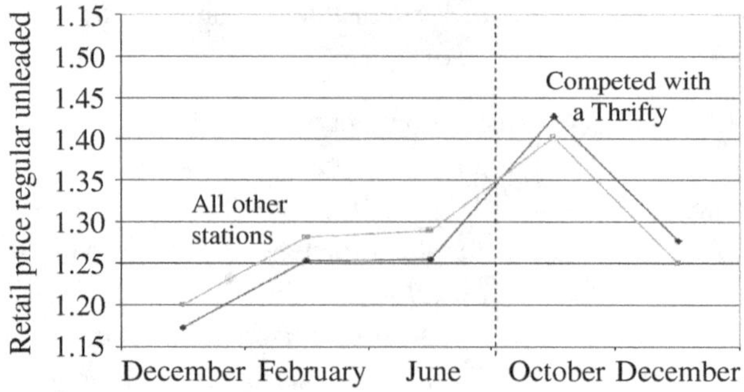

Figure 10.3. Los Angeles gas prices: treatment and control. *Source*: Hastings (2004).

gas stations that converted to company-owned gas stations and those that became dealer operated. These results suggest that vertical integration and the disappearance of an independent retailer is correlated with, perhaps even causes, higher prices in this particular market.[25]

Before we conclude that the vertical merger causes higher prices, Hastings first notes that a simple descriptive analysis such as that provided in figure 10.3 ignores the effect of changing conditions in the market. It could be that demand or costs increased in those areas where Thrifty was present, confounding the effect of the change in ownership structure. To control for this, Hastings runs the following fixed-effects regression:

$$p_{jt} = \mu + \alpha_j + \delta_{\text{City},t} + \phi c_{jt} + \theta z_{jt} + \varepsilon_{jt},$$

where μ is a constant, α_j is a station-specific effect, $\delta_{\text{City},t}$ are a set of city/quarter dummies, c_{jt} is an indicator of whether the station becomes a company operated station (as distinct from a dealer-operated station under lease), z_{jt} is an indicator of whether or not the station competes with an independent gas station, and ε_{jt} is the error term. The fixed effects control for potential omitted variables that determine prices and they turn out to be quite important in the regression, indicating that there are in fact many unobserved determinants of the price at the local level. The results of three variants of the regression are provided in table 10.1. The estimates in column 3 suggest that there is a 5 cent increase in retail prices when there is no longer an independent station in the market. There is no additional statistically significant effect of becoming a fully integrated company-operated gas station compared with becoming a dealer with a contractual relationship with the upstream company.

[25] While the direction of these results is not in contention, Taylor et al. (2007) argue that in their closely related data set the actual price difference appears to be considerably smaller, approximately 1 cent per gallon before and after the transaction, a net effect of 2 cents per gallon rather than Hastings's difference of 5 cents per gallon. Since the FTC paper is a relatively new one, the reader may find that Professor Hastings has subsequently responded to their paper. Whatever the resolution of that debate, the ideas behind Hastings's approach remain of substantial interest.

Table 10.1. Fixed-effects estimation of the effect of Thrifty's acquisition.

Variable	1	2	3
Intercept	1.3465	1.3465	1.3617
	(0.0421)	(0.0415)	(0.0287)
Company operated	0.1080	−0.0033	−0.0033
	(0.0107)	(0.0178)	(0.0122)
Independent	—	−0.1013	−0.0500
		(0.0143)	(0.0101)
LA[a] February	—	—	0.0180
			(0.0065)
LA[a] June	—	—	0.0243
			(0.0065)
LA[a] October	—	—	0.1390
			(0.0064)
SD[a] February	—	—	−0.0851
			(0.0036)
SD[a] June	—	—	−0.0304
			(0.0036)
SD[a] October	—	—	0.0545
			(0.0036)
Adjusted R^2	0.3772	0.3953	0.7181
F-test for no fixed effects:			
Numerator DF: 668			
Denominator DF: 1999			
F value: 3.262			Prob. > F: 0.000
Hausman test for random effects:			
Hausman's M value: 622.296			Prob. > M: 0.000

[a]Standard errors in parentheses. *Source*: Table II, Hastings (2004).

One area of particular concern arises from the fact that the merger results in a change of an unbranded product into a branded product and that may explain the price rise, once again independent of any effects of the vertical integration on prices. The potential importance of branding is fully explored in the paper. In an attempt to address this concern, Hastings breaks up the "treated group," those gas stations that were formerly competing with an independent station, into gas stations with a strong brand presence in California (Chevron, Shell, or Unocal), gas stations with medium brand presence (Exxon, Mobil, or Texaco), and gas stations with low brand presence (Beakon, Circle K, or Citgo). The effect of the disappearance of an independent competitor is stronger on those gas stations that have a lower brand presence and is smallest on the gas stations with established brands. That suggests that the branding effect may indeed be rather important in driving the price increase. Inasmuch as the structure of vertical ownership is changing the degree of product differentiation downstream, we could go so far as to argue that the increase in gasoline retail prices after the sale of Thrifty is a vertical effect. However, the empirical exercise leaves us with a distinctly more subtle question than the one we began with. Despite the apparently extremely clean natural experiment in the data, to evaluate the impact of the change in vertical structure on consumer welfare, in this case, because the vertically integrated firm already had a downstream brand we must evaluate whether the increase in branding (probably appropriately considered an aspect of product and/or service quality) is sufficiently valued to justify the price increase that we identified. We examine methods capable of evaluating such trade-offs in the next section.

10.2.2.2 Estimating the Effects of Vertical Integration in the Market for Cable TV

Another interesting attempt to empirically measure the effect of vertical integration examined the U.S. cable television industry and is provided by Chipty (2001). The paper looks at the effect of vertical integration between programming and distribution services in cable television. However, the essence of the paper uses two methodologies which may each generally be useful for assessing the way in which consumers trade off the various combinations of price and quality which may arise from vertical contracting. For example, a number of the models we examined in the first part of the paper found that vertical contracting arrangements may result in higher prices but also perhaps greater service provision. Such a defense would probably be easy for any company whose vertical restriction was in fact anticompetitive to at least allege. Chipty (2001) provides us with two approaches to assess this argument. First, she uses an approach which is familiar from earlier chapters, specifically she examines a reduced-form regressions of equilibrium outcomes, in this case a measure of quality and a measure of price, on demand and cost variables together with variables that capture the extent of vertical integration. In doing so she hopes to capture the independent effect of vertical integration on equilibrium outcomes. Second, she suggests a method for at least telling whether consumers do in fact sufficiently value the services being provided to make consumers better off in vertically integrated markets all else equal. Each of these pieces of evidence are provided from an industry where there was at least anecdotal evidence that vertical integration of cable system companies and content providers was resulting in refusals by cable operators to carry rival programming services.

Before discussing these two methods, it is worthwhile spending a few moments providing a little background on the industry. To that end, the vertical structure of the cable television industry in the United States is broadly as follows. Producer companies such as Paramount or Universal sell their media productions (films, TV shows) to program service providers such as HBO or AMC, which in turn sell the program content to cable system operators. Those cable operators are typically local monopolies in their markets.[26] They provide the final consumers with different sets of packaged channels at given prices. Chipty considers the vertical integration of service providers such as HBO (upstream) with cable system operators such as Comcast or TCI (downstream).

One very nice feature of this market for empirical work is that there are lots of distinct local markets for cable providers. Moreover, those local markets exhibit different degrees of vertical integration between the program services and the cable system operators.

Chipty (2001) wishes to investigate the actual effect of vertical integration on foreclosure, a difficult problem in a context where there is no one–zero classification for markets which have been "foreclosed." Instead of attempting to construct such a variable and perform a regression analysis, she proposes to study the way that observed market outcomes at the retail level vary across vertically integrated and nonvertically integrated markets. In doing so she hopes to consider in the round the effect of vertical integration on outcomes and ultimately consumer welfare. She uses 1991 data from the Television and Cable Factbook. The database comprises 11,039 cable franchises in the United States that are operated by 1,919 cable systems, which are in turn owned by 340 cable system operators, which may own more than one cable system brand. The data provide information on the structure of ownership, the channel capacity, the number of homes with access to cable in the franchise area, the cable system's program offer, the price, and the quantity of subscribers. There are also data on 133 program services (excluding pay-per-view and satellite) including eight premium services such as movies, one general entertainment, and two sport programming services. Data on the demographics of the market such as population size, fraction over 65 years old, or household size were taken from the 1988 City and County Data Book and USA Counties 1994.

Vertical integration occurs in this context when the cable operator owns any part of a program service that serves the franchise area. In principle, vertical integration could lead to foreclosure and harm to consumers from increases in the prices of the final good. On the other hand, it could increase product quality since there is a higher incentive by the cable provider to offer premium channels as they will also get the profits from the sale of that more expensive content.

The data used in Chipty (2001) show that, on average, a cable system provider offers fifteen basic service channels and slightly more than three premium content channels. Chipty uses the term "Basic system" to mean a cable system that is integrated with a basic content provider. Such vertically integrated basic systems offer twenty basic channels and four premium channels on average. Cable systems integrated with premium content providers (which Chipty calls premium systems) offer nineteen basic channels and slightly fewer than three premium channels. A simple look at these descriptive statistics therefore suggests that integration with basic

[26] More recently, some companies have undertaken a process of "overbuilding" cable franchise areas so that there are duopolies in some market areas.

content providers increases the variety of the supply of both basic and premium channels. Integration with suppliers of premium content providers increases the supply of basic channels but slightly reduces the retail supply of premium content.

First, Chipty considers whether these results hold once we control for other factors that affect demand and supply, and that could potentially also be spuriously correlated with the ownership structure. The approach will be familiar from earlier chapters and involves running a reduced-form regression of the equilibrium outcome (e.g., price or number of channels) on demand and cost factors as well as an indicator variable for vertical integration. Variables such as the system age and size, the size of the market, local population income, density, and age structure are considered. Two proxies for quality are examined, so that the reduced-form regressions are estimated for both the number of basic services (channels) offered and also the number of premium services offered. In addition, Chipty considers the effect of vertical integration on prices and penetration rates.

Chipty uses OLS so that no direct attempt is made in the specification to address any potential endogeneity concerns that may arise due to the fact that vertical integration and the number of channels are both decisions made by the firm. Naturally, it may be very difficult to find an appropriate instrument for vertical integration and Chipty's reduced-form results are therefore subject to the standard and potentially important endogeneity critique that Hastings (2004) hopes to avoid with her difference-in-differences approach.

While we do worry about endogeneity, at least such a reduced-form regression specification could presumably be motivated by a sufficiently rich version of the two-stage game we studied in chapter 5. Specifically, here we could motivate such a reduced-form regression equation by making the vertical integration decision the first stage of a game and the second stage generating the equilibrium outcomes of shorter-run decisions including the number of basic and premium channels. In each case it will be necessary to consider carefully the variables which are potentially endogenous. As always, doing so involves considering the factors which, from documents, industry knowledge, and often quite "soft" information obtained during the investigation may be determinants of the equilibrium variable being studied (e.g., number of channels) and which are not included through variables in the regression model. Any such omitted or imperfectly proxied variables may be in the residual of the model. It then remains to consider whether those omitted variables will be uncorrelated with the explanatory variables that are included in the model.[27]

Chipty finds that, vertical integration with basic content providers significantly increases the number of basic channels (one additional channel) and does not significantly affect premium content provision. The reduced-form regression results suggest that integration with a premium content provider results, on average, both

[27] Recall that OLS is only valid if $E[\varepsilon \mid x] = 0$, where ε is the error term in the model and x is the explanatory variables that are included in the model.

in fewer basic channels (one to two) and in one fewer premium channel (in partial contrast to the results suggested by a raw comparison of means). By looking at the channels actually provided, Chipty (2001) establishes that in fact premium systems carry fewer rival premium channels and are also less likely to carry basic service channels that may compete with premium content. This observation is consistent with a foreclosure story, but since we have not yet examined prices, it is only one element of such a story.

Next Chipty uses the reduced-form approach to examine the effect of vertical integration on prices. Looking at the price effects, there appears to be an ambiguous effect of vertical integration by both basic and premium systems. Integration with premium content providers sharply decreases the price of basic services but also sharply increases the price of premium content. Integration with basic content providers has the opposite effect but the price effects are much smaller in magnitude.

Since both prices and the number of channels change following vertical integration, whether (and, if so, which) consumers are better off will clearly depend on their relative value of the various price and quality of service effects that appear to arise from vertical integration.

On other occasions reduced-form analysis may provide a clearer-cut answer. If vertical integration, for example, led to lower service provision and higher prices, then it seems unlikely that vertical integration (or vertical contracting) has solved an externality problem and in doing so resulted in desirable outcomes for consumers. In this case, however, we are faced with informative results that do not provide a clear indication of foreclosure and simply cannot provide an outright answer as to whether the outcomes are desirable or not. Many case teams would probably stop at this stage and conclude that the case is unproven. However, Chipty (2001) attempts to go further and evaluate the net consumer welfare effects by estimating a structural model of consumer demand. Doing so moves us toward explicit modeling of the various agents in a market, though in her case only of consumers. For that reason we discuss the method in the next section under the general title of structural models.

10.2.3 Structural Modeling

Structural modeling requires that we specify demand and/or structural pricing equations or other supply-side decision equations. Doing so implies making assumptions regarding the shape of consumers' preferences and/or the nature of the competitive environment. Where those assumptions are crucial in determining the results, one must be sufficiently confident that they fit reality well. A particular problem with using structural models in determining the effect of vertical contracts is that several of the factors that determine and motivate those contracts are not well captured by off-the-shelf models. For example, it is not easy to measure sales effort or to model the mechanisms through which a change in price affects heterogeneous consumers.

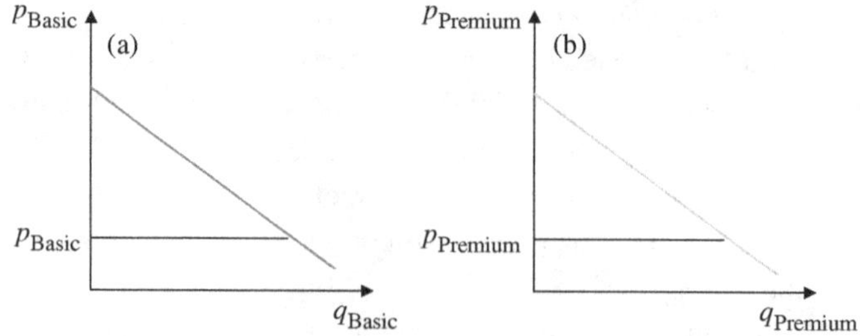

Figure 10.4. The interconnected demand equations for (a) basic $q_{\text{Basic}}(p_{\text{Basic}}, p_{\text{Premium}}; s_{\text{Basic}}, s_{\text{Premium}})$ and (b) premium $q_{\text{Premium}}(p_{\text{Basic}}, p_{\text{Premium}}; s_{\text{Basic}}, s_{\text{Premium}})$ cable.

Still, some attempts have been made to use structural models in order to identify the effect of vertical arrangements.

10.2.3.1 Measuring Effects on Consumer Welfare

Evaluating the effects of market outcomes on consumer welfare generally requires estimating demand function(s) since consumer welfare is often defined as the area below the demand curve (see the discussion in chapter 1).

If we have information on prices and qualities with and without vertical integration, we can compare the two situations and examine the effect of vertical integration on consumer surplus. Chipty (2001) estimates a demand system (illustrated in figure 10.4) with two demand functions, one for each of basic and premium cable. The variable measuring quantity demanded is the penetration rate. The specification also includes population variables affecting demand, the price of the service, and the price of the complementary service (either premium or basic respectively). System characteristics (system age and size) are used as identifying instruments. The results of the estimation are presented in table 10.2.

The results produce negative own-price elasticities as predicted by the theory. The price elasticity of basic cable is higher than that for premium cable, which may reflect differences in the preferences between the "average" basic consumer and the "average" basic plus premium consumer. If the latter are relatively inelastic demanders, then this result is intuitive.

Chipty (2001) uses a particularly simple (but approximate) calculation of the consumer surplus by adding the consumer surplus of the two different types of customers in each case: those that buy basic and premium and those that buy basic cable.[28]

[28] To calculate consumer welfare, there are various debates that must be addressed. First, whether one should use a Hicksian demand curve, which keeps utility constant along the curve as opposed to income, which is the variable kept constant along the most commonly used Marshallian demand curve. In this case, because the income effect is assumed to be small, the author argues that both demands are practically equivalent. Second, the fact that customers choose different options when faced with the same prices

Table 10.2. Demand estimates.

	Panel A: with channel capacity			
	Basic penetration rate		Premium penetration rate	
Variable	Coeff.	*t*-stat.	Coeff.	*t*-stat.
Constant	2.673	1.949	−0.933	1.076
Price of basic cable	−0.255	4.459	−0.021	0.892
Price of premium cable	−0.012	0.215	−0.046	1.698
Basic services offered	0.158	4.275	0.048	1.034
Basic program duplication	−2.232	3.757	−0.595	0.776
Offer AMC in the basic package (1 = yes, 0 = no)			−0.291	1.673
Natural log of income	0.267	2.132	0.131	3.575
Natural log of population density	−0.120	3.808	0.005	0.294
Younger viewership	−0.190	0.120	0.177	0.307
Older viewership	−2.337	2.871	−0.622	1.403
Nonwhite viewership	0.145	0.873	0.023	0.425
Household size	−0.413	2.056	−0.039	0.550
Natural log of television households	0.196	2.643	0.088	1.950
Area of dominant influence rank	0.289	2.422	0.108	1.763
Omnibus test for instruments		10.042 (0.123)		

Source: Chipty (2001).

The penetration rate in each case gives the fraction of individuals in each group for the markets that are vertically integrated and those that are not. Note that within each group of consumers, consumers are assumed to be homogeneous. This is imposed by the simple linear specification of the demand curve.[29] The results of the consumer surplus calculation are shown in table 10.3.

In summary, Chipty (2001) finds that vertical integration increases consumer surplus and that this increase is larger when there is vertical integration with a

and qualities since some people will have only basic services and some people will have both basic and premium. Heterogeneous demand also may complicate the calculation of consumer welfare since there is no longer one single demand curve. That said, in fact the issue may fairly easily be solved, at least in principle, by (for example) estimating demand curves for the various major types of consumers. Chipty notes that his approximate calculation requires that the utility provided by basic and premium cable is additively separable for consumers. This means that an increase in the utility obtained from basic cable does not affect the utility obtained from premium. This assumption would probably be wrong if, for example, we were considering the demand for beer and pizza and consumers usually found pizza more enjoyable with a beer. However, it seems a strong but reasonable approximation here, although those who prefer "exact" estimates may prefer a more sophisticated approach. Chipty (2001) also uses the results from Hausman (1981) to estimate consumer surplus exactly in this model.

[29] Chapter 9 provides a discussion of the assumptions underlying particular demand specifications.

Table 10.3. Consumer surplus estimates with and without vertical integration.

($ per month per consumer)	Unintegrated	Integration with basic service	Integration with premium service
Consumer surplus	$1.47	$1.69	$1.87

Source: Chipty (2001).

premium content provider. Note that the differences across markets of the three types appear because of differences in prices and service levels across the different types of markets and not because the demand model suggests that consumers care for some reason about vertical integration per se. Patterns in penetration rates appear to suggest that they are greater in markets with the kinds of price–service trade-offs that emerge from vertical integration. Since such factors will result in the demand curve being further out toward the right, for any given price we will tend to generate higher estimates of consumer surplus, although the amount of consumer surplus could easily be reduced if consumers faced high prices in those markets.

Crawford (2000) provides an alternate model of demand for basic and premium cable using a similar data set allowing for consumer heterogeneity while Shum and Crawford (2007) add a supply side to the model, allowing for firms to pick both price and quality in a way designed to implement second-degree price discrimination (see also Crawford 2005). We refer the reader to these papers to examine their authors' structural approach to this problem while we turn to another structural paper examining the case for the removal of territorial restraints in the sale of cars.

10.2.3.2 Estimating the Effect of Territorial Restraints

Brenkers and Verboven (2006)[30] use a structural approach to analyze the effects of the European car market liberalization; in particular, they want to estimate the effects of the removal of territorial restraints[31] and exclusive dealership arrangements on prices, consumer welfare, and profits. Until 2002, car manufacturers in Europe were allowed to select authorized dealers and grant them territorial exclusivity. The European Commission relaxed these exemptions in 2002 by preventing car manufacturers from applying both selectivity and territorial exclusivity. This means that, although manufacturers are still entitled to grant territorial exclusivity to a network of "official" dealers, these dealers can now sell cars to non "official" dealers or resellers within the country. They can also sell directly to customers in another country. The intention was to promote within-brand competition (across dealerships) both within a country and across countries in the European Union.

[30] For closely related models of vertical competition, see also Dubois and Bonnet (2008), Villas-Boas and Zhao (2005), and Villas-Boas (2007a,b).

[31] For a structural analysis of exclusive dealing using similar techniques to those described in this section, see Asker (2005).

Territorial restraints allow a manufacturer to price discriminate across countries. If, in addition, market power is granted to the retailer at national level, double marginalization can help soften competition among manufacturers (Rey and Stiglitz 1995). Liberalizing the car market and suppressing the price discrimination that is possible with national market segmentation may have ambiguous welfare effects as those consumers who had higher prices will be better off but those who benefited from cheaper prices will be worse off. On the other hand, if exclusivity prevents retailer competition at the national and cross-country level, then removing it will tend to decrease prices and benefit consumers, absent other efficiency effects of the vertical agreement.

In order to empirically assess the net effect of eliminating the restrictions, Brenkers and Verboven estimate a full structural model for the pre- and post-liberalization scenarios. To do so they use data including list prices, sales, and car characteristics of all car models sold in five European markets during 1970 to 1999. They also have national population and GDP data. They first estimate a nested multinomial logit (NMNL) demand system for cars. For each market m, the conditional indirect utility of individual i for car j takes the form,

$$u_{ij} = x_j\beta + \xi_j - \alpha_i p_j + \varepsilon_{ij},$$

where x_j are product-specific characteristics such as horsepower and size and ξ_j is a product-specific error component that captures product characteristics unobserved to the analyst such as the brand image. The price parameter α_i is defined as $\alpha_i = \alpha/y_i$, where y_i is the individual's income. The authors assume that ε_{ij} follow the assumptions of a two-level nested logit model (see chapter 9 for a discussion of the one-level NMNL model). The two-level NMNL model allows an investigator to "group" products and consider the consumers' choice problem as made up of a sequence of steps. First, consumers are assumed to choose between groups of cars. In Brenkers and Verboven, the car groups are defined as subcompact, compact, intermediate, standard, luxury, and an additional group is the outside good in case the consumer decides not to purchase a car. Given a group, the consumer is then assumed to choose between subgroups of domestic and imported cars. Finally, within each of the subgroups, the demand model assumes that consumers choose which model of car to purchase, at that stage choosing only between different members of the subgroup.

This two-level nested structure, whose assumption can be imposed by making particular choice on the distribution of ε_{ij}, allows an individual's probability of choosing car j, which is within a group of cars g and a subgroup h, to be expressed as

$$s_{ij} = \frac{\exp((x_j\beta + \xi_j - \alpha_i p_j)/(1-\sigma_{hg}))}{\exp(I_{ihg}/(1-\sigma_{hg}))} \frac{\exp(I_{ihg}/(1-\sigma_g))}{\exp(I_{ig}/(1-\sigma_g))} \frac{\exp(I_{ig})}{\exp(I_i)},$$

where

$$I_{ihg} = (1 - \sigma_{hg}) \ln \sum_{j=1}^{Jhg} \exp\left(\frac{x_j\beta + \xi_j - \alpha_i p_j}{1 - \sigma_{hg}}\right),$$

$$I_{ig} = (1 - \sigma_g) \ln \sum_{h=1}^{Hg} \exp\left(\frac{I_{ihg}}{1 - \sigma_g}\right),$$

$$I_i = \ln \sum_{g=1}^{G} \exp(I_{ig}),$$

and σ_{hg} and σ_g are the nesting parameters which are allowed to vary for the different groups and subgroups. As always, aggregate demands for a given product are calculated by integrating over the demands of each consumer type, here y_i. Thus, predicted sales for a given product are the weighted average of individual choice probabilities where the weights are by the density of the income distribution of the population. The parameters to be estimated are the K parameters for the product characteristics in x_j, the five group parameters σ_g, the ten subgroup parameters σ_{hg}, and the price parameter, α. The number of parameters to be estimated is therefore $K + 5 + 10 + 1$. For estimation, we need at least as many instruments as we have parameters in the model in order for the model to be identified. For estimation, the authors use a very slightly amended version of the BLP methodology described in chapter 9.

To obtain the instruments necessary for identification of the demand system, the authors first assume that the observed product characteristics x_j are uncorrelated with the unobserved component in demand, ξ_j. This assumption is familiar from OLS-style models and provides K instruments. It is also standard in the literature although the reason is probably because there are generally few better alternatives rather than because the assumption is obviously an entirely valid one. In addition, Brenkers and Verboven determine "markup shifter" variables that can be used as additional instruments. Those are the number and characteristics of the other products sold by the firm in a particular subgroup, the number and characteristics of the competing products in a particular subgroup, the number and characteristics of a firm's products within the same group, and the number and characteristics of competing products within the same group. Those constructed variables are supposed to capture the nature of the competitive interaction and therefore to affect margins while being uncorrelated with the unobserved product characteristic in demand. This approach to instrumentation is similar to that advocated by Berry et al. (1995).

Thus, so far, we have progressed from Chipty (2001) only to the extent that we have changed the type of demand system being estimated. However, in addition to demand, Brenkers and Verboven also estimate pricing equations using data from the pre-liberalization situation. To do so, they assume a two-stage game in which manufacturer f sets w_j a wholesale price for product j and then the retailer r sets the retail price p_j for product j given w_j. They solve the model by backward induction and calculate first the retailer's optimal pricing equation as a function of the wholesale prices of all cars. They normalize the retailers' operating marginal costs to 0. Instead of writing down a particular model of retailer pricing based on a particular model of conduct, they work with a general form of the retailer pricing equation which encapsulates several potential models of retailer conduct (competitive, monopoly pricing, etc.). Specifically, Brenkers and Verboven note that each model will generate a structural retailer pricing equation of the form

$$p = p(w),$$

where the subgame equilibrium retail prices will depend on the wholesale prices of all cars. We give some of their specific examples of the subgame below but for now notice that the move-order imposed on the game, where manufacturers set prices and then retailers compete, does nonetheless subsume important assumptions about the respective bargaining power of manufacturers and retailers. Namely this move order endows manufacturers with a first-mover advantage and the consequent bargaining power.

Following the process of backward induction, at the first stage of the game we must solve for the equilibrium wholesale prices that will be chosen by manufacturers and offered to retailers. In this model, the wholesale prices are chosen in the full knowledge that retailers will go on to set retail prices in a fashion dependent on the wholesale prices at stage two. We assume that each manufacturer chooses the wholesale prices of its product range to maximize the joint profits of all its own products $\Im_f$ taking into account retailers pricing behavior and demand:

$$\Pi_f(w) = \sum_{j \in \Im_f} (w_j - \mathrm{mc}_j) q_j(p(w)).$$

Note that this structural model is in fact essentially just the model typically used to study double marginalization (see the last section of chapter 9). Upstream manufacturers set wholesale prices and downstream retailers may subsequently find it profitable to charge markups. Thus, while the algebra may look complex, the basic framework is just the same as our standard double marginalization problem, albeit with two important differences: (1) product differentiation and (2) there may be an oligopoly at each of the retailer and manufacturer stages instead of just a monopoly manufacturer and a monopoly retailer.[32]

[32] One anonymous reviewer of this book noted that in many texts a treatment of vertical integration and vertical restraints would come earlier in many competition books. The reason is probably that books often treat such topics as largely analyzing either (i) upstream and downstream monopolies or (ii) monopoly at one level and competition at the other. We choose to treat vertical topics last primarily because in the real-world markets that competition agencies must analyze such settings are generically more complex

Returning to the manufacturer's problem, the first-order conditions for each product j are

$$q_j(p(w)) + \sum_{k \in \Im_f} (w_k - \text{mc}_k) \left(\frac{\partial q_k(p)}{\partial p_1} \frac{\partial p_1(w)}{\partial w_j} + \cdots + \frac{\partial q_k(p)}{\partial p_J} \frac{\partial p_J(w)}{\partial w_j} \right) = 0.$$

A small increase in the wholesale price of product j increases the manufacturer's profits by the amount of the market share of that product but that increase is then adjusted by the demand effects that the price increase has on each of the firm's models suitably adjusted by the way in which the retailer responds to the wholesale price increase of any given model.

Brenkers and Verboven consider two scenarios. In the first they assume intense retailer competition, so that the retail price is always equal to the wholesale price since that is the retailer's marginal cost and retail prices are just set equal to retailer's marginal costs under intense competition.[33] In that case we have a standard model of a manufacturer of various differentiated products. More specifically, the model is exactly the model we were able to study analytically with linear demands in chapter 8 except that we are using a more sophisticated differentiated product demand system and that makes the pricing equations nonlinear. The terms $\partial p_k(w)/\partial w_j$ will be 1 for $k = j$ and 0 for $k \neq j$. In this case, manufacturer marginal cost can be retrieved by subtracting the wholesale price from the observed retail price.

In the second scenario, where retailers have market power, retailers maximize profits over their set of products R_{r}. Retailers could have market power, for example, if retailers are granted exclusive territories which make their product range perhaps only a relatively poor substitute for another retailer's product range in the eyes of final consumers. The first-order conditions that arise from the retailer's problem are then

$$q_j(p) + \sum_{k \in R_{\text{r}}} (p_k - w_k) \frac{\partial q_k(p)}{\partial p_j} = 0.$$

After either some algebraic manipulation or computation, one can express the equilibrium retail prices p as a function of the wholesale prices, w. Computationally, given $p(w)$, one can then solve for the manufacturer's preferred wholesale prices taking into account the subsequent reactions of retailers. However, if we do not observe wholesale prices but we know from company documents that uniform prices appropriately approximate reality, then we can use this equation to solve for w given observed pricing behavior by retailers, i.e., given p. Knowing w and $p(w)$ we may then go back to the manufacturer's problem and use the now "observed"

---

than, say, evaluating a horizontal merger. In particular, analyzing vertical restraints or mergers means defining markets at various levels of the supply chain, analyzing the horizontal competition within each of them, and in particular how horizontal and vertical dimensions of competition interact. Such an activity is inherently more complex than looking at a single horizontal merger.

[33] For simplicity this model assumes that retailers require only one unit of input to generate one unit of output so that the manufacturer's demand is exactly that number of units required by retailers.

wholesale prices to facilitate the estimation of manufacturer's marginal costs of production. Thus, for a given set of demand estimates we can solve for the ws and mcs which explain the retail pricing data that we have. Obviously, such an approach relies extremely heavily on both the demand system estimates and also requires that we have correctly specified the model generating the observed retail prices. While such assumptions are strong ones, they are testable. For example, it would be possible to use out-of-sample data and/or accounting data cost estimates at both the retail and wholesale level to provide at least "reality checks." Similarly, cross-checks would often also be available using other evidence including testimony and company documents.

In addition to having written down the model of double marginalization plus product differentiation and oligopoly at each stage of the game in the pre-liberalization world, Brenkers and Verboven would like to amend the model so they can evaluate what will happen when the market is liberalized. Predicting what will happen is, of course, difficult, not least because the world is a counterfactual one so that, for example, they do not have estimates of consumer substitution patterns from a liberalized world where consumers and/or dealers have additional choices available. In fact, they model the post-liberalization situation by introducing constraints to the model that the markup differentials across countries should not exceed cross-country trade costs. They argue that this reflects the idea that intermediaries will act as arbitrageurs and hence tend to encourage margins to converge across markets. (As distinct from liberalization encouraging consumer switching behavior per se.) They also assume that, after liberalization, a reasonable approximation is that perfect retail competition is established so that retail price is exactly equal to wholesale price. Specifically, the pricing equations are assumed to be provided by the solution to the following constrained profit maximization problem:

$$\Pi_{fm}(p_m) = \sum_{m=1}^{M} \sum_{j \in F_f} (p_{jm} - \mathrm{mc}_{jm}) q_{jm}(p_m)$$
$$\text{subject to} \quad (1+\tau)(p_{jn} - \mathrm{mc}_{jn}) - (p_{jm} - \mathrm{mc}_{jm}) \geqslant 0,$$

where m are the markets in which the manufacturer operates and τ is the percentage increase in cost from transporting a car from country n to country m. Reasonable people can have a reasonable discussion about whether this fully captures the post-liberalization scenario.

Once equilibrium prices for the pre-liberalization and post-liberalization scenarios are estimated, the change in welfare can also be determined. As always, the change in consumer welfare can be calculated as the weighted average of the change of individual welfare. For the particular demand model above, the change in individual consumer surplus can be shown to be equal to the analytic formula

$$\Delta \mathrm{CS}_{im} = \frac{I_i(p_m^{\mathrm{Post}})}{\alpha_i} - \frac{I_i(p_m^{\mathrm{Pre}})}{\alpha_i},$$

where $I_i(p_m)$ is the nested logit inclusive value defined above. The change in producer surplus (profits) can also then be computed as

$$\Delta\text{PS}_m = \sum_{f=1}^{F} \Pi_{fm}(p_m^{\text{Post}}) - \sum_{f=1}^{F} \Pi_{fm}(p_m^{\text{Pre}}).$$

In addition, the change in total welfare is the sum of the change in consumer and producer surplus as well as the change in retailer surplus in the scenario where retailers enjoyed market power pre-liberalization. Clearly, given a well-understood "standard" demand system such as this and a fully specified model of firm behavior, we can always compute producer surplus, consumer surplus, and therefore total welfare.

We will not present Brenkers and Verboven's results in detail, but in brief they find that the total welfare gains from liberalization are likely to come from the increase in retailer competition at the national level generated by the possibility to supply nonofficial dealers, and find little evidence of total consumer welfare gains from the elimination of territorial exclusivity alone. They also find that increasing dealer competition at the national level and reducing double marginalization would in fact increase manufacturer profits suggesting that there may be unmeasured efficiency reasons for the system of authorized dealership, which are not captured in this model.

Finally, we note that such a vertical structural model cannot immediately be applied to the analysis of vertical mergers, at least without understanding the assumptions involved in doing so. To see why, consider an industry where some firms are vertically integrated and others are not. Before we could apply the model outlined above, we would need to be careful to define which are in fact "upstream" and which are "downstream" firms. This point was made in Salinger (1989) when reflecting on his earlier paper, Salinger (1988). In that paper, he had assumed that unintegrated upstream firms were first movers and then downstream producers of both the integrated and unintegrated varieties moved second. Such a specific move-order is not obviously uncontroversial and yet can affect the predicted effects of mergers materially.

In this section we have presented two structural models. First, Chipty's model examined just a final consumer demand-side model. Second, we saw Brenkers and Verboven's model that presented both a demand-side model for final consumers together with a model of retailer competition. This in turn generated an upstream "derived" demand model which they put together with a pricing model for manufacturers. Thus we have seen two variants of the structural approach. That said, we could certainly enrich the structural model further. For example, we could, at least in principle, happily introduce competition between retailers in service provision, along with spillover effects across retailers to capture free-riding effects. Doing so would extend this base model of territorial restrictions and double marginalization to allow for service and pricing externalities, thereby facilitating an evaluation of the incentives described at the start of this chapter.

The use of structural models is extremely appealing in principle since it allows us to estimate all the market outcomes and perform counterfactual policy experiments—such as what will happen to this market if we stop a particular form of vertical restraint being used. However, before rushing to embrace the approach it is vital to keep at the forefront of your mind that structural estimation of rich models is usually a complex and time-consuming exercise and therefore a costly one. In addition when we write down explicit models of behavior we usually need to make rather strong assumptions about the way consumers and firms behave and such assumptions are easily criticized by parties appealing decisions by competition authorities. In the context of an investigation, those potential drawbacks must be weighed against the use and additional value of the information obtained through the structural estimation. If theory produces unambiguous answers or if a reduced-form approach can be taken because of an available natural experiment, then the latter approach may well be preferable. On the other hand, structural estimation may be extremely useful when (1) theoretical predictions are ambiguous and depend in particular on the parameter values of the model, (2) when we are interested in some kind of explicit quantification, and (3) we are interested in modeling what equilibrium outcomes will look like in a world which does not currently exist; perhaps because a vertical restraint is currently used ubiquitously and an authority is considering stopping its use. Thus, structural estimation may be necessary if we wish to perform quantitative analysis and yet we cannot get information on outcomes with and without the practice. Horizontal merger simulation is similar in that regard—we do not see the world with the merger when we need to evaluate whether it should be allowed. In the cases where we are only interested in the effect of a practice on market outcomes and we have information on the world with and without the practice, simpler reduced-form approaches can often produce favorable results. Reduced-form approaches will, however, only be effective if we have an appropriate identification strategy. One very important source of identification can come from "natural experiments" and we return to that topic for the next section, where we turn to the empirical analysis of tying and bundling.[34]

10.2.4 Natural Experiments

A natural experiment is a technique that takes advantages of changes in behavior that are randomly forced upon some of the firms or individuals whose behavior we want to examine. By "randomly" we mean that the changes are not in any way determined by the subjects but happen due to external factors, such as an institutional change or the weather, on which the market players have no influence.

[34] We do not mean to suggest to the reader that there are not structural models of bundling, there are (see, for example, Crawford 2000). Rather, with the background in the book as a whole, our hope and expectation are that readers will be able to go to the literature and understand the now rich variety of models, including those structural models of bundling.

"Natural experiments" mimic actual experiments in a laboratory in which a random sample of individuals is given a "treatment" and the rest of the population is used as a "control group," providing a benchmark against which to compare those who were treated. For experiments to succeed, it is essential that the "treated group" is randomly selected so that that subgroup provides an accurate representation of the population.[35] In economics, one cannot always run actual experiments since market operators make their own decisions about what to do and, for example, there is no way to select a group of companies at random and impose, say, vertical integration on them. Nonetheless, economists can take advantage of exogenous factors that produce results similar to an experiment because when such a "natural experiment" occurs, we can observe its effects on firm conduct or market outcomes. Earlier in the chapter we considered Hastings (2004), whose event study involved the natural experiment arising because an elderly owner of an independent gas station chain decided to retire. Another, common, source of "natural experiments" involve changes in legislation and we now turn to a recent illustration of how this can be done using changes in legislation affecting funeral services in the United States.

10.2.4.1 Estimating the Effect of Bundling

Chevalier and Scott Morton (2008) use a natural experiment framework to determine the effect of bundling practices in the funeral industry. It turns out that some U.S. states require that only licensed funeral homes can sell caskets, which are the containers that bodies are buried in. Legislation on this matter varies greatly between states and in other states there are no restrictions imposed on the sales of caskets. Thus their paper uses variation in the legal environment for funeral homes across and within U.S. states as the "natural experiment" and uses it to see how equilibrium outcomes, particularly prices, are affected by the change in the regulatory environment.

To begin we note that funeral services include embalming, laying out the body, and arranging the funeral ceremony. Caskets and funeral services are close to being perfect complements since they are normally purchased in fixed one-to-one proportions. Every funeral requires a casket and also some associated funeral services. In a vertical-restraints context one might consider the restriction that only licensed funeral homes can sell caskets as potentially facilitating customer foreclosure. However, the restriction could alternatively be considered largely horizontal in nature and if so, then this should be interpreted as a study of the effect of tying (or bundling) of complements on prices since often the restriction will result in the bundling of caskets with funeral services.

The authors' aim is to evaluate tying and along the way to also evaluate the "one-monopoly-profit" argument from the Chicago school of thought, which the

[35] There are, of course, some techniques that soften this stringent requirement and essentially they involve designing a sampling frame that can be appropriately "undone" when analyzing the results.

reader will recall argued that if funeral service providers already have monopoly power, they cannot increase their profits further by undertaking activities like tying in an attempt to monopolize the complementary product market for caskets. The intuition is that when caskets are provided at close to marginal cost by a competitive industry, funeral service providers can nonetheless extract the full monopoly rent by way of the prices they set for funeral services. The Chicago school of thought goes on to assert that if there are bundling practices, they must arise only from efficiency considerations since they cannot be motivated by an attempt to extract a monopoly rent. On the other hand, others have argued that there may be instances where bundling does exactly this and therefore has, by way of strategic foreclosure of complementary product markets, an anticompetitive effect.

The data used for the analysis include data from six states. There is one state with casket sales restrictions (Virginia), two states with casket sales restrictions that are removed during the time frame of the data (South Carolina and Tennessee), and three states that never had casket sales restrictions (Kansas, Michigan, and North Carolina). The authors exploit the exogenous change in regulation in two states to identify the consequences of restrictions. The data set includes price data from individual funeral homes. The U.S. Federal Trade Commission states that all individual funeral homes must have "Generalized Price Lists" (GPL) itemizing the prices for goods and services. Surveys are carried out by the local affiliates of the Funeral Consumers Alliance. The authors use the prices for a direct burial—a simple burial service and casket with no embalming, no viewing, and no ceremony with body present—as a reference. Unfortunately, many surveys do not report separately the price of the funeral services and the price of the casket. Instead, they report the total price of direct burial, which is the sum of the two, and the authors use that price in their regressions.

The authors design the following reduced-form regression equation:

$$p_{it} = \alpha_i + \gamma \, \text{Casket}_{it} + \beta \, \text{Restrict}_{it} + \delta(\text{Restrict}_{it} \times \text{Casket}_{it}) + \lambda \, \text{Year}_t + \varepsilon_{it},$$

where p_{it} is the price of the direct burial funeral service (including casket) in funeral home i at time t, α_i is a funeral home fixed effect, Casket_{it} is a dummy variable for whether the casket is included in the bundle. This provides an estimate of the price of the casket since it is the additional amount that the customer must pay if the casket is included. Restrict_{it} is a dummy for whether the regulation is in place and captures the effect of the regulation on the prices of funeral services. The interaction term provides an estimate of the effect of the regulation on the price of the bundled casket. The regression included year dummies and an error term ε_{it}. No demand or cost shifters are explicitly included in the regression and thus the model implicitly assumes that such effects on prices must be subsumed in the funeral home fixed effect; they are assumed not to vary too much across time for a given funeral home, clearly a strong assumption. Alternatively, one might argue that demand and supply conditions are reasonably homogeneous across funeral homes and just vary across

Table 10.4. Price of direct burial.

	1	2	3
Price includes casket	793.0	877.0	689.8
	(70.2)	(132.2)	(60.0)
Restrictive	−251.7	−335.28	−196.30
	(134.1)	(147.8)	(128.17)
Restrictive × price includes casket	261.0	253.6	265.9
	(109.2)	(108.9)	(114.0)
Observations	1,437	1,437	1,516
Year dummies?	Yes	Yes	Yes
Funeral home dummies?	Yes	Yes	Yes
R^2	0.78	0.77	0.78
Means of dependent variable if without casket	$1,432		

Dependent variable is price of direct burial either including or not including a cloth-covered wooden casket. Standard errors are in parentheses. Standard errors in the third column are robust to clustering with funeral home-years. Construction of the price variable differs across the columns as described in the text.
Source: Chevalier and Scott Morton (2008).

time, in which case the time fixed effects will provide effective control for them. Again, that is clearly a rather strong assumption.

The net impact of the regulation on prices of funeral services is given by $\beta + \delta$. Because of the funeral home fixed effect, the impact of the regulation on prices is measured from "within funeral home" price variation, that is, from the price variation over time of those funeral homes for which there was a change in regulation during the sample period. (See the discussion of fixed-effects estimation in chapter 2.) The change of regulation is the natural experiment that imposes a change in behavior in the market where those funeral homes operate. Effectively, the removal of the regulation opens up the casket market to competition, while those funeral homes where the regulatory environment does not change will provide the benchmark against which to measure the effect of the regulation. The results of the regression are presented in table 10.4 for a variety of constructions of the price variable from the numerous local surveys.

In each column, we see that regulation appears to decrease the price of funeral services and increase the price of caskets. The third column provides estimates allowing for correlation in the error terms across funeral homes within a given year. The results suggest that when funeral homes lose the monopoly on the caskets, the price of caskets drops ($\delta > 0$) and the price of funeral services increases by almost the same amount ($\beta < 0$ with $\beta + \delta \approx 0$). If the net effect is close to zero, this would mean that the one monopoly rent does approximately hold in this case and if so then the change in regulation does not particularly change the profitability of funeral homes. Chevalier and Scott Morton (2008) also test this argument by looking at the effect of the changes in regulation on the expected profitability of the funeral homes concerned. Since event studies can provide a useful empirical tool for competition authorities, this technique is described in the next section first in the context of Chevalier and Scott Morton's paper and subsequently in the context of Ippolito and Overstreet's (1996) investigation into resale price maintenance (RPM).

10.2.5 Stock Market Event Studies

Unlike regressions, stock market event studies do not attempt to measure the effect of a conduct on the actual market outcomes.[36] Instead, they focus on the implications that certain practices will have on the perceived profitability of the firms. Specifically, event studies look at the investor's valuation of companies as approximated by the stock market valuation of the companies' shares or less frequently by the valuation of its bonds.[37] In fact such studies can potentially be useful for a whole variety of reasons from evaluating mergers to testing propositions about market definition. We illustrate with some examples how event studies can be useful but also their limitations.[38] (See also the discussion of event studies in chapter 2, where we focus on the econometric techniques used in stock market event studies.)

10.2.5.1 Estimating the Effect of Bundling (Continued)

Chevalier and Scott Morton (2008) examine the effect of the removal of legal restrictions on entry in the market for caskets on the stock market valuation of selected funeral companies. Specifically, they look at the stock valuation of a portfolio of four publicly traded funeral home firms (SCI, Stewart, Carriage, and Alderwood).

---

[36] Other industrial organization papers using stock market event studies include Eckbo (1983), Stillman (1983), Duso et al. (2006a,b), Aktas et al. (2007), and Kokkoris (2007).

[37] For a recent example of a case where a bond market event study was used, see the U.K. Competition Commission's investigation into the completed merger between Mid-Kent Water and South-East Water during 2006–7. The report is available at www.competition-commission.org.uk/inquiries/ref2006/water/index.htm and the particularly relevant paragraphs are in the final report, 5.129–5.131 while the details are provided in appendix E to the report.

[38] Conversations with various colleagues indicates that there appears to be a considerable divergence of views between finance professors and professionals on the one hand (many of whom believe that a fundamental function of markets is to aggregate information so that stock market event studies may provide useful additional information) and many industrial organization professors and professionals on the other (many of whom are rather more comfortable with the observation that competition agencies have more information than is available to the market). Other colleagues express concern about the robustness of the identification strategy in particular cases. For example, when attempting to identify problematic horizontal mergers using rivals' stock market reactions (according to the simple identification story, a positive reaction of rivals' stocks to a merger announcement means it is likely to be a problematic merger). The former point, the proposition that markets aggregate information, appears to be a fairly fundamental tenet of finance. The second concern is serious, but is perhaps not unlike the concern raised about every other piece of evidence in a merger inquiry. In reality, there is no perfect piece of information that will always identify problematic mergers, whether that information is market shares, profits, or stock market reactions.

They also look at the value of the Alderwood stock alone, since it is the one with the largest set of operations accounted for by the funeral homes in the states that have a restriction (23% of total sales). The authors use a three-day "event window" around the day of the legal events as the period during which to capture abnormal changes in expected returns and company valuation. Picking the length of the event window can be a challenging practical aspect of event studies. On the one hand, it may take time for news to be fully digested and understood by investors, and that pushes toward consideration of longer event windows, but on the other hand longer event windows potentially mean more news may arise in both the general market and also about the specific company or sector.

The legal timeline was as follows. On August 21, 2000, the District Court for the Eastern District of Tennessee removed legal restrictions on the market for caskets in the state. On December 12, 2002, the District Court of the Western District of Oklahoma decided to uphold legal restrictions on the market for caskets in the state. On August 23, 2004, the Tenth Circuit Appeals Court upheld the Oklahoma law. On June 12, 2002, the Sixth Circuit Appeals Court upheld the District Court decision to strike down the restriction law in Tennessee. The Supreme Court subsequently decided not to review these cases and in doing so let the inconsistent judgments coexist.

The regression explains the returns of the funeral home portfolio on the value-weighted total NYSE/AMEX stock market return obtained from the Center for Research in Securities Prices (CRSP). On the right-hand side, the authors include dummy variables for various three-day event windows: (1) that centered on the District Court's decision in the Tennessee case, (2) that centered on the District Court's decision in the Oklahoma case, (3) that centered on the Appeals Court's decision in the Tennessee case, and (4) that centered on the Appeals Court's decision in the Oklahoma case. The authors include daily returns for this portfolio for the 300 trading days before the first decision through December 31, 2004. The results of their regression are reported in the first column of table 10.5.

The results suggest that absolutely none of the legal events had any effect on the stock market valuation of the funeral homes concerned. This means the evidence in total would indicate that the restrictive sales laws on caskets, if repealed, would lead to lower prices of caskets due to entry in that market but at the same time funeral homes would start charging higher prices for funeral services. The pricing regressions and the stock market evidence are therefore in this instance consistent with the Chicago school "one-monopoly-profit" theory. Of course, the results also suggest that there is also a considerable amount of market power being exerted by funeral homes in their provision of funeral services, since they are able to recover all the profits lost to competition in the casket market with an increase in the prices of funeral services in a way that leaves their net profits virtually unchanged. In addition, because the final price of the direct burial is practically unchanged, there

Table 10.5. Event study results.

	(1) Funeral homes	(2) Alderwoods
Beta	0.69 (0.05)	0.86 (0.10)
Tennessee court	−0.0007 (0.0145)	
OK court	−0.0021 (0.0145)	−0.0053 (0.0179)
Tenth Circuit	−0.0014 (0.0145)	0.0114 (0.0180)
Sixth Circuit	0.0061 (0.0145)	0.0862 (0.0990)
Constant	−0.0001 (0.0007)	−0.0001 (0.0011)
R^2	0.11	0.09
Observations	1,397	754

Source: Chevalier and Scott Morton (2008).

seems to be no particular efficiency rationale, or inefficiency disadvantage, for the practice of bundling the casket to the funeral service.

10.2.5.2 Assessing Resale Price Maintenance

Ippolito and Overstreet (1996) perform an event study on changes in the law regarding resale price maintenance. Minimum RPM was made per se illegal in the United States in 1911[39] and that status was only recently reversed by the Supreme Court's Leegin decision in 2007.[40] They examine a famous RPM case from the 1970s. The company under investigation was Corning Glass Works, which sold household glass products such as Pyrex, Corning Ware, and Corelle. Corning sold to 360 wholesalers, who in turn sold to 50,000 retailers. Corning gave wholesalers presigned contracts which they were required to get their retailers to sign. Those contracts were direct contracts between Corning and the retailers and they included clauses imposing price floors, that is, minimum RPM. This practice lasted for about twenty years until the Federal Trade Commission (FTC) first challenged it in 1971. Corning's rationale for the contract can be summarized as follows:

> Our lab has developed a new glass ceramic with remarkable qualities, but to sell it we have to rely not on our dealer's reluctant acquiescence but on their active collaboration. They will have to display it and talk about it. And they won't do that

[39] *Dr. Miles Medical Co. v. John D. Park & Sons*, 220 U.S. 373 (1911).

[40] *Leegin Creative Leather Products Inc. v. PSKS Inc.*, Case no. 06-480. The decision is available at www.supremecourtus.gov/opinions/06pdf/06-480.pdf.

> if they believe that once they've built up the product some downtown store will take the business away by advertising it at a lower price. We cannot afford to become a target for stores which base their promotional appeal on someone else's name, the best known name they can lay their hands on.[41]

Clearly, Corning's view was that RPM in this case was geared toward reducing horizontal externalities between retailers of the form that led to bad outcomes for the manufacturer. In particular, the incentive to free-ride on rivals' provision of service combines poorly with the lack of incentive to take into account the effects on rival's sales if I undercut their prices. Absent the service dimension, the horizontal pricing externality between competitors is the main force we think of as driving good outcomes for consumers. On the other hand, with the service dimension added, providing a second horizontal externality between retailers, the net effects of the externalities on overall welfare are less clear cut. Finally, the manufacturer, Corning, will clearly be affected by such decisions being made downstream so there are important vertical externalities here.

The timeline of events was as follows. On October 8, 1971, the FTC announced a "price fixing" challenge to Corning's RPM policy. On January 16, 1973 the FTC issued a press release saying that an administrative law judge (ALJ), the FTC's hearing examiner, had ruled in Corning's favor on all counts. This was subsequently appealed by the FTC complaint counsel. On June 17, 1973 the full FTC announced their appeal decision, which reversed the administrative law judge's initial decision on the central RPM issue. On January 29, 1975, the U.S. Court of Appeals upheld the FTC decision.

Ippolito and Overstreet argue that stock market evidence may have the power to distinguish between a number of basic hypotheses about the role of RPM in this market.

(i) If the resale price maintenance was a device to cartelize the market at the retail level, a prohibition of RPM would increase the profits of all glass houseware producers.

(ii) An increase in retail competition (downstream) would increase the total profits of all manufacturers (upstream). If on the other hand RPM was an attempt to cartelize the industry at the manufacturer level, the prohibition of the practice would cause profits for all manufacturers to decrease.

(iii) Finally, if, as Corning claimed, the practice was only trying to elicit services from retailers, the end of RPM would hurt the profits of Corning as well as that of competitors that were using RPM. It would either have a zero or a positive effect on competitors that were not using RPM. This was the case of Anchor Hocking, Corning's closest competitor.

[41] Quoted in Ippolito and Overstreet (1996, p. 291).

Table 10.6. Predicted effect of eliminating Corning's use of RPM.

Economic theory	Corning	Anchor Hocking	Other competitors
Dealer collusion/ anticompetitive pricing	+	0 or +	0 or +
Manufacturer collusion/ anticompetitive pricing	−	−	−
Principal–agent theories	−	0 or +	− if using RPM + if not using RPM

Source: Ippolito and Overstreet (1996).

The table below shows Ippolito and Overstreet's predicted effects of a successful FTC case on stock values under alternative theories of resale price maintenance.

In reality, the prediction of the elimination of RPM on competitors in the case where RPM induces promotional and sales effort is not so obvious. For example, it could be that promotional efforts to promote Corning glassware increase the total demand for glassware positively, affecting Anchor Hocking's sales in the process. In such cases, where the marginal consumer reacting to the promotion is more the person who does not buy glassware as opposed to the person who is already a glassware customer from another brand, Corning's close competitors might be hurt by the end of the practice and the promotional effort it elicited. The effect of an end to RPM on competitors can therefore be ambiguous depending on the distribution of consumer preferences and the relative importance and effect of the price and advertisement efforts. Finally, if Corning and Anchor Hocking are branded substitutes, the decrease in the price of one of them after the elimination of RPM may trigger the decrease of the price of the other since the two goods will be strategic complements. This is another reason why we might in truth expect to see close competitors be hurt by the elimination of RPM.

Such concerns around the identification of harm (or otherwise) from RPM are serious and it is not immediately clear that the identification strategy always (or even often) works to tell apart a use of RPM that serves as a manufacturer's collusive mechanism from the use of RPM that has the simple purpose of increasing retailer's sales effort. On the other hand, as will be clear from our discussion at numerous points in this book, unambiguous identification results are rare and generally empirical exercises can be useful to undertake even if in order to place evidential weight on the results they need to be complemented with other pieces of evidence. Here, for example, we note that the extent of advertising spillovers is quantifiable and so that explanation of the results can be tested or at least a qualitative judgement made.

Ippolito and Overstreet (1996) estimate whether firms had an abnormal return around the day of events that ruled for or against resale price maintenance. They run the following regression:

$$R_{it} = a_i + b_i R_{\text{mt}} + c_i D_t + e_{it},$$

where a_i is a firm-specific effect, R_{it} is the percentage return of firm i on day t, R_{mt} is the percentage return of a value-weighted portfolio of the New York Stock Exchange (NYSE) and American Stock Exchange (ASE) stocks on day t, D_t is a dummy variable that takes the value 1 for the days in the event window and 0 otherwise, and e_{it} is a random error term for firm i on day t. The event window covers three to four days before and after the actual event. The motivation for this equation can be found in the capital asset pricing models (CAPMs) described in most finance books and we do not reiterate that here (see, for example, Campbell et al. 1997). Note that the coefficient c_i is the average per day of abnormal returns. With this specification, cumulative abnormal returns are calculated using

$$\text{CAR}_t = c_i \text{ Days in event window}_t.$$

The regression results on the effect of the events on the value of the Corning stock are presented in table 10.7. There is a negative effect on the valuation of the company after the FTC's announcement of the investigation. The interim reversal had a very small positive effect. The FTC reversal and upholding of the case had another negative effect on the firm valuation and the decision of the Seventh Circuit Appeals Court had no particular effect on the stock prices.

The cumulative abnormal return is a negative 12% in the five days before the announcement of the FTC investigation. Trading volumes presented in the paper do show abnormal activity right before the FTC announcement which, in the absence of other news at the time, appears to be highly suggestive that some traders were operating based on inside information. In the case of the second event, the CAR show a positive effect on the benefits of Corning, which the authors report is particularly marked after the decision to dismiss the charges was published in the *Wall Street Journal*.

The event study using Corning stock data indicates that investors in Corning value RPM as having a positive impact on the profits of Corning. However, such an observation is consistent with either RPM acting to facilitate downstream price fixing (reduction in intrabrand competition) or simply solving the free-rider problem in service provision. In order to attempt to discriminate between these stories we need to (at least) look at what happens to the expected profits of competitors. A positive effect of the demise of RPM on Corning's competitors could be consistent with the principal–agent theory. On the other hand, a negative effect of the elimination of RPM could be consistent with either a price-fixing world (or perhaps a situation in which competitors derive positive externalities from Corning's investment in services and promotion).

The results (reported in table 10.8) indicate that RPM by Corning was perceived to also favor its nearest competitor Anchor Hocking. The FTC reversal of the ALJ

Table 10.7. Changes in Corning stock value at events in FTC case.

	Cumulative abnormal return			
	1-day	3-day	5-day	10-day
1. FTC announces complaint:[a]				
Press release B	−0.016	−0.049**	−0.122**	−0.160**
(October 8, 1971)	(−1.17)	(−2.09)	(−4.13)	(−3.74)
2. ALJ dismisses case:				
Decision filed A	0.032**	0.018	0.012	0.068*
(December 27, 1972)	(2.68)	(0.86)	(0.42)	(1.73)
Wall Street Journal story B	−0.001	0.006	0.034	0.064
(January 17, 1973)[b]	(−0.08)	(0.29)	(1.23)	(1.62)
3. FTC reverses ALJ:				
Decision filed B	−0.014	−0.017	−0.055*	−0.110**
(June 5, 1973)	(−1.05)	(−0.776)	(−1.86)	(−2.62)
Wall Street Journal story B	0.003	−0.015	0.008	0.014
(June 18, 1973)[b]	(0.25)	(−0.64)	(0.26)	(0.31)
One day after *Journal*	−0.023*			
Journal story	(−1.74)			
4. Seventh Circuit upholds FTC:				
Decision date A	0.021	−0.015	−0.042	0.021
(January 29, 1975)[c]	(0.79)	(−0.32)	−0.72	(−0.25)

Notes: t-statistics are in parentheses. FTC, Federal Trade Commission; ALJ, Administrative Law Judge. "B" indicates that the window for the cumulative average return begins the required number of days *before* the event and ends with the event day. "A" indicates windows beginning at the event day with the required number of days *after* the event.

[a]The *Washington Star* carried the story on Friday afternoon, and the *Wall Street Journal* on Monday, October 11.

[b]Federal Trade Commission press releases were issued on the day before the *Wall Street Journal* stories.

[c]There was no *Wall Street Journal* story for this event.

*Significant at the 90% level of confidence.

**Significant at the 95% level of confidence.

Source: Ippolito and Overstreet (1996).

decision in favor of Corning (i.e., a finding against RPM) is associated with a 7.6% decline in returns for Anchor Hocking. Such a result is inconsistent with Corning's RPM only benefiting Corning. To help tell apart the potential explanations for this finding, Ippolito and Overstreet present another interesting piece of evidence. Specifically, they show that after the Appeals Court decision in 1975 declaring Corning's RPM activities illegal, Corning sharply increased its advertising expenses. That response is consistent with a story where RPM was serving to provide demand-enhancing services that were replaced with advertisement following the judgment. Rather strikingly, Anchor Hocking's advertisement activities remained largely unchanged.

Table 10.8. Results of the event study regression on Anchor Hocking stock.

	Cumulative abnormal return			
	1-day	3-day	5-day	10-day
1. FTC announces complaint:[a]				
Press release B	0.001	0.033	0.032	0.077
(October 8, 1971)	(0.09)	(1.32)	(0.99)	(1.64)
2. ALJ dismisses case:				
Decision filed A	−0.015	−0.03	−0.041	−0.063
(December 27, 1972)	(−1.08)	(−1.24)	(−1.32)	(−1.41)
Wall Street Journal story B	0.016	−0.008	−0.026	−0.041
(January 17, 1973)[b]	(1.16)	(−0.34)	(−0.85)	(−0.92)
3. FTC reverses ALJ:				
Decision filed B	0.013	−0.075**	−0.076**	−0.053
(June 5, 1973)	(0.76)	(−2.62)	(−2.02)	(−0.99)
Wall Street Journal story B	−0.007	0.004	0.020	0.042
(June 18, 1973)	(−0.41)	(0.12)	(0.49)	(0.72)
One day after *Wall Street Journal* story	−0.012			
	(−0.64)			
4. Seventh Circuit upholds FTC[b]:				
Decision date A	0.037	0.023	0.010	−0.071
(January 29, 1975)	(1.69)*	(0.60)	0.19	(−1.01)

Notes: t-statistics are in parentheses. FTC, Federal Trade Commission; ALJ, Administrative Law Judge. "B" indicates that the window for the cumulative average return begins the required number of days *before* the event and ends with the event day. "A" indicates windows beginning at the event day with the required number of days *after* the event.

[a]Except as reported for the Seventh Circuit Decision, no other events related to Anchor Hocking were reported in the *Wall Street Journal* or the *New York Times* near the case events.

[b]On February 28, 1975, Anchor Hocking agreed to acquire Amerock Corp., which was reported by the *Wall Street Journal* on March 5. This event may confound the interpretation of the Seventh Circuit Appeals decision.

*Significant at the 90% level of confidence.

**Significant at the 95% level of confidence.

Source: Ippolito and Overstreet (1996).

10.2.6 Discussion

This chapter has examined a relatively small number of recent or classic pieces of empirical work in the arena of vertical restraints and vertical integration. While our review has necessarily been a focused one, the literature on vertical restraints is neither large nor comprehensive at this point. Our aim has been to provide enough substance and detail about a small number of papers to help investigators move from these empirical examples to both the rest of the literature and perhaps more importantly toward designing and undertaking such analyses for bespoke projects.

Doing so is by no means an easy task. We hope that the material in this chapter (i) helps the reader to understand the kinds of approaches will be useful in evaluating vertical restrictions, (ii) provides sufficient introduction to encourage case handlers that there are helpful contributions available from the academic and case literature, and (iii) that there is certainly some exciting research in this area yet to come (e.g., around empirical effects of vertical integration on service provision or the appropriate approach to resale price maintenance, exclusive territories, or exclusive dealing).

Lafontaine and Slade (2005) provide a complementary review of the current empirical literature on vertical restraints. While we have focused on the empirical tools that have proven useful in a range of papers, they provide an important contribution by pulling together the limited evidence currently available in the literature. They argue that, at least in industries where academics have undertaken work—mostly the beer, gasoline, and auto-distribution industries—the empirical evidence from the academic literature suggests that vertical restraints are generally associated with positive net welfare effects.[42] Thus, the balance of work on vertical restraints and mergers does not suggest a general policy stance that is hostile toward them. At the same time, agencies will want to remain vigilant since we now have coherent economic theory suggesting that on occasion vertical restraints and vertical mergers may be welfare reducing.

Competition policy conferences across the world, like Lafontaine and Slade, have in recent years noted that there are currently rather a small number of such studies, and that there is no doubt that there remains a great deal that we have yet to learn. In terms of the balance of evidence (and experience) we note somewhat of a difference between past antitrust intervention, where, in the round, agencies appear to have found problems with at least some vertical mergers and restraints and the message from Lafontaine and Slade summarizing the available academic literature. Wherever the debate eventually rests, we hope that the material in this chapter encourages more and better empirical work, some of which should occur within the context of casework or *ex post* reviews.

10.3 Conclusions

- The effect of vertical restraints on the market may be captured using reduced-form regressions whenever there is enough relevant variation in the data to identify the effect. Natural experiments such as the prohibition of a practice can also provide good opportunities for useful regression analysis.
- Structural estimation allows us to model a world without the practice even if that world does not currently exist, much as we do when estimating the

[42] For a rare and very welcome examination of the relationship between vertical integration and productivity, see also Syverson and Hortascu (2007).

effect of anticipated horizontal mergers. Exactly the same caveats regarding the validity of the structural assumptions and the need for reality checks apply to the analysis of vertical mergers as those which apply to horizontal mergers. However, here generally the caseworker has far more work to do (multiple market definitions, some efficiency analysis (e.g., the likely extent of reduction in double marginalization), as well as an evaluation of the effectiveness of giving a rival market power on driving sales to your downstream division). As a result, robustness checks in analysis may well need to be even more extensive.

- Event studies focusing on the time when an investigation of a practice is announced may shed light on the markets' appreciation of the profitability of the practice. Such studies may under specific assumptions be sufficient to discriminate between potential pro- and anticompetitive motivations for vertical restraints.
- The theory of vertical restraints and/or vertical mergers suggests that there are many efficiency-based reasons to vertically integrate or use vertical restraints. Namely, such restrictions may decrease transaction costs or solve vertical or horizontal externality problems such as those caused by double marginalization or vertical service externalities or free-riding in the provision of service by retailers.
- In many instances, different types of vertical restraints can be used to solve externality problems. Economic theory does not typically provide unambiguous predictions about whether a given vertical practice is likely to be good or bad for consumer welfare. Predictions about the impact of vertical mergers on prices, for example, are fundamentally ambiguous whenever own costs fall (say, because of a decline in transactions costs or double marginalization) but the opportunity of, for instance, using full or partial foreclosure strategies means there is a potential for vertically integrated firms to "raise rivals' costs." This is a direct contrast in particular to the theoretical prediction about the price effect of a horizontal merger between firms producing substitutes. In casework, the ambiguity means that sometimes both pro- and anticompetitive explanations are consistent with the available evidence on the effect of a given vertical restraint and agencies may need to undertake a considerable amount of work to tell apart the two stories.

Conclusion

Since competition policy is now largely "effects" based, it is vital that the competition policy and economics communities continue to develop ways in which we can empirically evaluate the actual effect of potentially anticompetitive but also potentially desirable practices. Throughout this book, we have attempted to carefully examine both of the two main approaches to undertaking such empirical work in economics. Along the way, and equally importantly, we have tried to provide a clear statement of the basis for each of the approaches that emerges from economic theory.

The first general method we have looked at involves the estimation of reduced-form regressions of equilibrium market outcomes on factors that determine those equilibrium outcomes including some indicator variable for a practice of interest. We have generally argued that reduced-form approaches are ideally informed by some kind of experiment in the data that constitutes an appropriate "natural experiment" for the issue being studied. We noted that reduced-form approaches to estimating the impact of a practice, in the last chapter a vertical practice, on equilibrium outcomes generally requires being able to compare outcomes in a situation with and without the practice. In addition we must be sure that there are no systematic differences between the two samples that we are comparing except for the difference in the conduct that we are assessing, or at least as sure as we can be. The chances of being able to do so are best when we have a natural experiment which exogenously imposes or eliminates a conduct and also probably some form of local markets.

The second general method we have looked at involved a structural approach, building explicit models of consumer and/or firm behavior. One great advantage of structural modeling is that it enables us to develop predictions for what might happen in a world not yet observed. That is the very essence of policymaking. However, we have also noted that structural models will typically rely heavily on assumptions which must be sound and justifiable, at least as reasonable approximations to behavior in the world, in order for the results of any prediction exercise to be credible. We also emphasized throughout that the use of structural models can only go hand in hand with a process of "reality checking" and model testing in order to carefully evaluate and ultimately ideally verify the performance of the model being used. The bottom line on structural modeling is perhaps unsurprising: (1) if a model is a poor approximation of the world, it will probably provide a poor basis for making forecasts, and (2) modeling the world is what economists can and should do and while models are always approximations, the reality is that in industrial organization the models have improved substantially over the last few decades.

Which methodology to use will be a matter of judgment by the economist on a case team, ideally informed by her colleagues about such things as potentially appropriate natural experiments. The best method will greatly depend on the details of the case, the data available, and the question(s) which must be answered. Attempting to undertake a sound empirical exercise will often be informative even if analysts do not get so far as to build a sophisticated economic model. We often learn far more about an industry by examining data sets carefully than we would by listening to anecdotes from a variety of commentators on that industry. In terms of the variety of evidence we receive during investigations, cold hard numbers are attractive for competition authorities and probably many authorities do not currently do as much as they could to fully exploit the useful information available from market-, firm-, and consumer-level data. We hope this book will provide at least a small contribution to encourage agencies to do more.

References

Abrantes-Metz, R. M., L. Froeb, J. Geweke, and C. Taylor. 2006. A variance screen for collusion. *International Journal of Industrial Organization* 24:467–86.

Abreu, D. 1986. Extremal equilibria of oligopolistic supergames. *Journal of Economic Theory* 39:191–225.

Abreu, D., D. Pearce, and E. Stacchetti. 1990. Toward a theory of discounted repeated games with imperfect monitoring. *Econometrica* 58:1041–63.

Ackerberg, D., K. Caves, and G. Frazer. 2006. Structural identification of production functions. UCLA Working Paper.

Aghion, P., and R. Griffith. 2008. *Competition and Growth: Reconciling Theory and Evidence*. Cambridge, MA: MIT Press.

Aigner, D., and S. Chu. 1968. On estimating the industry production function. *American Economic Review* 58:826–39.

Aktas, N., E. Bodt, and R. Roll. 2007. Is European M&A regulation protectionist? *Economic Journal* 117:1096–121.

Amir, R. 1996. Cournot oligopoly and the theory of supermodular games. *Games and Economic Behaviour* 15:132–48.

Anderson, K., M. Lynch, and J. Ogur. 1975. The sugar industry. FTC Report. Washington, DC: U.S. Federal Trade Commission.

Anderson, T. W. 1958. *Introduction to Multivariate Statistical Analysis*. Wiley.

Andrews, D. 1994. Empirical process methods in econometrics. In *Handbook of Econometrics* (ed. R. F. Engle and D. McFadden), volume 4, pp. 2247–94. New York: North-Holland.

Angrist, J. 2004. Treatment effect heterogeneity in theory and practice. *Economic Journal* 114:52–83.

Angrist, J., K. Graddy, and G. W. Imbens. 2000. Instrumental variables estimators in simultaneous equations models with an application to the demand for fish. *Review of Economic Studies* 67:499–527.

Angrist, J., G. Imbens, and D. Rubin. 1996. Identification of causal effects using instrumental variables. *Journal of the American Statistical Association* 91:444–55.

Ashenfelter, O., D. Ashmore, J. Baker, and D. Hosken. 2006. Econometric analysis of pricing in *FTC v. Staples*. *International Journal of the Economics of Business* 13:265–79.

Ashurst. 2004. Study on the conditions of claims for damages in case of infringement of EC competition rules. Part 2. Analysis of economic models for the calculation of damages. Study prepared for the European Commission.

Asker, J. 2005. Diagnosing foreclosure due to exclusive dealing. Working Paper, Stern School of Business at NYU.

Aslanbeigui, N., and M. Naples. 1997. Scissors or horizon: neoclassical debates about returns to scale, costs, and long-run supply, 1926–1942. *Southern Economic Journal* 64:1926–42.

Athey, S., and P. Haile. 2002. Identification of standard auction models. *Econometrica* 70: 107–40.

Bailey, E. 1981. Contestability and the design of regulatory and antitrust policy. *American Economic Review* 71:179–83.

Bailey, E., and A. Friedlander. 1982. Market structure and multiproduct industries. *Journal of Economic Literature* 20:1024–48.

Bain, J. S. 1950 Workable competition in oligopoly: theoretical considerations and empirical evidence. *American Economic Review* 40:35–47.

——. 1951. Relation of profit rate to industry concentration: American manufacturing 1936–1940. *Quarterly Journal of Economics* 65:293–324.

——. 1956. *Barriers to New Competition*. Cambridge, MA: Harvard University Press.

Bajari, P., and L. Ye. 2001. Competition versus collusion in procurement auctions: identification and testing. Working Paper 01001, Department of Economics, Stanford University.

Bajari, P., and G. Summers. 2002. Detecting collusion in procurement auctions: a selective survey of recent research. *Antitrust Law Journal* 70:143–70.

Baker, J. B. 1989. Identifying cartel policing under uncertainty: the U.S. steel industry, 1933–1939. *Journal of Law & Economics* 32(2):47–76.

——. 1996. Identifying horizontal price fixing in the electronic marketplace. *Antitrust Law Journal* 65:41–55.

——. 1999. Econometric analysis in *FTC vs. Staples*. *Journal of Public Policy and Marketing* 18:11–21.

Baker, J. B., and T. Bresnahan. 1985a. Estimating the elasticity of demand facing a single firm: evidence on three brewing firms. Stanford University Economics Research Paper 54.

——. 1985b. The gains from merger or collusion in product differentiated industries. *Journal of Industrial Economics* 33:427–44.

——. 1988. Estimating the residual demand curve facing a single firm. *International Journal of Industrial Economics* 6:283–300.

Baker, J., and R. Pitofsky. 2007. A turning point in merger enforcement: *Federal Trade Commission v. Staples*. In *Antitrust Stories* (ed. E. Fox and D. Crane). Foundation Press.

Baker, J., and C. Shapiro. 2008. *Reinvigorating Horizontal Merger Enforcement*. In *Where the Chicago School Overshot the Mark: The Effect of Conservative Economic Analysis on Antitrust* (ed. R. Pitofsky). Oxford University Press.

Bakos, Y., and E. Brynjolfsson. 1998. Bundling information goods: pricing, profits and efficiency. NBER Working Paper 11488. (Available at http://ssrn.com/abstract=11488.)

Baldwin, L., R. Marshall, and J.-F. Richard. 1997. Bidder collusion at forest service timber sales. *Journal of Political Economy* 105:657–99.

Baltagi, B. 2001. *Econometric Analysis of Panel Data*, 2nd edn. Wiley.

Banerjee, A., J. Dolado, J. Galbraith, and D. Hendry. 2003. *Co-integration, Error Correction, and the Econometric Analysis of Non-Stationary Data*. Oxford University Press.

Banker, R. D., A. Charnes, and W. Cooper. 1984. Some models for estimating technical and scale inefficiencies in data envelopment analysis. *Management Science* 30:1078–92.

Banks, J., R. Blundell, and A. Lewbel. 1997. Quadratic Engel curves and consumer demand. *Review of Economics and Statistics* 79:527–39.

Barten, A. P. 1969. Maximum likelihood estimation of a complete system of demand equations. *European Economic Review* 1:7–73.

——. 1977. The systems of consumer demand functions approach: a review. *Econometrica* 45:23–51.

Baumol, W., J. Panzar, and R. Willig. 1982. *Contestable Markets and the Theory of Industry Structure*. New York: Harcourt Brace Jovanovich.

Bennion, E. 1952. The Cowles Commission's "simultaneous equation approach": a simplified example. *Review of Economics and Statistics* 34:49–56.

Berndt, E. 1991. *The Practice of Econometrics: Classical and Contemporary*. Reading, MA: Addison-Wesley.

Berndt, E., and N. E. Savin. 1975. Estimation and hypothesis testing in singular equations with autoregressive disturbances. *Econometrica* 43:937–57.

Bernheim, B. D. 2002. Expert report of B. Douglas Bernheim in RE: Vitamins Antitrust Litigation, M.D.L. no. 1285, United States District Court for the District of Columbia, May 24.

Bernheim, B. D., and M. Whinston. 1990. Multi-market contact and collusive behaviour. *RAND Journal of Economics* 21:1–26.

——. 1998. Exclusive dealing. *Journal of Political Economy* 106:64–103.

Berry, S. T. 1992. Estimation of a model of entry in the airline industry. *Econometrica* 60: 889–917.

——. 1994. Estimating discrete-choice models of product differentiation. *RAND Journal of Economics* 25:242–62.

Berry, S., and P. Reiss. 2007. Empirical models of entry and market structure. In *Handbook of Industrial Organization*, volume 3. Amsterdam: North-Holland.

Berry, S. T., J. Levinsohn, and A. Pakes. 1995. Automobile prices in market equilibrium. *Econometrica* 63:841–90.

Berry, S., O. Linton, and A. Pakes. 2004. Limit theorems for estimating the parameters of differentiated product demand systems. *Review of Economic Studies* 71:613–54.

Bertrand, J. 1883. Théorie mathématique de la richesse sociale. *Journal des Savants* 67:499–508.

Binmore, K. 1983. *Calculus*. Cambridge University Press.

Blumenthal, W. (ed.). 1985. *Horizontal Mergers: Law and Policy*. American Bar Association Section of Antitrust Law Monograph 12. American Bar Association.

Bolotova, Y., J. M. Connor, and D. J. Miller. 2008. The impact of collusion on price behavior: empirical results from two recent cases. *International Journal of Industrial Organization* 26:1290–307.

Bond, R., and W. Greenberg. 1976. Industry structure, market rivalry, and public policy: a comment. *Journal of Law and Economics* 19:201–4.

Bonnet, C., P. Dubois, and M. Simioni. 2006. Two-part tariffs versus linear pricing between manufacturers and retailers: empirical tests on differentiated products markets. CEPR Working Paper 6016.

Borenstein, S., and A. Shepard. 1996. Dynamic pricing in retail gasoline markets. *RAND Journal of Economics* 27:429–51.

Borenstein, S., J. Bushnell, and F. Wolak. 2002. Measuring market inefficiencies in California's restructured wholesale electricity market. *American Economic Review* 92: 1376–405.

Bowlin, W., W. Charnes, W. Cooper, and H. Sherman. 1985. Data envelopment analysis and regression approaches to efficiency estimation and evaluation. *Annals of Operations Research* 2:113–38.

Box, G., and D. Cox. 1964. An analysis of transformations. *Journal of the Royal Statistical Society* B 26:211–64.

Boyd, J., and K. Mellman. 1980. The effect of fuel economy standards on the U.S. automotive market: a hedonic demand analysis. *Transportation Research* 14:367–8.

Brenkers, R., and F. Verboven. 2005. Market definition with differentiated products: lessons from the car market. CEPR Discussion Paper 5249.

——. 2006. Liberalizing a distribution system: the European car market. *Journal of the European Economic Association* 4(1):216–51.

Breslaw, J., and J. B. Smith. 1995. A simple and efficient method for estimating the magnitude and precision of welfare changes. *Journal of Applied Econometrics* 10:313–27.

Bresnahan, T. F. 1981. Duopoly models with consistent conjectures. *American Economic Review* 71:934–45.

——. 1982. The oligopoly solution concept is identified. *Economics Letters* 10:87–92.

——. 1987. Competition and collusion in the American automobile market: the 1955 price war. *Journal of Industrial Economics* 35:457–82.

——. 1989. Empirical studies of industries with market power. In *Handbook of Industrial Organization* (ed. R. Schmalensee and R. Willig), volume 2, 1st edn, pp. 1011–57. Amsterdam: North-Holland.

Bresnahan, T., and P. Reiss. 1990. Entry in monopoly markets. *Review of Economic Studies* 57:531–53.

——. 1991a. Entry and competition in concentrated markets. *Journal of Political Economy* 99:977–1009.

——. 1991b. Empirical models of discrete games. *Journal of Econometrics* 48(1–2):57–81.

Brock, W., and J. A. Scheinkman. 1985. Price setting supergames with capacity constraints. *Review of Economic Studies* 52:371–82.

Brown, S., and J. Warner. 1985. Using daily stock returns: the case of event studies. *Journal of Financial Economics* 14:3–31.

Bultez, A. V., and P. A. Naert. 1975. Consistent sum-constrained models. *Journal of the American Statistical Association* 70:529–35.

Cameron, A. C., and P. K. Trevedi. 2005. Microeconomics: methods and applications. Cambridge University Press.

Campbell, J., A. Lo, and C. MacKinlay. 1997. *The Econometrics of Financial Markets*. Princeton University Press.

Campos, J., N. Ericsson, and D. Hendry. 2005. General to specific modelling: an overview and selected bibliography. International Finance Discussion Paper 838, Board of Governors of the Federal Reserve System (U.S.).

Capps, C., D. Dranove, S. Greenstein, and M. Sattherthwaite. 2001. The silent majority fallacy of the Elzinga–Hogarty criteria: a critique and new approach to analyzing hospital mergers. NBER Working Paper 8216.

Cardell, N. S. 1997. Variance component structures for the extreme-value and logistic distributions with applications to models of heterogeneity. *Econometric Theory* 13: 185–213.

Cardell, N., and F. Dunbar. 1980. Measuring the societal impacts of automobile downsizing. *Transportation Research* 14:423–34.

Carhart, M. 1997. On persistence in mutual fund performance. *Journal of Finance* 45(5): 57–82.

Carlton, D., and M. Waldman. 2002. The strategic use of tying to preserve and create market power in evolving industries. *RAND Journal of Economics* 33:194–220.

Castanias, R., and H. Johnson. 1993. Gas wars: retail gasoline price fluctuations. *Review of Economics and Statistics* 75:171–74.

Chamberlain, G. 1982. Multivariate regression models for panel data. *Journal of Econometrics* 18:5–46.

——. 1984. Panel data. In *Handbook of Econometrics* (ed. Z. Griliches and M. Intrilligator), volume 2. Amsterdam: North-Holland.

Charnes, A., W. Cooper, and E. Rhodes. 1978. Measuring the efficiency of decision making units. *European Journal of Operations Research* 2:429–44.

Chowdhury, P. 2002. Limit-pricing as Bertrand equilibrium. *Economic Theory* 19:811–22.

Chevalier, J. A., and F. M. Scott Morton. 2008. State casket sales and restrictions: a pointless undertaking? *Journal of Law and Economics* 51:1–23.

Chipty, T. 2001. Vertical integration, market foreclosure, and consumer welfare in the cable television industry. *American Economic Review* 91:428–53.

Chissick, M., and A. Kelman. 2002. *Electronic Commerce: Law and Practice*, 3rd edn. Sweet and Maxwell.

Choi, J. P. 2004. Tying and innovation: a dynamic analysis of tying arrangements. *Economic Journal* 114:83–101.

Christensen, L., and W. Greene. 1976. Economies of scale in U.S. power generation. *Journal of Political Economy* 84:655–76.

Chu, S. H. 1978. On the statistical estimation of parametric frontier production functions: a reply and further comments. *Review of Economics and Statistics* 60:479–81.

Church, J. 2004. The impact of vertical and conglomerate mergers. Mimeo, Directorate General for Competition, European Commission.

——. 2008. Vertical mergers. *Issues in Competition Law and Policy* 2:1455 (ABA Section of Antitrust Law).

Clarke, R., S. Davies, and M. Waterson. 1984. The profitability-concentration relation: market power or efficiency. *Journal of Industrial Economics* 32:435–50.

Coase, R. 1988. *The Firm, the Market and the Law*. University of Chicago Press.

Cobb, C., and P. H. Douglas. 1928. A theory of production. *American Economic Review* 18: 139–65.

Coelli, T., P. Rao, C. O'Donnell, and G. Battesse. 2005. *An Introduction to Efficiency and Productivity Analysis*. Springer.

Comanor, W., and H. Frech. 1985. The competitive effects of vertical agreements. *American Economic Review* 75:1057–62.

Competition Commission. 2000. Nutreco Holding NV and Hydro Seafood GSP Ltd: a report on the proposed merger.

——. 2007. Greif Inc. Blagden Packaging Group—Final report summary. (Available at www.competition-commission.org.uk/inquiries/ref2007/blagden/index.htm.)

Compte, O., F. Jenny, and P. Rey. 2002. Capacity constraints, mergers and collusion. *European Economic Review* 46(1):1–29.

Connor, J. M. 2000. Archer Daniels Midland: price-fixer to the world. Department of Agricultural Economics, Purdue University Staff Paper 00-11.

——. 2001. *Global Price Fixing: Our Customers Are Our Enemy*. Boston, MA: Kluwer Academic Press.

——. 2004. Global cartels redux: the amino acid lysine antitrust litigation. In *The Antitrust Revolution* (ed. J. E. Kwoka Jr. and L. J. White), 4th edn. Oxford University Press.

——. 2005. Collusion and price dispersion. Purdue University, Department Staff Paper 10-14.

——. 2008. Forensic economics: an introduction with special emphasis on price fixing. *Journal of Competition Law and Economics* 4(1):31–59.

Cooper, D., and K.-U. Kühn. 2009. Communication, renegotiation, and the scope for collusion. Mimeo, University of Michigan.

Cooper, W., L. Seiford, and K. Tone. 2007. *Data Envelopment Analysis: A Comprehensive Text with Models, Applications, References and DEA-Solver Software*. Springer.

Corts, K. 1999. Conduct parameters and the measurement of market power. *Journal of Econometrics* 88:227–50.

Cournot, A. 1938. *Recherche sur les Principes Mathématiques de la Théorie des Richesses*. Paris: Gerard Jorlan Ed.

Cowling, K., and M. Waterson. 1976. Price cost margins and market structure. *Economica* 43:267–74.

Crawford, G. 2000. The impact of the 1992 Cable Act on household demand and welfare *RAND Journal of Economics* 31:422–50.

——. 2005. The discriminatory incentives to bundle in the cable television market. *Quantitative Marketing and Economics* 6(1):41–78.

Crooke, P., L. M. Froeb, S. Tschantz, and G. J. Werden. 1999. Effects of the assumed demand system on simulated postmerger equilibrium. *Review of Industrial Organization* 15(3): 205–17.

Dalkir, S., and F. R. Warren-Boulton. 1999. Prices, market definition, and the effects of merger: Staples–Office Depot (1997). In *The Antitrust Revolution* (ed. J. E. Kwoka Jr. and L. J. White), 3rd edn, pp. 143–64. Oxford University Press.

d'Aspremont, C., J. J. Gabszewicz, and J. F. Thisse. 1979. On Hotelling's "stability in competition." *Econometrica* 47:1145–50.

Davidson, C., and R. Deneckere. 1990. Excess capacity and collusion. *International Economic Review* 31(3):521–41.

Davis, P. 2000. Empirical models of demand for differentiated products. *European Economic Review* 44(4-6):993–1005.

——. 2002. Estimating multi-way error components models with unbalanced data structures. *Journal of Econometrics* 106(1):67–95.

——. 2005. The effect of local competition on admission prices in the U.S. motion picture exhibition market. *Journal of Law and Economics* 48:677–707.

——. 2006a. Spatial competition in retail markets: movie theaters. *RAND Journal of Economics* 37: 964–82.

——. 2006b. The discrete choice analytically flexible (DCAF) model of demand for differentiated products. CEPR Discussion Paper 5880.

——. 2006c. Estimation of quantity games in the presence of indivisibilities and heterogeneous firms. *Journal of Econometrics* 134(1):187–214.

——. 2006d. Identification of the oligopoly solution concept in a differentiated product industry: necessary and sufficient conditions. Mimeo, London School of Economics.

——. 2006e. Measuring market expansion and business stealing effects of entry in the U.S. motion picture exhibition market. *Journal of Industrial Economics* 54:293–321.

——. 2006f. Coordinated effects merger simulation with linear demands. Mimeo, U.K. Competition Commission.

Davis, P., and C. Huse. 2009. Coordinated effects merger simulation in the network server market. Mimeo, U.K. Competition Commission.

Davis, P., and P. Sabbatini. 2009. Coordinated effects merger simulation. Mimeo.

Deaton, A., and J. Muellbauer. 1980a. An almost ideal demand system. *American Economic Review* 70:312–26.

——. 1980b. *Economics and Consumer Behaviour*. Cambridge University Press.

Debreu, G. 1974. Excess demand functions. *Journal of Mathematical Economics* 1(1):15–21.

Demsetz, H. 1973. Industry structure, market rivalry, and public policy. *Journal of Law and Economics* 16:1–9.

Deneckere, R., and C. Davidson. 1986. Long-run competition in capacity, short-run competition in price and the Cournot model. *RAND Journal of Economics* 16:404–15.

Deprins, D., and H. Tulkens. 1984. Measuring labor inefficiency in post offices. In *The Performance of Public Enterprises: Concepts and Measurements* (ed. M. Marchand, P. Pestieau, and H. Tulkens). Amsterdam: North-Holland.

Dickey, D., and W. Fuller. 1979. Distribution of the estimators for auto-regressive time series with a unit root. *Journal of the American Statistical Association* 74:427–31.

Diewert, E. 1976. Exact and superlative index numbers. *Journal of Econometrics* 46:115–45.

Dobson, P., and M. Waterson. 1996. Vertical restraints and competition policy. U.K. Office of Fair Trading, Research Paper 12.

Domowitz, I., G. Hubbard, and B. Petersen. 1988. Market structure and cyclical fluctuations in U.S. manufacturing. *Review of Economics and Statistics* 70:55–66.

Dorfman, R., and P. Steiner. 1954. Optimal advertising and optimal quality. *American Economic Review* 44:826–36.

Doyle, J., E. Muehlegger, and K. Samphantharak. 2008. Edgeworth cycles revisited. NBER Working Paper 14162.

Dubin, J., and D. McFadden. 1984. An econometric analysis of residential electric appliance holdings and consumption. *Econometrica* 52:345–62.

Dubois, P., and C. Bonnet. 2008. Inference on vertical contracts between manufacturers and retailers allowing for non-linear pricing and resale price maintenance. IDEI Working Paper 519.

Dunne, T., M. Roberts, and L. Samuelson. 1988. Patterns of firm entry and exit in U.S. manufacturing industries. *RAND Journal of Economics* 19:495–515.

Duso, T., K. Gugler, and B. Yurtoglu. 2006a. Is the event study methodology useful for merger analysis? A comparison of stock market and accounting data. Mimeo, Wissenschaftzentrum Berlin für Sozialforschung SP-II 2006-19.

Duso, T., D. Neven, and L. H. Röller. 2006b. The political economy of European merger control. *Journal of Law and Economics* 50:455–89.

Eccles, R. H. 1981. The quasi-firm in the construction industry. *Journal of Economic Behaviour and Organization* 2:335–58.

Eckbo, B. E. 1983. Horizontal mergers, collusion, and stockholder wealth. *Journal of Financial Economics* 11:241–73.

Efron, B., and R. Tibshirani. 1994. *An Introduction to the Bootstrap*. Chapman & Hall.

Eichenwald, K. 1997. The tale of the secret tapes. *New York Times*, November 16, 1997.

——. 1998. Videotapes take star role at Archer Daniels trial. *New York Times*, August 4, 1998.

Elzinger, K., and T. Hogarty. 1973. The problem of geographic market delineation in antimerger suits. *Antitrust Bulletin* 18:45–81.

——. 1978. The problem of geographic market delineation revisited: the case of coal. *Antitrust Bulletin* 23:1–18.

Engle, R., and C. Granger. 1987. Co-integration and error correction: representation, estimation and testing. *Econometrica* 55:251–71.

Ericson, R., and A. Pakes. 1995. Markov-perfect industry dynamics: a framework for empirical work. *Review of Economic Studies* 62:53–82.

Evans, D. S., and J. Heckman. 1984a. A test for subadditivity of the cost function with an application to the Bell system. *American Economic Review* 74:615–23.

——. 1984b. Multiproduct cost function estimates and natural monopoly test for the Bell system. In *Breaking Up Bell* (ed. D. S. Evans). Amsterdam: North-Holland.

——. 1986. A test for subadditivity of the cost function with an application to the Bell system: erratum. *American Economic Review* 76:856–58.

Fama, E., and K. French. 1993. Common risk factors in the returns on stocks and bonds. *Journal of Financial Economics* 33:3–56.

——. 1996. Multifactor explanations of asset pricing anomalies. *Journal of Finance* 51(1): 55–84.

Fare, R., S. Grosskopf, and C. Lovell. 1995. *Production Frontiers*. Cambridge University Press.

Farrell, J. 1957. The measurement of productive efficiency. *Journal of the Royal Statistical Society* 120(3):253–90.

Farrell, J., and C. Shapiro. 1990. Horizontal mergers: an equilibrium analysis. *American Economic Review* 80:107–26.

Finkelstein, M., and H. Levenbach. 1983. Regression estimates of damages in price fixing cases. *Law and Contemporary Problems* 46(4):145–69.

Fisher, F. 1980. Multiple regression in legal proceedings. *Columbia Law Review* 80(4):702–36.

——. 1986. Statistics, econometrics and adversary proceedings. *Journal of the American Statistical Association* 81:277–86.

Fisher, F., and J. McGowan. 1983. On the misuse of accounting rates of return to infer monopoly profits. *American Economic Review* 73:82–97.

Fisher, R. A. 1925. Applications of Student's distribution. *Metron* 5:90–104.

Fisher-Box, J. 1981. Gosset, Fisher and the *t*-distribution. *The American Statistician* 35(2).

Foster, L., J. Haltiwanger, and C. Syverson. 2008. Reallocation, firm turnover, and efficiency: selection on productivity or profitability? *American Economic Review* 98:394–425.

Friedman, J. 1971. A non-cooperative equlibrium for supergames. *Review of Economic Studies* 38:1–12.

Frisch, R. 1936. Annual survey of general economic theory: the problem of index numbers. *Econometrica* 4:1–38.

Froeb, L. M., and G. J. Werden. 1991. Residual demand estimation for market delineation: complications and limitations. *Review of Industrial Organization* 6:33–48.

——. 1992. The reverse cellophane fallacy in market delineation. *Review of Industrial Organization* 7:241–47.

FTC and DOJ. 2004. Improving health care: a dose of competition. Report by the Department of Justice and Federal Trade Commission.

Gal-Or, E. 1991. Vertical restraints with incomplete information. *Journal of Industrial Economics* 39:503–16.

Gandhi, A. K., L. M. Froeb, S. T. Tschantz, and G. J. Werden. 2005. Post-merger product repositioning. Vanderbilt University Law and Economics Working Paper 05-19

Garcés, E., D. Neven, and P. Seabright. 2009. The ups and downs of the doctrine of collective dominance: using game theory for merger policy. In *Cases in European Competition Policy: The Economic Analysis*. Cambridge University Press.

Gasmi, F., J. J. Laffont, and W. W. Sharkey. 2002. The natural monopoly test reconsidered: an engineering process-based approach to empirical analysis in telecommunications. *International Journal of Industrial Organization* 20(4):435–59.

Geary, R. 1949. Determination of linear relations between systematic parts of variables with errors of observation the variances of which are unknown. *Econometrica* 17:30–58.

Genakos, C., K.-U. Kühn, and J. van Reenen. 2006. The incentives of a monopolist to degrade interoperability: theory and evidence from PCs and servers. Mimeo, London School of Economics.

Genovese, D., and W. Mullin. 1998. Testing static oligopoly models: conduct and cost in the sugar industry 1890–1914. *RAND Journal of Economics* 29:355–77.

Geroski, P. 2005. Profitabilty analysis and competition policy. In *Essays in Competition Policy* (ed. P. Geroski). London: Competition Commission. (Available at www.competition-commission.org.uk/our_peop/members/chair_speeches/pdf/geroski_oxera_080205.pdf.)

Geroski, P., and R. Griffith. 2003. Identifying antitrust markets. IFS Working Paper 03/01.

Gil, R., and W. Hartmann. 2007. Why does popcorn cost so much at the movies? An empirical analysis of metering price discrimination. Mimeo, Stanford University.

Godfrey, L. G. 1989. *Misspecification Tests in Econometrics: The Lagrange Multiplier Principle and Other Approaches.* Cambridge University Press.

Goldfine, D., and K. M. Vorrasi. 2004. The fall of the Kodak aftermarket doctrine: dying a slow death in the lower courts. *Antitrust Law Journal* 1:209–31.

Gorman, T. 1956. The demand for related goods: a possible procedure for analyzing quality differentials in the egg market. Journal Paper 2319, Iowa Experimental Station. Printed belatedly in *Review of Economic Studies* (1980) 47:843–56.

Gorman, W. M. 1959. Separable utility and aggregation. *Econometrica* 27:469–81.

——. 1995. *Separability and Aggregation: Collected Works of W. M. Gorman* (ed. C. Blackorby and A. Shorrocks). Oxford: Clarendon Press.

Gowrisankaran, G. 1999. A dynamic model of endogenous horizontal mergers. *RAND Journal of Economics* 30:56–83.

Granger, C. W. J., and P. Newbold. 1974. Spurious regression in econometrics. *Journal of Econometrics* 2:111–20.

Green, E., and R. Porter. 1984. Non-cooperative collusion under imperfect price information. *Econometrica* 52:87–100.

Greene, W. H. 1997. Frontier production functions. In *Handbook of Applied Econometrics*, volume II. *Microeconomics* (ed. M. Pesaran and P. Schmidt). Oxford: Blackwell.

——. 2000. *Econometric Analysis*, 4th edn. Pearson Education.

——. 2007. *Econometric Analysis*, 6th edn. Pearson Education.

Greenslade, J., and S. G. Hall. 2002. On the identification of cointegrated systems in small samples: a modelling strategy with an application to UK wages and prices. *Journal of Economic Dynamics and Control* 26(9/10):1517–37.

Grilliches, Z. 1957. Hybrid corn: an exploration in the economics of technological change. *Econometrica* 25:501–22.

Grossman, P. (ed.). 2004. *How Cartels Endure and How They Fail: Studies in Industrial Collusion*. Cheltenham: Edward Elgar.

Grossman, S., and O. Hart. 1986. The costs and benefits of ownership: a theory of vertical and lateral integration. *Journal of Political Economy* 94:691–719.

Hall, R., and V. Lazear. 1994. Reference guide on estimation of economic losses in damages awards. In *Reference Manual on Scientific Evidence*. Washington, DC: Federal Judicial Center.

Hall, S. G., and M. J. Stephenson. 1990. An algorithm for the solution of stochastic optimal control problems for large nonlinear econometric models. *Journal of Applied Econometrics* 5(4):393–99.

Haltiwanger, J., and J. E. Harrington Jr. 1991. The impact of cyclical demand movements on collusive behavior. *RAND Journal of Economics* 22:89–106.

Hansen, L. 1982. Large sample properties of generalised method of moment estimators. *Econometrica* 50:1029–54.

Harberger, A. 1954. Monopoly and resource allocation. *American Economic Review* 44: 77–87.

Harrington, J. 2003. Cartel pricing dynamics in the presence of an antitrust authority. Johns Hopkins Department of Economics Working Paper 487.

——. 2008. Detecting cartels. In *Handbook in Antitrust Economics* (ed. P. Buccirossi). Cambridge, MA: MIT Press.

Harris, B. C., and J. J. Simons. 1989. Focusing market definition: how much substitution is necessary? *Research in Law and Economics* 12:207–26.

Hart, O. 1995. *Firms, Contracts and Financial Structure*. Oxford: Clarendon Press.

Hart, O., and J. Moore. 1990. Incomplete contracts and renegotiation. *Econometrica* 56: 755–85.

Hart, O., and J. Tirole. 1990. Vertical integration and market foreclosure. Brookings Papers on Economic Activity: Microeconomics, pp. 205–76.

Hastings, J. 2004. Vertical relationships and competition in the retail gasoline markets: an empirical evidence from contract changes in Southern California. *American Economic Review* 94:317–28.

Hausman, J. A. 1978. Specification tests in econometrics. *Econometrica* 46:1251–71.

——. 1981. Exact consumer's surplus and deadweight loss. *American Economic Review* 71: 662–76.

Hausman, J. A., and D. McFadden. 1984. Specification tests for the multinomial logit model. *Econometrica* 52:1219–40.

Hausman, J. A., and W. Newey. 1995. Non-parametric estimation of exact consumers surplus and deadweight loss. *Econometrica* 63:1445–76.

Hausman, J. A., G. Leonard, and J. Zona. 1994. Competitive analysis with differentiated products. *Annales d'Economie et de Statistique* 34:159–80.

Heckman, J., and E. Vytlacil. 2005. Structural equations, treatment effects, and econometric policy evaluation. *Econometrica* 73:669–738.

Hendel, I. 1999. Estimating multiple-discrete choice models: an application to computerization returns. *Review of Economic Studies* 66:423–46.

Hendel, I., and A. Nevo. 2004. Intertemporal substitution and storeable products. *Journal of the European Economic Association* 2(2/3):536–47.

——. 2006a. Measuring the implications of sales and consumer inventory behaviour. *Econometrica* 74:1637–73.

——. 2006b. Sales and consumer inventory. *RAND Journal of Economics* 37:543–61.

Hendry, D. F. 1995. *Dynamic Econometrics*. Oxford University Press.

Hicks, J. R. 1956. *A Revision of Demand Theory*. Oxford University Press.

Hosken, D., D. O'Brien, D. Scheffman, and M. Vita. 2002. Demand system estimation and its application to horizontal merger analysis. FTC Working Paper 246.

Hotelling, H. 1929. Stability in competition. *Economic Journal* 39:41–57.

——. 1938. The general welfare in relation to problems of taxation and of railway and utility rates. *Econometrica* 6:242–69.

Hsiao, C. 1986. *Analysis of Panel Data*, Econometric Society Monograph no. 11. Cambridge University Press.

——. 2003. *Analysis of Panel Data*. Econometric Society Monograph no. 11, 2nd edn. Cambridge University Press.

Huber, P. J. 1967. The behavior of maximum likelihood estimates under non-standard conditions. In *Proceedings of the Fifth Berkeley Symposium on Mathematical Statistics and Probability* (ed. L. M. LeCam and J. Neyman), volume 4, pp. 221–33. Berkeley, CA: University of California Press.

Hurwicz, L., and H. Uzawa. 1971. On the integrability of demand functions. In *Preferences, Utility and Demand* (ed. J. Chipman, L. Hurwicz, M. Richter, and H. Sonnenschein). New York: Harcourt.

Imbens, G., and J. Angrist. 1994. Identification and estimation of local average treatment effects. *Econometrica* 62:467–75.

Ippolito, P., and T. Overstreet. 1996. Resale price maintenance: an economic assessment of the Federal Trade Commission's case against the Corning glass works. *Journal of Law and Economics* 39:285–328.

Irvine, I., and W. Sims. 1998. Measuring consumer surplus with unknown Hicksian demands. *American Economic Review* 88:314–22.

Ivaldi, M., and S. Lorincz. 2005. A full equilibrium relevant market test: application to computer servers. CEPR Discussion Paper 4917.

——. 2009. Implementing relevant market tests in antitrust policy: application to computer servers. Mimeo.

Ivaldi, M., and F. Verboven. 2005. Quantifying the effects from horizontal mergers in European competition policy. *International Journal of Industrial Organization* 23:669–91.

Ivaldi, M., B. Jullien, P. Rey, P. Seabright, and J. Tirole. 2003. The economics of horizontal mergers: unilateral and coordinated effects. Report for DG Competition, European Commission.

Jensen, J. B., S. Redding, and P. Schott. 2007. Firms in international trade. *Journal of Economic Perspectives* 21(3):105–30.

Johansen, S. 1995. *Likelihood-Inference in Cointegrated Vector Auto-Regressive Models*. Oxford University Press.

Johnston, J., and J. Dinardo. 1997. *Econometric Methods*, 4th edn. McGraw-Hill.

Joskow, P. 1985. Vertical integration and long-term contracts. *Journal of Law, Economics, & Organization*1:33–88.

Joskow, P., and E. Kahn. 2001. A quantitative analysis of pricing behavior in California's wholesale electricity market during summer 2000. *Power Engineering Society Summer Meeting: IEEE* 1:392–94.

Jullien, B., and P. Rey. 2008. Resale price maintenance and collusion. *RAND Journal of Economics* 38:983–1001.

Just, R., and W. Chern. 1980. Tomatoes, technology and oligopsony. *Bell Journal of Economics and Management Science* 11:584–602.

Kalai, E., and W. Stanford. 1985. Conjectural variations strategies in accelerated Cournot games. *International Journal of Industrial Organization* 3:133–52.

Katz, M., and C. Shapiro. 2003. Critical loss: let's tell the whole story. *Antitrust Magazine*, Spring.

Kehoe, T. 1985. Multiplicity of equilibria and comparative statics. *Quarterly Journal of Economics* 100(1):119–47.

Kim, D. 2005. Measuring market power in a dynamic oligopoly model: an empirical analysis. Mimeo, International University of Japan.

Kim, D., and C. Knittel. 2006. Biases in static oligopoly models? Evidence from the California electricity market. *Journal of Industrial Economics* 54(4):451–70.

Klein, B. 1988. Vertical integration as organizational ownership: the Fisher Body–General Motors relationship revisited. *Journal of Law, Economics, & Organization* 4:199–213.

Klein, B., R. Crawford, and A. Alchian. 1978. Vertical integration, appropriatable rents, and the competitive contracting process. *Journal of Law and Economics* 21:297–326.

Klepper, S. 1996. Entry, exit, growth, and innovation over the product life cycle. *American Economic Review* 86:562–83.

Klepper, S., and K. Simons. 2000. The making of an oligopoly: firm survival and technological change in the evolution of the U.S. tire industry. *Journal of Political Economy* 108:728–60.

Kloek, T. 1981. OLS estimation in a model where a microvariable is explained by aggregates and contemporaneous disturbances are equicorrelated. *Econometrica* 49:205–7.

Kokkoris, I. 2007. A practical application of event studies in merger assessment: successes and failures. *European Competition Journal* 3(1):65–99.

Konüs, A. 1939. The problem of the true index of the cost of living. *Econometrica* 7:10–29.

Kovacic, W., R. Marshall, L. Marx, and S. Schulenberg. 2007. Coordinated effects in merger review: quantifying the payoffs from collusion. In *International Antitrust Law and Policy: Fordham Competition Law 2006* (ed. B. Hawk). New York: Juris.

Kreps, D., and J. Scheinkman. 1983. Quantity precommitment and Bertrand competition yield Cournot outcomes. *Bell Journal of Economics* 14:326–37.

Krueger, A., and Angrist, J. 2001. Instrumental variables and the search for identification: from supply and demand to natural experiments. *Journal of Economic Perspectives* 15(4): 69–86.

Kühn, K.-U. 2001. Fighting collusion by regulating communication between firms. *Economic Policy* 16:169–204.

——. 2004. The coordinated effects of mergers in differentiated product markets. CEPR Discussion Paper 4769.

Kumar, S., and R. Russell. 2002. Technological change, technological catch-up and capital deepening: relative contributions to growth and convergence. *American Economic Review* 92:527–48.

Kumbhakar, S., and C. Knox-Lovell. 2000. *Stochastic Frontier Analysis*. Cambridge University Press.

Lafontaine F., and M. Slade. 2005. Exclusive contracts and vertical restraints: empirical evidence and public policy. (Forthcoming in *Handbook of Antitrust Economics* (ed. P. Buccirossi). Cambridge, MA: MIT Press.)

Lancaster, K. 1966. A new approach to consumer theory. *Journal of Political Economy* 74: 132–57.

Landes, W., and R. Posner. 1981. Market power in antitrust cases. *Harvard Law Review* 94: 937–96.

Lau, L. J. 1982. On identifying the degree of competitiveness from industry price and output data. *Economics Letters* 10:93–99.

Leibenstein, H. 1950. Bandwagon, snob, and Veblen effects in the theory of consumers' demand. *Quarterly Journal of Economics* 64(2):183–207.

——. 1966. Allocative efficiency vs. X-efficiency. *American Economic Review* 56:392–415.

Levenstein, M., and V. Suslow. 2006. What determines cartel success? *Journal of Economic Literature* 44(1):43–95.

Levinsohn, J., and A. Petrin. 2003. Estimating production functions using inputs to control for unobservables. *Review of Economic Studies* 70:317–41.

Lewbel, A. 1989. Exact aggregation and a representative consumer. *Quarterly Journal of Economics* 104:621–33.

——. 2003. A rational rank four demand system. *Journal of Applied Econometrics* 18(2): 127–35.

Lind, J. 1753. Treatise on the scurvy. In *Lind's Treatise on the Scurvy* (ed. C. P. Stewart and D. Guthrie). Edinburgh University Press (1953).

Lintner, J. 1965. The valuation of risk assets and the selection of risky investments in stock portfolios and capital budgets. *Review of Economics and Statistics* 47:13–37.

MacKinlay, C. 1997. Event studies in economics and finance. *Journal of Economic Literature* 35:13–39.

Maddala, G. S. 1983. *Limited Dependent and Qualitative Variables in Econometrics*. Cambridge University Press.

——. 1989. *Introduction to Econometrics*. New York: Macmillan.

Makowski, L. 1987. Are "rational conjectures" rational? *Journal of Industrial Economics* 36: 35–47.

Manning, A. 2005. *Monopsony in Motion: Imperfect Competition in Labor Markets*. Princeton University Press.

Manski, C., and D. McFadden. 1981. *Structural Analysis of Discrete Data and Econometric Applications*. Cambridge, MA: MIT Press.

Mantel, R. 1974. On the characterization of aggregate excess demand. *Journal of Economic Theory* 7:348–53.

Markides, C., and P. Geroski. 2005. *Fast Second*. San Francisco, CA: Jossey-Bass.

McGahan, A. 2004. *How Industries Evolve: Principles for Achieving and Sustaining Superior Performance*. Cambridge, MA: HBS Press.

Marshall, A. 1890. *Principles of Economics*. Macmillan.

Martin, S. 1984. The misuse of accounting rates of return: comment. *American Economic Review* 74:501–6.

Martin, S., H. T. Normann, and C. M. Snyder. 2001. Vertical foreclosure in experimental markets. *RAND Journal of Economics* 32:466–96.

Mas-Colell, A., M. D. Whinston, and J. R Green. 1995. *Microeconomic Theory*. Oxford University Press.

Maskin, E., and J. Tirole. 1988a. A theory of dynamic oligopoly. I. Overview and quantity competition with fixed costs. *Econometrica* 56:549–69.

——. 1988b. A theory of dynamic oligopoly. II. Price competition, kinked demand curves, and Edgeworth cycles. *Econometrica* 56:571–99.

Mathewson, G. F., and R. A. Winter. 1987. The competitive effects of vertical agreements: comment. *American Economic Review* 77:1057–62.

Matzkin, R. 2008. Identification in nonparametric simultaneous equations. *Econometrica* 76: 945–78.

Mazzeo, M. 2002. Product choice and oligopoly market structure. *RAND Journal of Economics* 33:221–42.

McAfee, R. and M. Williams. 1988. Can event studies detect anticompetitive mergers? *Economics Letters* 28:199–203.

McDowell, E. 1992. American Airlines cuts some fares in half. *New York Times*, May 28, 1992.

McFadden, D. 1973. Conditional logit analysis of qualitative choice behavior. In *Frontiers in Econometrics* (ed. P. Zarembka). Academic Press.

——. 1978. Modeling the choice of residential location. In *Spatial Interaction Theory and Applications* (ed. A. Karlgvist et al.). Amsterdam: North-Holland.

——. 1981. Econometric models of probabilistic choice. In *Structural Analysis of Discrete Data and Econometric Applications* (ed. C. Manski and D. McFadden). Cambridge, MA: MIT Press.

——. 1989. A method of simulated moments for estimation of discrete response models without numerical integration. *Econometrica* 57:995–1026.

Mercenier, J. 1995. Non-uniqueness in applied general equilibrium models with scale economies and imperfect competition. *Economic Theory* 6(1):161–77.

Meyer, B. 1995. Natural and quasi-experiments in economics. *Journal of Business & Economic Statistics* 13(2):151–61.

Milgrom, P., and J. Roberts. 1990. Rationalizability, learning, and equilibrium in games with strategic complementarities. *Econometrica* 58:1255–77.

Milyo, J., and J. Waldfogel. 1999. The effect of advertising on prices: evidence in the wake of 44 Liquormart. *American Economic Review* 89:1081–96.

Modigliani, F., and M. Miller. 1958. The cost of capital, corporation finance and the theory of investment. *American Economic Review* 48:261–97.

Moulton, B. 1986. Random group effects and the precision of regression estimates. *Journal of Econometrics* 32:385–97.

——. 1990. An illustration of a pitfall in estimating the effects of aggregate variables on micro units. *Review of Economics and Statistics* 72:334–38.

Mundlak, Y. 1978. On the pooling of time series and cross section data. *Econometrica* 46: 69–85.

Nakamura, A., and M. Nakamura. 1981. On the relationships among several specification error tests presented by Durbin, Wu and Hausman (with A. Nakamura). *Econometrica* 49:1583–88.

Nakanishi, M., and L. G. Cooper. 1974. Parameter estimate for multiplicative interactive choice model: least squares approach. *Journal of Marketing Research* 11:303–11.

Nalebuff, B. J. 1999. Bundling. Yale ICF Working Paper 99-14.

Nerlove, M. 1963. Returns to scale in electricity supply. In *Measurement in Economics* (ed. C. Christ). Stanford University Press.

——. 2002. *Essays in Panel Data Econometrics*. Cambridge University Press.

Nevo, A. 1998. Identification of the oligopoly solution concept in a differentiated product industry. *Economics Letters* 59(3):391–95.

——. 2000. A practitioner's guide to estimation of random coefficients logit models of demand. *Journal of Economics & Management Strategy* 9(4):513–48.

Newey, W., and J. Powell. 2003. Instrumental variable estimation of non-parametric models. *Econometrica* 71:1565–78.

Nickell, S. 1996. Competition and corporate performance. *Journal of Political Economy* 104: 724–46.

Nocke, V., and M. Whinston. 2007. Sequential merger review. CEPR Working Paper 6652.

Noel, M. 2007. Edgeworth price cycles: evidence from the Toronto retail gasoline market. *Journal of Industrial Economics* 55:69–92.

Norman, H. T. 2007. Vertical mergers, foreclosure and raising rivals' costs—experimental evidence. Mimeo, Max Planck Institute, Goethe University Frankfurt.

Novshek, W. 1985. On the existence of Cournot equilibrium. *Review of Economic Studies* 52:85–98.

O'Brian, B. 1992. AMR's bid for simpler fares takes off. *Wall Street Journal Online*, April 10, 1992.

O'Brien, D., and A. Wickelgren. 2003. A critical analysis of critical loss analysis. FTC Working Paper 254.

Ofcom. 2007. Wholesale call termination statement, March 2007. Available at www.ofcom.org.uk/consult/condocs/mobile_call_term/statement/statement.pdf.

Office of Fair Trading. 2003. Assessing profitability in competition policy analysis. OFT Working Paper 657 (prepared by Oxera). (Available at www.oft.gov.uk/shared_oft/reports/comp_policy/oft657.pdf.)

Oi, W. 1971. A Disneyland dilemma: two-part tariffs for a Mickey Mouse monopoly. *Quarterly Journal of Economics* 85:77–96.

Olley, S. G., and A. Pakes. 1996. The dynamics of productivity in the telecommunications equipment industry. *Econometrica* 64:1263–97.

Ordover, J., G. Saloner, and S. C. Salop. 1990. Equilibrium vertical foreclosure. *American Economic Review* 80:127–42.

——. 1992. Equilibrium vertical foreclosure: reply. *American Economic Review* 82:693–704.

Pakes, A. 2003. A reconsideration of hedonic price indexes with an application to PCs. *American Economic Review* 93:1578–96.

Pakes, A., and P. Maguire. 1994. Computing Markov–perfect Nash equilibria: numerical implications of a dynamic differentiated product model. *RAND Journal of Economics* 25: 555–89.

——. 2001. Stochastic algorithms, symmetric Markov perfect equilibrium, and the curse of dimensionality. *Econometrica* 69:1261–81.

Pakes, A., and D. Pollard. 1989. Simulation and the asymptotics of optimization estimators. *Econometrica* 57:1027–57.

Panzar, J. C., and R. D. Willig. 1981. Economies of scope. *American Economic Review* 71: 268–72.

Pedraja-Chaparro, F., J. Salinas-Jimenez, and P. Smith. 1999. On the quality of data envelopment analysis. *Journal of the Operational Research Society* 50:636–44.

Pelzman, S. 1977. The gains and losses from industrial concentration. *Journal of Law and Economics* 20:229–63.

Perloff, J., and E. Shen. 2001. Collinearity in linear structural models of market power. Mimeo, University of Berkeley.

Pesendorfer, M. 2000. A study of collusion in first price auctions. *Review of Economic Studies* 67:381–411.

Pollak, R. and T. J. Wales. 1992. *Demand System Specification and Estimation.* Oxford University Press.

Porter, M. 1980. *General Electric vs Westinghouse* in large turbine generators. HBS Case 9-380-128.

Porter, R. H. 1983. A study of cartel stability: the joint executive committee, 1880–1886. *Bell Journal of Economics* 14:301–14.

——. 2005. Detecting collusion. *Review of Industrial Organization* 26(2):147–67.

Porter, R. H., and J. D. Zona. 1993. Detection of bid rigging in procurement auctions. *Journal of Political Economy* 101:518–38.

——. 1999. Ohio school milk markets: an analysis of bidding. *RAND Journal of Economics* 30:263–88.

Post, T., L. Cherchye, and T. Kuosmanen. 2002. Non-parametric efficiency estimation in stochastic environments. *Operations Research* 50:645–55.

Press, W., S. Teukolsky, W. Vetterling, and B. Flannery. 2007. *Numerical Recipes: the Art of Scientific Computing*, 3rd edn. Cambridge University Press.

Pudney, S. 1989. *Modelling Individual Choice: the Econometrics of Corners, Kinks and Holes.* Oxford: Blackwell.

Puller, S. 2006. Estimation of competitive conduct when firms are efficiently colluding: addressing the Corts critique. Mimeo, Texas A&M University.

Ramsey, F. 1927. A contribution to the theory of taxation. *Economic Journal* 37:47–61.

Ramsey, J. B. 1969. Tests for specification errors in classical linear least squares regression analysis. *Journal of the Royal Statistical Society* B 32:350–71.

Rasmusen, E., M. Ramseyer, and J. Wiley. 1991. Naked exclusion. *American Economic Review* 81:1137–45.

Ravenscraft, D. 1983. Structure-profit relationships at the line of business and industry level. *Review of Economics and Statistics* 65:22–31.

Reiersol, O. 1945. Confluence analysis by means of sets of instrumental variables. *Arkiv fur Matematik, Astronomi Och Fysik* 32(4):1–119.

——. 1950. Identifiability of a linear relation between variables which are subject to error. *Econometrica* 18:375–89.

Rey, P. 2003. The economics of vertical restraints. In *Handbook of Industrial Organization* (ed. M. Armstrong and R. Porter), volume 3. Amsterdam: North-Holland.

Rey, P., and J. Stiglitz. 1995. The role of exclusive territories in producers' competition. *RAND Journal of Economics* 26:431–51.

Rey, P., and J. Tirole. 2005. A primer on foreclosure. *Handbook of Industrial Organization* (ed. M. Armstrong and R. Porter), volume 3. Amsterdam: North-Holland.

Riordan, M. 1988. Anticompetitive vertical integration by a dominant firm. *American Economic Review* 88:1232–48.

Riordan, M., and O. Williamson. 1985. Asset specificity and economic organization. *International Journal of Industrial Organization* 3:365–78.

Röller, L.-H. 1990a. Proper quadratic cost functions with an application to the Bell System. *Review of Economics and Statistics* 72:202–10.

Röller, L.-H. 1990b. Modelling cost structure: the Bell system revisited. *Applied Economics* 22:1661–74.

Rotemberg, J., and G. Saloner. 1986. A supergame-theoretic model of business cycles and price wars during booms. *American Economic Review* 76:380–407.

Ryan, D., and T. Wales. 1999. Flexible and semiflexible consumer demands with quadratic Engel curves. *Review of Economics and Statistics* 81:277–87.

Sabbatini, P. 2006. How to simulate the coordinated effect of a merger. Collana Temi e Problemi, Autorità Garante della Concorrenza e del Mercato.

Salant, S., S. Switzer, and R. Reynolds. 1983. Losses from horizontal merger the effects of an exogenous change in indstry structure on Cournot–Nash equilibrium *Quarterly Journal of Economics* 98:185–99.

Salinger, M. 1988. Vertical mergers and market foreclosure. *Quarterly Journal of Economics* 103:345–56.

——. 1989. The meaning of "upstream" and "downstream" and the implications for modeling vertical mergers. *Journal of Industrial Economics* 37:373–87.

Salop, S. C. 1979. Monopolistic competition with outside goods. *Bell Journal of Economics* 10(1):141–56.

Salop, S. C., and Scheffman, D. 1983. Rising rivals costs. *American Economic Review* 73: 267–71.

Salvanes, K. G., and S. Tjøtta. 1998. A note on the importance of testing for regularities for estimated flexible functional forms. Department of Economics, University of Bergen Working Paper 177. (Available at http://ideas.repec.org/s/fth/bereco.html.)

Salvo, A. 2007. Inferring conduct under the threat of entry: the case of the Brazilian cement industry. Mimeo, Northwestern University, Kellogg School of Management. (Available at www.kellogg.northwestern.edu/faculty/salvo/htm/research.htm.)

Sargen, J. 1958. The estimation of economic relationships using instrumental variables. *Econometrica* 26:393–415.

Scarf, H. 1973. *The Computation of Economic Equilibria*. New Haven, CT: Yale University Press.

Schaumans, C., and F. Verboven. 2008. Entry and regulation: evidence from health care professions. *RAND Journal of Economics* 39:949–72.

Scheffman, D., and M. Coleman. 2003. Quantitative analyses of potential competitive effects of a merger. *George Mason Law Review* 12(2):319–69.

Scheffman, D., and P. Spiller. 1987. Geographic market definition under the U.S. Department of Justice merger guidelines. *Journal of Law and Economics* 30:123–47.

——. 1996. Econometric market delineation. *Managerial and Decision Economics* 17:165–78.

Scherer, F. M. 1980. *Industrial Market Structure and Economic Performance*. Chicago, IL: Rand McNally.

Scherer, F. M., A. Beckenstein, E. Kaufer, and R. D. Murphy. 1975. *The Economics of Multiplant Operations*. Cambridge, MA: Harvard University Press.

Schmalensee, R., and R. Willig (eds). 1989. *Handbook of Industrial Organization*, 1st edn, volume 2. Elsevier.

Schmidt, P. 1976. On the statistical estimation of parametric frontier production functions. *Review of Economics and Statistics* 58:238–39.

——. 1978. On the statistical estimation of parametric frontier production functions: rejoinder. *Review of Economics and Statistics* 60:481–82.

Schwartz, M. 1987. The competitive effects of vertical agreements: comment. *American Economic Review* 77:1063–68.

Segal, I., and M. Whinston. 2000. Exclusive contracts and protection of investment. *RAND Journal of Economics* 31:603–33.

Seim, K. 2006. An empirical model of entry with endogenous product-type choices. *RAND Journal of Economics* 37:619–40.

Shapiro, C., and W. Kovacic. 2000. Antitrust policy: a century of economic and legal thinking. *Journal of Economic Perspectives* 14(1):43–60.

Sharpe, W. 1964. Capital asset prices: a theory of market equilibrium under conditions of risk. *Journal of Finance* 19:425–42.

Sherman, H. 1984. Data envelopment analysis as a new managerial audit methodology: test and evaluation. *Auditing: A Journal of Practice and Theory* 4:35–53.

Sherwin, R. 1993. Comments on Werden and Froeb: correlation, causality and all that jazz. *Review of Industrial Organization* 8:355–58.

Shin, R. T., and J. S. Ying. 1992. Unnatural monopolies in local telephone. *RAND Journal of Economics* 23:171–83.

Shum, M., and G. Crawford. 2007. Monopoly quality degradation in cable television. *Journal of Law and Economics* 50:181–209.

Silverman, B. 1989. *Density Estimation for Statistics and Data Analysis*. London: Chapman & Hall.

Simar, L., and P. Wilson. 1998. Sensitivity analysis of efficiency scores: how to bootstrap in nonparametric frontier models. *Management Science* 44(1):49–61.

Simpson, J., and A. Wickelgren. 2007. Naked exclusion, efficient breach, and downstream competition. *American Economic Review* 97:1305–20.

Slade, M., J. Pinkse, and C. Brett. 2002. Spatial price competition: a semiparametric approach. *Econometrica* 70:1111–53.

Small, K., C. Winston, and J. Yan. 2005. Uncovering the distribution of motorists' preferences for travel time and reliability. *Econometrica* 73:1367–82.

Sonnenschein, H. 1973. Do Walras' identity and continuity characterize the class of community excess demand functions? *Journal of Economic Theory* 6:345–54.

Spengler, J. 1950. Vertical integration and antitrust policy. *Journal of Political Economy* 58: 347–52.

Sraffa, P. 1926. The laws of returns under competitive conditions. *Economic Journal* 36:535–50.

Stennek, J., and F. Verboven. 2001. Merger control and enterprise competitiveness: empirical analysis and policy recommendations. Research Institute of Industrial Economics, Stockholm, Working Paper 556.

Stigler, G. 1964. A theory of oligopoly. *Journal of Political Economy* 72:44–61.

Stigler, G., and K. Boulding. 1950. *Readings in Price Theory*. Chicago, IL: Irwin.

Stigler, G., and R. Sherwin. 1985. The extent of the market. *Journal of Law and Economics* 28:555–85.

Stillman, R. 1983. Examining antitrust policy towards horizontal mergers. *Journal of Financial Economics* 11(1–4):225–40.

Stock, J. 1987. Asymptotic properties of least-squares estimators of cointegrating vectors. *Econometrica* 58:1035–56.

Stock, J., and M. Watson. 2006. *Introduction to Econometrics*. Addison-Wesley.

Stone, R. 1954. Linear expenditure systems and demand analysis: an application to the pattern of British demand. *Economic Journal* 64(255):511–27.

Student (pseudonym for W. S. Gosset). 1908. The probable error of a mean. *Biometrica* 6(1): 1–25.

Sueyoshi, T. 1991. Estimation of stochastic frontier cost function using data envelopment analysis: an application to the AT&T divestiture. *Journal of the Operational Research Society* 42:463–77.

Sueyoshi, T., and P. C. Anselmo. 1986. The Evans and Heckman subadditivity test: comment. *American Economic Review* 76:854–55.

Suslow, V., and M. Levenstein. 2006. What determines cartel success. *Journal of Economic Literature* 44(1):43–95.

Sutton, J. 1991. *Sunk Costs and Market Structure*. Cambridge, MA: MIT Press.

——. 1998. *Technology and Market Structure*. Cambridge, MA: MIT Press.

Syverson, C., and A. Hortacsu. 2007. Cementing relationships: vertical integration, foreclosure, productivity, and prices. *Journal of Political Economy* 115:250–301.

Taylor, C. T., N. Kreisle, and P. Zimmerman. 2007. Vertical relationships and competition in retail gasoline markets: comment. FTC Working Paper 291.

Taylor, J., and M. Yokell. 1979. *Yellowcake: The International Uranium Cartel*. Pergamon Press.

Telser, L. 1960. Why should manufacturers want fair trade? *Journal of Law and Economics* 3:86–103.

Thanassoulis, E. 1993. A comparison of regression analysis and data envelopment analysis as alternative methods for performance assessments. *Journal of the Operational Research Society* 44:1129–44.

Theil, H. 1953. Repeated least squares applied to complete equation systems. Mimeographed memorandum of the Central Planning Bureau, The Hague.

Tirole, J. 1993 *The Theory of Industrial Organization*. Cambridge, MA: MIT Press.

Topkis, D. 1998. *Supermodularity and Complementarity*. Princeton University Press.

Triplett, J. 1992. Economic theory and BEA's alternative quantity and price indexes. Report, Bureau of Economic Analysis, Department of Commerce.

Van Dijk, T., and F. Verboven. 2007. Quantification of damages. In *Issues in Competition Law and Policy* (ed. W. D. Collins). Chicago, IL: ABA Publications.

Varian, H. R. 1992 *Microeconomic Analysis*, 3rd edn. New York: NW Norton.

Vartia, Y. 1983. Efficient methods of measuring welfare change and compensated income in terms of ordinary demand functions. *Econometrica* 51:79–98.

Vasconcelos, H. 2005. Tacit collusion, cost asymmetries and mergers. *RAND Journal of Economics* 36:39–62.

Verboven, F. 1996. The nested logit model and representative consumer theory. *Economics Letters* 50(1):57–63.

Verboven, F., and L. Bettendorf. 2001. Incomplete transmission of coffee bean prices: evidence from the Netherlands. *European Journal of Agricultural Economics* 27(1):1–16.

Verboven, F., and R. Brenkers. 2006. Liberalizing a distribution system: the European car market. *Journal of the European Economic Association* 4(1):216—51.

Verboven, F., and T. van Dijk. 2007. Cartel damages claims and the passing-on defense. CEPR Discussion Paper 6329.

Verouden, V. 2005. Vertical agreements: motivation and impact. In *Issues in Competition Law and Policy* (ed. W. D. Collins). American Bar Association.

Vickers, J., and M. Waterson. 1991. Vertical relationships: an introduction. *Journal of Industrial Economics* 39:445–50.

Villas-Boas, J. M., and Y. Zhao. 2005. Retailer, manufacturers, and individual consumers: modeling the supply side in the ketchup marketplace. *Journal of Marketing Research* 42(1):83–95.

Villas-Boas, S. 2007a. Vertical relationships between manufacturers and retailers: inference with limited data. *Review of Economic Studies* 74:625–52.

——. 2007b. Using retail data for upstream merger analysis. *Journal of Competition Law and Economics* 3(4):689–715.

Viner, J. 1931. Cost curves and supply curves. In *Zeitschrift für Nationalökonomie*, volume 3, pp. 23–46. (Reprinted in Stigler and Boulding (1950).)

Vives, X. 1990. Nash equilibrium with strategic complementarities *Journal of Mathematical Economics* 19(3):305–21.

Vuong, Q. 1989. Likelihood ratio tests for model selection and non-nested hypotheses. *Econometrica* 57:307–33.

Walker, M. 2005. The potential for significant inaccuracies in merger simulation models. *Journal of Competition Law and Economics* 1(3):473–96.

Ward, R. 1975. Revisiting the Dorfman–Steiner static advertising theorem: an application to the processed grapefruit industry. *American Journal of Agricultural Economics* 57: 500–504.

Werden, G. 1981. The use and misuse of shipments data in defining geographic markets. *Antitrust Bulletin* 26:719–35.

Werden, G., and L. Froeb. 1993a. Correlation, causality and all that jazz: the inherent shortcomings of price tests for antitrust market delineation. *Review of Industrial Organization* 8:329–53.

——. 1993b. The effects of mergers in differentiated products industries: structural merger policy and the logit model. *Journal of Law, Economics, & Organization* 10:407–26.

——. 2005. Unilateral competitive effects of horizontal mergers: theory and application through merger simulation. In *Handbook of Antitrust Economics* (ed. P. Buccirosi). Cambridge, MA: MIT Press.

Werden, G., L. Froeb, and D. Scheffman. 2004. A Daubert discipline for merger simulation. Report, Federal Trade Commission. (Available at www.ftc.gov/be/daubertdiscipline.pdf.)

Whinston, M. D. 1990. Tying, foreclosure, and exclusion. *American Economic Review* 80: 837–59.

——. 2003. On the transactions cost determinants of vertical integration. *Journal of Law, Economics, & Organization* 19(1):1–23.

Whish, R. 2003. *Competition Law*, 4th edn. Reed Elsevier.

White, G. I., A. C. Sondhi, and D. Fried. 2001. *The Analysis and Use of Financial Statements*, 3rd edn. Wiley.

White, H. 1980. A heteroskedasticity-consistent covariance matrix estimator and a direct test for heteroskedasticity. *Econometrica* 48:817–38.

——. 2001. *Asymptotic Theory for Econometricians*. Academic Press.

——. 2005. Estimating the effects of natural experiments. Mimeo, University of California, San Diego.

Williamson, O. 1975. *Markets and Hierarchies*. New York: Free Press.

——. 1977. Economies as an antitrust defense revisited. *University of Pennsylvania Law Review* 125(4):699–739.

Williamson, O. 1979. Transaction cost economics: the governance of contractual relations. *Journal of Law and Economics* 22:3–61.

——. 1985. *The Economic Institutions of Capitalism*. New York: Free Press.

Winter, R. 1993. Vertical control and price versus nonprice competition. *Quarterly Journal of Economics* 108:61–76.

Wooldridge, J. 2007. *Econometric Analysis of Cross Section and Panel Data*, 2nd edn. Cambridge, MA: MIT Press.

Wright, P. G. 1928. *The Tariff on Animal and Vegetable Oils*. Macmillan.

Yule, G. U. 1926. Why do we sometimes get nonsense-correlations between time-series? A study in sampling and the nature of time-series. *Journal of the Royal Statistical Society* 89(1):1–63

Zhou, L. 1994. The set of Nash equilibria of a supermodular game is a complete lattice. *Games and Economic Behaviour* 7(2):295–300.

Copyright Acknowledgments

Index

CPSIA information can be obtained
at www.ICGtesting.com
Printed in the USA
BVHW030812110422
633957BV00001B/33

9 780691 142579